W9-DAB-769

Man's Most Dangerous Myth

Man's Most Dangerous Myth

The Fallacy of Race

SIXTH EDITION

Ashley Montagu

ALTAMIRA

PRESS

AltaMira Press
A Division of Sage Publications, Inc.
Walnut Creek • London • New Delhi

For information address:

AltaMira Press
A Division of Sage Publications, Inc.
1630 North Main Street, Suite 367
Walnut Creek, CA 94596
explore@altamira.sagepub.com

SAGE Publications Ltd.
6 Bonhill Street
London EC2A 4PU
United Kingdom

SAGE Publications India Pvt. Ltd.
M-32 Market
Greater Kailash 1
New Delhi 110 048 India

PRINTED IN THE UNITED STATES OF AMERICA

98 99 00 01 02 03 04 05   7 6 5 4 3 2 1

Library of Congress Cataloging-in-Publication Data

Montagu, Ashley, 1905–
    Man's most dangerous myth : the fallacy of race / Ashley Montagu.
    —6th ed.
        p.   cm.
    Includes bibliographical references and index.
    ISBN 0-8039-4647-3 (cloth). — ISBN 0-8039-4648-1 (pbk.)
    1. Race. 2. Race relations. I. Title.
GN280.M59   1998
599.97—dc21   97-21132
                                                                                                    CIP

Typeset by Letra Libre

Cover design by Joanna Ebenstein

Contents

Acknowledgments

To Leonard Lieberman, Professor of Anthropology at Central Michigan University, my heartfelt thanks for his devoted reading of and commentary on every chapter of this book, and for his always helpful suggestions. I am similarly indebted to Professor of Sociology Larry T. Reynolds at Central Michigan University. To John Stanfield, Professor of Sociology at the University of California at Davis, I am similarly obliged. Their gentle ministrations have made this book a much better one than it would have otherwise been. To Elaine and Harry Mensh I am indebted for their help in the revision of chapter 6; to Troy Johnson of the American Indian Studies Program at California State University, Long Beach for his admirable revision of chapter 18 on the status of the American Indian.

To Louise Schaeffer, Librarian of the Biology Library at Princeton University, I am greatly indebted for bibliographical help; also to Mary Chaikin, Librarian of the Psychological Library at Princeton; to the reference librarians at Firestone Library of Princeton University; to Louise Yorke, Librarian of the Princeton Medical Center; to the reference librarians at the Princeton public library, all for their bibliographical help so generously given.

To Mitch Allen, my editor and publisher, I am most grateful for his advice and patience beyond the call of duty. To Erik Hanson I am similarly grateful. To Pattie Rechtman, my copyeditor, I am enormously indebted for her microscopic eye, and for keeping me in order, much to the benefit of this book.

Above all, my gratitude goes to my wife, Marjorie, for her heroic endurance, over the course of six years in the making of this revision, of the colossal untidiness of my study and its overflow into the adjoining dining room.

Ashley Montagu
Princeton, New Jersey
September 1997

About the Author

ASHLEY MONTAGU (1905–) ranks as one of the most influential public intellectuals of the twentieth century. Of British origin but an American resident since 1930 and a naturalized citizen since 1940, Montagu has written or edited over 80 books, many in multiple editions, and thousands of research articles, magazine pieces, book chapters, letters, commentaries, and lectures in a career that has spanned three-fourths of this century. Among his best known book-length works are *The Natural Superiority of Women, Touching,* and *The Elephant Man,* but he has also authored key professional volumes and textbooks in physical anthropology, cultural anthropology, human evolution, and anatomy. His intellectual contributions also have been felt in an enormous range of other fields including prenatal and infant development, aging, the role of culture in evolution, the evolutionary development of human behavior, the basic behavioral needs, human nature and genetics, education, history of science, human-animal relations, sociobiology, American culture, emotions, computers, and nuclear disarmament.

In the area of race relations, it can be argued that Ashley Montagu is the most important theorist of the twentieth century. The initial publication of *Man's Most Dangerous Myth,* at the height of Nazism in 1942, radically challenged the idea that race was a determinant of human behavior, a position he championed almost alone for decades until it became accepted wisdom. Through subsequent editions of the book, his other works on race, and his authorship of the seminal UNESCO *Statement on Race,* Montagu's work has become foundational for those who study the learned dimensions of human behavior.

Ashley Montagu received a Ph.D. from Columbia University, taught anthropology at New York University, Harvard University, Princeton University, Rutgers University, and other places, and is the recipient of honorary awards and degrees from organizations around the globe.

Foreword to the First Edition, 1942
by Aldous Huxley

Dr. Ashley Montagu's book possesses two great merits, rarely found in current discussions of human problems. Where most writers over-simplify, he insists on the principle of multiple and interlocking causation. And where most assume that "facts will speak for themselves," he makes it clear that facts are mere ventriloquists' dummies, and can be made to justify any course of action that appeals to the socially conditioned passions of the individuals concerned.

These two truths are sufficiently obvious; but they are seldom recognized, for the good reason that they are very depressing. To recognize the first truth is to recognize the fact that there are no panaceas and that therefore most of the golden promises made by political reformers and revolutionaries are illusory. And to recognize the truth that facts do not speak for themselves, but only as men's socially conditioned passions dictate, is to recognize that our current educational processes can do very little to ameliorate the state of the world. In the language of traditional theology (so much more realistic, in many respects, than the "liberal" philosophies which replaced it), most ignorance is voluntary and depends upon acts of the conscious or subconscious will. Thus, the fallacies underlying the propaganda of racial hatred are not recognized because, as Dr. Montagu points out, most people have a desire to act aggressively, and the members of other ethnic groups are convenient victims, whom one may attack with a good conscience. This desire to act aggressively has its origins in the largely unavoidable frustrations imposed upon the individual by the processes of early education frustrations imposed upon the individual by the processes of early education and later adjustments to the social environment.

Dr. Montagu might have added that aggressiveness pays a higher dividend in emotional satisfaction than does cooperation. Cooperation may produce a mild emotional glow; but the indulgence of aggressiveness can be the equivalent of a drinking-bout or sexual orgy. In our industrial societies, the goodness of life is measured in terms of the number and intensity of the excitements experienced. (Popular philosophy is molded by, and finds expression in, the advertising pages of popular magazines. Significantly enough,

11

the word that occurs more frequently in those pages than any other is "thrill.") Like sex and alcohol, aggressiveness can give enormous thrills. Under existing social conditions, it is therefore easy to represent aggressiveness as good.

Concerning the remedies for the social diseases he has so penetratingly diagnosed, Dr. Montagu says very little, except that they will have to consist in some process of education. But what process? It is hoped that he will answer this question at length in another work.

Foreword to the Sixth Edition
by C. Loring Brace

Well over half a century ago—two full generations—the world was in the midst of the colossal armed conflict of World War II. The instigator of its European manifestation was Germany under the leadership of Adolf Hitler and his Nazi Party. The basic motive behind Germany's actions was the belief, repeatedly articulated by Hitler, that Germans were a "master race" which had the right to take precedence over their neighbors because of their innate superiority.[1] In this regard, World War II was a resumption of the aspirations that had led to the outbreak of World War I in 1914 and which had not been extinguished by the German defeat of 1918. In Germany, there had been no sense that their role in generating World War I had been unjustified, and there was a comparable failure to face the fact that the war had been fairly lost. Instead, the scenario was constructed that their inability to continue generating the weaponry and personnel necessary for victory had been caused by a "stab-in-the-back" on the part of the "international financial community," a code name for "the Jews," themselves stigmatized as an "inferior race."[2]

Adolf Hitler took full advantage of this current of "racial" mythology and, in a masterfully murderous ploy of mass psychology, mobilized the German state to cleanse itself from "the enemy within"—the Jews—and charge forth in an attempt to gain control of the rest of the world. As a part of this overall plan, Jews were rounded up and shipped to concentration camps in the eastern part of Germany, in Czechoslovakia, and especially in Poland where they were killed by the millions. The whole appalling phenomenon came to be known as "The Holocaust."[3] This marked the first time in human history that a whole segment of the human species was earmarked for systematic extermination solely on the basis of what was perceived to be its "race."

At the very time that this was being carried out, Ashley Montagu produced the first edition of what is arguably his most important book, *Man's Most Dangerous Myth: The Fallacy of Race*.[4] In this work, Ashley Montagu was the first to articulate in fully developed fashion the fact that, despite almost universal belief to the contrary, the concept of "race" as applied to

13

the picture of human biological diversity had absolutely no scientific justification. Among those who had checked the manuscript prior to publication was America's premier anthropologist, Franz Boas, who had been the
author's doctoral dissertation mentor at Columbia University in the mid-
1930s. Launched with a Foreword by Aldous Huxley, the author who subsequently became celebrated for his *Brave New World,* the book rode a
wave of public reaction fueled by a growing awareness of the pervasive evil
manifest in the Nazi uses of "race."

There is a curious double irony to this whole situation. First, when
Montagu wrote the book, neither he nor the public for which he was writing had more than a partial realization of the magnitude of that lethal
enormity being enacted by the Nazis. When the full extent of the Holocaust became known as the war came to an end three years later (1945),
Man's Most Dangerous Myth, then in its second edition, achieved well-de-
served public recognition as a warning against the horrors that could result
from a belief in and application of the concept of "race."

The second irony is to be found in the fact that the public, while giving
Ashley Montagu due credit for having raised the alarm, never really took to
heart the fact that the foundation for that warning was located in his
demonstration that "race" was invalid from the perspective of basic biology.
At most, readers were willing to grant the fact that Jews are not really a definable biological unit, but they were not yet ready to face the fact that
there simply is no valid biological entity that corresponds to what is meant
by the term "race." They certainly recognized the inhumane consequences
of the political usage of the concept, but they tended—then and since—to
assume that the objections raised in *Man's Most Dangerous Myth* were solely
based on the social and political stance of the author.[5]

This is not to say that it avoided any expression of social and political
values. Far from it. The social values articulated were explicit and humanitarian, and were presented with forthright expressions of admiration for
the democratic ideals contained in the United States Constitution and particularly in the wording of the Declaration of Independence. He also recalled, from his own childhood in London before the outbreak in 1914 of
World War I, the furor caused by the publication of a glorification of war
and an exhortation to Germany to embark on a campaign of conquest for
the greater glory of people who were "racially" German and for the German nation. This was written by the former Prussian officer, Friedrich von
Bernhardi, who had led the triumphal march of the conquering army into
Paris in 1871 symbolizing the defeat of France in the Franco-Prussian War.[6]
The unresolved issues that were left by that conflict led directly to the two
world wars of the succeeding century. Among those issues was the belief
that human "races" not only constitute real entities but also that they can
be ranked in a hierarchy of worth, and that such differences warrant differ-

ences in treatment. The assumption that human groups must differ in cognitive as well as visually recognizable attributes can be designated "racialism," and the conversion of such beliefs into differential behavior directed towards such groups is what counts as "racism." As Todorov has recently concluded, "When . . . racism uses racialism to justify itself, the results are catastrophes: this was precisely the case with Hitler's racism."[7]

This was clearly understood by those who had prevailed over Hitler's intentions in World War II, and it was exactly this that earned Ashley Montagu such a sympathetic readership for *Man's Most Dangerous Myth* in the years immediately following the conclusion of that colossal conflict. Consistent with his admiration for the ideals expressed by Thomas Jefferson, he has regularly quoted the views of the latter in regard to those of varying background: "whatever be their degree of talent it is no measure of their rights."[8] This is the stance that underlay the political ideology of Jefferson's *Declaration of Independence*,[9] it was explicitly echoed by Abraham Lincoln at the time of the American Civil War, and it has been repeated in all five previous editions of this Ashley Montagu's most important book. Almost certainly this is why so many have felt that his position was based on political ideals alone.[10] It takes nothing away from the fundamental significance of his expressed ideals to note that there is a basic biological issue that often has been overlooked in the process.

That biological issue was at the bottom of the first edition of *Man's Most Dangerous Myth* in 1942, and Ashley Montagu's appreciation of it was so far ahead of his time that the anthropological world is only just now beginning to catch up. This is the idea that biological variation in a widespread species, where there is reproductive continuity from one group to another throughout the entire extent of the species range, is best understood by looking at the gradients in distribution of traits taken one at a time. The graded distribution of each such trait will be controlled by the distribution of the selective force to which it represents a response. In humans, the most easily perceived of such traits is the color of the skin. The descendants of populations who had resided in the tropics for a prolonged period of time will have heavily pigmented skin. The skin pigment, melanin, represents a defense against the cancer-causing effect of the intensive ultraviolet radiation in tropical sunlight. The degree of reduction in human skin pigmentation will be in proportion to the length of time that a given human group has lived north (and also south) of the portions of the earth included between the Tropic of Cancer and the Tropic of Capricorn. The selective force that controls the degree of skin pigmentation is the intensity of ultraviolet radiation which is at its maximum in the Tropics.[11]

Other traits, such as blood groups for example, will be controlled by selective forces such as diet and disease that are distributed without any regard to the distribution of ultraviolet intensity.[12] The configuration formed by the intersection of such traits then will have no meaning in and of itself. In fact, if we focus on such configurations rather than the distribution of each trait separately and in terms of its own selective force, then we will have lost the ability to make any kind of sense out of the meaning of human biological variation.[13]

Ashley Montagu understood this in theory in 1942, although the full range of basic biological data necessary to sustain such a theory had yet to be collected. The idea was not entirely original with him as he was the first to note. As he explicitly pointed out, the viewpoint was laid out by Lancelot Hogben over a decade earlier,[14] and it was also behind the stance taken by Alfred Cort Haddon and Julian Huxley in their insightful work, We Europeans.[15] Right after that book had appeared, Julian Huxley—the literate scientist brother of the scientifically literate writer, Aldous—articulated the concept of "cline" which went on to become the biological foundation to the "non-racial" outlook that has characterized the work of Ashley Montagu from that time hence.[16] A cline is simply the gradient in the response of a trait to the graded intensity of the selective force that controls its appearance, and, as Huxley clearly indicated, it was just a further consequence of looking at the nature of biological variation from a thoroughly Darwinian perspective along with an understanding of the way in which genetics contributes to the physical development and appearance of a given organism.

Of course, speaking from the basis of the purely theoretical in the absence of supporting data is never as compelling as it is when one can actually point to the assembled evidence of continent-wide distributions of this or that. This is always the case when a new theoretical position is first proposed. Not only is the stance still not crystal clear in the minds of the proposers, but, in the absence of illustrative examples, it can often strike the reader as just so much empty verbiage. This was largely the situation when the first edition of Man's Most Dangerous Myth appeared in print. Still, the social message concerning the misapplication of the concept of "race" to the human scene was so compelling that the book went through three editions before biologists began to make the first tentative steps towards catching up with the biological theory on which the critique was established.

By 1949, it was clear that the geographic distribution of the common leopard frog in the eastern part of North America from Canada to the Gulf of Mexico was best portrayed in terms of gradients of adaptive characters.[17] Subsequently, it was realized that the attempt to depict variation in terms of "subspecies" or "races" in creatures as diverse as butterflies,[18] the North American marten,[19] and the zebras of Africa[20] were doomed to failure as biologically indefensible. It was the growing perception that cases such as this represent the norm for the biological world that led to the realization that the presumed existence of units such as "subspecies"—or "races" in the human realm—derived more from the traditions of medieval theology than from an assessment of how the biological world is actually put together. The demonstration that such a concept does more harm than good in the everyday business of trying to make sense out of variation in ordinary biological species was first articulated by E. O. Wilson, the Harvard entomologist later to become famous for his promotion of *Sociobiology*.[21]

Ashley Montagu, of course, had long since documented the harm that could be done in the name of "race" as it was applied to the human world. Biological anthropologists in the field had begun to collect data that, from the perspective of traditionalists, showed a disconcertingly non-racial kind of distribution. Obviously, human beings have done a lot of moving about during the last 10,000 years, particularly those whose numbers have expanded as a result of the adoption of an agricultural way of life. Still, it has been possible to test the distribution of genetically controlled traits over large, continuously occupied areas, and it has become clear that these distributions can only be understood after the concept of "race" is dropped. The late Joseph Birdsell plotted gene distributions in aboriginal Australia, and showed that the genes for given traits changed in frequency from one part of the continent to another with relatively little regard for what the genes for other traits were doing.[22] Finally, late in the 1950s, the first major effort was made to trace the distribution of an inherited human trait—in this case, the form of the hemoglobin responsible for sickle-cell anemia—according to what could be reconstructed of population history in relation to the relevant selective force—malaria in this instance—that influenced the prevalence of the trait. This yielded a picture in which the frequency of the sickle-cell gene was determined solely by the intensity of the forces of selection and not at all by locality as such.[23]

The theoretical implications dawned upon the author of this study—Frank B. Livingstone—and led him to create his famous aphorism, "There are no races, there are only clines."[24] This, of course, fit in perfectly with the stance defended twenty years earlier by Ashley Montagu, and, hardly surprisingly, Montagu quickly solicited Frank Livingstone's presentation as a centerpiece for a collection of essays by those who were adopting clinal thinking as the appropriate way to go about dealing with the nature of human biological variation. This was published under the title *The Concept of Race*, which appeared in 1964, the same year as the fourth edition of *Man's Most Dangerous Myth*.[25]

I remember the era well. I had been a student when Joe Birdsell's study of Australian gene frequencies had been published, and, steeped in the standard racialist assumptions of the time, I recall being baffled by the seemingly senseless gene distributions he had plotted. Then as it became clear that variation in frogs, butterflies, pine martens, and human beings was characterized by trait gradients that crossed each other in completely independent fashion, it became evident that those gradients were responding to the distribution of separate and unrelated gradients of selective forces—in the fashion of human hemoglobins responding to the distribution of malaria—and the whole non-racial nature of biological variation came into focus for me for the first time. The biological justification for Ashley Montagu's denunciation of race as *Man's Most Dangerous Myth* was patently obvious, and I was honored to be included as one of the contributors to his 1964 volume, *The Concept of Race*.[26]

A decade earlier, the Supreme Court had ruled that schools that were "racially" segregated were inherently unequal.[27] By 1964, Title VII of the Civil Rights Act had belatedly prohibited employers from engaging in discrimination based on "race," color, religion, sex, or national origin, although there has been a continuing reluctance to accept this prohibition.[28] Even at that moment, the candidate for United States Senator in Texas offered his opposition to the Civil Rights Act as one of his qualifications for being elected. Subsequently the perception that he was indeed opposed to eliminating the results of the legacy of unequal treatment for minorities was sufficient to boost his aspiration for the office of President of the United States, although it was not enough to earn him re-election. That figure was the one-term President, George Bush.[29]

But 1964 was a third of a century ago. The "brave new world" that we hoped was dawning arrived in largely stillborn fashion. To be sure, the pursuit of genocide in the name of "race" is universally regarded as completely indefensible, but that should have been as much a foregone conclusion as was the realization emerging from the American Civil War a century earlier that perceptions of "race" were no justification for treating people as property—i.e., that the institution of slavery was incompatible with a recognition of human status. However, even an enlarged and reinforced fifth edition of *Man's Most Dangerous Myth* in 1974, over three decades after the appearance of the first, failed to affect the entrenched public assumption that the artificial American situation with population segments recently derived from three widely separate and locally circumscribed portions of the globe, juxtaposed and assigned different social status initially by force of arms, is a proper model from which to generalize about the nature of human variation in the world as a whole.

What happened instead was a kind of intellectual stasis or even backsliding. This seems to have been a recurring centennial phenomenon in America. Right after the ringing ideals phrased in the Declaration of Independence and the United States Constitution, the promise inherent in those words was denied to those who displayed evidence of African ancestry. Then after Abraham Lincoln signed the Emancipation Proclamation in 1863 and lost his life soon thereafter, the first Civil Rights Act in 1866 was passed over the veto of his successor, Andrew Johnson. Over the succeeding thirty years, the scope of those rights was whittled down in case after case until, in Plessy *v.* Ferguson in 1896, the Supreme Court ruled that there was no federal remedy for private discrimination.[30] In effect, this allowed the reinstitution of what amounted to slavery in everything except the name.[31] There things remained until the Court's decisions were reversed in 1954, and explicit civil rights legislation was enacted in 1966.

As was true for each previous instance of official attempts to undo the effects of the racism of the past, the most recent effort has been met with the same kind of maneuverings to preserve the privileges of those who have benefited from the long-lasting traditions of unequal conditions accorded to those who are perceived as belonging to different "races." Prominent among these are the ponderous attempts to "prove" that the lower average IQ scores achieved by Americans of African origin have nothing to do with the ubiquitous conditions of social deprivation under which they are born and raised.[32] The most notorious of these recent representatives of racism is *The Bell Curve* by the late psychologist Richard J. Herrnstein and the political scientist Charles Murray,[33] which has been called "a massive manifestation of genteel bigotry."[34] Other equally racist tracts are continuing to be produced where the basic nature of and circumstances surrounding human biological variation are distorted beyond recognition and old-fashioned "racial" prejudice emerges in all its traditional ugliness.[35]

As the end of the current millennium approaches and we contemplate the dawn of another, it is clear that entrenched and traditional attitudes towards "race" remain alive and well, continuing to make life miserable for millions of people. The time is obviously ripe for the administration of another dose of Dr. Montagu's medicine which is as topical and apt as it was when it was first formulated over half a century ago. Now in his tenth decade, the author remains as much on top of the situation as ever. All the points that had been made in earlier editions are polished and brought up to date, and the wholly new sixth chapter—"The Mythology of Race: For Whom the Bell Tolls"—is a crowning gem that can stand by itself. In effect it represents one of the most definitive rebuttals of that widely popular manifestation of American racism, *The Bell Curve*, mentioned above.[36] The very popularity of that work is a testimonial to the fact that "race" remains a powerful myth in the world of today. As much as anything else, that popularity is a measure of our need for an Ashley Montagu to help the public see the error of its ways.[37]

Several years ago, it was my honor to be able to present to him, on behalf of the American Association of Physical Anthropologists, the Charles Darwin Award for Lifetime Achievement. On that occasion, I declared, "It is no exaggeration to say that Ashley Montagu is the world's one and only free-lance physical anthropologist."[38] Just as he did in the dark days of World War II, now again in our hour of need he has sallied forth once more as our St. George to combat the continuing threat of what he has most aptly identified as *Man's Most Dangerous Myth: The Fallacy of Race*. We can only hope that, this time, the world will take his lesson to heart.

C. Loring Brace
Ann Arbor, Michigan
18 September 1996

Notes

1. *Mein Kampf,* by Adolf Hitler, originally published in Munich, 1925; translated by Ralph Manheim (Boston, Houghton Mifflin, 1943); Robert Cecil, *The Myth of the Master Race: Alfred Rosenberg and Nazi Ideology* (New York: Dodd, Mead, 1972).

2. Geoffrey G. Field, *Evangelist of Race: The Germanic Vision of Houston Stewart Chamberlain* (New York: Columbia University Press, 1981); Robert Kuttner, "Writers on the Grassy Knoll: A Reader's Guide," *New York Times Book Review,* 2 February 1992, 23–25; Richard Bessel, *Germany After the First World War* (Oxford: Clarendon Press, 1993); and see the continuity of the same views in the writings of that opponent of religious tolerance, Pat Robertson in *The New World Order* (New York: Word Publishing, 1991) and the assessment of its sources in "The Crackpot Factor," in his 'Abroad at Home,' column by Anthony Lewis, *New York Times,* 14 April 1995, p. A11, as they had been discussed in detail by Michael Lind, "Rev. Robertson's Grand International Conspiracy Theory," *The New York Review of Books* 42(3), 2 February 1995, 21–25; his "On Pat Robertson: His Defenders," *The New York Review of Books* 42(7), 20 April 1995, 67–68, and Jacob Heilbrunn, "On Pat Robertson: His Anti-Semitic Sources," in *The New York Review of Books* 42(7), 20 April 1995, 68–71.

3. Gerald Fleming, *Hitler and the Final Solution* (Berkeley: University of California Press, 1984); Irving Abrahamson, ed., *Against Silence: The Voice and Vision of Elie Wiesel,* 3 vols. (New York: Holocaust Library, 1986); Israel Gutman, editor-in-chief, *Encyclopedia of the Holocaust,* 4 vols. (New York: Macmillan, 1990); Christopher R. Browning, *The Path to Genocide: Essays on Launching the Final Solution* (New York: Cambridge University Press, 1993); Daniel Jonah Goldhagen, *Hitler's Willing Executioners: Ordinary Germans and the Holocaust* (New York: Alfred A. Knopf, 1996).

4. Ashley Montagu, *Man's Most Dangerous Myth* (New York: Columbia University Press, 1942).

5. The most recent reincarnation of this canard is in *The Evolution of Racism: Human Differences and the Use and Abuse of Science,* by Pat Shipman (New York: Simon and Schuster 1994), in which a discussion of the "evolution of racism" is conspicuous by its absence, and the abuse of science is on the part of the author and not the figures accused, Ashley Montagu being prominently included among the latter. For a documentation of the gaffes in Shipman's treatment, see my review in *The American Journal of Physical Anthropology* 96(2) (1995): 204–10.

6. F. Friedrich von Bernhardi, *Germany and the Next War* translated by Allen H. Powles (London: Longmans Green, 1911); A. Montagu, *Dangerous Myth,* 153.

7. Tsvetan Todorov "'Race,' Writing and 'Culture," in *"Race," Writing, and Difference* ed. Henry Louis Gates (Chicago: University of Chicago Press, 1985), 372.

8. Letter to Abbé Grégoire in 1809, in *Basic Writings of Thomas Jefferson,* ed. Philip S. Foner (New York: Halcyon House, 1950), 682.

9. Garry Wills, *Inventing America: Jefferson's Declaration of Independence* (Garden City, NY: Doubleday, 1978).

10. See Shipman *Evolution of Racism,* 190–91.

11. These matters are treated at length in *Biological Perspectives on Human Pigmentation,* by Ashley H. Robins (New York: Cambridge University Press, 1991).

12. William C. Boyd, *Genetics and the Races of Man, An Introduction to Modern Physical Anthropology* (Boston: Little, Brown and Company, 1950); Arthur E. Mourant, A. C. Kopec and K. Domaniewska-Sobczak, *Blood Groups and Disease: A Study of the Association of Diseases with Blood Groups and Other Polymorphisms* (New York: Oxford University Press, 1978).

13. Elsewhere I have urged the treatment of the distribution of inherited traits in terms of the history and distribution of the controlling selective forces as a general approach, see C. Loring Brace, "A Non-Racial Approach Toward the Understanding of Human Diversity," in *The Concept of Race,* ed. Ashley Montagu (New York: The Free Press of Glenco, 1964), 103–152, and C. Loring Brace "A Four-Letter Word Called "Race," chapter 7 in *Race and other Misadventures: Essays in Honor of Ashley Montagu in His Ninetieth Year,* eds. Larry T. Reynolds and Leonard Lieberman (Dix Hills, NY: General Hall Publishers, 1996) 106–41. Specific examples of how this can be applied are demonstrated in "Who Gave Whom Hemoglobin S: The Use of Restriction Site Haplotype Variation For the Interpretation of the Evolution of the (^{s}-globin gene," by Frank B. Livingstone, *American Journal of Human Biology* 1 (1989): 289–302; and "What Big Teeth You Had Grandma! Human Tooth Size, Past and Present," by C. Loring Brace, Shelley L. Smith, and Kevin D. Hunt, in *Advances in Dental Anthropology* eds. Marc A. Kelley and Clark S. Larsen (New York Wiley-Liss 1991), 33–57.

14. This had been done in the brilliant chapter, "The Concept of Race" in Lancelot Hogben's *Genetic Principles in Medicine and Social Science* (London: Williams and Norgate, 1931), 122–44.

15. *We Europeans: A Survey of "Racial" Problems,* by Alfred Cort Haddon and Julian S. Huxley (New York: Harper, 1936).

16. Julian Huxley, "Clines: An Auxiliary Taxonomic Principle," *Nature* 142 (1938): 219–20.

17. John A. Moore, "Geographic Variations of Adaptive Characters in *Rana pipiens* Schraber," *Evolution* 3(1)(1943): 1–23.

18. F. Martin Brown "Studies of Nearctic Coenonympha tullia," *Bulletin of the American Museum of Natural History* 105(4)(1955): 361–409; Nicholas W. Gillham "Geographical Variation and the Subspecies Concept in Butterflies," *Systematic Zoology* 5(3)(1956): 110–20.

19. Edwin M. Hagmeier, "Inapplicability of the Subspecies Concept to North American Marten," *Systematic Zoology* 7(1)(1958): 1–7.

20. R. E. Rau "Additions to the Revised list of Preserved Material of the Extinct Cape Colony Quagga and Notes on the Relationship and Distribution of Southern Plains Zebras," *Annals of the South African Museum* 77(2)(1978): 27–45.

21. E. O. Wilson and William L. Brown, Jr., "The Subspecies Concept and its Taxonomic Application," *Systematic Zoology* 2(3)(1953): 97–111; E. O. Wilson, *Sociobiology: The New Synthesis* (Cambridge: Belknap Press of Harvard University Press, 1975).

22. Joseph B. Birdsell, "Some Implications of the Genetical Concept of Race in Terms of Spatial Analysis," *Proceedings of The Cold Spring Harbor Symposia on Quantitative Biology* 15 (1951): 259–311.

23. Frank B. Livingstone, "Anthropological Implications of Sickle Cell Gene Distribution in West Africa," *The American Anthropologist* 30(3)(1958): 533–62.

24. Frank B. Livingstone, "On the Non-Existence of Human Races," *Current Anthropology* 3(3)(1962): 279.

25. Ashley Montagu, ed., *The Concept of Race* (New York: The Free Press of Glencoe, 1964).

26. C. Loring Brace, "A Non-Racial Approach Towards the Understanding of Human Diversity," in *The Concept of Race*, 103–52.

27. This was the landmark Brown *v.* Board of Education case, and it is treated in full in *From Brown to Bakke: The Supreme Court and School Integration, 1954–1978*, by Harvie Wilkinson III (New York: Oxford University Press, 1979); and in *The Burden of Brown: Thirty Years of School Desegregation*, by Raymond Wolters (Knoxville: University of Tennessee Press, 1984).

28. Kathleen Hall Jamieson, *Dirty Politics, Deception, Distraction, and Democracy* (New York: Oxford University Press, 1992).

29. While he did indeed continue to support the position that represented the survival of the traditions of "racial" discrimination, it was more a stance of window dressing than of genuine conviction. As one perceptive commentator noted, "The clothes have no emperor. There is no there there." In "No There There," by Anna Quindlan, in her column, "Public & Private," *New York Times*, 6 May 1992, A19.

30. "The Unhappy History of Civil Rights Legislation," by Eugene Gressman, in *Michigan Law Review* 50(8): 1323–58; and *Judicial Enigma: The First Justice Harlan*, by Tinsley E. Yarbrough, reviewed in, "The Great Dissenter," by William H. Chafe, *New York Times Book Review*, 28 May 1995, 14.

31. Gressman, "Unhappy History," 1324.

32. For instance, Arthur R. Jensen, "How Much Can We Boost IQ and Scholastic Achievement?" *Harvard Educational Review* 39(1)(1969): 1–123, in which the author implies that the answer to the question in his title is "none," and Arthur R. Jensen, *Bias in Mental Testing* (New York: The Free Press, 1980), in which he claims that there is no bias in mental tests themselves, but he then unwittingly provides a conclusive demonstration that there is a massive amount of bias among those who create them and assume that their results tell us anything about the average inherited capacities of the groups from which the testees are derived.

33. Richard J. Herrnstein and Charles Murray, *The Bell Curve: Intelligence and Class Structure in American Life* (New York: The Free Press, 1994). This work has provoked an enormous number of reviews and comments. So far, at least three collections have been assembled in book form: *The Bell Curve Wars: Race, Intelligence, and the Future*, ed. Steven Fraser (New York: Basic Books, 1995); *The Bell Curve Debate: History, Documents, Opinions*, eds. Russell Jacoby and Naomi Glauberman (New

York: Times Books, 1995); *Measured Lies: The Bell Curve Examined,* eds. Joe L. Kincheloe, Shirley R. Steinberg and Aaron D. Gresson III (New York: St. Martin's Press 1996). Two reviews deserve special attention. "Curveball" by Stephen Jay Gould, *New Yorker,* 28 November 1994, 139–49, has shown that the treatment of the massive data compilation assembled in *The Bell Curve* could practically serve as a textbook example of how to lie with statistics. And "The Tainted Sources of the Bell Curve" by Charles Lane, *New York Review of Books,* 1 December 1994, 14–19, documents the extent of the racist taint in the sources used by Herrnstein and Murray to support their preconceived stance.

34. C. Loring Brace, "Review of *The Bell Curve,*" *Current Anthropology* 37(Supplement)(1996): S156-S161, S161.

35. For example, J. Philippe Rushton, *Race, Evolution, and Behavior: A Life History Perspective* (New Brunswick: Transaction Publishers, 1995). My own review of this, entitled "Racialism and Racist Agendas," appeared in *The American Anthropologist* 98(1)(1996): 36–37, and it concluded that, "Quite evidently, it is a manifestation of blatant bigotry" (p. 37). Other reviewers have used considerably stronger and less temperate language, for example, David P. Barash in *Animal Behaviour* 49(4)(1995): 1131–33.

36. The overwhelming consensus of the reviewers is that the work represents a continuation of the same attitudes that created and defended American slavery in the past. It does have its defenders, prominent among them being that product of the apartheid society of South Africa, J. Philippe Rushton, illustrated by his review in *Current Anthropology* 37 (Supplement): S168–S172.

37. In order to document and strengthen the position he has maintained for the last half century and more, I am currently in the process of preparing a work entitled *Race Is a Four-Letter Word.* It is dedicated to Ashley Montagu.

38. The text of that presentation is recorded in the "Proceedings of the Sixty-Third Meeting of the American Association of Physical Anthropologists in Denver, April, 1994," *American Journal of Physical Anthropology* 95(4): 456–57, and the quote is from page 456.

Preface to the Sixth Edition
by John H. Stanfield II

The other day I noticed something quite promising. While scanning over an application form I was surprised and impressed to find not only the usual *racial status* boxes but one called *"multiracial."* Even though the word racial perpetuated THE MYTH, at least the new box was a well overdue acknowledgment of the complexities of human identity. The *multiracial* box was also an indicator of how much the ethnic identity questioning that characterizes the 1990s as the temporal anteroom to the twenty-first century has finally begun to influence the red-tape aspects of public policy.

The materialization of the multiracial box on the application form certainly symbolizes why Ashley Montagu's *Man's Most Dangerous Myth* is not only still relevant over fifty years after its publication, but, more importantly, why it is that the text will become even more important as we cross the threshold into the next century. The next century, which is already here in so many ways, will be a time in which the traditional methods of drawing sociological distinctions among human beings will crumble. We see this already in the late twentieth century American and more global movements that have begun to radically redefine the status positions and official and subjective identities of historically marginized and excluded populations such as women, indigenous peoples, colonized people of color, homosexuals and lesbians and physically disabled persons. The breakdown and breakup of national and empire boundaries and the growing acknowledgment of transnational identities, kinship networks, and economic modes of production have made the already cumbersome issue of human status and identity issues even more cumbersome, complex, and paradoxical.

In the midst of these revolutionary movements of human place and consciousness are the efforts of many Americans and other global residents to call into question the racial definitions imposed on them through official state invented categories and social and cultural traditions and stereotypes. We have seen in the 1990s, for instance, a number of biographical accounts of Americans who have written about their multiethnicity which do not easily fit into neat racialized boxes. The emerging lobbying effort to include a multiracial status box on the 2000 United States Census is another example of the growing awareness of the limitations of singular racial boxes, which symbolize a mythology losing its relevance.

Montagu's *Man's Most Dangerous Myth* is an indispensable background text for anyone interested in the historical development and use of the fallacy of race in public policy-making and in social life. Though over the years several excellent books have been published on the fallacy of race, none surpasses *Man's Most Dangerous Myth* in intellectual brilliance and in level of comprehensive analysis. Even though some of the examples Montagu refers to date to earlier times, the spirit behind his bold articulations still holds.

It should be pointed out that Ashley Montagu in his usual thorough way gives credit to those who proceeded him and influenced his thinking about the fallacy of race. Indeed, the vast array of extensive endnotes that anchor the minute details of his arguments stand alone as a lasting significant contribution to the study of the fallacies of race thinking and acting. As much as Montagu gives exhaustive credit to others, he distinguishes himself from his intellectual predecessors in the depth of his analyses and the interdisciplinary creative insights he uses to discredit the dangerous myth of race in various disciplines such as genetics, physiology, psychology, anthropology, and sociology. It is Montagu's profound depth of inquiry into the intricacies of the fallacies of race thinking with such brilliant reconsideration and re-interpretations about what we know about the fallacies of race-thinking that makes Montagu's *Man's Most Dangerous Myth* a seminal piece of scholarship that has yet to be surpassed.

This book is a must read for anyone interested in the first comprehensive text in what is now called postmodern race theory. In more extensive interdisciplinary frameworks than found anywhere in the postmodern race theory literature, Montagu offers a social constructionist (socialization) approach to the study of the myth of race. It is an approach that is much more thorough and convincing than contemporary texts such as Stephen Gould's *The Mismeasure of Man* and Cornell West's *Race Matters*. Indeed, neither of those works, nor others published in the post-1970s, offer the depth that Montagu presents in his masterful work. This is especially the case when it comes to how Montagu grounds his socialization approach in a critique of genetic and biological folklore that is either ignored or watered down in post-1970s attempts at postmodern race theory. The depth and breadth of Montagu's historical discussions on the idea of race in biology, genetics, and in the social sciences is a synthetic review and critique missing in contemporary critical race theory. This is especially the case among cultural studies of racism published by scholars who may grasp the importance of socialization approaches to race study but who lack the biological and genetic sciences background necessary to critique biological and genetic folklore in their scholarship.

The recent responses to Richard Herrnstein's and Charles Murray's *The Bell Curve* by progressive cultural studies scholars demonstrates how much more work must be done to understand the wisdom of Ashley Montagu's *Man's Most Dangerous Myth*. As much as such scholars have fought a good fight against the alleged scientific claims of Herrnstein and Murray about the cognitive deficiencies of black people, they like the men they oppose assume that race is a real category. So, we have had reams of published studies debunking *The Bell Curve* through calling attention to research which puts blacks as a ethnic in a more favorable light.

If it were up to Montagu, adjectives such as black and white would no longer be used. Race as a myth is a distorting variable that convolutes and in other ways distracts attention from the variables that really matter in understanding how and why human beings think, act, and develop as they do. The extent to which race does exist, it is an experience, it is not phenotype real or imagined. This takes us back to the fact that race is social; that is, it is learned. If we can learn race, we can unlearn race. It means that people with different cultural backgrounds can under certain historically grounded social, economic, and political conditions be made to feel like a particular "race." The usual way that "race" feeling becomes sustained is through people being segregated geographically on institutional, community, societal, and world-system levels. It is possible, as Montagu so aptly points out in his discussion on whites captured by nineteenth-century Indians becoming Indians in identity, for people of different phenotypical characteristics to become members of a different "race" through socialization or re-socialization. We see this happening with Korean children growing up in predominantly black and Latino neighborhoods in Los Angeles who go off to college and find they have more in common with black and Latino than with Korean classmates. We see it with black suburban kids in predominantly white neighborhoods who find themselves identifying more with the political and cultural values and priorities of their affluent white playmates than with their ethnic brothers and sisters in the inner-city.

The growing mixed race movement in the United States and its increasing impact on U. S. Census policies and elsewhere are also indicators of how much race is a experience. More and more Americans are beginning to insist on being called more than one "race" and are maintaining their transnational identities publicly as well as privately. These movements remind us that singular racialized categories do nothing more than oversimplify the complexities of ethnicity and culture. When it comes to self-identity and how it becomes sustained and important in building institutions, communities, and societies, ethnic and cultural background, especially when it is multiethnic and multicultural, certainly matters more than a singular imposed identity called race. When we converge issues of age, regionalism, gender, religion, and class with ethnicity, culture, multiethnicity, and multiculturalism, we begin to understand how much singular race categorization is a dangerous myth that encourages derogatory prejudgements that drain human beings of their complexity while placing emphasis on irrelevant distinctions.

As much as there are cracks showing in the use of singular race categories to identify self and others in the United States, most American citizens and residents continue to be trapped in this irrelevant way of viewing human qualities and potential. By this point in American history, the emotional energy invested in race as a means to define and organize social life has been the major barrier to dispensing with the use of the term in everyday language. It is not because there is something biological or natural about race that prevents the dismantling of the term and its use to define self and others.

As the United States continues to become defined as a multiethnic society with transnational tentacles, it is going to become increasingly difficult to maintain race as a legitimate form of emotional investment. We reside in a nation-state and a world in which demographically non-white fertility is much higher than white fertility. Most of the people who control the wealth and power in the world are non-English speakers and non-whites. Most of the children born in the United States have parents who speak English as a second language. Even though the present anti-affirmative action movements in California and elsewhere may be picking up steam, the demographic, economic, and political changes occurring in this country and world are demanding that we become much more inter-culturally competent, and quickly. It is a matter of casting away race as an increasingly obsolete and dysfunctional way to distinguish human beings and make life decisions.

Even though it is true that the ethnic demographic transformation may not bear obvious fruit in terms of significant power shifts in American life for many years to come, the fact of the matter is, the wheels are already in motion. Those groups that are preaching racial exclusion from the left and right and among non-whites as well as whites will not help but be left behind in the dust of a nation-state in a global community struggling with the meaning of a society and world which is ethnically plural inside out.

As people continue to come out of their balkanized racialized shells as power arrangements continue to shift west to east; from Europe and America to Asia; and as significant regional and ecological pockets of the United States become significantly non-white, sensible men and women will begin to search for paradigms to decide the best ways to deracialize. It is in this way that Montagu's *Man's Most Dangerous Myth* will once again find itself in the middle of the action. While its first appearance met great resistance and scorn in a world still rigidly embracing notions of white supremacy, now it reappears in a time of searching for ways to get along in a time when the rules of traditional racial hierarchies simply no longer hold even a spoonful of water.

The profound depth of Montagu's statement on the mythology of race makes it a timeless contribution to intellectual history and for those interested in designing a socially just society and world. It was here before postmodern theorizing about race as social construction and will be here for many years to come after postmodern theorizing is a footnote in some future history of late twentieth-century western social thought. That is why we all need to pause and drink deeply from the wells of what this extraordinary scholar and magnificent human being has to tell us about what has been indeed the most dangerous myth invented by *Homo sapiens*.

John H. Stanfield II
Director, The Research Program on
Racial, Ethnic, and Immigration Studies
University of California at Davis

Introduction to the Sixth Edition

More than half a century has passed since this book was first published in 1942, and more than a generation has gone by since the fifth edition was published in 1974. In spite of those five new editions, each larger than the one before, the race problem, like a malady that will not go away, seems to have grown more troubling than ever. And yet, true as that may be on a quantitative basis, qualitatively the evidence indicates that there are many more people today than ever before who believe in the right of all Americans to life, liberty, and the pursuit of happiness. But racism, by action or inaction, constitutes the denial of that right, and in that sense there appear to be many more racists than ever before.

The purpose of the present, sixth edition is to make use of the scientifically established facts to show that the term "race" is a socially constructed artifact—that there is no such thing in reality as "race;" that the very word is racist; that the idea of "race," implying the existence of significant biologically determined mental differences rendering some populations inferior to others, is wholly false; and that the space between an idea and reality can be very great and misleading.

Speaking of "space," I have never before put what is wrong with the idea of "race" in the form of a formula. Let me do so here. What the formula shows, in simplified form, is what racists, and others who are not necessarily "conscious" racists, believe to be the three genetically inseparable links which constitute "race:" The first is the phenotype or physical appearance of the individual, the second is the intelligence of the individual, and the third is the ability of the group to which the individual belongs to achieve a high civilization. Together these three ideas constitute the concept of "race." This is the structure of the current conception of "race" to which most people subscribe. *Nothing could be more unsound, for there is no genetic linkage whatever between these three variables.* And that is what this book is designed to discuss and make clear.

As a student of anthropology, at University College and the London School of Economics, in the early 20s, I inherited the established view of "race" from my teachers and the books I read, to the effect that human populations were separable into different varieties in which the hierar-

chy of difference led from the most advanced to the most backward
"races."

During the first half of the century, both English and American anthropologists, generally, continued to teach the nineteenth-century traditional view of "race," as if it were a demonstrable reality.[1] Indeed, the whole
of anthropology seemed to stem from the concept of "race." Like everyone
else, I took it for granted that such entities as were enshrined in terms like
"lower races," "inferior races," "superannuated races," "backward races,"
"mongrel races," "mixed races," "primitive peoples," "savages," and the
like, corresponded to actual realities. In fact one of my teachers, Sir Arthur
Keith, held that racial antagonisms are deeply seated in the "primitive organization of the brain."[2] For that view there was no more evidence then
than there is today, although it was implicit in the views of most anthropologists of the nineteenth and early twentieth centuries.

I can think of no better way of describing the intellectual atmosphere
in which I lived and learned than to quote from the viewpoint of a great
and unusually versatile scientist, Karl Pearson (1857–1936). Pearson was a
professor of applied mathematics at University College (University of London) and a principal founder of modern statistics and biometry, as well as a
proponent of eugenics and an intimate friend of Francis Galton, the
founder of eugenics, of whom he wrote a magnificent biography.[3] Pearson
became the first Galton Professor of National Eugenics at University College. A prolific author, at the age of 35 he published a brilliant book entitled *The Grammar of Science* in 1892.[4] This soon became a classic, and has
been in print in several editions to this day and remains completely en-
grossing. Finally, it should be said that Pearson's great and enduring
achievement was to make of the application of mathematical statistics a factor of utmost importance in many fields of scientific inquiry. And this, too,
should be said: In spite of some eccentricities Pearson had a great and noble mind.[5]

As a young man Pearson was an active socialist and wrote much on
politics and ethics, as well as folklore. As he grew older he became more
conservative, and in the field of research on intelligence, in the name of
statistics, as late as 1925 he was capable of committing the most egregious
of follies.[6] Statistics and prejudices, whether declared or undeclared, do
not go well together. In defense of Pearson, and before quoting the following passage from his *The Grammar of Science,* it should be pointed out
that virtually every scientist writing during the nineteenth century was,
like Pearson, caught in an inexorable web of racist beliefs. I have chosen
Pearson's presentation of those beliefs as typical because he stated them
so clearly, and because he spoke as a distinguished scientist. Yet in all fairness, it should be noted that there was generally no rancor involved in the
views in Pearson's writings or those of his contemporaries. The trouble

with nineteenth-century scientists was that they simply did not have available to them the research in genetics and anthropology of the first half of the twentieth century, facts that would have enabled them to deduce what was wrong with the customary arbitrary typological methods in the classification of the so-called "races of mankind." Addicted to their classificatory schemes, they saw them as confirming the "natural" stratification of the castes and classes of their own society. This was comforting because, among other things, it was powerfully reinforced by the ecclesiasticism of the day.[7]

I remember, as a small boy at school, singing with some feeling, the lovely hymn, *All Things Bright and Beautiful,* the final words of which put it all in a nutshell; although it was not until many years later that I understood what they meant.

> The rich man in his castle,
> The poor man at his gate,
> God made them high or lowly,
> And ordered their estate.
> —Cecil Frances Alexander 1818–1895

Such ideas were the common currency of the descendants of Calvinistic individualism, with its doctrine of the elect, and of the Puritans with their belief in wealth as an evidence of divine grace, and poverty as a proof of moral error.

After Darwin, many scientists were no longer comfortable with the idea of the divine ordering of nature, and felt that "natural selection" was a more efficient notion. Pearson was a firm believer in "natural selection," and his writings had a considerable influence well into the twentieth century, typifying the work and thinking of virtually every authority on the subject of "race." Here, then, are Pearson's views on "the races of mankind":

'The whole earth is mine, and no one shall rob me of any corner of it,' is the cry of civilized man. No nation can go its own way and deprive the rest of mankind of its soil and its mineral wealth, its labour-power and its culture—no nation can refuse to develop its mental or physical resources—without detriment to civilization at large in its struggle with organic and inorganic nature. It is not a matter of indifference to other nations that the intellect of any people shall lie fallow, or that any folk should not take its part in the labour of research. It cannot be indifferent to mankind as a whole whether the occupants of a country leave its fields untried and its natural resources undeveloped. It is a false view of human solidarity, a weak humanitarianism, which regrets that a capable and stalwart race of white men should replace a dark-skinned tribe which can neither utilize its land to the full benefit of mankind, nor contribute its quota to the common stock of human knowledge.[8]

This passage is followed by a footnote which reads: "This sentence must not be taken to justify a brutalizing destruction of human life. The anti-social effects of such a mode of accelerating the effects of the survival of the fittest may go far to destroy the preponderating fitness of the survivor. At the same time there is cause for human satisfaction in the replacement of the aborigines throughout America and Australia by white races of far higher civilization."

The best comment on this, I believe, was made at the time by one of Pearson's contemporaries in England, Alice James, the remarkable sister of William and Henry James, and like the latter permanently settled in England, who in February 1890 wrote in her diary of the English "profound ineradicable in the bone and sinew conviction that outlying regions are their preserves, that they alone of human races massacre savages out of pure virtue, it would ill-become an American to reflect upon the treatment of aboriginal races, but I never heard it suggested that our hideous dealings with the Indians was brotherly love masquerading under the guise of pure cussedness."[9]

Pearson's rigid application of the doctrine of the "survival of the fittest"—not Darwin's phrase, but Herbert Spencer's—and his "satisfaction in the replacement of the aborigines throughout America and Australia by white races of far higher civilization," may today make us shudder at its inhumanity and wrongheadedness, but in a very real sense the Victorian age was devastatingly inhuman. Pearson inherited a full share of its insensitivities. In his day the great divide was between the privileged and the poor or "the lower orders of society," as they were called, whose poverty and dreadful birth and mortality rates, were considered sins for which they were being punished.[10] It was therefore not difficult for thinkers like Pearson to apply such views to the extinction of the majority of the indigenous cultures not only of America, but of all the Americas, as well as to the aborigines of Australia and Tasmania, in which the extermination was virtually complete.

Reflecting upon the imminent extinction of the Tasmanian aborigines in 1836, the Reverend Thomas Atkins wrote, "Indeed, from a large induction of the facts, it seems to be a universal law in the Divine government, when savage tribes who live by hunting, fishing, and on the wild herbs, roots, and fruits of the earth, come into collision with civilized races of men . . . the savage tribes disappear before the progress of civilized races."[11]

And there we have it, the pietistic rationalization for the massacre and destruction of "savage tribes." It was clearly God's will, the divine dispensation, for were it not, He could hardly have permitted such a denouement.

And then there was Adolf Hitler, who said, "What good fortune for those in power that people do not think," who by utilizing the idolatry of "race" brought about the death and destruction of millions of innocent men, women, and children. During World War II approximately between fifteen and twenty million military personnel were killed in action, along with about twenty-five million civilians.[12]

It would take too long to tell the story of the manner in which, over the course of the years, and thanks to the work of many scientists in the biological and social sciences, I came to understand how wrong such beliefs as Pearson's were.

It was not so much through my biological and physical anthropological studies, as through my cultural anthropological ones that I began to comprehend what an important role culture—the way of life of a people—plays in producing the behavioral differences between societies. It gradually became clear to me that the most important setting of human evolution is the human social environment, and that the adaptive responses to the challenges of different environments can influence evolutionary changes through the media of mutation, natural selection, social selection, genetic drift, and hybridization. These views were first set out in *Science,* 6 June 1947,[13] by my friend Professor Theodosius Dobzhansky, a geneticist, and myself, a biosocial anthropologist. The paper, slightly revised for style, constitutes Chapter 5 of the present volume.

It was not until many years later that I found support for my conviction that everything a human being comes to know and do *as human being* has to be learned from other human beings, from the social environment.[14] Especially great support came from *The Social Construction of Reality: A Treatise in the Sociology of Knowledge* (1966) by sociologists Peter Berger and Thomas Luckmann.[15] What Berger and Luckmann showed is that everything that passes for knowledge in human society, particularly the "common sense knowledge" that constitutes the reality of everyday life, is socially determined. Following that demonstration, the authors proceeded to an equally convincing analysis of society as a dialectical process between objective and subjective reality.

In such a society one may readily understand how the unreal may often become more real than the real, a case in point being the idea of "race." In this connection one may recall Stephen Ullmann's remark, "Words certainly are the vehicles of our thoughts, but they may be far more than that: they may acquire an influence of their own, shaping and pre-determining our processes of thinking and our whole outlook."[16]

In pursuing the study of "race" my purpose has been not to prove or disprove anything, but to state the facts as they are; to identify error and faults; and, in the light of the evidence, to make the necessary corrections. Added to this one must, of course, discuss the significance of one's findings, conscious always that facts do not speak for themselves, but are often at the mercy of any juggler who chooses to play tricks with them, and above all bearing always in mind that falsification begins with language.

It was largely the distressing world in which I lived that sparked my interest in "race." The London of my childhood during World War I was characterized by an atmosphere of unbounded nationalistic belligerence, the shattering realities of death of loved ones, and the incomprehensibility of war. The postwar period was one of cynicism and depression. The feeling was of betrayal and abandonment, as if one had been emptied of all that one formerly believed to be the regularities of civilized life. But it was also a period of artificial gaiety, which gave one time furiously to think, among other things, about class differences, and pejorative nationalistic stereotypes. The latter, as through a glass darkly, caused me slowly to work my way toward some understanding that stereotypes and racism were inextricably related. World War II reinforced the suspicion that nationalism was but another form, even more dangerous, of racism. During what I came to see as the kleptomaniac period of imperialism, England had been engaged in expropriating other peoples' lands, usually by force and uninvited occupation, in either case the final effects, for the most part, were the same—the decimation of the indigenous peoples and the destruction of their cultures.

The gradual growth of my knowledge concerning the impact of civilized man upon so-called "primitive peoples," or "savages," validated by science and more than countenanced by the church, together with the arbitrariness and erroneousness upon which their views were based, led ultimately to the publication of the articles which together formed the first edition of *Man's Most Dangerous Myth: The Fallacy of Race* in 1942. To Julian Huxley, biologist, and Alfred Cort Haddon, physical and cultural anthropologist, I owed a great debt for the clarification of my thinking about "race" from the reading of their important and stimulating book, *We Europeans: A Survey of "Racial" Problems* (1936).[17] I owed a similar debt to Lancelot Hogben, for his chapter on "The Concept of Race," in his seminal book *Genetic Principles in Medicine and Social Science* (1931).[18] But before these books I had been greatly influenced by Franz Boas, cultural and physical anthropologist, whose writings on "race," beginning in the last decade of the nineteenth century, were made generally available in his book *The Mind of Primitive Man* (1911),[19] and subsequent editions, as well as in later books and articles on "race." Boas was one of those great scientists who never received a Nobel Prize. It would be difficult to think of anyone who was more worthy of that kind of recognition for his contribution to the understanding of the diversity and the cultural and physical development of humankind.

The first work I read on "race," began with a most unlikely title, *Christianity and the Race Problem*,[20] by J. H. Oldham, Secretary of the International Missionary Council, published by the Student Christian Movement, London, in May 1924. Highly informative, the book impressed me greatly for its humanity and reasonableness, while its Christianity was not in the least obtrusive. It is the kind of book that is worth rereading from time to time for the sheer pleasure of the author's fine mind. Beautifully written as it is, it remains one of the most quotable of books, and its influence stays with me to this day.

Now for some words concerning the sixth edition of *Man's Most Dangerous Myth: The Fallacy of Race*. It seems to me that the myth, the danger, and the fallacy remain, there are more people today who understand that racism is wrong, that there is no right way to do what is wrong, and that what is morally wrong cannot be politically right. But there are also more racists today than ever. This includes the morally apathetic as well as the active racists consisting largely of the generality of people, the least educated being the most racist. Today we are also faced with the new phenomenon of black leaders who, having learned from Hitler how well racism works, incite their people against "the enemy," "the Jews."

It is understandable in the light of the unspeakable wrongs that have been committed, and continue to be committed, against blacks, that many blacks should so easily fall victim to the demagoguery of unscrupulous leaders. Yet, it is sadly ironic to have to note that it has largely fallen to the lot of Jews to be the most earnest defenders of the rights of blacks, as well as the most active workers in the struggle to secure those rights. Jews have created foundations devoted exclusively to assist blacks to achieve their rights, and have helped in numerous other ways, in organizations or as individuals to break through the formidable wall of prejudice.

How can one forget that the friend and most active collaborator of the great black leader, W. B. Du Bois, in the founding of the National Association for the Advancement of Colored People, was an American Jew? Joel Spingarn, a charming personality who, at about this time, had resigned his professorship of comparative literature at Columbia University in protest against the wrongful dismissal of a colleague. Spingarn was a member of the Board and Chairman of the NAACP, and its most active speaker throughout the country, advancing the cause of the organization.[21] To list the foundations, funds, institutions, and benefactions created by Jews to improve the welfare of blacks would take a sizable volume.

The rise of anti-Semitism, the burning of dozens of black churches in the South, the growth of racist militias, various extremist movements, and innumerable hate groups, constitute a challenge to complacency, underscoring the urgency of understanding the nature of the "race problem." When that has been done, and more has been done than said, we may simultaneously proceed to the re-education of education, for what we have today that passes for education, is not education, but instruction, the technologization of education, a world in which we congratulate ourselves on making machines that think like human beings, mindless of the fact that for some time we have been creating human beings who think like machines. Until we understand that, and understand what needs to be done, we shall go on muddling through till we have exterminated ourselves, for we have become the most self-destructive species on this earth.

In 1920 H. G. Wells, in his magnificent work *The Outline of History*, remarked that "Human history becomes more and more a race between education and catastrophe."[22]

Since Wells wrote those words they have become even more apposite to our own times. I shall have more to say on that throughout this volume.

The unprincipled leaders of Serbia in 1991, in what has come to be known as the Yugoslav War, following the example of Hitler have, in the name of what they called "ethnic cleansing," committed the most unspeakable crimes against the Croat and Muslim populations of Bosnia and Herzegovina. Their "ethnic cleansing," which represented an extreme Nationalistic racism, permitted the Serbs to expel and massacre Croats and Muslims from Serb controlled areas, in the course of which they created some three million homeless refugees, all of them affected by the same vicious racism.

In November 1995 the Institute of Race Relations (London) published in its *European-Race Bulletin* a digest of reports on the rise of racism in thirty European countries.[23]

Clearly the demonology of "race," in its various forms, is very much with us elsewhere in the world, but no more so than in the United States. That being so it was thought that a new edition of *Man's Most Dangerous Myth* might be useful. Added to that, a number of anthropological friends felt that the book was of historic importance; and because a new generation of readers would relish savoring something of the flavor of the book that wrought some change in the thinking of anthropologists, as well as in the minds of various others, the call for a new edition seemed to be plausible. I have tried to bring the book up-to-date, and have retained most of the references which figured in the fifth edition. Some of them may appear to be out-of-date, but in fact very few, if any, of them are, for they refer to works which were built on solid ground. Bringing the book up-to-date meant casting a very wide net over the relevant literature, as the expanded bibliography will testify.

One of the great problems is that so much valuable research, discussion, debate, and works on "race" and "racism" exists—not by any means a surfeit, but in such numbers in quality so high and enlightening that it is quite impossible to read more than a fraction of them. So I take this opportunity to apologize to all those authors whose works I have been unable to read, and reference, much as I would have wished to. Time, alas, is the enemy and wounds us with its days. In any event I hope the bibliography, available in the unabridged edition, will be of use to the reader.

For the rest, the making of this new edition has been a great and refreshing, as well as a challenging adventure. I hope the reader may find the book so too.

Ashley Montagu
Princeton, New Jersey
September 1997

Notes

1. George W. Stocking, *Victorian Anthropology* (New York: The Free Press, 1987).

2. Arthur Keith, *Race and Nationality* (The Boyle Lecture, 1919), 17; Arthur Keith, *A New Theory of Human Evolution* (London: Watts, 1948).

3. Karl Pearson, *The Life, Letters and Labours of Francis Galton,* 3 vols in 4 (Cambridge: Cambridge University Press, 1914–1930).

4. Pearson, Karl, *The Grammar of Science* (London: Walter Scott, 1892), Final revised edition, (London: J. M. Dent, 1937).

5. Egon S. Pearson, *Karl Pearson: An Appreciation of Some Aspects of his Life and Work* (Cambridge: University Press, 1938).

6. Karl Pearson, and Margaret Moul, "The Problem of Alien Immigration into Great Britain, Illustrated by an Examination of Russian and Polish Children," *Annals of Eugenics,* vol. 1 (1925): 5–91, 126–7.

7. This was the period when Oxford and Cambridge were referred to as seminaries of the Church of England. It was not until 1871 that an Act of Parliament was passed abolishing the requirement to subscribe to any article or formulary of faith before reading for a degree.

8. Karl Pearson, *The Grammar of Science* (Everyman edition), 310.

9. Alice James, *The Diary of Alice James,* edited by Leon Edel (New York: Dodd, Mead, 1964), 88.

10. Patricia James, *Thomas Malthus: His Life and Times,* (London: Routledge & Kegan Paul, 1979), 130 sq.; [Joseph Townsend), *A Dissertation on the Poor Laws: By a Well-Wisher to Mankind* (London: C. Dilly, 1786). Reprinted with Foreword by Ashley Montagu. and Afterword by Clark Neuman (Berkeley: University of California Press, 1971).

11. Clive Turnbull, *Black War: The Extermination of the Tasmanian Aborigines* (Melbourne: F. W. Cheshire, 1948); Lyndall Ryan, *The Aboriginal Tasmanians* (Vancouver: University of British Columbia Press, 1953); H. Ling Roth, *The Aborigines of Tasmania* (Halifax, England, F. King & Sons, 1899); Alfred W. Crosby, Jr., *The Columbian Exchange: Biological and Cultural Consequences of 1492* (Westport, CT: Greenwood, 1972), Robert Hughes, *The Fatal Shore: The Epic of Australia's Founding*

(New York: Alfred A. Knopf, 1987); Alan Moorhead, *The Fatal Impact: An Account of the Invasion of the South Pacific* 1767–1840 (New York: Harper & Row, 1966); W. H. R. Rivers, ed., *Essays on the Depopulation of Melanesia* (Cambridge: Cambridge University Press, 1922); Lloyd Robson, *A History of Tasmania* (Melbourne: Oxford University Press, 1983); C. D. Rowley, *The Destruction of Aboriginal Society*, vol. 1 (Canberra: Australian National University Press, 1970); C. D. Rowley, *Outcasts in White Australia*, vol. 2 (Canberra: Australian National University Press, 1971); C. D. Rowley, *The Remote Aborigines*, vol. 3 (Canberra: Australian National University Press, 1971); Gary Witherspoon, *Language and Art in the Navajo Universe* (Ann Arbor: University of Michigan Press, 1977).

12. Louis L. Snyder, *World War II*, Academic American Encyclopedia, vol. 29 (Danbury, CT 1996), 280.

13. Theodosius Dobzhansky, and Ashley Montagu, "Natural Selection and the Mental Capacities of Mankind," *Science* 105 (1947): 587–90.

14. Ashley Montagu, *The Direction of Human Development*, 2nd ed. (New York: Hawthorn Books, 1970); Geoffrey Cowley, "It's Time to Rethink Nature and Nurture," *Newsweek*, 27 March 1955, 52–53.

15. Peter L. Berger, and Thomas Luckmann, *The Social Construction of Reality: A Treatise in the Sociology of Knowledge* (London: Penguin Press 1967).

16. Stephen Ullmann, "The Prism of Language," *The Listener* (London), 22 July 1954, 131–132.

17. Julian S. Huxley, and Alfred C. Haddon, *We Europeans: A Survey of "Racial" Problems* (New York: Harper & Bros. 1936).

18. Lancelot Hogben, "The Concept of Race," in his book *Genetic Principles in Medicine and Social Science* (London: Williams & Norgate, 1931), 122–124.

19. Franz Boas, *The Mind of Primitive Man* (New York: Macmillan, 1911, 1924, 1938); Franz Boas, *Race, Language and Culture* (Macmillan, 1940).

20. J. H. Oldham, *Christianity and the Race Problem* (London: Student Christian Movement, 1925).

21. David L. Lewis, *W. E. B. Du Bois: Biography of a Race* (New York: Henry Holt, 1993).

22. H. G. Wells, *The Outline of History* (London: Newnes, 1920).

23. Institute of Race Relations (London): *European Race Audit Bulletin No. 16*, November 1995.

1

The Origin of the Concept of Race

The idea of "race" represents one of the most dangerous myths of our time, and one of the most tragic. Myths are most effective and perilous when they remain unrecognized for what they are. Many of us are happy in the complacent belief that myths are what uncivilized people believe in, but of which we ourselves are completely free. We may realize that a myth is a faulty explanation leading to social delusion and error, but we do not necessarily realize that we ourselves share in the mythmaking faculty with all people of all times and places, or that each of us has his own store of myths derived from the traditional stock of the society in which we live, and are always in ready supply. In earlier days we believed in magic, possession, and exorcism; in good and evil supernatural powers; and until recently we believed in witchcraft. Today many of us believe in race. Race is the witchcraft, the demonology of our time, the means by which we exorcise imagined demoniacal powers among us. It is the contemporary myth, humankind's most dangerous myth, America's Original Sin.[1]

In our own time we have lived to see the myth of race openly adopted by governments as an expedient fiction. Myths perform the double function of serving both as models of and models for cultural attitudes and behavior. Thus myths reflect the beliefs and give sanction to the actions of society, while at the same time providing the forms upon which belief and conduct are molded. Built, as they are, into the structure of social relationships, racial myths often have a force which exceeds even that of reality itself, for such myths, in addition to the social encouragement they receive, draw upon both false biology and even worse theology for their sustenance. As Calas has said, myths are idealizations of social conditions, so that with regard to the matter of inequality, the main function of myths is to explain the origin of differences in ways that satisfy the needs of the group.[2] In short, the functional role of the myth is to provide a sanction for a course of action. Myths that account for social differences correspond to,

41

and often have the force of, legal fictions, while legalistic attempts to justify the status quo endow the myth with an aura of historical sanctity. As such, myths are almost impervious to rational thought, for it is the nature of myth to be elaborated, but never proved. Myths, therefore, are of great value since they make thinking, as a problem-solving exercise, unnecessary.

The monstrous myths that have captured the emotions of people and shackled their minds still afflict the minds of millions in so-called civilized societies. The ambiguities and uncritical use of our language give rise to ambiguities of their own and constitute the compost upon which myths proliferate and are sustained. In the reality of the mythologies which every society creates for itself, the unreal becomes more real than the real, ritual investing them with an importance that renders them sacred. Developing as they do, myths achieve an integrity, a validity, a power, which is quite impregnable to any attempted demonstration of the unreliability of their component parts. We realize that many people have different investments in their beliefs, that humans are governed more by emotion, custom, and precedent, than by logic and reason, that errors and illusions, serving some explanatory purpose, frequently become endemic myths shared in common in the world of unreason and political fantasy. Myths that at one time may have served a socially useful purpose may live on into a time when they have not only become useless, but thoroughly baneful, decayed, degraded, and degrading. As Paul Gaston has said, in his admirable book, *The New South Creed,*

> Myths are not polite euphemisms for falsehoods, but are combinations of images and symbols that reflect a people's way of perceiving truth. Organically related to a fundamental reality of life, they fuse the real and the imaginary into a blend that becomes a reality itself, a force in history.[3]

And as George Tindall put it, charged with values, aspirations, ideals and meanings,

> Myths may become the ground for either loyalty and defense on the one hand or hostility on the other. In such circumstances, a myth itself becomes one of the realities of history, significantly influencing the course of human action, for good or ill. There is, of course, always a danger that in ordering one's vision of reality, the myth may predetermine the categories of perception, rendering one blind to things that do not fit into the mental image.[4]

The function performed by myths is akin to that of religion, namely, the unification and intelligibility of experience. Racism often has its roots in religion, and like religion, can easily be accommodated to many diverse situations.[5]

The belief in race, as in Nazi Germany, became a secular religion whose myths recreated reality. The systematic murder of millions of human beings in the name of race was the final expression of the hideously brutal power of racial myths, of demonological mindedness.

The power of myths and their related ideologies lies not in their objective truth but in their being perceived as true. Of the myth of race it may be said that everyone seems to know, and is only too eager to tell. All but a few persons take it completely for granted that scientists have established the "facts" about race and have long ago satisfactorily recognized and classified the races of humankind. Scientists in the past did little to discourage this view, and, indeed, in most cases were even more wrongheaded than the layman on the subject. Exalted in their citadels of infallibility, scientists by their consensus gave security and comfort to those who believed in a hierarchy of races. Under such circumstances, it is not difficult to understand why so many people continue to believe that race is a reality, a fact, that some "races" are superior to others.

A scientific fact has been defined as a collective judgment of a specialized community. But the collective judgment of the specialized community of anthropologists during the nineteenth, and well into the twentieth, century was abysmally wrong concerning the "fact" of race. For this the scientists who subscribed to the concept of race cannot be faulted, for it was a product of a social environment which, through the distorting glass of prejudice, saw people divided by caste and class, and segregated by race. In a society that segregated people by caste and class, "race" was the term that categorized the most visibly distinguishable groups of people. As Lancelot Hogben, the eminent social biologist and early critic of the concept of race, remarked in 1932:

> Geneticists believe that anthropologists have decided what a race is. Ethnologists assume that their classifications embody principles which genetic science has proved to be correct. Politicians believe that their prejudices have the sanction of genetic laws and the findings of physical anthropology to sustain them.[6]

In reality, none of them had any grounds for such beliefs other than those which emanated prejudices.

In some nations, for example in Hitler's Third Reich, the myth of race also functioned as an ideology and continues to do so most prominently in such countries as South Africa, Australia, Brazil, and the United States of America, where it has come to be known as "the great divide."

An ideology is a prescriptive doctrine or system of belief that is not supported by rational argument, and flourishes in an environment of adverse political and social conditions. An ideology often originates with a charismatic leader or elite claiming exclusive authority as representing something like revealed truth; as such, an ideology may determine the lives and conduct of a whole population, providing its members with justifications, conviction, and moral fervor for their actions, regardless of the course of events.[7]

The myth of race refers not to the fact that physically distinguishable populations of humans exist, but rather to the belief that races are populations or peoples whose physical differences are innately linked with significant differences in mental capacities, and that these innate hierarchical differences are measurable by the cultural achievements of such populations, as well as by standardized intelligence (IQ) tests. This belief is thoroughly and dangerously unsound. It is the belief of racists and racism. Caught up in the vicious circle of prejudice, words become things, things become weapons—and the more weapons one has, the more convinced one is of the right to use them. But this is to anticipate.

It was as long ago as 1848 that John Stuart Mill wrote, in his *Principles of Political Economy,* "Of all the vulgar modes of escaping from the consideration of the effect of social and moral influences on the human mind, the most vulgar is that of attributing the diversities of conduct and character to inherent natural differences."[8] And even more forcibly, twenty-five years later in 1873, in his *Autobiography,* Mill wrote,

> I have long felt that the prevailing tendency to regard all the marked distinctions of human character as innate, and in the main indelible, and to ignore the irresistible proofs that by far the greater part of those differences, whether between individuals, races, or sexes, are such as not only might but naturally would be produced by differences in circumstances, is one of the chief hindrances to the rational treatment of great social questions, and one of the greatest stumbling blocks to the human improvement.[9]

Another political economist, Walter Bagehot, in 1869, similarly wrote: "When a philosopher cannot account for anything in any other manner, he boldly ascribes it to an occult quality in some race."[10]

Writing in 1915, Lord Bryce, author of *The American Commonwealth,* put the matter clearly: "No branches of historical inquiry," he wrote,

> have suffered more from fanciful speculation than those which relate to the origin and attributes of the races of mankind. The differentiation of these races began in prehistoric darkness, and the more obscure a subject is, so much the more fascinating. Hypotheses are tempting, because though it may be impossible to verify them, it is, in the paucity of data, almost equally impossible to refute them.[11]

Such views in the course of the years have had their effects, but nothing like the effect that the persisting myth of race has had upon the ignorant and the ill-educated. Taking it for granted that different populations could be classified into distinct groups—so-called "races"—anthropologists, on the basis of such differences as head shape, hair form, skin color, and similar traits drew up long lists of races. It was a game the classifiers played in all seriousness as if it were anything other than the postprandial indulgence it was, and the compilations of races that resulted numbered from half a dozen to two hundred.[12] Though taken seriously for a time were, these lists were ultimately a complete failure, primarily because they were based on a fundamental misconception of the nature and variability—and intractability—of the materials they attempted to put into some kind of order.

It was easy to see that an African black and a blonde Swede must have had a somewhat different biological history, and the difference in appearance considered sufficient to distinguish them as belonging to two different races. In biology a "race" has been customarily defined as a subdivision of a species that inherits physical characteristics distinguishing it from other populations of the species. By that definition then, do not "Blacks" and Swedes belong to different races? The answer, as we shall see, is that even in terms of the biological definition, they do not.

Is there a "black" race, or a Swedish race? There is not, any more than that there is a "white" race, a "yellow" race, or a "red" race. Both "black" and "Swede" are collective terms which lump together groups and individuals who differ from each other in physical and often in cultural traits. Furthermore, the variability in physical traits *within* any population is usually greater than it is *between* populations, while even more interesting and significant is the strikingly small number of gene differences between such populations, a fact evident in the gradational or climal variability which characterizes the populations of humankind.

For example, Richard Lewontin, professor of genetics at Harvard University, has carried out a most important investigation of genetic diversity in the human species. Taking the blood groups and various enzymatic traits for which the genetics is known, by means of a mathematical-genetic analysis Lewontin found that the mean proportion was 85.4 percent. The difference between populations within a race accounted for less than 8.3 percent, so that only 6.3 percent is accounted for by racial classification. Lewontin concludes,

> It is clear that our perception of relatively large differences between human races and subgroups, as compared to the variation within these groups, is indeed a biased perception and that, based on randomly chosen genetic differences, human races and populations are remarkably

similar to each other, with the largest part by far of human variation being accounted for by the differences between individuals.

Human racial classification is of no social value and is positively destructive of social and human relations. Since such racial classification is
now seen to be of virtually no genetic or taxonomic significance either, no
justification can be offered for its continuance.[13]

Such facts render the concept of race and the continuance of race classification erroneous and obsolescent—important subjects we shall discuss
in detail. For such reasons, among others, modern biologists find that the
use of the concept of race should be discontinued.[14]

The truth is that the "deceptively clear label," as Lucien Febvre called
the concept of race,[15] obscures and renders divisible what is indivisible.
This is not to say that there are no genetic or physical differences between
various populations, but it is to say that they are by no means as large or significant as most scientists once supposed. Misleading simplifications em-
bodied in word-labels, especially when they are given the respectability of
long-usage and established authority, tend to be accepted uncritically, and
do not constitute a substitution for critical examination and. We must constantly be on our guard against subscribing to a lexicon of unsound terms
of which we elect ourselves the guardians, and make ourselves the prisoners of our own vocabularies.

In the biological sense there do, of course, exist distinctive human
populations that exhibit an interesting variety of physical differences.
These differences are superficial, and far fewer in number than the traits
we have in common. It is well to remember that what makes us alike is very
much more important than what makes us different. In a racist society
which segregates people by race and divides them by class, in which exclusiveness is the unstated rule, it is not surprising that the classifiers would,
often without being aware of it, bring their class-structured ways of thinking to the classifications of the "races of mankind." The consciousness of
class and classificatory schemes were closely related. Embedded in this, of
course was the tacit assumption that with the biological ranking there naturally went a socio-cultural grading, which combined with the physical ranking, from "high" to "low," or superiority to inferiority, enabled one to assign populations and individuals to their "proper" levels. "The higher
races" were "superior," and "the lower races" were "inferior." In this way
was established the basic axiom of physical anthropology, namely, the belief that distinctive human characteristics and abilities are determined by
race, a view that was and is essentially racist. Since the meaning of a word is
the action it produces, this was racism.

Racism is conduct based on the belief that physical and behavioral differences characterizing individual members of different groups or popula-

tions are determined by genetic, that is, innate factors, and that these differences enable one to rank each individual and group in the scale of humanity according to the attributed predefined values of those differences. The implication is that in such individuals and groups the genes that are supposed to determine their physical traits, such as skin color, hair form, head shape, and the like, are linked with the genes that determine the qualities and limits of their mental capacities or abilities, and that linked with these traits is the ability of the population or group to achieve a high level of civilization. Thus, three criteria are involved in the racist view: (1) physical traits, (2) mental capacities and abilities, and (3) the ability to achieve a high level of civilization. To put it briefly, the racist believes that physical characteristics, capacity, and creativity, are genetically related, fixed and unchangeable. He may never have formulated his belief in these words but in this own mind, however, vaguely this is what it amounted to.

This is the triad that constitutes the basic belief of the racist, and it is entirely unsound, for there is absolutely no genetic linkage between genes for physical traits, mental capacities, or civilization-building abilities. As we shall see, human beings are born everywhere with potentialities or capacities which must be stimulated and guided by learning if they are to become abilities. A capacity is a potentiality. An ability is a trained capacity. Allowing for individual differences existing in every population, the full range of abilities that has been developed in any society—given the same opportunities for development—is within the capability of every human population, for educability is the species trait of humanity. What human beings have learned to do in any culture, human beings can anywhere learn. We shall discuss these matters more fully in later pages.

Here it should be pointed out that the very word "race" is itself a racist term not simply because it represents a congeries of errors, or that it is a spurious "reality" with no objective existence, but in addition, and most importantly, because its baleful influence constitutes a threat to the very existence of humanity, much of which has already vanished as a direct result of racism. In a large number of cases it has led to wars and unjustifiable conquests, costing the lives of many millions, and the destruction of untold numbers together with their cultures in their own homelands. Such destructive conduct continues to the present day in North and South America, Australia, Africa, India, Sri Lanka, Ethiopia, the Middle East, the Philippines, in Poland, the Balkans, and the former USSR, now Russia and the independent republics of Eastern Europe and Northern Asia.

To summarize then, humankind may be regarded as comprising of a number of populations or peoples the members of which often differ physically and superficially from one another. These differences have come about as a result of the long isolation of such populations during which the physical differences have evolved. The cultural differences have come about as the result of differences in the history of experience to which each population has adaptively responded. Both the physical and the cultural differences are neither fixed nor permanent, but are subject to change. We see this occurring very rapidly when boundaries that formerly separated people are reduced and populations come into contact. In spite of occasional appearances to the contrary, humanity is moving toward unity without uniformity, toward the condition in which the differences that today separate humanity will be regarded as points of interest and value, not as excuses for fear and discrimination, but as no more important than the differences which separate the members of the same family.

The classificatory definition of humanity as *Homo sapiens,* properly interpreted, is appropriate because it gives quite accurate status to a unique class of creatures—human beings—characterized by an educability, a capacity for wisdom and intelligence approached by no other creature. These traits, *not* the external physical traits constitute the principal, the distinctive qualities, that make *Homo sapiens* human. When human beings are defined on the basis of the differences in physical traits we narrow the definition of their humanity. And that is, perhaps, the most telling criticism of the concept of race.

It is nŏt that the classifiers of race were uninfluenced by their awareness of the cultural status of the groups they were classifying, ostensibly on the basis of their physical characters, for they could hardly have avoided introducing their prejudices when comparing the physical traits of "primitive" peoples with those of "civilized" peoples.

Even the term "civilized" has become a racist term because it has acquired the meaning that "civilized" people are superior, more advanced, than uncivilized peoples, that the "scale" of being is yet another racist term, for what it represents is a survival of a time when animals and humans were arranged on "the scale of nature" on the rungs of a ladder with the "higher" occupying the "highest," and the lower occupying the "lowest" position. All the peoples of Western Europe are arbitrarily bracketed with the same loosely-termed "Caucasoid major group," and the populational variability within this group simply represents small local differences arising from their circumscribed inbreeding or crossbreeding with members of adjacent populations. In Eastern Europe, among the Slavic-speaking peoples, the influence of "Mongoloid" admixture is to this day discernible in a number of them, even those far removed from the geographic habitat of the "Mongoloids." But this admixture does not make such Slavic-speaking peoples members of a distinct race. In Russia and in Poland, as in America, there are many different local types of men, but the majority of these belong to the white or "Caucasoid major group" of humans.

In Russia and Poland some are more or less obviously of Mongoloid origin, and in America some are clearly of black origin, but in both countries it is often difficult to say whether a person is of one major group or another. It is frequently just such difficulties as these that render it impossible to make the sort of racial classifications some anthropologists and others have attempted.[16] The fact is that all human beings are so much mixed with regard to origin that between different groups of individuals intergradation and "overlapping" of physical traits is the rule. It is for this reason, among others, that it is difficult to draw up more than a few hard and fast distinctions between even the most extreme types. As Huxley and Haddon have remarked,

> The essential reality of the existing situation . . . is not the hypothetical sub-species or races, but the mixed ethnic groups, which can never be genetically purified into their original components, or purged of the variability which they owe to past crossing. Most anthropological writings of the past and many of the present fail to take account of this fundamental fact.[17]

We may describe *ethnic group* here as follows: An ethnic group represents part of a population in process of undergoing genetic and socially, genetically unrelated, cultural differentiation, it is a group of individuals capable of hybridizing genetically and culturally with other groups to produce further genetic and cultural differentiation.

The classifiers of the races of mankind who have devised the various classificatory schemes during the past hundred years have mostly agreed in one respect—they have unexceptionally taken for granted the one thing which they were attempting to prove, namely, the existence of human races. Commencing with the assumption that "extreme" *types* of humankind, such as "Negro," "White," and "Mongol," could clearly be recognized as races, they proceeded to refine these grosser classifications by attempting to fit local groups of humans into similar racial schemes. Thus, to take a striking example, the late Professor Carleton Coon in his monumental two volumes *The Origin of Races* (1962) and *The Living Races of Man* (1965), created a large number of new European races and subraces upon the basis, principally, of slight differences in the physical traits of the head exhibited by different groups of Europeans, and this in spite of the fact that it has been repeatedly shown that the form of the head is not as constant a character as was at one time supposed.[18] It is true that some biologists have seen fit to create new subraces among lower animals on the basis of such single slight characters as differences in pigmentation of the hair on a part of the tail. Such a procedure would be perfectly justifiable if it were taxonomically helpful. Nor would it be necessary to stipulate that animals in other groups shall not exhibit this character, but one would have to insist that almost all members of one or both sexes of the new subrace shall exhibit it. No such requirement is fulfilled by the races and subraces that Coon created.[19] Coon simply assumed that within any group a certain numerical preponderance of heads of specified diameters and, let us say, noses of a certain form and individuals of a certain stature, are sufficient to justify the creation of a new race or "subrace." Few biologists would consider such a procedure justifiable, and there are few anthropologists who would. Yet this kind of overzealous taxonomy, which has its origin principally in the desire to force facts to fit preexisting theories, does not even require the sanction of facts to be put forward as such. In this sense the concept of race represents one of the worst examples we know of a viewpoint which from the outset begs the whole question. Anderson[20] has offered a practical example, which is quite typical of the way in which populations have in the past been classified by rule of thumb or authority in the most arbitrary manner. The Sami, a "Caucasoid" people, formerly referred to as Lapps, have for almost two centuries been forced into the mythical status of "Mongoloids," because in 1795, the father of physical anthropology, Johann Gottfried Blumenbach, said that they belonged to "the Mongolian variety."[21]

As Anderson remarks,

> In this day when scientists are entering precipitously into world council chambers, the history of Lapp racial classification reminds us anew that even venerable conclusions or the opinions of experts may be no more than scientific myths, perhaps useful in the development of ideas, but irresponsible bases for policy or administration.[22]

The very failure of ambitious anthropological attempts at classification strongly suggests that human populations do not, in fact, exist in anything like the embodiment the classifiers have given them. Indeed, all such attempts have been defeated by the intractability of the variability they sought to discipline.

For the purposes of convenience in referring to aggregates of humankind characterized by a relatively high frequency of distinctive physical traits, it has been the custom to refer to "Blacks," "Whites" or "Caucasoids," and "Mongoloids." These aggregates have been called "major groups," and in so calling them there has been no implication of a hierarchic difference in either physical or mental capacities. However, because the term "major" suggests some sort of superiority, it is better to use the term "extended," which rather more closely approaches the reality, for the extended groups are widely distributed and do not constitute an assemblage occupying a common territory. The populations that are part of the extended groups are best referred to as *ethnic groups*.[23]

The use of the term "extended group" is purely arbitrary and is merely calculated to indicate that the likenesses in certain traits exhibited by the members of some populations appear to link them in some respects more closely than to other populations. Nothing more is implied in the term than that.

Within the four extended groups of humans there exist many local types, but most of these local types are much mixed, so that only in a relatively small number of cases is it possible to distinguish distinctive local types or ethnic groups among them. Every honest attempt to discuss such types or ethnic groups within the larger parent groups or major groups deserves the fullest encouragement.

Truth will not be advanced by denying the existence of large population groups characterized, more or less, by distinctive inherited physical traits. Such physical differences are found in geographic and genetic populations of animals and plants in a state of nature, and in many varieties of domestic animals and cultivated plants. They are, to a certain extent, also found in the human species, but in a much more fluid condition, since human biological development and diversification has proceeded upon quite different lines from that of animals and plants. With the exception of the domesticated animals and plants, few if any other living forms have had a comparable history of migration and hybridization, and this is the fundamentally important fact to be remembered when comparisons are made between humans and other living forms. Not one of the "major groups" is unmixed, nor is any one of its ethnic groups pure; all are, indeed, much mixed and of exceedingly complex descent. Nor is there any scientific justification for overzealous or emotional claims that any one of them is in any way superior to another.

As Darwin put it a century ago,

> Although the existing races of man differ in many respects, as in color, hair, shape of skull, proportions of the body, &c., yet if their whole structure be taken into consideration they are found to resemble each other closely in a multitude of points. Many of these are of so unimportant or of so singular a nature, that it is extremely improbable that they should have been independently acquired by aboriginally distinct species or races. The same remark holds good with equal or greater force with respect to the numerous points of mental similarity between the most distinct races of man.[24]

The differences between the four extended groups of humans and between the ethnic groups they comprise merely represent a distribution of variations which, for reasons that may be fairly clearly understood, occur more frequently in one group than they do in another. We shall deal with these reasons later. Laughlin, who uses the term "race" as a synonym for population, points out that such populations are simply groups between which restricted gene flow has taken place.[25]

It has already been stated that in biological usage a race has been conceived as a subdivision of a species that inherits the physical characteristics serving to distinguish it from other populations of the species. In the genetic sense a race has been defined as a population that differs in the incidence of certain genes from other populations, one or more genes of which it is exchanging or is potentially capable of exchanging across whatever boundaries (usually geographical) that may separate them.[26] If we are asked whether in this sense there exist a fair number of ethnic groups in the human species, the answer is that there do. It is, however, more than questionable whether such a narrow definition of an ethnic group can be profitably employed in relation to humankind. Furthermore, this is not the sense in which racists and many race classifiers employ the term. For them race represents a unity of physical, mental, personality, and cultural traits which determines the behavior of the individuals inheriting this alleged interconnection. Nowhere was this false creed of the racist more exploited than in Nazi Germany from 1933 to 1945, with fatal consequences for millions of human beings.

The foundation upon which the Nazi view of humanity was based was the concept of race. Let us see, as a typical example, what a leading exponent of Nazi "race science," Dr. Lothar G. Tirala, had to say upon this subject. Writing in 1935, he begins by asserting that it is "a well-grounded view that it is highly probable that different human races originated independently of one another and that they evolved out of different species of apemen. The so-called main races of mankind are not races, but species."[27] Far from being "well-grounded," this is a view which no biologist and no anthropologist with whom I am familiar would accept.[28] It was generally agreed then as it is today that all humans belong to the same species, that all were probably derived from the same ancestral stock, and that all share in a common heritage.

Dr. Tirala's principal argument was that "the voice of blood and race operates down to the last refinements of thought and exercises a decisive influence on the direction of thought." Hence, "race science" proves that there exist irreconcilable differences in soul, mind, and blood between the numerous races which German "race scientists" have recognized. And, of course, that the German, or "Aryan," race was "superior," the "master race." Precisely similar views were expounded by a well-known German anthropologist in a work published in 1951.[29]

As early as 1931 Ludwig Schemann, professor of physical anthropology at the University of Freiburg put the matter very simply when he wrote that "race defines a definite physical type which is common to a larger national and tribal circle of men, and maintains itself by hereditary descent . . . Race is the alpha and omega of the life of nations in its entirety."[30]

In an article, published in 1939, entitled "Race: A Basic Concept in Education," Alfred Baeumler, a leading Nazi "philosopher," clearly presented the racist conception of the individual. "History," he wrote,

> has shown, and daily shows anew, that man can be trained to be nothing that he is not genuinely, and from the beginning, in the depths of his being; against this law, neither precept, warning, punishment, nor any other environmental influence avails. Realism in the study of man does not lie in attributing evil tendencies to him, but in recognizing that all that man can do emerges in the last resort from himself, from his innate qualities.[31]

Herr Baeumler modestly describes this as thinking "Copernically" when most others so far as such matters are concerned are still thinking "Ptolemaically"—an unfortunate slip on the part of Herr Baeumler, in view of the fact that Copernicus belonged to an allegedly "subhuman race," for Copernicus was Polish.

In 1933 the professor of New Testament at the University of Tubingen, Gerhard Kittel, welcomed National Socialism as "a renewal movement based on a Christian moral foundation," an antidote to the decadence and immorality of the Weimar republic. In a public lecture he delivered on "The Jewish Question," Kittel defended Hitler's anti-Semitic legislation, on the ground, among other things, that the Scriptures themselves teach such rejection. By rejecting Christ the Jews had themselves incurred rejection.[32]

Divine sanction for "purity of race" was most forcefully expressed by Hitler's fanatical Christian supporters, the Deutsch Christen, who described race, nationality, and nation, as "orders of life given and entrusted to us by God." God's law required them to resist all admixture, "the danger of racial mixture and bastardization."

The Nazi view of race, in all its starkness, could not have been more succinctly described than in a thesis by Hans Puvogel in 1936. In his discussion of the precepts of the Nazi Party, Puvogel wrote,

> The guideline for German criminal law in the future is recognizing the idea of race, which is the basis of the National Socialist conception of life.
>
> An individual's worth in the community is measured by his racial personality. Only a racially valuable person has a right to exist within the community. Someone who is useless for the community because of his inferiority, or even harmful to it, is to be eliminated.[33]

There is a certain irony in the fact that in later years, under Hitler, Hans Puvogel became the Justice Minister of the State of Lower Saxony, and did not resign his post until March 1978, on the grounds that although he had "no Nazi past," he did not wish to embarrass West Germany's Christian Democratic Party.

A new twist was added to the idea of race by Señor Perón, the dictator of Argentina. On 12 October 1947, in a speech on the "Day of Race," he put Argentina right on the side of Torquemada. On that occasion he said:

> For us, race is not a biological concept. For us, it is something spiritual. It constitutes a sum of the imponderables that make us what we are and impel us to be what we should be, through our origin and through our destiny. It is that which dissuades us from falling into the imitation of other communities whose natures are foreign to us. For us, race constitutes our personal seal, indefinable and irrefutable.

Lest it be thought that these mystical and mythical conceptions of race are a peculiarity of the Germans, we may turn to what a Greek professor of anthropology, John Koumaris, wrote in a respected English anthropological journal in the year 1948.

> The Greek race has almost uniform physical characteristics, physical and psychical, inherited in its descendants, it has all the characteristics of the basic elements, which are all Greek and indigenous in spite of the variety of types. If the British, for instance, with their various nuclei, form one race,[34] the Greeks have a greater right to be so considered. This race is distinguished today by a kind of 'fluid constancy,' with its own soul and especially with its own variety, dating from prehistoric times. Races exist and will continue to exist; and each one defends itself. Because every infusion of new 'blood' is something different and because children of mixed parents belong to no race, the Greek race, as all others, has to preserve its own 'fluid constancy' by avoiding mixture with foreign elements.
>
> The Greek race was formed under the Acropolis Rock, and it is impossible for any other to keep the keys of the sacred rock, to which the Greek Soul is indissolubly linked.[35]

The racist views presented in the above sampling represent those held by untold numbers of every kind, and with varying degrees of virulence are to be encountered in almost every civilized land in the world.

In America discrimination against Blacks is of long standing. No American needs to be told that racism is scarcely moribund in the United States. He may, however, be surprised to learn that at the present day there are in the United States over one thousand organizations, more than one hundred of them on a national basis, whose declared purpose is the suppression of "foreigners." In addition there are a large number of hate groups that operate out of private homes and are secretly organized, and others that are actively violent and dangerous.[36]

In the legislatures of the United States there has been a long tradition of actively open and clandestine racist members. The truth is, of course, that racism is endemic in the United States, and affects every one of its institutions, including its churches, which have a shameful record in their failure to speak out against racism, even when their own ministers were actively promoting it.[37] The demonological mindedness of the average American remains a psychosis and an outrage, the social costs of which are beyond calculation.

American writers such as Lothrop Stoddard, Madison Grant, Henry Fairfield Osborn, Ruggles Gates, Henry Garrett, and Carleton Putnam have freely espoused racist views of the most reactionary kind. Osborn, in his preface to Madison Grant's widely read book, *The Passing of the Great Race* (1921), writes,

> Race has played a far larger part than either language or nationality in moulding the destinies of men; race implies heredity, and heredity implies all the moral, social, and intellectual characteristics and traits which are the springs of politics and government.[38]

By the simple device of identifying biological traits with cultural or social traits, Osborn was able to make "hereditary" the carrier and determinant of both. As Chorover has said of sociobiologists,

> When they attempt to 'explain' why people behave in a certain way, they do not generally examine the structure of their own society but rather make an effort to graft selected patterns of behavior onto a biological core. In this way the selected pattern can be made to appear as if it results not from modifiable social conditions but from fixed biological causes. The effect of such 'explanations', of course, is implicitly to justify a given form of behavior by locating its origins outside the social order.[39]

Endlessly shuffled and reshuffled, the typical statement of the racist position is that something called "race" is the prime determiner of all the important traits of body and soul, of character and personality, of human beings and nations. And it is further alleged that this thing called "race" is a fixed and unchangeable part of the germ plasm, which, transmitted from generation to generation, unfolds in each people as a characteristic expression of personality and culture.

The gallery of race concepts set out above has no basis in scientific or any other kind of demonstrable fact; these concepts are compounded of socially acquired muddy myth—the tragic myth of our era. Tragic, because it is believed and made the basis for action, in one way or another, by so many people in our time. It is principally this idea of race that is examined in the following pages.

The modern understanding of race owes its widespread diffusion mainly to the white man. Wherever he has gone he has carried it with him. The rise of racism as an endemic disorder is associated with slavery and the growing opposition to it, so that it is not until the second half of the eighteenth century that one begins to encounter its development. This is not to say that discrimination against persons or groups on the basis of skin color or difference did not exist in the ancient world. There is plenty of evidence that it did.[40] But it is to say that such views never became the officially established doctrine, upon any large scale, of any ancient society.

The ancient Egyptians considered foreigners to be rustic and uninitiated, and indeed, distinguished between themselves as "men" and Libyans or Asiatics or Africans. Not that foreigners were not human, but the Egyptian simply considered himself more human than others. However, as John A. Wilson makes clear,

> The Egyptian isolationist or nationalist feeling was a matter of geography and of manners rather than of racial theory and dogmatic xenophobia. 'The people' were those who lived in Egypt, without distinction of race or color. Once a foreigner came to reside in Egypt, learned to speak the language, and adopted Egyptian dress, he might finally be accepted as one of 'the people' and was no longer the object of superior ridicule.[41]

Libyans, Asiatics, Africans, foreigners of every kind, once they had become acculturated, could obtain Egyptian citizenship and achieve the highest positions. Indeed, they might rise to the most elevated position of all, that of the god-king who possessed the nation.[42]

Caste and class differences certainly were made the basis for discrimination in many societies, and in ancient Greece some attempt was even made to find a biological foundation for such discrimination, but this was of a limited nature and never gained general acceptance.[43] When, in the fourth century, the institution of slavery in Greece began increasingly to come under attack, it fell to Aristotle to develop the necessary theoretical bases upon which to justify its existence. His justification consists of nothing but the most ill-founded rationalizations, and shows Aristotle—as it does every man, when he rationalizes—at his weakest. The slave, Aristotle argued in the *Politics,* was but a partial man, lacking the governing element of the soul and therefore needed to be ruled by those possessing this element. In short, that some men were more fitted by nature to be slaves than others.[44]

Before Aristotle, Plato had deliberately proposed a piece of disingenuous fiction concerning the innate differences existing between men, calculated to convince the workers that there were people who by nature were better qualified to rule than they.[45] But this "Phoenician lie," as Plato called it, failed to germinate.[46] Most serious scholars are agreed that, with the exception of the lone Aristotle, while the Greeks affected to despise the barbarian, they did so on purely cultural grounds, never on biological ones.[47] The Greeks, indeed, as Isocrates (436–338 B.C.) put it, thought of Hellenism as a thing of the spirit rather than of race. "So far," he wrote, "has Athens distanced the rest of mankind in thought and in speech that her pupils have become the teachers of the rest of the world; and she has brought it about that the name 'Hellenes' is applied rather to those who share our culture than to those who share a common blood."[48] Menander (342–291 B.C.), the Attic poet and playwright, put the general feeling thus: "For me no man who is good is a foreigner. The same nature have we all, and it is character that makes men kin."

The Greeks, as also the Romans, were singularly free of anything resembling race prejudice.[49] The Roman view was succinctly put by Terrence (ca. 195–150 B.C.) the writer of comedies who had been a slave. Borrowing from Menander he wrote in a play *The Self Tormentor:* "I am a man: nothing human is alien to me." For the modern racist that sentiment takes the form of a complete turnabout, "I am a man: nothing alien is human to me."

A study of both ancient and recent cultures and literatures shows us that the conception that there are natural or biological races of humankind that differ from one another mentally as well as physically is an idea that was not developed until the latter part of the eighteenth century. In this connection, Lord Bryce, after surveying conditions in the ancient world, the Middle Ages, and modern times up to the French Revolution, arrived at the following conclusions, which he regarded as broadly true. The survey of the facts, he wrote,

> has shown us that down till the days of the French Revolution there had been very little in any country, or at any time, of self-conscious racial feeling ... however much men of different races may have striven with one another, it was seldom any sense of racial opposition that caused their strife. They fought for land. They plundered one another. . . . But strong as patriotism and national feeling might be, they did not think of themselves in terms of ethnology, and in making war for every other sort of reason never made it for the sake of imposing their own type of civilization. . . . In none of such cases did the thought of racial distinctions come to the front.[50]

The justification and divine sanction for slavery appear with the very year of its European birth. Gomes Eannes de Azurara, in his *Chronicle of the Discovery and Conquest of Guinea* (1453), for example, after commenting on the "happy" condition of the kidnapped Africans, writes,

> And so their lot was not quite contrary to what it had been; since before they had lived in perdition of soul and body; of their souls, in that they were yet pagans, without the clearness and the light of holy faith; and of

their bodies, in that they lived like beasts, without any custom of reasonable beings—for they had no knowledge of bread or wine, and they were without the covering of clothes, or the lodgement of houses; and worse than all, through the great ignorance that was in them, in that they had no understanding of good, but only knew how to live in a bestial sloth.[51]

The black skin of the African was not only ugly, but was also the symbol of moral taint and turpitude. The African was the descendant of Ham, and thus accursed, and designed to be of service to his master, the white man.[52]

Christianity has much to answer for in the development of race prejudice. As Katherine George has pointed out, "Raw nature, 'fallen' nature, which for the Greek was disorder, is for the Christian even worse: it is sin." Far from eliminating the consciousness of class, caste, and other hierarchical divisions, Christianity, she writes, "collaborated with such hierarchies and more frequently than not strengthens instead of weakening them— though it did introduce the complicating idea of a possible restatement of human relations in the society of another world. The availability of salvation to all properly indoctrinated souls alike, despite bodily inequalities" is afforded by Christianity.[53] But does this lessen prejudice? It does not. On the contrary, it extols, as morally virtuous, conduct which is, by any means, designed to bring the pagan and the infidel into the arms of the Church. The justification for slavery then takes the form of the imposition of vassalage upon the savage for the good of his soul. The modern form of race prejudice is in the direct line of descent from this medieval Christian concept of the relation of Christians to their inferiors. In 1740 David Hume, the Scottish philosopher, wrote in his *Treatise on Human Nature:*

> I am apt to suspect all negroes, and in general all other species of men . . . to be naturally inferior to the white. . . . No ingenious manufactures amongst them, no arts, no sciences. . . . Such a uniform and constant difference could not happen, in so many countries and ages, if nature had not made an original distinction between these breeds of men. Not to mention our colonies, there are negro slaves dispersed all over Europe, of which none ever discovered any symptoms of ingenuity.[54]

It was a complacent assumption which Hume shared with many others. "No ingenious manufactures . . . no arts, no sciences." It was as simple as that. And if "symptoms of ingenuity" were occasionally exhibited, they were rare enough to prove the rule. If Hume had ever looked at an African woodcarving he would have called it primitive. Had he listened to the music the slaves had brought with them from Africa he would have branded it barbarous. Had he ever heard a West African Anansi story he would undoubtedly have held it to be childish. A critic has remarked upon the comforting relief afforded the conscience by Hume's speculative observation:

The Negroes were not beasts, but neither were they quite men. They added another link to the Great Chain of Being, strengthening it. They were designed to be subordinates, with faculties proper to their station. They were meant to hew and delve, and the gentleman and his lady need have no qualms as their voices floated in from the fields or up from the kitchen. The British public could go merrily ahead rattling the coins in a full pocket and relishing the taste of sugar. And as for those who had begun agitating on the Negroes' behalf, they could spare themselves the trouble. Were the slaves to be released and hoisted out of their rank, they would quickly drop back again to where they belonged. They simply lacked the innate abilities of the whites.[55]

It is not to be thought that ethnocentrism did not exist before the eighteenth century. It did. As Katherine George has said, "To be born into a culture has generally implied being supported by it, being upheld, as it were, on a pedestal, from which one might look down with varying degrees of disinterest or antagonism upon other, alien cultures."[56] The observer of alien cultures has tended to be prejudiced in favor of his own culture, and to view the alien and unfamiliar as barbaric and inferior. The Greeks divided the world into themselves and barbarians, but with a benevolence that has not been characteristic of later societies.

From the earliest times, the emotional attitude that one's own ethnic group, nation, or culture is superior to others, has been a concomitant of virtually every culture. Within any society, in earlier times, men might be persecuted or made the object of discrimination on the grounds of differences in religion, culture, politics, or class, but never on any biological grounds such as are implied in the idea of racial differences. In Europe during the Middle Ages and also during the Renaissance the Jews, for example, were singled out for discrimination and persecution, but this was always done on social, cultural, or religious grounds. The Jews, it was urged, had killed Christ; they were accused of murdering Christian children and using their blood for ritual purposes; they were infidels, anti-Christians, usurers; they were almost everything under the sun;[57] but whatever was held against them was never attributed to clearly defined biological reasons. The racial interpretation is a modern "discovery." That is the important point to grasp. The objection to any people on racial or biological grounds is virtually a purely modern innovation. That is the basic sense in which modern group antagonism differs from that which prevailed in earlier periods. It is perfectly true that in ancient Rome, as in ancient Greece and elsewhere, the suggestion was sometimes heard that other peoples were more stupid than they and that occasionally an attempt was made to link this difference with biological factors; but this idea, at no time clearly or forcefully expressed, seems, as we have already said, never to have taken root. On the other hand, in a stratified society based upon slavery, in which birth was operatively related to social status, it can readily be understood how the notion of the biological character of social classes, as of the persons comprising them, could have originated. Yet so far as the Western world is concerned anything remotely resembling such an idea was held by no more than a handful of Greek and Roman thinkers, and never for a moment extended beyond the boundaries of their own esoteric circles. In the year 1455 by papal decree approval was given for the subjugation of infidels by Christians. The net effect of this decree was the official sanction for the enslavement of Blacks, indigenous Americans, and other "infidels," for their benefit, of course: the salvation of their souls and their admission into God's Kingdom.

It was only among peoples who had themselves for centuries been emancipated from serfdom and slavery, but who themselves kept slaves, that the hereditary or biological conception of race differences was developed. What is of the greatest interest and importance for an understanding of this matter is that the concept developed as a direct result of the trade in slaves by European merchants. It is of even greater interest and importance to note that as long as the trade was taken for granted and no one raised a voice against it, or at least a voice that was heard, the slaves, though treated as chattels, were nonetheless conceded to be human in every sense but that of attainments. This may well be seen in the treatment accorded to slaves in Portugal and Spain, where many of them rose to high positions in church and state, as was the case in ancient Greece, Rome, and Arabia. Portugal, it should be remembered, initiated the African slave trade as early as the middle of the fifteenth century. A study of the documents of the English and American slave traders down to the eighteenth century also serves to show that these men held no other conception of their victims than that by virtue of their position as slaves, or potential slaves, they were socially their captors' caste inferiors. But that was not all, for many of these hardheaded, hardbitten men recorded their belief that their victims were often quite clearly their own mental equals and superior to many at home.[58] Similarly, almost all seventeenth-century observers agree in their high opinion of the abilities and intelligence of the American Indians.[59] All that they lacked was education and instruction, wrote Father Le Jeune more than three hundred years ago:

> I naturally compare our Savages with certain villagers, because both are usually without education; though our Peasants are superior in this regard; and yet I have not seen anyone thus far, of those who have come to this country, who does not confess and frankly admit that the Savages are more intelligent than our ordinary Peasants.[60]

Indeed, it was no less a person than the discoverer of America himself, Christopher Columbus who, in his famous letter to Ferdinand and Isabella announcing his discoveries, wrote, in March, 1493, of the great friendliness of the Indians and of their "excellent and acute understanding." Columbus described them as "a loving, uncovetous people, so docile in all things that there is no better people or better country . . . They loved their neighbors as themselves and they had the sweetest and gentlest way of speaking in the world, and always with a smile."[61]

Virtually everywhere the story is the same, the intruding, uninvited Europeans being made welcome by the trusting natives. So friendly were the natives at one place off the southeast coast of Africa where Vasco da Gama's ships first anchored, that the country was named by the Portuguese Terra da Boa Gente (Land of Good People).[62]

By the middle of the sixteenth century the Spaniards had decided that these same Indians were "lazy, filthy pagans, of bestial morals, no better than dogs, and fit only for slavery, in which state alone there might be some hope of instructing and converting them to Christianity." More than two centuries later, when voices began to make themselves heard against the inhuman traffic in slaves, and when these voices assumed the shape of influential men and organizations, that, on the defensive, the supporters of slavery were forced to look about them for reasons of a new kind to controvert the dangerous arguments of their opponents. The abolitionists argued that those who were enslaved were as good human beings as those who had enslaved them. To this, by way of reply, the champions of slavery could only attempt to show that the slaves were most certainly not as good as their masters. And in this highly charged emotional atmosphere there began the doleful recitation of the catalogue of differences which were alleged to prove the inferiority of the slave to his master.[63] When they had quoted at them the clear injunction from Exodus 21:16, "And he that stealeth a man, and selleth him, or if he be found in his hand, he shall surely be put to death," the proslavers could make reply, as the South still often does today, that the "Negro" was not a man, or by twisting meaning quote Scripture against Scripture, and the Bible as their authority for slavery.[64]

I have thus far only had in mind the literature published in England during the latter half of the eighteenth century. Much of this literature found its way to the American colonies, and after the successful conclusion of the War of Independence a certain amount of controversial literature was published in this country. In France and in Holland similar works were making their appearance. It is also well to remember that it was during this period that the conception of "the noble savage" was born in France and that the romantics were not slow to capitalize upon the new-found theme in such novels as Bernardin de Saint-Pierre's *Paul et Virginie* (1788).[65] In Germany, during this period, we have such distinguished thinkers as Kant,[66] Hardenberg, Herder, Goethe, and Novalis, not to mention many others, emphasizing the unity of humankind. Herder, in particular, foresaw the danger of those loose and prejudiced utterances of the defenders of the institution of slavery, and in a memorable passage of his remarkable book *Ideen zur Philosophie der Geschichte der Menschheit*, he writes:

> I could wish the distinctions between the human species, that have been made from a laudable zeal for discriminating science, not carried beyond due bounds. Some for instance have thought fit to employ the term races for four or five divisions, originally made in consequence of country or complexion: but I see no reason for this appellation. Race refers to a difference of origin, which in this case does not exist, or in each of these countries, and under each of these complexions, comprises the most different races. . . . In short, there are neither four or five races, nor exclusive varieties, on this Earth. Complexions run into each other: forms follow the genetic character: and upon the whole, all are at last but shades of the same great picture, extending through all ages, and over all parts of the Earth. They belong not, therefore, so properly to systematic natural history, as to the psysico-geographical history of man.[67]

This was written in 1784, and I have quoted from the English translation of 1803. That Herder was able to write so clearly and sensibly was, I suspect, principally due to the publication, in 1775, by a young countryman of his, of a work entitled *De generis humani varietate* (that is to say, "On the Natural Variety of Mankind"). In this work the author, Johann Friedrich Blumenbach (1752–1840), the founder of physical anthropology, who was in his twenty-third year, in his thesis for the M.D. degree, set out to classify the varieties of humankind and to show what significance was to be attached to the differences, physical and mental, which were supposed to exist between them. He insisted at the outset that no sharp distinctions could be made between peoples. Thus, he writes:

> Although there seems to be so great a difference between widely separate nations, that you might easily take the inhabitants of the Cape of Good Hope, the Greenlanders, and the Circassians for so many different species of man, yet when the matter is thoroughly considered, you see that all do so run into one another, and that one variety of mankind does so sensibly pass into the other, that you cannot mark out the limits between them. Very arbitrary indeed both in number and definition have been the varieties of mankind accepted by eminent men.[68]

A statement which stands with quite as great force today as when it was written nearly two centuries ago.

In the greatly enlarged and revised third edition of this work, published in 1795, Blumenbach concluded that "no variety of mankind exists, whether of color, countenance, or stature, etc., so singular as not to be connected with others of the same kind by such an imperceptible transition, that it is very clear they are all related, or only differ from each other in degree." Not only did Blumenbach make clear the essential unity of humankind, but he also clearly recognized and unequivocally stated the fact that all classifications of the so-called "varieties" of mankind are arbitrary. "Still," he remarked, "it will be found serviceable to the memory to have constituted certain classes into which the men of our planet may be divided."[69]

Almost echoing the words of Blumenbach, Emerson, writing of *English Traits* in 1856, observed that:

> The individuals at the extremes of divergence in one race of men are as unlike as the wolf to the lapdog. Yet each variety shades down imperceptibly into the next, and you cannot draw the line where a race begins or ends. . . . We must use the popular category as we do the Linnaean classification, for convenience, and not as exact and final.[70]

Yet with few exceptions most writers on the subject, with complete conviction, maintained their belief in the physical and mental inferiority of Blacks.[71]

The history of physical anthropology, after the middle of the nineteenth century, may be described in terms of the gradual inversion of this genetic approach to the problem of the variety of humankind. The investigation of causes steadily gave way to the description of effects, as if the classification of humankind into as distinctive groups as possible were the proper function of a science of physical anthropology. The Darwinian conception of evolution, understood as dealing with continuous materials which, without selection, would remain unchanged, led anthropologists to believe that taxonomic exercises in the classification of humankind, both living and extinct, would eventually succeed in elucidating the relationships of the various groups of humankind to one another. We now know, however, that the materials of evolution are not continuous, but discontinuous, and that these materials are particulate, independent genes, which are inherently variable and unstable. Thus, classifications based on the shifting sands of morphological characters and physique can be extremely misleading.[72] Just how misleading may be gathered from the fact that in nature there actually exist many groups of individuals in different phyla which are distinct species in every sense but the morphological one.[73] The converse also is true, that is, individuals of the same species may exhibit morphological differences which the taxonomist would be led to assign to different specific rank. Such classificatory efforts belong to the pre-Mendelian era.[74] Then, as now, the concept of the continuity of species and the existence of transitional forms was associated with a belief in missing links. The anthropologist conceived his task to be to discover these links so that when they were all joined together we should have a complete Great Chain of Being leading from the most "primitive" to the most "advanced" forms of humans.[75] In this manner was established a racial anthropology which sought to identify some of these links among existing peoples on the basis of the physical differences that averaged groups of them were supposed to exhibit. As Linton has remarked, "unfortunately, the early guesses on these points became dogmas which still have a strong influence on the thought of many workers in this field."[76]

It may be noted here that at the beginning of the nineteenth century Cuvier had clearly foreseen the danger of such arbitrary procedures, and in the preface to his *Le Regne animal* (Paris, 1817), he explained:

> It formed no part of my design to arrange the animated tribes according to gradations of relative superiority, nor do I conceive such a plan to be practical. I do not believe that the mammalia and the birds placed last are the most imperfect of their class; still less do I think that the last of the mammiferous tribes are superior to the foremost of the feathered race or that the last of the mollusca are more perfect than the first of the annelides or zoophytes. I do not believe this to be, even if we understand the vague term perfect in the sense of 'most completely organized.' I have considered my divisions only as a scale of resemblance between the individuals classed under them. It is impossible to deny that a kind of step downward from one species to another may occasionally be observed. But this is far from being general, and the pretended scale of life, founded on the erroneous application of some partial remarks to the immensity of organized nature, has proved essentially detrimental to the progress of natural history in modern times.[77]

Throughout Blumenbach's great work and the several editions that followed the author carefully examined and rebutted, point by point, many of the arguments that had been brought forward to prove the inequality of the varieties of man, and most convincingly showed that there was no good reason to believe anything other than that they were essentially equal. Thus the treatise, which is properly regarded as having laid the foundations of the science of physical anthropology, stood foursquare for the essential relative mental and physical equality of man. The writings which such works inspired were many and important.

For example, Blumenbach's pupil, the remarkable Alexander von Humboldt (1769–1859), wrote:

> Whilst we maintain the unity of the human species, we at the same time repel the depressing assumption of superior and inferior races of men.

There are nations more susceptible of cultivation, more highly civilized, more ennobled by mental cultivation than others—but none in themselves nobler than others. All are in like degree designed for freedom; a freedom which in the ruder conditions of society belongs only to the individual, but which in social states enjoying political institutions appertains as a right to the whole body of the community.

And then Alexander quotes his brother Wilhelm, who writes:

If we would indicate an idea which throughout the whole course of history has ever more and more widely extended its empire—or which more than any other testifies to the much contested and still more decidedly misunderstood perfectibility of the whole human race—it is that of establishing our common humanity—of striving to remove the barriers which prejudice and limited views of every kind have erected amongst men, and to treat all mankind without reference to religion, nation, or color, as one fraternity, one great community, fitted for the attainment of one object, the unrestrained development of the psychical powers. This is the ultimate and highest aim of society, identical with the direction implanted by nature in the mind of man towards the indefinite extension of his existence. He regards the earth in all its limits, and the heavens as far as his eye can scan their bright and starry depths, as inwardly his own, given to him as the objects of his contemplation, and as a field for the development of his energies . . . the recognition of the bond of humanity becomes one of the noblest leading principles in the history of mankind.[78]

Wilhelm von Humboldt, the older brother of Alexander, declared himself even more emphatically in his extraordinary book on the Kawi language of Java. "All humans are one species," he wrote.

Different as men may be in size, color, bodily form, and facial features, their mental qualities are the same. Assertions to the contrary are refuted by abundant evidence. Were it not for the greed to profit from the traffic in Negro slaves, or for the ludicrous pride of color, it would never have been seriously claimed that it is otherwise.[79]

Such ideas were part of the revolutionary atmosphere of the time. During the first part of the nineteenth century, the reverberations of the French and American revolutions, the wars of liberation in Latin American, the series of revolutions in Europe that broke out in rapid succession in 1848, the growing reaction to the continuing problems ensuing from the Industrial Revolution, had raised many serious questions in the minds of thinking men and women. It was a time in which the human rights, freedom, fraternity, equality, and the pursuit of happiness, were seen to be within the power of ordinary people to accomplish.[80] It was a time—in

1809—when Wordsworth wrote, on the French Revolution, "Bliss was it in that dawn to be alive,/ But to be young was very heaven."

It was a time during which many gifted men and women found their voices, and among the many movements they initiated was the founding of antislavery societies and similar organizations. The activities of the abolitionists eventually impressed upon public opinion, and in 1807 Britain abolished the slave trade, and America did so a year later. In 1833 Britain outlawed slavery altogether, but slavery survived as an institution in America for almost sixty more years, and during that period the issue it presented kept the subject of race differences always at a high temperature. In America the differences in ways of life and the better social and economic conditions in the South compared with the North, produced a deep rift between the North and the South. On 4 February 1861 the South seceded from the Union, and on 12 April the new Confederation of Southern States hastened the Civil War by firing the first shot at Fort Sumter.

Slavery had been an abrasive issue between the North and South for almost half a century during the antebellum period. The South increasingly saw the unrelenting attacks upon this pillar of their society as intolerable; these attacks eventually could only be met by secession and force. The result was four years of the bloodiest and most destructive conflict in which over six hundred thousand men died, and every principle of humanity sacrificed, on both sides, to the evils of expediency and revenge.

It was not until 1 January 1863, two years after Fort Sumter, that Lincoln issued the Emancipation Proclamation, which declared all slaves living in the rebel states "henceforward and forever free." Lincoln at this time was a white supremacist, who initially viewed the war as the desperate, and on his part reluctant, means for preserving the Union. It was the pressure for abolition in the country and in Congress that led him to a more sympathetic view, a view which showed Americans, and the world, that the war was now being fought to end slavery. As one of the world's largest slave-holding republics, the Southerners began the war pledged to protect the rights of the slaveowners. Slavery, however, was by no means ended by the Proclamation; indeed, fugitive slaves were usually returned to their masters, and many of them were held by the Confederate forces throughout the Civil War. The formal end of slavery did not come about until the 13th Amendment to the Constitution was passed on 18 December 1865, eight months after the end of the war on 9 April 1865, and Lincoln's tragic death five days later.[81]

The Civil War was fought neither for the emancipation of the human spirit, nor for the civil rights of Blacks, for more than a hundred years later the emancipation of the human spirit remained unachieved, and while the civil rights of Blacks was now the law of the land, it was not a law that whites cared to observe. As Barbara Field has said, "the Civil War is not over, it is in the present, not in the past." The North may have won the war, but from the standpoint of white supremacy it was the South that won the peace. The story of the ignominious treatment of Blacks in the postbellum period is one of the most disgraceful in the history of America, and in spite of small gains, for many it is no better today than it was then. It is necessary to understand this if one is to comprehend the nature of the racism that has stood as a forceful barrier against the African American's right to "life, liberty, and the pursuit of happiness."

With the loss of the war and the ruthless assault upon its way of life, followed by the equally ruthless exploitation by Northern invaders who contributed to its further humiliation and impoverishment, the South had a ready scapegoat upon whom it could readily wreak its wrath, the "Negro." It was the "Negro" who was to blame for the war. And with that supreme rationalization, in the tradition of many that flourished in the antebellum period, it was clear that there would have been no war if there hadn't been any "Negroes." It is this feeling, in great part, that explains the peculiarly bitter antipathy toward the "Negro," and antipathy which continues to the present day, only slightly, if at all, modified.

Harry Ashmore, the distinguished journalist, who was born to and grew up in a white family in the first half of the twentieth century in Greenville, South Carolina, in his book *The Man in the Middle,* tells with appropriate irony what it was like to live in the socially stratified environment of a racist society. "People came in two clearly defined castes," he writes,

> those who wore faded blue overalls to work in the factories and fields and tended to be shiftless. There was another group, too, but it did not count for much—Negroes, who handled menial chores and performed personal services and were to be treated with tolerance and even affection, but were not exactly people. Negroes, I understood, were inextricably bound up in the Southern Way, but in that simple time they had not even risen to the status of a Problem.[82]

"Not exactly people." The mythology which supported such beliefs and conduct served as an ideological reinforcement of "the Southern Way." Anyone who questioned it was considered outside the pale, or worse.

And so it is in some Southern places it lingers on.

To return to the beginning. When we examine the scientific literature of the seventeenth century with a view to discovering what beliefs were held concerning the diversity of humans, we find it was universally believed that humankind comprised a single species and that it represented a unitary whole. With one or two heretical exceptions, it was the accepted belief that all the children of humankind were one, and that all had a common ancestry in Adam and Eve. Physical differences were, of course, known to exist between groups of humankind, but what was unfamiliar was the notion that the differences exhibited by such peoples represented anything fundamental. Such differences, it was believed, could all be explained as due to the action of differing climatic and similar physiographic factors. Humankind was essentially one. Questions concerning the variety of humankind occurred to few thinkers during the seventeenth century. This was not because the known varieties of humankind were so few that they suggested no problem requiring solution, but principally, it would seem, because the conception of the "superiority" or "inferiority" of races that followed the increasing exploitation of other peoples had not yet developed to the point of creating a "race problem." It was not until the economic relations between Europe and peoples of other remote countries had given rise to the necessity of defining their place in nature that attempts were made to deal with this question. Such endeavors naturally first appeared toward the end of the eighteenth century. It was only then that Samuel Johnson, in *The Vanity of Human Wishes,* could write:

> Let observation with extensive view
> Survey mankind, from China to Peru.

By the middle of the nineteenth century racism had become an important ideological weapon of nationalistic and imperialistic politics.[83] During the whole of the seventeenth century only five discussions relating to the varieties of humankind were published, and toward the end of the century Leibnitz, the great mathematician, summed up the prevailing view concerning the nature of the peoples of the earth when he wrote:

> I recollect reading somewhere, though I cannot find the passage, that a certain traveler had divided man into certain tribes, races, or classes. He made one special race of the Lapps and Samoyedes, another of the Chinese and their neighbors, another of the Caffres or Hottentots. In America, again, there is a marvelous difference between the Galibs, or Caribs, who are very brave and spirited, and those of Paraguay, who seem to be infants or in pupilage all their lives. That, however, is no reason why all men who inhabit the earth should not be of the same race, which has been altered by different climates, as we see that beasts and plants change their nature and improve or degenerate.[84]

The work which Leibnitz had in mind was a brief anonymous essay published in the *Journal des Sçavans* in April, 1684, and which remained almost completely unnoticed.[85] Race was definitely not yet in the air. It was not until 1749 that Buffon introduced the word "race," in its zoological connotation, into the scientific literature.[86]

It is commonly stated that Buffon classified man into six races.[87] Buffon, who was the enemy of all rigid classifications, did nothing of the sort. What he did was to provide an account of all the varieties of man known to him in a purely descriptive manner. This is how he begins: "In Lapland, and on the northern coasts of Tartary, we find a race of men of an uncouth figure, and small stature." And this is the type of Buffon's description. Here the word "race" is used for the first time in a scientific context, and it is quite clear, after reading Buffon, that he uses the word in no narrowly defined, but rather in a general, sense.[88] Since Buffon's works were widely read and were translated into many European languages, he must be held at least partially responsible for the diffusion of the idea of a natural separation of the races of humankind, though he himself does not appear to have had such an idea in mind.

With the voyages of discovery of Bougainville (1761–66), of Wallis-Carteret (1766), of Captain Cook (1768–79), and others in the eighteenth century, there were opened up to the view of Europe many new varieties of humans—people hitherto undreamed of who thickly populated the islands of the South Seas, of Melanesia, and the Antipodes. Soon the inhabitants of the most distant parts of the world began to be described, pictured, and some of their skulls and handiwork collected and placed in museums. Meanwhile, the African slave trade had increased to enormous proportions. During the eighteenth century the slave trade was regarded as sanctioned by the Bible and as fully consistent with the good life.[89] "For what could be more godly than to deliver poor Negroes from heathen darkness and the certainty of damnation, by carrying them to a land where they would receive the 'blessings of Christianity.'"[90] The institution of slavery was not without its critics almost from the day the first twenty Africans arrived at Jamestown in 1619.[91]

Curiously enough, the first recorded use of the phrase "Negro slave" occurs in a document issued 30 March 1660, the date of an act designed to encourage the importation of "Negroes" by the Dutch.[92] George Fox, the first Friend, had become convinced of the evil of slavery as early as 1671, but it was not until the Society of Friends had weathered the years of persecution to which they had themselves been exposed and overcome their own internal difficulties that they opened the campaigne on slavery. By 1714 Friends had commenced pamphleteering against slavery, using the doctrine of the Divine presence in every man as their main argument.[93] John Wesley, the founder of Methodism, had declared himself against slavery in 1743. In his *General Rules* he prohibited "the buying or selling the bodies and souls of men, women, and children, with an intention to enslave them." And in 1774, in his *Thoughts Upon Slavery,* he excoriated the barbarous and inferior white men who put the noble savage in fetters. "It is impossible," he wrote, "that it should ever be necessary for any reasonable creature to violate all the laws of Justice, Mercy, and Truth. No circumstances can make it necessary for a man to burst asunder all the ties of humanity."[94] Wesley was read religiously by his followers, his ideas nurturing an antislavery sentiment which was to grow in moral force as the confrontation with the mother country made more explicit the principles of freedom upon which the rights of man depend. The American Revolution was brought about by men who justly considered themselves oppressed, the victims of repeated injuries and usurpations, and of an absolute tyranny, which they were resolved to bring to an end. The principles fought for, and set out in the Declaration of Independence, clearly included Blacks. By 1780 the Pennsylvania legislature initiated steps toward the abolition of slavery in that State, and by 1804 the end of slavery was ensured above the Mason and Dixon line. By the vision of Thomas Jefferson and Congress the institution of slavery had been preempted for the Northwest.[95] In 1780 the Methodists formally decided to work for the emancipation of the slaves on the grounds that the institution was contrary to divine, human, and natural justice, a violation of the Golden Rule, and inconsistent with pure religion.[96]

In 1790 Cesar de l'Escale de Verone, writing on the Blacks of the French colonies, warned against the infusion "into the very heart of our country of that thick, heavy, impure, black, crafty blood so unworthy of that which flows in your veins, the reason of which has covered the whole earth and eclipsed all that was ever acquired by the Greeks and Romans."[97]

In 1837 Victor Courtet de l'Isle provided a quite original "proof" of the black's inferiority, and at the same time of the value of slavery, when he made the measure of a people's ability to govern and dominate, the enslavement of other races, declaring that Blacks were at the bottom of the scale of humanity, and their absolute inferiority demonstrated, because of the fact that "they have enslaved no foreign races; they have only enslaved one another."[98]

Toward the end of the eighteenth century, when the traffic in slaves was increasingly being opposed and challenged, the question of the status and relation of the varieties of humans became the subject of acrimonious debate. Long-term residents of lands in which Blacks were held in slavery published their beliefs concerning the mental and physical qualities of Blacks and the social arrangements they considered desirable between whites and Blacks. Thomas Jefferson, for example, had originally thought Blacks poor in mental endowment, but believed in their emancipation, with the qualification that when freed they were "to be removed beyond the reach of mixture."[99] But with increasing experience of Blacks, Jefferson later several times repudiated his earlier statements which he freely acknowledged to be prejudices. In 1791, in a letter to Benjamin Banneker, of

Maryland, the slave-born black inventor and mathematician,[100] praising the latter's almanac, Jefferson wrote,

> No body wishes more than I do to see such proofs as you exhibit, that nature has given to our black brethren, talents equal to those of the other colors of men, and that the appearance of a want of them is owing merely to the degraded condition of their existence, both in Africa and America. . . .[101]

In the same year, as Secretary of State, Jefferson appointed Banneker a member of the three-man commission to survey the site for the national capital. Some seventeen years later, in 1809, Jefferson wrote in a letter to Henri Gregoire,

> Be assured that no person living wishes more sincerely than I do to see a complete refutation of the doubts I have myself entertained and expressed on the grade of understanding allotted to them [Blacks] by nature, and to find that in this respect they are on a par with ourselves. My doubts were the result of personal observation on the limited sphere of my own State, where the opportunities for the development of their genius were not favorable, and those of exercising it still less so. I expressed them therefore with great hesitation; but whatever be their degree of talent is no measure of their rights.[102]

Two years later, in 1811, Leigh Hunt, commenting on Paul Cuffee, the son of slaves, who arrived in England in his own vessel entirely manned by Blacks, writes, "Nobody who pretends to sense or decency, thinks any longer, that a difference of color in human beings implies inequality of rights, or that because we find men ignorant we ought to make them wretched."[103]

Edward Long's remarks on the black man, whom he compared to an orangutan [the contemporary name for the chimpanzee], were written after a five-year residence in Jamaica, and first published in England in 1774,[104] and in 1788 reprinted in *The Columbian Magazine*. Mentally, wrote Long, Negroes were void of genius, destitute of moral sense, and incapable of making progress in civilization or science. As plantation slaves they do their work "perhaps not better than an orang-outang might, with a little pains, be brought to do."[105]

There were innumerable publications of a similar kind during this period, as there were countless others presenting the opposite viewpoint. Perhaps the most remarkable of the latter was the Reverend Samuel Stanhope Smith's book, *An Essay on the Courses of the Variety of Complexion and Figure in the Human Species,* first published in 1787 and greatly enlarged in a second edition in 1810.[106] Smith was a Presbyterian clergyman who became professor of moral philosophy in 1779 at the College of New Jersey (afterwards Princeton University), and in 1795 seventh president of the college. Smith wrote,

> If we compare together only those varieties of human nature by which the several sections of mankind differ most widely from one another, the difference is so great that, on the first view, it might very naturally lead to the conclusion that they must belong to distinct species. But, when we come to examine more particularly the intermediate grades which connect the extremes, and observe by what minute differences they approach, or recede from, one another; and when we observe further, that each of these minute gradations can be traced to obvious and natural causes, forming so many links, as it were, in the great chain connecting the extremes, we are ready to call in question our first impressions, and perceive the necessity of subjecting them to a new and more vigorous examination.[107]

After citing evidence for the unity of the human species, Smith concluded "that the denial of the unity of the human species tends to impair, if not entirely to destroy, the foundations of duty and morals, and, in a word, of the whole science of human nature."[108] Smith goes on to say, "It is a debt we owe to humanity to recognize our brethren in every class of men into which society is divided, and under every shade of complexion which diversifies their various tribes from the equator to the poles."[109]

In the discussion of the origins of modern racism it is necessary to recall that in America there was in existence a long tradition of antipathy toward the native "savages," the American Indian. Unable to "civilize" them, their dispossessors determined to destroy them.[110] Of the American Indians Benjamin Franklin wrote in his *Autobiography,* "And indeed, if it be the design of Providence to extirpate these savages in order to make room for the cultivators of the earth, it seems probable that rum may be the appointed means."[111]

When the issue of emancipation was at last settled, in 1833, for the English colonies, it was far from being so for those of France and Holland. It was not until 1848 that the French emancipated their slaves, and not until 1863 that the Dutch liberated theirs. During all these years the monstrous race legend was continually being reinforced by the advocates of slavery, so that when the matter was finally settled in favor of the freedom of the slaves, the race legend nonetheless persisted. It served to solace the hearts of the aggrieved supporters of slavery, while now, more than ever, they saw to it that the myths and legends which they had served to popularize would be perpetuated.

The idea of race was, in fact, the deliberate creation of an exploiting class seeking to maintain and defend its privileges against what was profitably regarded as an inferior social caste. Ever since the commencement of the

slave trade there had been those who had attempted to justify their conduct
in it by denying the slaves the status of humanity. Montesquieu with devastating irony nicely put the view of such traders with their consciences as well as
their slaves: "It is impossible for us to suppose these creatures to be men, because, allowing them to be men, a suspicion would follow, that we ourselves
are not Christians."[112] Conversely, since they conceived themselves to be
Christians, it followed that the slaves could not be men. The notion does not
appear to have occurred to them that since men are equal in the sight of
their God they should also be equal in the sight of one another.[113]

More than two decades before the Civil War the most respected and influential Southern philosophers of slavery, Thomas R. Dew and William
Harper[114] codified, as it were, and openly avowed and defended what
Southern cotton planters had been thinking since the abolitionists had
first challenged the "rights" upon which their economy was based. Dew
and Harper were supported by the leading American physician-ethnolo-
gist, Josiah C. Nott,[115] of the University of New Orleans, who in his *Types of
Mankind* [1854], formulated, together with his co-author George Gliddon,
the principles of the natural inequality of man.

Like Dew, Harper attacked and repudiated the philosophy of equality
of Thomas Jefferson. "Is it not palpably nearer the truth," he writes, "to say
that no man was ever born free and that no two men were ever born
equal? . . . Man is born to subjection. . . . The proclivity of natural man is to
domineer or to be subservient." In the evolution of society each man or
class of men comes to find his proper place and level, and the resulting differences are then codified and given a definite form and legalized by society. Laws are instituted to prevent outbreaks against this established order
as well as to render the different classes contented and even ignorant—for
"if there are sordid, servile, and laborious offices to be performed, is it not
better that there should be sordid, servile, and laborious beings to perform
them?" As William E. Dodd put it, "Society in the lower South was to be the
realization unhindered of the social philosophy which began with the repudiation of the Declaration of Independence and ended with the explicit
recognition of social inequality."[116]

Thomas Cooper characterized the rights of man as "a great deal of
nonsense. Nothing can be more untrue; no human being ever was, now is,
or ever will be born free." Man has no inalienable rights," wrote another
Southerner, "not even those of life, liberty, and the pursuit of
happiness. . . . Instead of that 'glittering generality' which might serve as a
motto for the wildest anarchy, the truth is that men and races of men have
certain natural capacities and duties, and the right to use the one and discharge the other."[117]

After 1840, denials and attacks upon the principles of the Declaration
of Independence became a staple practice in the proslavery literature of

the South. A learned legal proslavery authority, Thomas Cobb, writing in 1858, cited such evidence as the following in order to contest the notion that slavery is contrary to the law of nature, that all men are free, and at birth entitled by nature to no higher rights and privileges than another:

> The red ant will issue in regular battle array, to conquer and subjugate the black or negro ant . . . these negro slaves perform all the labor of the communities into which they are brought. . . . Upon this definition, therefore, of the law of nature, negro slavery would seem to be perfectly consistent with that law."[118]

If, argues Cobb, the black were by nature equal to the white, enslavement of the black would be wrong, for the law of nature imposes upon man in relation to his fellow man the obligation,

> so to shape his course as to attain the greatest happiness, and arrive at the greatest perfection of which his nature is susceptible. Consequently, whatever interferes with the attainment of this happiness and perfection does violence to the law of his nature, and whatever promotes and is consistent therewith is sanctioned by the law of his nature. In this view, natural rights depend entirely upon the nature of the possessor, not of the right.[119]

It is, therefore, a matter of the greatest ease for Cobb to show that the nature of the black man is such that his best interests and greatest happiness are secured by his enslavement to the white man.[120] The master is as necessary to the slave as the pilot is to the ship. By citing most of the leading authorities of the day Cobb has no difficulty in supporting his thesis. Cobb is transparently a man of great character, honesty, and worth. His learned book is written with dignity and sincerity—he is no ignorant rabble-rouser, nevertheless his book is a treasure house of most of the myths that have ever been uttered about the black. "In mental and moral development," says Cobb, "slavery, so far from retarding, has advanced the Negro race."[121] "Contact with the Caucasian is the only civiliser of the negro, and slavery the only condition on which that contact can be preserved."[122]

As Norlin has so well said, the slaveholding aristocracy of the South

> rationalized their freedom to exploit and enslave. Even before the Civil War broke out, they had persuaded themselves that the institution of slavery was divinely ordained; that it was good for master and equally good for slave, and therefore worthy to be extended beyond the states where it was sanctified by law. They felt themselves to be the heaven-appointed shepherds of their flocks, being better able to care for their black wards than those outsiders who proposed by the tyranny of legislation to set bounds to their freedom of thought and action.[123]

They would see to it, as one Virginian slaveholder wrote, that they continued to hold their property, "and for the right thereto, to be called in question by an unphilosophical set of political mountebanks, under the influence of supernatural agency or deceit, is insufferable."[124]

Some there were, like William Andrew Smith, Methodist minister and president of Randolph-Macon College, who, in the 1850s, argued that all men are really slaves, even such institutions as the family and democratic government contain elements of slavery. Hence, slavery could be identified in principle with good order in society.[125]

The slaveholder's representative rationalization for slavery was stated clearly when, in 1856, George Fitzhugh claimed that slavery combined three advantages: it fostered paternalistic and loving interdependence; it placed human conduct under adequate governmental controls; and it relied on a highly decentralized version of authority.[126] It is not quite true to suggest, as R. H. Tawney has done, that the one thing these political philosophers omitted to ask themselves was on what grounds the view could be sustained that inequalities in intelligence or biology justified the penalty of slavery. The fact is that they were asked and asked themselves this question ceaselessly, and they made answer, as Aristotle had done before them, that some men were born to be masters and others to be slaves. Like Aristotle, they deliberately invented a theory to justify social discrimination. As early as the year 1700, we find the Puritan judge John Saffin of Boston writing,

> To prove that all men have equal right to Liberty, and all outward comforts of this life . . . [is] to invert the Order that God hath set in the World, who hath Ordained different degrees and orders of men, some to be High and Honorable, some to be Low and Despicable; some to be Monarchs, Kings, Princes and Governors, Masters and Commanders, others to be Subjects and to be Commanded; Servants of sundry sorts and degrees, bound to obey; yea, some to be born Slaves, and so to remain during their lives, as hath been proved.[127]

From 1830 to 1860 vigilance committees were established throughout the South to punish anyone who in any way exhibited antislavery or proemancipation tendencies. Russel Nye has given an account of such cases in his book *Fettered Freedom*. Here are but two typical cases from the month of January 1850. Elijah Harris, an itinerant schoolteacher, from Dunbarton, New Hampshire, was arrested on a writ issued by the justice of the peace of Clinton, Barnwell District, South Carolina. He was arraigned before the local committee of safety, and convicted of carrying in his trunk an antislavery sermon by a New Hampshire minister. The committee shaved his head, tarred and feathered him, and gave him twelve hours to leave town.[128] Robert Esmond, a resident of Charleston, South Carolina, during the same month, was tarred and feathered on suspicion of teaching Negroes to read.[129]

For the slaveholders the strategic elaboration of erroneous notions which had long been held presented no great difficulty. In order to bolster their self-appointed rights the superior caste did not have far to seek for reasons that serve to justify its conduct. The deliberately maintained illiteracy and the alleged spiritual benightedness of the slaves supplied abundant material for elaboration on the theme of their essential inferiority. Their different physical appearance provided a convenient peg upon which to hang the argument that this represented the external sign of more profound ineradicable mental and moral inferiorities. It was an easily grasped mode of reasoning, and in this way the obvious difference in their social status, in caste status, was equated with their obviously different physical appearance, which, in turn, was taken to indicate a fundamental biological difference. Thus was a culturally produced difference in social status converted into a difference in biological status. What had once been a social difference was now transformed into a biological difference which would serve, it was expected, to justify and maintain the social difference.[130]

This was a most attractive idea to many members of a society in which the classes were markedly stratified, and it was an idea that had a special appeal for those who were beginning to take an active interest in the scientific study and classification of the races of humankind.[131] For the term "race," taken over from Buffon with all the emotional connotations that had been added to it, had by now become established. It was with this term as a tremendous handicap that most anthropologists of the nineteenth century embarked on their researches. The question they had begged was the one which required to be proved, namely, that mental and moral differences were associated with racial external physical differences. As Wundt once remarked in another connection, "in the seventeenth century God gave the laws of Nature; in the eighteenth century Nature did this herself; and in the nineteenth century individual scientists take care of that task."[132] And we may add that in the twentieth century the tasks determine for the scientists, and others, what the laws of nature shall be.

The allegedly scientific presentation of the case for slavery was produced by Josiah C. Nott, and published in 1854 under the title *Types of Mankind*. This 738-page volume, which enshrined most of the prejudices and pseudoscience of the day, was embellished with an essay contributed by Louis Agassiz, professor of zoology at Harvard, in which he identified himself with the pluralist position of the authors, and thus lent them and their views the prestige of his great authority as a scientist.[133] This work was not without some influence in the world, and all of it for the worse. Henry

Schoolcraft, the great authority on the American Indians wrote, in September, 1854, of this work,

> The types are . . . the fruits of the mountain that was in labor. From one end of the land to the other subscribers have been drummed up for this work, and when it came forth it is a patchwork of infidel papers . . . if this be all that America is to send back to Europe . . . it were better that the Aborigines had maintained their dark empire undisturbed.[134]

As an independent student of the evidence has put it:

> When between the years 1859 and 1870, anthropological societies were established successively in Paris, London, New York, Moscow, Florence, Berlin and Vienna, the attention of anthropologists was in the first place directed mainly to the statement and exploration of problems of racial divergence and distribution. The need for such a preliminary investigation was great. Popular opinion drew a rough but ready distinction between men of white, black, yellow and red color, vaguely supposed to be native to the continents of Europe, Africa, Asia and America respectively. Differences of average stature, of physiognomy, of growth and texture of hair were recognized; certain combinations of these characters were supposed to be typical of certain ultimate stocks. There was the self-satisfied view, influenced by an uncritical acceptance of the Biblical account of the Creation, Flood, dispersion of its survivors, selection of a favored race, which either alone or [together] conspicuously expressed divine purpose, that divergence from European standard[s] should ultimately be explained in terms of degradation.[135]

It was not principally the scientific student of the varieties of man who influenced European thought along these lines, but an aristocrat of the Second Empire, an amateur orientalist and professional diplomat, Count Joseph Arthur de Gobineau. Gobineau was a reactionary littérateur who rejected the principles of the French Revolution,[136] and looked upon the egalitarian philosophy of the Revolution as the hopelessly confused expression of a degraded rabble. If the founders of the First Republic had believed in the liberty, equality, and fraternity of mankind, this scion of the Second Empire would show that, on the contrary, a man was not bound to be free, that the idea of the brotherhood of man was a vain and empty dream, a repugnant dream which could never be realized because it was based upon a fallacious belief in the equality of man.[137] These views were fully set out by Gobineau in his four-volume work entitled *Essai sur l'inégalité des races humaines* (Paris, 1853–55). In 1856 an American translation of the first two volumes under the title *The Moral and Intellectual Diversity of Races* was published at Philadelphia. This was the work of H. Hotz, of

Montgomery, the pious Alabama proslavery propagandist. At the invitation of either Gobineau or Hotz, Josiah C. Nott, the proslavery anthropologist, contributed an anthropological appendix to the translation. Gobineau returned the compliment by subscribing to Nott and Gliddon's *Indigenous Races of the Earth,* which appeared in the following year, 1857, from the same publishing house which had issued the translation of the Essai. As Finot has pointed out, Gobineau never attempted to conceal or dissimulate the motives which led him to write the Essai. For him,

> It was only a matter of bringing his contributions to the great struggle against equality and the emancipation of the proletariat. Imbued with aristocratic ideas . . . he thought it useful to oppose to the democratic aspirations of his time a number of considerations on the existence of natural castes in humanity and their beneficial necessity.[138]

Ever since their publication Gobineau's works have enjoyed a considerable readership among reactionaries and demagogues of every kind. Among others they gave the composer Richard Wagner a "scientific" basis for his racist prejudices, fortifying him and encouraging him in the production of his virulent and influential racist writings.[139]

Some forty-five years later the views originally expressed in Gobineau's works were taken over lock, stock, and barrel by Wagner's son-in-law, Houston Stewart Chamberlain, and elaborated in his *Grundlagen des neunzehnten Jahrhunderts* (1899). The English translation, *The Foundation of the Nineteenth Century,* was published in 1910.[140]

John Oakesmith, in his book *Race & Nationality* (1919), arguably one of the best and most readable books ever written on the subject, brilliantly anatomized Chamberlain's monstrosity at some length. Here, briefly, is his characterization of it:

> We can have no hesitation in describing it as one of the most foolish books ever written. It is false in its theories; ludicrously inaccurate in its assertions; pompous and extravagant in its style; insolent to its critics and opponents. It is so dominated by a spirit of stormy rhetoric that it contradicts itself with passion at every turn. It asserts as dogmas fancies of whose futility the author would have been aware, had he consulted his Jew-baiting baby.[141] He frequently uses the term 'lie' and 'liar' of others while claiming that he is himself constitutionally incapable of lying. He can never quote an opponent without covering him with abuses: his critics are 'shallow, venal, ignorant, babblers, slavish souls sprung from the chaos of peoples.' He is a twentieth century exaggeration of the pompous and vapid bully[142] who used to lord it in the *Quarterly* [*The Edinburgh Quarterly Review*] of the early nineteenth; he is a street-corner preacher now assuming the toga of Roman oratory, and now the robes of Christian ceremony; but

he is a violent and vulgar charlatan all the time. We say, and say it deliberately, that he is the only author we have read to whose work Sydney Smith's phrase, 'the crapulous eructations of a drunken cobbler,' could appropriately be applied.

A judgement, I believe, that all impartial critics would share.[143]

It is not surprising that early in January 1923 Hitler, who was greatly influenced by Chamberlain's racist thinking, enjoyed a mutually gratifying visit with his mentor at Bayreuth. Chamberlain was greatly taken with Hitler, and the following day, in a mood of religious exaltation, wrote him a long letter, telling his new found friend of his renewal of faith in the future of the Fatherland which Hitler had inspired in him. "You have immense achievements ahead of you . . . That Germany in its hour of greatest need has given birth to a Hitler is proof of vitality. . . . May God protect you!"[144] Thereafter whenever Chamberlain spoke or wrote of Hitler, it was with reverence and affection. It proved to be of great propaganda value to the Nazis in the development of their movement. When in January 1927 Chamberlain died, Alfred Rosenberg, the official Nazi philosopher, praised him as the pioneer and founder of the German Future."[145]

Chamberlain's book enjoyed an enormous popularity in Germany. Kaiser Wilhelm II, the principal architect of World War I, caller it "my favorite book," and distributed it widely among libraries, the military, the nobility, his friends, and schools. Both Gobineau and Chamberlain's works may be regarded as the spiritual progenitors of Hitler's *Mein Kampf.* In this connection the works of John Oakesmith, written during World War I, are of interest to all who, by forces similar to those which were operative then, have since been plunged into far more horrible wars. Oakesmith wrote:

> The essence of the racial theory, especially as exhibited by writers of the school of Houston Stewart Chamberlain, is profoundly immoral, as well as unnatural and irrational. It asserts that by virtue of belonging to a certain 'race,' every individual member of it possesses qualities which inevitably destine him to the realization of certain ends; in the case of the German the chief end being universal dominion, all other 'races' being endowed with qualities which as inevitably destine them to submission and slavery to German ideals and German masters. This essentially foolish and immoral conception has been the root-cause of that diseased national egotism whose exhibition during the war [World War I] has been at once the scorn and the horror of the civilized world.[146]

From the commencement of the nineteenth century the Germans, intoxicated by their Faustian romanticism, have been especially prone to the appeal of a magus who promises to exorcise the possessing evil spirits.[147]

Luther (1483–1546), to a large extent, had successfully destroyed the mythological element in Christianity for the Germans, and from 1517 onwards, when he posted the ninety-five articles on the door of the castle church at Wittenberg, to the advent of the Nazi Party, the Germans had been seeking for some new mythology wherewith to replace what they had lost. When Luther cleared the way for a more purely rational interpretation of the world, he failed to foresee that by withdrawing the experience of the mystical, the poetic, and metaphysical, and the dramatic, he was building for a time when the people would be glad to embrace a mythology whose barbarity would have appalled him. One may never deprive a people of its feeling of unity with the world, with nature, and with man without providing another set of such metaphysical beliefs—unless one is ready to brook disaster. We may recall the words of Ernest Renan, written in 1848:

> The serious thing is that we fail to perceive a means of providing humanity in the future with a catechism that will be acceptable henceforth, except on the condition of returning to a state of credulity. Hence, it is possible that the ruin of idealistic beliefs may be fated to follow hard upon the ruin of supernatural beliefs and that the real abasement of the morality of humanity will date from the day it has seen the reality of things. Chimeras have succeeded in obtaining from the good gorilla an astonishing moral effort; do away with the chimeras and part of the factitious energy they aroused will disappear.[148]

It is a fact worth remarking that throughout the nineteenth century hardly more than a handful of scientific voices were raised against the notion of a hierarchy of races. Anthropology, biology, psychology, medicine, and sociology became instruments for the "proof" of the inferiority of various races as compared with the white race. What H. G. Wells called "professional barbarity and braggart race-imperialism," played a major role in the rationalization justifying the disenfranchisement and segregation of "inferior races," and thus prepared the way for the maintenance of racial thinking and exploitation of "native" peoples, and the unspeakable atrocities of the nineteenth and twentieth centuries.[149]

After World War I the Germans found themselves particularly frustrated and alone. By providing them with a new mythology and making the Germans feel that they belonged to a "superior race," the "Herrenvolk," Hitler endowed them with a completely acceptable *Weltanschauung*. The fact that the Nazi race theories represented the most vicious mythology that had ever been perpetrated upon a people did not, as we know, prevent those myths from functioning as if they were perfectly true. "If one asks," as Bonger has done, whether these partisans are even partially successful in proving their thesis, then the answer must be a decided No. It is really no theory at all but a second-rate religion. Things are not proved but only alleged. It resembles the commonly witnessed phenomenon of persons who, quite without reason, fancy themselves (and often their families also) to be more exalted than others. But now it is carried out on a much larger scale, and with much greater detriment to society, since it affects wide-spread groups.[150]

What Hitler said about race is reported from a personal conversation by Hermann Rauschning. "I know perfectly well," Hitler said to Rauschning,

just as well as all those tremendously clever intellectuals, that in the scientific sense there is no such thing as race. But you, as a farmer and cattle-breeder, cannot get your breeding successfully achieved without the conception of race. And I as a politician need a conception which enables the order which has hitherto existed on historic bases to be abolished and an entirely new and anti-historic order enforced and given an intellectual basis. . . . With the conception of race, National Socialism will carry its revolution abroad and recast the world.[151]

Similar statements were made by Hitler to his confidant Otto Wagener.[152] Lord Bryce, writing in 1915 during World War I, remarked:

Whatever condemnation may be passed—and justly passed—upon reckless leaders and a ruthless caste that lives for and worships war, it is popular sentiment behind them, the exaggeration of racial vanity and national pretensions, that has been and is the real source of the mischief, for without such sentiments no caste could exert its baleful power. Such sentiments are not confined to any single nation, and they are even more widespread in the wealthier and more educated classes than in the humbler. As it is largely by the educated, by students and writers as well as by political leaders, that the mischief has been done, more or less everywhere, even if most conspicuously in one country, so it should be the function and the privilege of thinkers and writers as well as of practical men to enforce a broader, saner, and more sympathetic view of the world as a vast community, in which every race has much to give and much to receive, to point out that it is by the co-operation, unconscious but unceasing, by the reciprocal teaching and learning of the more gifted races, that all progress has been achieved. Perfection is obtained not by the ascendancy of any one form of excellence, but by the blending of what is best in many different forms.[153]

How much more true are these words today than when they were written. We all know only too well to what horrors the reckless "Führers" of the Axis nations and their ruthless conduct have led the world, and we have witnessed the exaggeration of racial vanity and national pretensions assuming the form of a national religion and serving as an incentive to the common people to follow wherever their "Führers" lead. We have seen the virus of the disease spread throughout the greater part of the civilized world in the form of racism, and in the United States we have heard the word race bandied about on radio and TV, on the screen, from the pulpit, in our houses of legislature, our Supreme Court, and used by demagogues in various mischievous ways. In the press, in books of all sorts, and in the magazines the same perverse looseness of usage is observable. Today, more than at any previous time in the history of man, it is urgently necessary to be clear as to what this term is and what it really means.

The fact is that the modern concept of race is a product of irrational emotional reasoning, and, as we have seen, from their inception racial questions have always been discussed in an emotional atmosphere. It might almost be called "the atmosphere of the scapegoat" or, possibly, "the atmosphere of frustration or fear of frustration." As a writer in the leading organ of British science, *Nature,* remarked:

> It is a matter of general experience that racial questions are rarely debated on their merits. In the discussion of the effects of inter-racial breeding among the different varieties of the human stock, the issue is commonly determined by prejudice masquerading as pride of race or political and economic considerations more or less veiled in arguments brought forward in support of a policy of segregation. No appeal is made to what should be the crucial factor, the verdict of science.[154]

And what is the verdict of science? It will be our purpose to make that verdict clear in the following pages. The members of the older school of anthropologists, some of whom are still with us, grappled with the problem of race unsuccessfully, and the great number of conflicting viewpoints they presented shows that they were, as a whole, never quite clear as to what was to be meant by the term. They were, indeed, something less than clear, if not altogether confused.[155] In the following chapter a brief attempt will be made to show how it came about that so many of the older anthropologists came to be confused upon the subject of race.

In using the term "anthropologist" in the succeeding chapter, I am mainly referring to the physical anthropologist as distinguished from the cultural or social anthropologist. Possibly because of their wider and more intimate acquaintance with a variety of different peoples, particularly in the more isolated parts of the world, cultural anthropologists have been somewhat more sound on the subject of race than have most physical anthropologists. Indeed, the physical anthropologist has virtually disappeared from the scene and been replaced by the biological anthropologist.

Notes

1. For excellent discussions of contemporary mythmaking and myths, see Barrows Dunham, *Man against Myth* (Boston: Little, Brown, 1947); Bergen Evans, *The Natural History of Nonsense* (New York: Alfred A. Knopf, 1964); Read Bain, "Man, the Myth-Maker," *Scientific Monthly* 65 (1947): 61–69; David Bidney, "The Concept of Myth and the Problem of Psychocultural Evolution," *American Anthropologist* 62 (1950): 16–26; D. H. Monro, "The Concept of Myth," *Sociological Review* 42 (1950): 115–32; Lewis S. Feuer, "Political Myths and Metaphysics," *Philosophy and Phenomenological Research* 15 (1955): 332–50; Harry A. Murray, ed., *Myth and Mythmaking* (New York: Braziller, 1960).

2. Nicholas Calas, "Myth and Initiation," *Chimera* 4 (1946): 21–24.

3. Paul M. Gaston, *The New South Creed: A Study in Modern Mythmaking* (New York: Alfred A. Knopf, 1970).

4. George M. Tindall, *The Ethnic Southerners* (Baton Rouge: Louisiana State University Press, 1976).

5. Alan Davies, *Infected Christianity: A Study of Modern Racism* (Kingston & Montreal: McGill Queen's University Press, 1988); Ervin Staub, *The Roots of Evil: The Origins of Genocide* (New York: Cambridge University Press, 1989); Michael Barkun, *Religion and the Racist Right: The Origins of the Christian Identity Movement* (Chapel Hill: University of North Carolina Press, 1994).

6. Lancelot Hogben, "The Concept of Race," in *Genetic Principles in Medicine and Social Science* (New York: Alfred A. Knopf, 1932), 122–44; see also L. Hogben, *Nature and Nurture* (New York: W. W. Norton, 1933).

7. Louis J. Halle, *The Ideological Imagination* (New York: Quadrangle Press, 1972). For an illuminating study of the causes of the ideological appeal of Naziism, see Peter H. Merkl, *Political Violence Under the Swastika: 581 Early Nazis* (Princeton: Princeton University Press, 1975); Paul Massing, *Rehearsal for Destruction* (New York: Harper & Brothers, 1949); George L. Mosse, *Toward the Final Solution: A History of European Racism* (Madison: University of Wisconsin Press, 1985).

8. John Stuart Mill, *Principles of Political Economy* (London: Longmans, 1848).

9. John Stuart Mill, *Autobiography*.

10. Walter Bagehot, *Physics and Politics* (New York: Alfred A. Knopf), 3; Ashley Montagu, "The Language of Self-Deception," in *Language in America*, eds. Neil Postman, Charles Weingartner, and Terence P. Moran (New York: Pegasus, 1969), 82–95.

11. James Bryce, *Race Sentiment as a Factor in History* (London: University of London Press, 1915), 3.

12. As an example see A. C. Haddon's *The Races of Man* (Cambridge: Cambridge University Press, 1924). This was a book by a very noble man, a great scholar and founder of the anthropology department at Cambridge University. For a sympathetic biography of Haddon (1955–1940) see A. Hingston Quiggin, *Haddon the Head Hunter* (Cambridge: Cambridge University Press, 1942). Among many hundreds of scholarly articles and some twenty books, Haddon was the co-author with Julian Huxley of the admirable and influential *We Europeans: A Survey of "Racial" Problems* (New York: Harper & Bros., 1935).

13. Richard Lewontin, "The Apportionment of Human Diversity," in *Evolutionary Biology*, vol. 6, eds. T. Dobzhansky, M. K. Hecht, and W. C. Steere (New York: Appleton Century-Cotts, 1972), 396–97.

14. See Ashley Montagu, *An Introduction to Physical Anthropology*, 3rd ed. (Springfield, IL: Thomas. 1960); A. Montagu, "A Consideration of the Concept of Race," *Cold Spring Harbor Symposia on Quantitative Biology* 15 (1950): 315–36; A. Montagu, "The Concept of Race," *American Anthropologist* 64 (1962): 929–45; Livingstone, "On the Non-Existence of Human Races," *Current Anthropology* 3 (1962): 279–81; A. Montagu, ed., *The Concept of Race* (New York: Free Press, 1964).

15. Lucien Febvre, *A Geographical Introduction to History* (New York: Alfred A. Knopf, 1925).

16. For an anthropological example of this fractionating method of race-making see Carleton Coon, *The Races of Europe* (New York: Macmillan, 1939); also Stanley Garn, *Human Races* (Springfield, IL: Thomas, 1969).

17. Huxley and Haddon, *We Europeans*, 114. In order to avoid possible misunderstanding of this passage, it is desirable to point out that by the words "genetically purified into their original components" the authors are not referring to pre-existing "pure races," but to the earlier states of the ancestral groups entering into the formation of the mixed ethnic groups as we know them today.

18. Franz Boas, *Changes in Bodily Form of Descendants of Immigrants* (New York: Columbia University Press, 1912); Harry L. Shapiro, *Migration and Environment* (New York: Oxford University Press, 1939); Walter Dornfeldt, "Studien über Schädelform und Schadelveranderung von Berliner Ostjuden und ihren Kindern," *Zeitschrift für Morphologie und Anthropologie* 39 (1941): 290–372; Marcus S. Goldstein, *Demographic and Bodily Changes in Descendants of Mexican Immigrants* (Austin: Institute of Latin-American Studies, 1943); on the absurdity of classification by head shape, see Franz Weidenreich, "The Brachycephalization of Recent Mankind," *Southwestern Journal of Anthropology* 1 (1945): 1–54; Gabriel Lasker, "Migration and Physical Differentiation," *American Journal of Physical Anthropology*, n.s., 4 (1946): 273–300.

19. Coon, *Races of Europe*.

20. Robert T. Anderson, "Lapp Racial Classifications As Scientific Myths," *Anthropological Papers of the University of Alaska* 11 (1962): 15–31.

21. Blumenbach, *De Generis Varietate Humani Nativa* (London, 1865).

22. Anderson, "Lapp Racial Classifications," 29–30.

23. For a further discussion of the term "ethnic group" and why it is to be preferred to "race" see Appendix A of this volume.

24. Charles Darwin, *The Descent of Man*, Chap. 7 (London, Murray, 1871).

25. William S. Laughlin, "Race: A Population Concept," *Eugenics Quarterly* 13 (1966): 327.

26. Dobzhansky, "On Species and Races of Living and Fossil Man," *American Journal of Physical Anthropology*, n.s., 2 (1944): 251–65. For a criticism of this viewpoint, see Livingstone, "On the Non-Existence of Human Races."

27. Lothar G. Tirala, *Rasse, Geist, und Seele* (Munich: Lehman's Verlag, 1935).

28. A contrary view was, indeed, expressed by Dr. R. Ruggles Gates, who claimed that many of the races of man must be regarded as belonging to different species. Such claims were rendered possible by the utter disregard and com-

plete violation of the principles of zoological taxonomy and the accepted definition of a species, principles and definitions which represent the judgment of
generations of scientists. For Gates's view see his "Phylogeny and Classification
of Hominids and Anthropoids," *American Journal of Physical Anthropology*, n.s., 2
(1944): 279–92. As Franz Wiedenrich has said, "raising the differences between
racial groups specific names is nothing but an attempt to exaggerate the dissimi-
larities by the application of a taxonomic trick," *Apes, Giants, and Man* (Chicago:
University of Chicago Press, 1946), 2. For the designation of "races" of humankind as "species," see John R. Baker, *Race* (New York: Oxford University
Press, 1974), 98.

29. Hans Weinert, *Der Geistige Aufstieg der Menschheit som Ursprung bis zur
Gegenwart* (Stuttgart: Ferdinand Enke, 1951). For an interesting account of the Nazi
application of the "methods" of "race science" in which the writer himself repeats
many of the favored Nazi doctrines, see Tage Ellinger, "On the Breeding of
Aryans," *Journal of Heredity* 33 (1942): 141–43. For replies to this article see Goldschmidt, "Anthropological Determination of 'Aryanism,'" *Journal of Heredity* 33
(1942): 215–16; and Ashley Montagu, "On the Breeding of 'Aryans,'" *Psychiatry* 4
(1943): 254–55. The term "Aryan" is frequently misused to describe a physical stock
of languages which are spoken by a wide variety of ethnic groups. It has nothing
whatever to do with physical characteristics.

30. Ludwig Schemann, *Die Rassenfrage im Schrifttum der Neuzeit* (Munich:
Lehman's Verlag, 1931).

31. Alfred Baeumler, "Race: A Basic Concept in Education" (trans. from the
original article in the *Internationale Zeitschrift für Erziehung* 8 [1939]), *World Education* 4 (1939): 506–9.

32. For an illuminating discussion of the role of German churchmen in the
cause of what they called 'positive Christianity,' see James Bentley, "The Most Irre-
sistable Temptation," *The Listener* (London), 16 November 1978, 635–37.

33. *The New York Times*, 15 March 1978, 3.

34. Which, of course, they do not.

35. John Koumaris, "On the Morphological Variety of Modern Greeks," *Man*
48 (1948): 126–7.

36. James Coates, *Armed and Dangerous* (New York: Hill & Wang, 1987);
Arnold Forster and Benjamin Epstein, *The Trouble Makers* (Garden City, NY: Doubleday, 1952); Arnold Forster and Benjamin Epstein, *Danger on the Right* (New York:
Random House, 1964); Donald A. Downs, *Nazis in Skokie* (Notre Dame: University
of Notre Dame, 1985); Robert C. Liebman and Robert Wuthnow, *The New Christian
Right* (New York: Aldine, 1983); Kevin Flynn and Gary Gerhardt, *The Silent Brotherhood* (New York: Free Press, 1989); Staub, *Roots of Evil;* Gary E. McCuen, *The Religious Right* (Hudson, WI: G. E. McCuen, 1989).

37. Davies, *Infected Christianity;* Forrest G. Wood, *The Arrogance of Faith: Christianity and Race in America from the Colonial Era to the Twentieth Century* (New York: Alfred A. Knopf, 1990).

38. Osborn, in Madison Grant, *The Passing of the Great Race*, 3rd ed. (New
York: Scribner, 1919), vii.

39. Steven L. Chorover, *From Genesis to Genocide: The Meaning of Human Behav-
oir and the Power of Behavior Control* (Cambridge: MIT, 1979), 107.

40. Cedric Dover, "Antar for the Anthropologist," *The Eastern Anthropologist* 5 (1952): 165–69. Dover showed that the famous Bedouin warrior-poet of the sixth century was very conscious of the social disability of being a mulatto. See also Ibn Khaldun, the fourteenth-century Arab scholar, who quoted and criticized those who had appealed to biological factors as explanatory of Negro behavior. *The Muquaddimah* 1.1, trans. by F. Rosenthal (New York: Pantheon Books, 1958), 175–76; Ashley Montagu, *The Idea of Race* (Lincoln: University of Nebraska Press, 1965).

41. John Wilson, "Egypt," in *The Intellectual Adventure of Ancient Man*, eds. H. & H. A. Frankfort et al. (Chicago: University of Chicago Press, 1946), 33–34.

42. S. Davis, *Race-Relations in Ancient Egypt* (New York: Philisophical Library,1952); T. J. Haarhoff, *The Stranger at the Gate* (New York, Macmillan, 1948).

43. John Baldry, *The Unity of Mankind in Greek Thought* (New York: Cambridge University Press, 1947).

44. "By nature, too, some beings command, and others obey, for the sake of mutual safety; for a being endowed with discernment and forethought is by nature the superior and governor; whereas he who is merely able to execute by bodily labour is the inferior and natural slave." Aristotle, *Politics*, 1.2. To this Rousseau made an excellent reply. "Aristotle said," he writes, "that men were not naturally equal, but that some were born for slavery, and others for domination. Aristotle was right, but he took the effect for the cause. Nothing can be more certain than that every man born in slavery is born for slavery. Slaves lose everything in their chains, even the desire to escape from them; they love servitude as the companions of Ulysses loved their brutish condition. If then, there are slaves by nature, it is because there have been slaves against nature. Force made the first slaves, and their cowardice perpetuated them." Rousseau, *The Social Contract*, 1.2.

45. Plato, *The Republic*, 547a.

46. Robert Eisler, "Metallurgical Anthropology in Hesiod and Plato and the Date of a 'Poenician Lie,'" *Isis* 11 (1949): 108–12. On Plato see Karl R. Popper, *The Open Society and Its Enemies* (Princeton: Princeton University Press, 1950). It is not for nothing that during the nineteenth century Plato was considered an indispensable part of the education of a gentleman, that is to say, of a person who relied upon others to do the job of earning a living for him.

47. For discussions of this subject see E. E. Sikes, *The Anthropology of the Greeks* (London: Nutt, 1914),69–89; Robert Schlaifer, "Greek Theories of Slavery form Homer to Artisotle," *Harvard Studies in Classical Philology* 47 (1936): 165–204; F. M. Snowden, Jr., *Blacks in Antiquity* (Cambridge: Harvard University Press, 1970); W. L. Westermann, "The Slave Systems of Greek and Roman Antiquity," *Memoirs of the American Philosophical Society* 40 (1995): xi–180; W. L. Westermann "Slavery and the Elements of Freedom in Ancient Greece," *Quarterly Bulletin of the Polish Institute of Arts and Sciences in America* 1 (1943): 332–47.

48. Isocrates, *Panegyricus*, 4.50. Trans. By George Norlin, pp.xxiv, 149.

49. Aubrey Diller, *Race Mixture Among the Greeks Before Alexander*, Illinois Studies in Language and Literature, vol. 20 (Urbana, 1937); Hertz, *Race and Civilization* (London: Kegan Paul, 1928): 137 ff.; Martin P. Nilsson, "The Race Problem of the Roman Empire" in *Hereditas* 2 (1921): 370–90; Frederick G. Detweiler, "The Rise of Modern Race Antagonisms," *American Journal of Sociology* 38 (1932): 738–47;

Matthew Thomas McClure, "Greek Genius and Race Mixture," in *Studies in the History of Ideas* 3 (1935): 25–33; Haarhoff, *Stranger at the Gate;* Davis, *Race-Relations in Ancient Egypt;* A. N. Sherwin-White, *Racial Prejudice in Imperial Rome* (London and New York: Cambridge University Press, 1968); M. I. Finley, "Prejudice in the Ancient World," *The Listener* 79, 1968, 146–7; Baldry, *Unity of Mankind.*

50. Bryce, *Race Sentiment,* 25–26.

51. Gomes Eannes De Azura, *The Chronicle of the Discovery and Conquest of Guinea* 1 (1453) (London: Hakluyt Society, 1896), 84–85.

52. It was not God, but the drunken Noah, who cursed Canaan the son of Ham, whose descendants occupied Africa, to be a "servant of servants unto his brethren" (Gen. 9). This was clearly in contradiction to the Divine Mind as expressed by Jesus of Nazareth: "One is your Master and all ye are brethren."

53. Katherine George, "The Civilized West Looks at Primitive Africa: 1400–1800. A Study in Ethnocentrism," *Isis* 49 (1958): 66.

54. David Hume, *Treatise on Human Nature,* 1720.

55. Anonymous, "Black Girl's Search." *Times Literary Supplement* (London), 19 January 1967, 46.

56. George, "The Civilized West," 62–72.

57. For a fully documented, pitiless revelation of the history of Jew-hating from the idea stage to that of mass murder see Malcolm Hay, *Europe and the Jews* (Boston: Beacon Press, 1960). See also Joshua Trachtenberg, *The Devil and the Jews* (New York: Meridian Books, 1961).

58. Elizabeth Donnan, ed., *Documents Illustrative of the History of the Slave Trade to America,* 4 vols., (Washington, D.C.: Carnegie Institution, 1930, pub. 409); Eric Williams, *Capitalism and Slavery* (Chapel Hill: University of North Carolina Press, 1944).

59. A. Irving Hallowell, "Some Psychological Characteristics of the Northeastern Indians," in *Man in Northeastern North America,* Papers of the R. S. Peabody Foundation for Archaeology, vol. 3 (1946): 195–225; Lewis Hanke, *Aristotle and the American Indians* (Bloomington: Indiana University Press, 1959).

60. "Le June, Quebec and Hurons: 1640," *Jesuit Relations* 19 (1898): 39, quoted from Hallowell, "Psychological Characteristics," 200.

61. Richard A. Newhall, *The Columbus Letter* (Williamstown, MA: Chapin Library, Williams College, 1953), 8.

62. E. G. Ravenstein, ed., *A Journal of the First Voyage of Vasco de Gama, 1497–1499* (London: Hakluyt, 1897), 17–18.

63. So far as I know, an historical study of this aspect of the subject has never been attempted. It would make a fascinating and highly desirable contribution to our better understanding of the period and of the antecedents of racism. For the early period see George H. Moore, *Notes on the History of Slavery in Massachusetts* (New York: Appleton, 1866). For the later period immediately preceding the Civil War there is the attractive little volume by William Dodd, *The Cotton Kingdom* (New Haven: Yale University Press, 1919). See also Lerone Bennett, Jr., *Before the Mayflower: A History of the Negro in America 1619–1962* (Chicago: Johnson Publishing, 1962); Eugene H. Berwanger, *The Frontier Against Slavery* (Urbana: University of Illinios Press, 1971); Robin Blackburn, *The Overthrow of Colonial Slavery, 1776–1848* (London and New York: Verso, 1988); John W. Blassingame, *The Slave Community*

(New York: Oxford University Press, 1979); Mary Cable, *Black Odyssey* (New York: Viking Press, 1971); David W. Cohen and Jack P. Greene, eds., *Neither Slave Nor Free* (Baltimore: John Hopkins University Press, 1972); Pete Daniel, *The Shadow of Slavery: Peonage in the South 1901–1969* (Urbana: University of Illinois Press, 1972); Basil Davidson, *Black Mother: The Years of the African Slave Trade* (Boston: Little, Brown, 1961); David Brian Davis, *The Problem of Slavery in Western Culture* (Ithaca: Cornell University Press, 1966); Carl N. Degler, *Neither Black Nor White: Slavery and Race Relations in Brazil and the United States* (New York: Macmillan, 1971); Martin Duberman, ed., *The Antislavery Vanguard* (Princeton: Princeton University Press, 1966); W. E. B. DuBois, *The Suppression of the African Slave-Trade to the United States of America 1638–1870* (Baton Rouge: Louisiana State University Press, 1969); Dwight L. Dumond, *Antislavery Origins of the Civil War in the United States* (Ann Arbor: University of Michigan Press, 1960); Robert F. Durden, *The Gray and the Black* (Baton Rouge: Louisiana State University Press, 1972); Stanley Elkins, *Slavery* (Chicago: University of Chicago Press, 1959); Stanley Feldstein, *Once a Slave: The Slaves' View of Slavery* (New York: Morrow, 1971); Betty Fladeland, *Men & Brothers* (Urbana: University of Illinios Press, 1972); Eric Foner, ed., *America's Black Past* (New York: Harper & Row, 1970); John Hope Franklin, *From Slavery to Freedom* (New York: Alfred A. Knopf, 1961); George M. Frederickson, *The Black Image in the White Mind* (New York: Harper & Row, 1971); L. Fuller, *The Crusade Against Slavery* (New York: Harper, 1960); Eugene D. Genovese, "The Slave South: An Interpretation," *Science & Society* 25 (1961): 320–37; Eugene D. Genovese, *The Political Economy of Slavery* (Middletown, CT: Wesleyan University Press, 1989); Eugene P. Genovese, *The World the Slaveholders Made* (New York: Pantheon Books, 1969); Thomas Gossett, *Race: The History of an Idea in America* (Dallas: Southern Methodist University Press, 1963); Douglas Grant, *The Fortunate Slave: An Illustration of African Slavery in the Eighteenth Century* (New York: Oxford University Press, 1968); Lorenzo J. Greene, *The Negro in Colonial New England* (New York: Atheneum, 1968); Herbert G. Gutman, *The Black Family in Slavery and Freedom, 1750–1925* (New York: Pantheon Books, 1976); Paul Jacob, Saul Landau, and Eve Pell, *To Serve the Devil*, 2 vols. (New York, Random House, 1971); Winthrop D. Jordan, *White over Black* (Chapel Hill: University of North Carolina, 1968); Herbert Klein, *Slavery in the Americas* (Chicago: University of Chicago Press, 1967); Aileen S. Kraditor, *Means and Ends in American Abolitionism* (New York: Pantheon, 1969); Lawrence Lader, *The Bold Brahmins* (New York: E. P. Dutton, 1961); Anne J. Lane, ed., *The Debate Over Slavery* (Urbana: University of Illinois Press, 1971); Leon F. Litwak, *Been in the Storm so Long: The Aftermath of Slavery* (New York; Alfred A. Knopf, 1979); John R. Lynch, *The Facts of Reconstruction* (Indianapolis: Bobbs-Merrill, 1970); Carelton Mabee, *Black Freedom: The Nonviolent Abolitionists from 1830 through the Civil War* (New York: Macmillan, 1970); Bernard Mandel, *Labor: Free and Slave* (New York: Associated Authors, 1955); Daniel P. Mannix, *Black Cargoes* (New York: Viking Press, 1962); Donald G. Mathews, *Slavery and Methodism* (Princeton: Princeton University Press, 1965); Howard McGary and Bill E. Lawson, *Between Slavery and Freedon* (Bloomington: Indiana University Press, 1992); Eric L. McKitrick, ed., *Slavery Defended: The Views of the Old South* (Englewood Cliffs, NJ: Prentice Hall, 1963); Melton A. McLaurin, *Celia: A Slave* (Athens: University of Georgia Press, 1991); Edgar J. McManus, *A History of Negro Slavery in New York* (Syracuse: Syracuse University Press, 1966); James M. McPherson, *The Struggle For*

Equality (Princeton: Princeton University Press, 1965). A bibliography on slavery in the Americas will be found in James M. McPherson et al. eds., *Blacks in America* (New York: Doubleday, 1971). See also August Meier and Elliot Rudwick, *From Plantation to Ghetto* (New York: Hill and Wang, 1966); Frederick Merck, *Slavery and the Annexation of Texas* (New York: Alfred A. Knopf, 1966); Randall M. Miller and John David Smith, eds., *Dictionary of African American Slavery* (Westport, CT: Greenwood Press, 1988); Wilbert E. Moore, *American Negro Slavery and Abolition* (New York: The Third Press, 1971); Michael Mullin, ed., *American Negro Slavery: A Documentary History* (Columbia: University of South Carolina Press, 1976); Charles H. Nichols, *Many Thousand Gone* (Leiden: Brill, 1963); Earl Ofari, *Let Your Motto Be Resistance* (Boston: Beacon Press, 1972); Ulrich B. Phillips, *American Negro Slavery* (Baton Rouge: Louisiana State University Press, 1966); James Pope–Hennessy, *Sins of the Fathers: A Study of the Atlantic Slave Traders: 1441–1807* (New York: Alfred A. Knopf); Benjamin A. Quarles, *Black Abolitionists* (New York: Oxford University Press, 1969); James A. Rawley, *Race and Politics: "Bleeding Kansas" and the Coming Civil War* (Philadelphia: Lippincott, 1969); J. Saunders Redding, *They Came in Chains* (Philadelphia: Lippincott, 1950); Donald E. Reynolds, *Editors Make War: Southern Newspapers in the Secession Crisis* (Nashville: Vanderbilt University Press, 1970); Leonard L. Richards, *Gentlemen of Property and Standing* (New York: Oxford University Press, 1970); David L. Robinson, *Slavery in the Structure of American Politics 1765–1820* (New York: Norton, 1979); Peter Rose, ed., *Old Memories, New Moods* (New York: Atherton, 1970); Peter Rose, ed., *Slavery and its Aftermath* (New York: Atherton, 1970); Willie L. Rose, ed., *A Documentary History of Slavery in North America* (New York: Oxford University Press, 1976); V. Freimarck Rosenthal and B. Rosenthal, eds., *Race and the American Romantics* (New York: Schoken, 1971); Clinton Rossiter, *The American Quest 1790–1860* (New York: Harcourt Brace Jovanovich, 1969); Louis Ruchames, *The Abolitionists: A Collection of Their Writings* (New York: Putnams, 1963); Louis Ruchames, ed., *Racial Thought in America* (Amherst: University of Massachussetts Press, 1969); A. G. Russell, *Colour, Race and Empire* (London: Gollancz, 1944); Lester B. Scherer, *Slavery and the Churches in Early America* (Grand Rapids: Eerdman's, 1975); Elbert B. Smith, *The Death of Slavery* (Chicago: University of Chicago Press, 1967); Kenneth Stampp, *The Peculiar Institution* (New York: Alfred A. Knopf, 1966); Robert S. Starobin, *Industrial Slavery in the Old South* (New York: Oxford University Press, 1970); James B. Stewart, *Holy Warriors: The Abolutionists and American Society* (New York: Hill & Wang, 1976); Charles S. Sydnor, *Slavery In Mississippi* (Gloucester, MA: P. Smith, 1965 [ca. 1933]); John L. Thomas, ed., *Slavery Attacked: The Abolitionist Crusade* (Inglewood Cliffs, NJ: Prentice Hall, 1965); Okon Edet Uya, *From Slavery to Public Service: Robert Smalls 1839–1915* (New York: Oxford University Press, 1971); Richard C. Wade, *Slavery in the Cities—The South 1810–1860* (New York: Oxford University Press, 1964); W. E. F. Ward, *The Royal Navy and the Slavers* (New York: Pantheon Books, 1969); Eric Williams, *Capitalism and Slavery* (Chapel Hill: University of North Carolina Press, 1944); Robin W. Winks, *The Blacks in Canada* (New Haven: Yale University Press, 1971); Harvey Wish, ed., *Ante-Bellum* (New York; Putnam's 1960); C. Vann Woodward, *American Counterpoint: Slavery and Racism in the North-South Dialogue* (Boston: Little, Brown, 1970); C. Vann Woodward, *The Strange Career of Jim Crow,* 2nd ed., (New York: Oxford University Press, 1966); Norman R. Yetman, *Voices From Slavery* (New York: Holt, Rinehart & Winston, 1970).

64. See, for example, Thomas R. R. Cobb, *An Inquiry into the Law of Negro Slavery in the United States of America* (Philadelphia: Johnson & Co., 1858).

65. For an account of the rise and development of the convention of the noble savage in French and, particularly, in English literature see Hoxie N. Fairchild, *The Noble Savage* (New York: Columbia University Press, 1928); see also Eva B. Dykes, *The Negro in English Romantic Thought* (Washington, D.C.: Associated Publishers, 1942).

66. Whose categorical imperative is seldom spelled out in our time. Here it is: "so act as to treat humanity, whether in thine own person or in that of another, in every case as an end withal, never as a means only."

67. Johann G. Von Herder, *Outlines of a Philosophy of the History of Man*, vol. 1, trans. by T. Churchill, (London: J. Johnson, 1803), 298. An attempt has been made to show that Herder was a racist; see Cedric Dover, "The Racial Philosophy of Johann Herder," *British Journal of Sociology* 3 (1952): 124–33.

68. Johann F. Blumenbach, *On the Natural Variety of Mankind*, trans. and ed. by Thomas Bendyshe in *The Anthropological Treatises of Johann Friedrich Blumenbach* (London: Anthropological Society, 1865), 98–99 ff.

69. Ibid., 100.

70. Ralph Waldo Emerson, "Race," in *English Traits* (Boston: Philips, Sampson & Co. 1856), 54.

71. Ibid., 62.

72. For a brilliant discussion of this subject see Lancelot Hogben, "The Concept of Race," in his *Genetic Principles in Medicine and Social Science* (New York: Alfred A. Knopf, 1931), 122–44. See also William C. Boyd, *Genetics and the Races of Man* (Boston: Little Brown, 1950); Lancelot Hogben, *Nature and Nurture* (New York: W. W. Norton, 1933).

73. W. H. Thorpe, "Biological Races in *Hyponemeuta Padella L.*," *Journal of the Linnaean Society (Zoölogy)* 36 (1928): 621; W. H. Thorpe, "Biological Races in Insects and Allied Groups," *Biological Reviews* 5 (1930): 177; W. H. Thorpe, "Ecology and the Future of Systematics," in *The New Systematics*, ed. Julian Huxley (Oxford: Clarendon Press, 1940), 358; Th. Dobzhansky and Carl Epling, *Contributions to the Genetics, Taxonomy, and Ecology of* Drosophila pseudoobscura *and Its Relatives,* Pub 554 (Washington, D.C.: Carnegie Institution, 1944).

74. For an admirable presentation of the new taxonomy see Ernst Mayr, *Systematics and the Origin of Species* (New York: Columbia University Press, 1970).

75. For a critical discussion of such terms as "advanced" and "primitive," see Ashley Montagu, "The Concept of 'Primitive' and Related Anthropological Terms: A Study in the Systematics of Confusion," in *The Concept of the Primitive,* ed. Ashley Montagu, (New York: Free Press, 1968), 148–68.

76. Ralph Linton, *The Study of Man* (New York: Appleton-Century, 1936), 22.

77. Georges Cuvier, *Le Regne Animal,* vol. 1 (Paris: Deterville, 1817), iv-vi.

78. Alexander von Humbolt, *Cosmos: A Sketch of a Physical Description of the Universe,* trans. from the German by E. C. Otté (London: Bohn: 1849), 368–69.

79. Wilhelm von Humboldt, *Über die Kawi-Sprach auf der Insel Java,* vol. 3 (Berlin: Königlichen Academie der Wissenschaften, 1836), 426.

80. David Brion Davis, *Revolutions: Reflections on American Equality and Foreign Liberation* (Cambridge: Harvard University Press, 1991).

81. Roger Bruns, ed., *Am I Not a Man and a Brother* (New York: Chelsea House, 1977); Robin Blackburn, *The Overthrow of Colonial Slavery: 1776–1848* (London: Verso, 1988; New York: Routledge, 1989); Terrence Brady and Evan Jones, *The Fight Against Slavery* (New York: W. W. Norton, 1977); Robert M. Cover, *Justice Accused: Antislavery and the Judicial Process* (New Haven: Yale University Press); Davis, *Reflections;* David Brion Davis, *Slavery and Human Progress* (New York: Oxford University Press, 1984); David Brion Davis, *The Problem of Slavery in Western Culture* (Ithaca: Cornell University Press, 1966); Morton L. Dillon, *Slavery Attacked: Southern Slaves and Their Allies, 1619–1865* (De Kalb: Northern Illinios University Press, 1990); Morton L. Dillon, *The Abolitionists* (De Kalb: Northern Illinois University Press, 1974); Duberman, ed., *The Antislavery Vanguard;* Louis Filler, *The Crusade Against Slavery: 1830–1860* (New York: Harper Bros., 1960); Eric Foner, *Reconstruction: America's Unfinished Revolution 1863–1877* (New York: Harper & Row, 1988); Eric Foner, ed., *America's Black Past;* John Hope Franklin, *From Slavery to Freedom: A History of Negro Americans* (New York: Alfred A. Knopf, 1961); George M. Frederickson, *The Arrogance of Race: Historical Perspectives on Slavery, Racism, and Social Inequality* (Middletown, CT: Wesleyan Univeristy Press, 1988); Frederickson, *Black Image;* Eugene Genovese, *The World The Slaveholders Made* (New York; Pantheon, 1969); Jack Greene and J. R. Pole, *Colonial British America* (Baltimore: Johns Hopkins University Press, 1984); J. Morgan Kouser and James M. McPherson, eds., *Region, Race, and Reconstruction* (New York: Oxford University Press, 1982); Duncan J. McLeod, *Slavery, Race and the American Revolution* (London, New York: Cambridge University Press, 1974); James M. McPherson, *The Abolitionist Legacy* (Princeton: Princeton University Press, 1975); James Oakes, *The Ruling Class: A History of American Slaveholders* (New York: Alfred A. Knopf, 1982); Orlando Patterson, *Slavery and Social Death* (Cambridge: Harvard University Press, 1982); Lewis Perry, *Radical Abolitionism* (Ithaca: Cornell University Press, 1973); James A. Rawley, *The Trans-Atlantic Slave Trade* (New York: Norton, 1981); Ruchames, ed., *Racial Thought;* Ruchames, *The Abolitionists;* Scherer, *Slavery and the Churches;* James B. Stewart, *Holy Warriors: The Abolitionists and American Slavery* (New York: Hill and Wang, 1976); Michael Tadman, *Speculators and Slaves* (Madison: University of Wisconsin Press, 1989); Larry E. Tise, *Proslavery: A History of the Defense of Slavery in America 1700–1840* (Athens: University of Georgia Press, 1988); Geoffrey Ward, Ric Burns and Ken Burns, *The Civil War* (New York: Alfred A. Knopf, 1990).

82. Harry Ashmore, *The Man in the Middle* (Columbia: University of Missouri Press: 1966), 24; H. Ashmore, *Hearts and Minds: The Anatomy of Racism from Roosevelt to Reagan* (New York: McGraw-Hill, 1982).

83. For a valuable discussion of this aspect of the subject, see Hannah Arendt, *The Origins of Totalitarianism* (New York: Harcourt Brace Jovanovich, 1951). "It is highly probable that the thinking in terms of race would have disappeared in due time together with other irresponsible opinions of the nineteenth century, if the 'scramble for Africa' and the new era of imperialism had not exposed Western humanity to new and shocking experiences. Imperialism would have necessitated the invention of racism as the only possible 'explanation' and excuse for its deeds, even if no race-thinking had ever existed in the civilized world," pp. 183–84. See also "Racism and Imperialism" in Richard Hofstadter, *Social Darwinism in American Thought, 1860–1915* (Philadelphia: University of Pennsylvania Press, 1944), 146–73;

Philip D. Curtin, "The Origin of the 'White Man's Burden,'" *The Listener* 66, 1961, 412–15; Christine Bolt, *Victorian Attitudes to Race* (London: Routledge & Kegan Paul, 1971); L. H. Gann and Peter Duignan, *Colonialism in Africa 1870–1960*, 3 vols. (London and New York: Cambridge University Press, 1969); Boris Gussman, *Out in the Mid-Day Sun* (New York: Oxford University Press, 1963); J. A. Hobson, *Imperialism: A Study* (London: Allen & Unwin, 1965); V. G. Kiernan, *The Lords of Human Kind* (Boston: Little, Brown, 1969); Philip Mason, *Patterns of Dominance* (New York, Oxford Univertisy Press, 1970); Louis Snyder, ed., *The Imperialism Reader* (Princeton: Van Nostrand, 1962).

84. Gottfried W. von Leibnitz, *Otium Hanoveriana; sive, Miscellanea* (Leipzig, 1718), 37.

85. [Bernier] "Nouvelle division de la Terre, par les différentes Especes ou races d'homme qui l'habitent, envoyée par un fameux Voyageur à Monsieur . . . à peu près en ces termes," *Journal des Sçavans,* 24 April, 1684, 85–89. In English translation this essay is reprinted in Bendyshe, "The History of Anthropology," in *Memoirs Read before the Anthropological Society of London,* I (1863–64): 360–64.

86. Georges Buffon, *Histoire naturelle, générale et particulière* (Paris, 1749), Natural History, General and Particular, trans. by William Smellie III, corrected by William Wood (London, 1812), 302 ff.

87. Ales Hrdlicka, for example, lists six varieties as purporting to be "Buffon's classification." See "The Races of Man" in *Scientific Aspects of the Race Problem,* ed. J. W. Corrigan (New York: Longmans, 1941), 174.

88. The word "race" is of obscure origin. In English many uses of the word are set out in the Oxford English Dictionary, but it is clear that it was already in use in the sixteenth century. In France, François Tant, in a book entitled *Thrésor de la langue française,* published in 1600, derived the word from the Latin *radix,* a root, and stated that "it aludes to the extraction of a man, of a dog, of a horse; as one says of good or bad race." See Paul Topinard, "La Notion de race en anthropologie," *Revue d'Anthropologie,* 2nd ser., 2 (1879): 590. Attempts have been made to derive the words from the Latin *ratio,* the Italian *razza* (fourteenth century), the Spanish and Portuguese *raza,* and even from the Arabic *ras.* See Cedric Dover, "Race," *Man,* art. 95 (1951): 1.

89. John Newton, captain of the slaver African in 1752, who afterwards aided Wilberforce in the campaign to abolish the trade, wrote, "During the time I was engaged in the slave trade I never had the least scruple as to its lawfulness." See Anne Holt, *Walking Together* (London: Allen & Ulwin, 1938), 155.

90. L. P. Jacks, *The Confessions of an Octogenarian* (London: Allen & Ulwin, 1942), 137–38.

91. Carl Bridenbaugh, *Jamestown 1544–1699* (New York: Oxford University Press, 1980); Stanley M. Elkins, *Slavery* (Chicago: University of Chicago Press, 1959), 38sq; Rose, ed., *Documentary History of Slavery in North America.*

92. Klein, *Slavery,* 45–46.

93. Mary Stoughton Locke, *Anti-Slavery in America From the Introduction of African Slaves to the Prohibition of the Slave Trade 1619–1808,* Gloucester, MA: P. Smith, 1965.

94. John Wesley, *Thoughts Upon Slavery* (London: n.p., n.d.), 35.

95. Dumond, *Anti-Slavery*.

96. Mathews, *Slavery and Methodism*.

97. Cesar de l'Escale De Verone, *Observations sur les Hommes Couleur des Colonies* (Paris, 1790).

98. Victor Courtet de l'Isle, *La Science Politique Fondee sur la Science de l'Homme*. (Paris, 1837).

99. Thomas Jefferson, *Notes on the State of Virginia*, in *The Complete Jefferson*, ed. Saul K. Padover, (New York: Tudor Publishing, 1943), 662. For by far the best study of Jefferson's views on Blacks and slavery see John C. Miller, *The Wolf By The Ears: Thomas Jefferson and Slavery* (New York: Free Press, 1977). See also the measured discussion of Jefferson's views in Dumas Malone's *Jefferson and His Time: The Sage of Monticello*, vol. 6 (Boston: Little, Brown, & Co., 1948), 316–27.

100. Silvio Bedini, *The Life of Benjamin Banneker* (New York: Schribner's Sons, 1972).

101. A facsimile of the original letter may be seen in Bedini, *Benjamin Banneker*, fig.17.

102. Thomas Jefferson, Letter of Henri Gregoire, 25 February 1809, in *Basic Writings of Thomas Jefferson*, ed. Philip Foner (New York: Halcyon, 1950), 682.

103. Leigh Hunt, "Negro Civilzation," *The Examiner*, 4 August 1811, No. 188.

104. Edward Long, *The History of Jamaica*, 3 vols. (London, 1774).

105. Edward Long, "Observations on thte Gradation in the Scale of Being Between the Human and the Brute Creation. Including Some Curious Particulars Respecting Negroes," *The Columbian Magazine or Monthly Miscellany* 2 (1788): 15.

106. Samuel S. Smith, *An Essay on the Causes of the Variety of Complexion and Figure in the Human Species*, reprint (Harvard University Press, 1965).

107. Ibid., 33.

108. Ibid.

109. Ibid., 34.

110. For an account of this aspect of the subject, see Roy H. Pearce, *The Savages of America*, revised (Baltimore: Johns Hopkins Press, 1965).

111. Albert H. Smyth, ed., *The Writings of Benjamin Franklin*, vol. 1 (New York: Macmillan 1907), 376. In passing, it may be noted that in 1760 Franklin was admitted to membership in the English Anti-Slavery Society, and that when he was eighty-one years old Franklin became the president of the Pennsylvania Abolition Society. Nevertheless, Franklin's own slaves were not freed until after his death.

112. Charles de Secondat Montesquieu, *The Spirit of the Laws*, book 15, chap. 5, trans. Thomas Nugent (New York: Hafner 1949).

113. Claudine Hunting, "The *Philosophes* and Black Slavery 1748–1765," *Journal of the History of Ideas* 39 (1978): 405–18.

114. Thomas Dew, *Review of the Debates in the Virginia Legislature of 1831–1832* (Richmond, VA: Randolph, 1832). Dew's discussion first appeared in pamphlet form in Richmond in May, 1832, and was widely noticed in the Southern press. See also William Harper, *A Memoir on Slavery* (Charleston: Burgess, 1838).

115. Josiah Nott, *Types of Mankind* (Philadelphia: Lippincott, 1854). In 1856 Nott contributed an appendix to Hotz's translation of Gobineau's *The Moral and Intellectual Diversity of Races*, in which he sought to provide the biological evidence for

the natural inequalities of the various branches of mankind. See Emmet B. Carmichael, "Josiah Clark Nott," *Bulletin of the History of Medicine* 22 (1948): 249–62.

116. Dodd, *Cotton Kingdom,* 146; see also chap. 3, "The Social Philosophy of the Cotton Planter."

117. Willliam S. Jenkins, *Pro-Slavery Thought in the Old South* (Chapel Hill: University of North Carolina Press, 1935), 125.

118. Cobb, *Inquiry,* 8–9.

119. Ibid., 16–17.

120. Ibid., 51.

121. Ibid., 49.

122. Ibid., 51.

123. George Norlin, *The Quest of American Life University of Colorado Studies,* Series B, Studies in the Humanities, vol. 2 (Boulder, 1945), ix.

124. Quoted from Herbert Apthekar, *Essays in the History of the American Negro* (New York: International Publishers, 1945), 139.

125. On Smith see Donald H. Meyer, *The American Moralists: Academic Moral Philosophy in the United States 1835–1880.* Unpublished Ph.D. dissertation, University of California, Berkeley, 1976, 34–366. Also Lewis Perry, *Radical Abolitionism* (Ithaca: Cornell University Press, 1973); Ann J. Lane, ed., *The Debate Over Slavery* (Urbana: University of Illinois Press, 1971).

126. George Fitzhugh, *Sociology for the South, or Failure of Free Society* (Richmond, VA: A. Morris, 1954.)

127. John Saffin, *A Brief and Candid Answer to a Late Printed Sheet, Entitled, The Selling of Joseph* (Boston, 1701). Quoted from Moore, *Notes on the History of Slavery,* 251. In our own time this doctrine has been even more efficiently preached by Protestant theologians of the Dutch Reformed Church of South Africa.

128. Russel Nye, *Fettered Freedom* (East Lansing: Michigan State College Press, 1949). For further reading, see *The National Anti-Slavery Standard,* 28 January 1850.

129. *The Anti-Slavery Bugle,* 12 January 1850.

130. It is of interest to note here that in what is undoubtedly the most important study of the problem of the American black that has ever been made, the author's independent analysis of the historical facts has led him to practically identical conclusions: "The biological ideology had to be utilized as an intellectual explanation of, and a moral apology for, slavery in a society which went out emphatically to invoke as its highest principles the ideas of the inalienable right of all men to freedom and equality of opportunity." Gunnar Myrdal, *An American Dilemma: The Negro Problem and Modern Democracy,* 2 vols. (New York: Harper, 1944), 83–89. "The correct observation that the Negro is inferior [i.e., socially inferior] was tied up to the correct belief that man belongs to the biological universe, and, by twisting logic, the incorrect deduction was made that the inferiority is biological in nature," ibid., 97. For a valuable discussion of the subject see John C. Greene, "The American Debate on the Negro's Place in Nature," *Journal of the History of Ideas* 15 (1954): 384–96.

131. We may refer, for example, to the case of the president of the Anthropological Society of London, Dr. James Hunt. On 17 November 1863, Dr. Hunt read a paper before the society entitled "The Negro's Place in Nature," in which he asserted the essential inferiority in every way of the Negro to the white man. "The Ne-

gro's Place in Nature," *Memoirs of the Anthropological Society* (London) 1 (1863), 1–64. This paper was discussed at the meeting in a very dignified manner by everyone but the egregious and insolent Dr. Hunt, who wound up his reply to his critics with the remark that "all he asked was that scientific evidence of this character should be met by scientific argument, and not by poetical clap-trap, or by gratuitous and worthless assumptions." *Anthropological Review* 1 (London, 1863): 391. The paper was the immediate cause of many acrimonious debates, and it was, of course, received with much applause by the proslavery party, especially in the United States. When, in 1869, Dr. Hunt died, a New York paper wrote that "Dr. Hunt, in his own clear knowledge and brave enthusiasm, was doing more for humanity, for the welfare of mankind, and for the glory of God, than all the philosophers, humanitarians, philanthropists, statesmen, and, we may say, bishops and clergy of England together." This last statement is taken from Alfred C. Haddon's *History of Anthropology* (London: Watts, 1934), 45.

132. Wilhelm Wundt, *Philosophische Studien*, vol. 3 (Leipzig: Englemann, 1883).

133. See Edward Lurie, "Louis Agassiz and the Races of Man," *Isis* 45 (1954): 227–42; William Stanton, *The Leopard's Spots: Scientific Attitudes Toward Race in America, 1815–59* (Chicago: University of Chicago Press, 1960); John S. Haller, Jr., *Outcasts From Evolution: Scientific Attitudes of Racial Inferiority* (Urbana: University of Illinois Press, 1971).

134. See C. L. Bachman, *John Bachman* (Charleston: Walker, Evans, and Coswell, 1888), 317.

135. T. S. Foster, *Travels and Settlements of Early Man* (London: Benn, 1929), 31.

136. For an account of Gobineau and a distillation of the essence of Gobineauism by an apostle of both Gobineau and Nietzsche, Dr. Oscar Levy, see Count Joseph A. de Gobineau, *The Renaissance*, trans. by Paul V. Cohn (London: Allen & Unwin, 1927). The introductory essay of some sixty pages by Dr. Levy is an amazing thing. See also Michael Biddiss, ed., *Gobineau: Selected Political Writings* (New York: Harper & Row, 1970).

137. Observe how, from the same motives, this reaction expresses itself in the more recent writings of one of the most confused of American racists, namely in Madison Grant's *The Passing of the Great Race*. He writes: "There exists to-day a widespread and fatuous belief in the power of environment, as well as of opportunity, to alter heredity, which arises from the dogma of the brotherhood of man, derived in turn from those loose thinkers of the French Revolution and their American mimics. Such beliefs have done much damage in the past, and if allowed to go uncontradicted, may do much more serious damage in the future" (p. 14).

138. Jean Finot, *Race Prejudice* (New York; Dutton, 1907), 7. For a brilliant analysis of Gobineau and his views see Ernst Cassirer, *The Myth of the State* (New Haven: Yale University Press, 1946), 225–47.

139. For a valuable account of these writings and their influence, see Leon Stein, *The Racial Thinking of Richard Wagner* (New York: Philosophical Library, 1950).

140. Houston Chamberlain, *Die Grundlagen des neunzehnten Jahrunderts* (1899), trans. by John Lees as *The Foundations of the Nineteenth Century* (London and New York: Lane, 1910).

141. This refers to Chamberlain's statement that "it frequently happens that children who have no conception of what 'Jew' means . . . begin to cry as soon as a genuine Jew or Jewess comes near them."

142. This is probably John Wilson (pseudonym Christopher North) whose lifelong friend wrote the works which Wilson passed off as his own. See Elsie Swann's *Christopher North* (Edinburgh: Oliver Boyd, 1934).

143. John Oakesmith, *Race and Nationality* (London: Heinemann, 1919), 58.

144. William L. Shirer, *The Rise and Fall of the Third Reich* (New York: Simon and Schuster, 1960).

145. For Chamberlain see Geoffrey E. Field's fascinating biography, *Evangelist of Race* (New York: Columbia University Press, 1981); for Chamberlain's letter see pp. 436–437.

146. Oaksmith, *Race and Nationality,* 50.

147. Mary Butler, *The Tyranny of Greece Over Germany* (Cambridge: Cambridge University Press, 1935); Leon Poliakov, *The Aryan Myth* (New York: Basic Books, 1974); Louis L. Snyder, *German Nationalism: The Tragedy of a People* (Harrisburg, PA: Stackpole 1952).

148. Ernest Renan, *The Future of Science* (London: Chapman and Hall, 1891), xviii. Almost a hundred years later we find Sigmund Freud writing, a little queriously, "Because we destroy illusions, we are reproached with endangering ideas."

149. Michael D. Biddiss, ed., *Images of Race* (Leicester: Leicester University Press, 1979); William Stanton, *The Leopard's Spots: Scientific Attitudes Toward Race in America 1815–59* (Chicago: University of Chicago Press, 1960): Haller, *Outcasts From Evolution;* Ruchames, ed., *Racial Thought;* Nancy Stepan, *The Idea of Race in Science: Great Britain 1815–1800–1960* (New York: Anchor Books, 1982); Daniel Gasman, *The Scientific Origins of National Socialism* (New York: Basic Books, 1974); Elazar Bakan, *The Retreat of Scientific Racism* (Cambridge: Cambridge University Press 1991); Audrey Smedley, *Race in North America: Origin and Evolution of a World View* (Denver: Westview Press, 1993).

150. Willem A. Bonger, *Race and Crime* (New York: Columbia University Press, 1943), 11. On the invasion of Holland by the Nazis, Bonger became one of their first victims. For an admirable account of the rise of racism in Germany see Massing, *Rehearsal for Destruction.*

151. Hermann Rauschning, *The Voice of Destruction* (New York: Putnam, 1940) 232; George W. Stocking, Jr., *Victorian Anthropology* (New York: Free Press, 1987); Walter E. Houghton, *The Victorian Frame of Mind 1830–1870* (New Haven: Yale University Press, 1957).

152. Henry Turner Jr., ed., *Hitler: Memoirs of a Confidant* (New Haven: Yale University Press, 1985), 201–15.

153. James Viscount Bryce, *Race Sentiment as a Factor in History* (London: University of London Press, 1915), 31. For an excellent study of the "mischief" done by educated writers see Frederic E. Faverty, *Matthew Arnold the Ethnologist* (Evanston, IL: Northwestern University Press, 1951).

154. "Miscegenation in South Africa," *Nature* 3698 (1940): 357. The above remarks refer to the official report of the commissioners appointed by the Union of South Africa under the title Report of the Commission on Mixed Marriages in

South Africa (Pretoria, Government Printer, 1939). This document provides an interesting case study of "race" prejudice in action at a high governmental level. American precedents, laws, and decisions relating to intermarriage are heavily drawn upon. So was the way prepared for apartheid.

155. See the UNESCO Report *The Race Concept*. See also, Ashley Montagu, *Statement on Race,* revised (New York: Oxford University Press, 1972), and Appendix A of the unabridged edition of this volume.

2

The Fallaciousness of the Older Anthropological Conception of Race

At the famous 1860 meeting of the British Association for the Advancement of Science at Oxford, just a few months after the publication of Charles Darwin's *The Origin of Species,* the redoubtable young Thomas Henry Huxley scored a resounding victory over Bishop Wilberforce, who led the forces opposed to Darwin's new theory of evolution, and attempted to make a monkey of Huxley, whereupon the younger man rose to the occasion, turned the tables, and made a monkey out of the Bishop. It is told that when the Bishop of Worcester returned home he communicated the intelligence to his wife that the horrid Professor Huxley had stated that man was descended from the apes, whereupon the good lady exclaimed: "Descended from the apes! My dear, let us hope that it is not true. But if it is, let us pray that it will not become generally known."

More recently, the attempt to deprive the older generation of physical anthropologists of their belief in race was construed by its members as an affront akin to that which sought to deprive the Bishop's wife of her belief in the doctrine of special creation. Throughout the nineteenth century and well into the first half of the twentieth there was hardly a scientist who did not fully subscribe to the concept of race.[1] Indeed, the older anthropological conception of race and the belief in special creation have much in common, for race is, to large extent, the special creation of the physical anthropologist. Most physical anthropologists until recently took it for granted that race corresponded to some sort of physical reality in nature. Indeed, the concept of race was one of the fundamental ideas with which the physical anthropologist habitually worked. To question the validity of this basic concept upon which he was intellectually nurtured as if it were an axiom was something which never occurred to him. One doesn't question the axioms upon which one's science and one's activity in it are based—at least, not usually. One simply takes them for granted.

But in science, as in life, it is good practice to attach from time to time a question mark to the facts one takes most for granted, to question the fundamental postulates or facts which require no demonstration; for a fact as a postulate is largely the opinion of those who *should* know—and being human those who *should* know are sometimes fallible, and therefore liable to err. In science such questioning is important, because without it there is a very real danger that certain erroneous or arbitrary ideas, which may originally have been used merely as a convenience, may become so fortified by technicality and so dignified by time that their original infirmities may eventually be wholly concealed.

So it was with the older or classical anthropological conception of race. It was, indeed, nothing but a whited sepulcher, a conception which in the light of modern field and experimental genetics proved utterly erroneous and meaningless; "an absolutist system of metaphysical beliefs," as it has been called.[2] As such, it has been suggested that the term be dropped from the anthropological as well as from the popular vocabulary, for it is a tendentious term which has done an infinite amount of harm and no good at all.

The development of the anthropological conception of race may be traced from the scholastic naturalization of Aristotle's doctrine of the predicables of genus, species, difference, property, and accident. From the Middle Ages through the seventeenth century it may be followed to the early days of the Age of Enlightenment, when Linnaeus, in 1735, took over the concepts of class, genus, and species from the theologians to serve him as systematic tools.[3] As we have already seen, the term "race" was first introduced into the literature of natural history by Buffon in 1749. But Buffon did not use the term in a classificatory sense; this was left to Blumenbach (1752–1840) the founder of physical anthropology.[4]

As used by Blumenbach, the term "race" merely represented an extension of the Aristotelian conception of species; that is to say, it was a subdivision of a species. Like Buffon, Blumenbach recognized, as did Linnaeus, that all human beings belong to a single species and considered it merely convenient to distinguish between certain geographically localized groups of humankind. Thus, when with Blumenbach, in the late eighteenth century, the term assumed a classificatory value, it was understood that that value was purely arbitrary and no more than a simple convenience. It had no other meaning than that. The Aristotelian conception of species, the theological conception of special creation, and the natural history of the Age of Enlightenment, as represented particularly by Cuvier's brilliant conception of unity of type, namely, the idea was that animals can be grouped and classified upon the basis of assemblages of structural characters which, more or less, they posess in common. These three conceptions fitted together extremely well and yielded the idea of the fixity of species, an idea which, in spite of every indication to the contrary in the years which followed, was gradually extended to the typological concept of race, namely, that certain people or populations existed who were characterized by physical types that distinguished them from all other peoples or populations.

The Darwinian contribution showed that species were not so fixed as was formerly believed and that under the action of natural selection one species might give rise to another; that all animal forms might change in this way. It is, however, important to remember that Darwin conceived of evolution as a process involving continuous materials which, without the operation of natural selection, would remain unchanged. Hence, under the Darwinian conception of species it was still possible to think of species as relatively fixed and immutable, with the modification that under the slow action of natural selection they were capable of change. For the nineteenth-century physical anthropologist, therefore, it was possible to think of race or races, not as Blumenbach did in the eighteenth century, as an arbitrary convenience in classification, but as Cuvier did at the beginning of the nineteenth century for all animals, as groups which could be classified on the basis of the fact that they possessed an aggregate of common physical characters, and, as Darwin later postulated, as groups which varied only under conditions of natural selection, which otherwise remained unchanged.

This is essentially a scholastic conception of species with the one fundamental difference that a species is considered to be no longer fixed and immutable. As far as the older physical anthropological conception of race is concerned, a few anthropologists, still unaware of the significance of the findings of modern genetics, continued to think of race as the scholastics thought of species, as a knowable, even though mutable, fixed whole, the essence of which could be defined *per genus, species, propria, differentia, et accidens.* In fact, the physical anthropologist had simply taken over a crude eighteenth-century notion which was originally offered as a general term with no more than an arbitrary value—a convenient aid to the memory in discussing various groups of humankind—and, having erected an emmense terminology and methodology about it, deceived himself in the belief that he was dealing with an objective reality.[5]

Anthropologists failed in their vision because they neglected to subject to rigorous examination the presuppositions upon which their concept of race was based. With the exception of T. H. Huxley, Franz Boas, Julian Huxley, and Alexander and Wilhelm Humboldt, especially during the period of kleptomaniac imperialism of the nineteenth century, when good reasons had to be found to justify the conquest and exploitation of the "inferior races" one could hardly question what was so "clear" to everyone.

An illuminating reflection of a vanishing physical anthropological viewpoint occurs in an attractive book by a field student of physical anthropology. In explaining the object of her investigations, she wrote:

The purpose of these anthropometric measurements is the establishment of various physical types. The more generalized characteristics of any one locality can be determined, the resemblances to and differences from their near and remote neighbours, the ideal being to discover the various strains which are there combined. In anthropology there is as much information to be gathered from these physical measurements as from the study of social habits and customs.[6]

This represents a fair statement of the older anthropological viewpoint: "the purpose of these anthropometric measurements is the establishment of various physical types."

For more than a century physical anthropologists directed their attention principally toward the task of establishing criteria by means of which races of humankind might be defined—a diverting postprandial occupation in which by arbitrarily selecting the criteria one could nearly always make the races come out exactly as one thought they should. As Boyd wrote,

> Those of the proposed criteria which were adopted are evidently those which were found to give 'reasonable results'—that is, they brought home the bacon; so that in cases where the anthropologist was convinced race differences ought to exist, these criteria proved that they did. Unobliging criteria that seemed to show no differences between races 'obviously' distinct, or which indicated differences within groups 'obviously' homogeneous, have been tactfully related to the scrap heap.[7]

In this observation we probably have the crux of the whole problem. Only those methods of race classification which indicated the "right sort" of race differences were encouraged and utilized.

Most physical anthropologists took completely for granted the one thing required to be proved, namely, that the concept of race corresponded to a reality that could actually be measured and verified and descriptively set out so that it could be seen to be a fact.[8] In short, they took for granted that the anthropological conception of race was verifiably true, and showed that in nature there exist groups of human beings comprising individuals each of whom possesses a certain typical aggregate of characters which individually and collectively serve to distinguish them from the individuals in all other groups.

Plainly stated, this is the conception of race that most physical anthropologists held and practically everyone else, even some geneticists, accepted. When, in the light of accumulating criticism in recent years, a growing number of physical anthropologists have admitted that the concept cannot be strictly applied in any systematic sense, they have thought to escape the consequences of such an admission by calling the term a "general" one and have proceeded to play the old game of blindman's bluff with a sublimity which is almost enviable. For it is not vouchsafed to everyone completely to appreciate the illusory grandeur of the doctrine here implied. The feeling of dissatisfaction with which the older physical anthropologists had viewed the many laborious attempts at classification of human groups had not, on the whole, succeeded in generating the disloyal suspicion that something was probably somewhere wrong. If there was a fault, it was generally supposed, it lay not with the anthropologist, but with the refractory material, with the human beings themselves who were the subject of classification, and who always varied so much that it was difficult to put them into the group where they were conceived properly to belong. This was distinctly a nuisance, but, happily, one which could be overcome by the simple expedient of "averaging"—the principal occupation of the self-appointed authorities on race.

Race: A Conceptual Omelet

The process of averaging the characters of a given group, of knocking the individuals together, giving them a good stirring, and then serving the resulting omelet as a race was essentially the anthropological process of race-making. It may have been good cooking, but it was not science, since it served to confuse rather than to clarify. When an omelet is done it has a fairly uniform character, though the ingredients which have entered into its making have been varied. So it was with the anthropological conception of race. It was an omelet that corresponded to nothing in nature: an indigestible dish conjured into being by an anthropological chef from a number of ingredients which were extremely varied in character. This omelet conception of race had no existence outside the statistical frying pan in which it had been reduced by the heat of the anthropological imagination; it was a meaningless concept because it is inapplicable to anything real. When anthropologists began to realize that the proper description of a group does not consist in the process of making an omelet of it, but in the analysis and description of the character of the variability of the elements entering into it—its ingredients—they discovered that the fault lay not with the materials but with the conceptual tool with which they had approached their study. *In passing, it is a good idea not to accept any concept until the presuppositions upon which it is based have been thoroughly examined.*

It is a sobering thought that as early as 1836, when the English were busily exterminating the Tasmanian aborigines, and elsewhere, the English anthropologist, James Cowles Prichard (1786–1848), in his book *Researches Into the Physical History of Man*, clearly pointed out the dangers of such thinking: "Races," he wrote, are properly successions of individuals propagated from any given stock; and the term should be used without any involved meaning that such a progeny or stock has always possessed a particular character. The real import of the term has often been overlooked, and the word race has been used as if it implied a distinction in the physical character of a whole series of individuals. By writers in anthropology who adopt this term, it is often tacitly assumed that such distinctions were primordial, and that their successive transmission has been unbroken. If such were the fact, a race so characterized would be a species in the strict sense of the word, and it ought to be so termed.[9]

There were a few others who saw this clearly, especially Franz Boas (1858–1942), the founder of anthropology in the United States, who, recalling his earliest days as a physical anthropologist in the 1890s wrote, "When I turned to the consideration of racial problems I was shocked by the formalism of the work. Nobody had tried to answer the questions why certain measurements were taken, why they were considered significant, whether they were subject to other influences."[10]

That many differences exist between different groups of human beings is obvious; but the older anthropological conception of these was erroneous, and the traditional anthropological approach to the study of their relationships was unscientific and pre-Mendelian.[11] Taxonomic exercises in the classification of assemblages of phenotypical, that is, observable traits produced in conjunction with the environment, will never succeed in elucidating the relationships of different groups of humankind to one another, for the simple reason that it is not assemblages of traits that undergo change in the formation of the individual and the group, but rather the single complex units, the genes, which are physiologically associated with those traits. One of the great persisting errors involved in the anthropological conception of race was due to the steady refusal to recognize this fact. The truth is that it is not possible to classify the various groups of humankind by means of the traits the older anthropologists customarily used, because those traits do not behave as complexes; they behave instead in a totally different manner: as the expression of many independent units, linked and unlinked, in interaction with the environment, that have entered into their formation.

The parallel in the history of biology is striking here, and was well illustrated by Dobzhansky, who, in his classic book *Genetics and the Origin of Species* wrote:

> Many studies on hybridization were made before Mendel, but they did not lead to the discovery of Mendel's laws. In retrospect, we see clearly where the mistake of Mendel's predecessors lay: they treated as units the complexes of characteristics of individuals, races, and species, and attempted to find rules governing the inheritance of such complexes. Mendel was first to understand that it was the inheritance of separate traits, and not complexes

of traits, which had to be studied. Some of the modern students of racial variability consistently repeat the mistakes of Mendel's predecessors.[12]

The materials of evolution are not represented by continuous aggregates of traits, but by discontinuous packages of chemicals, each of which is more or less independent in its action and may be only partially responsible for the genes, situated mostly within the chromosomes, structures with which many physical anthropologists were until recently scarcely on bowing acquaintance. The genes retain both their independence and their individual character more or less indefinitely, although probably they are all inherently variable, are known to jump around, are subject to many influences, and, in time, may undergo mutation. For these reasons any conception of race which operates as if inheritance were a matter of transmitting gross aggregates of traits is both erroneous and confusing. To quote Dobzhansky once more:

> The difficulty . . . is that . . . the concept is obviously outmoded and incapable of producing much insight into the causative factors at work in human populations. Although the genic basis of relatively few human traits is known, it seems that following up the distribution of these traits could tell us more about the 'races' than a great abundance of measurements.[13]

A typical example of the prevailing views at the time among physical anthropologists were those of Professor Earnest A. Hooton, Chairman of the Department of Anthropology at Harvard University, and the most amiable teacher of many later able anthropologists. In the Vanuxem Lectures delivered at Princeton University and published in 1940 by its press as *Why Men Behave Like Apes and Vice Versa,* Hooton averred that

> We must rid ourselves of the false prophets of cultural salvation and the witless preachers of human equality. The future of our species does not hang upon forms of government, economic adjustment, religious or social creeds, and purely environmental education. The future of man is dependent upon biology.

Such views were the expression of a physical anthropology unenlightened by a knowledge of genetics or evolutionary biology, pronouncements which led to the buttressing of a pseudoscientific eugenics and devastating governmental immigration policies.[14]

Evolution, Genes, and Race

The principal agencies of evolutionary change in humans are primarily gene variability and gene mutation. Evolutionary changes are brought about through the rearrangements in the combination of genes in consequence of the operation of many secondary factors, physical and cultural, and changes in the character of genes themselves. In order to appreciate the meaning of the variety presented by humankind today it is indispensably necessary to understand the manner in which these agencies work. Thus, in humans it is practically certain that some forms of hair and skin color are due to mutation, while still other forms are due to various combinations of these mutant forms with one another, as also with nonmutant forms. The rate of mutation for different genes in humans varies. It has been calculated that the gene for normal clotting mutates, for example, to the gene for hemophilia in one out of less than 10,000 males per generation. It is highly probable, for example, that such a mutation occurred in the person of Queen Victoria's father, a fact which in the long run may perhaps constitute both his and her chief claim to fame.[15] The rate of mutation of the blood group genes, however, appears to be low. Mutation of skin-color genes also is infrequent, while mutation of hair-form genes is somewhat more frequent. If anthropologists are ever to understand how the different groups of humankind came to possess such traits as distinguish the more geographically isolated of them, and those of the less isolated, more recently mixed, and therefore less distinguishable groups, it should be obvious that they must cease making omelets of the very ingredients, the genes, which it should be our purpose to isolate and to map. What must be studied are the frequencies with which such genes occur in different groups of populations. The gene frequency method for the study of the distribution of human genes is a simple one and has now been available for some time, as likewise has been the method for the study of genetic linkage in man.

If, roughly speaking, one gene be arbitrarily assigned to every component of the body, it should be fairly clear that as regards the structure of man we are dealing with many thousands of genes. In the fruit fly *Drosophila melanogaster,* in which there are four pairs of chromosomes, it has been estimated that there are no less than 5,000 genes. Humans have 23 pairs of chromosomes, with one member of each pair being inherited from each parent, the theoretical possible combinations between the 23 chromosomes of the male parent and those of the female parent in the production of sperm or ovum are 8,388,608, or 2 raised to the 23rd power. The offspring produced by the parents can be genetically different by $7x10^{13}$, or 70,000,000,000,000. It will be seen that the different combinations that a 46 chromosome system can take reach a stupendous figure. This is on a purely numerical basis. Earlier and by totally different methods Spuhler arrived at the figure of about 34,000 genes in humans,[16] and Evans at an estimate of between 10,000 and 100,000 genes in humans.[17] Most sources currently agree on 100,000 genes. If we consider the newer concepts, which recognize that the adult individual represents the end point in the interaction between all these genes, under the influence of the environments in which they have undergone development, the complexities become even greater.[18]

The morphological characters that anthropologists in the past have relied on for their racial classifications have been few indeed, involving a minute fraction of the great number of genes it would actually be necessary to consider in attempting to make any real—that is to say, genetically analytic—classification of humankind.

The reality is that within a region or over a geographical area populations grade into each other. Such gradation is called a *cline* (Gr. *klinein,* to incline, slope or bend), and refers to a measurable gradation of physical traits such as hair, color, body form, gene frequencies, and the like. In other words, it is a *process* of *direction* in which a trait varies. Also, interbreeding usually occurs at intergrading zones.

To sum up, the indictment against the older, or traditional, anthropological conception of race is that: (1) it was artificial, (2) it did not correspond to the facts, (3) it led to confusion and the perpetuation of error, and finally, (4) for all these reasons it was scientifically unsound, or rather, more accurately, that it was false and misleading. Based as it was on unexamined facts and unjustifiable generalizations, it were better that the term "race," corrupted as it is with so many deceptive and dangerous meanings, be dropped altogether from the vocabulary.

If it be agreed that the human species is one and that it consists of a group of populations which, more or less, adjoin each other geographically or ecologically and of which the neighboring ones intergrade or hybridize wherever they are in contact, or are potentially capable of doing so,[19] then it should be obvious that the task of the student interested in the character of these populations must be to study the frequency distribution of the genes which characterizes them—not misconceived and misconstrued entities.

In 1942 when this chapter was first written, I wrote that physical anthropologists must recognize that they have unwittingly played no small part in the creation of the myth of race, which in our time has assumed so dangerous a form. It is encouraging to be able to say that since the appearance of the first edition of this book in 1942 an increasing number of anthropologists have seen their responsibility clearly and the newer generation of students of humankind are taking active steps to exorcise the monster of race and deliver the thought and conduct of our species from its evil social consequences.[20]

In 1944 Dr. G. M. Morant, in delivering the address on physical anthropology at the centenary meeting of the Royal Anthropological Institute, made the important point clearly. "It seems to me," he said, that the time has come when anthropologists must fully recognize fundamental changes in their treatment of the problem of racial classification. The idea that a race is a group of people separated from all others because of the distinctive ancestry of its members is implied whenever a racial label is used, but in fact we have no knowledge of the existence of such populations today or in any past time. Gradations between any regional groups distinguished, and an absence of clear-cut divisions, are the universal rule. Our methods have never been fully adapted to deal with this situation.[21]

Notes

1. John Haller, Jr., *Outcasts From Evolution* (Urbana: Universtity of Illinois Press, 1971), 3 sq.

2. Gunnar Myrdal, *An American Dilemma: The Negro Problem and Modern Democracy* (New York: Harper & Bros., 1944), 116.

3. Linnaeus, *Systema naturae.*

4. Stephen Jay Gould, "The Geometer of Race," *Discover* 15 (1994): 64–69.

5. Franz Boas, "History and Science in Anthropology: a Reply," *American Anthropologist* 38 (1936): 137–51.

6. Charis Crockett, *The House in the Rain Forest* (Boston: Houghton Mifflin, 1942), 29.

7. William C. Boyd, *Genetics and the Races of Man* (Boston: Little, Brown, 1950), 195.

8. T. H. Huxley, in his essay, published in 1865, "On the Methods and Results of Ethnology" reprinted in *Man's Place in Nature and Other Anthropological Essays* (New York: Appleton & Co., 1890], refused to use the terms "stocks," "varieties," "races," or "species" in connection with man, "because each of these last well-known terms implies, on the part of its employer, a preconceived opinion touching one of those problems, the solution of which is the ultimate object of the science; and in regard to which, therefore, ethnologists are especially bound to keep their minds open and their judgments freely balanced."

9. James Cowles Prichard, *Researches Into the Physical History of Man*, 3rd ed. (London: Ballière, 1836), 359.

10. Franz Boas, "History and Science in Anthropology: A Reply," *American Anthropologist* 38 (1936): 140; also Franz Boas, *Race, Language and Culture* (New York: Macmillan, 1940).

11. Edmond Demolins, *Anglo-Saxon Superiority: To What is it Due*, 10th ed. (New York: R. F. Frenno, 1898).

12. Theodosius Dobzhansky, *Genetics and the Origin of Species* (New York: Columbia University Press, 1937), 62.

13. Ibid.

14. J.B.S. Haldane, *Heredity and Politics* (New York: Norton, 1938), 88; Michael R. Cummings, *Human Heredity: Principles and Issues* (St. Paul: West, 1991), 97.

15. For a clear exposition of the facts see William C. Boyd, *Genetics and the Races of Man* (Boston: Little, Brown, 1950); Curt Stern, *Principles of Human Genetics*

(San Francisco: Freeman, 1973); L. L. Cavalli-Sforza and W. P. Bodmer, *The Genetics of Human Populations* (San Francisco: Freemana, 1971); L. L. Cavalli-Sforza, Paolo Menozzi, and Albert Piazza, *The History and Geography of Human Genes* (Princeton: Princeton University Press, 1994); M. Levitan and A. Montagu, *Textbook of Human Genetics* (New York: Oxford University Press, 1971; 3rd ed. 1983); Daniel J. Kevles, *In the Name of Eugenics* (New York: Alfred A. Knopf, 1985); Mark H. Haller, *Eugenics: Hereditarian Attitudes in American Thought* (New Brunswick: Rutgers University Press, 1963); Donald K. Pickens, *Eugenics and the Progressives* (Nashville: Vanderbilt University Press, 1968); Hamilton Cravens, *The Triumph of Evolution: American Scientists and the Heredity-Environment Controversy 1900–1941* (Philadelphia: University of Pennsylvania Press, 1978); Kenneth Ludmerer, *Genetics and American Society* (Baltimore: Johns Hopkins University Press,1972), 1075; Audrey Smedley, *Race in North America* (Boulder: Westview Press, 1993); Richard C. Lewontin, Steven Rose, and Leon Kamin, *Not in Our Genes* (New York: Pantheon Books, 1984).

16. James N. Spuhler, "An Estimate of the Number of Genes in Man," *Science* 108 (1948): 279.

17. Robley D. Evans, "Quantitative Inferences Concerning the Genetic Effects of Radiation of Human Beings," *Science* 109 (1949): 299–304; W. F. Bodmer and L. L. Cavalli-Sforza, *Genetics, Evolution, and Man* (San Francisco: W. H. Freeman, 1976); Michael R. Cummings, *Human Heredity: Principles and Issues* (St. Paul, MN: West, 1991), 37.

18. See Ashley Montagu, *Statement on Race*, 2nd ed. (New York, Oxford University Press, 1972); Ernst Mayr, *Populations, Species, and Evolution*, (New York: Columbia University Press, 1970); Ernst Mayr, *The Growth of Biological Thought* (Cambridge: Harvard University Press, 1982); Ernst Mayr, *Systematics and the Origin of Species*, (New York: Columbia University Press, 1942), 154ff.

19. Ernst Mayr, "Speciation Phenomena in Birds," *Biological Symposia* 2 (1941): 66, and *Systematics*, 154 ff.; Ernst Mayr, *Animal Species and Evolution* (Cambridge: Harvard University Press, 1963).

20. Leonard Lieberman, Blaine W. Stevenson, and Larry T. Reynolds, "Race and Anthropology: A Core Concept Without Consensus." *Anthropology and Education Quarterly* 20 (1989): 67–73; Alice Littlefield, Leonard Lieberman, and Larry T. Reynolds "Redefining Race: The Potential Demise of a Concept in Physical Anthropology," *Current Anthropology* 23 (1982): 641–655; Frank B. Livingstone, "On the Non-Existence of Human Races," *Current Anthropology* 3 (1962), 279–281; C. Loring Brace and Ashley Montagu, *An Introduction to Biological Anthropology*, 2nd ed. (New York: Macmillan, 1977); Ashley Montagu, ed., *The Concept of Race*, (New York: Free Press, 1964); Ashley Montagu, *The Idea of Race* (Lincoln: University of Nebraska Press, 1965); Ashley Montagu, *An Introduction to Physical Anthropology* (Springfield, IL: C.C. Thomas, 1945, 2nd ed. 1951, 3rd ed. 1960); Joseph B. Birdsell, *Human Evolution: An Introduction to the New Physical Anthropology*, 2nd ed. (New York: Rand McNally, 1975); Elazar Barkan, *The Retreat of Scientific Racism*, (Cambridge: Cambridge University Press, 1991).

21. Geoffrey M. Morant, "The Future of Physical Anthropology," *Man* 44 (1944).

3

The Genetical Theory of Race

The traditional anthropological practice of describing the end effects of complex variations without attempting to consider the nature of the conditions responsible for them could never lead to any understanding of their real meaning. In order to understand the end effects with which the physical anthropologist of the past was so much concerned it is necessary to investigate the causes producing them, and this can only be done by studying the conditions under which they come into being, for it should be obvious that it is the conditions producing the end effects which must be regarded as their efficient causes.

Comparing numerous series of metrical and nonmetrical traits relating to different groups of humankind may produce some notion of their likenesses and differences or tell us something of the variability of their traits; this may be desirable, but no amount of detailed description and comparison will ever tell us how such groups came to be as we now find them, unless serious investigation is made to discover the causes involved in their production.

Such causes are at work before our eyes at the present time. In America and in many other parts of the world where members of different racial groups have met and cohabited, determinate sequences, if not the actual mechanism, of physical change may be studied. The discoveries of geneticists concerning the manner in which genetic changes are brought about in other organisms and what is known of human genetics render it perfectly clear that the genetic systems of all living things behave fundamentally according to the same laws. If this is true, it then becomes possible, for the first time in the history of humankind, to envisage the possibility of an evolution in genetical terms of the stages through which humans, as a variable species, must have passed in order to attain its present variety of form and also, in the same terms, to account for that variety.

The principles involved in the genetic approach to the study of the evolution of the variety of humankind cannot be discussed here fully,

111

because such a discussion would demand a treatise in itself, and because such treatises already are available in great number.[1]

Here we have space only for a very condensed statement of the genetical theory of race. The conception of "ethnic group differences" proposed here is based upon the following fundamental postulates: (1) that the original ancestral population was genetically relatively heterogeneous; (2) that by migration away from this original ancestral group, individual families became dispersed; (3) that some of the groups thus dispersed became geographically isolated from one another and remained so isolated for a relatively significant period of time; (4) that upon all these isolated groups several of the following factors came into play as conditions leading to evolutionary change: (a) the random genetic drift or inherent variability of the genotypic materials of each member of the group, as compared to the parent population, and (b) physical change in the action of a gene associated, in a partial manner, with a particular trait, that is, gene mutation.

Genetic drift describes the fact that given a genetically heterogeneous or heterozygous group, spontaneous random fluctuations in gene frequencies will, especially in small populations, in the course of time, occur, so that such originally relatively homogeneous groups will come to exhibit certain differences from other isolated groups which started with a similar genetic equipment.

Mutation defines the condition in which a particular gene undergoes a permanent change of some sort, so that its physiological expression differs from that of the older form of the gene, and its action may express itself in the appearance of a new trait or new form of an old one. Mutations have almost certainly occurred independently in different human isolate groups, at different times and at different rates, and have affected different traits. Thus, for example, in one part of a population mutant dominant genes leading to the development of kinky hair may have appeared and have ultimately become scattered throughout the population, as among Blacks. We cannot, however, make a similar assumption for all or many of the traits which distinguish the various groups of humankind from one another. Skin color, for example, cannot be so simply explained, for the probabilities are high that even in early humans there were already in existence variations in skin color and also, incidentally, hair color.[2] Selection has undoubtedly played an important role here.

Up to this point we have seen that it is possible to start with a genetically heterogeneous population, from which independent groups have migrated and become isolated for a time from one another. By random variation in gene frequencies and the change in the action of genes themselves—disregarding for the moment the operation of such factors as selection of various sorts—new genetic combinations of traits have appeared in various groups, thus defining the differences existing between such groups. Such differences occur as gradients in each group and are called *clines*. In brief, random variation in gene frequency and the action of mutant genes are the primary agencies responsible for the production of physical differences between human groups. It has been estimated that some eighty mutations occur in every individual in a mating population. In fact, these constitute the basic processes in the evolution of all animal forms. But there are also other factors involved which, though secondary in the sense that they act upon the primary factors and influence their operation, are not less important in their effects than the primary factors. Indeed, these secondary factors, ecological, natural, social, and sexual selection, inbreeding, outbreeding, or hybridization, and so forth, have been unremitting in their action upon the primary factors, but the nature of that action has been highly variable. The action of these secondary factors does not require any discussion here; I wish here to emphasize principally that in the character of the action of the two primary factors, genetic drift and gene mutation, we have the clear demonstration that the variation of all human groups is a natural process that is constantly proceeding. The genetic and physical differences that characterize populations, the mislabeled races, merely represent an expression of the process of genetic change over a definite ecologic range. An ethnic group represents a dynamic, variable condition, characterized by potential for continuous change; populations become static and classifiable only when a taxonomically minded scientist arbitrarily fixes the process of change at his own temporal level.

In short, so-called races are populations that merely represent different kinds of temporary mixtures of genetic materials common to all humankind. As Shelley wrote,

> Man's yesterday may ne'er be like his morrow;
> Naught may endure but mutability.

Over a sufficient length of time, it is probable that all genes will mutate. Most mutations are known to be harmful, but useful mutations also occur, relative to ecology and timespan. The frequency with which various genes have undergone change or mutation in human populations is at present unknown, but when anthropologists address themselves to the task of solving the problem of gene variability in different human populations, important discoveries are to be expected. What is known is that in many cases and conditions it can be rapid.[3] The immediate task of the physical anthropologist interested in the origins of human diversity should be to investigate the problem presented by that diversity, not as a taxonomist but as a geneticist, since the diversity which is loosely termed race is a process which can be described accurately only in terms of the frequencies with which individual genes occur in groups representing adequate geographic isolates.

If between populations variability can best be described in terms of gene frequencies, then one of the most important tasks of the anthropologist must be the discovery of the roles played by the primary and secondary factors in producing that variability. The approach to the solution of this problem is twofold: first, through the analysis of the nature of the variability itself in localized groups; and, second, through the study of the effect of "ethnic" mixture among living peoples. Such studies as those of Boyd, Birdsell, and Garn, have already shown what can be achieved by means of the genetic approach.[4] As Dobzhansky pointed out, "the fundamental units of racial variability are populations and genes, not complexes of characters which connote in the popular mind a racial distinction."[5]

In humans the process of differentiation between populations is genetically best understood in terms of the frequency with which certain genes become differentiated in different groups derived from an originally somewhat heterogeneous species population and subsequently undergo independent development. We have already seen that the mechanisms involved in differentiating a single collective genotype into several separate genotypes, and the subsequent development of a variety of phenotypes within these genotypes, are primarily genetic drift or gene variability and gene mutation, and secondarily, the action of such factors as environment, natural, social, and sexual selection, inbreeding, outbreeding, and the like.

Perhaps the wisest thing ever said about the genetics of human variability is R. A. Fisher's admonition in one of the greatest scientific classics of the twentieth century, his *The Genetic Theory of Natural Selection* (1930), that

> While genetic knowledge is essential for the clarity it introduces into the subject, the causes of the evolutionary changes in progress can only be resolved by an appeal to sociological, and even historical facts. These should at least be sufficiently available to reveal the more powerful agencies at work in the modification of mankind.[6]

It is the failure of IQ testers to understand the powerful role that social factors play in the development of human behavior that renders their findings invalid. And the same is, of course, true of the arguments of racists generally.

Many of the physical differences existing between living human populations probably originally represent the end effects of small gene mutations fitting harmoniously into gene systems which remain relatively unaltered. Judging from the nature of their likenesses and differences, and from the effects of intermixture, the number of genes involved would appear to be relatively small, each being for the most part independent in its action. The processes involved are akin to those practiced in the production of domestic breeds of animals from wild types, in whom generic, specific, and population traits which, under natural condition, in the secular period of time concerned, would have remained stable, are rendered markedly unstable, as in our artificially produced varieties of cats, dogs, horses, and other domesticated animals. Considering the roles of mutation, inbreeding, crossbreeding, and selection in the evolution of other animals, the great geneticist Sewall Wright arrived at a judgment concerning the conditions for evolution based on the statistical consequences of Mendelian heredity which, allowing for the modifying effects of the secondary factors arising out of human social activities, may be applied to humans.

> The most general conclusion is that evolution depends on a certain balance among its factors. There must be gene mutation, but an excessive rate gives an array of freaks, not evolution; there must be selection, but too severe a process destroys the field of variability, and thus the basis for further advance; prevalence of local inbreeding within a species has extremely important evolutionary consequence, but too close inbreeding leads merely to extinction. A certain amount of crossbreeding is favorable, but not too much. In this dependence on balance the species is like a living organism. At all levels of organization life depends on the maintenance of a certain balance among its factors.
>
> More specifically, under biparental reproduction a very low rate of mutation balanced by moderate selection is enough to maintain a practically infinite field of possible gene combinations within the species. The field actually occupied is relatively small though sufficiently extensive that no two individuals have the same genetic constitution. The course of evolution through the general field is not controlled by direction of mutation and not directly by selection, except as conditions change, but by a trial and error mechanism consisting of a largely nonadaptive differentiation of local populations (due to inbreeding balanced by occasional crossbreeding) and a determination of longtime trend by intergroup selection. The splitting of species depends on the effects of more complete isolation, often made permanent by the accumulation of chromosome aberrations, usually of the balanced type. Studies of natural species indicate that the conditions for such an evolutionary process are often present.[7]

Precisely similar conditions have been operative in the evolution and diversification of humankind. The variety of traits exhibited by different ethnic groups almost certainly owe their being to the operation of the factors so well described by Wright. The common definition of race, however, is based on an arbitrary and superficial selection of traits, a statement which applies when the term is used by animal breeders as well as in connection with humans. As Kalmus has pointed out,

> Breeders of the old school rarely distinguish between the characters which are due to single gene differences and those which are due to many, and their use of the word race still remains rather vague. The term used by modern geneticists to take the place of race is strain, which has a more precise meaning; it is applied to forms which differ from the commonly found wild type by one or several precisely defined hereditary characters which usually breed true.[8]

Attempts have been made to define race as a group of individuals of whom an appreciable majority, taken at a particular time level, is characterized by the possession through a common heredity of a certain number of genes phenotypically (that is, on the basis of certain observable or measurable traits) selected as marking "physical" boundaries between them and other groups of individuals of the same species population not characterized by so high a degree of frequency of these particular genes.

This is, however, granting the common conception of race too much credit for either significance or intelligibility, for it should be obvious that such a definition represents a rather fatuous kind of abstraction, a form of extrapolation for which there can be little place in scientific thought. What, for instance, does "an appreciable majority" refer to? What are the traits which are to be exhibited by this "appreciable majority"? And upon what grounds are such traits to be considered as significantly defining a race? As Dobzhansky points out, "the geographical distributions of the separate genes composing a racial difference are very frequently independent."[9] Thus, blood group distributions are independent of skin color or cephalic index distributions, and so forth.

What aggregation, then, of gene likenesses and differences constitutes a race or ethnic group?

There is no point to an attempt at redefinition of the term "race," for that term is so embarrassed by unsound and inhumane meanings that its preservation would only defeat any hope of a better understanding of people than the term *ethnic group*. It is better to adopt the recommendation of Huxley and Haddon in their 1936 book *We Europeans* as well as by the UNESCO *Statement on Race* (1950) to replace the term "race" by the term *ethnic group* (see Appendix A in the unabridged edition).

In conformity with the genetic facts an ethnic group may be defined as a population in process of undergoing genetic and social differentiation; it is a group of individuals capable of hybridizing and intergrading with other such ethnic groups to produce further genetic recombination and differentiation.[10]

An example will perhaps help to clarify this definition. When American Blacks mate with other Blacks, their children more closely resemble other American Blacks, as well as Blacks elsewhere in the world, than they do American or other whites. This merely means that the offspring have drawn their genes from a local group in the population in which certain genes, say for skin color, were present that were not present in other local groups of the American population. The manner in which such genes are distributed within a population such as the United States is determined not so much by biological factors as by social ones. This may be illustrated by means of a homely example. Were the social barriers to intermixture be abrogated, the physical differences between Blacks and whites would eventually be completely eliminated. That this has not occurred to any great extent is due principally to the maintenance of social barriers opposed to such admixture. Such social and caste barriers tend to keep the stock with genes for black skin color separate from those who carry genes for lighter skin color. In this way such barriers act as isolating mechanisms akin to geographic isolating conditions, which have the same effect in maintaining the homogeneity of genetic characters within the isolated group.

It is clear, then, that the frequency distributions of one or more genes within a population that differ from those of other populations, for the most part, represent the effects of the action of different isolating agents upon a common stock of genetic materials. Such agencies as natural, social, and sexual selection result in the different gene frequencies among local groups and populations,result in gradational effect, and are called *clines*. Such, from the standpoint of the anthropologist, is an ethnic group.

It will be observed that such a definition emphasizes the fact that so-called racial differences simply represent more or less temporary or episodic expressions of variations in the relative frequencies of genes in different parts of the species population and rejects altogether the all-or-none conception of race as a static immutable process of fixed differences. It denies the unwarranted assumption that there exist any hard and fast genetic boundaries between any groups of humankind and proclaims the common genetic unity of all groups, a unity without uniformity. Such a conception of race cuts across all national, linguistic, religious, and cultural boundaries and thus asserts their essential interaction of social and genetic factors.

We may conclude with the words of the distinguished geneticist, Professor Albert Jacquard: "The geneticist has a definite answer if questioned about the content of the word 'race.' It is that in the case of the human species the term does not correspond to any objectively definable entity."[11]

Notes

1. L. L. Cavalli-Sforza, P. Menozzi, and A. Piazza, *The History and Geography of Human Genes* (Princeton: Princeton University Press, 1994); W. F. Bodmer and L. L. Cavalli-Sforza, *Genetics, Evolution, and Man* (San Francisco: Freeman, 1976); Max Levitan and Ashley Montagu, *Textbook of Human Genetics*, 3rd ed. (New York: Oxford University Press, 1988); G. Harrison et al., *Human Biology*. 2nd ed. (New York: Oxford University Press, 1977), Ashley Montagu, *Human Heredity* (New York: New American Library, 1963); Jonathan Marks, *Human Biodiversity: Genes, Race, and History* (Hawthorne: Aldine, 1994).

2. Among apes of the present day, for example, one encounters animals that are almost completely white skinned, other that are completely black or brown skinned; still others are mixed or differently colored, thus the face and hands and feet may be black and the remainder of the body white or brown. The hair on the crown of a young gorilla's head may contain almost every primary color that is to be found among humans today.

3. For mutation rates in humans, see Max Levitan and Ashley Montagu, *Textbook of Human Genetics*, 2nd ed. (New York: Oxford University Press, 1977). Mutations, it should be mentioned, do not direct development, but for the most part replenish the gene pool.

4. William C. Boyd, *Genetics and the Races of Man* (Boston: Little, Brown, 1950); Joseph B. Birdsell, "Some Implications of the Genetical Concept of Race in Terms of Spatial Analysis," *Cold Spring Harbor Symposia on Quantitative Biology* 15 (1950): 259–314; Joseph B. Birdsell, "The Problem of the Early Peopling of the Americas as Viewed from Asia," in *Papers on the Physical Anthropology of the American Indian*, ed. William S. Laughlin (New York: The Viking Fund, 1951), 1–68a; Carleton Coon, Stanley Garn, and Joseph B. Birdsell, *Races: a Study of the Problems of Race Formation in Man* (Springfield, IL: Thomas, 1950); Curt Stern, *Principles of Human Genetics* (San Francisco: Freeman, 1973); L. L. Cavalli-Sforza et al., *The History and Geography of Human Genes;* Marks, *Human Bioiversity;* Ashley Montagu, "Genetics and the Antiquity of Man in the Americas," *Man* 43 [nos. 103–124] 105: 131–35.

5. Th. Dobzhansky, *Genetics and the Origin of Species*, 3rd ed. (New York: Columbia University Press, 1951), 177; Th. Dobzhansky, *Mankind Evolving* (New Haven: Yale University Press, 1962); Richard Lewontin, *Human Diversity* (New York: H. Freeman, 1982); M. Levitan and A. Montagu, *Textbook of Human Genetics,* 3rd ed. (New York: Oxford University Press, 1988); Th. Dobzhansky, Francisco J. Ayala, G. Ledyard Stebbins, and James W. Valentine, *Evolution* (San Francisco: W. H. Freeman, 1977); Eviator Nevo, "Genetic Diversity and the Evolution of Life and Man, *Racism, Science and Pseudo Science* (Paris: UNESCO, 1981), 77–92; Albert Jacquard, "Science and Racism," *Racism, Science and Pseudo Science* (Paris: UNESCO, 1981), 15–49; Th. Dobzhansky, *Evolution, Genetics, and Man* (New York: Wiley & Sons, 1955); Steven Rose, ed., *Against Biological Determinism* (London: Allison & Busby, 1982).

6. Ronald A. Fisher, *The Genetical Theory of Natural Selection* (Oxford: Clarendon Press, 1930), 174. See also Games F. Crow, "Mechanisms and Trends in Human Evolution," in *Evolution and Man's Progress*, eds. Hudson Hoagland and Ralph W. Burhoe (New York; Columbia University Press, 1962), 6–21; Frank G. Livingstone

and James N. Spuhler, "Cultural Determinants in Natural Selection," *International Social Science Journal* 17 (1965): 118–20; Ashley Montagu, ed., *Culture and the Evolution of Man* (New York: Oxford University Press, 1962); George G. Simpson, "Behavior and Evolution," in Ann Roe and George G. Simpson *Behavior and Evolution* (New York: Yale University Press, 1958), 597–635; Frank G. Livingstone, "Anthropoligical Implications of Sickle Cell Gene Distribution in West Africa," *American Anthropologist* 60 (1958): 533–62.

    7. Sewall Wright, "The Roles of Mutation, Inbreeding, Crossbreeding, and Selection in Evolution," *Proceedings of the Sixth International Congress of Genetics* 1 (Ithaca, New York, 1932), 356–66; Cavalli-Sforza et al., *The History and Geography of Human Genes.*

    8. H. Kalmus, *Genetics* (London: Pelican Books, 1948), 46.

    9. Dobzhansky, *Genetics*, 2nd ed., p. 77.

    10. The conception of an ethnic group was clearly stated as early as 1844 by Alexander von Humboldt. He writes: "The distribution of mankind is . . . only a distribution into varieties, which are commonly designated by the somewhat indefinite term races. As in the vegetable kingdom, and in the natural history of birds and fishes, a classification into many small families is based on a surer foundation than where large sections are separated into a few but large divisions; so it also appears to me, that in the determination of races a preference should be given to the establishment of small families or nations. Whether we adopt the old classification of my master, Blumenbach . . . or that of Prichard . . . we fail to recognize any typical sharpness of definition, or any general or well established principle, in the division of these groups. The extremes of form and colour are certainly separated, but without regard to the races, which cannot be included in any of these classes." *Cosmos: A Sketch of a Physical Description of the Universe* (London, 1849), 365–66.

    11. Albert Jacquard, "Science and Racism," in *Racism, Science, and Psuedo Science* (Paris: UNESCO, 1983), 15.

4

The Biological Facts

Concerning the origin of the living varieties of humans we can say little more than that there are many reasons for believing that a single stock gave rise to all of them. All humans belong to the same species and have the same remote ancestry. This is a conclusion to which all the relevant evidence of comparative anatomy, paleontology, serology, and genetics, points. On genetic grounds alone it is virtually impossible to conceive of the varieties of humankind as having originated separately as distinct lines from different anthropoid ancestors. Genetically the chances against such a process ever having occurred are, in terms of probability, of such an order as to render that suggestion inadmissible. On purely physical grounds it is, again, highly improbable that starting from different ancestral stocks the varieties of humans would have independently come to resemble one another as closely as they do. This is demanding too much from convergence.

In October, 1962, Professor Carleton S. Coon published a book entitled *The Origin of Races,* in which he attempted to trace the evolution of five races which he called Australoids, Mongoloids, Caucasoids, Capoids, and Congoids. The theory he presented is that

> At the beginning of our record, over half a million years ago, man was a single species, *Homo erectus,* perhaps already divided into five geographic races or subspecies, *Homo erectus* then evolved into *Homo sapiens* not once but five times, as each subspecies, living in its own territory, passed a critical threshold from a more brutal to a more *sapient* state.[1]

The reference to the "more brutal" state of the assumed five subspecies of *Homo erectus* as compared with their descendants of sapient state is capable of several meanings in such a context, and when juxtaposed to "sapient" perpetuates pejorative and odious comparisons which are out of place in scientific discussions, unless they can be justified. There are absolutely no grounds for believing that early humans were any more brutal, even though morphologically and culturally "less" developed, than contemporary humans. It is a question whether early humans were, in fact, brutal at all.

The idea that five subspecies or geographic races of *H. erectus* (which refers to early humans of the pithecanthropine type), in isolation from one another, "evolved independently into *Homo sapiens* not once but five times," at different times and in different places, is a very dubious one. The theory simply doesn't square with the biological facts. Species and subspecies simply don't develop that way. The transmutation of one species into another is a gradual process, and the development of the subspecies reflects the biological history of the species as a whole. However few or many subspecies of *Homo erectus* there may have been, all of them, at one time or another, probably participated in the development of *sapiens* subspecies. Subspecies of one species do not usually become transformed into subspecies of another single species. On the contrary, independent subspecies of a single species, as incipient species, tend to speciate into different species.

If Coon had been right the living so-called races or subspecies of humans would present the most remarkable example of parallel or convergent evolution in the history of animated nature. The human species is a species because all its members have shared a more or less common biological history-making allowance for all the differences in that history which each population or so-called race, subspecies, or cline, has undergone. Coon implied that that history has been essentially and independently different for his five assumed races, and further implied that in isolation the genetic direction of *H. erectus* was predetermined—that each of the subspecies occupying their separate ecologic niches would inevitably have developed into *sapiens*. But the evolutionary process, even for humankind, the cultural creature, does not work that way, as is abundantly testified by the biological history of humanity itself. For had the subspecies of humankind developed in the kind of independent isolation Coon postulated, it would have exhibited, owing, among other things, to the inherent variability of the genetic constitution, far greater differences in their earlier and more recent forms than they in fact, have.

What is so remarkable about the varieties of humankind is their likenesses, not their differences. It would be putting too much of a strain upon, and demanding too much of, any theory to require it to make out a case for an independent or parallel and convergent evolution of varieties of any kind as like one another as are the miscalled "races" of humankind.

Were this all, Coon's theory could be written off as just another of those monumental flawed attempts that are made from time to time to unravel the tangled skein of humankind's biological history, and rejected on the ground of its improbability, were it not for the fact that the author of

The Origin of Races delivered himself, *ex cathedra,* of opinions as if they were facts, and these of a kind which are likely to be misunderstood by the unwary, or understood for what they are not, and misused by racists and others for their own nefarious purposes. Since its publication Coon's book has given aid and comfort to many academic racists and demagogues.

From the very first page of his book Coon made statements of the following kind: "Each major race had followed a pathway of its own through the labyrinth of time. Each had been molded in a different fashion to met the needs of different environments, and each had reached its own level on the evolutionary scale."[2] There can be no doubt about the meaning here: Each of the races occupies a different evolutionary level on the ladder of development, for that is what "evolutionary scale" means. That implied, of course, as we shall see, that some "races" stand higher in the scale of evolution than others. Indeed, this is exactly what Coon meant.

Coon regretted that "dead men can take no intelligence tests," thus revealing a rather misplaced faith in the value of intelligence tests, and an obvious failure to understand their worthlessness when applied cross-culturally or "racially." "However," he went on to say,

> It is a fair inference that fossil men now extinct were less gifted than their descendants who have larger brains, that the subspecies that crossed the evolutionary threshold into the category of *H. sapiens* the earliest have evolved most, and that the obvious correlation between the length of time a subspecies has been in the *sapiens* state and the levels of civilization attained by some of its populations may be related phenomena.[3]

This, again, reveals a rather naive faith in the value of brain size as a measure of mental capacity. Was Neanderthal man, with a mean cranial capacity of 1550 cc, brighter than contemporary humans with a mean cc of 1400? If not, then why should white men be any more gifted than many of their extinct ancestors with smaller brains than theirs? The statement that the subspecies which has been in the *sapiens* state longer than another—allowing for a moment that such a statement makes any sense at all—must therefore have evolved the most and have a correspondingly higher level of civilization is just the kind of thing that was being said by racist anthropologists a hundred years ago. Professor Coon is in the direct line of descent of Nott and Gliddon. Altogether apart from the fact that there are differences in biological rates of development, and that there is such a thing as "cultural" or "social time,"[4] facts which would alone be sufficient to dispose of Coon's "fair inference"(s), there is not the slightest ground for believing that any of the varieties of humankind attained the *sapiens* state either earlier or later than any other. Supposing one subspecies had arrived at the *sapiens* state later than any other, such a subspecies could very well, under favorable conditions, have far outdistanced the earlier subspecies in cultural development. The fact is that grandchildren have a way of sometimes outliving their grandparents! But this is all an argument *in vacuo*.

Since, according to Coon, "Congoids" (blacks) were the last of the subspecies of *H. erectus* to be transformed into *sapiens*,[5] the level of civilization attained by them is "explained"—they simply did not have as long a history as *sapiens*, as do Caucasoids, and, interestingly enough, nor have the so-called archaic Australoids (Australian aborigines, Papuans, Melanesians, Negritos, and the like), so it is not to be wondered at that we are as *we* are, and they are as *they* are. And if the reader desired to observe what one of the latest to be developed *sapientes* looked like, when compared with one of the earliest to be developed *sapiens* types, he had only to consult Plate 32, in which he would see the photographic reproduction of an Australian aboriginal woman above and of a Chinese scholar below. The captions read as follows: "The Alpha and Omega of *H. sapiens:* An Australian aboriginal woman with a cranial capacity of under 1,000 cc (Topsy a Tiwi); and a Chinese sage with a brain nearly twice that size (Dr. Li Chi, the renowned archaeologist and director of Academia Sinica)."

"Alpha and Omega," the first and the last, "Obviously," Topsy just growed, and is what she is, a poor benighted Australian aboriginal, primarily because she has a brain of under 1000 cc, and Dr. Li Chi is primarily what he is because he has a brain nearly twice as big. Of course, there are cultural differences, but the implication is clear: no matter what cultural advantages Topsy or any of her children had been afforded, neither she nor they could have achieved what Dr. Li Chi had achieved.

This seems to me a really shocking example of scientific illiteracy. Apart from the demonstrable biologistic fallacies involved in this sort of argument, does it really have to be re-proven again and again that brain size within the normal range of variation characteristic of the human species at the *sapiens* level, and characteristic of every human population, in which a brain size of 850 cc. in a perfectly normally intelligent European is occasionally encountered,[6] in a land area in which one may also encounter an Anatole France with a brain size no larger than Topsy's, has nothing whatever to do with mental capacity?[7] But then, according to Coon, the Australian aborigines "come closest of any living peoples, to the *erectus-sapiens* threshold."[8] So they ought to be "less gifted" than Caucasoids and the large-brained Mongoloids. And by the same token (though Coon omitted any reference to this), the large-brained Mongoloids, having larger brains, on the average, than Caucasoids, ought to be "more gifted" than the latter.

"The genetic basis for high intelligence," Coon announced, "has been acquired independently in different taxonomic categories of primates. There is no evidence that the most successful populations within several different human races have not also become bright independently."[9] In other words, different human "races" are likened to the different monkeys, orangutans, chimpanzees, and gorillas, and there is "no evidence" that just as these different "taxonomic categories of primates" had independently acquired their different mental capacities, that the different human "races" had not independently done likewise. It hardly needs to be pointed out that the "races" of humankind are not equatable with the "different taxonomic categories of primates," and that, in any event, the evolution of man's intelligence has proceeded upon very different lines from that of any other taxonomic category of primate. This is a subject to which we shall return in the next chapter.

Coon also found that "Human beings vary in temperament. It is a common observation among anthropologists who have worked in many parts of the world in intimate contact with people of different races that racial differences in temperament also exist and can be predicted."[10] This was news to many anthropologists, among whom it was the common observation that the more one gets to know "people of different races" the more fundamentally alike they appear to be beneath the surface of the superficial differences. It is the present belief of many anthropologists and others that this discovery constitutes one of the principal contributions made by anthropology to the understanding of the richness of human diversity.

African blacks—Coon's "Congoids"—would almost seem to have been specially created, according to Coon's reading of the evidence. "As far as we know now," he wrote, "the Congoid line started on the same evolutionary level as the Eurasiatic ones in the Early Middle Pleistocene and then stood still for half a million years, after which Negroes and Pygmies appeared as if out of nowhere."[11]

Of course, the joker in this particular pack lies in the "As far as we know now." And what we know now is precisely so unilluminatingly little relating to the physical evolution of blacks, that the half a million years of standing still, mentioned by Coon, represents nothing more than the reflection of the paucity of our knowledge concerning black physical evolution. Even the surface of the subject has not yet been scratched, for the materials which would enable us to reconstruct the barest outline of black evolution or, for that matter, that of any other ethnic group, are simply not available. In any event, "the top-drawer people" didn't originate in "the Dark Continent." "The Children of Light" originated elsewhere. "If Africa was the cradle of mankind," we are told, "it was only an indifferent kindergarten. Europe and Asia were our principal schools."[12] In other words, those who remained in Africa never developed as did those who went on to Europe and Asia. "Genes in a population," Coon held, are in equilibrium if the population is living a healthy life as a corporate entity. Racial intermixture can upset the genetic as well as the social equilibrium of a group, and so, newly introduced genes tend to disappear or to be reduced to a minimum percentage unless they possess a selective advantage over their local counterparts.[13]

The population genetics of these statements are entirely erroneous, in fact they are preposterous, and far from reflecting the facts, the truth is that under the ordinarily prevailing conditions newly introduced genes can establish themselves rapidly, especially within small breeding populations. As for racial intermixture upsetting the genetic equilibrium of a group, the evidence of everyday experience throughout the world and field investigations is entirely contrary to this statement.

Coon finally concluded that had it "been in the evolutionary scheme of things, and had it not been advantageous to each of the geographical races for it to retain, for the most part, the adaptive elements in its genetic *status quo*" we would all have been "homogenized" by now.[14]

It is a common practice of humans to identify their prejudices with the laws of nature. It would appear that Coon was guilty of the same error. In any event, he was not a reliable guide to "the evolutionary scheme of things." "The evolutionary scheme of things" is not some mystical process which has kept people apart from one another, from being "homogenized," to use Coon's exceedingly unpleasant word. The evolutionary process has no scheme, and it has not schemed to keep humans apart for adaptive or any other reasons. What has kept people apart has been physiographic and social barriers, principally the former, and this is why the so-called "geographical races" being separated by geography and similar barriers, have not been "homogenized."

Since the publication of Coon's anachronistic book the anthropological conception of "race" has pretty much yielded to genetic pressure. The future of what used to be called the study of "race" lies, in my view, largely in the direction of microevolutionary studies and population genetics. The older anthropological conception of "race" still occasionally lingers on, suggesting that in some cases it is perhaps beyond the reach both of scientific judgment and mortal malice. Insofar as the genetic approach to the subject is concerned, some anthropologists are, as it were, self-made men and only too obviously represent cases of unskilled labor. However, my feeling is that they should be praised for trying rather than blamed for failing. The new anthropology is on the right track. Garn and Coon have attempted to adapt the terms "geographic race," "local race," and "microgeographical race" for use in the human species. They define, for example, "a geographical race" as, "in its simplest terms, a collection of (race) populations having features in common, such as a high gene frequency for blood group B, and extending over a geographically definable area."[15]

In this definition I think we can see, in high relief as it were, what is wrong with the continuing use of the term "race." The term "geographical race" immediately delimits the group of populations embraced by it from others, as if the so-called geographical race were a biological entity "racially" distinct from others. Such a group of populations is not "racially" distinct, but differs from others in the frequencies of certain of its genes. It was suggested by the UNESCO group of geneticists and physical anthropologists that such a group of populations be called a "major group."[16] This suggestion was made precisely in order to avoid such difficulties as are inherent in the term "geographical race." Since Garn and Coon themselves admit that "geographical races are to a large extent collections of convenience, useful more for pedagogic purposes than as units for empirical investigation,"[17] it seems to me difficult to understand why they should have preferred this term to the one more closely fitting the situation, namely, "groups." It is a real question whether spurious precision, even for pedagogical purposes, or as an "as if" fiction, is to be preferred to a frank acknowledgment, in the terms we use, of the difficulties involved. Garn and Coon are quite alive to the problem, but it may be questioned whether it contributes to the student's clearer understanding of that problem to use terms which not only do not fit the conditions, but which serve to contribute to making the student's mind a dependable instrument of imprecision, especially in view of the fact that a more appropriate term is available.

The principle of "squatter's rights" apparently applies to words as well as to property. When people make a heavy investment in words they are inclined to treat them as property, and even to become enslaved by them, the prisoners of their own vocabularies. Stone walls may not a prison make, but technical terms sometimes do. This, I would suggest, is another good reason for self-examination with respect to the use of the term "race," and the recognition that definitions are obstinate.

Commenting on Garn's views on race, Dr. J. P. Garlick has remarked,

The use of 'race' as a taxonomic unit for man seems out of date, if not irrational. A hierarchy of geographical, local and microraces is proposed, with acknowledgments to Rensch and Dobzhansky. But the criteria for their definition are nowhere made clear, and in any case such a scheme could not do justice to the many independent fluctuations and frequency gradients shown by human polymorphic characters. Surely physical anthropology has outgrown such abstractions as 'Large Local Race. . . . Alpine the rounder-bodied, rounder-headed, predominantly darker peoples of the French mountains, across Switzerland, Austria, and to the shores of the Black Sea.'[18]

Garn and Coon do not define "local races" but say of them that they "can be identified, not so much by average differences, but by their nearly complete isolation." In that case, as Dahlberg[19] long ago suggested, why not call such populations "isolates"? However, today the proper term to describe such populations is *clines,* that is, populations characterized by gradient differences in the frequency of genes for physical traits as between one population and another.

Taxonomies and terms should be designed to fit the facts, and not the facts forced into the procrustean rack of pre-determined categories. If we are to have references, whether terminological or taxonomical, to existing or extinct populations of humankind, let the conditions as we find them determine the character of our terms or taxonomies, and not the other way round.

At present, no satisfactory classification of the varieties of humans has been devised, and it is greatly doubted whether such classification is possible in any manner resembling the procedure of the purely botanical or zoological taxonomist. The reason for this is that all human varieties are much more mixed than are plant or animal forms, hence there is a greater dispersion or scattering of traits, which has the effect of producing a considerable amount of intergrading between ethnic groups or varieties. The more or less great variability of all ethnic groups constitutes a genetic proof of their mixed character. From the biological standpoint the physical differences which exist between the varieties of humankind are so insignificant that when properly evaluated they can be described mainly in terms of a particular expression of an assortment of genes common to humankind as a whole. At most, human varieties probably differ from one another only in the distribution of a comparatively small number of genes, and at the phenotypic level by clinal differences. This one may say much more definitely of humans than one could say of the differences exhibited by any of our domesticated varieties of cats, dogs, or horses. There are numerous varieties of cats, dogs, and horses, many of which represent highly selected strains of animals which have been developed as more or less homogeneous strains and domesticated by humans. Humankind, too, is to some extent a self-domesticated species but, unlike our domestic animals, humans exhibit varieties that are much mixed and far from representing homogeneous breeds.

The range of variation in humans is considerably greater than that exhibited by any group of animals belonging to a comparatively homogeneous breed. All the evidence indicates that the differences between the so-called races to a large extent represent a random combination of variations derived from a common source, which, by inbreeding in isolated groups, have become scattered and more or less stabilized and hereditary in a large number of the members of such groups. Furthermore, the evidence suggests that such selection of variations as has occurred in different groups has been primarily restricted to physical traits. There is no evidence among the ethnic groups of humankind that any process of mental selection has ever been operative which has acted differentially upon them to produce different types of mind (see Chapter 5).

The conception of differential selection for mental qualities seems to be a peculiarly modern one, adapted to modern prejudices. The evolution of human mental capacities and traits is discussed in the next chapter. Humans have bred dogs for certain temperamental qualities useful in the hunt for many centuries. The Irish setter, for example, is almost always red-haired, but his red hair has no connection whatever with his temperamental qualities. The Irish setter has the same kind of temperament as the English setter, but the hair color of the English setter is white or black. The only difference between the white, the black, the white and black, and the red setters is in their coat color; there are no significant differences in their mental or temperamental qualities. No one ever asks whether there are mental and temperamental differences between white, black, or brown horses—such a question would seem rather silly. When, however, humans are involved, the prejudice of anyone who has ever made the statement that skin color is associated with mental capacity is accepted as gospel. For such an assumption there is about as much justification as there would be for the assumption that there exist substantial differences between different hair color varieties of setters. We know this to be false concerning setters only because we seem to have paid more unprejudiced attention to the mental qualities of dogs than we have to those of human beings. But those of us who have paid some attention to the character and form of the behavior of peoples belonging to different ethnic groups and to different cultures have satisfied ourselves by every scientific means at our disposal that significantly or innately determined mental differences between the ethnic groups have thus far not been demonstrable. It may be that some such differences do exist, but if they do they have so far successfully eluded every attempt to prove their existence. There is every reason to believe that such mental differences as we observe to exist between the different ethnic groups are due principally to factors of a cultural nature and are in no demonstrably significant manner inseparably related to biological factors. We shall presently refer to the nature of the mental differences alleged to exist between different ethnic groups.

Whether ethnic groups have a common origin or not is strictly a matter which need concern us little, in view of the fact that structurally and functionally, in spite of superficial differences, they are all so much alike. There are few physical traits which are limited to any particular ethnic group. Perhaps it is nearer the truth to say that different ethnic groups show higher frequencies in the possession of certain physical traits than others. Such differences in the distribution of the frequencies of physical traits in different human groups may mean that at some time in the past individuals of different heredity interbred, and in isolation continued to do so with the result that a new combination of traits became more or less evenly distributed throughout the group. In this way a new ethnic group was produced. The probability that such factors as isolation and hybridization have played a large part in the evolution of most human groups is suggested not only by what we know of human intermixtures today—particularly the American black—and the behavior of other animal groups, but also by the presence in all human beings of by far the most substantial majority of traits most frequently found in any one group. The fundamental genetic kinship of all the ethnic groups of this world would, therefore, seem to be clear.

Le Gros Clark, the distinguished anatomist and physical anthropologist of Oxford University, made the important point that

> From the purely anatomical point of view, there are already available certain elementary observations on the physical anthropology of race which, though well-known to anatomists, are not, I think, widely enough recognized by those who are concerned with the social problems of race. At first sight, the contrast in appearance between such extreme types of mankind as the 'Negroid,' 'Mongoloid' and 'Caucasoid' might suggest fundamental constitutional differences. In fact, however, a close anatomical study seems to show that the physical differences are confined to quite superficial traits. I may best emphasize this by saying that if the body of a black were to be deprived of all superficial features such as skin, hair, nose, and lips, I do not think that any anatomist could say for certain, in a isolated case, whether he was dealing with the body of a black or a European. Naturally, such a test, being limited to the rather crude evidence of gross anatomy, is not by itself to be taken as a final demonstration of the constitutional equivalence of one race with another. Nor does it take account of statistical differences of a relatively minor trait. But it does suggest very strongly indeed that the somatic differences of race may after all not be of a very fundamental nature.[20]

With respect to the nature of those physical traits in the frequency distribution of which various groups differ from one another, it needs to be said that not one can be classified as either "higher" or "lower," "superior" or "inferior," in the scale of development. Every normal physical trait must be appraised as equally valuable for the respective functions which it is called upon to perform. Whatever its origin; a black skin is undoubtedly a trait of adaptive value, for there is some evidence that it enables its possessor to withstand the effects of prolonged exposure to sunlight. It is known that under such conditions the black skin is less liable to sunburn and cancer than is the white.[21] Hence, for groups living in areas of intense sunlight black skin would, by the measure of natural selection, in general be superior to white skin.

By definition all members of the human species belong to the same classificatory and evolutionary rank, and the ethnic groups, for the most part, merely represent the expression of successful attempts at adaptation to the environment or habitat in which they have been isolated. It is not altogether an accident that we find dark skins associated with regions of high temperatures and intense sunlight and light skins associated with cooler climates and moderate degrees of sunlight. In this same connection, compare the habitat of the white bear with that of the black or brown bear; also, the frequency of black insects in deserts. Gloger's rule states the fact that melanin (black) pigmentation in mammals and birds increases in warm and humid regions, and lighter pigmentation increases in arid regions. Lukin finds that darkly pigmented races of insects are found in regions whose climate is humid, and lightly pigmented races of insects are found in regions with arid climates.[22] Black skin appears to represent a trait of adaptive value which in some groups followed upon the loss of the body covering of hair. Thus, most apes and monkeys that possess an abundant hairy coat have white skin beneath the hair. It might, therefore, be assumed that the skin of the earliest humans was probably white; but the opposite assumption may be equally true, that is, some groups of the earliest humans may have been black. In that case we would have to say, disregarding for the moment all other considerations, that white-skinned peoples have a reduced distribution of pigment in their skin merely because the shift from the birthplace of their ancestors, which there is good reason to believe was Africa south of the Sahara, to the cooler regions of Europe gradually resulted in a decrease in the distribution of pigment in their skin, so that in the course of time, by means of selection of genes for low pigmentation, this has become considerably reduced.[23] The pigmentary difference is not one of kind but of degree. The same chemical pigments are present in the skin of all humans (with the exception of albinos, who have no pigment at all), varying only in its diffusion throughout the body rather than in quality.

The principal pigment, melanin, is produced in pigment cells known as melanocytes, by a reaction between the amino acid tyrosine and oxygen. The enzyme tyrosinase in the melanocytes acts on tyrosine to produce and control the speed of production of melanin. Exposure to the ultraviolet rays of sunlight, for example, activates tyrosine to convert tyrosine into melanin. There are no differences in the number of melanocytes in the different ethnic groups. Differences in pigmentation in populations and in individuals, as also in different parts of the body, are due to differences in the dispersion and distribution of melanin particles in the melanocytes.

This is in part under genetic, and in part under environmental, control. To the present day, exposure to the intense sunlight will bring about the production of an increased amount of pigmentation in many whites, so that depending upon the degree of exposure the skin may turn dark—even black. This latter phenomenon will occur more readily in brunets than in blonds, simply because brunets possess a greater amount of the substances required for the production of pigment, whereas blonds possess them in much lower proportion.[24]

It should be obvious that black and white skins are, in their own ways, traits of physiological importance for the survival of the individual. In hot, humid climates those individuals would be most favored who possessed skins sufficiently dark to prevent heat loss at too rapid a rate, and thus avoid heat exhaustion. In cool climates in which the humidity is relatively low, those individuals would be at a advantage—that is, over a considerable period of time—who were characterized by a lesser amount of pigment in the skin. For the white skin, less abundantly supplied with sweat glands than the black, acts as a good insulator against heat and cold.

Albinos, individuals whose skin tissues are completely devoid of any pigment, suffer intensely when exposed to sunlight. Their pigmentless tissues are incapable of making the necessary adjustments to the rays of the sun; in other words, they have no adaptive mechanism to protect them from the effects of solar radiation. In so far as they lack such a mechanism they are biologically unadapted to meet efficiently the demands of their environment and to that extent they are adaptively inferior to those of their fellows who are so adapted. But there is no evidence of any associated mental inferiority in such cases. Blacks are much better adapted to meet the demands of the conditions of intense sunlight and high temperatures to which their ancestors were born than are whites,[25] just as whites are better adapted to meet the requirements of the cooler climates of their adopted homelands. Is the one therefore superior or inferior to the other? Is the white superior to the black because he has lost so much of his pigment? Because biologically his organism has not required its presence under the conditions in which he has lived? And is the black superior (or inferior) because he is the descendant of ancestors who were able to survive by virtue of the selective value of their darkly pigmented skins? Clearly, there can be no question here of either inferiority or superiority. Both black and white have survived because they and their ancestors possessed traits of adaptive value which, under the respective conditions of their differing environments, enabled them to survive. Traits of adaptive value, whatever form they may take, are usually desirable, because from the standpoint of the organism and of the group they enable it to survive under the unremitting action of the challenges of natural selection.

Is there any reason, then, for devaluing a person because of the color of his skin, that selfsame color which probably enabled the ancestral group that gave him birth to surmount the challenges of this world? Of course there is none, and there can be none from any possible point of view. The same is true of hair and eye color. But, as racists insist, it is not only the color of the skin which counts; what of the other differences, such as in hair, lips, or nose? These, surely, are all marks of inferiority? We may well ask: "Marks of inferiority in what sense? In the cultural or in the biological sense?" If the statement is made from the cultural point of view, there can be no argument, for what a community or person considers culturally satisfying in such connections is purely an arbitrary matter of taste, and concerning taste it is notorious there can be no disputing. Even blacks when educated in Western cultures, as in North America, owing to the cultural norms which are everywhere set before them as standards or values, frequently come to consider that straight hair and light skin are to be preferred to kinky hair and black skin.[26] But if the statement is made in the biological sense as meaning that such black physical traits are marks of biological inferiority, then it can be demonstrated that such a statement stands in complete contradiction to the facts.

The three traits in question, namely, tightly curled hair, thick lips, and general lack of body hair, are not marks of inferiority, but are, unequivocally, in the biological sense, examples of traits which have progressed further in development than have the same physical structures in whites. In these very traits the black is from the evolutionary standpoint more advanced than the white; that is, if we take as our criterion of advancement the fact of being furthest removed from such conditions as are exhibited by the existing anthropoid apes, such as the gorilla and chimpanzee. If racists would take the trouble to visit their local zoo and for a moment drop their air of superiority and take a dispassionate look at either one of these apes, they would find that the hair of these creatures is lank, that their lips are thin, and their bodies are profusely covered with hair. In these traits the white man stands nearer to the apes than does the black. Is the white, then, for this reason, to be judged inferior to the black? Surely not.

We do not know why the black's head hair, body hair, and lips have developed as they have or why whites have more nearly retained the primitive condition of these traits.[27] But we can be certain that biologically there is a good functional reason responsible in both cases, which in the system of values involved in biological judgments must be appraised as equally valuable for the respective functions which each is called upon to perform. It has been suggested that the broad nose of the black is adapted to meet the requirements of air breathed at relatively high temperatures, whereas the comparatively long, narrow nose of the white is adapted to breathing air at relatively low temperatures.[28] From the standpoint of aesthetics, a much stronger case could be made out for the black nose than for that of the white. The bone, cartilage, and soft tissue that juts out from the face of the white like a peninsula, with its stretched skin, which becomes shiny as soon as the sweat begins to break through its enlarged pores, is really something of an atrocity. At least, any ape would think so (as, indeed, the apes in *The Planet of the Apes* did). Let us try to imagine, for a moment, such an outgrowth from the middle of one's face. In such a case, we would regard this structure from our present aesthetic standards, as an unsightly abnormality. But were the nose growing out of the middle of one's forehead the usual thing, we would, of course, find it perfectly acceptable, and even a thing of beauty. Cultural habituation and social standards of beauty are all. We have all grown used to our noses and take them very much for granted.

All that one can say is that biologically the form of the black nose and the form of the white nose are each, in their own way, perfectly capable of performing the functions to which they appear to be equally well adapted in all environments. That being so, there can be no question of either superiority or inferiority. Whether such traits are due to adaptation, natural selection, social selection, or a combination of such factors is uncertain. What is certain is that such traits do enable individuals possessing them to meet the demand their environments have made upon them and those that were made on their ancestors.[29] They have adaptive value, and this may be said for most, possibly all, the normal characters of humankind.

There is one trait of the human body which has been cited more frequently than any other as a "proof" of the inferiority of blacks to whites. This is the size of the brain. The size or volume of the brain is usually estimated from the capacity of the brainpan of the skull in terms of cubic centimeters. The material available upon which to base a discussion of the value of the size of the brain as related to mental capacity is far from satisfactory. We do not possess sufficient series of thoroughly controlled measurements on numerically adequate samples taken upon the brains of skulls of different human groups; it is possible for anyone with the intention of proving a particular case to prove it in precisely the terms he desires. But upon the basis of the available facts the scientist can come to only one conclusion, and that is that since there is no demonstrable difference in the structure, gross or microscopic, of the brains of the members of different ethnic groups, and since the variability in the size of the brain is such that there is no demonstrable relationship between cultural and intellectual status and brain size, there is therefore no significance to be attached to brain size as a mark of cultural or intellectual development. Let us briefly consider the facts.

The cranial capacity of the Paleolithic Neanderthal was, on the average, 1,550 cc. What an extraordinary situation! So-called primitive Neanderthal man, who lived more than 50,000 years ago, had a larger brain than the average white man of today. Strange that this elementary fact has been so consistently overlooked. Are we to assume, then that Neanderthal man was culturally and intellectually superior to the average modern white man? Blacks are reported to have an average cranial capacity of 1,300 cc, 50 cc less than the white, whereas the modern white has a cranial capacity lower than that of the Neandertal by about 200 cc. Are we, then, to conclude that the modern white is intellectually four times as much or at least as much inferior to Neandertal man as the black is to the white? We believe not.

We know that Neandertal was hardly as highly developed culturally as the modern black or white. But that he possessed the same capacities for cultural and intellectual development as do modern humans seems highly probable. Neandertals were neither inferior nor superior to modern humans because of their larger brains—they were inferior culturally to modern humans for the simple reason that the opportunities for cultural and technological development open to them were not of the kind that have been open to us later peoples, but vastly more challenging, they responded admirably to meet all the needs of their time and place in the small bands with which they harmoniously lived. The Neandertal brain almost certainly was as good as that of modern humans, and had nothing whatever to do with the technologically undeveloped state of his culture.

The brain is essentially the organ that coordinates or integrates nervous activities, and to a large extent it performs that coordination or integration according to the educative pattern in which it is conditioned. That pattern is always culturally determined. Therefore, it depends to a considerable extent on the sort of cultural experience to which an individual has been exposed and caused to coordinate or integrate within his nervous system, whether he is capable of functioning at the necessary integrative level or not. The material bases of those structures which are eventually organized to function as *mind* are to a large extent inherited precisely as are all other structures of the body. This is an assumption, but it seems a perfectly legitimate one to make. The qualification "to a large extent" is introduced for the reason that in humans the nervous system continues to develop long after birth and is therefore appreciably influenced by the experience of the individual.[30] There is every reason to believe, as Edinger first pointed out, "that in certain parts of the nervous mechanism new connections can always be established through education."[31] And, as Ranson has put it, "the neurons which make up the nervous system of an adult man are therefore arranged in a system the larger outlines of which follow an hereditary pattern, but many of the details of which have been shaped by the experiences of the individual."[32]

It is evident that experience must play a considerable role in the development of the structure and functioning relations of the nervous system, and it is also clear that that aspect of the functioning of the body or nervous system which we know as *mind* is dependent upon the interaction of several factors; these are, primarily: the inherited, *incompletely developed*, structure of the nervous system; and the nature of the *external developing* influences. There can be little doubt that the material bases of mind are inherited in much the same manner as are the other structures of the body. While the organization of the structures of the body is appreciably influenced by external factors, the resulting effects appear to be incomparably fewer and less complex than are those capable of being produced through the organization of those nervous structures which functioned as mind.[33]

While it is possible—though it has never been demonstrated—that in different ethnic groups the nervous system differs in some of its structural details, it is certain that if such differences exist, they are of the most insignificant kind. Summarizing the findings of science, Professor W. E. Le Gros Clark, one of the most distinguished neuroanatomists and physical anthropologists of the day, is quite positive upon this point. He writes that "in spite of statements which have been made to the contrary, there is no macroscopic difference by which it is possible for the anatomist to distinguish the brain in single individuals of different races."[34] The measurable mental traits of different human groups strongly suggest that between such groups there exist no differences whatever that can be attributed to the nervous system alone. Furthermore, the mental differences that occur between human groups would appear to be much less considerable than those found to exist between individuals of the same group. In the light of our present knowledge, the evidence indicates that within the limits of normal, brain weight, cranial capacity, head size, or the gross structure and form of the brain, there is no relation of any kind to the qualities of the mind, as between individuals of the same or different ethnic groups.[35] As Professor C. Judson Herrick has remarked, "mental capacity cannot be measured in avoirdupois ounces on the scales." Nor is there any biologically determined association between certain ethnic group traits and certain kinds of mentality.[36]

Since mental functions are so largely dependent upon experience, upon cultural conditions, it is impossible to draw any inferences as to the equivalence or nonequivalence of mental potentialities as between ethnic groups or peoples among whom the cultural conditions are not strictly comparable. In short, no statement concerning the mentality of an individual or a group is of any value unless it is accompanied by a specification of the conditions of the cultural environment in which that mentality has developed. No discussion of "racial" mental traits can be countenanced which neglects full consideration of the associated cultural variables. For it is evident that it is precisely these cultural variables that play the most significant role in producing mental differences between groups. As I have already indicated, it is more than probable that genetically influenced mental differences do exist between *individuals* of the same and different ethnic groups, but there is absolutely no evidence that significant mental differences determined by any genetic factors exist between any two *ethnic groups*. It is, of course, possible that future researches may reveal that in some ethnic groups there exist differences in the frequency distribution of genes which exercise limiting effects upon some potentialities. It would, however, be very surprising if it were found that such differences were anything more than differences in the frequency with which such genes occur in such groups, genes which are common to all humankind. The evidence, as we know it, indicates that all human groups possess all the gene potentialities that all other human groups possess, but that there are differences, between groups, in the manner in which such gene potentialities are both distributed and environmentally conditioned. At the present time we know what amounts to absolutely nothing concerning the gene frequency distribution of such potentialities in any of the groups of humankind. It is quite possible that we never shall. In any event, the important point is this: While on theoretical grounds we may be interested in the gene frequency distribution of such potentialities in populations, we are in actual practice concerned with the expression of the potentialities of the individual. As human beings we are not, and should not, be concerned with groups, but with individual human beings, with persons. "Do not speak to me of mankind," said Goethe, "I know only men." We must judge each person on his own merits, and in making our judgments we must be careful not to attribute to genes what may be, and usually is, for the most part largely developmentally influenced by the environment in interaction with the genes.

Professor L. H. Snyder has summarized this view very clearly. He writes,

> Among the findings emerging from the study of population genetics is the conclusion that human populations differ one from the other almost entirely in the varying *proportions* of alleles of the various sets and not in the *kinds* of alleles they contain. The manifold combinations of traits which in turn derive from manifold combinations of genetic and environmental influences result in the almost infinitely diverse range of human individuality—a range which we are just beginning to comprehend.[37]

A range in which the ethnic groups of humankind are to be regarded as so many variations on a common theme. As we have already said, apparently it is principally, if not entirely, due to differences in cultural experience that individuals and groups differ from one another culturally, and it is for this reason that, where the cultural experience has appreciably differed, cultural achievement is an exceedingly poor measure of the mental value, genetically speaking, of an individual or of a group. For all practical purposes, therefore, and until further evidence to the contrary be forth-coming, we can safely take cultural achievement to represent the expression chiefly of cultural experience, not of biological potentiality.

As long ago as 1935, Professor Otto Klineberg, our then leading authority in the field of "racial" or ethnic psychology, after considering the evidence from every standpoint, offered the following important conclusion: "We may state with some degree of assurance that in all probability the range of inherited capacities in two different ethnic groups is just about identical."[38] Most authorities today thoroughly agree.

The environmental plasticity of mental traits is so great that when the evidence is all in, it will almost certainly show that the average differences between ethnic groups will be smaller than the amplitude of the differences to be found within each of the ethnic groups themselves. The brain does not secrete cultural or intellectual power in the same way that the liver secretes bile. One is not born with the ability to think brilliantly. Such an ability can be brought about only by exposure of the brain and nervous system to, and education in, the appropriate conditions.

Two thousand years before the birth of Christ the people of what is to-day England were living in an Early Bronze Age phase of cultural development. Long before this period the civilization of the Egyptians, as represented by the Old Kingdom (III–IV dynasties, 2780–2270 B.C.), had reached one of its most splendid periods. As a people the Egyptians had long been in contact with other peoples who had acted upon them as so many cross-cultural fertilizing agents, unlike the Britons who had been isolated from the main course of such contacts. Well might the Egyptians at this time have looked upon the Britons as a "primitive people."

Were the brains of the Britons in the Early Bronze Age made of such inferior stuff that they could only assume efficient qualities by an infusion of new genes? Clearly, genes and brain had nothing to do with the matter; on the other hand, the cultural stimulation which came to them increasingly after the Early Bronze Age, and particularly after the Iron Age, when Julius Caesar landed on their shores in 54 B.C., had everything to do with the development which eventually, in the fifteenth century, culminated in that great cultural efflorescence which has been called the Greece of the modern world.

Even so, it took the Britons some 1,500 years following the Roman Conquest to begin popping. Invasions and settlement by Scandinavians, Celts, Angles, Jutes, Saxons, and Normans, extending over a period of more than 1,000 years, following an occupation by the Romans of some 500 years, had produced very little effect. It would have been easy and even reasonable to conclude that the Britons were not an especially well-endowed people. Following such intensive and prolonged contacts with such highly civilized peoples, the Britons, after 1,500 years, had very little to show for it. And then, all of a sudden, it seemed, there was such an explosion of genius as the world had not witnessed since Periclean Athens. The pyrotechnical display of genius which illuminated the hitherto relatively empty English firmament, has brought light, and warmth, and joy to the whole of the literate world. Shakespeare, John Donne, Thomas Heywood, George Chapman, Ben Jonson, Thomas Dekker, Philip Massinger, Christopher Marlowe, Francis Bacon, Gilbert of Colchester, George Eliot, Jane Austen, the Brontës, as well as numerous other luminous spirits in the arts and sciences who followed in a continuous succession of new stellar births, would have been considered highly improbable by most of Britain's conquerors. These men and women were, of course, exceptional. They were men and women of genius. But it is customarily by the achievements of such individuals that we measure a society's or ethnic group's quality. Apparently certain specific conditions are necessary and must be present in every culture before the latent potentialities for achievement in each population can be expressed.

The English until very recently were the most notoriously unmusical people of our age. Yet in Elizabethan times they were among the most musical in Europe. What had happened? Had the "musical part" of the English brain atrophied? We can be certain that it had not. The cultural and economic development of the English had simply led in a direction away from such interests to other pursuits. Brain has nothing to do with the matter, culture everything. In short, it is culture which makes "brains"; not brains, culture. If this were not so, then the Amahosa of Africa, who have few cultural opportunities but more brains by size than whites, with 1490 cc as compared with 1400 cc for European males and 1350 cc for females, would be culturally and intellectually superior to whites, as would the Buriats, 1496 cc; the Iroquois, 1519 cc; the Eskimos, 1563 cc; and the Mongols, 1570 cc.[39] If we are to hold that blacks are mentally inferior to whites because their brains have, on the average, a volume of 50 cc less than that of whites, then by the same token we must hold that Amahosa, Eskimos, Mongols, and many other peoples are superior to whites. This we have reason to believe is untrue. There is no evidence that any people is either biologically or mentally superior or inferior to any other people in any way whatever. What we do know is that there exist considerable cultural differences between peoples and that these cultural differences are readily explained upon purely historical grounds, not upon any biological ones.

Differences in brain size have about as much relation to intelligence and cultural achievement as have differences in body size; that is to say, within the limits of normal variation absolutely none, either between groups of individuals or between individuals of the same group. In short, the concept of "race" which holds that the physical differences between peoples are reflections of underlying significant mental differences is an idea which, on the existing evidence, cannot be scientifically substantiated. It is, in fact, a myth and a delusion.

The average person in our society observes that certain other persons belonging to different ethnic groups possess physical and mental traits which differ from his own. He concludes that these physical and mental traits are somehow linked together, and these traits are inborn, and that they are immutable.[40] Vague notions about a unilinear evolution "from monkey to man" encourage him to believe that such "races" are "lower" in the "scale" of evolution than is the group to which he belongs; that there exists a natural hierarchy of "races." From such a starting point as "prehistoric man" he envisages a continuous progression upward, culminating in the final development of his own "race" or group. Between "prehistoric man" and himself stand, in an intermediate position, all the other peoples of humankind. "Race" is a definite entity to him, and all the intellectual supports for his conception of it are ready at hand. Newspapers, periodicals, books, radio, TV, publicists, politicians, and others tell him much the same story. The significance of "race" for him emotionally is, as we shall soon see, of considerable importance. Therefore, "race" exists. Such is the conception of "race" with which we have to reckon. We have seen that there are no scientific grounds whatever for such a belief.

Notes

1. Carleton Coon, *The Origin of Races* (New York: Alfred A. Knopf, 1962), 657.

2. Ibid., vii.

3. Ibid., ix–x.

4. Ashley Montagu, "Social Time: A Methodological and Functional Analysis," *American Journal of Sociology* 44 (1938): 282, 284.

5. Coon, *Origin of Races*, 655–56.

6. Bella Hechst, "Über einen Fall von Mikroencephalie ohne Geistigen Defekt," *Archiv für Psychiatrie und Nevenkrankheiten* 97 (1932), 64–76. See also G. C. Van Walsem, "Ueber das Gewicht des Schwersten bis jetzt Gescriebenen Gehirns," *Neurologisches Centrallblatt* (1899): 578–80.

7. Donald G. Paterson, *Physique and Intellect* (New York: Century, 1930), 80–123; P. Guillaume-Louis and Louis Dubreuil-Chambardel, "Le Cerveau d'Anatole France," *Bulletin de l'Academie de Medecine* (Paris) 98 (1927): 328–36.

8. Coon, *Origin of Races*, 427.

9. Ibid., 184.

10. Ibid., 116.

11. Ibid., 658.

12. Ibid., 656.

13. Ibid., 661.

14. Ibid., 662.

15. Stanley Garn and Carleton Coon, "On the Number of Races of Mankind," *American Anthropologist* 67 (1955): 997.

16. See Appendix A, *Ethnic Group and Race.*

17. Garn and Coon, *"On the Number of Races,"* 1,000.

18. J. P. Garlick, "Review of Human Races and Readings on Race by S. M. Garn," *Annals of Human Genetics* 25 (1961): 169–70.

19. Gunner Dahlberg, *Race, Reason, and Rubbish: A Primer of Race Biology* (New York: Columbia University Press, 1942).

20. W. E. Le Gros Clark, *Fitting Man to His Environment* (Newcastle-upon-Tyne: King's College, 1949), 19.

21. Harold Blum, "The Physiological Effects of Sunlight on Man," *Physiological Reviews* 25 (1945): 524; Harold Blum, "Does the Melanin Pigment of Human Skin Have Adaptive Value?" *Quarterly Review of Biology* 36 (1961): 50–63.

22. Th. Dobzhansky, "Rules of Geographic Variation," *Science,* 99 (1944): 137–28; Julian Huxley, ed., *The New Systematics* (New York: Oxford University Press, 1940): 213–14; Farrington Daniels Jr., "Man and Radiant Energy: Solar Radiation," in *Adaptation to the Environment,* eds. D. B. Dill et al. (Washington, D.C.: American Physiological Society, 1964): 969–87.

23. For a further speculative discussion of skin color see Carleton S. Coon, Stanley M. Garn, and Joseph Birdsell, *Races: A Study of the Problems of Race Formation in Man* (Springfield: Thomas, 1950), 51–55; and Blum, "Menlanin Pigment,"; M. L. Thomson, "Relative Efficiency of Pigment and Horny Layer Thickness in Protecting Skin of Europeans and Africans Against Solar Ultraviolet Radiation," *Journal of Physiology* 127 (1955): 236–46.

24. T. Edwards and S. Quimby Duntley, "The Pigments and Color of Living Human Skin," *American Journal of Anatomy* 65 (1939): 1–33. The darkening of white skin under sunlight has, of course, no effect on the genes for white skin. Any permanent change in skin color could only come about by the selection of genes for more pigmentation. See Thomas B. Fitzpatrick, M. Seiji, and David McGugan, "Melanin Pigmentation," *New England Journal of Medicine* 265 (1961): 328–32, 374–78, 430–34.

25. Julian H. Lewis, *The Biology of the Negro* (Chicago: University of Chicago Press, 1942), 94–6.

26. For the preferences of African Americans in these and other respects see Margaret Brenman, "Urban Lower-Class Negro Girls," *Psychiatry* 6 (1943): 311–12.

27. For some interesting conjectures see Coon, Garn, and Birdsell, *Races.*

28. Arthur Thompson and L. H. Dudley Buxton, "Man's Nasal Index in Relation to Certain Climatic Conditions," *Journal of the Royal Anthropological Institute of Great Britain and Ireland,* 52(1923): 92–122.

29. For an excellent discussion of this subject see Lewis, *Biology of the Negro,* 77–81; Paul T. Baker and J. S. Weiner, eds.), *The Biology of Human Adaptability* (Oxford: Clarendon Press, 1966); Emilio F. Moran, *Human Adaptability: An Introduction to Ecological Anthropology* (Belmont, CA: Wadsworth, 1979); Jane H. Underwood, *Human Variation and Human Microevolution* (Englewood Cliffs, NJ: Prentice-Hall, 1979); Valerius Geist, *Life Strategies, Human Evolution, Environmental Design: Toward a Biological Theory of Health* (New York: Springer Verlag, 1978).

30. Margaret A. Kennard and John F. Fulton, "Age and Reorganization of the Central Nervous System," *Journal of the Mount Sinai Hospital* 9 (1942): 594–606; E. Tobach, L. R. Aronson, and E. Shaw, eds., *The Biopsychology of Development* (New York: Academic Press, 1971).

31. Ludwig Edinger, *Vorlesungen über den Bau der nervüsen Zentralorgane des Menschen und der Tiere* (Leipzig: Vogel, 1911).

32. Marian Diamond, *Enriching Heredity: The Impact of Environment on the Anatomy of the Brain* (New York: Free Press, 1988); Paul Ranson, *The Anatomy of the Nervous System* (Philadelphia: Saunders, 1939), 41.

33. It should be clearly understood that while mind is an aspect of the functioning body it is also a great deal more than that, and that in man it is at least as much a product of culture as of genes. See Leslie A. White, *The Science of Culture* (New York: Farrar, Straus, 1949); Ernst Cassirer, *An Essay on Man* (New Haven: Yale University Press, 1944); Gilbert Ryle, *The Concept of Mind* (New York: Barnes and Noble, 1949); Peter Laslett, ed., *The Physical Basis of Mind* (New York: Macmillan, 1950); Asley Montagu, ed., *Culture and the Evolution of Man* (New York: Oxford University Press, 1962).

34. Le Gros Clark, *Fitting Man to His Environment*, p. 19; for a thoroughgoing discussion see Phillip V. Tobias, "Brain Size, Grey Matter and Race—Fact or Fiction?" *American Journal of Physical Anthropology* 32 (1970): 3–26; Phillip V. Tobias, *The Brain in Hominid Evolution* (New York: Columbia University Press, 1971); Samuil Blinkov and Il'ya M. Glezer, *The Human Brain in Figures and Tables* (New York: Basic Books, 1968).

35. On these matters see Karl Pearson, "Relationship of Intelligence to Size and Shape of the Head and Other Mental and Physical Characters," *Biometrika* 5 (1906): 105–46; Raymond Pearl, "On the Correlation between Intelligence and the Size of the Head," *Journal of Comparative Neurology and Psychology* 16 (1960): 189–99; K. Murdock and Louis R. Sullivan, "A Contribution to the Study of Mental and Physical Measurements in Normal Children," *American Physical Education Review* 28 (1923): 209–15, 278–88, 328; R. R. Reid and J. H. Mulligan, "Relation of Cranial Capacity to Intelligence," *Journal of the Royal Anthropological Institute of Great Britain and Ireland* 53 (1923): 322–32; Paterson, *Physique and Intellect* (1930); S. P. Pickering, "Correlation of Brain and Head Measurements and Relation of Brain Shape and Size to Shape and Size of the Head," *American Journal of Physical Anthropology* 15 (1931): 1–52; Gerhardt von Bonin, "On the Size of Man's Brain, as Indicated by Skull Capacity," *Journal of Comparative Neurology* 59 (1934): 1–28.

36. Steven Jay Gould, *The Mismeasure of Man* (New York: Norton, 1981).

37. Lawrence H. Snyder, "The Genetic Approach to Human Individuality," *Science*, 108 (1948): 586.

38. Otto Klineberg, "Mental Testing of Racial and National Groups," in *Scientific Aspects of the Race Problem*, ed. J. W. Corrigan, (New York: Longmans, 1941), 284; see also Otto Klineberg, "Race Differences: The Present Position of the Problem," *International Social Science Bulletin* (UNESCO), 2 (1950), 460–66; Richard Bergland, *The Fabric of the Brain* (New York: Viking, 1986); Diamond, *Enriching Heredity;* Herbert L. Leff, *Experience, Environment, and Human Potentials* (New York: Oxford University Press, 1978); R. D. Lund, *Development and Plasticity of the Brain* (New York: Oxford University Press, 1978); Steven Rose, *The Conscious Brain* (New York: Alfred A.

Knopf, 1973); Tobias, *The Brain in Hominid Evolution;* Russell Tuttle, *The Functional and Evolutionary Biology of Primates* (Chicago/New York: Aldine, 1972).

39. For a list of cranial capacites in fossil and living man, as well as in fossil and living apes, see Ashley Montagu, *An Introduction to Physical Anthropology* (Springfield, IL: Thomas, 1960). 458–59.

40. "We are apt to construct ideal local types which are based on our everyday experience, abstracted from a combination of forms that are most frequently seen in a given locality, and we forget that there are numerous individuals for whom this description does not hold true." Franz Boas, "Race and Progress," *Science* 74 (1931): 1.

5

Natural Selection and the
Mental Capacities of Humankind*

The biological heredity of humankind is transmitted by mechanisms similar to those encountered in other animals as well as in plants. Similarly, there is every reason to believe that the evolutionary factors which led up to the development of our species were of much the same nature as those which have been operative in the evolution of other forms of life. The evolutionary changes that occurred before the prehuman could become human, as well as those which supervened since the attainment of the human estate, can be described causally only in terms of mutation, selection, genetic drift, and hybridization—common processes throughout the living world. This reasoning, indisputable in the purely biological context, becomes a fallacy, however, when used, as it often has been, to justify narrow biologism in dealing with human development.

The specific human features of the evolutionary pattern of *Homo sapiens* cannot be ignored. Humankind is a unique product of evolution in that human beings, far more than any other creatures, have escaped from the bondage of the physical and biological into the integratively higher and more complex social environment. This remarkable development introduces a third dimension, a challenging new zone of adaptation, in addition to those of the external and internal environments—a dimension many biologists, in considering the evolution of humankind, have tended to neglect. The most important setting of human evolution is the human social environment. The human social environment can influence evolutionary changes only through the media of mutation,

---

*This chapter is based on the article originally written in collaboration with Theodosius Dobzhansky, and published in *Science* 105 (1947): 587–90, with the title "Natural Selection and the Mental Capacities of Mankind."

natural selection, social selection, genetic drift, and hybridization. There can be no genuine clarity in our understanding of humankind's biological nature until the role of the social factor in the development of the human species is understood.

In the words of R. A. Fisher, author of *The Genetical Theory of Natural Selection*, "For rational systems of evolution, that is, for theories which make at least the most familiar facts intelligible to the reason, we must turn to those that make progressive adaptation the driving force of the process."[1] It is evident that humankind, by means of its reasoning abilities, has achieved a mastery of the world's varying environments quite unprecedented in the history of organic evolution. The system of genes which has permitted the development of the specifically human mental capacities has thus become the foundation and the paramount influence in all subsequent evolution of the human stock. An animal becomes adapted to its environment by evolving certain genetically determined physical and behavioral traits; the adaptation of humans consists chiefly in developing their inventiveness, a quality to which their physical heredity predisposes them, and which their social heredity provides them with the means of realizing. To the degree to which this is so, humankind is unique. As far as physical responses to the world are concerned, humans are almost wholly emancipated from dependence upon inherited biological dispositions, uniquely improving upon the latter by the process of learning everything their social heredity (culture) makes available to them. The individual possesses much more efficient means of achieving immediate or long-term adaptation than the member of any other biological species, namely, through learned responses or novel inventions or improvisations.

In general, two types of biological adaptation in evolution can be distinguished. One is genetic specialization and genetically controlled fixity of traits. The second consists in the ability to respond to a given range of environmental situations by evolving traits favorable in these particular situations; this presupposes genetically controlled plasticity of traits. It is known, for example, that the composition of the blood which is most favorable for life at high altitudes is somewhat different from that which is characteristic at sea level. A species that ranges from sea level to high altitudes on a mountain range may become differentiated into several attitudinal varieties, each having a fixed blood composition favored by natural selection at the particular altitude at which it lives; or a genotype may be selected which permits an individual to respond to changes in the atmospheric pressure by determinate alterations in the composition of the blood. It should always be remembered that every aspect of our biology is at some level the product of the environment. The responses may be more or less rigidly fixed, so that approximately the same traits develop in all environments in which life is possible. On the other hand, the responses may differ in different environments. Fixity or plasticity of a trait is, therefore, genetically controlled.

The biological makeup of humans provides one with the *capacity* to learn, the emergence of the *ability* to make choices is largely shaped by the environment, by culture, the human-made part of the environment, the culture of which one is a member—the culture that is the work of many minds, and a more or less long history.

Whether the evolutionary adaptation in a given phyletic line will occur chiefly by way of genetic fixity or by was of genetically controlled plasticity of traits will depend on circumstances. In the first place, evolutionary changes are compounded of mutational steps, and consequently the kind of change that takes place is always determined by the composition of the store of mutational variability which happens to be available in the species populations. Secondly, fixity or plasticity of traits is controlled by natural selection. Having a trait fixed by heredity and hence appearing in the development of an individual regardless of environmental variations is, in general, of benefit to organisms whose milieu remains uniform and static except for rare and freakish deviations. Conversely, organisms inhabiting changeable environments benefit from having their traits plastic and modified by each recurrent configuration of environmental agents in a way most favorable for the carrier of the trait in question.

Comparative anatomy and embryology show that a fairly general trend in organic evolution seems to be from environmental dependence toward fixation of the basic features of the bodily structure and function. The appearance of these structural features in the embryonic development of higher organisms is, in general, more nearly autonomous and independent of the environment than in other forms. The development becomes "buffered" against environmental and genetic shocks. If, however, the mode of life of a species happens to be such that it is, of necessity, exposed to a wide range of environments, it becomes desirable to vary some structures and functions, in accordance with the circumstances that confront an individual or a strain at a given time and place. Genetic structures that permit adaptive plasticity of traits become, then, obviously advantageous for survival and so are fostered by natural selection.

The social environments that human beings have created everywhere are notable not only for their complexity but also for the rapid changes to which immediate adjustment is demanded. Adjustment occurs chiefly in the mental realm and has little or nothing to do with physical traits. In view of the fact that from the very beginning of human evolution the changes in the human environment have been not only rapid but diverse and manifold, genetic fixation of behavioral traits in humans would have been decidedly unfavorable for survival of the individual as well as of the species as a whole. Success of individuals in most human societies has depended and continues to depend upon their ability to rapidly evolve behavior patterns which fit them to the kaleidoscopic conditions they encounter. Individuals are best off if they submit to some, compromise with some, rebel against or avoid others, or escape from still other situations. Those who display a relatively greater fixity of response than their fellows suffer under most forms of human society and tend to fall by the way. Suppleness, plasticity, and, most important of all, ability to profit from experience and education are required. No other species is comparable to *Homo sapiens* in its capacity to acquire new behavior patterns and discard old ones in consequence of training. Considered socially as well as biologically, humankind's outstanding capacity is its educability. The survival value of this capacity is manifest, and therefore the possibility of its development through natural selection is evident. Natural selection on the human level favors gene complexes which enable their possessors to adjust their behavior to any condition in the light of previous experience. In short, it favors educability.

The replacement of fixity of behavior by genetically controlled plasticity is not a necessary consequence of all forms of social organization. Attempts to glorify insect societies as examples deserving emulation ignore the fact that the behavior of an individual among social insects is remarkable precisely because of the rigidity of its genetic fixation. The perfection of the organized societies of ants, termites, bees, and other insects is indeed wonderful, and the activities of their members may strike an observer forcefully by their objective purposefulness. The purposefulness is retained, however, only in environments in which the species normally lives. The ability of an ant to adjust its activities to situations not encountered in the normal habitats of its species is limited. On the other hand, social organizations on the human level are built on the principle that an individual is able to alter his or her behavior to fit any situation, whether previously experienced or new.

This difference between human and insect societies is not surprising. Adaptive plasticity of behavior can develop only on the basis of a vastly more complex nervous system than is sufficient for adaptive fixity. The genetic differences between human and insect societies furnish a striking illustration of the two types of evolutionary adaptations—those achieved through genetically controlled plasticity of behavioral traits and those attained through genetic specializations and fixation of behavior.

The genetically controlled plasticity of mental traits is, biologically speaking, the most typical and uniquely human characteristic. It is probable that the survival value of this characteristic in human evolution has been considerable for a long time, as measured in terms of human historical scales. Just when this characteristic first appeared is, of course, conjectural. Here it is of interest to note that the most marked phylogenetic trend in the evolution of humans has been the special development of the brain, and that the characteristic human plasticity of mental traits seems to be associated with the exceptionally large brain size. The brain, for example, of the Middle Pleistocene fossil forms of man was, grossly at least, scarcely distinguishable from that of modern man. The average Neandertaloid brain of the Upper Pleistocene was somewhat larger than that of modern man. More important than the evidence derived from brain size is the testimony of cultural development. The Middle Acheulian handiwork of Swanscombe man of three hundred thousand years ago, the Tayacian handiwork of Fontéchevade man of 160,000 years ago, and the beautiful Mousterian cultural artifacts associated with Neandertal man of 100,000 years ago, indicate the existence of minds of a high order of development.

The cultural evidence suggests that the essentially human organization of the mental capacities emerged early in human evolution. However that may be, the possession of the gene system, which conditions educability rather than behavioral fixity, is a common property of all living humans. In other words, educability is truly a species character of *Homo sapiens*. This does not mean, of course, that the evolutionary process has run its course and that natural selection has introduced no changes in the genetic structure of the human species since the attainment of human status. Nor is there any implication that no genetic variations in mental equipment exist at our own time level. On the contrary, it seems likely that with the attainment of human status the part of the human genetic system related to mental potentialities did not cease to be labile and subject to change.

This brings us face to face with the old problem of the likelihood that significant genetic differences in the mental capacities of the various ethnic groups exist. The physical and, even more, the social environments of people who live in different countries are quite diversified. Therefore, it has often been argued, natural selection would be expected to differentiate the human species into local groups or races differing in mental traits. Populations of different regions may differ in skin color, head shape, and other bodily characters. Why, then, should they be alike in mental traits?

As Kenneth Mather has put it,

Many non-European peoples, especially savages, have been regarded as genetically inferior because their level of social development was below that of the European, and this view has drawn strength from these people's obvious genetical departures from the European in colour and physical characteristics. The existence of one genetical difference makes it easier to impute another. The falsity of such an argument is self-evident. Since genes can recombine, their effects can be reassociated, so that differences in the genetic determinants of one character do not imply differences in the determinants of another.[2]

It will be through investigation rather than speculation that the problem of the possible existence of genetic differences in the mental make-up of human populations of different geographical origins will eventually be settled. Arguments based on analogies are precarious, especially where evolutionary patterns are concerned. If so-called human races differ in structural traits, it does not necessarily follow that they must also differ in mental ones. Ethnic group differences arise chiefly because of the differential action of natural selection on geographically separated populations. In the case of humans, however, the structural and mental traits are quite likely to be influenced by selection in different ways.

We are not directly concerned here with the problem of ethnic differentiation of structural traits. Suffice it to say that ethnic differences in such traits as the blood groups may conceivably have been brought about by genetic drift, that is, the random fixation of genes, in populations of limited effective size, as well as by selection. Other ethnic traits are genetically too complex and too consistently present in populations of some large territories to be accounted for by genetic drift alone.

In agreement with the views here expressed, George Gaylord Simpson, the distinguished paleontologist, wrote,

> There are biological reasons why significant racial differences in intelligence, which have not been found, would not be expected. In a polytypic species races adapt to differing local conditions but the species as a whole evolves adaptations advantageous to all its races, and spreading among them all under the influence of natural selection and by means of interbreeding. When human races were evolving, it is certain that increase in mental ability was advantageous to *all* of them in approximately equal degrees. For any one race to lag definitely behind another in overall genetic adaptation, the two would have to be genetically isolated over a very large number of generations. They would, in fact, have to become distinct species; but human races are all interlocking parts of just one species.[3]

Differences in skin color, hair form, nose shape, and so on, are almost certainly products of natural selection.[4] The lack of reliable knowledge of the adaptive significance of these traits is perhaps the greatest gap in our understanding of human evolutionary biology. Nevertheless, it is at least a plausible working hypothesis that these and similar traits have, or at any rate had in the past, differential survival value in the environments of different parts of the world. By contrast, the survival value of a higher development of mental capacities in humans is obvious. Furthermore, natural selection seemingly favors such a development everywhere. In the ordinary course of events in almost all societies those persons are likely to be favored who show wisdom, maturity of judgment, and ability to get along with people—qualities that may assume different forms in different cultures. Those are the qualities of the plastic personality, not a single trait but a general condition, and this is the condition which appears to have been at a premium in practically all human societies.

In human societies conditions have been neither rigid nor stable enough to permit the selective breeding of genetic types adapted to different statuses and forms of social organization. Such rigidity and stability do not prevail in any society. On the other hand, the outstanding fact about human societies is that they do change and do so more or less rapidly. The rate of change was possibly comparatively slow in earlier societies, as the rate of change in present-day indigenous societies may be when compared to the rate characterizing western societies. In any event, rapid changes in behavior are demanded of the person at all levels of social organization even when the society is at its most stable. Life at any level of social development in human societies is a pretty complex business, and it is met and handled most efficiently by those who exhibit the greatest capacity for adaptability, flexibility.

It is this very plasticity of their mental traits that confers upon humans the unique position which they occupy in the animal kingdom. Its acquisition freed humankind from the constraint of a limited range of biologically predetermined reactions. Humans became capable of acting in a more or less regulative manner upon their physical environment instead of being largely regulated by it. The process of natural selection in all climes and at all times has favored genotypes which permit greater and greater educability and plasticity of mental traits under the influence of the uniquely social environments to which humans have been continuously exposed.

As Muller has pointed out, "racial genetic differences . . . may well be insignificant in comparison with the individual ones, owing to the lack of any substantial difference in the manner of selection of most of these characters in the major part of the past history of the various human races." And, again, as Simpson has put it, "Human races all belong to the same species and have generally had enough interbreeding so that genetic progress, as distinct from local adaptation, could and evidently did spread through the entire species."[5] Finally, as Hiernaux has said,

> If we . . . consider man's place in nature, what made him so successful on earth is his genetic capacity for culture. This major distinction is so essential for his survival in any environment that, in the light of current knowledge at least, all populations seem to be equal in this respect. Adaptation to local environment was and still is a paramount factor in the genesis of genetical or 'racial' differences between human populations, both these differences are minor and unessential compared with man's general physiological adaptability and his general capacity to find

non-biological means of coping with the variations of his environment, including the new biological challenges which cultural evolution itself unceasingly generates.[6]

Whether or not we are reasonably justified in assuming that there has been little if any significant change in the mental potentialities of humans during the major part of their past history, this does seem to be reasonably clear—namely, that the effect of natural selection in humans has probably been to render genotypic differences in personality traits, in mental traits, in genetic potentialities, as between individuals and particularly as between ethnic groups or races, relatively unimportant compared to their phenotypic plasticity. The human genotype is such that it makes possible the development of the widest possible range of behavioral adjustments and adaptations. Instead of having genetically fixed responses as in other animal species, *Homo sapiens* is the only species that invents its own responses, and it is out of this unique ability to invent, to improvise, his responses that his cultures develop.

There is every good reason to believe that natural selection has been operative upon traits making for educability in much the same way from the earliest beginnings of man's history, and in all human groups, no matter how long isolated they may have been from one another. It should be obvious that under any and all forms of social organization, as David and Snyder put it,

> Flexibility of behavioral adjustment to different situations is likely to have had a selective advantage over any tendency toward stereotyped reactions. For it is difficult to conceive of any human social organization in which plasticity of response, as reflected by ability to profit from experience (that is, by intelligence) and by emotional and temperamental resilience, would not be at a premium and therefore favored by natural selection. It therefore seems highly improbable that any significant genetic differentiation in respect to particular response patterns, populations or races has occurred in the history of human evolution.[7]

And that is the conclusion of this chapter; or, to put it more positively, the evidence considered in this chapter points to the conclusion that in human evolution natural selection has placed, as it were, a high premium upon flexibility or educability, that it has done so nondifferentially, and that for these reasons it becomes highly probable that the mental capacities of humankind are everywhere pretty much of a muchness.[8] This does not mean that all humans have become exactly alike; such a statement would be demonstrably untrue. Human beings differ from one another in many traits, and there can be little doubt that mental traits are influenced by many genes, and that as long as this remains the case people will always differ from each other—more so within groups than between groups. What this statement does mean is that the selection pressures to which the human species has been subject since its origin has been nondifferential selection for educability, "i.e., for the capacity to modify one's behavior under the influence of experience and reasoning."[9] This seems to have had the effect of allowing for individual differences, of bringing all human groups up to pretty much the same mental level.

Finally, it is becoming increasingly clear that intelligence, from the genetic standpoint, is not so much a product of major genes, that is, of single genes producing a large effect, but rather of polygenes, that is of many genes each of which produces a small individual quantitative effect. This being the case it is highly improbable that differences in intelligence could have been brought about in the small, separated populations of humankind by genetic drift. This would require the assumption of so many correlated changes in positive-acting or negative-acting genes as to render such an effect quite out of the question.[10]

Let us then, always remember that from the very earliest beginnings of the arrival at the human estate the development of humanity has involved a feedback process between genotype and environment, the social environment, and the recreative organization of his experience and the world by the individual himself.[11]

Notes

1. R. A. Fisher, *The Genetical Theory of Natural Selection* (Clarendon Press: Oxford, 1930).

2. Kenneth Mather, *Human Diversity* (Edinburgh: Oliver and Boyd, 1964).

3. George Gaylord Simpson, *Biology and Man* (New York: Harcourt, Brace & World, 1966),104.

4. For suggestive treatment of this subject see Carleton Coon, Stanley M. Garn, and Joseph Birdsell, *Races, a Study of the Problems of Race Formation in Man* (Springfield, IL: Thomas). See also Th. Dobzhansky, *Mankind Evolving* (New Haven: Yale University Press, 1962); W. E. Howells, ed., *Ideas on Human Evolution* (Cambridge: Harvard University Press, 1962); Ashley Montagu, ed. *Culture and the Evolution of Man* (New York: Oxford University Press, 1962); James N. Spuhler, ed., *The Evolution of Man's Capacity for Culture* (Detroit: Wayne State University Press, 1959); Anne Roe and George G. Simpson, eds., *Behavior and Evolution* (New Haven: Yale University Press, 1958); Marshall Sahlins and Elmin R. Service, eds., *Evolution and Culture* (Ann Arbor: University of Michigan Press, 1960); Sherwood Washburn, ed., *Social Life of Early Man* (Chicago: Quadrangle Press, 1961); Ashley Montagu, *The Human Revolution* (New York: World Publishing, 1965); Ashley Montagu, ed., *Culture: Man's Adaptive Dimension* (New York: Oxford University Press, 1968); Th. Dobzhansky, *Genetic Diversity and Human Dignity* (New York: Basic Books, 1973); Jonathan Marks, *Human Biodiversity* (New York: Aldine de Gruyten, 1995); Weston La Barre, *The Human Animal* (Chicago: University of Chicago Press, 1954); E.

Moran, *Human Adaptability* (Belmont, CA: Wadsworth, 1979); P. T. Baker and J. S. Weiner eds., *The Biology of Human Adaptability* (Oxford: Clarendon Press, 1966).

5. George G. Simpson, "The Biological Nature of Man," *Science* 152 (1966), 474.

6. Jean Hiernaux, "Adaptation and Race," *Advancement of Science* (1967), 658–62.

7. Paul David and Lawrence Snyder, "Genetic Variability and Human Behavior," in *Social Psychology at the Crossroads,* eds. J. H. Rohrer and M. Sherif (New York: Harper, 1951), 71.

8. Th. Dobzhansky and A. Montagu, "Natural Selection and the Mental Capacities of Mankind," *Science* 105 (1947), 587–90.

9. Th. Dobzhansky, "The Genetic Nature of Differences among Men," in *Evolutionary Thought in America,* ed. S. Persons (New Haven: Yale University Press, 1962), 154.

10. J. L. Fuller, *Nature and Nurture: A Modern Synthesis* (New York: Doubleday, 1954), 27–28.

11. Richard Lewontin, Steven Rose, and Leon Kamin, *Not in Our Genes: Biology, Ideology, and Human Nature* (New York: Pantheon Books, 1984), 272–73.

6

The Mythology of Race, or "For Whom the Bell Tolls"

Old myths never die. Nor do they fade away. Not, certainly, if they are related to "race" and its boon companion "IQ."

For millions of people the terms "race" and "IQ" seemingly possess a clear and well-defined meaning. This common usage implies the users' belief in a reality beyond question. When, on occasion, the suggestion is made that these terms constitute an amalgam of erroneous and stultifying ideas of the most damaging kind, the suggestion is apt to be received with blank incredulity or derision. Despite the fact that "race" and "IQ" correspond to no verifiable reality whatever, they have been made the basis for social and political agendas of the most heinous kind. The most recent example of this phenomenon is *The Bell Curve*, by Richard J. Herrnstein and Charles Murray.[1]

When Murray was seeking a publisher for *Losing Ground* (1984), he stated in his proposal that: "[A] huge number of well-meaning whites fear that they are closet racists, and this book tells them they are not. It's going to make them feel better about things they already think but do not know how to say."[2] This is surely a perfect description of *The Bell Curve*. Not only has *The Bell Curve* (which more than made up for the sales the earlier book failed to attain) told numbers of "well-meaning" whites that it is perfectly permissible for them to voice what they already thought about "race" and "intelligence" (if, indeed, they were not already doing so). It also assured such book buyers that their preexisting beliefs are "scientifically" sound and should therefore prevail in the policy-making arena.

Involved in the concept of "race" intrinsic to *The Bell Curve* is the assumption that first there *is* such a thing as "race," and second that what is so obvious and beyond question is that the physical differences which allegedly mark off the "races" from one another are inseparably linked with individual and group achievement. Some "races," it is held, from this point of view, are in all significant respects inferior to others. Hence, all that is necessary to arrive at a proper estimate of an individual's abilities is to identify, usually by external appearance, his or her "racial" membership. This method will at once tell one the limits of that individual's capacities, what he or she is likely to be able to accomplish, and, furthermore, what his or her particular "race" will be able to achieve.

This "manifest reality"—in which physical appearance, individual ability, and group achievement are inseparably linked by heredity—is what is generally understood by "race." It is, in other words, the popular, or social, concept of "race."[3]

What is wrong with the social or racist view of "race" is that, among other things, there happens to be no genetic association or linkage between genes for physical appearance, individual behavior, and group achievement. Nevertheless, believers in the doctrine of "race" choose to take it for granted that such linkage exists.

As an exponent of the "race" doctrine, Murray is understandably sympathetic to the plight of whites who "fear they are closet racists" because social pressures presumably cause them to hide their views. And Murray is all the more sympathetic because he and Herrnstein actually engaged in such behavior before their book was published: "Some of the things we read to do this work, we literally hide when we're on planes and trains. We're furtively peering at this stuff."[4] What could they have been hiding?

"Surely the most curious of the sources he and Herrnstein consulted is *Mankind Quarterly* . . . ," observes Charles Lane. Cited in *The Bell Curve*'s bibliography, Lane points out, are no less than seventeen researchers who have contributed to this "notorious journal of 'racial history' founded, and funded, by men who believe in the genetic superiority of the white race." Five articles from the journal itself are also listed in *The Bell Curve*. One of Herrnstein and Murray's advisors is Richard Lynn, an associate editor of *Mankind Quarterly* (the authors list twenty-three of his works). The causes that *Mankind Quarterly*'s editors and contributors have supported range from apartheid in South Africa to "eugenically minded" attacks on school desegregation in this country. The journal has also published works by individuals who conducted research in Nazi Germany.[5] Another of *The Bell Curve*'s sources is Frank C. J. McGurk, who surfaced in the mid-1950s as a "scientific" opponent of school desegregation. He was also a leader of the International Association for the Advancement of Ethnology and Eugenics, whose executive committee "reflect[ed] an alliance between American segregationists and neo-Nazi elements abroad."[6]

The Bell Curve has been treated by its supporters as a ground-breaking work, but its authors essentially recycle the claims Jensen made in "How Much Can We Boost IQ Scores and Scholastic Achievement?" (1969) and other works. Herrnstein and Murray bestow high praise on their predecessor, who, they say, is "respected for his meticulous research."[7] The "meticulous research" in Jensen's 1969 monograph was linked to claims that created a media sensation in their time and returned biological determinism to center stage.

According to Jensen, it is "a not unreasonable hypothesis that genetic factors are strongly implicated in the average Negro-white intelligence difference."[8] But Jensen's hypothesis *is* unreasonable: it requires that one share his assumptions that the black-white scoring difference on IQ tests represents a black-white intelligence difference, and that 80 percent of the scoring difference is attributable to genetic differences.

In justifying his claims, Jensen made much of his heritability measures.[9] But the truth is that the so-called heritability coefficient is an especially undependable measure when applied to the human species. It has been criticized from its very inception by mathematical geneticists such as R. A. Fisher, as well as others. Fisher, one of the founders of modern statistics and mathematical and population genetics, referred to the coefficient of heritability "as one of those unfortunate short-cuts which have emerged in biometry for lack of a more thorough analysis of the data."[10] And David Layzer devastatingly showed that Jensen's 80/20 percent estimate belongs to numerology rather than science.[11]

Herrnstein and Murray also offer a heritability estimate. Without saying how they arrived at the estimate, they reduce Jensen's 80/20 to 60/40. One may safely assume that the reduction was made to lend their argument an aura of reasonableness, but the gaping difference between their percentages and Jensen's merely reveals once again the capriciousness of heritability estimates—that they are, as another critic observes, "little more than a hollow quantification."[12] This is hardly surprising, given that the genetic contribution to intelligence, let alone test scores, is unknown both for individuals and populations. Thus, even though Herrnstein and Murray's central argument treats a genetic component in test scores as established fact (e.g., "Recent studies have uncovered other salient facts about the way IQ scores depend on genes"), they also hedge on the genetic argument: "ethnic" differences in test scores "May well include some (*as yet unknown*) genetic component" (italics added).[13]

Herrnstein and Murray present no "theoretical" justification for the claim that different physical characteristics among "races" bespeak different mental characteristics. Perhaps the authors dispensed with this matter because of the attention that Jensen and other contemporary biological determinists had already devoted to it. Jensen, for instance, states that he held discussions with a number of geneticists; these discussions, he says, revealed rather consistent agreement on several points, including the following: "genetic differences are manifested in virtually every anatomical, physiological, and biochemical comparison one can make between representative samples of identifiable racial groups (Kuttner, 1967). There is no reason why the brain should be exempt from this generalization."[14] The first generalization is quite unsound, the second blatantly wrong.

Jensen's reference to Kuttner as his authority for the second statement is not supported by the latter's own paper which is restricted to a review of the biochemical differences between so-called races.[15] (Jensen's misconstruction of Kuttner's paper could hardly have displeased Kuttner, who is an arch-segregationist and a former associate editor of *Mankind Quarterly*.)[16] In any event, Jensen sees only differences between "racial" groups in virtually every anatomical, physiological, and biochemical trait, when in fact the likenesses in all these classes of traits are far greater than the differences. Differences in these areas of structure and function exist, but to argue that therefore differences must also exist for the genetic distribution of mental functioning among "races" is to call in the ambiguity of language to add to the confusion of thought.

Jensen sees no reason why the brain "should be exempt from the generalization" that genetic differences exist in virtually every organic trait between "races." But contrary to his conclusion, there is every reason why the brain should be exempt from this generalization. To begin with, by "brain" Jensen presumably means the neural circuitry which under the processes of socialization and their organization will function as mind. Since the brain is an organic structure, it can easily be slipped into Jensen's generalization and quite erroneously equated with "mind." Certainly the brain has undergone considerable evolutionary change, but the pressures of natural selection have not acted directly on it but indirectly through its functions, especially capacities for culturally-acquired functions. The complexity and size of the human brain represent the end-effects of the action of selection on the functions of human behavior in human environments. What has been under selective pressure is not the brain as an organ, *but the skill in using it and its competence in responding as a culturally adaptive organ.*

This aspect of the manner of humanity's unique mental evolution was fully dealt with by Dobzhansky and Montagu as long ago as 1947,[17] and may well be reemphasized here in the words of the distinguished paleontologist George Gaylord Simpson, who has explained in his book *Biology and Man* how it would have come about that from a biosocial viewpoint the mental abilities of humanity should everywhere have developed alike in response to the complex challenges of the environment. Simpson writes: "There are biological reasons why significant racial differences in intelligence, which have not been found, would not be expected. In a polytypic species races adapt to differing local conditions but the species as a whole evolves adaptations advantageous to all its races, and spreading among them all under the influence of natural selection and by means of interbreeding. When human races were evolving, it is certain that increase in the mental ability was advantageous to *all* of them. It would, then, have tended over the generations to spread among all of them in approximately equal degrees. For any one race to lag definitely behind another in overall genetic adaptation, the two would have to be genetically isolated over a very large number of generations. They would, in fact, have to become distinct species; but human races are all interlocking parts of just one species."[18]

To this may be added the words of two other biologists, Paul David and L. H. Snyder, when they wrote that

"flexibility of behavioral adjustment to different situations is likely to have had a selective advantage over any tendency toward stereotyped reactions. For it is difficult to conceive of any human social organization in which plasticity of response, as reflected by ability to profit from experience (that is, by intelligence) and by emotional and temperamental resilience, would not be at a premium and therefore favored by natural selection. It therefore seems to us highly improbable that any significant genetic differentiation in respect to particular response patterns, populations or races has occurred in the history of human evolution."[19]

The anthropologists Sherwood L. Washburn and C. S. Lancaster state, "To assert the biological unity of mankind is to affirm the importance of the hunting way of life. It is to claim that however such conditions and customs may have varied locally, the main selection pressures that forged the species were the same."[20]

The foodgathering-hunting way of life was pursued by the human species the world over during the greater part of its evolutionary history. However, the importance of hunting in early human evolution has perhaps been overemphasized. A more likely view of the facts, but one which surely includes hunting within its purview, is expressed in the latest survey of evidence from a number of scholars. This evidence indicates that human beings are and always have been a species of generalists, whose adaptive advantage lies in their ability to exploit all facets of their environment.[21] This view gives women an equal or even greater role in the provisioning of the group, and thus the basis for sharing in the opportunities for the development of intelligence.

Professor Jensen also thinks it not unlikely that

different environments and cultures could make differential genetically selective demands on various aspects of behavioral adaptability... Europeans and Africans have been evolving in widely separated areas and cultures for at least a thousand generations, under different conditions of selection which could have affected their gene pools for behavioral traits just as for physical characteristics."[22]

Here Jensen has confused two different phenomena; that is, he fails to distinguish between the environmental pressures of widely separated and diverse geographic areas upon the physical evolution of the human species, and the virtually identical cultural pressures upon the mental development of people living as adaptive generalists. Again contrary to Jensen, the challenges to humanity's problem-solving abilities were essentially of a social nature—and as of a very different order from those which eventually resulted in differences in skin color, hair texture, breadth of nose, and so on. While physical environments have varied considerably, humanity's cultural environments during the whole of its history, right up to the present period, have been fundamentally alike, namely, that of omnivorous generalists.[23] Thus, the important fact that Jensen fails to understand is that while the differences in the physical environments may have been extreme, the conditions of selection under which humanity's mental evolution occurred were everywhere alike.

Jensen's "scientific" theorizing about genetic differences in intelligence among "races" lent a seemingly sophisticated aura to the hereditarian argument, which had traditionally been advanced in manifestly crude ways. Once the argument was modernized, new twists could be added that might make hereditarians appear as objective, unbiased researchers. Jensen himself supplied such an addition or variation in 1973, when he alleged that East Asians are in all likelihood genetically superior in intelligence to whites.[24] Herrnstein and Murray followed suit.

That Herrnstein and Murray's decision to reiterate the Asian-superiority thesis was not prompted by the nature of the available data is apparent: "Only two studies sampled Asians in America, and they were inconclusive," states Margaret Cohn. Five other studies made comparisons between Asians in Asia and white Europeans or white Americans.

A scientist who is testing for the effect of genes independently of environment could not think of a worse study than one which compares groups in radically different cultures," Cohn notes, adding: "comparing Asians in Asia to whites in America is like comparing apples to oranges—not to mention the fact that IQ is to intelligence as apples are to zebras." Pointing to the reason why Herrnstein and Murray assert that Asians may well be the most intelligent "race," Cohn states: "Once they establish a super human or 'good' minority, then there can't be any racism in their research.[25]

Other researchers who preceded Herrnstein and Murray in promoting the Asian-superiority myth include Richard Lynn and J. Philippe Rushton. Rushton is notorious for his claim that a correspondence exists between brain size and "race" and penis size and "race"—with Asians at the top in the first category, whites slightly below, and blacks far below, and a reverse ranking in the second category. Herrnstein and Murray, defending Rushton against charges of "crackpot" and "bigot," assert that he has "strengthened the case for consistently ordered race differences . . ."[26]

By comparing the times in which each was published, one can see in yet another way that *The Bell Curve* is an extension of Jensen's monograph. Jensen's article appeared in the *Harvard Educational Review* not long after the civil rights movement had won major victories. His approach was, one might say, microcosmic: he attacked one new program, Head Start. In doing so, it was evident, he placed a range of other programs in jeopardy. By the time *The Bell Curve* was a work in progress, the social climate had so drastically changed that its authors could not only engage in a macrocosmic attack on educational and social programs, but feel confident that this would help make their book a best seller.

Among Herrstein's and Murray's many targets is Head Start, whose growth had long been severely curtailed. Using statistics generated during the years since Jensen's attack, the authors repeat the by now standard criticism of the program: Head Start, whose goal is to "boost IQ's," has failed. At first the children show significant scoring gains, but by the time they reach the third grade, the gains are "usually gone"; by the sixth, the scoring gains have "vanished from aggregate statistics."[27]

In other words, according to this argument, if the children's intelligence had actually been boosted, their IQ scores would not rise only to decline; the gains would be permanent. This interpretation fails to explain either the rise or fall in the children's scores. The scoring pattern is, in fact, inexplicable if IQ tests are regarded as measures of intelligence. But if the tests are recognized as instruments whose covert standard is school performance, the reason for the scoring pattern is evident: When the children's aggregate scores increased, it was because Head Start allowed them to acquire scholastic-type skills to which they would not otherwise have had access. But skills acquired in pre-school will not earn a child high marks in the third grade, let alone the sixth. When the children's scores declined, it was because their education had regressed; after leaving Head Start, they were relegated to the inferior schools provided for poor children, particularly black ones.

One might well contend that the logic of the initial increase in the children's scores called for upgrading their education after they left Head Start. But IQ tests serve to justify racial and class inequities in education, not to help eliminate them. If inferior, segregated schools had been deemed the problem, Head Start would have been seen as the first step in upgrading the children's education, not as a program designed to "boost IQs." Although it is now all but forgotten, the reason Head Start was given the objective of "increasing" the children's intelligence—which, it was held, had been stunted by their family environments—was so that they could go on to end the "cycle of poverty." So, by placing the blame for their poverty on poor people rather than on the society, the concept underlying Head Start also put the onus for deficient school performance on the children rather than on deficient schools.

Implicit in the Head Start concept is the assumption that individuals are mere products of their environment. But human development is determined neither by genes nor environment. Nor is the process of development, as a variant of these views holds, simply a matter of interaction between environment and genes. This process is instead the reorganization of that interaction by the developing organism. As R. C. Lewontin, Steve Rose, and Leon J. Kamin stress, it is not a question of

> organism and environment insulated from one another or unidirectionally affected, but of a constant and active interpenetration of the organism with its environment. Organisms do not merely receive a given environment but actively seek alternatives or change what they find."

While this applies to organisms in general, it applies prepotently to humans: "Humans above all are constantly and profoundly making over their environment in such a way that each generation is presented with quite novel sets of problems to explain and choices to make; we make out own history, though not in circumstances of our own choosing."[28]

The concept that humans are simply products of their environment and that mental processes develop in one kind of environment rather than another—thus overlooking that individuals are active agents in their own development who, in every environment, must explain problems and make choices—has long been influential, and is reflected in a variety of contemporary studies. For instance, the Coleman Report (1966) found that the quality of schooling has little effect on scholastic performance because the children's intelligence or cognitive abilities, as measured by IQ tests, is essentially set by the family environment at levels that vary with the family's race and socioeconomic status.[29] Despite criticism of the report on matters ranging from crude statistical methods to reliance on administrators' claims that schools for blacks were separate but equal, it has been used for three decades to justify the "savage inequalities" in education for African American and other minority children.[30] Jensen's monograph leaned heavily for its data on the environmentalist Coleman Report, and Herrnstein and Murray also use it to argue that equalizing education along racial and class lines is futile.

Among the justifications Herrnstein and Murray present for applying the genetic thesis to social matters is the following: Proceeding from the incontestable premise that environmentalists as well as hereditarians interpret the black-white scoring gap as an intelligence gap, the authors assert that even if it were discovered "tomorrow" that "the B/W difference in measured intelligence is entirely genetic in origin," they can think of "*no legitimate argument why any encounter between individual whites and blacks need be affected . . .*" (italics in the original).[31]

That no discovery will be made tomorrow or at any other time linking black-white differences in IQ scores to genes is beside the point (as is Herrnstein's and Murray's notion of what constitutes a "legitimate argument"). The *assumption* that such a difference exists is sufficient to affect behavior. Take Herrnstein and Murray's behavior: Although they admitted that the existence of a genetic component in the black-white scoring gap is "as yet unknown," they did not hesitate to use the genetic argument to influence public opinion and policy in the direction they wanted it to go.

Herrnstein and Murray, however, deny that the genetic argument affects policy making: "The *existence* of the difference [in black-white intelligence] has many intersections with policy issues. The *source* of the difference has none that we can think of, at least in the short term."[32] The qualifying phrase "at least in the short term" is the prelude to an argument ostensibly concerned with the uselessness of long-range environmentalist programs aimed at boosting IQs, but the real message is in the subtext, which signals the uselessness of allocating funds for pre-school or any other level of education for poor children, particularly if they are African American. This position is not exclusive to hereditarians but, as the Coleman Report attests, is also shared by conservative environmentalists.

But the phrase "at least in the short term" has other ramifications: it is a reminder of the long-term intersections between biological determinism and public policies and/or practices ranging from slavery, "eugenic" sterilization, and Nazi genocide to the Herrnstein-Murray vision of groups with low IQ scores being placed on reservations. The authors' amnesia regarding the fact that the genetic argument has historically served as the justification for the most brutal policies and practices is so appalling that it may easily distract attention from a point that calls for the most careful consideration: that the *assumption per se* of a black-white intelligence differential does indeed determine the outcome of a host of policy decisions, as well as innumerable individual encounters.

For instance Herrnstein and Murray—posing a supposedly hypothetical question—state that if employers were to use "ethnicity" as their hiring standard, they would do so because of a "difference in observed intelligence regardless of whether the difference is genetic."[33] It would be difficult indeed to argue that employers who reject African American applicants care whether the presumed black-white intelligence gap is the product of heredity or environment. It is the presumption of inferiority that justifies discriminatory hiring practices and, at the same time, inflames opposition to affirmative action—which was not designed to compensate for allegedly inferior intelligence but to combat centuries-old discrimination. The same principle applies to segregation and discrimination in every area, including the classroom, where IQ scores, not the way in which they are interpreted, determine a child's destiny. Thus, while the environmentalist interpretation of a supposed African-American intelligence deficit may sound benign, particularly when compared with the alternate interpretation, the *assumption of inferiority* is the opposite of benign.

The assumed black-white "difference in observed intelligence," which was first "observed" during slavery, has been "confirmed" by IQ tests for most of this century. Almost from the start, test use was joined by test criticism. An early critic was Walter Lippmann, the most brilliant journalistic and political commentator of his time. In a trenchant anatomy of IQ testing, he pointed to a fatal flaw: That intelligence testers had "no clear idea of what intelligence means."[34]

To answer this recurring charge, the testers have often asserted that "Intelligence is what the tests test."[35] Such a circular definition is hardly likely to advance our understanding of intelligence, although it can be interpreted as making a point, namely, that IQ tests don't measure intelligence, for the simple reason that no one knows what it is.

Still, it might be thought that the tests provide a rough estimate of certain problem-solving abilities. But abilities represent trained capacities, that is, skills, and therefore experience and learning enter substantially into their development. Since the tested ability/skill represents to a large extent the trained expression of a capacity of capacities, the "measurement" of the skill can tell us nothing about the original quality of the capacity.

Although the creators of IQ tests had no definition of intelligence, they nonetheless "knew" that school performance is a measure of intelligence and that different races and classes have superior or inferior intelligence. Because they constructed their tests of problems that call for scholastic-type skills and information and because quality of education varies along racial and class lines, their tests appeared to support their assumptions.

The early testers also "knew" that their tests measured "innate" intelligence, despite the fact that, even today, our knowledge of the genetics of intelligence is virtually non-existent. Intelligence is clearly a function of many genes in interaction not only with the environment but, as has been stressed, with the verdicts of the organism itself. The fact that we have no idea how many genes may be involved would not in itself constitute a sufficient impediment to the study of the genetics of intelligence were we able to separate the contribution made by the environment from the action of the organism itself toward influencing the expression of intelligence. But we are unable to do that, and the best authorities agree that it does not seem likely that we shall ever—even though "ever" is a long time—be able to make such a separation. But, to repeat the point that cannot be too often repeated, since genes never function in isolation, but always in interaction with the environment and the active organism, it does not appear likely that we shall ever be able to say to what extent intelligence is due on the one hand to genes and on the other to organismal and environmental factors.

It is quite clear that there are many unknowns involved in the development of intelligence, as for example, aspects of physiological, biochemical, neurological, neurohumoral, molecular, and social conditions—conditions which are never taken into account because they are unknown. All of which leads to the conclusion that those who tell us that IQ tests measure intelligence by that very statement make it evident that they simply do not understand the complexity of the problem. In claiming to have solved the problem and making recommendations based on specious evidence, they deceive both themselves and those who rely upon their judgment. They perceive cause and effect relations between variables such as test scores and assumed genetic or environmental determinants, when in fact no such cause and effect relations exits.

Given that they are alleged to measure what has not even been defined, it is not surprising that criticism of IQ tests has mounted over the years. The criticism, particularly of the tests' ethnocentric and class biases, reached a peak after Jensen published his 1969 article.[36] To defend the tests, Jensen published *Bias in Mental Testing* (1980);[37] his defense is reiterated in *The Bell Curve*. This defense maintains, accurately enough, that the tests are not biased according to the test makers' own criterion. By this criterion—a statistical one that has nothing to do with what test critics mean by bias—an IQ test is bias-free if it has "predictive validity," that is, if its prediction for the school performance of each tested group correlates to the same degree with the group's performance. Not only would the results of a test whose biases match those of the schools be expected to correlate with school performance, but the test makers "confirm" the predictive validity of IQ tests by "achievement" tests, which are constructed of the same kinds of items as the IQ tests.

Jensen, Herrnstein, and Murray also maintain that the tests are free of "cultural bias." To support this view, the trio relies on Frank McGurk's dissertation (1951).[38] According to Jensen, the work is a "pioneer doctoral study" that tests the "hypothesis that the poorer performance of blacks, as compared with that of whites, on most mental tests, is the result of cultural bias in the tests."[39] But rather than investigating a hypothesis regarding test bias, as Jensen claims, McGurk set out to uphold the hereditarian interpretation of IQ tests.

To "prove" that black-white scoring differentials do not result from test bias but from black-white genetic differentials in intelligence, McGurk constructed his study so that it would appear to rule out any other explanation.

He selected as his subjects 213 black-white pairs of high school seniors; the members of each pair, he claimed, had been matched for socioeconomic status, including education. His socioeconomic indices were probably adequate for making rather crude intra-group distinctions, but only a researcher who wanted to deny that racial discrimination affects socioeconomic status would use them for a black-white comparison.[40]

Take, for instance, McGurk's claim that the members of each black-white pair were matched for education. The students were drawn from seven different high schools in New Jersey and Pennsylvania, with the members of each pair said to have attended the same high school for four years. One hundred ninety-five pairs had reportedly been enrolled in the same school *districts* since first grade; however, the black and white members of a pair were not said to have been enrolled in the same *school*—a crucial distinction, since the schools the blacks attended would by no means have matched those the whites went to. That the black and white members of each pair would have arrived at high school with significant differences in preparation is further illustrated by the remaining eighteen pairs: The members of each attended grade school in entirely different areas.

The subjects of the study were tested on IQ items that had been rated from "least cultural" to "most cultural" by seventy-eight judges. Allowed to define "cultural" as each saw fit, the judges ranked items calling for vocabulary and/or information "most cultural," and those calling for scholastic-type skills "least cultural." (Of course, McGurk saw nothing untoward in convening a white panel to decide if items were biased against blacks.)[41] Because blacks did better on the "most cultural" than the "least cultural," McGurk reported that there was "no evidence" that "culturally weighted test material discriminates against the Negro."[42]

Thus, to support a predetermined conclusion, McGurk compared *black* averages on two *different* types of items. Had he made the appropriate comparison—namely, between black *and* white averages on the *same* type, he would, by his own comparative standard, have demonstrated that the culturally-loaded items *were* biased against blacks: Whites as well as blacks did better on them, but the white average was higher than the black one.

Perhaps, one might argue, McGurk should have said that the "most cultural" items were less biased against blacks because the black-white scoring gap was smaller than on the "least cultural" ones. But in terms of the IQ method, this is a meaningless distinction. On an IQ test, each type of item (vocabulary, analogy, and so forth) plays its part in bringing about a predetermined result. Although this means that the black average for each category must be lower than the white one, it does not mean that the racial scoring differential for each item contributes to the desired outcome (items that do not are dropped during a test's tryout period).[43] Thus McGurk, who supposedly aimed to discover if culturally-loaded items discriminate against blacks, was "investigating" a matter that the testers had resolved decades earlier. (Culturally-loaded items that discriminate against blacks could be replaced with culturally-loaded items that discriminate against whites, but this would of course reverse the desired results.) McGurk seems to have had at least two reasons for limiting his "investigation" of test bias to culturally-loaded items. By doing so, he dismissed even the possibility that other types of items could be biased. At the same time, by emphasizing that blacks did better on "most cultural" items, while passing over that fact that whites did too, his study seemed to support the hereditarian claim that the reason for the larger black-white scoring gap on the "least-cultural" (for instance, those involving mathematical problems) is that these items test an "innate" quality, that is, what hereditarians call "g," or "general intelligence." In reality, what these items test are skills that come with a quality education; the more difficult the problem, the higher quality of schooling required to deal with it. Thus these items, as well as the culturally loaded ones, reflect the inherent bias of a test whose measure is school performance.

McGurk's ambitious project had yet another object: to revive the hereditarian interpretation of the black-white scoring differential on the much-criticized World War I Army Mental Tests. To this end, he charged that the studies refuting this interpretation had used "extreme methods of selection." The reality is quite different: where the hereditarians claimed that the difference in the national black and white averages reflected a difference in "innate" intelligence, the refutations uncovered hidden scoring patterns that told another story.

An early refutation, which McGurk does not name, was published in 1924 by Horace Mann Bond.[44] Bond noted that if the tests were measures of "native and inherent ability," whites from Georgia should score as high as whites from Oregon. In ranking the whites from each state by their median score on the Alpha, the test for literates, he found an almost 50 percent difference between the white scores in the top- and bottom-ranked states. He also compared the whites' median score for each state with the state's rank according to the amount it spent per pupil, on teachers' salaries, and related indices. There was a strikingly high (almost 75 percent) correlation between the two sets of rankings, with southern states at the bottom for both test scores and education. Bond also compared black median scores from four northern states with white median scores from four southern ones; he found, for instance, that blacks from Illinois outranked whites from several southern states. The "boasted superiority of the white over the Negro stock does not seem so impressive when the Negroes of Illinois" outscored whites in "at least four Southern states," Bond observed.[45]

One of the studies that McGurk accuses of using "extreme methods of selection" is Ashley Montagu's (1945).[46] When Ashley Montagu found, two decades after the Bond study, that no additional black-white medians had been computed, he set out to calculate them for the remaining states. As it turned out, there were no statistics for blacks in twenty-five states, but he computed black and white Alpha medians for nineteen more states and the District of Columbia. The results showed that blacks from four northern states outscored whites from nine *southern* ones. Ohio blacks did better than whites from nine *northern* states.

The distribution of scores over the states, Ashley Montagu found, showed that for both African Americans and whites, "the deeper the South the lower the score":

> The depressed socio-economic state of the South as compared with the greater part of the rest of the United States is an unfortunate fact. It is, therefore, not surprising that both Negroes and whites in the South should do worse on the tests than their fellows in any other part of the Union; and, since conditions are invariably worse for Negroes than for whites, that the Negroes should do worse than the whites.[47]

The combined findings of the Ashley Montagu and Bond studies also point to an extension of this conclusion: that is, to a connection between the fact that, although northern states with better socioeconomic conditions spent more for educating whites than blacks, and the fact that the white median for each state was higher than its black counterpart.

Ashley Montagu also calculated medians for the Beta, the test for nonliterates, which showed a generally high correspondence with Alpha rankings. Comprehensive medians for the draftees who took the Alpha plus the Beta, an individual examination, or all three tests, also demonstrated that northern blacks did better than whites from many southern states. The explanation for the consonance between the Alpha and Beta medians may lie in the fact that in states with better socioeconomic conditions, nonliterate draftees would have had more opportunities to acquire information, both through broader experiences and more contact with literates, who would have formed a larger percentage of the population in those states.

Since the fact that northern blacks outscored southern whites could not be denied outright, it was hidden from a public that had been deluged with claims that the WWI scores were proof of African-American inferiority. Had the testers acknowledged that, by their own standards, northern blacks were more intelligent than southern whites, they would have shown simple fairness. But such a declaration, while no more nor less unscientific than the claim of white mental superiority, would of course have been heretical.

In addition to refuting present as well as past hereditarian interpretations, the state-by-state analyses of the WWI scores have other implications.

Certainly they counter the Coleman Report's claim that the quality of schooling has little effect on tests scores. They also counter other environmental interpretations, such as the one that attributes the black-white scoring gap to the "legacy of slavery." As the records left by the slaves (and in some cases by their masters) attest, devastating as it was, slavery did not stunt the slaves' cognitive processes. In most cases the black WWI draftees would have been the grandchildren, if not the children, of slaves. Northern blacks could not have outscored the southern whites had the legacy of slavery—the supposedly deleterious effects of racism and segregation on cognitive, or problem-solving, abilities—affected their aptitude for acquiring knowledge according to the opportunities available to them.

When the false claim that the legacy of slavery has arrested blacks' mental processes is rejected, it becomes possible to consider the actual psychological burdens this legacy places on African Americans. For example, black test takers are confronted with doing well on the very instruments used to "prove" their inferiority. These test takers, including the relatively small percentage with a quality education, are subject to what Claude Steele, a professor of social psychology, calls "stereotype vulnerability." This phenomenon, Steele has found, has an adverse effect on test scores. This is not, he stresses, because these students accept, consciously or unconsciously, the pervasive claim that they are inferior in intelligence, but that they must contend with it at the very moment they are under intense pressure to counter it. Steele also stresses that stereotype vulnerability is a "patient predator" that affects African Americans in every aspect of their academic life.[48]

Testing's crucial role in sustaining black stereotypes in white minds is in itself critical evidence that Jensen's 1969 article and *The Bell Curve* do not simply misuse worthwhile data, as has often been contended. The data flaunted by such as Jensen, Herrnstein, and Murray are provided by tests that "validate" the separation of children by "race." The statistical treatment of these data may at times be quite unexceptionable, but when unexceptional statistical methods are applied to the analysis of unsound data, based on assumptions that are equally unsound, one can only end up with conclusions that are thoroughly unsound. Such are the erroneous constructs of "race" and "IQ."

Notes

1. Richard J. Herrnstein and Charles Murray, *The Bell Curve: Intelligence and Class Structure in American Life* (New York: Free Press, 1994).

2. Quoted in Jason DeParle, "Daring Research or 'Social Science Pornography'?," *New York Times Magazine*, 9 October 1994, 50.

3. Ashley Montagu, ed., *The Concept of Race* (New York: Free Press, 1964).

4. Quoted in DeParle, "Daring Research or 'Social Science Pornography'?," 51.

5. Charles Lane, "The Tainted Sources of *The Bell Curve*," *New York Review of Books*, 1 December 1994, 14–19; 14.

6. William H. Tucker, *The Science and Politics of Racial Research* (Urbana: University of Illinois Press, 1994), 173. For more information on McGurk's opposition to school desegregation, see pp. 152–53, 168; for McGurk's connections to the International Association for the Advancement of Ethnology and Eugenics, see p. 249.

7. Herrstein and Murray, *The Bell Curve*, 13.

8. Arthur Jensen, "How Much Can We Boost IQ and Scholastic Achievement?," *Harvard Educational Review* 39 (Winter 1969): 1–123; 82.

9. Heritability is the proportion of the genetic to the total phenotypic variance. It is a group or population measure, and cannot be determined on an individual. For any particular trait in a specified population H (Heritability) is obtained by genetic variance divided by phenotypic variance, that is, in the present instance the observable trait yielded as the IQ score and called "intelligence," as $H = VG/VP$ or $VG + VE$ (VG = genetic variance; VP = phenotypic variance; VE = environmental variance). Genetic variance denotes the portion of the phenotypic variance which is caused by variation in the genetic constitution of the individuals in a population.

10. R. A. Fisher, "Limits to Intensive Production in Animals," *British Agriculture Bulletin* 4 (1951): 317–18.

11. David Layzer, "Science or Superstition? A Physical Scientist Looks at the IQ Controversy," in N. J. Block and Gerald Dworkin, *The IQ Controversy: Critical Readings* (New York: Pantheon, 1976): 194–241.

12. Vernon W. Stone, "The Interaction Component is Critical," *Harvard Educational Review* 39 (1969): 628–39, 629.

13. Herrnstein and Murray, *The Bell Curve*, 108, 312.

14. Jensen, "How Much Can We Boost IQ," 80.

15. Robert E. Kuttner, "Biochemical Anthropology," in *Race and Modern Science*, ed. Robert E. Kuttner (New York: Social Science Press, 1967), 197–222.

16. For more on Kuttner's views and activities, including his neo-Nazi connections, see Tucker, *Science and Politics of Racial Research*, 170–72, 173, 175, 178, 180, 182, 190, 257, 262, 263.

17. Theodosious Dobzhansky and Ashley Montagu, "Natural Selection and the Mental Capacities of Mankind," *Science* 105 (1947): 587–90.

18. George Gaylord Simpson, *Biology and Man* (New York: Harcourt, Brace, & World, 1969), 104.

19. Paul David and Laurence H. Snyder, "Genetic Variability and Human Behavior," in *Social Psychology at the Crossroads*, eds. John H. Rohrer and Muzafer Sherif (New York, Harper & Bros., 1951), 71.

20. Sherwood L. Washburn and C. S. Lancaster, "The Evolution of Hunting," in, *Man the Hunter*, eds. Richard B. Lee and Irven De Vore (Chicago: Aldine, 1968), 303.

21. Robert S. O. Harding and Geza Teleki, eds., *Omnivorous Primates* (New York: Columbia University Press, 1981); Tim Ingold et al., eds., *Hunters and Gatherers*, 2 vols. (Oxford: Berg, 1988).

22. Arthur R. Jensen, *Educability and Group Differences* (New York: Harper & Row, 1973), 24.

23. Richard B. Lee and Irven De Vore, eds., *Man the Hunter* (Chicago: Aldine Publishing Co., 1968); Elman R. Service, *The Hunters* (Englewood Cliffs, NJ: Prentice-Hall, 1966); Tim Ingold et al., eds., *Hunters and Gatherers*, 2 vols. (Oxford: Berg, 1988).

24. Jensen, *Educability and Group Differences*, 289–90.

25. Margaret Cohn, "The Truth About Asian Americans," in *The Bell Curve Debate: History, Documents, Opinions*, eds. Russell Jacoby and Naomi Glauberman (New York: Times Books, 1995), 239. The article first appeared as "About Asian Americans: False Flattery Gets Us Nowhere," *New York Newsday*, 28 October, 1994. For further analyses of the data related to the Asian-superiority myth, see Lane, "Tainted Sources," 17; and Barry Sautman, "Theories of East Asian Superiority," in *The Bell Curve Debate*, eds. Jacoby and Glauberman, 210–21.

26. Herrnstein and Murray, *The Bell Curve*, 642–43.

27. Ibid., 402–44.

28. R. C. Lewontin, Steve Rose, and Leon J. Kamin, *Not in Our Genes: Biology, Ideology, and Human Nature* (New York: Pantheon, 1984), 12, 13. This is a fundamental work that presents the whole matter of genes, environment, organism, and reality with clarity and authority. See also Peter L. Berger and Thomas Luckmann, *The Social Construction of Reality* (New York: Penguin, 1971).

29. James S. Coleman et al., *Equality of Educational Opportunity* (Washington, D.C.: U.S. Government Printing Office, 1966).

30. The reference is to Jonathan Kozol's *Death at an Early Age: The Destruction of the Hearts and Minds of Negro Children in the Boston Public Schools* (New York: Houghton Mifflin, 1967), a devastating critique of the flagrantly unequal education the school systems provide along racial and class lines.

31. Herrnstein and Murray, *The Bell Curve*, 642–43.

32. Ibid., 313.

33. Ibid.

34. Walter Lippmann, "The Mystery of the 'A' Men," in *The IQ Controversy: Critical Readings*, eds. N. J. Block and Gerald Dworkin, (New York: Pantheon, 1976), 9. The article, one of six on testing by Lippmann, was originally published in the *New Republic*, 1 November 1922. The other five articles, which also appeared in the New Republic, are: "The Mental Age of Americans," 25 October 1922; "Tests of Hereditary Intelligence," 22 November 1922; "The Future of the Tests," 29 November 1922. All the articles, together with the debate that followed between Lippmann and Lewis M. Terman, the hereditarian creator of the Stanford-Binet IQ test, as well as the replies by those criticized, are included in Block and Dworkin. It is a fundamental, and fair, presentation of the whole subject. See also John L. Rury, "Race, Region, and Education: An Analysis of the Black and White Scores on the 1917 Army Alpha Test," *Journal of Negro Education*, 57 [1] (1988): 51–65; Stephen J. Gould, *The Mismeasure of Man* (New York: Norton, 1981), 192–233

35. Edwin G. Boring, quoted in Richard J. Herrnstein, *I.Q. in the Meritocracy* (Boston: Atlantic Monthly Press/Little Brown, 1973), 107. Herrnstein provides a rather tortured justification for Boring's remark, which was first published in the *New Republic* in 1923.

36. See Ken Richardson, David Spears, and Martin Richards, eds., *Race, Culture, and Intelligence* (Baltimore: Penguin Books, 1972); Evelyn Sharp, *The IQ Cult* (New York: Coward, McCann & Geoghegan, 1972); Carl Senna, ed., *The Fallacy of the IQ* (New York: Third Press, 1973); John Garcia, "IQ: The Conspiracy," *Psychology Today* (September 1972), 40–43, 92–92; Peter Watson, ed., *Psychology and Race* (Chicago: Aldine, 1974); Robert L. Williams, "Scientific Racism and IQ: The Silent Mugging of the Black Community," *Psychology Today* (May 1974), 32–41, 101; Elaine and Harry Mensh, *The IQ Mythology: Class, Race, and Inequality* (Carbondale: Southern Illinois University Press, 1991).

37. Arthur R. Jensen, *Bias in Mental Testing* (New York: Free Press, 1980).

38. Frank C. J. McGurk, *Comparison of the Performance of Negro and White High School Seniors on Cultural and Noncultural Psychological Test Questions* (Washington, D.C.: Catholic University Press, 1951) (Microcard) 12 July 1996.

39. Jensen, *Bias in Mental Testing*, 524.

40. McGurk used a revised Sims Record Card for ranking the students according to socioeconomic status. They were matched by such criteria as parents' education, wage earner's occupation (the question assumes only one wage earner), personal bank account, amount of dental care, family's attendance at concerts, mother's membership in clubs, private music lessons, number of books and magazines in the home. To illustrate why black-white differences are hidden by such questions, take Occupation: even if a black and white wage earner were in the same general occupation, the white would in almost all cases have had a higher-paying position (McGurk further blurred economic distinctions by reducing Sims' five occupational categories to two). Moreover, even in those cases where black income would have matched white income, the blacks as a rule would have lived in different areas, with different schools and cultural institutions.

41. The subjects of the study are identified by "race," the judges (who included psychology and sociology professors, teachers, and graduate students) are not. Given that McGurk would have considered whites the "norm" group, it would not have occurred to him to identify the judges by race.

42. Frank C. J. McGurk, "On White and Negro Test Performance and Socioeconomic Factors," *Journal of Abnormal and Social Psychology* 48[3] (1952): 448–50; 450; Frank C. J. McGurk, "Socio-economic and Culturally-Weighted Test Scores of Negro Subjects," *Journal of Applied Psychology* 37[4] (1953): 276–77.

43. McGurk's test was a composite of items from three different IQ tests. Although the items would not have performed statistically in the same way as in their original contexts, they produced the results McGurk required because they retained their original biases.

44. Horace M. Bond, "What the Army 'Intelligence' Tests Measured," in Jacoby and Glauberman, eds., *The Bell Curve Debate*, 583–98. Originally published in the *Crisis*, July 1924.

45. Ibid., 597.

46. M. F. Ashley Montagu, "Intelligence of Northern Negroes and Southern Whites in the First World War," *American Journal of Psychology* 58 (April 1945): 161–88. See Appendix D, this volume.

47. Ibid., 186. Clearly, McGurk constructed his study so it could be alleged that it countered Montagu's conclusion: Montagu's study, McGurk asserted, was

not an experimental project but one based on the author's knowledge of differences in North-South socioeconomic conditions. Since an almost needless amount of data is available to support what is common knowledge about North-South socioeconomic conditions of that period only an individual determined to uphold biological-determinist claims at any cost (in this case by means that included spurious iindices for comparing black and white socioeconomic status) would try to cast doubt on the validity of the North-South comparison in Montagu's study. See Elaine Mensh and Harry Mensh, *The IQ Mythology* (Carbondale: Southern Illinois University, 1991).

48. Claude Steele, quoted in Ethan Waters, "Claude Steele Has Scores to Settle," *New York Times Magazine,* 17 September, 1995, 44–47; 6. For instance, together with Joshua Aronson of the University of Texas, he conducted an experiment on two groups of black and white Stanford undergraduates that involved the most difficult verbal skills questions from the Graduate Record Exam. One group was told that the project's purpose was simply to research "psychological factors involved in solving verbal problems"; the other was told that the exam was "a genuine test of your verbal abilities and limitations" (ibid., 45). The blacks who thought they were merely being asked to solve problems performed as well as the whites (whose performance was the same in both situations). But the test performance of blacks who were told that their intellectual potential was being measured was significantly worse than that of the other test takers.

In Steele's experiment, when stereotype vulnerability was eliminated the black students' academic preparation allowed them to perform equally with the white ones on a test of scholastic performance. In real-life situations, most blacks come to the tests with unequal academic preparation, so stereotype vulnerability would not be *the* factor lowering their scores but an *added* one.

Clearly, stereotype vulnerability is the product of a vast array of racist pressures and practices in and out of the schools, all of which are legitimated by IQ and IQ-type tests. To put it another way, white stereotyping, with which blacks must constantly contend, is justified by spurious tests that assign greater mental worth to whites than to blacks.

7

Race and Society

No activity of man, whether it be the making of a book, the contraction of a muscle, the manufacture of a brick, or the expression of an idea, can be understood fully without a knowledge of the history of that activity in so far as it has been socially determined. For, obviously, any neglect to take into consideration the relations of the social framework can only lead to an incomplete and defective understanding of such events. The social construction of reality is created for us from the moment we are born, and as we grow and acquire the knowledge, "the common-sense knowledge" of everyday life, our perceptions are formed by the particular socialization process within which we have learned, been conditioned, to behave.

It should be clear that humankind develops in and through an environment that is social as well as physical. There is, perhaps, no subject and no event of which this is more conspicuously true than of that tendentious and reverberative word race. I say "event," because in a very real sense it would be preferable to speak of race as an "event," a thing, "for this is the process of reification, that is, the apprehension of a human phenomenon as if it were a thing."[1] Apart from the cells of a dead lexicographer's brain or the taxonomist's judgment, race in reality hardly ever functions as a word, but almost always as an event, an emotion, an experience, an action. In our society—and it is within the universe of our society that I am speaking—race is not merely a word which one utters but it is also an event that one experiences. The word itself merely represents a series of sounds which usually serve as a stimulus to set in motion a host of feelings and thoughts which, together, form an emotional experience; this generally, for most people, is what race is.

It is of the greatest importance that this fact be clearly understood, and in this chapter an attempt will be made, among other things, to inquire into the development of those psychological factors which tend to make this event possible. That such psychological factors exist is indisputably clear, but these factors are not so well known as they deserve to be.

"Race," in our society, is not a term that clearly and dispassionately defines certain real conditions which can be demonstrated to exist, but, as I have already said, the word acts more as a stimulus that touches off a series of emotional charges that usually bear as much relation to the facts as bees do to bonnets. Feelings and thoughts concerning such a concept as race are real enough, and so, it may be pointed out, are feelings and thoughts concerning the existence of unicorns, pixies, goblins, satyrs, ghosts, Jews, blacks, Catholics, and foreigners in general. Endowing a feeling or a thought about something with a name and thereby imputing to that something a real existence is one of the oldest diversions of humankind. Humans impose on nature the limitations of their own minds and identify their views with reality itself. Pixies, ghosts, satyrs, Aryans, and the popular conception of race represent real enough notions, but they have their origin in traditional stories, myths, or imagination.

Language especially seduces us into believing that every noun is a thing, and that things are enduring and permanent. Error, imagination, emotion, and rationalization are among the chief components of these notions. Facts, it should always be remembered, do not speak for themselves, but invariably through an interpreter. The word "fact" (*facere*) originally meant a thing made; we still make our own "facts," but fail to realize how much of ourselves we put into them or how much others have put into them. This is especially unfortunate in a century in which, as Ignazio Silone pointed out, words have been so much perverted from their natural purpose of putting man in touch with man as they are today.[2] The lesson necessary for all of us to understand and learn is that *the meaning of a word is the action it produces.* No matter if words and beliefs are false, if men define them as real, they will be real in their consequences.

Nothing, indeed, can be so real as the unreal. It is not here my purpose to show that concepts denoted by such a term as "ghost" or race do not, in the sense in which they are commonly used and understood, correspond to anything scientifically demonstrable as having a real existence. Madame de Staël once remarked, "I do not believe in ghosts, but I am afraid of them." Rationally convinced of the non-existence of ghosts, Madame de Staël nonetheless reacted irrationally and emotionally to the notion of ghosts for all the world as if they had a real existence. Most of us are familiar with such reactions. It is evident that in her early childhood Madame de Staël had been emotionally conditioned to believe in the existence of ghosts to such an extent that as an adult, in spite of the fact that she knew that such beliefs were quite irrational, she was quite unable to throw off the effects of that conditioning. That is what occurs, in most cases, with regard to race. Even though they may know it is nothing but a "ghost," most persons continue to be haunted by it. As Mussolini put it in his pre-racist days, "Race! It is a feeling, not a reality."[3]

Indeed, where matters of race are concerned feelings are likely to be involved. The fault, however, lies not so much in the emotional involvement, but in the refusal to recognize that involvement for what it is, and to exercise some measure of rational control over it.

There can be little doubt of the fact that in many parts of the world children are emotionally conditioned early to a belief in the existence of race differences.[4] In many parts of Europe, for example, where the larger number of troubles of state and person have traditionally been attributed to the Jews, such attributions can hardly have failed to escape the attention of most children. Indeed, they usually become aware quite early in their lives that hostility toward Jews is a socially sanctioned, even required, form of behavior. Such children would grow up to accept the existence of imputed race differences as real and would act upon such beliefs as if it were perfectly natural to do so. But just as Madame de Staël became rationally convinced that ghosts do not exist in spite of the acknowledged strength of the emotion attached to the idea, so, too, it is quite possible to produce a rational appreciation of the nature of their error among those who have been emotionally conditioned to accept the mythology of race as real. Indeed, nearly all of us have been to some extent so emotionally conditioned, yet many of us have been more or less able to emancipate ourselves from the effects of such conditioning by becoming acquainted with the facts relating to these matters. But with many others it cannot be as simple as that, for the roots of their prejudices go much deeper—as we shall soon see. But for those whose prejudices are more superficial an adequate discussion of the facts should suffice. Hence, one of the first requirements necessary for the production in the individual of an intelligent understanding of race problems must be the existence of a readily available body of adequately correlated scientific facts relating to every aspect of the race problem for use in the education or re-education of the individual. Moreover, these facts must be used, and they must be made available in a form for use. In this field science and knowledge are valueless unless they can be applied in a practical way to increase human happiness.

The dispassionate scientific collection and analysis of facts are activities of the first importance, but the end of such activities should not rest with their publication in learned journals. The ultimate purpose of these scientific activities must be recognized as having been defeated unless the most pertinent results are disseminated in such a manner as to increase the understanding of these matters in every human being, until correct understanding is translated into sound conduct.[5]

All who at present appear to be hopelessly confused upon the subject of race are not beyond redemption. Methods can be developed by means of which many persons who now superficially harbor myths and delusions concerning race may be reached and re-educated. Through the press, periodicals, popular lectures, books, film, radio, TV, school, the church, and many similar agencies, innumerable misguided persons can be reawakened to their true relation to their fellow humans. With respect to those who are more pervasively infected with the virus of racism, I am not so sure. But more important than these is the growing generation. Through the lower and upper grade schools the most significant work can be done in clarifying the minds of children concerning the facts relating to the fascinating variability of humankind and in educating them to think critically for themselves in the light of the evidence.[6] Let us teach geography, but instead of presenting the subject in a dry-as-dust manner, let us humanize its teaching and furnish its field with the living peoples who inhabit the earth.[7] Let us teach our children what we know about the peoples of the earth, and about their respective values for one another and for civilization as a whole. Let us emphasize their likenesses and create interest in the meaning of the differences, differences which enrich the common heritage of humanity and make the world the richly variegated experience it can be. Let us teach appreciation of the other person's point of view, the more so since, if it is unlike our own, it will require more sympathetic appreciation if it is to be understood.

Relations between other human beings and ourselves form the most important of all the experiences and situations of our lives. Nevertheless, in our society human beings are permitted to enter into such relations without being equipped with the most elementary understanding of what they mean.[8] No attempt is made to supply them with the facts relating to race as demonstrated by science. On the contrary, for the most part they are supplied with the kind of information that makes fertile ground for the development of race prejudices.[9]

Prejudices early acquired are notoriously difficult to eradicate. The child picks up attitudes long before he becomes familiar with the facts. What should be done is to see to it that, instead of such prejudices, the growing personalities in our schools are taught the facts which the anthropological and social sciences have made available. Our children should be taught that the physical features of people, however different, are all of equal value, and that readily understood they are of great interest and that the whole area of difference is an inexhaustibly exciting terrain to explore. Children are fascinated by the explanation of the nature and development of such differences. One of the great basic needs which the child strives to have satisfied is its curiosity, and nothing can be more gratifying than to have that need satisfied, and nothing can be more gratifying to the caregiver than to observe the resulting humanizing effect upon the child. To explain to a child that even the expression of the face, which is by many taken to be biologically determined, is not necessarily so, that facial expression, as well as bodily behavior, gestures, like the clothes one wears, are often strongly influenced by class or caste membership.[10] Children should be taught that there are never any grounds in the appearance of people for discrimination against them. For it should be obvious that, though some of us may not be particularly attracted to people who exhibit a certain type of physiognomy, the cause of our dislike lies not in their physiognomy but in the values, the culturally conditioned ideas, in our own minds which have taught us to react in this way to the perception of such physiognomies. The causes of such dislikes must be looked for in the cultural background of one's conditioning, not in the shape of the nose or the color of the skin of our neighbors. Physical differences are merely the pegs upon which culturally generated hostilities are made to hang, ending with the smug and empty conviction that a superior race is one that you look like and an inferior race is one that you don't look like. Here, then, is a most important field in which a great and valuable pioneer work remains to be done. Academic discussions alone will not carry us far. We must be willing to roll up our sleeves and set to work on this immense and pressingly important problem in human relations, until it is solved.[11]

Community projects for teaching sympathetic understanding of other peoples and ethnic groups have demonstrated to what an extent race prejudice can be handled. Treated like any other disease, race prejudice can be prevented where it has not yet become endemic and eliminated where it has. Each community should make itself responsible for ridding itself of a disease which makes for so much social wastage and distress. Each community should see to it that it thinks and acts, in its own cooperative interests, in the light of the soundest modern knowledge and the best human practice. Where there is a desire for just action it will be achieved, and where there is more than a hope of clarity, confusion will yield. Our communities often have departments of sanitation, departments of roadways, why not a department of human relations?

One of the first points to be grasped before much progress in this subject can be made is that, so far as human beings and as far as society and social development are concerned, race is not a biological problem at all; furthermore, that it does not even present any socially relevant biological problems. "Race" is a term for a problem created by special types of social conditions and by such types of social conditions alone. In terms of social relations so-called race problems are, in the modern world, essentially of the nature of caste problems.

Race and Caste

"Race," wrote Wyndham Lewis in his book *The Art of Being Ruled,* "is the queen of the 'classes.'"[12] We must recognize the fact that in our own society the "race problem" is essentially a problem of social relations and that it is, therefore, fundamentally a social problem, always in a political context. In the social context of America, to take an example with which we are all familiar, what is usually referred to as a race or racial group in reality often constitutes a caste. Thus, African Americans, Jews, Japanese Americans, and Native Americans are to varying degrees, and in different regions, treated very much, by the dominant white groups, as if they were members of specific castes, "untouchables."

A caste may be defined briefly as a specific, socially limited status group, or more fully as an hereditary and endogamous group, occupying a position of superior or inferior rank or social esteem in comparison with other such groups. The functions of the limiting factors of caste are, in effect, primarily to create barriers against sexual relations between members of the "superior" caste and those of the "inferior" castes and, secondarily, to regulate the social status, privileges, and social mobility of the members of the "inferior" castes. A class differs from a caste in that a greater degree of social mobility is, in all respects, permitted between the members of the upper and the lower social classes than is permitted between castes.

"The presence of caste is revealed by two crucial attitudes: (1) a sentiment against intermarriage; and (2) the practice of judging individuals on the basis of their group membership rather than their individual merits."[13] When we speak of the race problem in America, what we really mean is the caste system and the problems which that caste system creates in America.[14] To recognize this fact is to recognize and to effect a clarification and a change in conceptual approach to a problem upon which, perhaps more than any other in our time, clear thinking and accurate concepts are an urgent necessity.

Humphrey has suggested that "the term race should be discarded entirely in the cultural reference, and the more appropriate term caste employed in its stead."[15] This is a worthy suggestion. There can be no cultural races; there can only be cultural castes. But when Humphrey adds that "the term race should be retained in its biologic context as a taxonomic category for the delineation of types of mankind," we must, as the lawyers say, put in a demurrer, for the term "race," as we have seen, is embarrassed, and it is a question whether as a taxonomic category referring to humans it is not unrescuably compromised. Even geneticists today tend to avoid its use.

As Kalmus pointed out, "A very important term which was originally used in systematics is 'race.' Nowadays, however, its use is avoided as far as possible in genetics . . . The term used by modern geneticists to take the place of race is strain, which has a more precise meaning; it is applied to forms which differ from the commonly wild type by one or several precisely defined hereditary characters which usually breed true."[16] In a widely consulted dictionary of biology the term "race" was altogether omitted,[17] while in his 1951 authoritative work on evolution the author Carter made it quite clear that such terms as "'race,' 'variety,' and 'form' are used so loosely and in so many senses that it is advisable to avoid using them as infraspecific categories."[18]

Let us consider a little further what the meaning of this term "race," in the social sense, really is. In countries such as England, France, Germany, and Spain, in which class distinctions are well marked and there exist no significantly large ethnic groups other than the dominant national population, race prejudice is replaced by class prejudice. In fact, there is scarcely any difference between the two phenomena. Almost every condition encountered in the one is to be found in the other, even down to the imputed biological differences. In his beautiful novel, *Bread and Wine,* Ignazio Silone, writing of his native Abruzzi in Italy, describes the social identification of "class" with "race." He writes:

> Don Paolo was surprised to observe the role that mustaches, beards, and hair still played in differentiating the professional class from the peasants and the landlords. He realized also why the various classes were indicated in dialect by the word 'race'—the 'race' of husbandmen, the 'race' of 'artists' (artisans), the 'race' of landowners. The son of a petty landowner who studies, and therefore inevitably becomes a state or municipal employee, promptly tries to obliterate the fact that he comes of the 'race' of husbandmen by brushing his hair in the style of his new station.[19]

A similar phenomenon is encountered in Brazil, where straight, shiny hair and thin, pointed nose are often more important than skin color, and where there is also a saying, "The black man who is rich is white—the white man who is poor is black."[20]

In Brazil blacks make up at least half the nation, and it is the blacks who are the underclass. There is a myth which has long enjoyed support among some North Americans that Brazil enjoys a racial harmony which is unique in the Americas. This is not true. Brazil is not a racially harmonious society. Brazil discriminates against and subordinates its blacks and ensures that they will be kept in "their place" and live the fate of their class.[21]

Perhaps the best book, and the most readable, that has been written on Brazil's racial problems is Roger Bastide's *The African Religions of Brazil: Toward a Sociology of the Interpenetration of Civilizations* (1978). Here in his own words, is what Bastide says of race relations in Brazil:

> In a racial democracy the black is split. Split between rebellion against the white, who tends to reject him, and rebellion against himself, which intensifies his feeling of inferiority. Split between African militancy, and the desire to be assimilated, through miscegenation, into the great white mass. In the United States, the mulattos belong with the Negroes. In Brazil the mulatto escapes from the colored caste and turns against the blacks. It is he, not the white, who holds the deepest prejudices against his darkest brothers.[22]

The "annihilating prejudice" as Bastide calls it, is in many ways more complex than it is in the United States.

Almost everywhere the upper classes make much of "breeding," of "good family" or "birth" or "quality" or "ancestry," and will not, generally, marry out of their "class" or "quality."[23] To marry out of one's class is to lose "caste," or status not only socially but also, it is considered, biologically, for such a person's children can belong only to the class and caste of the "inferior" parent. There are, of course, many exceptions, but this is the general rule. This rule tends to be more strictly applied to women than to men. The upper-class male generally elevates the woman he chooses to marry to his own class; the lower-class male generally reduces his wife and children to his own class. In the Western world the biology and stratification of the classes are patrilineally determined; that is to say, they operate through, and in favor of, the male line. This is not the case where ethnic crossing is concerned, and it constitutes one of the few differences between the working of class and race prejudice. Thus, for example, should an upper-class white male marry a black female, the offspring will, in the United States at least, be relegated to the mother's caste, and not to that of the father.

The mechanism of this "caste" form of race prejudice is clearly seen at work in England. During the last several decades there has been an appreciable increase in the colored population in England, principally owing to the immigration of West and Asiatic Indians, and a concomitant appearance of race prejudice where formerly it was nonexistent. But as Banton[24] and others[25] have pointed out, the English form of race discrimination, is not really race prejudice, but an expression of the desire to avoid losing caste in one's own group by behaving as an equal to those who are for one reason or another regarded as of lower social status. Since "class" is largely determined by the people with whom one associates, and since a dark skin color, in England, is largely identified with formerly subject peoples, association with persons of color detracts from one's social standing. Banton in his study found that by far the majority of Britons felt sympathetically toward colored people, but the problem of caste bothered them. In a study of colonial students in London, Carey found that London landladies preferred white to colored lodgers mainly because of their fears about what other people might think. One boardinghouse landlady remarked: "Of course, I don't take blacks; I'm sorry for the darkies, that I am, but I know what the neighbors would say: 'Look at Mrs. So-and-So! She really has come down in the world.'"[26]

This kind of discrimination must be distinguished from race prejudice. It is not based on emotional or irrational prejudgments or on hostility, but represents a response to social situations, defined by considerations of social status. There can be little doubt that elsewhere in the world such factors enter into much that is called race prejudice. In the United States,

Westie has shown that the occupational status is a significant determinant of the response that whites make to a particular African American.[27] And as Liston Pope has put it, "The mill worker, with nobody else to 'look down on,' regards himself as eminently superior to the Negro. The colored man represents his last outpost against social oblivion."[28] A study, by Dr. William T. Liu, mainly of Catholics who had emigrated to Tallahassee, Florida, from other regions, principally the North, revealed that moral values, though important, did not decisively determine these persons' attitudes toward segregation. Residential stability and subjective identification with the Southern community seem to have been the critical factors.[29]

Blumer has drawn attention to the fact that the collective process through which a group position is formed, vis-à-vis other groups, is a potent factor in the genesis of race prejudice. "Race prejudice becomes entrenched and tenacious to the extent the prevailing social order is rooted in the sense of social position."[30] The process of group definition produces an abstract image of the subordinate groups, which spreads out far beyond the boundaries of contacts with individual members of such groups, and transcending any experience with them. The reaction or response to all members of such subordinate groups is not in terms of experience of them, but in terms of the abstract image of the group that has been built up of them, and into which they are made to fit.[31]

Among the strongest supporters of the view that the upper classes are not only socially but biologically superior to the lower classes are those who have themselves recently migrated from the lower into the ranks of the upper classes. Success in life is held to be not so much a matter of social opportunity as of biological quality. Such views are, of course, rationalizations, but once made they help to determine the attitudes not only of the upper but also of the lower classes. Indeed, as Polanyi has pointed out, the poorer classes of England a century ago were the detribalized, degraded natives of their time.[32] And, as Johnson has stated, the arguments used to justify the practice of child serfdom in England were identical with those used to justify the slave trade.[33]

It should be fairly evident that in societies in which there is an extreme division of the population into classes whose interests are necessarily opposed and in which the means of earning a living, the economic system, is organized upon an unequal or extremely competitive basis, there will be abundant opportunities for class or race antagonisms. This is a matter with which we shall deal in the next chapter.

The point I wish to bring out here is that race prejudice is merely a special case of class prejudice, a prejudice that will be developed, under certain conditions, where different ethnic groups are thrown together in significant numbers.[34] In the absence of such conditions—or in the absence of a variety of ethnic groups the prejudices of the upper classes against all members of the lower classes and their conduct toward the members of such classes will, in almost every respect, take the form usually associated with race prejudice. Wherever classes exist there exists class prejudice. In socially stratified class societies the shift from class prejudice to race prejudice is easily achieved and, in fact, amounts to little more than a change of names, for the race against which prejudice is now especially directed is but another class or caste, even though it may be regarded as something substantially different.

Race and class prejudices are simply particular kinds of the group phenomenon of which national prejudices, religious prejudices, sex prejudices, and the like are similar kinds. As MacCrone points out,

> We must not think of race prejudices as if they were a unique kind of group or social attitude; instead we must think of them in their proper context as simply one of a class of group or cultural phenomena, all of which are dependent upon the same kind of conditions, display the same basic characteristics, and serve the same functions.[35]

In the case of the American black it is necessary to understand that the original difference in his status was one of caste, not of biology. It was only later that the allegedly biological differences were attached to the difference in caste. An African or American black would be enslaved by virtue of the fact that he or she was considered to belong to the infidel slave class, not biologically but socially. American Indians were not usually enslaved, because they had established themselves as a class that did not adapt itself to slavery. White men, however, could be bought and sold if they belonged to the class born to servitude, the lowest class. The status of the black could be recognized at once by the color of his skin, which was a great convenience, but nothing more than that. It was only afterward that the obvious physical differences were utilized to reinforce the strength of the arguments in favor of the necessity of continuing the depressed social status of the black.

Thus, in the case of peoples showing any physical differences distinguishing them from the dominant class or caste, the mechanism of exclusion works both ways: one may oppose such peoples on the ground of their social inferiority and one may oppose them on the basis of their biological inferiority, the physical differences being taken to signify the latter. One may then proceed to adopt the view that such peoples are socially inferior because they are physically or biologically inferior, and since the physical or biological difference was believed to be constant, the social difference would always remain so. In this way one could not only have one's cake but one could also cut it into thin slices and eat it too. Imperialism, itself a racist idea, extended this conception of human relations to all peoples.[36]

Looking back now at the history of the nineteenth century, it seems fairly clear that the drive to find differences in the races of humankind grew out of, among other things, the general social climate of the day. A natural stratification of the races mirrored the social stratification of the classes, and in the light of the baleful doctrine of "the survival of the fittest" sanctioned and justified the exploitation and oppression of both.

Most authorities at the present time entertain no doubts as to the meaninglessness of the older anthropological conception of race. They do not consider that any of the existing concepts of race correspond to any reality whatever; the general opinion is that these concepts are usually nothing but poor substitutes for thought. But they do consider that the persistence of the term and the concept has been responsible for much confused thinking and, what is worse, has rendered possible much confused and confusing action resulting in the most tragic consequences for millions of human beings. Race has, indeed, become a fratricidal word

> . . . And what if all-avenging Providence,
> Strong and retributive, should make us know
> The meaning of our words, force us to feel
> The desolation and the agony
> Of our fierce doings?
> —*S. T. Coleridge.*[37]

It is for these reasons, because the term, as it were, has been compromised, that a number of us, as biological and social anthropologists, have strongly urged that the term race be altogether dropped from the vocabulary. If we do no more than indicate our demotion of the term, this in itself will serve as a contribution to clear thinking, precisely as the banishment of the term "instinct" from psychological thought fifty years ago has had a most beneficial effect upon the development of the science of psychology. Not that there has been a loss of contact with what science means by "race," for many scientists are themselves far from clear as to what they mean when they use the term. In addition to that, some scientists who have concerned themselves with the problem have contributed to its confusion. "Verbal habits," remarked Ogden and Richards long ago, "overpower the sense of actuality even in the best of philosophers." And as Korzybski has stated,

> Because of the great semantic influence of the structure of language on the masses of mankind, leading, as it does, through lack of better understanding and evaluation to speculation on terms, it seems advisable to abandon completely terms which imply to the many the suggested elementalism, although these terms are used in a proper non-elementalistic way by the few.[38]

Huxley first suggested that "it would be highly desirable if we could banish the question-begging term 'race' from all discussions of human affairs and substitute the noncommittal phrase 'ethnic group.' That would be a first step toward rational consideration of the problem at issue."[39]

Since Huxley does not venture a definition of an "ethnic group," I shall offer one here: An ethnic group represents one of a number of populations, which grade into one another and together comprise the species *Homo sapiens,* but individually maintain their differences, physical and cultural, by means of isolating mechanisms such as geographic and social barriers. Such gradient differences will vary as the power of the geographic and social barriers vary. Where these barriers are of low power, or loose-jointed, as it were, neighboring ethnic groups will intergrade or hybridize with one another. Where these barriers are of high power, such ethnic groups will tend to remain more or less different from each other or replace each other geographically or ecologically.

From this definition or description of an ethnic group it will be seen that the problem of ethnic variation is in part a geographic problem involving the physical mobility of populations and the consequences resulting therefrom. Thus, the problem of ethnic variation falls definitely within the purview of the student of the social life of humankind.

The term ethnic is derived from the Greek *ethnos,* meaning a number of people living together, a company, a body of people. In the *Iliad,* Homer variously uses the word to mean a band of comrades a tribe, a group. Pindar uses it in the sense of a family a nation, a people.

One of the most important advantages of the term "ethnic group"[40] is that it eliminates all question-begging emphases on physical factors or differences and leaves that question completely open, while the emphasis is now shifted to the fact—though it is not restricted to it—that man is predominantly a cultural creature. The change in emphasis seems to me highly desirable. It does not exclude the consideration of the possible significance of physical traits, but it leaves the question of the latter open for further dispassionate analysis, omitting any suggestion that the physical traits are determined, fixed, or definable, or that they are in any way connected with mental or cultural traits. This is not to replace one term by another, but constitutes a significant shift in emphasis based on a fundamental difference in point of view. It is the point of view of the person who is desirous of taking a mature, responsible view of the words he uses and who is anxious to avoid the consequences of thinking in "fuzzy" terms.

If, then, we can eliminate the outmoded concept of race by presenting the advantages of the concept of "ethnic group," we shall have secured a real clarification and change in conceptual approach to a problem whose urgency requires no emphasis here. The sociologist will then be able to proceed with the study of the problem of caste, intra- and intersocially, with the clear consciousness of the fact that, as far as he is concerned, the problem is entirely a social problem and that for him, at any rate, it has no biological relevance whatever, but that, in so far as it is necessary for him to take cognizance of the biological evidence, the old concept of race has no more scientific justification for use in the field of human biology than it has in the field of human sociology.

Were we to pay attention to the realities of the situation in the cultural reference, the term race would be entirely discarded and the term "caste" would be employed in its stead; while the term race would, in popular parlance, be replaced by the term "ethnic group" in the biologic or social context with reference to humankind.

Notes

1. For an interesting discussion of the meaning of the word along these lines see S. I. Hayakawa, "Race and Words," *Common Sense* 12 (1934): 231–35; Reuven Bar-Levan, *Thinking in the Shadow of Feelings,* (New York: Simon & Schuster, 1988); Peter L. Berger and Thomas Luckmann, *The Social Construction of Reality* (New York: Penguin, 1971); J. Dan Rothwell, *Telling It Like It Isn't* (Englewood Cliffs, NJ: Prentice-Hall, 1982).

2. Ignazio Silone, *Bread and Wine* (New York: Penguin Books, 1946), 158.

3. In the spring of 1932, during his conversations with Emil Ludwig, Mussolini declared: "Of course there are no pure races left; not even the Jews have kept their blood unmingled. Successful crossings have often promoted the energy and beauty of a nation. Race! It is a feeling, not a reality; ninety-five percent, at least, is a feeling. Nothing will ever make me believe that biologically pure races can be shown to exist today . . . No such doctrine will ever find wide acceptance here in Italy . . . National pride has no need of the delirium of race." Emil Ludwig, *Talks with Mussolini* (Boston: Little, Brown, 1933), 69–70. In 1939, under the influence of his Axis partner, Hitler, he completely reversed himself and introduced racist measures of great severity. See Martin Agronsky, "Racism in Italy," *Foreign Affairs* 17 (1939): 391–401.

4. On this subject see Bruno Lasker, *Race Attitudes in Children* (New York: Holt, 1929); Mary E. Goodman, *Race Awareness in Your Children* (Cambridge, MA: Addison Wesley Press, 1952); H. G. Trager and M. R. Yarrow, *They Learn What They Live* (New York: Harper); Kenneth Clark, *Prejudice and Your Child* (Boston: Beacon Press, 1955); McDonald, *Not By the Color of Their Skin* (New York: International Universities Press, 1970); Judith D. R. Porter, *Black Child, White Child* (Cambridge: Harvard University Press, 1971); Florence Halpern, *Survival: Black/White* (New York: Pergamon Press, 1973); Jean D. Grambs, *Group Processes in Intergroup Education* (New York: National Council of Christians and Jews, 1953); David L. Kirp, *Just Schools: The Idea of Racial Equality in American Education* (Berkeley: University of California Press, 1982); David Milner, *Children and Race* (Harmondsworth: Penguin, 1975); David Milner, *Children and Race, Ten Years On* (London: Ward Lock Educational, 1983).

5. This is a task which has been undertaken by UNESCO. See Ashley Montagu, *Statement on Race* (New York: Oxford University Press, 1972), 361–71.

6. Excellent volumes along these lines published for the Bureau for Intercultural Education by Harper & Brothers, New York, are the following: William E. Vickery and Stewart G. Cole, *Intercultural Education in American Schools* (New York: Harper, 1943); Hortense Powdermaker, *Probing Our Prejudices* (New York: Harper, 1944); Spencer Brown, *They See for Themselves* (New York: Harper, 1944); Theodore Brameld, *Minority Problems in the Public Schools* (New York: Harper: 1946); Ina C. Brown, *Race Relations in a Democracy* (New York: Harper, 1949); William Van Til, et al., *Democracy Demands It* (New York: Harper, 1947); H. G. Trager and M. R. Yarrow, *They Learn What They Live* (New York: Harper, 1952). See also Goodwin Watson, *Action for Unity* (New York: Harper, 1947); Curriculum Office, Philadelphia Public Schools, *Open-Mindedness Can Be Taught* (Philadelphia, 1946); Kenneth Clark, *Prejudice and Your Child* (Boston: Beacon Press, 1955); Lillian Smith, *Now Is the Time* (New York: Dell, 1955); John P. Dean and Alex Rosen, *A Manual of Intergroup Relations* (Chicago: University of Chicago Press, 1955); James Martin and Frank R. Westie, "The Tolerant Personality," *American Sociological Review* 24 (1959): 521–28; Muzafer Sherif and Carolyn W. Sherif, *Groups in Harmony and Tension* (New York: Harper, 1953).

7. See, for example, the admirable book by Richard J. Russell and Fred B. Kniffen, *Culture Worlds* (New York: McMillan, 1951); Margaret Mead, *Peoples and Places* (Cleveland and New York: World Publishing Co., 1959); Ashley Montagu, *Man: His First Two Million Years* (New York: Columbia University Press,1969); Ashley Montagu, *The Science of Man* (New York: Odyssey Press, 1964); Ashley Montagu, *The Human Revolution* (New York: Bantam Books, 1965).

8. See Ashley Montagu, *On Being Human* (New York: Hawthorn Books, 1969); Ashley Montagu, *The Direction of Human Development* (New York: Hawthorn Books, 1970); Ashley Montagu, *Education and Human Relations* (New York: Grove Press, 1958); Ashley Montagu, *Growing Young* (Westport, CT: Bergin and Garvey, 1989).

9. See Emily V. Baker, "Do We Teach Racial Intolerance?" *Historical Outlook* 24 (1933): 86–89; Marian Radke and Helen Trager, "Children's Perceptions of the Social Roles of Negroes and Whites," *Journal of Psychology* 29 (1950): 1–33.

10. Weston La Barre, "The Cultural Basis of Emotions and Gestures," *Journal of Personality,* 16 (1947), 49–68; Leo Silbermann and Betty Spice, *Colour and Class in Six Liverpool Schools* (Liverpool: University of Liverpool Press, 1951).

11. See note 6, this chapter; also Helen P. Mudgett, *Democracy for All* (Minneapolis: General Extension Division, University of Minnesota, 1945). See also *Teaching Biologist* 9 (1939): 17–47.

12. Wyndam Lewis, *The Art of Being Ruled* (New York: Harper Bros., 1926), 234.

13. John H. Cooley, Robert R. Angell, and Julliard Carr, *Introductory Sociology* (New York: Schribner's Sons), 287. See Pitirim Sorokin, "What Is a Social Class?" *Journal of Legal and Political Sociology* 4 (1946): 15–28; Arthur Richmond, "Memories of South Africa," *The Listener* 60 (1958), 736—39.

14. The same is true for most other areas of the world. See: J. H. Hutton, *Caste in India* (New York: Cambridge Unversity Press, 1946); Ernest Beaglehole, "Race, Caste and Class," *Journal of the Polynesian Society,* 52 (1943): 1–11; Norman

Humphrey, "American Race and Caste," *Psychiatry* 4 (1941): 159–60; Ashley Montagu, "Race, Caste and Scientific Method," *Psychiatry* 4 (1941): 337–38; John Dollard, *Caste and Class in a Southern Town* (New Haven: Yale University Press, 1937); W. Lloyd Warner and Allison Davis, "A Comparative Study of American Caste," in E. T. Thompson, ed., *Race Relations and the Race Problem,* (Durham: Duke University Press, 1939): 219–45; Allison Davis, Burleigh Gardner, and Mary R. Gardner, *Deep South: A Social Anthropological Study of Caste and Class* (Chicago: University of Chicago Press, 1941); Liston Pope, *The Kingdom Beyond Caste* (New York: Friendship Press, 1967); Anthony de Rueck and Julie Knight, eds., *Caste and Race: Comparative Approaches* (New York: Little, Brown, 1967).

15. Humphrey, "American Race and Caste."

16. H. Kalmus, *Genetics* (London: Pelican Books, 1948) 45–46.

17. M. Abercombie, C. J. Hickman, and M. L. Johnson, *A Dictionary of Biology* (London and New York: Penguin Books, 1951).

18. G. S. Carter, *Animal Evolution: A Study of Recent Views of its Causes* (London: Sidgwick and Jackson; New York: Macmillan, 1951), 163. See also W. T. Calman, *The Classification of Animals* (New York: Wiley, 1949), 14; Cedric Dover, "The Classification of Man," *Current Science* 21 (1952): 209–13; Lionel Penrose, "Review of Dunn and Dobzhansky's Heredity, Race and Society," *Annals of Eugenics,* 17(1952): 252–53; J. P. Garlick, "Review," *Annals of Eugenics,* 25(1961): 169–70; P. A. Parsons, "Genetic Determination of Behavior (Mice and Men)," in *Genetics, Environment, and Behavior,* eds. Lee Ehrmann, Gilbert Omenn, and Ernst Caspari (New York: Academic Press, 1972), 4; L. L. Cavelli-Sforza, Paolo Menozzi and Albert Piazza, *The History and Geography of Human Genes* (Princeton: Princeton Unviversity Press, 1994); Jonathan Marks, *Human Biodiversity* (New York: Aldine, 1995).

19. Silone, *Bread and Wine,* 151.

20. Donald Pierson, *Negroes In Brazil,* (Chicago: University of Chicago Press, 1942); Charles Wagley, ed., *Race and Class in Rural Brazil.* (Paris: UNESCO, 1952).

21. Jeff H Lesser, "Brazil Pretends to Have no Race Problem," *The New York Times,* 10 Oct 1991, A26: Douglass G. Glasgow, "Brazil's Black Underclass: Almost Half a Nation," *The New York Times,* 30 November 1984, A30.

22. Roger Bastide, *The African Religions of Brazil: Toward a Sociology of the Interpenetration of Civilizations* (Baltimore: Johns Hopkins University Press, 1978), 307.

23. For some pithy remarks on this subject see Hogben, "Race and Prejudice," in his *Dangerous Thoughts* (New York: Norton, 1940), 45–58. "There is of course a parochial distinction between Rassenhygiene and its sister cult in Britain. In Germany the Jew is the scapegoat. In Britain the entire working class is the menace" (p. 51). To the same effect see R. H. Tawney, *Equality* (New York: Harcourt Brace, 1952).

24. Michael Banton, "Beware of Strangers!" *The Listener,* 3 April 1958, 565–67.

25. Kenneth Little, *Negroes in Britain* (London: Kegan Paul, 1948); Arthur Richmond, *The Colour Problem* (New York: Penguin Books, 1955); Michael Banton, *White and Coloured* (London: Cape, 1959); Maurice Freedman, ed., *A Minority in Britain* (Lonton: Valentine, Mitchell, 1955); Sydney Collins, *Coloured Minorities in Britain* (London: Lutterworth Press, 1957); Sydney Collins, "The Status of Coloured People in Britain," *Phylon* 18(1957): 82–87; Michael Banton, *Race Relations* (New York: Basic Books, 1967); John Rex, *Race, Colonialism and the City*

(London and Boston: Routledge & Kegan Paul, 1973). R. Moore, *Racism and Black Resistance in Britain* (London: Pluto Press, 1975); A. Dummet, *A Portrait of English Racism* (London: Penguin, 1973).

26. Alexander Timothy Carey, *Colonial Students* (London: Secker & Warburg, 1956). See especially Sheila Patterson, *Dark Strangers* (London: Tavistock, 1963).

27. Frank Westie, "Negro-White Status Differentials and Social Distance," *American Sociological Review* 17(1952): 550–58.

28. Liston Pope, *Millhands and Preachers* (New Haven: Yale University Press, 1942), 69.

29. William T. Liu, "The Community Reference System, Religiosity, and Race Attitudes," *Social Forces* 39 (1961): 324–28.

30. Herbert Blumer, "Race Prejudice as a Sense of Group Position," in *Race Relations*, eds. Jitsuichi Masuoka and Preston Valien, 217–27.

31. Angus Campbell, *White Attitudes Towards Black People* (Ann Arbor: Institute for Social Research, 1971); Bert T. King and Elliott McGinnies, eds., *Attitudes, Conflict and Social Change* (New York: Academic Press, 1972); George Frederickson, *The Black Image in the White Mind* (New York: Harper & Row, 1971); Morris Dees, with Steve Fiffer, *A Season for Justice: The Life and Times of Civil Rights Lawyer Morris Dees* (New York: Scribner's Sons, 1991).

32. Karl Polanyi, *The Great Transformation* (New York: Rinehart, 1944), 290.

33. Charles S. Johnson, "Race Relations and Social Change," in Thompson, ed., *Race Relations and the Race Problem*, 274.

34. For an account of the absence of race problems among ethnic groups of the same population see John Gillin, "'Race' Relations without Conflict: A Guatemalan Town," *American Journal of Sociology* 53 (1948): 337–43; Robert Redfield, "Culture Contact without Conflict," *American Anthropologist* 41(1939): 514–17; Robert Redfield, "Race and Class in Yucatan," in *Cooperation in Research* (Washington, D.C.: Carnegie Institution of Washington, 1938), 511–32.

35. I. D. MacCrone, *Group Conflicts and Race Prejudice* (London: Oxford University Press, 1937), 7.

36. B. Ashcroft, G. Griffiths, and H. Tiffin, eds., *The Post-Colonial Studies Reader* (London and New York: Routledge, 1995); E. Barker *National Character*, 4th ed. (London: Meuthen, 1948); Philip D. Curtin, "The Origins of the 'White Man's Burden,'" *The Listener* 66 (1961): 412–15; L. Greenfield, *Nationalism* (Cambridge: Harvard University Press, 1992); B. Gussman, *Out in the Mid-day Sun* (New York: Oxford University Press, 1963); J. A. Hobson, *Imperialism: A Study*, 2nd ed.(London: Allen & Unwin, 1965); R. A. Huttenback, *Racism and Empire* (Ithaca: Cornell University Press, 1976); M. Ignatieff, *Blood and Belonging: Journeys into the New Nationalism* (New York: Viking, 1993); O. Mannoni, *Prospero and Caliban: The Psychology of Colonization* (New York: Praeger, 1956); J. Rex, *Race, Colonialism, and the City* (London & Boston: Routledge & Kegan Paul, 1971); L. L. Snyder, *Encyclopedia of Nationalism* (New York: Paragon House, 1990); Louis L. Snyder, *The Imperialism Reader* (Princeton: Von Nostrand, 1964); T. Todorov, *On Human Diversity: Nationalism, Racism, and Exoticism in French Thought* (Cambridge: Harvard University Press, 1993); Ernest Gellner, *Conditions of Liberty: Civil Society and its Rivals* (New York: Penguin Press, 1994); Ernest Gellner, *Nations and Nationalism* (Ithaca: Cornell University Press, 1983).

37. From "Fears in Solitude," 1798.

38. Alfred Korzybski, *Science and Sanity,* 2nd ed. (Lancaster: Science Press, 1941), 31.

39. Julian Huxley, "The Concept of Race," in *Man Stands Alone* (New York: Harper, 1941), 126.

40. E. E. Sikes, *The Anthropology of the Greeks* (London: Nutt, 1914); R. R. Marret, ed., *Anthropology and the Classics* (Oxford: Clarendon Press, 1908); Joseph B. Gittler, ed., *Social Thought Among the Early Greeks* (Athens: University of Georgia Press, 1941); Louis Gernet, *The Anthropology of Ancient Greece* (Baltimore: Johns Hopkins University Press, 1981); John L. Myres, *Who Were the Greeks?* (Berkeley: University of California Press, 1930).

8

Biological and Social Factors

The problem of the origin and development of different physical types is as artificial and unreal a problem as is the study of race, for neither types nor races are anything more than abstractions which are believed and are treated as if they had a real existence, when in fact the only reality is the artificial construction of the terms and the meanings that have been given to them. It should be clearly understood that the meaning of a word is the action it produces. Because loaded words are capable of exploding with disastrous effects it is extremely important that we teach children to develop the habit of questioning every word for its meaning. We must be especially careful about the terms we use, for unsound terms like "race" and the systematics of race and human "types" lead directly to the systematic "extermination" of millions of human beings. It is necessary to be particularly cautious about so-called scientific and technical terms.

Goethe, in his play *Faust,* makes Mephistopheles say, "Where an idea is wanting a word can always be found to take its place, and a whole system of philosophy built thereon." The reign of such words may be long or short, but whatever their duration, their damage can be considerable.

The study of human variability is a fascinating one, and is part of the larger problem of discovering how we all come to be the way we are; that, too, is a social problem, and only arbitrarily, and in a limited technical sense, is it a biological problem. Humans are outstandingly the one animal species in which "biological" development has, from the earliest times, been substantially influenced by the operation of social factors—and this, ever increasingly, continues to be the case. The biological development of humans cannot be considered apart from their social development, for humans are, more or less, domesticated, self-domesticated, animals.[1]

Domestication is a social or cultural process by means of which biological changes are produced in animals. Such changes, to some extent, represent the socially preferred expression of genetic rearrangements of traits common to all humans. The chief agencies in the production of such changes are social, but the scientific study of such social agencies has only

193

just begun. Thus far, the emphasis has for the most part been upon the biological aspect of such changes, while there has been an almost complete failure to recognize the role that social influences may have played in their development.[2]

The biological aspects of the subject are important, but only in so far as they render possible an understanding of the physiological and genetic mechanisms underlying the actual process of change. R. A. Fisher has remarked:

> While genetic knowledge is essential for the clarity it introduces into the subject, the causes of the evolutionary changes in progress can only be resolved by an appeal to sociological, and even historical facts. These should at least be sufficiently available to reveal the more powerful agencies at work in the modification of mankind."[3]

When the mechanism of these physiological and genetic changes is understood, it is then fully realized that "race" is a term that refers to a process representing a series of genetically active temporary or episodic conditions, always in process of change. It then becomes clear that the stage at which one catches this process depends upon the segment of time which one arbitrarily delimits from the space-time continuum in which the process is occurring. Neither races of men nor races of lower animals are immutable; they seem to become so, but then only conceptually, when an anthropologist or a taxonomist follows the traditional practice of pinning his specimens down for study and classification. It is erroneous to conceive of any animal group, particularly human groups, as static and immutable. It is an error to do so in the case of humans in particular, because the facts of prehistory and those of more recent times indicate the flexibility and variability of which humankind is capable. In this process social factors play a considerable role. Upon recognizing this fact we must further recognize that in our own society the problem of race is essentially a problem of caste and class relations and that it is, of course, fundamentally a social problem.

In our own society, explanations of the race problem have been offered in terms of economic forces, social stratification, biological differences, or all three. Such explanations have never been altogether convincing. The causes motivating human behavior are complex, and human behavior is hardly ever to be explained in terms of single processes, which in themselves are complicated enough, such as the economic, the biological, or the purely social. In all cases, in order to understand the nature of any event it is necessary to discover and to relate all the conditions entering into its production. In other words, what is required is a specification of all the necessary conditions which together then form the sufficient cause of the event into whose nature we are inquiring.

While it may be true, for instance, that certain conditions arising out of our present economic organization of society are responsible for maintaining and exacerbating the "problem of race," it is by no means certain that a reorganization of our economic system would automatically result in a solution of that problem, although it is probable that it would help. It is quite conceivable that race problems may exist under ideal economic conditions. These problems, indeed, are far from simple, and it is therefore necessary to approach them by the use of such methods as are calculated to reduce them. It would obviously be an egregious error to approach the study of race from the standpoint of the economic determinant alone, precisely as it would be an error to approach the study from the viewpoint solely of biology or of sociology.

This brings us to what I consider to be an extremely important methodological aspect of the whole problem. It is the matter of the person who discusses the subject of race. Hitherto, practically anyone with the ability to develop a hoarse throat, with arrogance and effrontery in place of erudition, has been able to set himself up as an authority on race. We need only recall the names of Gobineau, Stoddard, Houston Stewart Chamberlain, Madison Grant, Adolf Hitler, and their like,[4] to discover that the principal equipment necessary to qualify one as an authority on race consists in a well-rounded ignorance, a considerable amount of viciousness, and an unshakable confidence. To listen to such "tangled oracles which ignorantly guide" is to suffer a positive increase in one's ignorance. With the passing of the above-mentioned individuals the nuisance is not abated, for there are always others ready to take their place.[5] In the universe of science the situation, though incomparably better, is not by any means—as we have already seen—all that could be desired. Until very recently little progress had been made in the scientific study of race. This had been chiefly due to the fact that the subject had been dealt with in a piecemeal manner and by specialists with an insufficient grasp of the complexities of the subject. Thus, psychologists failed to take into account the sociological and biological factors (if only to dismiss the latter as of no significance); while sociologists have in the past failed to give adequate consideration to the psychological and anthropological factors. Finally, and worst of all, the physical anthropologists restricted their studies almost entirely to the morphological aspects of the subject. The complexity of the problem is today recognized by most students, and thanks to the increasing volume and quality of their work, we today see that problem much more clearly than we did a generation ago. Nevertheless, we still need more students who will combine the best qualities of the psychologist, the sociologist, the biologist, and both the cultural and physical anthropologist.[6]

Racism as an ideological phenomenon has its origins and being in social and political forces. Its motivations are never the discovery of what *is*, of the *facts*, but of what, according to its proponents, ought to be. And what ought to be is determined by the political and social necessities of the moment. These will vary at different times and in different places, but in general these necessities are interpreted to mean that the differences which characterize various races determine a hierarchy of values. These values are always distinguished in terms of "superiority" and "inferiority." The recognition of these values then determines the manner in which the "superior" must conduct themselves in relation to the "inferior," and vice versa. The racist is not interested in the scientific facts, except to the extent to which, in some special form, they may serve his purposes. Because he is not interested in the facts, but in an ideology, it is quite impossible to demonstrate the fallacy of his views to the racist. Any attempt to reason with racists on the basis of the facts is rather more than a waste of time. Anyone who has had experience of these persons will know how unspeakably vicious they can be. The whole history of racism testifies to that fact.

Let us recall the ringing words of William Lloyd Garrison, "With reasonable men I will reason; with humane men I will plead; but to tyrants I will give no quarter, nor waste arguments where they will certainly be lost."

As Manning Nash has pointed out, the skeletal form of any racial ideology may be stated in six propositions: as (1) the attempt to flout natural law by man-made edicts about race relations, (2) the races differ in their capacities to embrace the complexities of civilization, (3) the level of cultural achievement of races indicates their relative innate capacities, (4) left on their own, inferior races tear down a cultural heritage, (5) the fight against racial equality is the fight for truth in the interests of all people, and (6) those who favor equality are undesirables.[7]

The scientist is put in the position of having to make available the facts, for the benefit of those who may wish to judge the evidence for themselves. But, again, it needs to be said that human rights are not dependent upon the facts of science or the assertions of racists or of any other kind of statement. Those rights rest squarely and firmly upon an ethical principle, the principle that by virtue of their humanity humans have the right to the fullest development of their capacities, to realize their potentialities, to fulfill themselves. No one or group has the right to stand in the way of another's development. Such conduct is evil. It is a social evil, and it is only by social means that it will ever be eradicated. Race, it should always be remembered, is an abstraction, an arbitrary label of a human grouping culturally defined in a given society. Race prejudice is a system of reciprocal relations of stereotyping, discrimination, and segregation existing between human groupings that are considered as races.

Since, as I have already pointed out, facts do not speak for themselves, but are at the mercy of whoever chooses to give them a meaning, it is obviously of the first importance that the meaning which they shall receive be given them by those who have made themselves thoroughly acquainted with the facts. As Henry A. Wallace said:

> For the combating of 'racism' before it sinks its poison fangs deep in our body politic, the scientist has both a special motive and a special responsibility. His motive comes from the fact that when personal liberty disappears scientific liberty also disappears. His responsibility comes from the fact that only he can give the people the truth. Only he can clean out the falsities which have been masquerading under the name of science in our colleges, our high schools and our public prints. Only he can show how groundless are the claims that one race, one nation, or one class has any God-given right to rule.[8]

In the modern world, racial problems, as I have already said, are essentially social problems. But no student of human society can ever hope to assist in the solution of these problems without acquiring an adequate understanding of what the biologist, the psychologist, and the psychoanalyst can alone supply, namely, an appreciation of the nature of the fundamental facts of physical and mental development as well as their pathological materialization. Obviously, what we need is more human ecologists, liaison officers between the sciences of humankind.[9]

The Economic Factor and the Factor of Social Stratification

Our society is a socially stratified one, and social stratification in our society is determined principally by the manner in which our society is economically structured. It is usually possible to migrate from one social stratum or class to another only by means of the economic process. By the acquisition of economic power one rises in the social hierarchy; by the loss of economic power one falls. Groups and persons who are denied effective participation in the economic process clearly cannot rise above the lower social strata, while the only way to exclude groups and persons who have not been denied an effective participation in the economic process from rising and maintaining their places socially is to erect barriers against them, to deprive them, in various ways, of their economic rights. We need hardly go farther back than our own time for the evidence with which to prove the truth of this statement. In those parts of Europe under Nazi domination in World War II such barriers were deliberately created in the form of a mythological racial dogma which was imposed upon whole peoples—a dogma which, in operation as a barrier, deprived all those who were not mythical "Aryans" of the right to earn a living and to keep even the little they had. No more telling or painful example than this could be cited of the blatant economic motivation underlying the creation and practice of this mythology, which leads so effectively to the social and economic disfranchisement of powerless groups.

In the United States there are several ready examples that may be cited as illustrating the relationship between the economic factor and the presence of racial barriers. Along the Pacific coast, where the Japanese and Chinese constituted an appreciable competitive group, there was considerable race prejudice against them. With the increase in the number of Filipinos entering the United States within recent years, despite the heroic resistance of their compatriots against the Japanese in the Philippines during World War II and their loyalty to the United States, racial prejudices were rapidly transferred to them.[10] Along the Atlantic coast, where the numbers of these ethnic groups are comparatively small and they cannot possibly be conceived to constitute economic competitors, there has been relatively little prejudice against them, apart from that which was generated by war conditions. Similarly, in California, when Native Americans were numerous there was a great deal of prejudice against them. In the Midwest, where Native Americans are relatively few and under "control," there is little prejudice against them. In the East a trace of Native American ancestry has some prestige value, for Native Americans are so rare that they are almost worth their weight in genes. In areas such as the South, where the social status of the African American is changing and he emerges as an economic competitor, the prejudices against the large population of blacks constitute a serious problem. In the North, where the economic situation is much better, the African American has always enjoyed a greater degree of social and economic freedom, limited as that social and economic freedom has always been in this divided society. In England, when there were few representatives of either of these groups, there was little active prejudice against them. In localities, however, in which there exists a concentration of members of such ethnic groups, prejudices are easily generated.[11]

In the days when Englishmen went out to the "colonies" to govern the native people, they soon learned that the natives "threatened" their own interests and those of their own people, and reactively, frequently developed the usual racial prejudices. This lead to an exclusiveness and a capacity for making the local people feel second rate in their own land. This in turn produced that bitterness and loathing for their invaders that the stolid Englishman usually found unaccountable. Today, with the immigration into England of thousands of people, Englishmen no longer have to go abroad to develop race prejudice.

Sir Arthur Richmond, who as a young man was sent out to serve under Lord Milner in South Africa in 1901, recounts how without his being aware of it race prejudice crept up on him. He writes,

Before the Boer war no Kaffir had been allowed to walk on the side-walk in a town. He had to walk in the roadway. I had not particularly noticed that they always, women as well as men, walked in the middle of the road when, one day, a Kaffir came towards me striding along the side-walk of the principal street in Pretoria. Instantly I felt a surge of indignation. I had not before been conscious of any colour prejudice; I hardly knew of the rule forbidding the use of the side-walk to black men, yet subtly and unconsciously I had been infected with the accepted view that blacks must not be allowed any kind of equality with whites. I was horrified by my automatic reaction, and its immediate effect was to make me feel intense sympathy for the black man and to realize how conscious I had to be of the difficulties inherent in the relationship between the black man and the white.[12]

Lord Milner, under whom Richmond served, was, though he does not say so, a calamity. As the supreme British race patriot of the period, it was Milner's avowed intention to obliterate, by a ruthless and obdurate policy of Anglicization, all traces of national identity in the Afrikaner. It was the fanatical zeal of Milner in the holy cause of empire, which precipitated the Boer War, and led to the razing of farmsteads and crops, as well as the creation of the first concentration camps by the British. It was Milner's conduct which provided the impetus by which the then loosely-knit politically unsophisticated Afrikaners were welded into an acutely race-conscious fervently nationalistic people, whose supreme hatred was for the British, and whose increasing anxiety was the non-white population. It was this misguided British imperial policy that was directly responsible for the hideous practice of apartheid.[13]

Without in the least underestimating the important role economic factors play in the creation of race prejudice in Western society generally, it may be observed that there is no absolutely necessary or sufficient relationship between economic conditions and racial problems. Just as it is possible to conceive of difficult racial problems existing under ideal economic conditions, so it is quite possible to conceive of perfect ethnic relations and mutual appreciation under the most difficult economic conditions.

So far as the individual is concerned, race prejudice is by no means a necessary concomitant of economic anxieties. For example, Bettelheim and Janowitz in a study of a group of World War II veterans found that there were quite a number who, in spite of a doubtful economic future, were sufficiently well integrated to be able to control any hostilities they may have had without the need to discharge them upon some scapegoat.[14] These were men who were secure in their personalities, who had been given emotional security in their childhood. Fundamentally, the problem is one of personality structure—and whatever it is that may contribute to that structure is an essential part of the problem; it is of no use dealing with the one without the other. Economic conditions may, of course, produce substantive changes in the personality. When children are brought up in families in which the economic conditions are satisfactory, the children are likely to be emotionally more secure than in families in which the economic conditions have been poor. But whatever the economic conditions in the family, if the child is made to feel secure, he will not need to indulge in irrational discharges of hostility against the members of an outgroup. The problem, then, is fundamentally not one of economics, though improving economic conditions will help. The problem is really one of emotional integration and security, a problem of parent-child relationships, a problem of human relations.[15]

The fact is that in our own society the regrettable discovery has been made that by utilizing the physical and cultural differences existing between groups and individuals, it is relatively simple to disguise the motives and evade the consequences of one's own conduct by attributing existing and potential evils to the conduct of some other group or to utilize those differences for the most ignoble political purposes. In this way, by setting groups of people against one another, attention is diverted from the real sources of evil. The discovery is, in fact, an old one. As a device for moving people it is extremely well grounded in that it caters to a deep-seated tendency which many persons have acquired during their early conditioning to find a scapegoat outside themselves upon which to blame their troubles or release their aggressive, frustrated feelings. As long ago as the second century A.D., the early father Tertullian of pagan Rome was fully aware of the fact that the persecution of the Christian minority was merely being used as a device to divert the attention of the people from the real causes of corruption within the Roman state. Says Tertullian, "If the Tiber rose to the walls of the city, if the inundation of the Nile failed to give the fields enough water, if the heavens did not send rain, if an earthquake occurred, if famine threatened, if pestilence raged, the cry resounded: 'Throw the Christians to the lions!'" In this manner the Roman populace was provided, as later peoples have been, with a socially sanctioned outlet for their frustration. And that is the important point to grasp about the nature of race prejudice, namely, that it is a socially sanctioned and socially learned attitude. It is a ready-made and culturally accepted outlet for various forms of hostility and feelings of frustration. In the South, race hatred has long been kept alive and fanned to white heat at the instigation of unscrupulous industrialists and politicians, ever ready to capitalize on baseless popular superstitions, prejudices, and beliefs, because there is no issue more useful than race as a political platform for securing votes. Tell the poor whites, and others not so poor, that their status is due to, and continually threatened by, the competition of the blacks, and they will vote for anything to which such an issue is tied in promised favor of themselves.

Things have not changed much in more than half a century in the South, when in 1943 Thomas Sancton wrote:

> There are millions of white and black men in the South, and their children, on blighted farms and in the slums, who live a more bearable life because of what the Roosevelt administration made possible. But these are the poor and ignorant, and their race hate, kept alive for years just as Governor Dixon and the Alabama capitalists are keeping it alive now, makes them vulnerable. Of the millions of people whom the New Deal aided, the blacks cannot vote, and most of the whites who can have been poisoned by the belief that the President and Mrs. Roosevelt are trying to wipe out all racial barriers under the war emergency; the Dixons are now in the saddle; they seem to be able to foist upon the disfranchised masses anything they want to; and once more the white man's fear of the Negro has made it possible. It is no mystery why the South's congressman, elected by a small and privileged proportion of its population fight so hard to defeat an anti-poll-tax bill: and it is no mystery, come to think of it, why reactionary Northern members, their blood brothers, by one subterfuge and another let them get away with it.[16]

More than half a century later, things have changed somewhat for the better, but not nearly enough. The granting of statehood to the territories of Alaska and Hawaii had been opposed and blocked since 1916, largely by Southern Democrats who feared that the potentially incoming four Senate votes would bring about the advancement of civil rights. These territories are now full states within the Union. The fears of the Southern Democrats appear to have been groundless. In the November elections of 1966 racism won the ballot of a majority of white voters. The reaction against civil rights legislation and black demonstrations made the victory of Southern segregationists a foregone conclusion, and not without its considerable effect elsewhere throughout the land.[17]

The church in the South, which is largely Protestant, reflects the beliefs of its parishioners. Religion says no more to society than society says to itself. In the South, and in this the South is not alone, Jehovah is a tribal god. He serves the interests of the people. Hence, scripture is quoted in support of ideas, institutions, and practices, which to outsiders appear to be the very antithesis of Christianity.[18]

When we apply the measure of determining what people believe, by observing what they do—not by what they say, then Christianity has not only been one of the great failures of history, in not practicing what it preached, but has been a powerful source of racist propaganda. What is even worse, the church through its great power has failed to assume the leadership in speaking out against tyrants and demagogues wherever they may occur, and take active nonviolent measures where it ought. In The

Sermon on the Mount (Matthew 5–7), which sets forth the principles of the Christian ethic, the most important of these principles is "All things whatsoever ye would that men should do to you, do ye even so to them: for this is the law and the prophets." This also goes by the modern label, "The Golden Rule." A common phrasing is, "Do to others as you are done by." It was in the New Testament that the doctrine was developed that "the essential nature of God is love."[19]

Whether God is Love, or Love is God; or whether one should love others more than we love ourselves, the truth is that Christianity from the days of the early Church Fathers to the present day has been in the forefront of those institutions which created, maintained, and fanned the hatreds directed especially against the Jews. This is a subject which has been fully dealt with in many scholarly works, and in none of them, with a few individual exceptions, is there any evidence, of the Church ever having shown much love for Jews. However that may be, anyone who wishes to understand the origins of racism should read *The History of Anti-Semitism*, by Leon Poliakov; it is the most readable and scholarly work on the subject.[20]

A short work on the same subject is by Alan Davies, professor of religious studies at the University of Toronto entitled *Infected Christianity: A Study of Modern Racism*. In this admirable work focusing on five different Christs, the Germanic, Latin, Anglo-Saxon, Afrikaner, and black, Davies shows how the Christian church succumbed to the infection of racist ideas. He takes the reader through the steps which led from the myths of race and nation to become "sacred" myths and histories, and how infected Christianity in Germany and South Africa served to legitimate ruling racist elites. Davies traces the course of fascism to its roots in the religious, cultural, and intellectual history of western civilization and to its culmination in the formation of the European white supremacist Aryan myth. Racialized Christianity in this way became a powerful agency in the transmission of the virus of racism, the support of nationalist and imperialist ambitions, and the governmental control of "undesirable" elements.[21]

The Catholic Church has a long history of antisemitism. This has been dealt with admirably by Davies, who has shown how easy it was for the Church to adopt the language of racialism when it was expedient, or to remain silent when one might have expected it to speak out. There were always a number of popes, archbishops, bishops, priests, convents, and monasteries that failed to protest and to give shelter to their fellow human beings. Pope Pius XII, and the Vatican, found it expedient during the reign of Hitler to utter not a word.[22]

The Protestant press in the United States, from 1933 onwards, took note, if only in brief references and short new items, of what was happening to the Jews in Germany. At the end of the war in Europe its concern was chiefly what was happening to the churches in Germany. Robert Ross, professor of religious studies at the University of Minnesota, has discussed all this in his moving book *So It Was True: The American Protestant Press and the Nazi Persecution of the Jews.* Professor Ross concludes,

> The press reported far more extensively than has generally been thought to be the case. The accepted view is that the press had said little or nothing. Clearly, this was not true. It must be said, then, that American Protestant Christians did know, for, if the people read, the people knew. But the editors and writers of the American Protestant press tried to deal with the mass extermination of the Jews of Germany and Europe as if it were part of an ordered, stable, normal world of fact. In fact, it happened in a world gone mad. In the end, editors and writers seemed unable to cope with something as unreal, among them six million Jews in an organized, bureaucratic, planned extermination. They could report this madness, this unreality, but, beyond the reporting and even beyond the expressed shock and horror over the discovery of the death camps, there remains the awful pall that hangs over the entire episode in modern history.[23]

The crimes committed by the Nazis against the Jews and other peoples in civilized Europe between the years 1933 and 1945 tell us that civilization is a very fragile thing, so that when attacked by hordes of barbarians, its openness can seldom provide a successful defense against them.[24]

By the skillful use of the myth of race and the labeling of the Jews as the "super-State power," and "world danger," Hitler hypnotized a whole nation, and was able to conquer the greater part of Western Europe in the declared aim to conquer the world, for the glory of "a Reich that would endure a thousand years." And very well he might have, had it not been for several of his fatal blunders, and the massive forces the Allies were at last able to put into the field. Hence, the importance of civilization making racism a crime against humanity, while at the same time through education raising children as humane beings who will fully understand why racism is a crime necessitating prompt application of the law wherever bigotry raises its ugly head. Such a law of nations is long overdue.

When in 1933 Hitler came to power, antisemitism was transformed from a personal obsession and propaganda weapon into a national policy. With the cunning of a psychopath Hitler systematically manipulated the mass psyche of the German people to provide them with a scapegoat they happened to be more familiar with and ready to embrace as the cause of all their problems—the Jews as an affliction that had to be eradicated from the body politic. As Leon Wieseltier put it,

> Nothing could more bountifully satisfy the demonological needs of the day than antisemitism. It would be all things to all Germans—a 'scientific' theory of race, a metaphysics, a philosophy of history, an explanation of

the modern world, a theodocy and a plan for national regeneration. It accounted for what went wrong and showed how to make it right."[25]

It is not to the common people alone that we need to apply our remedies, but also to those who have enjoyed the advantages of what is customarily called "a good education." The latter is generally acquired at the best private schools and Ivy League colleges from which the expensively uneducated regularly emerge in influential numbers, without having learned anything at all about the most important of all the arts and sciences, the art and science of being a human being. And, of course, this is true of virtually all educational enterprises in the United States, and elsewhere. From our educational institutions, our children, our only hope for the future, have received no training whatever in the art and science of learning to live as if to live and love were one.[26]

Governments and government officials who could have rescued the fleeing victims of Hitler's genocidal wrath virtually everywhere failed to respond to their need. This was especially true of the fleeing victims who in their extremity were rejected by the United States and Britain, an attitude fairly summed up in the remark of one high ranking official of the Foreign Office in September 1944: "In my opinion a disproportionate amount of the time of this office is wasted on dealing with these wailing Jews . . ."[27]

"These wailing Jews . . ." The unconcern and insensitivity of these "cold fish" was shocking, but what was even worse was the chilling indifference, the utter heartlessness, and obstruction by high government officials who, on the basis of one pretext after another, even deceit, declined to grant asylum to those fleeing from Hitler's murderous pursuit. The world stood by even when, watching their movie screens, the viewers saw shiploads of victims turned away from every shore where they sought refuge. After all, they were only Jews. If this phenomenon is to be given a name, it should be "The Great Betrayal," not only of the betrayers, but also of their humanity.[28] Did any people, with the exception of the Danes, rise up and plead for the victims? The answer is a staggering "No!"

For many years it was the official policy of the USSR to harass its Jewish population and liquidate its intelligentsia. The communists continued this policy in an inhuman manner by the imprisonment and execution of hundreds of leading Jewish intellectuals, writers, painters, musicians, critics, and others. They were accused of being "rebels, agents of American Imperialism, nationalist bourgeois Zionists, and enemies of the USSR."[29] Bent on destroying the last remnants of Jewish culture the communist government actively encouraged antisemitism.[30]

Under Khruschev the terror was relaxed, but the basic policy remained in force. The thinly disguised antisemitism which was exhibited by the Communist representatives at the United Nations Security Council was clearly a policy fixed at the highest levels. With the advent of Mikhail Gorbachev in the 1980s and the move toward greater "democracy" or "glasnost," and the opening up of the media to calls for freedom and justice, there simultaneously appeared a virulent antisemitism, with the Jews being held responsible for everything that had gone wrong over the last seventy years. Again, as elsewhere, the Jews were accused of being Russia's most dangerous enemies. Writing in support of an article by Irina Ginsburg in The New York Times, entitled "We Russian Jews Fear For Our Lives" (5 May 1990), John and Carol Garrard, who visited Moscow several times in the 1980s and talked with many Russians, wrote

> There is an obvious parallel between Soviet society today and German society prior to the rise of Hitler. Here again is a weak democracy—really a democracy in its infancy—where the leadership has no popular support, including Mikhail Gorbachev, economic collapse seems imminent. Just as Germany went through the hyper-inflation of the 1920s, so Russians find their rubles growing increasingly worthless . . . In the midst of the growing corruption, Russians feel frustrated and angry. We listened in Moscow apartments to fears of famine in the countryside within the year, accompanied by street demonstrations and riots in Moscow itself. Such exasperation over the denigration of Russian culture during much of the Soviet period makes many Russians give in to the all-too-human desire to find a scapegoat. Inevitable, the old belief in the Jew as the source of the Russians' troubles has re-emerged."[31]

The Union of South Africa, which openly supported Hitler during World War II, is the only government in the world which for many years consistently defined itself as the embodiment of white supremacy, and adopted racism as an official ideology. This made race discrimination a dominant part of daily life. This institutionalized policy went by the Afrikaans name of "apartheid," which means "apartness." Apartheid was widely condemned by much of the civilized world, but to no effect. The United Nations repeatedly passed resolutions against it, but the government of South Africa left the Commonwealth rather than modify its racial policies. A small white population cruelly continued to protect its economic and social privileges against any incursions which might be made upon it by its African, Coloured, Asiatic, and Jewish populations. The percentage representation of the various groups of the South African population is as follows: Africans, 69.8; Whites, 17.4; Colored, 9.3; and Asiatics, 2.9. The Jews form only 4.0 percent of the *total* population, and they have from the first proved themselves loyal and able citizens of the Union.

What, then, is the reason for the prejudice against the Jews? Is it fear of economic competition? In view of their small representation this cannot be the whole story. The fact, again, is that, while they themselves do not constitute an economic problem, the prejudice against them is utilized and, indeed, inspired by politicians and other interested parties for economic purposes. In a sympathetic and penetrating study of the Union, Lewis Sowden returned an answer to the question

> Why prejudice against the Jews? Simply this, that South Africa, like most other countries, has its Jewish problem kept alive by politicians for purposes of personal or party aggrandizement. The Nationalists used it in 1930 to strengthen their hold on the country and to embarrass General Smuts's opposition. Their Quota Act [aimed against the Jews] had the full support of their own people and many sympathizers among the other parties. General Smuts's men could not effectively oppose it for fear of being accused as 'pro-Jewish,' fatal, of course, for any politician.[32]

In May 1948, the Nationalist Party of Dr. Malan was returned to power in South Africa on a straight racist ticket. "The election was mainly fought on the propaganda slogan: 'Vote for a White South Africa.' All the emphasis was on the 'Black Menace.'"[33] At a conference of Protestant theologians held early in 1954 in South Africa the question of apartheid as a policy of permanent political separation of blacks and whites was discussed. Is apartheid untrue to the teachings of Christ? The South African Anglican bishops replied, "No." The leaders of the Dutch Reformed Church, whose members have vast material and political interests at stake, answered that cooperation between blacks and whites was sinful. Equal rights for all men, it was held, is a perversion of true Christian doctrine. "It is a misinterpretation of Scripture and therefore a defiance of the will of God." "We know," stated these Reformed theologians,

> God the Creator in Scripture as Hammabdil, as the Maker of Separations. To create a cosmos God separated things; light from darkness,[34] waters above the firmament, dry land from the sea. From the very beginning it was the intention of the Lord that mankind should live in separate nations. In his awful self-conceit man wished to frustrate this intention. . . . Therefore attempts at unification, the equalitarian idea, and a revival of the Babylonian spirit.[35]

As for the Dutch Reformed Church, its position was made abundantly clear some years ago when, one Sunday morning, three blacks desired to attend the service at a prominent church in Johannesburg. Apprised of their intention, a phalanx of sextons, aligned at the head of the steps, was ready to bar their way, and barred they were. Whereupon one of the would-be worshippers inquired, "Is not this the House of God?" To which the leading sexton emphatically replied, "It is *not*. This is the Dutch Reformed Church of South Africa."

A year prior to this at a meeting of theologians Prime Minister Malan declared that "the color question is the greatest and most urgent matter on which the election must hinge," and in April 1953, Malan's Nationalist party received an overwhelming majority at the polls.[36]

In South Africa there is a serious land problem for "poor whites." Sachs states that

> About a quarter of the Afrikaner farmers do not own the land they work and there has set in among them the kind of spiritual degeneration described in Erskine Caldwell's *Tobacco Road*. Hitlerism gave them a new hope, as it did to the 'Lumpen' in the Berlin tenement houses. The slogan, 'The Jews are our misfortune,' proved an acceptable and satisfyingly simple explanation of their misery and want.[37]

In 1966 the Assembly of the United Nations voted to end South Africa's League of Nations mandate over Southwest Africa, now known as Namibia. But it was only after a long and heroic struggle for independence by the many peoples of this southwest portion of Africa that the South African Government reluctantly withdrew from what is now an independent Namibia.

During the time of apartheid the outcome of racism in South Africa seemed to be very unpromising. A typical expression of the feeling among many South Africans was that of Professor P. V. Pistorius of the University of Pretoria:

> We see our doom inevitably approaching, but we are powerless to avert it. And it is a doom of our own making. . . . He who creates a tribal god will perish by the tribal gods of others. He who worships his own group and regards even injustices as good if it is thought to be in the interest of his group, will perish by the injustices perpetrated by other groups.[38]

It has been said that rulers and ruling classes never voluntarily surrender their power and privileges. This is quite true. However, political events in South Africa in recent years provide a welcome exception to this rule. The rigid system of racial segregation designed to maintain white supremacy, "apartheid," was officially put into effect in 1948 and was inhumanly enforced in the most barbarous of ways.[39] But several remarkable events occured in 1989: a stroke suffered by the oppressive incumbent President Pieter Botha, his subsequent resignation, and the election of Mr. F. W. de Klerk as President of the Union of South Africa. Mr de Klerk was expected to continue the oppressive policies of his predecessors, but to everyone's astonishment he immediately embarked upon a course of change that led to the abolition of apartheid and the establishment of a democratic order in South Africa.

One of de Klerk's first acts was the unconditional release of Nelson Mandela after twenty-seven years of imprisonment, as well as the release of other political prisoners. In 1991 the Population Registration Act, which classified people by race at birth, was repealed. The Convention for a Democratic South Africa, a broad black-led coalition met, and formally began negotiations towards the creation of a new constitution extending political rights to all ethnic groups. In February 1992, following the loss by the National Party, under de Klerk's leadership, of an election in the Transvaal to the reactionary Conservative Party, de Klerk boldly called a nationwide referendum of whites to seek a mandate for his policies of social and political reform, together with the sharing of power with blacks. The result was a resounding 68.7 percent of the vote in favor of his program. In 1993 de Klerk abandoned the idea of power sharing; Mandela also agreed to the postponment until 1999 of an undiluted one-man-one-vote majority rule. This is but a small catalog of changes wrought by de Klerk. On 10 May 1994 Mandela became the first black president of South Africa, de Klerk sharing the presidency with Mandela. In 1993 Mandela and de Klerk were awarded the Nobel Prize for their joint efforts to bring peace and democracy to South Africa. We see, then, that one person with the right ideas seizing the opportunity can change the world, or at least a part of it.[40] One does not necessarily have to wait until "the wicked shall have ceased from troubling and the weary are at rest."

It has often been pointed out that under difficult economic conditions in a diverse population racism is likely to become exacerbated. For example, in a study of race relations between blacks and whites in Liverpool, England, Richmond has shown that under conditions of economic stress, the coincidence of the three factors, insecurity, visibility, and stereotype, will help to produce a predominating attitude of prejudice and hostility among the members of the "in-group" toward the members of the "out-group." The intensity of expression of this attitude will vary according to any changes in one or other of the three predisposing factors. The more highly visible the "out-group" the more derogatory are the stereotypes, or the greater the degree of insecurity felt among the members of the "in-group," the greater will be the tension.

During the October 1964 General Election in England the "white backlash" played a considerable role in unseating several Labour incumbents and in defeating a number of Labour candidates for office. An on-the-scene reporter wrote of the defeat of the Labour incumbent for Smethwick, an industrial suburb of Birmingham, "There is little doubt in the country that Mr. Gordon Walker had been defeated by the whispered slogan, 'If you want a nigger neighbour, vote Labour.'"[41]

In Perry Barr, an electoral district in Birmingham's inner ring, the Labour incumbent was defeated on the purely racial issue. In West

Bromwich, which borders on Birmingham, the Labour incumbent's majority was pared by nearly 8,000 votes, and in Bradford, Yorkshire, it was halved. Here 1,200 Pakistanis had taken over whole shifts in some of the woolen mills. Losses in Labour votes occurred wherever immigrants of color had established themselves as a permanent working force.[42]

In the March 1966 General Election, racism was given a decisive setback. Mr. Peter Griffiths, who unseated Labour's Patrick Gordon Walker in 1964 by exploiting the feeling against immigrants of color, was thoroughly repudiated by the electors. Throughout the Birmingham area candidates who campaigned on color or immigration or accepted support from the forces of bigotry were mowed down. It should be fairly evident that race prejudice is easily generated in the societies of the Western world, when those societies are socially and economically so structured as to be continually productive of frustrations in the individual, from childhood on; these, in turn, produce an aggressiveness, a hostility, for which the individual must find expression in some way. However, the aggressiveness for which the individual must secure release is not entirely produced by economic factors. It also should be clear that the frustrative situations called into being by economic and social factors, while producing some aggressiveness in the individual, do not in themselves and need not necessarily lead to race prejudice. That the aggressiveness produced by such factors may lead to race prejudice is largely to be explained by the fact that race prejudice constitutes a socially sanctioned and encouraged or socially directed means of releasing aggressiveness. The aggressiveness may in part be produced by socioeconomic factors, but the form of the response which that aggressiveness takes is not necessarily linked with such factors. Alternative responses are available, but race prejudice is among the easiest and the psychologically most satisfying.

Merton has effectively described the frustrative situation which exists in Western societies. He writes:

> It is only when a system of cultural values extols, virtually above all else, certain common symbols of success *for the population at large*, while its social structure rigorously restricts or completely eliminates access to approved modes of acquiring these symbols for a considerable part of the same population, that antisocial behavior ensues on a considerable scale. In other words, our egalitarian ideology denies by implication the existence of noncompeting groups and individuals in the pursuit of pecuniary success. The same body of success-symbols is held to be desirable for all. These goals are held to transcend class lines, not to be bound by them, yet the actual social organization is such that there exist class differentials in the accessibility of these common success-symbols. Frustration and thwarted aspiration lead to the search for avenues of escape from a culturally induced intolerable situation; or unrelieved ambition may eventuate

in illicit attempts to acquire the dominant values. The American stress on
pecuniary success and ambitiousness for all thus invites exaggerated anxieties, hostilities, neuroses and antisocial behavior.[43]

The avenue of escape from such frustrative conditions is almost always
the same, through aggressiveness. The object to which that aggressiveness
may attach itself is culturally determined by what is rendered culturally
available.[44] Race, from an objective point of view, represents a cultural misunderstanding of certain facts, but from the point of view of the psyche of
the person (which is far from objective), it presents a most satisfactory solution of a particular problem, affording, as it does, both a convenient and a
suitable release for aggressiveness. It should, however, be clearly understood that the misunderstanding is psychological or cultural in origin, not
economic. The conception of race is a psychological or cultural artifact and
does not in itself lead to race prejudice. What leads to race prejudice is the
cultural manipulation of those psychophysical energies which, in most persons, overtly find expression in some form of hostility, no matter what the
underlying motivation of that manipulation may be. Economic factors represent but one group of conditions—and these are of the greatest importance—by means of which such aggressiveness may be called forth under
conditions and in situations in which it may be easily attached to race.[45]

Economic factors, in Western society, are certainly among the most important of the factors leading to situations in which race prejudice may be
caused to develop. But their dependence upon cultural factors for the direction they can be made to give to individual aggressiveness is proved by
the fact that the aggressiveness arising under those same economic conditions can also be directed toward the production of good-fellowship and
mutual aid between different ethnic and social groups. Such fellowship
and cooperation between different groups have been repeatedly witnessed
in times of war, when, for example, an alien nation has become the socially
sanctioned release-object for one's aggressiveness. In peacetime the repair
of some natural disaster, affecting the lives of all, frequently produces the
same effect, by providing a wholesome outlet for such aggressiveness. As
Freud remarked in this connection,

> It is one of the few noble and gratifying spectacles that men can offer,
> when in the face of an elemental catastrophe they awake from their mud-
> dle and confusion, forget all their internal difficulties and animosities,
> and remember the great common task, the preservation of mankind
> against the supremacy of nature.[46]

The attack upon some social problem requiring solution is in every way a
far more satisfactory outlet for aggression than an attack upon other hu-

man beings. Clearly, then, it is what is culturally offered as the most suitable object for the release of these aggressive tendencies that is the primarily important fact, the economic factors are only of secondary importance. As Dollard has put it, "Race prejudice seems, then, but a footnote to the wider consideration of the circumstances under which aggression may be expressed within a society."[47]

It is only under special kinds of conditions that worry, fear, and insecurity may be made to add up to race prejudice. Economic conditions are culturally utilizable, for good or for evil purposes, as each culture, or segment thereof, sees fit. If in some cultures the aggressiveness which arises under such conditions is made to discharge itself in hostile behavior toward some group, that can hardly be said to be due to economic conditions, but must clearly be held to be due to those factors which render possible the cultural manipulation of the situation to which such conditions give rise. In short, economic factors may provide some of the conditions in which race hostility may be generated but, unless those conditions are directed into channels leading to race hostility, there will be no race hostility, and the aggressiveness which must be released will have to find some other outlet. Under prosperous economic conditions, when the individual's feelings of security are at an optimum level, anxiety is not as likely to be aroused as under unfavorable economic conditions.

The history of prejudice against the Japanese in California affords a telling case study of the complexity of the factors involved. Here it would be an easy matter for the economic determinist to show that economic factors are chiefly responsible for that prejudice, but he would not be entirely correct. A study of the history of the prejudice against the Japanese in California proves that a large number of independent factors are involved. In the first place, Japanese immigration into California unfortunately coincided with the rise of Japan as a great power with territorial ambitions, hence Japanese immigrants came to be regarded as "the spearhead of Japanese invasion." Corrupt politicians, anxious to divert public attention from their own malpractices, and newspapers, supporting the latter or for their own particular purposes, have continually emphasized the danger that California might develop a race problem even worse than the color problem in the South. The continual emphasis on the inevitability of war with Japan, the fact that the Japanese present perceptible physical and cultural differences, their hard-won, but warmly resented, expansion into fields of commerce in which they have become "competitors" where whites formerly held the field exclusively, are important factors, among others, which together have been responsible for the development of race prejudice against the Japanese in California.[48]

The aggressive intentions of the Japanese government and fear of the development of another "color problem," two issues almost daily drummed into the ears of Californians, would alone have been sufficient to produce an acute case of race prejudice. Add to these the other factors already mentioned, and many others not mentioned, and it becomes clear that any explanation in terms of a single factor would do violence to the facts.

Many Californians disliked the Japanese, not because they constituted an economic threat but because they had been taught to believe that the Japanese were opposed to all that good Californians and good Americans stood for. This belief made it possible for the federal government to avail itself of racial discrimination as an instrument of national policy following the attack on Pearl Harbor. In February 1942 President Franklin D. Roosevelt signed Executive Order 9066 ordering the forcible removal from the area of the Western Defense Command of approximately 112,000 Japanese and Japanese Americans. 71,000 of these were American citizens. All were ruthlessly interned in concentration camps.[49] This was an act of naked racism. To this date not one single act of espionage, sabotage, or disloyalty has been traced to any person of Japanese descent either in Hawaii or on the mainland.[50] By this cruel, inhumane, and utterly illegal act, 112,000 men, women, and children were torn from their homes, schools, and employment, and imprisoned for more than four years, for the crime of race.

It is of interest to note that American citizens of German, Italian, Austrian, and Hungarian ancestry were subject to no restraints whatever. Can it be that it was due to their being racially indistinguishable from the rest of white America? In an article "Repay U.S. Japanese?" (*The New York Times,* 10 April 1983), protesting the government's belated intention to recompense the surviving prisoners of the concentration camp, John J. McCloy, an Assistant Secretary of War, who had played a leading role in persuading President Roosevelt to evacuate the Japanese American population justified the rounding up of everyone with common racial characteristics on the ground that "it was not feasible to carry out immediate personal evaluation . . ." and declared that it was the right thing to have done.

In spite of a sedulous search by many agencies, not a single act of disloyalty has ever been traced to a Japanese American, as such persons as Secretary of War Henry L. Stimson, Chief of the Federal Bureau of Investigation J. Edgar Hoover, and others have attested. Nevertheless a Public opinion survey conducted in 1946 revealed that two-thirds of the American public believed Japanese Americans had been guilty of such acts.[51]

Following the conclusion of World War II some Californians violently opposed the return of loyal American citizens of Japanese ancestry to their former homes in California. Scheming politicians declared that were they permitted to do so every Japanese seen on the streets would be killed, thus artfully inciting the public to riot and murder. What were the motives of these politicians? Obviously, what they have always been: to keep the race issue alive so that they might fully exploit it for their own and their friends' economic advantage. The California Alien Land Law which rendered Japanese Americans ineligible to own agricultural land and the California law barring Japanese from the fishing industry were clearly economically motivated, even though both were patently unconstitutional and in direct violation of the 14th Amendment, and in 1950 so declared by the Supreme Court of California, as "racism in one of its most malignant forms."[52]

An example of the little known many acts of mindless racism of the United States government is what happened to the peaceful Mongoloid inhabitants of the Aleutian Islands. Following the Japanese bombing of Dutch Harbor on the Aleutian Islands chain, in June 1942 all inhabitants of the Islands were forcibly removed from their villages to camps in southeastern Alaska. The two-year internment of these gentle people was described by Congressman Don Young as "a living nightmare." The "internment camps" were abandoned fish canneries and fishmeal plants, as was an abandoned gold mine in southeastern Alaska. Scores of people died from lack of proper shelter, poor sanitary conditions, and inadequate care. To this day there has been no adequate compensation paid to the survivors of the wrongs and massive losses suffered at the hands of the United States government.[53]

The details may vary where the members of different groups are involved and in different regions, but the general pattern of racism is the same wherever found and under whatever high-sounding name it may be disguised. Not one factor, but a complex of factors, is generally involved. Nevertheless, when this has been said and all the necessary conditions entering into the generation of race prejudice have been considered, it remains clear that economic conditions are among the most powerful. Our economic system, with all the frictions, frustrations, misery, and war which it brings, is a basic cause of racism and race situations. These, together, supply the motivation and a good deal of the aggressiveness expressed in race prejudice. Race prejudice is a socially sanctioned and socially channeled means of relieving aggressive tensions, because in our society there exist powerful groups of men who believe that in their own interest and in order to maintain their power or increase it they must maintain divisions between men. It is the domestic application of the formula "Divide and rule." What more simple than to produce such divisions between members of different ethnic groups within our society? They are "aliens," "foreigners," "the white man's burden," "the rising tide of color," "the yellow peril," "niggers," "the international Jew," "wops," "Greeks," "the lesser breeds without the law," and so on.[54]

In an economic organization of society which is frequently characterized by one crisis after another, with its attendant unemployment in the industries involved, the aggrieved part of the population is easily led to believe that if there were fewer people to be employed there would be employment and adequate wages for all. Race antagonism under such conditions is easily generated.

As Edward Reuter has put it,

> In the human as in the subhuman realm, the geographic distribution, the physical differences, the varying modes of life, and the mental traits and characteristics are, in large measure, the impersonally determined end results of the competitive struggle to live. Men live where they can secure the means of life, and they develop the physical, mental, and social characters that enable them to live in the area.[55]

One of the most serious "end results of the competitive struggle to live" in our society is race prejudice. It has been emphasized that the economic factor is not the sole condition involved in the causation of race antagonism; it is one of the conditions that facilitates the development of race prejudice, but it is not the only condition. It should, however, be quite clear that in our society the economic factor is a powerful condition in the causation of such antagonisms, a necessary condition without which—whatever we may be able to conceive to the contrary—such antagonisms would be much less likely to occur. Like good doctors, therefore, if we would prevent the disease we must eliminate or modify the principal condition or conditions that make it possible. In other words, we must attend to the conditions such as overpopulation and poverty of economic duress under which so many human beings are unjustly forced to live today.[56] By so doing we will have removed one of the most important breeding grounds in which the virus of race prejudice so readily grows; such other conditions as remain can then be dealt with efficiently. This is something to understand and to work for.

Notes

1. Upon this important subject see the following: Eduard Hahn, *Die Haustiere* (Leipzig: Dunckcker und Humbold, 1896); B. Klatt, "Mendelismus, Domestikation und Kraniologie," *Archiv für Anthropologie*, n.s., 18 (1921): 225–50; H. Friedenthal, "Die Sonderstellung des Menschen in der Natur," *Wege zum Wissen* 8 (1925); Eugen Fischer, "Rasse und Rassenentstehung beim Menschen," *Wege zum Wissen* 62 (1927): 1–137; Berthold Laufer, "Methods in the Study of Domestications," *Scientific Monthly* 25 (1927): 251–55; Melvile J. Herskovits, "Social Selection and the Formation of Human Types," *Human Biology* 1 (1929): 250–62; G. Renard, *Life and Work in Prehistoric Times* (New York: Alfred A. Knopf, 1929); Franz Boas, *The Mind of Primitive Man* (New York: Macmillan, 1938), 74–98; Franz Boas, ed., *General Anthropology* (Boston: Heath, 1938), 108; A. B. D. Fortuyn, "The Origin of Human

Races," *Science* 90 (1939): 352–53; Ashley Montagu, "The Socio-Biology of Man," *Scientific Monthly* 50 (1940): 483–90; J. B. S. Haldane, "The Argument from Animals to Men," in *Culture and the Evolution of Man*, ed. Ashley Montagu (New York: Oxford University Press, 1962), 65–83; Sherwood L. Washburn, ed., *Social Life of Early Man* (Chicago: Quadrangle Books, 1961); James Spuhler, ed., *The Evolution of Man's Capacity for Culture* (Detroit: Wayne State University Press, 1959); Melville J. Herskovitz, "Domestication," *Encyclopedia of the Social Sciences* 5 (1937): 206–8; Michael Banton, *Racial Theories* (New York: Cambridge University Press, 1987).

2. Montagu, "The Socio-Biology of Man"; Washburn, *Social Life*.

3. R. A. Fisher, *The Genetical Theory of Natural Selection* (Oxford: Clarendon Press, 1930), 174.

4. See Leo Lowenthal and Norbert Guterman, *Prophets of Deceit* (New York: Harper, 1949).

5. James Cook, *The Segregationists* (New York: Appleton-Century-Crofts, 1962); Benjamin Epstein and Arnold Forster, *The Troublemakers* (New York: Doubleday, 1952); B. Epstein and A. Forster, *The Radical Right* (New York: Random House, 1956); Neil McMillen, *The Citizens' Council: Organized Resistance to the Second Reconstruction, 1954–1964* (Urbana: University of Illinois Press, 1991); Gertrude Selznick and Stephen Steinberg, *The Tenacity of Prejudice* (New York: Harper & Row, 1969); A. Forster and B. Epstein, *Danger on the Right* (New York: Random House, 1964).

6. For an analysis of the problem of prejudice and discrimination, and a program of investigation and strategy, see Robert M. MacIver, *The More Perfect Union* (New York: Macmillan, 1948); also, Donald Young, "Techniques of Race Relations," *Proceedings of the American Philosophical Society* 91 (1947): 150–61; Gordon Allport, "Controlling Group Prejudice," *Annals,* American Academy of Political and Social Science (1946): 1–240, 244; Gordon Allport, *The Nature of Prejudice* (Cambridge, MA: Addison Wesley, 1953) and *Personality and the Social Encounter* (Boston: Beacon Press, 1960); Joseph B. Gittler, ed., *Understanding Minority Groups* (New York: Wiley, 1956); Philip Mason, *An Essay on Racial Tension* (London: Royal Institute of National Affairs, 1954); Arnold M. Rose, ed., *Race Prejudice and Discrimination* (New York: Alfred A. Knopf, 1951); Jacob Javits, *Discrimination–U.S.A.* (New York: Harcourt Brace, 1960); J. Masuoka and Preston Valien, eds., *Race Relations* (Chapel Hill: University of North Carolina Press, 1961); Irwin Katz and Patricia Gurin, eds., *Race and the Social Sciences* (New York: Basic Books, 1969).

7. Manning Nash, "Race and the Ideology of Race," *Current Anthropology* 3 (1962): 285–88; J. W. Vander Zanden, "The Ideology of White Supremacy," *Journal of the History of Ideas* 20 (1959): 385–402.

8. Henry Wallace, *The Genetic Basis for Democracy* (New York: American Committee for Democracy and Intellectual Freedom, 1939), 7. See also Henry Wallace, "Racial Theories and the Genetic Basis for Democracy," *Science* 89 (1939), 140–43.

9. A. Montagu, "A Cursory Examination of the Relations between Physical and Social Anthropology," *American Journal of Physical Anthropology,* 26 (1940): 41–61; A. Montagu, "Physical Anthropology and Anatomy," *American Journal of Physical Anthropology* 28 (1941): 261–71; John Gillin, ed., *For a Science of Social Man;* A. Montagu, *Man in Process* (Cleveland and New York: World Publishing. 1961); A. Montagu, *The Biosocial Nature of Man* (New York: Grove Press, 1956); Allan Mazur and Leon Robertson, *Biology and Social Behavior* (New York: Free Press, 1972).

10. "Unwanted Heroes," *New Republic* 106 (1942), 655; Carey McWilliams, *Brothers Under the Skin*, revised (Boston: Little, Brown, 1964). It is sad to have to record the fact that in the third week of September 1944, the Fourth Filipino Inter-Community convention held at New City, California, adopted as two of its objectives "the abolition of discriminatory legislation against Filipinos" and "permanent post-war exile of all Japanese from California" (reported in the *Pacific Citizen*, Salt Lake City, Utah, 23 September 1944, 3–4). The Filipinos apparently regarded the Japanese as serious economic competitors, and desired to eliminate their "competition" by this means. In a period of high feeling there was also the motive of jumping on the bandwagon of the most vocal California "patriots." In addition we may perceive here the mechanism of response to frustration of low status position in the scapegoating of another (even if temporarily) low status group. See Horace Miner, *Timbuctoo* (Princeton: Princeton University Press, 1953), 254.

11. Kenneth Little, *Negroes in Britain* (London: Kegan Paul, 1948); Michael Banton, *White and Coloured* (London: Cape, 1959); Anthony Richmond, "Racial Relations in England," *Midwest Journal* 3 (1951): 1–13; A. Richmond, *The Colour Problem* (New York: Penguin Books, 1955); Sheila Patterson, *Dark Strangers* (London: Tavistock, 1963).

12. Anthony Richmond, "Memories of South Africa," *The Listener* 60 (1958), 736–39.

13. Graham Greene, "African Chequerboard," *The Listener* 74 (1965), 421–22.

14. Bruno Bettelheim and Morris Janowitz, *Dynamics of Prejudice* (New York: Harper, 1950), 169–86.

15. Kenneth Clark, *Prejudice and Your Child* (Boston: Beacon, 1955); Ashley Montagu, *On Being Human* (New York: Hawthorn Books, 1969); A. Montagu, *The Direction of Human Development*, revised (New York: Hawthorn Books, 1970); Helen H. Davidson, *Personality and Economic Background* (New York: King's Crown Press, 1943); A. Montagu, *Growing Young*, 2nd ed. (Westport, CT: Bergen & Garvey, 1989); Report of the Joint Commission on Mental Health in Children: *Crisis in Child Mental Health: Challenge for the 1970's* (New York: Harper & Row, 1970); Charles V. Willie, Bernard M. Kramer, and Bertram S. Brown, eds., *Racism and Mental Health* (Pittsburgh: University of Pittsburgh Press, 1973); Mary E. Goodman, *Race Awareness in Young Children* (New York: Collier Books, 1964); Alice Miller, *For Your Own Good: Hidden Cruelty in Child-Rearing and the Roots of Violence* (New York: Farrar, Straus & Giroux, 1982); Jean S. Phinney and Mary J. Rotheram, *Children's Ethnic Socialization* (Thousand Oaks, CA: Sage Publications, 1987); David Milner, *Children and Race* (Thousand Oaks, CA: Sage Publications, 1965); Darlene P. Hopson and Derek S. Hopson, *Different and Wonderful: Raising Black Children in a Race-Conscious Society* (Englewood Cliffs, NJ: Prentice-Hall 1990).

16. Sancton, "Trouble in Dixie," *New Republic* 108 (1943), 51.

17. Paul Good, "Blue Notes From Dixie," *The Nation* 203 (196), 570–75.

18. Clyde L. Menschreck, "Religion in the South: Problems and Promise," in *The South in Perspective*, ed. Francis B. Simkins (Farmville, VA: Longwood College, 1959), 84–89; Harry S. Ashmore, *Hearts and Minds: The Anatomy of Racism From Roosevelt to Reagan* (New York: McGraw-Hill, 1982); Charles E. Wynes, ed., *Forgotten Voices: Dissenting Voices in an Age of Conformity* (Baton Rouge: Louisiana State University Press, 1967).

19. F. L. Cross and E. A. Livingstone, eds. *The Oxford Dictionary of the Christian Church*, 2nd ed. (New York, Oxford University Press).

20. Leon Poliakov, *The History of Anti-Semitism*, 4 vols. (New York: Vanguard Press, 1973–1983).

21. Alan Davies, *Infected Christianity: A Study of Modern Racism* (Kingston and Montreal: McGill-Queen's University Press, 1988).

22. Round Table Magazine, April 1954; David S. Wyman, *The Abandonment of the Jews: America and the Holocaust 1941–1945* (New York: Pantheon Books, 1984).

23. Robert W. Ross, *So It Was True: The American Protestant Press and The Nazi Persecution of the Jews* (Minneapolis: University of Minnesota Press, 1980), 300–301.

24. Hannah Arendt, *Eichman in Jerusalem* (New York: Viking Press, 1963); H. Arendt, *The Origins of Totalitarianism* (New York: Harcourt, Brace, 1951); Hans Askenasy, *Hitler's Secret* (Laguna Beach, Van Dyke Drive, 1984); David Barnow and Gerrold Van Der Stroom, eds., *The Diary of Anne Frank* Critical Edition (New York: Doubleday, 1989); Ruth Bondy, *Elder of the Jews* (New York: Grove Press, 1989); Lucy Dawidowicz, *The War Against the Jews* (New York: Holt, Reinhart and Winston, 1975); Lucy Dawidowicz, *The Holocaust and the Historians* (Cambridge: Harvard University Press, 1981); Terrence Des Pres, *The Survivor* (New York: Oxford University Press, 1976); Leonard Dinnerstein, *American and the Survivors of the Holocaust* (New York: Columbia University Press, 1982); Lucjan Dobroszycki, ed., *The Chronicle of the Lodz Ghetto 1841–1944* (New Haven: Yale University Press, 1984); Vaffa Elliach, *Hasidic Tales of the Holocaust* (New York: Oxford University Press, 1982); Helen Epstein, *Children of the Holocaust* (New York: Putnam, 1979); Richard J. Evans, *Hitler's Shadow: West German Historians and the Attempt to Escape From the Nazi Past* (New York: Pantheon Books, 1989); Helen Fein, *Accounting For Genocide* (New York: Free Press, 1979); Gerald Fleming, *Hitler and the Final Solution* (Berkeley: University of California Press, 1982); Martin Gilbert, *The Holocaust: A History of the Jews of Europe During the Second World War* (New York: Holt, Rinehart & Winston, 1986); Anton Gill, *The Journey Back From Hell* (New York: William Morrow, 1989); Leonard Gross, *The Last Jews of Berlin* (New York: Simon & Schuster, 1982); Peter Hayes, *Lessons and Legacies: The Meaning of the Holocaust in a Changing World* (Evanston, IL: Northwestern University Press, 1991); Raul Hilberg, *The Destruction of the European Jews*, 2nd ed. (New York: Holms & Meyer 1985); Jacob Katz, *From Prejudice to Destruction* (Cambridge: Harvard University Press, 1980); Hanna Krall, *Shielding the Flame* (New York: Henry Holt, 1986); Leo Kuper, *Genocide: Its Political Use in the Twentieth Century* (New Haven: Yale University Press, 1982); Leo Kuper, *The Prevention of Genocide* (New Haven: Yale University Press, 1981); Nora Levin, *The Holocaust* (New York: Crowell, 1968); Alfred D. Low, *Jews in the Eyes of the Germans: From the Enlightenment to Imperial Germany* (Philadelphia: Institute for the Study of Human Issues, 1979); Bert Mark, *Uprising in the Warsaw Ghetto* (New York: Schocken Books, 1975); Roger Maxwell and Heinrich Fraenkel, *The Incomparable Crime* (New York: Putnam, 1967); Judith Miller, *One, By One, By One: Facing the Holocaust* (New York: Simon & Schuster, 1990); Sarah Moskovitz, *Love Despite Hate: Child Survivors of the Holocaust and Their Adult Lives* (New York: Schocken Books, 1983); Benno Muller-Hill, *Murderous Science: Elimination by Scientific Selection of Jew, Gypsies, and Others, Germany 1953* (New York: Oxford University Press, 1988); Samuel Pisar, *Of Blood and Hope* (Boston: Little, Brown, 1980); Emanuel Ringelblum, *Notes From the Warsaw Ghetto* (New York:

McGraw-Hill, 1952); Alvin H. Rosenfeld, *A Double Dying: Reflections on Holocaust Literature* (Bloomington: University of Indiana Press, 1980); Alvin Rosenfeld and Irving Greenberg, eds., *Confronting the Holocaust: The Impact of Elie Wiesel* (Bloomington: University of Indiana Press, 1978); Michael Selzer, *Deliverance: The Last Days at Dachau* (Philadelphia: Lippincott, 1978); Jurgen Stroop, *The Stroop Report (The Official Nazi Report on the Destruction of the Warsaw Ghetto)* (New York: Pantheon Books, 1979); Rita Thalmann and Emanual Feinermann, *Crystal Night* (New York: Columbia University Press, 1971); Leonard Tusnet, *The Uses of Adversity* (South Brunswick: Thoman Yoseloff, 1966); Susan Zuccotti, *The Holocaust, the French, and the Jews* (New York; Basic Books, 1993).

25. Leon Wieseltier, "History and the Holocaust," *The Times Literary Supplement*, 25 February 1977, 220–221; see also Robert H. Abzug, *Inside the Vicious Heart* (New York: Oxford University Press, 1985); Omer Bartov, *Hitler's Army* (New York: Oxford University Press, 1992); Norbert Bromberg and Verna V. Small, *Hitler's Psychopathology* (New York: International Universities Press, 1983); Alan Bullock, *Hitler: A Study in Tyrany* (New York: Harper & Row, 1964); Robert Cecil, *The Myth of the Master Race: Alfred Rosenberg and Nazi Ideology* (New York: Dodd, Mead, 1972); Joan Coamy, *The Diaspora Story: The Epic of the Jewish People Among the Nations* (New York: Harper & Row, 1972); Charles B. Flood, *Hitler: The Path to Power* (Boston: Little, Brown, 1980); Karl Jaspers, *The Question of German Guilt* (New York: Dial Press, 1947); Sam Keen, *Faces of the Enemy* (New York: Harper & Row, 1986); Walter Laqueur, *The Terrible Secret: Suppression of the Truth About Hitler's Final Solution* (Boston: Little, Brown, 1980); Stein U. Larsen, Bernt Hagtvet, and Jan P. Myklebust, eds., *Who Were the Facists: Social Roots of European Fascism* (Bergen: Universitetsforlaget, 1980); Paul W. Massing, *Rehersal for Destruction: A Study of Political Anti-Semitism in Imperial Germany* (New York: Harper & Brothers, 1949); Paul R. Mendez-Flohr and Jehuda Reinharz, *The Jew in the Modern World: A Documentary History* (New York: Oxford University Press, 1980); Peter H. Merkl, *Political Violence Under the Swastika* (Princeton: Princeton University Press 1975); P. H. Merkl, *The Making of a Stormtrooper* (Princeton: Princeton University Press, 1980); Monty N. Penkower, *The Jews Were Expendable: Free World Diplomacy and the Holocaust* (Urbana: University of Illinois Press, 1984); William L. Shirer, *The Rise and Fall of the Third Reich: A History of Nazi Germany* (New York, 1960); Louis L. Snyder, *Encyclopedia of the Third Reich* (New York: McGraw-Hill, 1976); Hans Staudinger, *The Inner Nazi: A Critical Analysis of Mein Kampf* (Baton Rouge: Louisiana State University Press, 1981); Yavon Svoray and Nick Taylor, *In Hitler's Shadow* (New York: Doubleday, 1994); Peter Viereck, *Metapolitics: The Roots of the Nazi Mind* (New York: Capricorn Books, 1961); Binjamin Wilkomirski, *Fragments: Memories of a Wartime Childhood* (New York: Schocken Books, 1997).

26. Ashley Montagu, *On Being Human,* 2nd ed. (New York: Dutton, 1966); A. Montagu, *The Direction of Human Development,* 2nd ed. (New York: Hawthorn Books, 1970); M. A. R. Tuker, *Past and Future of Ethics* (London & New York: Oxford University Press, 1938). Tuker's book is certainly one of the most original and, probably, one of the best books of its kind ever written on the subject of human relations.

27. Bernard Wasserstein, *Britain and the Jews of Europe 1939–1945* (New York: Oxford University Press, 1979), 351; Leonard Dinnerstein, *America and the Survivors of the Holocaust* (New York: Columbia University Press, 1982); Martin Gilbert,

Auschwitz and the Allies (New York: Holt, Rinehart & Winston, 1981); Leo Goldberger, *The Rescue of the Danish Jews: Moral Courage Under Stress* (New York: New York University Press, 1987); William R. Perl, *The Four Front War: From the Holocaust to the Promised Land* (New York: Crown, 1978). Perl's fascinating and revelatory book is one of the most important accounts of the connivance of the British and other governments to prevent the entrance of refugees in flight from Hitler into Palestine. See also David S. Wyman, *Paper Walls: America and the Refugee Crisis 1938–1941* (New York: Pantheon, 1968); D. S. Wyman, *Abandonment of the Jews* (New York: Pantheon, 1984); Yitzhak Zuckerman, *A Surplus of Memory: Chronicle of the Warsaw Uprising* (Berkeley: University of California Press, 1993). This is the story, told in his own words, of one of the great heroes of history.

28. Ashley Montagu, *The Humanization of Man* (New York: World Publishing, 1962); A. Montagu and Floyd Matson, *The Dehumanization of Man* (New York: McGraw-Hill, 1983); A. Montagu, *On Being Human* (New York: Henry Schuman, 1950); Henry L. Feingold, *The Politics of Rescue* (New Brunswick: Rutgers University Press, 1970); Saul S. Friedman, *No Haven For the Oppressed* (Detroit: Wayne State University Press, 1973); Arthur D. Morse, *While Six Million Die: A Chronicle of American Apathy* (New York: Random House, 1967).

29. Robert Conquest, *The Great Terror* (New York: Viking, 1990); R. Conquest, *Stalin: Breaker of Nations* (New York: Viking, 1991).

30. Tibor Szamuely, "Jews in Russia: The Semi-Final Solution," *The Spectator,* 11 August 1969, 153–54.

31. John and Carol E. Garrard, "Glasnost Byproduct: Virulent Anti-Semitism," *The New York Times,* 27 May 1990; Irina Ginsburg, "We Russian Jews Fear for Our Lives," *The New York Times,* 5 May 1990.

32. Lewis Sowden, *The Union of South Africa* (New York: Doubleday, Doran, 1943), 216. See also John Burger, *The Black Man's Burden* (London: Gollancz, 1943); Russell, *Colour, Race and Empire* (London: Gollancz, 1944); Henry Gibbs, *Twilight in South Africa* (New York: Philosophical Library, 1950); Adamastor, *White Man Boss* (Boston: Beacon Press, 1951); Wulf Sachs, *Black Anger* (Boston: Little, Brown, 1947); "South Africa," *Time* 59 (1952), 32–38; "America and the Challenge of Africa," *Saturday Review* 36 (1953), 9–29; Patrick Van Rensburg, *Guilty Land: The History of Apartheid* (New York: Praeger, 1962); Muriel Horrell, *A Survey of Race Relations in South Africa* (Johannesburg: South African Institute of Race Relations, 1962); Norman Phillips, *The Tragedy of Apartheid* (New York: McKay, 1960); Peter Ritner, *The Death of Africa* (New York: MacMillan, 1960); Alfred Lowenstein, *Brutal Mandate* (New York: MacMillan, 1962); Leo Kuper, Hilstan Watts, and Ronald Davies, *Durban: A Study in Racial Ecology* (New York: Columbia University Press, 1958); T. Dunbar Moodie, *The Rise of Afrikanerdom* (Berkeley: University of California Press, 1975); Leonard Thompson and Jeffrey Butler, eds., *Change in Contemporary South Africa* (Berkeley & Los Angeles: University of California Press, 1975); Joseph Llelyveld, *Move Your Shadow* (New York: Basic Books, 1995).

33. T. C. Robertson, "Racism Comes to Power in South Africa," *Commentary* 6 (1948), 428; Herbert Adam, *Modernizing Racial Domination* (Berkeley: University of California Press, 1971); Douglas Brown, *Against The World* (New York: Doubleday, 1968); William A. Hance, ed., *Southern Africa and the United States* (New York; Columbia University Press, 1968); Jim Hoagland, *South Africa: Civilizations in Conflict*

(Boston: Houghton Mifflin, 1972); Trevor Huddleston, *Nought For Your Comfort* (New York: Doubleday, 1956); E. J. Kahn, Jr., *The Separated People* (New York: Ungar, 1967); Lowenstein, *Brutal Mandate;* Naboth Mokgatle, *The Autobiography of an Unknown South African* (Berkeley: University of California Press, 1971); Edward Roux, *Time Longer Than Rope: A History of the Black Man's Struggle for Freedom in Africa* (Madison: University of Wisconson Press, 1976); Benjamin Sacks, *South Africa: An Imperial Dilemma* (Albuquerque: University of New Mexico Press, 1967); Donald G. Mathews, *Law, Order and Liberty in South Africa* (Princeton: Princeton University Press, 1965); UNESCO, *Apartheid* (New York: Unipub., 1969); Pierre L. Van den Berghe, *South Africa: A Study in Conflict* (Middletown, CT: Wesleyan University Press, 1965); Albie Sachs, *Justice in South Africa* (Berkeley: University of California Press, 1973).

34. "Light from darkness," of course, means "white from black." See also Cross and Livingstone, eds., *Oxford Dictionary of the Christian Church.*

35. *Round Table Magazine,* April 1954.

36. Z. K. Matthews, "The Black Man's Outlook," *Saturday Review* 36 (2 May 1953) 13–14, 41–52; Alex La Guma, ed., *Apartheid: A Collection of Writings on South African Racism,* (New York: International Publishers, 1972); Robert W. Peterson, ed., *South Africa and Apartheid* (New York: Facts on File, 1975); UNESCO, *Apartheid: Its Affects on Education, Science, Culture, and Information,* 2nd ed. (New York: Unipub., 1972); William R. Frye, *In Whitest Africa: The Dynamics of Apartheid* (Englewood Cliffs, NJ: Prentice Hall; 1975); David Mermelstein, ed., *The Anti-Apartheid Reader: South Africa and the Struggle Against White Racist Rule* (New York: Grove Press, 1987); Nic Rhoodie, ed., *South African Dialogue: Contrasts in South African Thinking on Basic Race Issue* (Philadelphia: Westminster Press, 1972); John A. Marcum, *Education, Race, and Social Change in South Africa* (Berkeley: University of California Press, 1981); Leonard Thompson and Jeffery Butler, eds., *Change in Contemporary South Africa;* Leonard Thompson, *The Political Mythology of Apartheid* (New Haven: Yale University Press, 1985); Joseph Lelyveld, *Move Your Shadow: South Africa: Black and White* (New York: Time Books, 1985); Robert W. July, *A History of the African People,* 2nd ed. (New York: Charles Scribners, 1971); Robert Ross, *Cape of Torments: Slavery and Resistance in South Africa* (Boston: Routledge & Kegan Paul, 1983); Margo & Martin Russell, *Afrikaners of the Kalahari* (New York: Cambridge University Press, 1979); V. A. February, *Mind Your Colour: The Coloured Stereotype in South African Literature* (Boston: Kegan Paul, 1981).

37. Bernard Sachs, "South Africa: Life on a Volcano," *Commentary* 9 (1950), 536. For a full account of race problems in South Africa see Ellen Hellman and Leah Abrahams, *Handbook on Race Relations in South Africa* (London: Oxford University Press, 1949). See also John Laurence, *Seeds of Disaster* (London: Gollancz, 1968); Vincent Crapanzano, *Waiting: The Whites of South Africa* (New York: Random House, 1985).

38. Quoted in D. M. Paton, ed., *Church and Race in South Africa* (London: Student Christian Movement Press, 1958).

39. Stanley Meisler, "Our Stake in Apartheid," *The Nation* 201 (August 16, 1965), 71–73; B. Lapping, *Apartheid: A History* (London: Grafton, 1986); M. Meredith, *In the Name of Apartheid* (London: Hamilton, 1988); L. Thompson, *Political Mythology of Apartheid* (New Haven: Yale University Press, 1985); N. Worden, *Making of Modern South Africa* (Oxford and Cambridge MA: Blackwell, 1993).

40. Patti Waldmeir, *Anatomy of a Miracle: the End of Apartheid and the Birth of the New South Africa* (New York: W. W. Norton, 1997); Crocker, Chester A, *High Noon in Southern Africa: Making Peace in a Rough Neighborhood* (New York: W. W. Norton, 1992).

41. Lawrence Fellows, "Labourites Slate a Racial Inquiry," *New York Times* 17 October 1964, 9. "Tears streamed down the face of Mr. Gordon Walker last night when the election result was announced. 'This was the dirtiest election I ever fought,' he said."

42. Ibid. See also David Watt, "Colour and the Election," *The Spectator,* 28 August 1964, 261–62; Nicholas Deakin, *Colour and the British Electorate* (London: Pall Mall, 1965).

43. Robert K. Merton, "Social Structure and Anomie," *American Sociological Review* 3 (1938), 680. See also Edwaard McDill, "Anomie, Authoritarianism, Prejudice, and Socio-Economic Status: An Attempt at Clarification," *Social Forces* 39 (1961), 239–45.

44. For a development of the frustration-aggression hypothesis, see John Dollard et al., *Frustration and Aggression.* See also Leonard Berkowitz, *Aggression: A Social Psychological Analysis;* L. Berkowitz, ed., *Roots of Aggression* (New York: Atherton Press, 1969); E. F. M. Durbin and John Bowlby, *Personal Aggressiveness and War* (New York: Columbia University Press, 1939); Albert Bandura, *Aggression: A Social Learning Analysis* (Englewood Cliffs, NJ: Prentice-Hall, 1973).

45. Arthur Richmond, "Economic Insecurity and Stereotypes as Factors in Colour Prejudice," *Sociological Review,* 42 (1950), 147–70. See also Edward L. Ayers, *The Promise of the New South: Life After Reconstruction* (New York: Oxford University Press, 1991); Christopher Bagley and Gajendra K. Verma, *Racial Prejudice, the Individual and Society* (Lexington, MA: D.C. Heath, 1979); Rae Sherwood, *The Psychodynamics of Race* (Atlantic Highlands, NJ: Humanities Press, 1980); Gerald D. Berreman, *Social Inequality* (New York: Academic Press, 1978); T. A. Van Dijk, *Communicating Racism: Ethnic Prejudice in Thought and Race* (Thousand Oaks, CA: Sage Publications, 1987); Dorothy K. Newman, et al., Protest, Politics, and Prosperity (New York: Pantheon, 1978); Stephen Steinberg, *Turning Back: The Retreat from Racial Justice in American Thought and Policy* (Boston: Beacon Press, 1995); Richard L. Zweigenhaft and William Domhoff, *Blacks in the White Establishment* (New Haven, Yale University Press, 1991).

46. Sigmund Freud, *The Future of an Illusion* (London: Hogarth Press, 1928), 27.

47. John Dollard, "Hostility and Fear in Social Life," *Social Forces* 17 (1938), 15–26.

48. For an able analysis of the problem in California see McWilliams, *Brothers Under the Skin,* 147–75, and the same author's *Prejudice—the Japanese Americans: Symbols of Racial Intolerance* (Boston: Little, Brown, 1944); William Petersen, *Japanese Americans: Oppression and Success* (Washington, D.C.: Washington University Press, 1971).

49. For an objective account of conditions in these camps as experienced by internees see Mine Okubo, *Citizen 13660* (New York: Columbia University Press, 1925); Charles Kikuchi, *The Kikuchi Diary: Chronicle from an American Concentration Camp,* edited and with an introduction by David Modell (Urbana: University of

Illinois Press, 1992). The detailed story of the Japanese American evacuation is authoritatively told in Milton M. Grodzins' *Americans Betrayed* (Chicago: University of Chicago Press, 1949), and in Audrie Girdner and Anne Loftis, *The Great Betrayal* (New York: Macmillan, 1960). The socio-economic consequences are dealt with by Leonard Bloom and Ruth Riemer in their book *Removal and Return* (Berkeley: University of California Press, 1949); the social and psychological consequences by Dorothy Thomas and Richard S. Nishimoto, *The Spoilage* (Berkeley: University of California Press, 1946), George Jean Oishi, "The Anxiety of Being a Japanese American," *New York Times Magazine*, 28 April 1985, 54; and Alexander Leighton, *The Governing of Men* (Princeton: Princeton University Press,1945). For an account by four anthropologists who shared in the task of administering the camps see Edward Spicer et al., *Impounded People* (Tucson: University of Arizona Press, 1969).

50. In November 1946, the Privy Council of the government of England, the British Empire's highest court of appeals, upheld Canadian legislation forcing the deportation of citizens and resident aliens of Japanese ancestry. In short, the representatives of the British Empire ruled that a person's citizenship in one of its dominions may be revoked and that person exiled for no other reason than race. Against this may be set the achievement of the voters of Saskatchewan, Canada, who, on 1 May 1947, made it a punishable offense by law for anyone to infringe the right of any person "to obtain and retain employment; engage in business; own and occupy property; have access to public places, hotels, theaters, restaurants; to membership in professional and trade organizations; education and enrollment in schools and universities." Saskatchewan is the only Canadian province which has a Cooperative Commonwealth Federation government. Nevertheless the government of Canada made it very comfortable for Nazi war criminals to settle in Canada for the rest of their lives, with one deportation only, even though these murderers were receiving their pension checks regularly from the German government.

51. "Survey of the National Opinion Research Center of the University of Denver," *Pacific Citizen*, 21 (31 August 1946), 3.

52. For a full account see Frank F. Chuman, *The Bamboo People: The Law and Japanese Americans* (Del Mar, CA: Publishers Inc., 1976).

53. For further on this grim subject, see the comments of Senator Ted Stevens (R-Alaska) and Representative Don Young (R-Alaska), and editorial, "Aleuts WWII Tragedy," *Indian Affairs* 102, March 1981, 4.

54. See Michael Selzer, ed., *"Kike!"* (New York: World Publishing Co., 1972); Chang-Tsu Wu, *"Chink!"* (New York: World Publishing Co., 1972); Jay David and Elaine Crane, eds., *Living Black in White America* (New York: William Morrow, 1972); Norman Coombs, *The Black Experience in America* (New York: Twayne, 1972); William Brink and Louis Harris, *Black and White: A Study in U.S. Racial Attitudes Today* (New York: Simon & Schuster, 1967); H. Brett Melendy, *The Oriental Americans* (New York: Twayne, 1972); Leo Grebler, Joan Moore and Ralph Guzman, *The Mexican-American People* (New York: Macmillan, 1970); Matt S. Meier and Feliciano Rivera, *The Chicanos: A History of Mexican Americans* (New York: Hill & Wang, 1972); William Powell, *Tree of Hate: Propaganda and Prejudices Affecting United States Relations With the Hispanic World* (New York: Basic Books, 1971); Wayne Moquin and Charles van Doren, eds., *A Documentary History of the Mexican Americans* (New York: Praeger, 1973); Stan Steiner, *La Raza: The Mexican Americans* (New York: Harper & Row, 1970); William

G. Shade and Roy C. Herrenkohl, eds., *Seven on Black: Reflections on the Negro Experience in America* (Philadelphia: Lippincott, 1969).

55. Edward Reuter, "Competition and the Racial Division of Labor," in *Race Relations and the Race Problem,* ed. Edgar Thompson (Durham: Duke University Press, 1939), 49.

56. For a discussion of the facts and also for the necessary recommendations see Bruno Bettelheim and Morris Janowitz, *Dynamics of Prejudice* (New York: Harper, 1950), 174 et seq.; Robert M. MacIver, *The More Perfect Union* (New York: Macmillan, 1948); R. M. MacIver, ed., *Unity and Difference in American Life* (New York: Harper, 1947); Arnold Rose and Carolyn Rose, *America Divided* (New York: Alfred A. Knopf, 1948); David Spitz, *Patterns of Anti-Democratic Thought* (New York: Macmillan, 1949); Gerhart Saenger, *The Social Psychology of Prejudice* (New York: Harper, 1953); Andrew Lind, ed., *Race Relations in World Perspective* (Honolulu: University of Hawaii Press, 1955); Karl W. Bigelow, ed., *Cultural Groups and Human Relations* (New York: Columbia University Press, 1951); Muzafer Sherif and Carolyn Sherif, *Groups in Harmony and Tension* (New York: Harper, 1953); Stewart G. Cole and Mildred Wise Cole, *Minorities and the American Promise* (New York: Harper, 1953); Lillian Smith, *Now Is the Time* (New York: Viking, 1955); Philip Mason, *Common Sense About Race* (New York: Macmillan, 1961); Alfred J. Marrow, *Changing Patterns of Prejudice* (New York: Chilton, 1962); Melvin Conant, ed., *Race Issues on the World Scene* (Honolulu: University of Hawaii Press, 1955); George Abernethy, ed., *The Idea of Equality* (Richmond: John Knox Press, 1959); Paul Ramsey, *Christian Ethics and the Sit-In* (New York: Association Press, 1961); C. E. Silberman, *Crisis in Black and White* (New York: Random House, 1964); B. Brandt, ed., *Social Justice* (Englewood Cliffs, NJ: Prentice-Hall, 1962); Edward Budd, *Inequality and Poverty* (New York: W. W. Norton, 1966); Maurice Cranston, *Freedom* (New York: Basic Books, 1967); Frank Gell, *The Black Badge: Confessions of a Case Worker* (New York: Harper & Row, 1969); Alan Grimes, *Equality in America* (New York: Oxford University Press, 1964).

9

Psychological Factors

At this stage of our discussion I wish to focus attention on the general factor which is too frequently overlooked in discussions of the race problem. This is the factor of the normal psychological and psychophysical traits of the person—traits which are utilized in the generation of racial enmities and which have already been touched upon in the preceding chapter.

The one thing clear concerning racial hostility and prejudice is the ease with which persons are led to exhibit it. There are few persons in our society who have not, at one time or another, exhibited race prejudice. It would seem clear that most persons are capable of being brought to a state of mind in which they are glad of the opportunity of freely releasing their feelings against some group or person representing such a group. When society as a whole sanctions such provocations against any group, the free exercise of racial intolerance is enjoyed as a release for feelings that are ever ready to find expression. It is in the nature of such feelings—the nature of which we shall presently discuss—that they can be suitably directed against some person or particular group of persons, and it is for this reason that they can be so easily directed to the support and maintenance of race prejudices. People exhibit race prejudice because it affords them a means of easing certain tensions within themselves; because their tensions are reduced when they are most freely able to discharge those tensions. As far as the individual is concerned, the prejudice itself is unimportant, it merely provides the channel through which feelings are permitted necessary expression. Such feelings should, and for the sake of the health of the individual must, find expression. As I have already said, feelings will attach themselves to the most suitable object offered—whatever it may be. Such feelings are not feelings of race prejudice or any other kind of prejudice; and they are not inborn. On the contrary, such feelings are to a large extent generated during the early childhood development of almost every person. There can, however, be little doubt that the elementary forms of these affective states in their undifferentiated states are physiologically determined.[1] The

225

manner in which such feelings are generated has been discussed in great detail by psychoanalysts and others.[2]

The aggressiveness that adults exhibit in the form of race prejudice would appear to have universally the same origin. That is to say, the aggressiveness, not the race hatred, has the same origin universally and that aggressiveness is merely arbitrarily directed, in some societies, against certain groups. Under other conditions, this same aggressiveness could be directed against numerous different objects, either real or imagined. The object against which aggressiveness is directed is determined by particular conditions, and these we shall later briefly consider. If in racial intolerance and prejudice a certain amount of aggressiveness is always displayed, we must ask and answer two questions: (1) where does this aggressiveness originate, and (2) why is it exhibited? Briefly, a considerable amount of the aggressiveness adults exhibit is originally produced during childhood by parents, nurses, teachers, or whoever else participates in the process of socializing the child. By depriving the infant, and later the child, of the many means of satisfaction which it seeks—the breast, the mother's body, uncontrolled freedom to excrete and to suck, the freedom to cry at will, to stay up late, to do the thousand-and-one things that are forbidden—expected satisfactions are thwarted and frustration upon frustration is piled up within the child. Such frustrations lead to resentment, to fear, to insecurity, to hostility, and to aggressiveness. In childhood this aggressiveness or resentment is displayed in "bad temper" and in general "naughtiness." Such conduct almost invariably results in further frustration—in punishment. At this stage of his development the child finds himself in a state of severe conflict. He must either control the expression of his aggressiveness or else suffer the punishment and loss of love which his aggressiveness provokes. Such conflicts are usually resolved by excluding the painful situation from consciousness and direct motor expression—in short, by the repression of one's aggressive energies. These are rarely completely repressed, but only in so far as they permit a resolution of the original conflict situation, and the further the original derivatives of what was primarily repressed become detached from the latter, the more freely do these energies gain access to consciousness and the more available for use do they become.[3] The evidence renders it overwhelmingly clear that these energies are never to any extent destroyed or exhausted. As a part of the functioning total organism, they must, in one way or another, find expression, and the ways in which they can find expression are innumerable. Race hatred and prejudice merely represent familiar patterns of the manner in which aggressiveness may later express itself.[4]

Fear of those who have frustrated one in childhood and anxiety concerning the outcome of the situation thus produced leads to the repression of aggression against the original frustrators and thereby to the conditioning of an emotional association between certain kinds of frustrative or fear situations and aggressive feelings. As a result of such conditioning, any object even remotely suggesting such fear or frustrative situations provokes the aggressive behavior with which such fears and frustrations have become associated.

The aggressiveness, more or less common to most human beings, is not a cause of race prejudice, but merely represents an expression, a motive force or affective energy that can be attached, among other things, to the notion that other groups or races are hateful and may thus serve to keep such ideas supplied with the emotional force necessary to keep them going. Under such conditions race becomes important, not as a biological description or ethnic classification but as a means of projecting an unconscious conflict.

Since the infliction of mental, and even physical, pain, as well as the frustration and depreciation of others, is involved in the process of race prejudice, and since much of the aggressiveness of the individual owes its existence to early experiences of a similar kind, it is perhaps not difficult to understand why it is that so many persons are so ready to participate in the exercise of race prejudice. By so doing they are able to find an object for their aggressiveness which most satisfactorily permits the free expression of it by means almost identically resembling those which in childhood were indulged in against them. In this way the individual is enabled, as an adult, to pay off—quite unconsciously—an old score of childhood frustration. The later appreciable frustrations suffered in adolescence and adult life naturally add to the store and complexity of aggressiveness, and require no discussion here. At this point reference should be made to such important psychological mechanisms as "displacement," which defines the process whereby aggression is displaced from one object to another, and "projection," the process of attributing to others feelings and impulses originating in ourselves which have been refused conscious recognition.

When the release of aggression toward certain objects or agents is socially interdicted or otherwise made difficult, as in the case of parents, teachers, or employers, aggressiveness may then be displaced toward some more accessible target. The government, blacks, Jews, Catholics, foreigners and the like, will conveniently serve as such targets, and where such displacement of aggression occurs the object of it becomes the scapegoat. Collective displacement of this sort is a well-known phenomenon. Both on the individual and on the group level, forbidden thoughts and aggressions are by such means turned into socially acceptable activities. Humans in search of a target readily utilize social tension for the displacement of personal tension.[5] Since the displacement occurs from what is forbidden to that which is not, it would be a psychologically sound procedure to make the socially acceptable in this case socially unacceptable in demonstrable form such as by legal fiat. For the displacers displace because they are, among other things, great respecters of authority, and will displace their aggression only where it is socially permissible. This analysis is fully supported by a number of clinical studies which were instituted in order to discover what kind of persons adopt and become active carriers of antisemitic ideas, why they so readily become "scapegoat-addicts," and what function, if any, antisemitism serves in their personality structure.[6] A group of approximately 100 state university students, 76 of them women, provided the material for this study. Subjects giving evidence of a high degree of antisemitism were classified as "high extremes," those showing the contrary tendency were classified as "low extremes," and those with in-between attitudes, as "intermediate."

The high extremes were conservative in their attitudes, automatically tending to support the status quo; they were generally Republicans, although they showed few signs of having developed an organized social-political outlook; and there was a tendency to hold their own ethnic or social group in high esteem, to keep it unmixed and pure, and to reject everything that differed from it. The fathers' income was higher than that of the fathers of the average intermediate or low-extreme subjects, and the high-extreme girls appeared to be well groomed, very different from that of the low-extreme girls (almost all subjects were members of the middle class). On the surface these antisemitic girls appeared composed and untroubled. They seemed to have little familiarity with their inner lives, but were characterized rather by a generally externalized orientation. They were sensitive to any encroachment from the outside. On the surface they showed an uncritical devotion and obedience to their parents, and to authority in general. They were mostly interested in social standing, and in making an appropriate marriage.

The low extremes, on all these points, contrasted strongly with the high extremes, being nondescript in appearance, less at ease socially, possessed of varied interests, quite willing to talk about themselves and their situations, and able to make critical appraisals of their parents.

Examination of the results of tests and interviews revealed the fact that the high extremes were markedly characterized by unconscious aggressive drives of a destructive nature, the repression of basic impulses, ambivalent attitudes of love and hate toward their parents, basic insecurity. Both sexes in the high-extreme group tended to be intellectually underproductive, somewhat lower in intelligence, and lacking in creative imagination. They were less interested in human beings as individuals, and tended to be more hypochondriacal.

"The analysis of the content of their responses suggests that the adoption of an aggressive attitude towards outgroups may stem from frustrations received (mainly at the hands of the mother-figure) in childhood"—frustrations which appeared to have produced definite inferiority feelings.

The rigidity with which the high-extreme girl adhered to her conventional values or stereotypes of behavior and the anxiety which she exhibited in the presence of opposite tendencies afforded the clue to the sources of her behavior. Insecurity was the condition with which such girls were struggling. "The fear of losing status is associated with the fear that they will be tempted to release their inhibited tendencies in the way they believe Jews and proletarians do." Anti-semitism thus helps them to maintain their identification with the middle class and to ward off anxiety.

"Thus," the authors of this enlightening study go on to say,

> it is not so much middle class values themselves that we would call into question, but rather the rigidity with which they are adhered to. And in the individual case this appears to be the result of the manner in which they have been put across. The mischief is done when those trends which are taboo according to the class standards become repressed, and hence, no longer susceptible to modification or control. This is most likely to happen when parents are too concerned and too insistent with respect to their positive aims for the child and too threatening and coercive with respect to the 'bad' things. The child is thus taught to view behavior in terms of black and white, 'good' and 'evil'; and the 'evil' is made to appear so terrible that he cannot think of it as something in himself which needs to be modified or controlled, but as something that exists in other 'bad' people and needs to be stamped out completely.[7]

Parent-child relationships clearly need to undergo a substantial change in the direction of greater understanding and sympathy on the part of parents, in the dropping of "either-or" attitudes, for disjunctive commands give rise to disjunctive personalities. As Frenkel-Brunswik and Sanford say, if the kind of repression which they have uncovered in their high-extreme girls, and its consequences, are to be prevented, "there must be less fear of impulses on the part of parents. The parental attitude toward children must be more tolerant and permissive. Parents must learn that 'bad' impulses can be modified and controlled and that it is of crucial importance to invite the child's participation in these processes."[8] Parents must learn how to give their children the maximum degree of security consonant with the ideal of a socially fully integrated personality. Parents must develop a greater interest in the significance of the whole socialization process. In this task teachers must play almost as large a part as parents.[9]

Ackerman and Jahoda have made available the results of a study calculated to reveal the dynamic basis of antisemitic attitudes in a number of persons who have experienced psychoanalytic therapy. The material was collected from some thirty accredited psychoanalysts, and the conclusions both enlarge and confirm those of Frenkel-Brunswik and Sanford as well as those of other investigators.

Two extreme categories of anti-Semitic types were theoretically set up by the authors. The one is the antisemite whose attitude seems to be one of superficial conformity to the values, in this respect, of the dominant group; the other is the antisemite whose hostility derives from some definite disorder in his own personality structure to which his antisemitism has a specific relation. All the cases encountered fell between the two extremes, presenting both elements in varying proportions.

All these individuals suffered from anxiety. They were insecure in their group membership. They had a basic feeling of rejection by the world, a feeling of not belonging. They failed to form safe and secure personal attachments. They felt a continuous apprehension of injury to their integrity as individuals. They frequently suffered from an exaggerated sense of vulnerability. They did not seem able to derive support from their own identity as persons. Because of their insecurity, their confused and unstable image of themselves, they lacked direction and made erratic shifts in their group associations. Fundamentally they were weak, immature, passive, dependent, with the desire to control unrealized in the normal channels of constructive action. They endeavored to deny to consciousness the image of themselves as inferior and crippled.

> Overtly they have the urge to conform but unconsciously they resent the compulsory submission and react with destructive rebellion. At the unconscious level they have no hope of being able to repair their damaged identity as persons; basically they accept it as irreversible. However, this basic despair is concealed from consciousness, where they behave in exactly the opposite manner. The core of these character traits is the weak identity, the immaturity, the unconscious passivity, the intense sense of vulnerability to social injury—all of which are denied in consciousness where they are replaced by aggression.[10]

In relation to such a syndrome antisemitism plays a functionally well-defined role. It is a defense against self-hate, a displacement of the self-destroying trends of the character structure described. At the psychic level antisemitism assumes the function of a profound though irrational effort to restore the crippled self, and at the social level it constitutes a pattern producing secondary emotional gain. Were the antisemite to permit his internal conflict, between what he is unconsciously and what he thinks of himself as being consciously, to proceed to its logical conclusion, he would find the consequences unbearable. And so he escapes the dilemma by preoccupation with external events, thus achieving a spurious relief from tensions and the bogus satisfaction of being a member of a powerful, united group, an ingroup in whose program of action he can join. Nevertheless, the central conflict continues with unabated intensity.

To summarize: The prejudice pattern is created through the mobilization of the following series of mechanisms: *(a)* by denial of anxiety and substitution of aggression, *(b)* by an effort to reinforce affiliation with dominant social groups, *(c)* by the elaboration of a variety of reaction formations and compensatory emotional drives, and *(d)* by renunciation of parts of the person's image of self and the concomitant substitution of a borrowed identity. Associated with this there is a suppression and repression of anxiety-ridden impulses.

> Having submissively renounced parts of their own individuality they feel deep resentment against any one who does not do likewise. They demand that other people should conform to the same restrictions. The demand for conformity is thus a result of partial self-renunciation. The person who is forced to renounce his real self as the price of social acceptance is doubly sensitive to others who do not conform. Here lies the root of the excessive reaction to difference which characterizes our antisemitic patients. Every sign of nonconformity in another person is, as it were, an unwelcome reminder of the painful sacrifice that the prejudiced person has made by renouncing part of his self in the vain hope of achieving group identification. The fear of the 'different' is hence not in proportion to the extent of objective, measurable differences; rather it grows in proportion to the implied ego threat, in other words, to the degree to which the difference symbolizes the fruitless suppression of the self. All prejudiced people insist on conformity to the extent of trying to destroy the nonconformist. Since conformity denotes surrender of the individuality, a person who is 'different' symbolizes nonsurrender, and therefore, an individual who is strong, mature, independent, superior, able to stand up against others with his differences. The prejudiced person cannot bear the implied comparison. Because of the inherent weakness of his own self-image, the 'different' person represents a potential menace to his own integrity as an individual or whatever there is left of it. The inevitable response is to attack the menace, the person who symbolizes the difference.[11]

The elaborated and inconsistent picture of the stereotype Jew forms a perfect projective screen for the antisemite's irreconcilable impulses. The Jew is at once successful and low class; capitalist and communist; clannish, and an intruder into other people's society; highly moral, spiritual, and given to low forms of behavior such as greed, sharp business practices, and dirt; magically omnipotent and omniscient, and incredibly helpless and defenseless and therefore readily destroyed.

What any individual projects upon the Jew invariably represents unacceptable components of the self or components envied in others, at least unacceptable on the conscious level though unconsciously such attributes form an active part of the person's psychic drives.[12] Hence, the object which is consciously rejected, the Jew, may, at the unconscious level, be represented by a strong identification with him. This identification, because of the symbolic aspect of the Jew's weakness, his crippled, defenseless position, cannot be admitted, because to do so would be to endanger one's ego and social position. It is therefore denied and in its place there is substituted an identification with the attacker, in order to avoid being victimized and also to draw strength through identification. "Thus the Jew at one and the same time stands for the weakness or strength of the self; for conscience, for those parts of the person which blame and accuse the weakness of the self, and also for those primitive appetites and aggressions which must be denied as the price of social acceptance."[13]

It may be objected that inferences based on data obtained from patients who have been psychoanalytically treated cannot be justly applied to the analysis of the behavior of normal persons. To this objection several replies may be made. First, it is doubtful whether normal individuals are ever antisemitic in the disordered sense here described, and since a large proportion of persons give evidence of disordered character structure it is likely that the observations made and the conclusions drawn from them are valid for a great segment of the population of antisemites. Second, the inability to pay the fees of a psychotherapist is no mark of normality; and, third, in any event the study of the pathological is still one of the best ways of learning to understand the nature of the pathological, for antisemitism is a pathological disorder of individuals and of societies, carrying many pathogenic ideas.

Anti-Semitism is, of course, only one form of group prejudice, as is race prejudice in general.[14] Other kinds of group prejudice, such as religious prejudices, national prejudices, sex prejudices, class prejudices, and the like, as has already been pointed out, are merely special forms of the same general phenomenon of group prejudice. As soon as one becomes aware of group membership and identifies oneself with that group the ground is laid for the development of group prejudice in some particular form. The prejudice may be of the most benign kind and socially not make for the least disharmony. On the other hand, it may develop under certain conditions in so disoperatively strong a manner as to threaten the very existence of the society in which it appears. This happens to be the case in the United States as well as in some other lands. Awareness of this fact, together with our understanding of the psychodynamics of the development of such forms of behavior, suggests the immediate necessity of reconsidering our processes of socializing children in relation to the health of the social structure as a whole. Race prejudice is at its strongest where social maturity is at its weakest.

The teaching of the facts about race or race prejudice will not be adequate to solve the problem. The roots of prejudice are woven into the very psychic structure of the individual, and unless we attend to the soil from which they draw nourishment it will not help either the resulting plant or ourselves if we attempt to cure its sickness by lopping off the ailing leaves. The soil in which race prejudice grows is the social experience to which the developing individual is exposed, and it is to this that we must attend if we are ever to be delivered from the sickness which is race. As Bettelheim and Janowitz put it, "It seems reasonable to assume that as long as anxiety and insecurity persist as a root of intolerance, the effort to dispel stereotyped thinking or feelings of ethnic hostility by rational propaganda is at best a half-measure. On an individual level only greater personal integration combined with social and economic security seems to offer hope for better inter-ethnic relations."[15] These authors point out that on the social level a change of climate is necessary. Their subjects who accepted social controls and were more tolerant of other minorities were also less tolerant of the Black, because discrimination against blacks is more commonly condoned, both publicly and privately. They suggest, therefore, that this should lead, among other things, to additional efforts to change social practices in ways that will tangibly demonstrate that ethnic discrimination is contrary to the mores of society.

MacCrone, in a valuable study of the psychology and psychopathology of race prejudice in South Africa, has written that "the extra-individual conflicts between the two racial groups are but the intra-individual conflicts within the mind writ large, and until the latter are removed, reduced, or modified, they must continue to exercise their baleful influence upon the race relations and the race contacts of white and Black."[16]

It is these intra-individual conflicts, the psychological factor, the deep, early conditioned motive forces represented by the aggressiveness which is produced in so many human beings and is continually being augmented by the frustrations of adolescent and adult life, that must receive more attention than they have in the past. It is this aggressiveness that renders so easily possible the usual emotional and irrational development of race prejudice. A rational society must reckon with this, for since a certain amount of frustration is inevitable—and even desirable—in the development of the individual and a certain amount of aggressiveness is inevitably produced by some social controls, and by some is even considered a necessary part of the equipment of most human beings, the task of an intelligent society is clear.

At the adult levels society must provide outlets for individual aggressiveness that will benefit both to him or her, and by extension, society. Outlets for aggression which result in social friction and in the destruction of good relations between human beings must be avoided.

Frustrations in the early and subsequent development of the individual must be reduced to a minimum, and aggressiveness always directed toward ends of constructive value. But it is not through appeals to reason that the race problem will be solved, but by the provision of a healthy environment and a loving socialization of the child that will grow and develop into a warm, loving, human being. Indeed, as the writers of *The Authoritarian Personality* conclude, all that is really necessary is that children be genuinely loved and treated as human beings.[17] These are key words, the key to the solution of humanity's problems. But how are they to be made into living realities in a society so terribly disorganized as ours? How are we to learn to love in a cold climate, in which there is an absence of love behind the show of love? We shall attempt some answers in our final chapter.

The findings revealed in the studies of *The Authoritarian Personality* have been challenged as probably not applying to all classes of society. The subjects of that study were largely middle class. The findings and conclusions as a whole, however, have been supported by the independent studies of other investigators.[18]

A study by McCord, McCord, and Howard, based on interviews, in 1948, with 48 males aged 20 years of lower-class origin revealed that the apparently tolerant did not differ from the bigoted members of this small sample.[19] As Allport[20] and others have pointed out, not all prejudice is necessarily related to the personality as a whole, some prejudices are conformative or mildly ethnocentric. And as McDill has shown, in a study of 146 female and 120 male white non-Jewish adults in Nashville, Tennessee, anomie, the collapse of social stability, and authoritarian influences are equally important in accounting for intolerant attitudes toward minority groups.[21] The McCords and Howard incline to the belief that prejudice in the lower classes is based on a generally stereotyped culture, which is not related to specific personality needs or to unique familial environments. Prejudice in the lower classes appears to be the result of adult rather than childhood experiences, according to these investigators.

If this hypothesis is correct, and it would certainly appear to be so in many cases, then improvement in economic and educational opportunities and other social conditions would offer some hope of reducing the quantum of what we call bigotry.

Koenig and King, in a study of students on a coeducational campus in the Southwest, found that "Cognitively simple persons tend to overlook nuances and to classify experience into a few, inclusive categories. Unable to perceive the behaviors of others accurately, they project their own characteristics (including attitudes) onto others. This tendency is related to stereotyping and to intolerance or prejudice."[22] Such findings have been many times independently confirmed by other investigators.

Martin, in a study designed to determine whether some of the findings of *The Authoritarian Personality* would also obtain in a randomly selected adult sample drawn from a balanced urban community, Indianapolis, secured results which corroborated the California studies strikingly. The study involved visits to 668 households and preliminary interviews with 429 persons. The final study was reduced to 41 tolerant and 49 prejudiced individuals. Martin's well-described findings in the strongly prejudiced and strongly tolerant syndromes will be given here at some length.

In general, the strongly prejudiced person presents the following pattern or syndrome of traits and characteristics: he tends to be quite ethnocentric; he makes sharp distinctions between his in-groups and out-groups; he is a "social reductionist," in that his reference groups reflect an exclusive rather than an inclusive emphasis; he is unlikely to identify with "humanity," but prefers more exclusive levels of identification; he thrives on selective membership with himself on the "inside." Such an attitude provides a sustaining and compensating mechanism for psychological and social insecurity. Although typically obscure himself, he borrows prestige from his race, nation, whatever.

The prejudiced person tends to be suspicious, distrustful and extrapunitive. He attributes ulterior motives to blacks and other out-group members. The race problem is due to blacks, and if their lot is not to their liking then it is because they are at fault. He is afraid of contact with minority group members, and foresees dire consequences of intergroup interaction. Segregation is the political-social policy he urges and defends because he "knows" that blacks and whites cannot live peacefully together. He views the world as an arena of conflict, involving power struggles and competition among individuals and groups. Other people are not to be trusted in general, because everyone is seeking to maximize his own advantage at the expense of others. He prides himself on his "realism" and tends to regard "idealistic" people as naive and even dangerous, and he favors the "practical" over the "theoretical."

The strongly prejudiced person seeks certainty through the use of dichotomized absolutes. He does not think in relative terms; he keeps his fear of doubt repressed by the dogmatism he substitutes for it. He therefore views blacks and whites as being essentially and markedly different; a person is either good or evil, and a statement is either true or false.

The strongly prejudiced person favors obedience and submission to authority. This trait is congruent with his zeal for definiteness and his basic distrust of the impulses and motives of other people. He prefers order, discipline, and conformity in the social environment. He is likely to be conservative in his social attitudes and interests, and is often a vigorous supporter, at the verbal level, of conventional morality. He is moralistic, but distinctly unsentimental. Such a person evidently represses much and engages in considerable projection, particularly in connection with the matter of conventional moral norms and their violation.

The strongly prejudiced person also tends to be poorly endowed with imagination, humanitarianism, creativeness, and compassion. He tends to be fatalistic; he is pessimistic about the scientific study of human behavior. Superstition has a considerable appeal to him, as do the magical, the mystical, and the mysterious.

Compared with the tolerant type he tends to be more emotional and less rational, and he is more moralistic rather than ethical (in terms of the connotations of these two words). The strongly prejudiced individual is typically nonintellectual and frequently anti-intellectual; he is very often dogmatic in expression and angers easily when he meets with disagreement. He is likely to interpret intellectual disagreement as a personal affront.

In religion the bigot subscribes to the more fundamentalist, dogmatic, irrational, and authoritarian doctrines and beliefs. He is less likely to concur with ideals and values relating to brotherhood, basic humanity, and unselfish deeds. He is opposed to "modernism," and would appear to resent having to donate money to his religious group.

In terms of social characteristics, the prejudiced individual has less formal education, a lower occupational level, and perhaps a smaller circle of friends than the tolerant type, even though the latter may often have a lower income.

In general the very tolerant, or relatively unprejudiced individual presents the following pattern or syndrome of traits and characteristics: his tolerance tends to be general with respect to people; perhaps the only exception is his intolerance of persons who are bigoted. A conspicuous trait is his trust of other people. The tolerant individual is inclined to look for the best in people; he gives them the "benefit of the doubt." He tends to judge individuals as individuals, and rejects the practice of group stereotyping. He expects other people to be friendly, fair, and cooperative, and he is likely to suspend his judgment of others beyond the first impression.

The tolerant individual apparently feels reasonably secure, or at least he is not prone to exaggerate actual threats from other people. He may be neurotic but he is rarely paranoid. He is inclined to be rational, humanitarian, liberal in social attitudes, and intropunitive.

The tolerant individual is also characterized by a high degree of empathic ability, and is much more likely to be sympathetic and compassionate than the strongly prejudiced person. He is "sensitive" as distinct from being "tough"; he is opposed to cruelty, violence, and harsh discipline where the strongly prejudiced person would be likely to condone it. Whereas the bigoted male is often ultra-masculine (to the point of having almost no compassion), the tolerant male seemingly has no obsessive need to "prove" his masculinity, at least he is seldom "swaggering and arrogant" in his maleness.

The tolerant type is able to perceive variation accurately and realistically; thus he is less impelled to resort to stereotyping and dogmatism. He apparently realizes and recognizes that each individual is unique (though not radically different from other individuals), and that good and evil, shortness and tallness, darkness and lightness, stupidity and intelligence, are all relative concepts. He has no obsessive fear of being mistaken or wrong, he is willing to admit his own shortcomings and weaknesses.

The tolerant personality is not a highly rigid one. He is more likely to be witty and have a highly developed sense of humor than 'the bigot. For example, the tolerant person is capable of engaging in self-ridicule, whereas the image of a grim and rigidly serious expression is more plausibly associated with the bigot.

The tolerant individual is typically interested in and optimistic about the improvement of human society. He is likely to stress cooperation as against competition, conciliation rather than confrontation, in achieving human progress. He is often idealistic and utopian, and interested in intellectual matters. Likewise, the tolerant person values creative activities and is not so prone to stress the "practical" over the "theoretical." The tolerant type is much less of a "social reductionist." It is "humanity" that interests him. Being a member of an "exclusive" group has a weak appeal for him.

The unprejudiced person tends to be "kindhearted," if not "softhearted"; he is typically in sympathy with the underdog, and is not characterized by the "threat-competition orientation" so evident in highly intolerant people. This is readily observable in the religious values and beliefs of tolerance; there is an emphasis upon brotherhood, humanitarianism, charity, reason, and tolerance of personal deviation. Similarly, he is likely to be altruistic and somewhat sentimental, and be more appreciative of the aesthetic, as compared with the strongly prejudiced person.

Such a personality is more concerned with serving than leading; is likely to be relatively autonomous; does not have a strong need for dominance; is rarely ever obsessively conformist; and dislikes both subordination and superordination of any appreciable degree. He tends to view his social interaction and social relationships as possibilities for expression, mutual assistance, affective response, and so on, rather than as opportunities for exploitation and manipulation.

Socially speaking, the relatively unprejudiced person is almost certain to have more formal education than the highly intolerant person, and his occupational status is usually higher. Although it is not borne out by the reports of the subjects in this study, the investigators are of the opinion that the tolerant type usually experiences a childhood family environment characterized by an absence of harsh discipline and authoritarian parental control.

The child-rearing attitudes of the strongly prejudiced subjects certainly suggest that authoritarian discipline is actually applied by such parents, and one would assume that their offspring would show the effects of this conditioning in their intergroup attitudes. It is surmised that the tolerant individual would usually come from a more relaxed, secure, and lenient home environment, and would experience more affection and less rejection and hostility from parents than the highly intolerant individual.[23]

Race Prejudice and Classified Hostilities

Race prejudice in many cases may be regarded as one of a number of classified hostilities that are not a result of an immediate interpersonal relationship, but which arise out of the individual's need to fit his hostility into the dynamic framework of his personality structure, altogether apart from the presence of a direct and immediate stimulus situation.

In one very significant sense race prejudice arises from the individual's failure to make use of his own potentialities, particularly his powers to relate himself to other beings, to establish human ties. The failure to establish human ties on the basis of the integrity of the individuality of the self allows only one alternative—the adoption of attitudes which seek to justify to himself this failure. Race prejudice or the adoption of classified hostilities is one of the methods of trying to satisfy or complete the constellation of needs springing from this failure.

If the constellation of needs in itself arises from a failure to make use of one's powers to love, then there can be no satisfactory solution of the problem in any real sense. For the solution, as offered by rationalizing that there is no basis in reality to love, only succeeds in further stifling this potentiality.

Humans are born social beings who can reach their full development only through interaction with their fellows. The denial at any point of this social bond between humans brings with it disintegration. A major symptom of this denial is race prejudice. What is observed in this connection is not the failure to develop into that which the individual, the person, in the utmost sense, potentially is, but rather the failure to carry on the process of development. Race prejudice functions primarily as a barrier to the further development of the person, and ultimately a repudiation of humanity.

What is the alternative to holding such prejudices or rationalizations? What does it mean to the person to give up these rationalizations? In brief, what is the danger which the individual must face if he were to give up these prejudices? That there is a danger is apparent, otherwise people would not cling to ideas, however early formed and strongly held, that are demonstrably unsound.

All the evidence of research and inquiry indicates that the danger seems to lie in the fact that if rationalizations are perceived for what they are and abandoned, the individual faces the necessity of taking his own life seriously, and the essentiality of forming meaningful human relations on the basis of his personal integrity is challenged. He must give up the primary dependent ties. He is forced to see himself as an individual entity, and not as a part of another person either in the capacity of master or subject, ruler or ruled. He must be willing to bear the pain of isolation that is concomitant with mature independence.[24] He must recognize his actual position in the universe, feel his aloneness, and at the same time his power to overcome this through love on the basis of his own integrity.

The inability to give up the primary ties is crucial—the ties to the nurturing authority. Often people rationalize that they have given up what could be called their incestuous ties, when a closer examination will reveal that what they have done has been to transfer these ties to a more acceptable object. An interesting fact here is that when group affiliations are of this nature, that is, a source of power for the individual ("I am a member of this strong group"), we find that accompanying this group attachment is a complementary feeling of out-group hostility. That is to say, the stronger and more permanent the individual's attachment to the particular group, the stronger does his out-group hostility tend to be.

This particular consequence of group allegiances is one of the "services" the group performs for the person. If the group functions primarily as a transferred source of strength for the individual, a place of worship of power, this consequence will almost always follow. If, on the other hand, the group serves a cooperative function, if the individual on the basis of his integrity can lend support to efforts that cannot be accomplished on a personal basis, then the consequence of outgroup hostility is not a necessary result of such group relationships. It is evident that this problem can be manipulated in part by manipulation of the groups. In working with boys' clubs and children's groups, some of the hostility which is the side effect of in-group allegiance can be eliminated by reducing the strength of that allegiance. This can be done by making the groups less permanent and the membership more flexible.[25]

However, it is further clear that it is not the group as such which generates the out-group hostility, but rather the private and personal use to which the group is put by the persons constituting it. In a sense what develops is a vicious circle. If the group in some (usually disguised) way serves the person as a primary source of strength, a place where he can transplant his umbilical cord, where he can deny his individuality, then it becomes progressively necessary to develop the power of the group, but not his own strength. Since the group is a direct source of security, and since he cannot bear to have his security threatened, then progressively more and more effort must be supplied to this source of strength. But what happens is that the individual only more firmly binds himself to the nourishing mother. More and more it becomes clear to him that it is his position in the group that is of importance, and not his position in terms of his responsibility to himself. The greater the crippling of his own individualization, the greater the need to cripple it until at last we find men ready blindly to negate their own lives or even life in general in their efforts to protect and revere this source of strength.

The in-group has certain characteristics, too; it must be just that, an in-group. Its membership must be restricted and of relative permanency. For if its membership should be accessible to all (in actuality, not pretense), and if that goal were reached, this group could no longer serve as a source of strength. This kind of strength involves "power over" and there would no longer be any scapegoat to exercise this "power over."

In contrast to this vicious circle is the kind of group relationship where the effort is applied to achieving "power of"—power of thought, power of understanding, power of growth. The individual's relation to the group is one where his individuality is affirmed by his particular contribution to the group effort. Though the group here is also a source of power for the individual, it is a power that affirms life and his own identity. It is an affirmative strength that does not seek the negation of life itself, but rather the enhancement and growth of those conditions which lead to the fullest development of the individual's unique identity.[26]

The satisfactions yielded by and the epidemiology of hostility are interconnected phenomena. Thorne has investigated the epidemiology of hostility through family studies. He has shown that acute and chronic frustration-hostility states tend to be socially transmissible in epidemic form, because of the contagious, inescapable nature of the emotions involved. It is almost impossible to avoid the influence of a hateful person in one's environment, particularly when such a person can exercise great personal power to frustrate by control over money, work, family discipline, and the like. Such built-up hostilities have a contagious quality, and a tendency toward chain reactions. A further result of such hostilities is the building up of mutually suspicious paranoid attitudes.[27]

Attitudes of Mind

The problem of race in our society is social, and not biological in any but a vague technical tense.[28] Fairness toward other groups of persons or a person is a matter of simple human decency; and decency is an attitude of mind, for the most part culturally conditioned. Whether ethnic groups or castes are biologically equal is an utterly irrelevant consideration where fair-mindedness is concerned. In any event, it is not a matter of biological equality that is involved, but political and social equality. Whatever differences exist between peoples and however they may have been determined, the willingness to understand those differences and to act upon them sympathetically ought to increase in proportion to the magnitude of the differences believed to exist between ourselves and others. As Professor E. G. Conklin has so well put it:

> To the naturalist the differences between human races, subraces, and individuals are small indeed as compared with their manifold resemblances. Biology and the Bible agree that 'God hath made of one blood all nations of men.' Our common traits and origin and fate, our common hopes and fears, joys and sorrows, would call forth our common sympathy with all mankind, if it were not for the lessons of hate which have been cultivated and instilled by selfish and unscrupulous persons and social groups. These racial antagonisms are not the results of inexorable nature, nor of inherited instincts, but of deliberate education and cultivation.[29]

The plea for fairness in dealing with ethnic groups not our own is usually phrased in terms of "tolerance." But if we are to make progress in ethnic relations, it is desirable to recognize that tolerance is not good enough, for tolerance defines an attitude which constitutes a somewhat reluctant admission of the necessity of enduring that which we must bear, the presence of those whom we do not like. A New York high-school girl put the whole matter in a nutshell. "Tolerance," she said, "is when you put up with certain people but you don't like to have them around anyhow." That, it is to be feared, is the general nature of tolerance, the hand-washing indifference of the "superior" person who patronizingly condescends to ensure the co-existence of "inferior" beings on condition that they keep their "proper" distance. Tolerance is the attitude of mind of those who consider themselves not only different but superior. It implies an attitude toward different ethnic or minority groups, not of understanding, not of acceptance, not of recognition of human equality, but of recognition of differences which one must suffer—generally, not too gladly. We must be more than tolerant; we must be fair.

Tolerance is the best one can hope from bigots; fairness is the attitude of mind we look for in decent, humane people. By fairness, where ethnic relations are concerned, is meant the attitude of mind which takes it for granted, there being no actual evidence to the contrary, that for all their individual differences no human being is really superior to another by virtue of his group affiliation, and that, given the necessary opportunities, it is probable that the average person of any one group is capable of doing at least as well as the average individual of the culturally most advanced group. It is more than merely being willing to concede that the *others* are not inferior to us; it is readiness to accept the verdict that we are not superior to the *others*. One is not called upon to be magnanimous, still less is one called upon to condemn or condone, but one is called upon to attempt to be fair—to understand and then to act upon that understanding.[30] Until such an attitude of mind becomes part of the equipment of every individual, no amount of instruction in the facts concerning the biology of race will ever succeed in eliminating race prejudices.

Race prejudice is ultimately merely the effect of an inadequately developed personality—a personality that has failed to learn any of the simple fundamental facts concerning the nature of human nature and in the light of other human understanding to apply it not only to others, but also to oneself. A personality that has not achieved this is simply reacting to frustration by belaboring the object which it imagines has in some way been the cause of its frustration; it is a personality that is still projecting the blame on others for errors for which it alone is responsible. It is a personality that contrasts sharply with the mature personality which tries to understand and does not seek to wash its hands of its fellows by condemning or condoning their conduct and thus dismissing them from mind. The mature personality does not automatically resort to the infliction of punishment because it has been frustrated, but attempts to understand the cause of its frustration and then, in the light of that understanding, so to act that frustrations will not again be produced. He does not try to escape the exercise of understanding by emotionally letting off steam. He accepts responsibility for his own acts and is moved by the injustice of the acts of others to attempt to remedy the conditions which give rise to such conditions. He understands that no one's father is really bigger than anyone else's father, and that to act in a superior manner is merely an immature way of asserting one's desire to feel important, to feel that one amounts to something. He realizes that, on the other hand, the desire to feel that one belongs with all humankind and not above or below any group, to feel that one is of them and belongs with them, is the most satisfying and efficient way of living and thinking. He not only insists upon the right of everyone to be different, but rejoices in most of those differences and is not unsympathetically indifferent to those which he may dislike, that there are no strangers, only friends we have not yet met. He understands that if people are characterized by likenesses and differences, it is no argument against the likenesses to dwell on the differences, or that difference in any way implies inequality. He realizes that diversity is not only the salt of life but also the true basis of collective achievement, and he does everything in his power to further the purposes of that collective achievement.[31]

True culture has been defined as the ability to appreciate the other person. While this particular ability has many sources, it is generally derived from varied, sympathetic, and understanding contacts between people who differ from each other in several respects.[32]

If race prejudice is ever to be eliminated, society must assume the task of educating the individual—not so much in the facts of race as in the processes which lead to the development of a completely integrated healthy human being—one who is able to love, to work, to play, and to think critically. The solution here, as in so much else, lies in education; education for humanity first and with regard to the facts afterward. For of what use are facts unless they are intelligently understood and humanely used?

Suppose for a moment that significant differences did exist between different peoples which rendered one, in general, superior to the other; a reasonably developed human being would hardly consider such differences sufficient reason for withholding opportunities for social and cultural development from such groups. On the contrary, such a person would be the more anxious to provide them with such opportunities. Undeveloped personalities operate in the opposite manner and, creating most of the differences they condemn, proceed to intensify those differences by making it increasingly more difficult for the groups thus treated to avoid or overcome them.

Fromm writes:

> The implicit assumption underlying much reactionary thinking is that equality presupposes absence of difference between persons or social groups. Since obviously such differences exist with regard to practically everything that matters in life, their conclusion is that there can be no equality. When the liberals conversely are moved to deny the fact of great differences in mental and physical gifts and favorable or unfavorable accidental personality conditions, they only help their adversaries to appear right in the eyes of the common man. The concept of equality as it has developed in Judaeo-Christian and in modern progressive tradition means that all men are equal in such basic human capacities as those making for the enjoyment of freedom and happiness. It means, furthermore, that as a political consequence of this basic equality no man shall be made the means to the ends of another group. Each man is a universe for himself and is only his own purpose. His goal is the realization of his being, including those very peculiarities which are characteristic of him and which make him different from others. Thus, equality is the basis for the full development of difference, and it results in the development of individuality."[33]

It is or should be axiomatic that the natural inequality of endowment that exists between all human beings does not render equality of opportunity a contemptible principle. It is in our differences that our richness lies, that because you are different you are precious to me.[34]

There exist no really separative or divisive biological differences between ethnic groups; there are differences only between persons. In every group there will be found a large range of differences in the native endowment of its members, some individuals may be less capable than others in the realizable potentials of intelligence, in vigor, or in beauty. Such differences may, by some, be made the pretext for heaping contumely and humiliation upon those who are less fortunately endowed than their fellows; but it would be scarcely human to do so, and less than decent.

Furthermore, the common practice of attributing to individuals traits derived statistically from population studies is as deplorable as it is absurd. The individual is a unique entity and should never be regarded as someone describable as a statistical constant. The reverse practice is equally reprehensible, of attributing to a whole group or population traits, whether physical or psychological, that are seen in an individual.

The form of the mind and body are so dependent upon social conditions that when the latter are unequal for different groups, little or no inference can be drawn as to the mental and physical potentialities of these groups. As the great American anthropologist Alfred Louis Kroeber wrote many years ago, "Most ethnologists, at any rate, are convinced that the overwhelming mass of historical and miscalled racial facts that are now attributed to obscure organic causes or at most are in dispute, will ultimately be viewed by everyone as social and as best intelligible in their social relations."[35]

Race prejudice is a pigment of the imagination. It begins in the minds of men, but it doesn't end there. Until we have succeeded in producing emotionally secure, mature human beings, instead of emotionally insecure, immature human beings, until we have succeeded, by means of the appropriate educational methods,[36] in producing that cultivation of mind which renders nothing that is human alien to it, the race problem will never be completely solved. The means by which that problem may to some extent be ameliorated have already been indicated, and will be further discussed later. There is one more aspect of the psychology of race prejudice to which I should like to draw attention, that is, the process of rationalization, the process of finding reasons to justify emotionally held, essentially irrational beliefs, and the construction of one's "logic" to fit one's rationalizations.

We saw in Chapter 1 by what means race prejudice originally came into existence in the United States; that is, in large part as the stratagem by means of which the proslavery party attempted to overcome the arguments of the abolitionists that the slaves were men and brothers and should be free. The upholders of slavery avidly sought reasons with which to justify their interest in maintaining that institution, and they brought those reasons forward in force and from all sorts of sources, including the Bible. But no matter from what source they drew their arguments, they were nothing but the most patently fallacious.

Since race prejudice invariably rests on false premises, for the most part emotional in origin, it is not surprising to find that it is practically always rationalized. As Professor W. O. Brown pointed out:

> The rationalization is a moral defense. And the rationalizer is a moralist. The rationalization, in the nature of the case, secures the believer in his illusion of moral integrity. The morality of the rationalization is perhaps intensified by the fact that it represents an effort to make that which is frequently vicious, sordid, and inhumane rational, idealistic, and humane. The semi-awareness of the real nature of the attitude being rationalized intensifies the solemnity with which the rationalization is formulated. Securing moral values the rationalization naturally partakes of a moral quality. This fact explains, in part, perhaps, the deadly seriousness of the devotee of the rationalization. Its value lies in the fact that it removes the moral stigma attached to race prejudice, elevating this prejudice into a justified reaction.[37]

Practically every one of the arguments used by the racists to prove the inferiority of this or that race was not so long ago used by the antifeminists to prove the inferiority of that "lower race," the female of the species. In the case of these sexual prejudices one generation has suffered to show how completely unfounded they were.[38] It need not take longer to do the same for race prejudice. Since this subject provides an instructive and pertinently parallel case history, we shall devote the next chapter to its discussion.

The rationalization is not, of course, regarded as the expression of prejudice, but rather as an explanation of one's behavior—the reason for it. Few rationalizers are aware of the fact that their reasons are simply devices for concealing the real sources of their antipathies, many of which may be quite unconscious.[39] They fail to understand that thought is a means both of concealing and of revealing feelings and that a conviction in the rationality of one's conduct may signify little more than a supreme ability at self-deception. As Professor Brown remarks, "the rationalization is not regarded as cloaking antagonism, but is regarded as a serious interpretation of conduct. No good rationalizer believes that he is prejudiced." Hence, the stronger the reasons we hold for any belief the more advisable it is to inquire into the soundness of the supports upon which such beliefs rest. This is especially true when the beliefs are as strongly held as they are in connection with race prejudice. The prejudiced individual, constellating ahead of experience, is usually a conformist who worships institutions.

He cannot exist without his prejudices. He fashions an island of security for himself and clings to it. Any exceptions to his views or beliefs are regarded by him as nonrepresentative and dismissible, for they do not conform to his encrusted system of expectations. What is more, they make him uncomfortable and anxious. They must therefore be suppressed. As Oliver Wendell Holmes remarked, "The mind of a bigot may be compared to the pupil of the eye; the more light you pour on it the more it contracts."

When people have no moral justification for their beliefs or their conduct, they will invent them. Intelligence and humanity call for a tentative attitude, "for an attitude subject to change, 'good for this day only': prejudice is lack of plasticity. A tentative attitude decreases prejudice, for it replaces absolute with relative values . . . breadth of understanding decreases prejudice."[40] Seen through the filter of prejudice reality becomes distorted.

> Through the distorting glass of Prejudice
> All nature seems awry, and but its own
> Wide-warped creations straight; but Reason's eye
> Beholds in every line of nature—truth,
> Immortal truth, and sees a God in all.

Notes

1. Frank Fremont-Smith, "The Physiological Basis of Aggression," *Child Study* 15 (1938): 1–8, and "The Influence of Emotional Factors upon Physiological and Pathological Processes," *Bulletin of the New York Academy of Medicine* 15 (1939): 560–69; Hudson Jost, "Some Physiological Changes During Frustration," *Child Development* 12 (1941): 9–15; Melvin De Fleur and Frank R. Westie, "The Interpretation of Interracial Situations," *Social Forces* 38 (1959): 17–23, who found that autonomic physiological responses below the threshold of awareness indicated the degree of involvement; Roger N. Johnson, *Aggression in Man and Animals;* B. E. Eleftheriou and J. P. Scott, The *Physiology of Aggression and Defeat;* Richard E. Whalen, ed., *The Neurophysiology of Aggression* (New York: Plenum Press, 1974); Ashley Montagu, *The Nature of Human Aggression* (New York: Oxford University Press, 1976); Ashley Montagu, ed., *Learning Non-Aggression* (New York: Oxford University Press, 1978); Rae Sherwood, *The Psychodynamics of Race: Vicious and Benign Spirals* (Atlantic Highlands, NJ: Humanities Press, 1980); Peter Watson, ed., *Psychology and Race* (Chicago: Aldine, 1974); Morris Rosenberg and Ralph H. Turner, *Social Psychology: Sociological Perspectives* (New York: Basic Books, 1981).

2. Joel Kovel, *White Racism: A Psychohistory* (New York: Pantheon Books, 1970); Frank H. Tucker, *The White Conscience* (New York: Frederick Ungar, 1968); Gordon Allport, *The Nature of Prejudice* (Cambridge: Addison-Wesley, 1953); Isidore Pushkin and Thelma Veness, "The Development of Racial Awareness and Prejudice in Children," in *Psychology and Race,* ed. Peter Watson (Chicago: Aldine, 1974); Jean L. Briggs, "The Origins of Nonviolence: Aggression in Two Canadian Eskimo

Groups," in *The Psychoanalytic Study of Society,* vol. 6, eds. Warner Muensterberger and Aaron H. Esman (New York: International Universities Press, 1975), 134–203; Charles C. Hughes, *Eskimo Boyhood* (Lexington: University of Kentucky Press, 1974); Donald L. Horowitz, *Ethnic Groups in Conflict* (Berkeley: University of California Press, 1985); Christopher Bagley and Gajendra K. Verma, *Racial Prejudice: The Individual and Society* (Westmead, England: Saxon House, 1979); George B. de Huszar, ed., *Anatomy of Racial Intolerance* (New York: The H.W. Wilson Co., 1946); Hubert M. Blalock, Jr., *Toward a Theory of Minority Group Relations* (New York: John Wiley, 1967); Michel Barkun, *Religion and the Racist Right: The Origins of the Christian Identity Movement* (Chapel Hill: University of North Carolina Press, 1994); John L. Davidio and Samuel Gaertner, eds., *Prejudice, Discrimination, and Racism* (Orlando: Academic Press, 1986); V. Reynolds, Vincent S. E. Flager, and Ian Vine, *The Sociology of Ethnocentrism* (London: Croom Helm, 1987); Daniela Gioseffi, *On Prejudice: A Global Perspective* (New York: Anchor Books, 1993); Gustavus Myers, *History of Bigotry in the United States* (New York: Random House, 1943); Louis S. Snyder, *German Nationalism: The Tragedy of a People* (Harrisburg, PA: Stackpoole 1952).

3. T. W. Adorno et al., *The Authoritarian Personality* (New York: Harper, 1950).

4. For interesting treatments of this view see John Dollard et al., *Frustration and Aggression* (New York: Yale University Press, 1939); E. F. M. Durbin and John Bowlby, *Personal Aggressiveness and War* (New York: Columbia University Press, 1939); Lauretta Bender, *Aggression, Hostility, and Anxiety in Children* (Springfield, IL: Thomas); Lydia Jackson, *Aggression and Its Interpretation* (London: Metheun, 1954); Kurt Lewin, *Resolving Social Conflicts* (New York: Harper, 1948); Norman Maier, *Frustration* (Ann Arbor: University of Michigan Press, 1961); J. P. Scott, *Aggression* (Chicago: University of Chicago Press, 1958); Arnold Buss, *The Psychology of Aggression* (New York: Wiley, 1961); Leonard Berkowitz, *Aggression: A Social Psychological Analysis* (New York: McGraw Hill, 1962); Bruno Bettelheim and Morris Janowitz, *Social Change and Prejudice* (New York: Free Press, 1964); Hubert M. Blalock, Jr., *Toward a Theory of Minority-Group Relations* (New York: Capricorn Books, 1970); Donald L. Horowitz, *Ethnic Groups in Conflict* (Berkeley: University of California Press, 1985)); Alice Miller, *Prisoners of Childhood* (New York: Basic Books, 1981); Alice Miller, *For Your Own Good: Hidden Cruelty in Child-Rearing and the Roots of Violence* (New York: Farrar Straus, 1983); Alice Miller, *Thou Shalt Not Be Aware: Society's Betrayal of the Child* (New York: Farrar Straus, 1984); Alice Miller, *The Untouched Key* (New York: Doubleday, 1988); Ashley Montagu, *Nature of Human Aggression;* John E. Williams and J. Kenneth Morland, *Race, Color, and the Young Child* (Chapel Hill: University of North Carolina Press, 1976).

5. H. Hartmann, E. Kris, and M. Lowenstein, "Notes on the Theory of Aggression," *The Psychoanalytic Study of the Child* 3–4 (1949): 9–36.

6. Else Frenkel-Brunswik and R. Nevitt Sanford, "Some Personality Factors in Anti-Semitism," *Journal of Psychology* 20 (1945): 271–91.

7. Ibid., 289.

8. Ibid., 290. See also Bruno Bettelheim and Morris Janowitz, *Dynamics of Prejudice* (New York: Harper, 1950), 170, and Caleb Gattegno, *What We Owe Children* (New York: Avon Books, 1971).

9. See T. W. Adorno et al., *The Authoritarian Personality* (New York: Harper, 1950).

        10. Nathan W. Ackerman and Marie Jahoda, "Toward a Dynamic Interpretation of Anti-Semitic Attitudes," *American Journal of Orthopsychiatry* 18 (1948): 168.
        11. Ibid., 171.
        12. N. Ackerman, and M. Jahoda, "Anti-Semitic Motivation in a Psychopathic Personality," *Psychoanalytic Review* 34 (1947): 76–101.
        13. Ackerman and Jahoda, "Dynamic Interpretation" 173.
        14. For the material on antisemitism see N. Ackerman and M. Jahoda, "The Dynamic Basis of Anti-Semitic Attitudes," *Psychoanalytic Quarterly* 17 (1948): 240–60; Detlev Peukert *Germany: Conformity, Opposition, and Racism in Everyday Life* (New Haven: Yale University Press, 1987); Nathan W. Ackerman and Marie Jahoda, *Anti-Semitism and Emotional Disorder* (New York: Harper, 1950); Adorno et al. *Authoritarian Personality;* Jean Amery, *At the Mind's Limits: Contemplations by a Survivor on Auschwitz and its Realities* (Bloomington: Indiana University Press, 1966); Hannah Arendt, *The Jew as Pariah: Jewish Identity and Politics in the Modern Age* (New York: Grove Press, 1978); Salo W. Baron, *The Russian Jew Under Tsars and Soviets* (New York: Macmillan, 1976); Ratner Baum, *The Holocaust and the German Elite* (London: Croom Heim, 1981); N. C. Belth, ed., *Patterns of Discrimination Against Jews* (New York: Anti-Defamation League of B'nai B'rith, 1958); Bettelheim and Janowitz, *Dynamics of Prejudice;* Morton Borden, *Jews, Turks, and Infidels* (Chapel Hill: University of North Carolina Press, 1984); Hamida Bosmajian, *Metaphors of Evil: Contemporary German Literature and the Shadow of Nazism* (Iowa City: University of Iowa Press, 1979); Randolph L. Braham, ed., *The Origins of the Holocaust: Christian Anti-Semitism,* (New York: Columbia University Press, 1986); Joel Carmichael, *The Satanizing of the Jews* (New York: Fromm International, 1989); Davidio and Gaertner, eds., *Prejudice, Discrimination, and Racism;* Alan Davies, *Infected Christianity: A Study of Modern Racism,* (Kingston & Montreal: McGill-Queen's University Press 1988); Alan Davies, ed., *Antisemitism and The Foundations of Christianity* (Mahwah, NJ: Paulist Press, 1979); de Huszar, *Racial Intolerance;* Leonard Dinnerstein, *America and the Survivors of the Holocaust* (New York: Columbia University Press, 1982); Leonard Dinnerstein, *Anti-Semitism in America* (New York: Oxford University Press 1994); Alan Edelstein, *An Unacknowledged Harmony—Philo-Semitism and the Survival of European Jewry* (Westport, CT: Greenwood Press, 1982); Todd M. Endelman, *The Jews of Georgian England 1714–1830: Tradition and Change in a Liberal Society* (Philadelphia: The Jewish Publication Society of America, 1979); Benjamin R. Epstein and Arnold Forster, *Some of My Best Friends . . .* (New York: Farrar, Straus, & Cudahy, 1962); Helen Fein, *Accounting for Genocide: National Responses and Jewish Victimization During the Holocaust* (New York: Free Press, 1979); Louis Finkelstein, ed., *The Jews: Their History, Culture, and Religion,* 2 vols. (New York: Harper, 1949); Saul Friediander, *Nazi Germany and the Jews, vol. 1: The Years of Persecution, 1933–1939* (New York: Harper-Collins, 1997); Otto Friedrich, *Before the Deluge: A Portrait of Berlin in the 1920's* (New York: Harper & Row, 1960); John G. Gager, *The Origins of Anti-Semitism: Attitudes Toward Judaism in Pagan and Christian Antiquity* (New York: Oxford University Press, 1983); Daniela Gioseffi, *On Prejudice: A Global Perspective* (New York: Anchor Books, 1993); Benjamin Ginsberg, *The Fatal Embrace: Jews and the State* (Chicago: University of Chicago Press, 1993); Bernard Glassman, *Anti-Semitic Stereotypes Without Jews: Images of the Jews in England 1290–1700* (Detroit: Wayne University Press, 1975); Michel Goldberg, *Namesake* (New Haven: Yale University Press, 1982); Daniel J. Goldhagen, *Hitler's*

Willing Executioners: Ordinary Germans and the Holocaust (New York: Alfred A. Knopf, 1996); Isacque Graeber and Steuart Britt, eds., *Jews in a Gentile World* (New York: Macmillan, 1942); Leonard Gross, *The Last Jews in Berlin* (New York: Simon & Schuster, 1982); Yisrael Gutman and Michael Berenbaum, *Anatomy of the Auschwitz Death Camp* (Bloomington: Indiana University Press, 1994); Ben Halpern, *The American Jew: A Zionist Analysis* (New York: Schocken Books, 1983); Malcolm Hay, *Europe and the Jews* (Boston: Beacon Press, 1960); Peter Hayes, *Lessons and Legacies: The Meaning of the Holocaust in a Changing World* (Evanston: Northwestern University Press, 1991); Celia S. Heller, *On the Edge of Destruction: Jews of Poland Between Two World Wars* (New York: Columbia University Press, 1977); Raul Hilberg, *The Destruction of the European Jews,* 2nd ed. (New York: Holmes & Meir, 1985); Isaac Jules Isaac, *The Teaching of Contempt* (New York: Holt, Rinehart and Winston, 1964); Jacob Katz, *From Prejudice to Destruction: Anti-Semitism 1700–1933* (Cambridge: Harvard University Press, 1980); Jonathan Kaufman, *A Hole in the Heart of the World: Being Jewish in Eastern Europe* (New York: Viking, 1997); Leo Kuper, *Genocide: Its Political Use in the Twentieth Century* (New Haven: Yale University Press, 1981); Primo Levi, *Moments of Reprieve* (New York: Summit Books, 1986); Primo Levi, *Survival in Auschwitz* (New York: Collier Books, 1961); Deborah E. Lipstadt, *Denying the Holocaust: The Growing Assault on Truth and Memory* (New York: Free Press, 1993); Sigmund Livingston, *Must Men Hate?* (New York: Harper, 1948); Leo Lowenthal and Norbert Guterman, *Prophets of Deceit* (New York: Harper, 1949); Roger Manwell and Heinrich Fraenkel, *The Incomparable Crime: Mass Extermination in the Twentieth Century: The Legacy of Guilt* (New York: Putnam's, 1967); Paul W. Massing, *Rehearsal for Destruction: A Study of Anti-Semitism in Imperial Germany* (New York: Harper, 1949); Edward C. McDonagh, "Status Levels of American Jews," *Sociology and Social Research* 32 (1948): 944–53; Carey McWilliams, *A Mask for Privilege* (Boston: Little, Brown, 1944); Paul R. Mendes-Flohr and Jehuda Reinharz, eds., *The Jew in the Modern World: A Documentary History* (New York: Oxford University Press, 1980); Donald E. Miller and Lorna Touryan Miller, *Survivors: An Oral History of the Armenian Genocide* (Berkeley and Los Angeles: University of California Press, 1993); Judith Miller, *One by One: Facing the Holocaust* (New York: Simon and Schuster, 1990); Montagu F. Modder, *The Jew in the Literature of England: To the End of the 19th Century* (Philadelphia: The Jewish Publication Society of America, 1939); Sarah Moskovitz, *Love Despite Hate: Child Survivors of The Holocaust and Their Adult Lives* (New York: Schocken Books, 1983); Filip Muller, *Eyewitness Auschwitz: Three Years in the Gas Chambers* (New York: Stein and Day, 1979); Myers, *Bigotry;* I. A. Newby, *Challenge to the Court: Social Scientists and the Defense of Segregation, 1954–1966* (Baton Rouge: Louisiana State University Press, 1969); James Parkes, *An Enemy of the People: Antisemitism* (New York: Pelican Books, 1946); James Parkes, *Anti-Semitism: A Concise World History* (Chicago: Quadrangle Books, 1969); James Parkes, *The Jewish Problem in the Modern World* (New York: Oxford University Press, 1946); Nathan Perlmutter and Ruth Perlmutter, *The Real Anti-Semitism in America* (New York: Arbor House, 1982); Detlev J. Peukert, *Inside Nazi Germany* (New Haven: Yale University Press, 1987); Reynolds, et al., *Sociology of Ethnocentrism;* Alvin Rosenfeld and Irving Greenberg, eds., *Confronting the Holocaust: The Impact of Elie Wiesel* (Bloomington: University of Indiana Press, 1978); Theodore I. Rubin, *Anti-Semitism: A Disease of the Mind* (New York: Continuum, 1990); Abram L. Sachar, *Sufferance is the Badge: The Jew in the Contemporary World* (New York: Alfred A. Knopf,

1939); Maurice Samuel, *The Great Hatred* (New York: Alfred A. Knopf, 1948); Jean P. Sartre, *Anti-Semite and Jew* (New York: Schocken Books, 1965), also see Sartre, "Portrait of the Anti-Semite," *Partisan Review*, 13 (1946): 163–78; Gertrude L. Selznick and Stephen Steinberg, *The Tenacity of Prejudice: Anti-Semitism in Contemporary America* (New York: Harper & Row, 1969); Jorge Semprun, *The Long Voyage* (New York: Penguin Books, 1997); Ernst Simmel, ed., *Anti-Semitism: A Social Disease* (New York: International Universities Press, 1946); Snyder, *German Nationalism;* Ervin Staub, *The Roots of Evil* (New York: 1989); Charles H. Stember, ed., *Jews in the Mind of America* (New York: Basic Books, 1966); Samuel Tenenbaum, *Why Men Hate* (New York: Jewish Book Guild of America, 1947); Joshua Trachtenberg, *The Devil and the Jews* (New York: Meridian Books, 1961); Pierre Vidal-Naquet, *Assassins of Memory: Essays on the Denial of the Holocaust* (New York: Columbia University Press, 1992); Stephen J. Whitfield, *Jews in American Life and Thought* (Hamden, CT: Shoestring Press, 1984); Elie Wiesel, *Night* (New York: Avon Books, 1960); Forrest G. Wood, *The Arrogance of Power: Christianity and Race in America from the Colonial Era to the Twentieth Century* (New York: Alfred A. Knopf, 1990); David S. Wyman, *The Abandonment of the Jews: America and the Holocaust 1941–1945* (New York: Pantheon, 1984); Susan Zuccotti, *The Holocaust, the French, and the Jews* (Basic Books, 1993); Susan Zuccotti, *The Italians and the Holocaust* (New York: Basic Books, 1987); Yitzhak Zuckerman ("Antek"), *A Surplus of Memory: Chronicle of the Warsaw Ghetto Uprising* (Berkeley: University of California Press, 1993).

15. Bruno Bettelheim and Morris Janowitz, "Prejudice," *Scientific American,* 183 (1950): 13.

16. I. D. MacCrone, *Race Attitudes in South Africa* (London: Oxford University Press, 1937), 310.

17. Adorno et al., *The Authoritarian Personality,* 975; Ashley Montagu, *The Direction of Human Development* (New York: Harper 1970); Ashley Montagu, *On Being Human,* 2nd ed. (New York Dutton, 1969); Ashley Montagu, *Growing Young,* 2nd ed. (Westport, CT: Bergin & Garvey, 1989); Ashley Montagu and Floyd Matson, *The Human Connection* (New York, McGraw-Hill, 1989).

18. D. B. Harris, H. G. Gough, and W. E. Martin, "Children's Ethnic Attitudes: II, Relationships to Parental Beliefs Concerning Child Training," *Child Development* 21 (1950): 169–81; Else Frenkel-Brunswik, "Patterns of Social and Cognitive Outlook in Children and Parents," *American Journal of Orthopsychiatry* 21 (1951): 543–58; Ackerman and Jahoda, *Anti-Semitism.*

19. William McCord, Jane McCord, and Alan Howard, "Early Familial Experiences and Bigotry," *American Sociological Review* 25 (1960): 717–22.

20. Allport, *Nature of Prejudice,* 395, 408.

21. Edward McDill, "Anomie, Authoritarianism, Prejudice, and Socio-Economic Status: An Attempt at Clarification," *Social Forces* 39 (1961): 239–45.

22. Frederick Koenig and Morton B. King, Jr., "Cognitive Simplicity and Prejudice," *Social Forces,* 40 (1962): 220–22.

23. James G. Martin, "Tolerant and Prejudiced Personality Syndromes," *Journal of Intergroup Relations* 2 (1961): 171–75.

24. For a penetrating discussion of this, see Dostoyevsky, *The Brothers Karamazov* 5.5.

25. Kurt Lewin, *Resolving Social Conflicts* (New York: Harper, 1948); Muzafer Sherif and Carolyn W. Sherif, *Groups in Harmony and Tension* (New York: Harper,

1953); Edward Spicer, ed., *Human Problems in Technological Change* (New York: Russell Sage Foundation, 1952); Chris Argyris, *Personality and Organization* (New York: Harper, 1957); Norman Maier, *Principles of Human Relations* (New York: Wiley, 1952); George E. Simpson and J. Milton Yinger, *Racial and Cultural Minorities*, 5th ed. (New York: Plenum Press, 1985); *Report of the Joint Commission on Mental Health of Children, Crisis in Child Mental Health: Challenge for the 70's* (New York: Harper & Row, 1970); Ruth H. Munroe, Robert L. Munroe, and Beatrice Whiting, eds., *Handbook of Cross-Cultural Development* (New York; Garland Press, 1981).

26. I have a feeling that I am not altogether the author of the words or ideas in this section on classified hostilities. My notes, made long ago, indicate no outside source. If I have used someone else's ideas or words without individual acknowledgment, I hope this brief note will serve both as explanation and apology.

27. Frederick E. Thorne, "The Attitudinal Pathoses," *Journal of Clinical Psychology* 5 (1949): 1–21; F. E. Thorne, "The Frustration-Anger-Hostility States: A New Diagnostic Classification," *Journal of Clinical Psychology* 9 (1953): 334–39. See also Arnold H. Buss, *The Psychology of Aggression* (New York: Wiley, 1961); Saul Siegal, "The Relationship of Hostility to Authoritarianism," *Journal of Abnormal and Social Psychology* 52 (1956): 368–72; Jack Hokanson, "The Effects of Guilt Arousal and Severity of Discipline on Adult Aggressive Behavior," *Journal of Clinical Psychology* 17 (1961): 29–32; Teun A. van Dijk, *Communicating Racism: Ethnic Prejudice in Thought and Talk* (Thousand Oaks, CA: Sage Publications, 1987); Ian D. Suttie, *The Origins of Love and Hate* (New York: Julian Press, 1966); Erich Fromm, *The Anatomy of Human Destructiveness* (New York: Holt, Rinehart & Winston, 1973); Floyd W. Matson, *The Broken Image: Man, Science and Society* (New York: Braziller, 1964), Ashley Montagu, *The Nature of Human Aggression* (New York: Oxford University Press, 1976.)

28. This statement has been interpreted to mean that race in the biological sense in man has no existence. Much more is meant here than that, namely that, in so far as social action is concerned, the biological facts about population differences do not constitute the social problem of race. It is the social attitude toward race that constitutes the problem. Frederick E. Thorne, "Epidemiological Studies of Chronic Frustration-Hostility-Aggression States," *American Journal of Psychiatry* 112 (1957): 717–21.

29. Edwin G. Conklin, "What Is Man?" *Rice Institute Pamphlet* 28 (1941): 163.

30. This is what Oscar Wilde meant when he said that "it is only by the cultivation of the habit of intellectual criticism that we shall be able to rise superior to race prejudices." "The True Function and Value of Criticism," *Nineteenth Century* 28 (1890): 123–47.

31. For a valuable discussion of this aspect of the subject see Henry A. Davidson, "The Anatomy of Prejudice," *Common Ground* 1 (1941): 3–12; and Julian Huxley, *Man Stands Alone* (New York: Harper); see also Henry A. Myers, *Are Men Equal?* (New York: Putnam, 1945)); David Thompson, *Equality* (London and New York: Cambridge University Press, 1949); Lyman Bryson et al., eds., *Aspects of Human Equality* (New York: Harper, 1956); R. H. Tawney, *Equality*, 4th ed. (London: Allen & Unwin, 1952); Michael Lewis, *The Culture of Inequality* (Amherst: University of Massachusetts Press, 1978); Christopher Jencks, *Inequality* (New York: Basic Books, 1972); William Ryan, *Blaming the Victim* (New York: Pantheon Books, 1971); William Ryan, *Equality* (New York: Pantheon Books, 1981); George L. Abernethy, *The Idea of Equality: An Anthology* (Richmond: John Knox Press, 1959); Donald M. Levine and

Mary Jo Bane, *The 'Inequality' Controversy: Schooling and Distributive Justice* (New York: Basic Books, 1975); Gerald D. Berreman, ed., *Social Inequality: Comparative and Developmental Approaches* (New York: Academic Press, 1981); Harvard Educational Review, *Equal Educational Opportunity* (Cambridge: 1969); Leonard Broom et al., *The Inheritance of Inequality* (London & Boston: Routledge & Kegan Paul, 1980); Ronald Dworkin, *A Matter of Principle* (Cambridge: Harvard University Press, 1985).

32. Donald R. Taft, "Cultural Opportunities through Race Contacts," *Journal of Negro History* 14 (1929): 19; Robin M. Williams, Jr., *The Reduction of Intergroup Tensions* (New York: Social Sciences Research Council, 1947): 69–73; Kurt Lewin, *Resolving Social Conflicts* (New York: Harper, 1948); Bryson et al., eds., *Approaches to Group Understanding* (New York: Harper, 1947); Wallace Stegner, *One Nation* (Boston: Houghton Mifflin, 1945); Alfred Marrow, *Living Without Hate* (New York: Harper, 1951); Robert M. MacIver, ed., *Unity and Difference in American Life* (New York: Harper, 1947); Ernest F. Johnson, ed., *Foundations of Democracy* (New York: Harper, 1947); Oscar Handlin, *Race and Nationality in American Life* (Boston: Little, Brown, 1957); Leonard Bloom, *The Social Psychology of Race Relations* (Cambridge, MA: Schenckman, 1949); Ina C. Brown, *Understanding Race Relations* (Englewood Cliffs NJ: Prentice-Hall, 1973); David Loye, *The Healing of a Nation* (New York: W. W. Norton, 1971); Mary C. Waters, *Ethnic Options: Choosing Identities in America* (Berkeley: University of California Press, 1990).

33. Erich Fromm, "Sex and Character," *Psychiatry* 11 (1943): 23.

34. Albert Jacquard, *In Praise of the Difference: Genetics and Human Affairs* (New York: Columbia University Affairs, 1984); David Hawkins, *The Science and Ethics of Equality* (New York: Basic Books, 1977).

35. Alfred Kroeber, "The Superorganic," *American Anthropologist* 19 (1917): 163–213.

36. See Ashley Montagu, *On Being Human*, 2nd ed. (New York: Hawthorn Books, 1969); A. Montagu, *The Direction of Human Development*, revised (New York: Hawthorn Books, 1970); Hugh Miller, *The Community of Man* (New York: Macmillan, 1949); Lawrence K. Frank, *Nature and Human Nature* (New Brunswick: Rutgers University Press, 1951); Robert Ulich, *The Human Career* (New York: Harper, 1955); C. H. Waddington, *The Ethical Animal* (New York: Atheneum, 1960); Loren Eiseley, *The Firmament of Time* (New York: Atheneum, 1960); Gilbert Highet, *Man's Unconquerable Mind* (New York: Columbia University Press, 1954); Ashley Montagu, "Education, Humanity, and Technology," in *Advances in Telematics*, vol. 2, 1–15, ed. Jarice Hanson (Norwood, NJ: Ablex Publishing, 1994).

37. W. O. Brown, "Rationalization of Race Prejudice," *International Journal of Ethics* 63 (1933): 305.

38. Ashley Montagu, *The Natural Superiority of Women*, 3rd ed. (New York: Macmillan, 1974).

39. Chester Alexander, "Antipathy and Social Behavior," *American Journal of Sociology* 51 (1946): 288–92.

40. Wilson Wallis, "Some Phases of the Psychology of Prejudice," *Journal of Abnormal and Social Psychology* 24 (1930): 426.

10

The Creative Power
of Ethnic Mixture

One of the most strongly entrenched popular superstitions is the belief that interbreeding or crossing between races, miscalled "miscegenation,"[1] results in inferior offspring and that the greater number of such crossings lead to degeneration of the stock. The commonly employed stereotype is that the "half-caste" inherited all the bad and none of the good qualities of the parental stocks. These bad qualities the "half-breed" was said to transmit to the offspring, so that there was produced a gradual but definite mental and physical deterioration within the group, finally resulting in complete infertility. Not only has the dying out of peoples been attributed to this cause by racist writers, but it was also held to be responsible for "the chronic unrest of eastern Europe, the so-called 'eastern question'" being, it was alleged, "only the ferment of mixed bloods of widely unlike type."[2] In our own day it was the official Nazi doctrine that race mixture was responsible for the decay of the great civilizations of the past.[3] This belief constitutes the stock-in-trade of contemporary racists, and is widely shared by many people.

An influential book, written by a New York Park Avenue "aristocrat," Madison Grant, entitled *The Passing of the Great Race,*" and published in 1916, asserted that the threat of race mixture would lead to the extinction of the native American of colonial stock, who "will not bring children into the world to compete . . . with the Slovak, the Italian, the Syrian, and the Jew. The native American is too proud to mix socially with them, and is gradually withdrawing from the scene, abandoning to these aliens the land which he conquered and developed."[4]

Here we perceive that it is the fear of race mixture, of race contamination, together with a sense of pride in the "purity" of one's "own" stock which, according to Grant, was leading to the decline of the Old American stock.

As is the case with most of the evils that have been attributed to so-called miscegenation, or race mixture, there is no truth whatever in any of these statements. Such facts as they may have reference to are in every case demonstrably due to social factors. The colonial stock from which Grant's long-headed, blond, blue-eyed native American was supposed to have descended was far from being the homogeneous mythical "Nordic" stock which he and Henry Fairfield Osborn, President of the American Museum of Natural History, who wrote the approving preface to Grant's book, believed it to be.

It was left to one of those scorned lowly "Slovaks" of tainted ancestry, who had come to these shores as a poor immigrant boy, the American physical anthropologist Aleš Hrdlička, of the Smithsonian Institution, to show that the colonial stock was a very mixed lot indeed. The evidence indicates that only a few of them could have been blondes and that, for what the cephalic index is worth, which is nothing whatever, the round-headed were distinctly more numerous than the long-headed.[5]

We have already encountered a Greek professor of anthropology, John Koumaris, stating that since "children of mixed parents belong to no race" existing races must perceive their "own 'fluid constancy' by avoiding mixture with foreign elements."[6] To belong to no race was, of course, to be beyond the pale.

The fact that "half-castes" often impressed those who were disposed to judge them unfavorably as mentally and morally inferior to their parental stocks, was reinforced by the fact that such hybrids were often acceptable neither to the maternal group, on the one hand, nor to the paternal group, on the other. That, indeed, is the precise significance implied in the term "half-caste." In most instances the half-castes found it extremely difficult to adjust to conditions which were themselves the cause of maladjustment in others. Generally it has been their lot to live under conditions of the most depressing kind and to occupy an anomalous and ambiguous position in society.[7]

One of the earliest scientific commentators on this subject, William E. Castle, Professor of Biology at Harvard, wrote in 1926,

Since there are no biological obstacles to crossing between the most diverse human races, when such crossing does occur, it is in disregard of social conventions, race pride and race prejudice. Naturally therefore it occurs between antisocial and outcast specimens of the respective races, or else between conquerors and slaves. The social status of children is thus bound to be low, their educational opportunities poor, their moral background bad. . . . Does the half-breed, in any community of the world in which he is numerous, have an equal chance to make a man of himself, as compared with the sons of the dominant race? I think not. Can we then fairly consider him racially inferior just because his racial attainments are less? Attainments imply opportunities as well as abilities.[8]

The environment in which the half-caste was trapped constitutes a conspicuous example of the action exclusively of socially depressing conditions, and of the effects of biological ones. The truth seems to be that far from being deleterious to the resulting offspring and the generations following them, interbreeding between different ethnic groups is from the biological, and virtually every other standpoint, highly advantageous to humankind.

Just as the fertilizing effects of the contact and mixing of cultures led to the growth and development of the older forms of culture and the creation of new ones within it, so, too, does the continuing intermixture of different ethnic groups lead to the healthy growth and development of the physical stock of humankind. It is through the agency of intermixture that nature, in the form of man's genetic system, shows its creative power. Not so long ago, when it was the custom to personify nature and to speak somewhat metaphysically of "her" as the purposive mother of us all, we should have said that "crossing" is one of nature's principal devices for the uninterrupted production of ever new and more vigorous types of life.

As Emerson wrote in *English Traits* in 1856,

> We are piqued with pure descent, but nature loves inoculation. A child blends in his face the faces of both parents and some feature from every ancestor whose face hangs on the wall. The best nations are those most widely related; and, navigation, as effecting a world-wide mixture, is the most potent advancer of nations.
>
> The English composite character betrays a mixed origin. Everything English is a fusion of distant and antagonistic elements. The language is mixed; the names of men are of different nations—the currents of thought are counter: contemplation and practical skill; active intellect and dead conservatism; worldwide enterprise and devoted use and wont; aggressive freedom and hospitable law with bitter class-legislation; a people scattered by their wars and affairs over the face of the earth, whole and bitter to a man; a country of extremes—dukes and chartists, Bishops of Durham and naked heathen colliers—nothing can be praised in it without damning exceptions and nothing denounced without salvos of cordial praise.
>
> Neither do this people appear to be of one stem, but collectively a better race than any from which they are derived. Nor is it easy to trace it home to its original seats. Who can call by right names what races are in Britain? Who can trace them historically? Who can discriminate them anatomically, or metaphysically?[9]

Of no land is what Emerson wrote in 1856 of the English more true than it is of America in the twentieth century, a land that clearly owes its physical vigor and cultural efflorescence to the influx of innumerable ethnics of every creed, culture, color, and complexion. America is the out-standing example of the land in which intermixture has occurred on a grand scale, before our very eyes, with resulting differentiation which is most beautiful to behold, and on a less visible scale characterized by many significant biological and social changes. Hybridization is one of the funda-mental processes of evolution. In plants one readily sees that it is a univer-sal and continuous phenomenon; in animals it is regularly occurring[10] while in humans it is an age-old process unquestionably operative among our protohuman ancestors.[11] Indeed, if there were any truth in the sugges-tion that hybridization results in degeneration or decadence, humans should have died out long ago or else sunk to the level of deformed idiots, for humans are an example of one of the most highly hybridized creatures on earth. The advantages of hybridization over any other process in the de-velopment of new human types should be obvious. Evolution, by the way, is another word for development. Evolution by mutation, is a slow and incal-culable process compared with evolution by hybridization. Furthermore, far from causing any existing stocks to die out, the infusion of new genes into old stocks may have been the means which not only saved them from extinction but also served to revitalize them. Populations consisting of in-bred family lines need not be genetically any better or worse than popula-tions that are not mixed; but if, on the whole, we compare the advantages of inbreeding with those of outbreeding, the advantages are chiefly with the latter. Inbreeding is not in itself a bad thing, and under certain condi-tions may be favorable for the production of speedy evolutionary changes, but there is sometimes a danger of unfavorable effects arising from the emergence of concealed deleterious recessive genes. In outbreeding, on the other hand, since the chances of rare deleterious genes coming to-gether are lowered, this danger is reduced to a minimum or altogether canceled. In general, outbreeding serves to increase physical vigor and vi-tality. Depending upon the size of the population, inbreeding in small pop-ulations tends to produce a relative homogeneity of traits; outbreeding, on the other hand, tends to produce a heterogeneity of traits and to increase variability. The phenomenon of increased vigor following upon hybridiza-tion has been long recognized by biologists and is known as *heterosis,* or hy-brid vigor.[12]

As early as 1859 Darwin, in Chapter 9 of *The Origin of Species,* fully rec-ognized the phenomenon of hybrid vigor when he wrote "It seems that, on the one hand, slight changes in the condition of life benefits all organic be-ings, and on the other hand, that slight crosses, that is, crosses between the male and females of the same species, which have been subject to slightly different conditions, or have slightly varied give vigour and fertility to the offspring." By "hybrid vigor" is meant the phenomenon frequently ob-served as a result of the crossing of the members of two distinct inbred lines derived from different species, varieties, or groups. The hybrid, that is, the offspring resulting from the union of a sperm and an egg which differ in one or more genes, surpasses both parents in size, fecundity, resistance, or other adaptive qualities and genetically is known as heterozygous advantage.[13]

From this discussion it will be perceived that all possible matings between human beings must result in hybrids, since all potential human matings, whether they occur in the same or in different ethnic groups, are necessarily between individuals who differ from one another in many genes. In practice, however, the term "hybrid" is used to refer to the offspring of two individuals who differ from each other in their genetic constitution for one or more distinctive traits or qualities. The essential difference between these two conceptions of a hybrid is an important one; we shall return to it. In what follows we shall abide by the latter conception of a hybrid because it is the sense in which the term is most commonly used.

Evidence of hybrid vigor in humans is difficult to obtain because the gene differences between human ethnic groups for the majority of traits are insufficiently marked. For the same reason we would not expect, and do not find, any degeneration, disharmonies, or infertilities in so-called "race crosses." Inbred plants and animals, on the other hand, constitute highly homozygous strains, often characterized by different chromosome numbers and other genetic differences, which frequently produce genetic disharmonies in the offspring. But this is not the case in humans, for the human varieties are characterized by a high degree of heterozygosity. Heterozygotes are characterized, on the whole, by greater stores of both genotypic and phenotypic plasticity and variability. It has been suggested that hybrid vigor, in the form of benefits which accrue to the offspring and eventually to the group as a result of crossing, occurs because each parent supplies dominant genes for which the other parent may be recessive. As Scheinfeld put it,

> Suppose some desirable trait . . . were dependent for its production on a four-gene combination, 'A-B-C-D.' If, then, only two of the genes, 'A' and 'B,' were common in one racial stock, while the genes 'C' and 'D' were common in the other stock, crossbreeding would bring together the required four genes and prove advantageous. Similarly, where two racial stocks each carry combinations of harmful genes not found in the other stock, intermarriage would reduce the incidence of these combinations and the defects resulting from them.[14]

Everyone is acquainted with the offspring of one or more varieties of ethnic unions. Such offspring show the physical characters, as it were, "blended" of their parental stocks.

The new types which emerge in this way generally exhibit something more than merely the blended sum of the properties of the parental types. That is, they show some traits and qualities which are in their way somewhat novel, traits not originally possessed by, although potentially present in, the groups from which the parents were derived. In this development we perceive the emergence of novelty, the emergents of hybrid syntheses.

Penrose presented evidence indicating that hybrid vigor is not expressed by metrical overdominance in such traits as stature, weight, limb length, and the like, but by changes in fertility connected with subtle mechanisms such as potential resistance to disease. He pointed out that genes responsible for immunity to infection, if they are dominant or intermediate in their effects, are likely to bestow considerable advantages upon the hybrid.[15] Bridges, for example, tells us that in Tierra del Fuego it was the unmixed natives who succumbed to measles, whereas the hybrids were able to resist the disease.[16] In some cases it is possible that the responsible protective factor was not simply genetic but also immunological, for example the conceptus of a woman can actually acquire measles in utero without either of the parents necessarily manifesting the disorder. Such a child would be born with a lasting immunity.[17] The probabilities are high, however, that hybrid vigor was the responsible factor among the hybrids of Tierra del Fuego for their immunity. A clear example of the mechanism at work is sickle-cell anemia, which, in the homozygous state, is exhibited in an absence of normal hemoglobin and a resulting severe anemia, which is frequently fatal. Hybridization with normal hemoglobin carriers would result in an obviously immediate advantage, since none of the offspring would suffer from sickle-cell anemia even though they carried the gene for it, and their hemoglobin was not altogether normal. Homozygotes are very susceptible to subtertian malaria, whereas heterozygotes have a strong natural immunity to the disorder.[18] Yet one racist writer has seen fit to cite sickle-cell anemia as an example of the disadvantages of race mixture![19]

Penrose also brought forward convincing evidence that suggested that levels of intelligence are prevented from declining because of the more or less continuous process of hybridization within the same ethnic group. Both the differences in fertility and in intelligence as well as in resistance to disease may be due to the slight heterotic effects of many individual genes which in combination serve to produce the improvement.[20]

As might have been expected among mixed populations characterized by a relatively greater heterozygosity than less mixed populations, the hybrids show a highly significant lower incidence of congenital malformations. Thus, as Murphy showed for American blacks in Philadelphia, the malformation rate is 5.7 per 1,000 white babies born, as compared with 3.2 per 1,000 Black babies born. The significantly lower malformation rate among American blacks may reflect the influence of a heterotic process, the result of admixture with whites.

The heterotic factor is almost certainly reflected in the findings of Saldanha on the genetic effects of immigration into a rural community some eighty-five miles northwest of São Paulo, Brazil. The population of Capivari consisted of some 89 percent whites, 2 percent mulattos, and 9 percent blacks. Some 6,742 individuals were examined for, among other things, seven congenital abnormalities. The percentage of abnormalities in the descendants of Brazilians was 5.0 percent, in descendants of Italians 3.3 percent, in the descendants of other nationalities 6.9 percent, and in the descendants of admixture between Brazilians and Italians there was only a single instance of abnormality, of 0.6 percent. In the latter case the individual exhibited Down's syndrome, probably a function of maternal age. This strikingly low incidence of congenital malformations in the hybrid group constitutes testimony to the beneficial effects of hybridization.[21]

Hulse has shown that exogamous Swiss from the Canton of Ticino, in which marriage within the Canton (endogamy) has traditionally been the rule, results in significant increases in height, sitting height, chest depth, head breadth, and prolongation of growth period. The endogamous sedentes are smaller and have a shorter growth period than both the endogamous and exogamous migrants from Ticino to California, but the exogamous migrants significantly exceed the endogamous migrants in stature and duration of growth period. The indications, therefore, are that hybrid vigor is the explanation of this favorable difference.[22] Hiernaux and Heintz in a study of Franco-Vietnamese children found some evidence for heterosis in a later weight increase during growth.[23]

The adult stature of the population of Martinique, according to Benoist, is probably the result of heterosis consequent upon admixture of Africans and Europeans.[24]

The observation by Schull of the depressed growth of Japanese children who were the offspring of consanguineous parents, as compared with the more vigorous growth of children whose parents were not related, but who were themselves offspring of consanguineous parents, points to heterosis as the responsible factor in the latter cases.[25]

Strouhal in a study of an Egyptian population in Fadidja in Nubia, which was characterized by a high rate of endogamy, but in which exogamy also occurred, found a possible heterotic effect in all twenty-nine anthropometric and functional features measured.[26]

In hybridization the inbreeding rate is reduced, and as a consequence the availability or possible conjunction of rare recessive traits is reduced, while at the same time the increase in heterozygote frequency of new combinations of genes serves both to reduce the frequency of abnormalities and increase the frequency of heterotic traits. King has suggested that the heterotic effect of hybridization is probably due to the increase in the frequency of non-identical genes.[27]

Reviewing the *Report of the Commission on Mixed Marriages in South Africa* (1939) in *Nature* (14 September) 1940, the reviewer wrote

> It is a matter of general experience that racial questions are rarely debated on their merits. In the discussion of the effects of inter-racial breeding among the different varieties of the human stock, the issue is commonly determined by prejudice masquerading as pride of race or political and economic considerations more or less veiled in arguments brought forward in support of a policy of segregation. No appeal is made to what should be the crucial factor, the verdict of science.[28]

It is, indeed, a sorry commentary upon the present condition of Western man that when it is a matter of supporting his prejudices he will distort the facts concerning hybridization so that laws are caused to be enacted making it an offense against the state. But when it comes to making a financial profit out of the scientifically established facts he will employ geneticists to discover the best means of producing hybrid vigor in order to increase the yield of some commercially exploitable plant or animal product.

Utilizing the knowledge of hybrid vigor, animal geneticists have succeeded in producing offspring that for particular desired characters are in every way superior to the parental stock, while plant geneticists have succeeded, by the same means, in producing enormous increases in sugar cane, corn, fruits, vegetables, and other economically important foodstuffs.[29] Such hybrids are clearly in no way inferior to their parents, but exhibit qualities superior to those possessed by either of the parental stocks. They are so far from being weakly that they will frequently show, as in the case of certain kinds of maize, an increase in yield between 150 and 200 percent. They are usually larger, stronger, fitter, and better in almost every way than their ancestral parental stocks. As a rule hybridization takes place only between the members of the same species, although interspecific crosses and even intergeneric crosses do occasionally occur.[30]

The best-known example of an inter-specific cross is the mule, which is the hybrid of a cross between the horse (*Equus caballus*) and the donkey, or ass (*Equus asinus*). The mule combines most of the good qualities of its parental stocks. From the horse it inherits its speed, size, strength, and spiritedness; from the donkey, its surefootedness, lack of excitability, endurance, and ability to thrive on little food. Because of these qualities it is able to adapt itself to conditions in which both the horse and the donkey would fail. Hence, the mule fetches a higher market price than do animals of either of its parental stocks. The mule, however, is itself usually sterile.

Knowledge of this fact has, perhaps, been responsible for the notion that hybridization generally results in sterility. This is, of course, quite erroneous except, for the most part, in those comparatively rare cases in which interspecific crosses are involved.

All human ethnic groups belong to the same species, and all are mutually fertile, as are the resulting offspring of mating between the members of such groups. The evidence, though by no means conclusive, suggests that among human beings, as among other forms of life, anything resembling hybrid vigor is most markedly characteristic of the first generation of hybrids. In plants and in some animals there would appear to be a gradual decline in vigor, possibly owing to the re-establishment of a relative homozygosity by inbreeding. Thus, one of the principal means of revitalizing any group of living forms is by hybridization, by introducing new genes or increasing the frequency of new combinations of genes having adaptive value. This is precisely what has occurred, from the earliest times, in humans. For early humans, in process of evolution, we have a probable example of evolution by hybridization in the Neanderthaloid people, whose fossil remains were discovered in 1931–32 at Mount Carmel in Palestine.[31] The variability presented by the skeletal remains of the Carmelites suggests hybridization even though that hybridization may have occurred between their ancestors long before.[32]

Inbreeding tends to stabilize the type and in the long-run may produce a decrease in vigor. Outbreeding, on the contrary, tends to increase the variability of the type and, at least temporarily, to augment its vigor. This is particularly significant in the case of small breeding groups in which the rate of homozygosis is likely to be more rapid than in larger populations. It has already been suggested that one of the principal agencies in the production of new human types has been in the past, as it is in the present, hybridization. In fact, at all times in human evolutionary history humans have unconsciously conducted their reproductive lives in a manner that would undoubtedly win the approval of the professional stockbreeder.

Thus, in a treatise on stockbreeding, one of the world's foremost geneticists, Professor Sewall Wright, summarized the facts relating to hybridization in these words:

> By starting a large number of inbred lines, important hereditary differences in these respects are brought clearly to light and fixed. Crosses among these lines ought to give full recovery of whatever vigor has been lost by inbreeding, and particular crosses may be safely expected to show a combination of desired characters distinctly superior to the original stock, a level which could not have been reached by selection alone. Further improvement is to be sought in a repetition of the process—isolation of new inbred strains from the improved crossbred stock, followed ultimately by

crossing and selection of the best crosses for the foundation of the new stock.[33]

This, by and large, is actually the way in which new human ethnic groups and varieties have come into being and evolved. First, by isolation and inbreeding and the action of various selective factors, then, by contact with other groups and crossbreeding with them, followed once more by isolation and inbreeding. This process has, of course, occurred with various degrees of frequency in different human groups, but that it has occurred in some degree in all is virtually certain. The evidence indicates, as Julian Huxley has put it, that "The essence of man's success as an organism is that he has not evolved as a set of separated specialized types, but has kept all his genes in a common interbreeding pool."[34] As Lord Bryce said in his Romanes Lecture in 1902, "All the great peoples of the world are the result of a mixing of races."[35]

All that we know of human history points to constant migration and the intermingling of peoples. Today over the greater part of the earth human hybridization is proceeding at rates more rapid than at any period in our history, and a vastly greater number of peoples are involved in the process at one and the same time. The tragedy, however, is that, while the genes combine to produce new types that are often recognizably superior in some traits to their parental stocks and often novel, the prejudices of humans for the most part conspire to render those novel traits embarrassments and their possessors miserable. In many parts of the world where people of color live under the domination of whites the hybrid is, by the whites, usually regarded as something of an outcast—"outcast" and "half-caste" being regarded as synonymous terms—a biological and social error viewed with unconcealed disgust. There have been and will continue to be some exceptions to this kind of attitude, but on the whole it will be agreed by those who are at all familiar with the facts that the hybrid has been cruelly received by whites. When, instead of being ostracized by whites, hybrid children and adults are given an opportunity to show what they can do, the results have often been so disconcerting to their alleged superiors that everything possible has been done either to suppress or to distort the facts.[36] It is certainly unequivocally clear to those who are capable of viewing the evidence dispassionately that biologically the offspring of mixed unions are, on the whole, at least as good human beings in most respects, and better in some, than their parents. Did we not have good reason to believe this from our daily experience of such offspring, we should expect it upon the grounds of such genetic evidence as we have already discussed. Here we may briefly cite the evidence, such as it is, for existing populations whose mixed ancestry is known and which have been the subject of anthropological studies.

Polynesian-White Crosses

In the year 1790, nine English sailors and about twelve Tahitian women and eight Tahitian men landed on Pitcairn Island in the mid-Pacific. The English sailors were the remnant of the mutineers of the English warship *Bounty* who had made their escape to this lonely island. The story is now well known; the descendants of the English mutineers and the Tahitian women are to this day living on Norfolk and Pitcairn island. Shapiro, who studied both groups in their island homes, found that the offspring of the initial white-Tahitian unions were numerous, being 11.4 children per female on Pitcairn and 9.1 on Norfolk Island.[37] A large proportion of these hybrids were long-lived, and they have had unusually long-lived descendants. The modern Norfolk and Pitcairn Islanders were taller than the average Tahitian or Englishman, were more vigorous, robust, and healthy, and mentally they were perfectly alert. The general conclusion was that after five generations of inbreeding these descendants of Polynesian-white unions showed little if any diminution of the vigor of the kind which sometimes follows crossbreeding in the later hybrid generations.

Hybridity may have little, and environmental factors a great deal, to do with the vigor of these people. One thing, however, is certain: the physical type of these populations is in every respect perfectly harmonious, with white traits predominating. As Shapiro concluded:

> This study of race mixture on the whole rather definitely shows that the crossing of two fairly divergent groups leads to a physical vigor and exuberance which equals if not surpasses either parent stock. My study of the Norfolk islanders shows that this superiority is not an ephemeral quality which disappears after the F_1 or F_2 generation, but continues even after five generations. Furthermore, the close inbreeding which the Norfolk hybrids have practiced has not led to physical deterioration.
>
> This conclusion regarding the physical vigor of the Norfolk hybrids applies also to their social structure, which on Pitcairn was not only superior to the society instituted by the Englishmen themselves, but also contained elements of successful originality and adaptability. Although the Norfolk Island society is much influenced by European contacts, it has maintained itself—a fact which acquires increased significance in view of the deterioration of the fiber of Polynesian life as a result of European influences.[38]

This conclusion also holds good for the Pitcairn Islanders.

As far as the evidence goes, then" writes Shapiro, "the Pitcairn experiment lends no support for the thesis that race mixture merely leads to degeneration or at best produces a breed inferior to the superior parental race. In fact, we see in this colony some support for heightened vigor, for an extended variation and for a successful issue of the mingling of two diverse strains.[39]

Maori-White Mixture

Perhaps the best effects of human hybridization under favorable social conditions are seen in the character and achievements of the offspring of Maori-white unions and their descendants in New Zealand. Both physically and culturally the hybrids combine the best features of both ethnic groups.[40] Native as well as hybrid Maoris have shown themselves in every way as capable as whites. Maoris are active members of parliament, and one has been acting prime minister of New Zealand, while several others have been ministers of high rank in government. A distinguished anthropologist, physician, and the foremost authority on Polynesian ethnology, the late Te Rangi Hiroa (Sir Peter Buck), was the son of a Maori mother and a white father. "I can truly say," he wrote, "that any success I may have achieved has been largely due to my good fortune in being born a mongrel. I am absolutely certain that I could not have accomplished what I have if I had been born a full Maori or a full pakeha [white]."[41]

The achievements of Maoris have been rendered possible by the fact that discrimination and the color bar, except in a few local areas, have never been intensely developed in New Zealand.[42]

Australian-White Mixture

Social conditions could not be more unfavorable for the offspring of aboriginal-white crosses than they are in Australia, an abysmally racist society, yet all unprejudiced observers agree that the offspring of such intermixtures represent an excellent physical type, and that both the aborigines and the hybrids are possessed of considerable mental ability.[43] There can be little doubt that were the aborigines and their mixed offspring treated as they deserve to be, they would do quite as well as the Maori or any other people. Cecil Cook, the chief protector of aboriginals in the Northern Territory of Australia, in an official report on the subject made to his government in 1933, stated:

> Experience shows that the half-caste girl can, if properly brought up, easily be elevated to a standard where the fact of her marriage to a white will not contribute to his deterioration. On the contrary under conditions in the Territory where such marriages are socially accepted amongst a certain section of the population, the results are more beneficial than otherwise since the deterioration of the white is thereby ar-

rested and the local population is stabilized by the building of homes. It is not to be supposed that such marriages are likely to produce an inferior generation. On the contrary a large proportion of the half-caste female population is derived from the best white stock in the country whilst the aboriginal inheritance brings to the hybrid definite qualities of value—intelligence, stamina, resource, high resistance to the influence of tropical environment and the character of the pigmentation which even in high dilution will serve to reduce the at present high incidence of Skin Cancer in the blonde European.[44]

The "half-caste" males are, of course, to be bred back to "full-blood" aboriginal women. From Dr. Cook's report it is evident that the "half-caste," in the Northern Territory at least, in spite of a vicious and endemic racism is considerably advantaged by his aboriginal biological heritage. This is undoubtedly true of all "half-castes" in Australia.[45] In terms that Western peoples readily understand, such facts as the following should not be unimpressive.

Writing in 1899, the Reverend John Mathew states:

In schools, it has often been observed that aboriginal children learn quite as easily and rapidly as children of European parents. In fact, the aboriginal school at Ramahyuck, in Victoria, stood for three consecutive years the highest of all state schools of the colony in examination results, obtaining one hundred percent of marks.[46]

Elspeth Huxley, reporting on the status of the Australian aborigines in 1965, writes in connection with the schooling of the children, "The teachers I spoke to were emphatic that Aborigines are in no way intellectually inferior, in the fundamentals, to white children of the same age. What they lack is background: a knowledge of the material objects (pencils, paper, mugs, shoes, coat pegs, toys) we take for granted, and experience of a way of living, thinking and reasoning."[47] In May 1926, an aboriginal, Jacob Harris, defeated the draughts (checkers) champion of New South Wales and Western Australia, being himself subsequently defeated by the champion of Victoria. Harris had learned the game at the mission station by watching over the shoulders of the players and was entirely self-taught.[48] The extraordinary abilities of Australian aborigines to draw and paint in Western style is now well known. Aboriginal children are especially gifted. The book by Miller and Rutter, *Child Artists of the Australian Bush,*[49] contains painting after painting by children, for the most part under the age of 14, which have to be seen to be believed. The story of the remarkable artistic abilities of Australian aborigines is instructive because for many years their highly stylized, mature and beautiful ethnocentric art incomprehensibly impressed many observers as being rather primitive, and was used by some as yet another evidence of the aborigine's behavioral inca-pacities.[50] But capacities require opportunities for development if they are to be converted into abilities, as the story of the Australian aborigines' la-tent capacities for artistic creation so strikingly illustrate. The remarkable paintings, done in the style of the white man's world, by the self-taught aboriginal artist Albert Namatjira, are famous throughout the world.[51] But aboriginal art gives access to a world which is as powerful as any European abstract painting we know.

Tindale, who has made a survey of the "half-caste" problem in Aus-tralia, cites a number of cases which suggest that increased vigor is the rule in aboriginal-white unions. Tindale also gives it as his opinion that the re-productive and survival rates of the latter are probably higher than among whites. He concludes:

> There seems little evidence to indicate that the difficulties of adjustment mixed breeds may have at present are particularly the result of marked ethnic inferiority. Physically many are of fine type, and have shown their physical superiority for example in sports such as running, football and boxing—their disabilities seem to be lack of education and home-training and the discouragement implicit in belonging to an outcast stock. There may be no mixed blood geniuses, but there are also on the other hand rel-atively few of markedly inferior mental calibre. The majority are of a mediocre type, often but little inferior to the inhabitants of small white communities which have, through force of circumstances remained in poverty, ignorance or isolation.[52]

Ethnic Mixture in Hawaii

Hawaii has afforded investigators an excellent opportunity for the study of the effects of the mixture of different ethnic groups. Here native Hawai-ians, who are, of course, Polynesians, have intermixed with whites of many nationalities, with Japanese, Filipinos, Chinese, Koreans, Puerto Ricans, and others. All these have intermixed with each other, so that in Hawaii there are literally scores of varieties of mixed types. They are all in process of amalgamating, and were immigration to cease the people of Hawaii would become a more or less distinctive ethnic group. In Hawaii is being repeated what has undoubtedly taken place on both greater and lesser scales innumerable times elsewhere in the world. In 1976 somewhat more than a third of all marriages in Hawaii occurred across ethnic lines.[53] Here the evidence is clear that the descendants of the mixed Hawaiian unions are in many ways superior to their Hawaiian and non-Hawaiian progeni-tors. The part-Hawaiians have a much higher fertility rate than all the other ethnic groups, and they are more robust, while in height, weight, and in their physical characters, as well as mental traits, they appear to be intermediate between their Hawaiian and non-Hawaiian forebears.[54] The native Hawaiian is inclined to be over-heavy, a disadvantageous trait which tends to be reduced in the part-Hawaiian. The distribution of physical traits in the crosses follows the Mendelian laws of segregation and of independent assortment. That is to say, the children of crosses of the same ethnic groups, in a single family, segregate in their characters—some around the parents, while others resemble the stocks of the grandparents; furthermore, it has been observed that single hereditary traits are often inherited independently of each other.

As a result of six years of intensive study of the Hawaiian population, Dr. William Krauss has shown that not the slightest evidence of any disharmonies is to be found in the hybrids of their descendants and that, while there is no particular evidence of hybrid vigor, the mixed offspring are in every way satisfactory physical and mental types.[55] Similar conclusions were reached by Morton and his coworkers.[56] Throughout Oceania, including the islands of Melanesia and Polynesia, aboriginal-white hybridization has been proceeding for centuries.[57] Handy, a careful student of Oceanic affairs, declares that throughout Polynesia the mixed breed "is one of the greatest assets which govern a community, both white and native phases," and that the mixed breed is "one of the most solid bonds between the white and the native."[58] This is also the conclusion stated by Krauss for the special case of Hawaii.

In concluding this section on Polynesian-Hawaiian ethnic matings, it is of interest to quote the comment of the former bishop of Honolulu, S. Harrington Littell:

> In my opinion the peoples of Hawaii have gone farther than elsewhere in appreciating the contributions which men of all races and colors are bringing to cosmopolitan thinking and to interracial understanding and good will. They are not perfect, but they have made a good start toward the noble ideal of right and brotherly relationships within the family of God.[59]

Ethnic Mixture Between American Indians and Whites

In 1894 Professor Franz Boas published the results of a pioneer study on the "half-blood" American Indian, in which he showed that the latter was taller and more fertile than the parental Indian and white stocks. In many of his physical traits, as was to be expected, the hybrid Indian presented an intermediate appearance.[60] Since increases in stature and fertility are among the most characteristic marks of hybrid vigor throughout the plant and animal kingdoms, it would be possible to claim hybrid vigor for the offspring of Indian-white crosses. A similar conclusion might be drawn from

Sullivan's analysis of Boas's data on mixed and unmixed Siouan tribes.[61] In a study of Indian-white crosses in northern Ontario, involving Ojibway Indians, Cree Indians, Frenchmen, and Englishmen, Gates found the descendants to be of an admirably hardy type. "They appear to have the hardiness of the native Indians combined.... They push the fringe of civilization farther north than it would otherwise extend, and help to people a territory which would otherwise be nearly empty." The evidence derived from this study, the author concludes, "serves to show that an intermediate race may be more progressively adapted to the particular conditions than either of the races from which it springs."[62]

Williams' study of Maya-Spanish crosses in Yucatan, where much crossing and recrossing have gone on for almost four centuries, shows that after some twelve or thirteen generations the Maya-Spanish population, judged by any standard of biological fitness, is a vigorously healthy one.[63]

Goldstein's observations on the mestizo population of Mexico, which is largely a mixture of Indian and Spanish, found that the mestizos were taller than the original parental stocks and more fertile. They were in every way a thoroughly vigorous group biologically, in spite of the debilitating effects of chronic poverty and primitive living conditions.[64]

The trihybrid Seminole Indians of Oklahoma are, as is well known, the recent descendants of a mixture between runaway Creek Indians, African slaves, and whites. The Oklahoma Seminoles have never been studied from the point of view of ethnic mixture, but they have been studied anthropometrically as a single population by Krogman.[65] From Krogman's observations and those of his colleagues it is evident that the modern Seminole population exhibits, in varying degrees, the traits of all three ancestral types that have gone into its making. The physical types were, on the whole, good, and often beautiful. There was not the slightest evidence of degeneration or disharmony in development.

The same may be said of the Moors and Manticokes of Delaware, the Brass Ankles of North Carolina, the Jackson Whites of New York and New Jersey, the Melungeons of Tennessee, and the Red Bones of Louisiana, who are similarly the descendants of Indian, Black, and white admixture. Furthermore, these groups have been inbreeding for more than two centuries with no observable ill effects; on the contrary, they appear to be hardy indeed, who have managed to make a place for themselves under the most untoward conditions which have been forced upon them by their "white Christian" neighbors.[66]

Black-White Unions

The American Black is, of course, the most obvious and best-known example of the Black-white admixture. Because of the clear-cut differences in pigmentation, hair color and form, and eye color, the offspring of Black-white unions and of their descendants afford scientists an excellent opportunity of judging the effects of such hybridization and shuffling and reshuffling of genes. The studies of Herskovits on the American Black,[67] of Davenport and Steggerda on the Jamaican Black,[68] and of Little on the English Black,[69] conclusively show that in their physical traits the admixed offspring show every evidence of hybrid vigor, and that in the American population we are witnessing the development of a genetic enrichment, the like of which the world has perhaps never before experienced. And if by hybrid vigor we understand greater vigor in terms of growth, survival and fertility, the evidence is all about us, even though it may be in a context of a high degree of social disorganization, but that is another thing.

The Black population, in spite of devastating oppressive social conditions, entirely due to an endemic racism, has survived, increased in number, held its own in fertility, though contrary to the current myth, has not exceeded that of whites.[70]

Claims have been made in the past, and continue to be implicit in racist thought, that "miscegenation"—the very word sounds ominous (see Appendix C)—leads to physical disharmonies of various sorts. There is no truth whatever in such claims.

Charles B. Davenport (1866–1944), Director of the Station for Experimental Evolution at Cold Spring Harbor, N.Y., zoologist and eugenist, claimed that hybridization sometimes produces disharmonies, and also asserted that he had discovered such disharmonies in some of the mixed Jamaicans who were examined and measured by his associate, Morris Steggerda, a physical anthropologist who had no part in the writing of the book. In a work in which a simple table was headed "Traits in Which Browns Are *Inferior* to blacks and Whites," when the word "intermediate" would more accurately have described the facts recorded in the table, one is not surprised to discover that the findings upon which this assertion rested were most strangely exaggerated. More revealing of Davenport's attitude of mind were the following remarks, which surely, as more than one critic has observed, deserve a prize of some sort. Davenport wrote:

> The blacks seem to do better in simple mental arithmetic and with numerical series than the Whites. They also follow better complicated directions for doing things. It seems a plausible hypothesis, for which there is considerable support, that the more complicated a brain, the more numerous its 'association fibers,' the less satisfactorily it performs the simple numerical problems which a calculating machine does so quickly and accurately.[71]

Even when blacks did better than the whites an utterly absurd argument had to be devised whereby their achievement was turned into yet an-

other evidence of their well-known "inferiority." This is a cautionary example of how a respected scientist's prejudices could affect his mind! Some of
the hybrids measured by Steggerda showed a combination of "long arms
and short legs." "We do not know," wrote Davenport, "whether the disharmony of long arms and short legs is a disadvantageous one for the individuals under consideration. A long-legged, short-armed person has, indeed,
to stoop more to pick up a thing on the ground than one with the opposite
combination of disharmony in the appendages."[72]

Three out of four brown (hybrid) Jamaicans were cited in support of
this generalization, a generalization which was made by Davenport as if it
applied to his own findings on the Jamaican browns as compared to the Jamaican blacks and whites. Professor H. S. Jennings, a leading geneticist,
adopted this generalization and made it part of the basis of a discussion on
the possible ill effects of hybridization which constitutes the only unsatisfactory section in an otherwise admirable book.[73] Professor W. E. Castle
has cogently disposed of both Jennings and Davenport's generalizations by
stating the plain facts as represented by Davenport and Steggerda's own
figures. Here are the figures:

TABLE 10.1

LIMB PROPORTIONS AND STATURE IN JAMAICANS

	Black	Brown	White
Arm length in cm.	57.3±0.3	57.9±0.2	56.8±0.4
Leg length in cm.	92.5±0.4	92.3±0.3	92.0±0.4
Total stature in cm.	170.6±0.6	170.2±0.5	172.7±0.7

It will be seen from these figures that the arm length of the browns is,
on the average, .6 cm greater than in blacks and 1.1 cm greater than in
whites, and the leg length of the browns is .2 cm less than in blacks. It is
here that the alleged "disharmony" is presumably to be found. It should be
obvious that the order of the differences in total stature is so small—at
most not more than 2.5 cm (1 inch) between brown and white—that it
would not make the slightest practical difference in the efficiency of stoop-
ing. As Castle has said:

> We like to think of the Negro as an inferior. We like to think of Negro-
> white crosses as a degradation of the white race. We look for evidence in

support of the idea and try to persuade ourselves that we have found it even when the resemblance is very slight. The honestly made records of Davenport and Steggerda [measurements in text were made by Steggerda and the text was written by Davenport] tell a very different story about hybrid Jamaicans from that which Davenport and Jennings tell about them in broad sweeping statements. The former will never reach the ears of eugenics propagandists and Congressional committees; the latter will be with us as the bogey men of pure-race enthusiasts for the next hundred years.[74]

In an investigation of the offspring of Black-white unions conducted in the seaports of England and Wales, Fleming found that 10 percent of the hybrids showed a disharmonic pre- or postnormal occlusion of teeth and jaws. The palate was generally well arched, while the lower jaw was V-shaped and the lower teeth slipped up outside the upper lip, seriously interfering with speech; this disharmony "resulting where a well arched jaw was inherited from the Negro side and a badly arched one from the white side."[75] No other "disharmonies" were observed. Fleming states that a "badly arched" jaw was inherited from the white side. In other words, the disharmony was not due to the effects of crossing but to the fact that it was transmitted from the white parent to the child. Such "disharmonies" were limited to only 10 percent of the cases. It is also possible that, while some of these cases merely represent the expression of inherited defects, not necessarily exhibited in the jaws of the parents themselves, still others were due to malnutrition, and that the defect actually bears no relation whatever to the fact that one parent was Black and the other white. If this were not so, it would be expected that more than 10 percent of the hybrids would exhibit "disharmonies" of occlusion.

Little, who examined 220 children of Black-English parentage in the seaports of Liverpool, Cardiff, and Hull, found no disharmonies of any kind. Only twelve children showed greater or lesser degrees of crowding of the teeth.[76] He did, however, find evidence of increased vigor in the greater stature and weight of these children as compared with unmixed English children of the same class and locality.[77]

As an anatomist and biological anthropologist, I am fully convinced that the whole notion of disharmony as a result of ethnic crossing is a myth. Certainly there is some evidence of occasional asymmetric inheritance in hybrids, but this is rare, and it is more than doubtful whether such asymmetries occur any more frequently in the general population than they do among hybrids. The fact seems to be that the likenesses between human groups so far outweigh any differences that such differences as do exist are quite insufficient to produce any disharmonies whatever.

As a typical example of the loose kind of speculative argumentation which has marred the discussion of human hybridization, reference may be made to a typical pronouncement upon the subject by an anatomist, Professor Charles Stockard. Since prejudices have a great deal to do with latitude and longitude, it should perhaps be mentioned that for many years Professor Stockard lived in a predominately Black area of the South. In an elaborate work, supported by a large grant from the Rockefeller Foundation, allegedly designed to throw some light upon the effects of hybridization among artificially produced breeds of dogs, Stockard wrote as follows:

> Since prehistoric time, hybrid breedings of many kinds have occurred at random among the different races of human beings. Such race crossings may have tended to stimulate mutations and genic instability, thus bringing about freak reactions and functional disharmonies just as are found to occur among dogs. The chief difference has been that in dogs a master hand has selected the freak individuals according to fancy and purified them into the various dog breeds. No such force regulates the mongrel mixing of human beings, and dwarf, giant, achondroplastic and acromegalic tendencies have not been selected out or established in pure form. On the contrary, individuals carrying different degrees of these tendencies are constantly being absorbed into the general human stock, possibly to render the hybridized races less stable and less harmonious in their structural and functional complexes than were the original races from which they were derived. Mongrelization among widely different human stocks has very probably caused the degradation and even the elimination of certain human groups; the extinction of several ancient stocks has apparently followed very closely the extensive absorption of alien slaves. If one considers the histories of some of the south European and Asia Minor countries from a strictly biological and genetic point of view, a very definite correlation between the amalgamation of the whites and the negroid slaves and the loss of intellectual and social power in the population will be found. The so-called dark ages followed a brilliant antiquity just after the completion of such mongrel amalgamation. Contrary to much biological evidence on the effects of hybridization, racially prejudiced persons, among them several anthropologists, deny the probability of such results from race hybridization in man.[78]

The astonishing conclusion, drawn from crosses between monstrously formed dogs which have not the slightest counterpart in humans, that the disharmonies observed in such crosses offer no "encouragement to the indifferent attitude frequently expressed towards crossing and hybridizing the various human stocks,"[79] has been adequately dealt with by Castle. He comments upon this statement: "What human stock, it may be asked, is characterized by monstrous body form, like that of the long inbred dachshund or the Boston terrier? What occasion for alarm about the physical consequences of human crosses have we, other than the actual results of such crosses as shown by anthropological and sociological studies?" Castle goes on to criticize Stockard's suggestion, without any evidence which justifies it, that racial degeneration among humans is a necessary consequence of racial crosses. No human racial crosses have ever been made or can be made which involve gene controlled differences such as exist between short-legged and bull-dog types of dogs, the reason being that such differences, though they may exist in certain families of various human races, do not characterize any race as a whole, to which Stockard extends by implication his caution against human racial crosses.[80]

As for the alleged ill effects of the "absorption of alien slaves," Castle points out that this is a pure assumption. "Besides, slave making in antiquity did not involve racial diversity but only social or political status. Hence his [Stockard's] argument involves a complete *non sequitur.*"[81]

In short, the idea that hybrids from widely differing breeds of dogs are often deformed, sometimes infertile, or even unviable constitutes an unsound analogy when extrapolated to humans. As the geneticist Kalmus has pointed out:

> In the first place breeds in dogs are not adaptations to natural conditions, but are usually products of fancy breeding, and are often already biologically unbalanced, especially so far as their endocrines are concerned. Secondly, the differences in such characters as size, hairiness and form of skeleton (skull and pelvis) that are found in the various breeds are infinitely greater than those found in the human races, where in numerous mixed populations no signs of incompatibility in mating have been observed.[82]

Stockard's reference to "some of the south European and Asia Minor countries" presumably relates to some of the lands bordering upon the Mediterranean Sea, extending from Portugal and Spain on the west to Turkey on the east. The major lands in this region in which any appreciable "absorption of alien slaves" has occurred are Portugal and Spain. What are the facts? Interestingly enough, while the populations of the Iberian Peninsula are of exceedingly complex descent, North African blacks have, from the earliest times, made only a relatively minor contribution to that descent. Phoenicians, Celts, Romans, Carthaginians, Teutons, Goths, Normans, Moors of Arab and Berber origin, and Jews, together with North African blacks and some West African blacks, have in various regions in differing numbers gone into the making of the populations of the Iberian Peninsula. Far more blacks were probably absorbed into some of those populations in prehistoric times than have been since, and Black genes were probably more widely distributed throughout the populations of Spain and Portugal when both these nations were at the height of their power than were absorbed by them after they had embarked upon the slave trade in the middle of the fifteenth century.

On the basis of such reasoning as Stockard's, the people of Portugal and Spain should never have been capable of attaining anything like the degree of civilization which characterized them up to the middle of the seventeenth century, if black genes could possibly exert a deleterious effect upon a population and its cultural activities. In reality the absorption or nonabsorption of Black genes had nothing whatever to do with the yielding to others of the political and social leadership which Portugal and Spain had maintained in Europe. An unprejudiced review of the evidence will show that this was entirely due to the far-reaching changes in the political and social fortunes of Europe as a whole, changes over which neither of these nations could exercise adequate control, and also to the peculiar social and economic organization of the peoples of the Iberian Peninsula itself.[83]

The loss of the Spanish Armada, as a result of its ill-timed attempt to sink the English fleet, for example, seriously undermined both the power and the prestige of Spain. The fortunate intervention of a storm saved Britain from being reduced to a vassal state and almost instantly reversed the fortunes and status of the two nations. Did genes have anything to do with the storm? Possibly there are some who would maintain that they did.

There is good evidence that appreciable admixture occurred between blacks and early Egyptian populations,[84] an admixture which in no way appears to have prevented the rise of the great civilization of Egypt. When Carleton Putnam asks, "What great civilization . . . ever arose after an admixture of Negro genes?" we may safely reply, "Dynastic Egypt."[85]

Another case in point, to which Stockard does not refer, is ancient Greece, for its history constitutes an excellent exemplification of the benefits of hybridization. More than a hundred and fifty years of research by scholars have shown that the formative influences which entered into the making of classical Greece, both culturally and genetically, were of appreciable diversity. The rise of Greek genius in the years between 600 and 400 B.C., and especially the fifth century, saw the most distinguished intellectual achievements in the arts, literature, architecture, drama, mathematics, sculpture, philosophy, natural history, political theory, government, law, morality, ethnic relations, and much else that eventually became the principal humanizing legacy of the Western World.[86]

It is fairly well established that Bronze Age civilization came to Greece from the more advanced East beginning about 3000 B.C. This resulted in some biological as well as cultural admixture with the indigenes of the Greek mainland. By about 1550 B.C. the Greeks had already been much influenced by the highly developed culture of Crete, and would seem gradually to have wholly assimilated it. The admixture of Cretans with the population of Greece was well known in antiquity. Crete, with its large fleet, traded with Egypt, Mesopotamia, Libya, the Hittite empire of Anatolia, and the Canaanite Phoenicians; with their network of colonies; and with the inhabitants of the many sea-indented lands skirting that veritable vortex and ferment of activity, the shores of the Mediterranean Sea. Additional biological and cultural contributions came from the inhabitants of many of the Cyclades and Sporades, the more than two hundred sea-girt islands of the Greek Archipelago. The migration from these sources over the course of the years must have been appreciable. A major feature of the Aegean is that from land no ship could have been long out of sight, a circumstance which undoubtedly encouraged migration.[87]

Evidence of admixture can also be found in the known foreign origins of such luminaries as Demosthenes, Thucydides, Pausanias, Hipparchus, Pittacus, Antisthenes, and many others. There is also evidence of the Greek language—the roots of which are clearly Indo-European—as well as its many dialects, especially those of the Helladic period, that is, the Bronze Age prior to 1100 B.C. There are also suggestions of some Asiatic biocultural contributions. All this points to a much mingled ancestry.

Indeed, the evidence is unequivocally clear that the Greeks were the product of a much hybridized lineage, a fact which seems clearly to have contributed significantly to the development of their magnificent cultural achievement, the first *thinking* civilization in the world; the first civilization to have established the independence of rational thought as an independent discipline of the mind, and among other qualities, freedom from prejudice (eutrapelia).[88]

The gainsayers, when they pejoratively speak of "miscegenation," or "mongrelization," would, no doubt, maintain that the ethnic elements that entered into the making of the fifth century Greeks were of a "desirable" kind. But by what standard is "desirability" to be measured? The eugenists and racists would certainly not have approved of some of the elements that entered into the pedigree of Socrates, Plato, Aristotle, or Pericles. In addition, it is highly probable that their ancestry included Eurafrican and Alpine elements. It should be clear, then, that any judgment of desirability must be made on the objective basis of the *results* of hybridization.[89] By that measure the facts more than suggest that there is no form of human intermixture which by objective standards is undesirable, except, of course, in the rare case of mating individuals who carry defective genes. It is not race crossing that is responsible for a genetic defect in the offspring, but the fact that one or both genitors carried the defective gene. As William Castle, the Harvard geneticist, wrote in a series of papers as long ago as 1926, "suppose that a white man who was affected with Huntington's chorea should marry a Negro woman and half their children should prove to be choreic (as in all probability they would), could we ascribe this unfortunate occurrence to race mixture? By no means, the same result would have followed had the wife been a white woman."[90]

Those who take the view that intermixture between different ethnic groups is undesirable haven't a leg to stand upon. In rare individual cases certain unfavorable combinations of genes may occur, but such combinations are no more likely to occur in any ethnic group than in any random mating population.

Surveying the rise and development of great civilizations it becomes increasingly evident that they often experienced a history of ethnic intermixture, thus providing a striking endorsement of the benefits of ethnic intermixture.

In passing, it is worth noting here that the prejudices of the eugenists and racists blinded them to the role that alien elements and their progeny played in the making of their civilization. To this day American racist writers have failed to perceive a relationship between the extraordinary development of their own society and the contributions of those who, in many cases overcame great obstacles, in order to become loyal citizens of the United States.

In the latter half of the nineteenth century, and especially during the twentieth century, America, had become a talisman, a haven and a home for the "huddled masses yearning to breathe free," this "paradise," as one such immigrant, Albert Einstein, expressed it. On both sides there was a willingness of the heart and promises to be kept, a collaboration richly fulfilled which made America what it is today: one of the greatest cultural, scientific, and technological centers of the world. Surely, never before in human history have immigrants of so many different ethnic groups been so drawn to a land, bringing with them their own cultural backgrounds, ideas, and skills, as well as new genes, to contribute to the making of America.

America may not be a "melting pot," but what is abundantly clear is, in spite of its many unsolved problems, that the commingling of so many varying genotypes, each contributing to the gene pool of the population, has proceeded on a scale so considerable, and at a rate so rapid, the world has perhaps never before witnessed anything quite like it.[91]

It matters not how few the new genes each individual brings to the gene pool as long as they differ somewhat from each other on the homologous chromosomes on which they are situated for them to produce an heterotic effect, an effect known to geneticists as *heterozygote advantage*.

Stockard, who was a native of the South, failed to understand that unlike plants and dogs human populations are not even a relatively purebred line or species, such as the breeder produces. Nor are the peoples of the earth genetically sufficiently different to generate the kinds of extreme or undesirable effects which frequently occur in the crossing of specially bred lines of plants and dogs. The genetic differences between human populations are simply not extreme enough, a truth which is itself proved by the fact of daily experience that the offspring of unions between members of different ethnic groups show no more disharmonies or undesirable traits than do the off-spring of unions between members of the same ethnic group.

To associate defectiveness with race is a common device of the racist, but it is no more than a specious invention which is thoroughly contraverted and discredited by the facts. An unprejudiced examination of any number of unselected American blacks shows that they carry no more defective genes than do whites, and that there is no question that they abundantly meet every test of biological fitness.[92]

Further discussion of American blacks will be continued in Appendix D, but the reader should also see the eight UNESCO volumes on the *General History of Africa*, 1981.[93]

One of the earliest studies on human Black-white hybridization was published in 1913, by Eugen Fischer, a German anthropologist. This was an investigation of the descendants of Reheboth Hottentot-Dutch and Low German peasant admixture. Fischer reported no disharmonies whatever, stating that the hybrids were admirably developed and exhibited something very like hybrid vigor, being, among other things, taller, than their parental stocks.[94]

Were one to be asked to name the two human physical types that would seem to stand at opposite extremes to each other we would probably place the Bushmen and Hottentots, or Khoisan as they are jointly called, at one end and whites at the other. The Khoisan are short, have peppercorn head hair, are rather free of body hair elsewhere, have small ears, broad noses, small flat faces, a yellowish loose wrinkled skin, in many cases overhanging middle upper eyelid folds, and in women large protruding buttocks (steatopygia), as well as a heavy deposit of fat on the thighs (steatomeria).

Sometime in the 1950s Professor Phillip Tobias of the University of Witwatersrand in South Africa photographed the daughter of a union between a Bushman woman and a white man, and the offspring of her daughter's union with a white man, shown holding their daughter. In two generations every trace of Bushman ancestry had completely disappeared in the grandchild; the genes from the white male and the the hybrid mother produced a blue-eyed blonde-haired child, free of any "disharmonies."

More recently (1996), Professor Tobias has written me of a family in which a South African man of European origin had had six Bushman wives, partly consecutively and partly concurrently, who had produced ten children. Professor Tobias managed to track down all the members of this family over a spread of some 100 square miles of Kalahari terrain in Botswana. He also managed to photograph all the members of the family, and perceived no disharmonies in any of them. He hopes to publish an account of this family together with the photographs in the near future.

The truth is that in the long history of unions between blacks and whites in the Americas I have never heard of a single case of a genetic disorder in the descendants. Claims to the contrary are nothing but racist myths.

When we turn from Stockard's *arbiter dicta* on the evils of hybridization to his so-called experimental work upon which his conclusions are supposed to be based, we discover that this suffers from the serious defect that many of his animals represented highly selected artificial strains to begin with, a number of which were well-known hereditary defectives, such, for example, as the dachshund, the bulldog, and the Pekinese. The crossing of such defective stocks with normal breeds would certainly result in a number of defective progeny, and there would generally be as much disharmony as was present in the original progenitors. To jump from such effects to Stockard's general conclusion that "race crossing may have tended to stimulate mutations and genic instability, thus bringing about freak reactions and functional disharmonies just as are found among dogs," is to abandon the last vestiges of scientific method for the hobbyhorse of prejudice.

In any event, such defective animals would have become extinct within a short time, since they could not have survived under natural conditions. Here it should be emphasized once more that there are no "pure races," for if there ever were any they would have ceased to exist long ago, as a consequence of their overload of identical genes. The more homozygous a population becomes the more vulnerable it becomes to the challenges of the environment. Isolation and inbreeding together, especially in a small population result in the accumulation of too many homozygotes. A striking living example of the dangers of homozygote overload is the cheetah, whose numbers are rapidly diminishing to a hardly sustainable population. A genetic study has revealed that the highly inbred cheetah suffers from an almost complete heterozygosity, accompanied by a high susceptibility to infectious diseases, a considerable increase in defective sperm, and a markedly reduced reproductivity.[95]

The deleterious effects of inbreeding have been known for millennia, and have been abundantly confirmed by genetic studies from fruit flies to humans. In human societies marriage between "blood relatives" has often been strictly forbidden, on the ground of the possible ill-effects of such unions.

In America the physical effects of this intermixing of genes is, in both sexes, most pleasing to behold, in differentiation, the accompaniment of immunological benefits, health, and expectation of life. Added to the genetic benefits which physical intermixing produces, there are the socio-cultural benefits which produce a cultural heterosis in every area of human creativity. The waves of new immigrants have continually remolded the bodily and cultural physiognomy of Americans, and have imparted a dynamic quality to its society which is unsurpassed.[96]

Clearly genetic *variability*, that is, heterozygosity, is beneficial both for the individual and for the group or population, disproving racist claims that intermixture of people of different origins leads to deterioration. Whether covert or overt in everyday life, and at any level, prejudice becomes institutionalized as the "politically correct" idolatry of race. The consequences of race mixture or "miscegenation" (see Appendix C) which the would-be purifiers of race fear, lead not to deterioration but to increased vigor and differentiation, to unity, without uniformity, but to the biocultural diversity and our own hybridity that constitutes the riches of humanity.

Fischer's findings were fully confirmed on a much larger variety of inhabitants of South Africa by Lotsy and Goddijn. These investigators studied the crosses of Bushmen, Basutos, Fingos, "Kaffirs," Mongoloids, Indians, whites, and many others, and their evidence unequivocally disproves any suggestion of the development of any ill effects from such crossings. It proves, on the contrary, that perfectly harmonious and often strikingly beautiful types develop as a result of such matings.[97]

Archdeacon Watts of Swaziland, South Africa has written of the Swazi-white "half-castes": "The half-caste becomes immoral, perhaps, in immoral surroundings, but, in good surroundings, he brings out the virtues of both races as well as their vices—the energy and ability of the European with the lack of greed, the natural obedience and the love of order of the Native . . . These half-castes should be the natural leaders of the Native in the years to come."[98]

In Brazil, where blacks are conservatively estimated to constitute 44.5 percent of the population, crossing between blacks, Indians, and whites has been proceeding for more than four hundred years. The mixed population has increased enormously. The physical type of the descendants of such hybrid unions is in every respect biologically efficient and harmonious. Many Brazilians of mixed ancestry have attained the highest distinction in every walk of life. Bastide makes it quite clear

> that Brazilian society is composed of social classes in which skin color symbolizes one's position in a hierarchy of privilege and in which racial prejudice continues more or less hypocritically to impede the collective rise of a colored group which is conceived to pose a threat to another group's key positions within the global society.[99]

Summarizing his studies and those of his colleagues on race mixture in Brazil, Professor Arthur Ramos, the Brazilian anthropologist, writes, "Nothing justifies the idea that the Brazilian mestizos have any character of inferiority."[100]

Pourchet in his investigation of Indian-white-Black intermixture in Brazil[101] concludes, with Freyre,[102] that "Everything leads us to believe that miscegenation was a valuable contributing factor in the formation of the Brazilian, creating that ideal type of the modern man for the Tropics, the European with Negro or Indian blood to revive his energy."

Similarly, in Cuba, where conditions somewhat approximate those existing in Brazil, the descendants of Black-white admixture are generally recognized to be of particularly fine physical type and socially among the most progressive.[103]

East Asian or Mongoloid-White-Black Intermixture

In a study of the hybrid population of the island of Kisar in the Timor Archipelago, involving the product of admixture between Mongoloid, Indo-Malayan, Oceanic Black, and European whites, Rodenwaldt found its members to be perfectly harmonic in form. There was not the slightest evidence of any developmental disharmonies. In their physical and cultural traits the Kisarese were intermediate between the native islanders and the whites, and with 7.3 children per marriage, were considerably more fertile than either.[104]

Chinese-White Intermixture

Studies of French-Annamite hybrids in Vietnam and Tonkin by Bonifacy,[105] and also by Holbé,[106] Abel,[107] Huard and Bigot,[108] and Tao,[109] and Hiernaux and Heintz,[110] pay tribute to the biologically "beautiful results" of the admixture. Tao, for example, studied the offspring of 32 Chinese-French marriages and of 13 Chinese-German marriages in which, in almost every case, the father was Chinese. In each case the offspring were perfectly healthy, exhibiting no disharmonies.

Fleming examined 119 children who were the offspring of Chinese fathers and white English mothers. In only one instance was there any evidence of any asymmetric or disharmonious physical character in the hybrid. In a 14-year-old boy, "One orbit was Chinese in shape, the eye dark opaque brown and the Mongoloid [epicanthic fold]fold marked. The other orbit was English in type, eye color the gray with a brown net so common in English people, and there was no Mongolian fold."[111] Such abnormalities of inheritance are obviously extremely rare, as is suggested both by Fleming's findings and by experience, and almost certainly were not related to the fact that the parents were members of different ethnic groups.

Among the statements sometimes encountered regarding the alleged disharmonic effects of race mixture is that owing to differences in head shape of the races involved, as well as to differences in the form of the female pelvic outlet, "an important disharmony might result," that is, a baby inheriting the large head of the race of one parent might find itself in difficulties getting born to a mother of a race with a narrow pelvic outlet.[112] In the face of the extremely low maternal and infant mortality rates of the Hawaiian population, in which so many offspring of mixed marriages are born, and in the light of the American Black-white experience such statements are without the slightest foundation. Investigation of the matter by the United States Army Medical Corps in Japan, in 500 cases where a Japanese woman was married to a white, led to the firm conclusion that "The Japanese woman married to a Caucasian was found to present no greater difficulties in obstetric management than the Caucasian counterpart."[113]

Japanese-white, Malayan-white, East Indian and white, Arab-white, and Egyptian-white intermixtures have not been at all thoroughly studied, but such evidence as we have indicates strongly that the hybrids and the mixed-breeds resulting from these mixtures are in every way satisfactory, and frequently very beautiful.[114]

Conclusions

The evidence summarized in the preceding pages, unequivocally indicates that human hybridization and ethnic mixture lead, on the whole, to effects which are advantageous to the offspring and to the group. Harmful effects, physical disharmonies of various alleged kinds, are of the greatest rarity, and cannot be attributed to intermixture, nor is there the slightest evidence of degeneration following upon intermixture. In this connection it has been said that one cannot get out of a mixture more than one puts into it. This is not true. When we combine oxygen and hydrogen, we obtain water, which is more than each element alone could yield. When we combine zinc and copper, we obtain an alloy, bronze, which has far greater strength, and numerous other superior qualities, than the unalloyed metals comprising it; that is certainly getting more out of a mixture than was put into it. When two purebred varieties of plants or animals unite to produce offspring, the latter often show many more desirable qualities and traits than the stocks from which they were derived. Surely the varieties which humankind present in its varying ethnic forms would suggest that something more has been obtained out of the mixture of the elements than was originally brought into association. To maintain the contrary would be to subscribe to a genetic fallacy. All offspring of unions between human beings represent the expression of a unique association of genes. Some of these combinations may result in individuals who in one respect or another are superior or inferior or similar to the parents, but invariably one always obtains something different out of the mixture than whatever originally entered into it.

As Nabours has put it:

> In a considerable number of hybrids, to be sure, especially among the higher animals and man, some of the respective characteristics may be blended or arranged in mosaics in such manner as to indicate certain of the qualities of the component races. Even so, such composites generally exhibit, in addition, qualities extraneous to any shown by the original organisms, and at the same time some of the properties of the latter are lost in the process. In this category probably belongs the mulatto, many of whose qualities, in spite of certain degrees of blending, are superveniently different from the mere sum or mosaic of the several characteristics of the white and Black races. The respective properties of the ass and horse would not, by simple addition, or mosaically, make a mule, and the cattalo is far from displaying nothing but the sum or mosaics of the several attributes of buffalo and cattle. Nearly all the higher plants and animals when hybridized—and which are not?—exhibit extraneous qualities such that they largely, or completely effect the dissimilitude of the qualities of their several, contributive, primary races.[115]

All this, of course, does not mean that the emergent is independent of the genes that have entered into its making; it is, in fact, upon the genes contributed by each parent that, other conditions being equal, the combinations into which they enter to create the new individual will depend. It should be remembered that gene distributions are not so much a matter of the distribution of genes of individuals as of the distribution of genes within populations. It is not, therefore, a matter of speaking of two individuals who, characterized by either a superior or a mediocre assortment of genes, transmit their genes to their offspring, but of the continuous interchange and shuffling and reshuffling of every kind of gene within a population to yield a large number of gene combinations. Some of these will be superior to others; in fact, there will be every possible form of variation within the limits set by the genetic equipment of the population. This is true of all populations. No population has a monopoly of good genes, and no population has a monopoly of bad genes; normal and defective genes are found in all populations of human beings. Furthermore, it is most unlikely that the kind of defective genes distributed in one population will be found to occur in anything like as great a frequency, if at all, in another population or ethnic group.

As Jennings has put it:

> In view of the immense number of genes carried by individuals of each race, and their separate history up to the time of the cross, the relatively

few defects that have arisen are almost certain to affect genes of different pairs in the two. Hence, when the races cross, the individuals produced will receive a normal gene from one parent or the other in most of their gene pairs; and since the normal gene usually manifests its effect, the offspring of the cross will have fewer gene defects than either of the parents.[116]

In a later work Jennings adds: "Thus the offspring of diverse races may be expected to be superior in vigor, and presumably in other characteristics . . . Data on this point are not abundant, but it is probable that hybrid vigor is an important and advantageous feature of race crosses in man."[117]

Genes peculiar to each group are contributed by the parents to the offspring, and these genes express themselves in new traits not possessed by either of the parents or their stocks. It is in this process that the creative power of race mixture shows itself. The fact is that all ethnic groups and varieties are characterized by biologically fit qualities. Were this not so, they could not possibly have survived to the present time. Hence, when they do intermix, it is not surprising that the hybrids should show qualities capable of passing every test of biological fitness and efficiency. True hybrids are, of course, only the first filial generation of intermixture; but since all human hybrids are polyhybrids—that is, hybrid for a very large number of genes—hybridization in mixed human populations will often extend over a period of many generations. Thus, because of such polyhybridization over several generations, the tendency will be to add more and more new genes to the common stock and for a considerable number of generations (depending upon the size of the population) to maintain a high degree of variability or heterogeneity. Certainly some poor combinations of genes will occur in individual cases, resulting in some mediocre individuals, but these will take their chances with the rest, contributing perhaps a genius or two, or perhaps a few politicians, to the population before passing on their way or else being selectively eliminated. Ernst Kretschmer, the distinguished student of human constitutional typology, found in his study of genius that most geniuses were of mixed ethnic ancestry.[118]

He goes on to say:

One may assume, with some probability, that the rise of lofty civilizations, blossoming with genius, at other times and in other races and nations, was caused by a similar biological process of cross-breeding. For an individual human biology too, suitable cross-breeding gives rise to richly-developed 'hybrids' who easily outgrow the parental types from which they have sprung. The breeding of genius is thus assimilated to the same process which, in specialist biology, is known as the 'luxuriation' of hybrids [hybrid vigor]. Hence highly developed civilizations are usually produced within a definite time interval after the migrations of peoples and the invasions of conquering tribes which have gradually mixed themselves with the native populations.[119]

Kretschmer points out that it is an error to assume that the immigrating or invading group, as such, has brought genius with it, but rather that the blossoming of a new civilization is due to hybridization alone. This view would, however, tend to make the progress of culture dependent on biological factors, whereas it should be evident that it is cultural hybridization, not biological hybridization, which is principally, if not entirely, responsible for such blossomings of culture. The transition from tribalism to civilization in the ancient civilizations was largely a result of the foundation of these states and empires by migrating peoples. This intermingling of peoples and cultures occurred all along the Fertile Crescent, the very birthplace of civilization, with wave after wave of migrating and conquering peoples participating. As Murphy points out, one of the most striking examples of the effects of cultural hybridization is the culture of England. In England, Celts, Angles, Jutes, Saxons, Normans, and Danes, "crossing with an Alpine and Mediterranean substratum, mingled with each other so as to produce after a few hundred years that great outburst of intellectual vigor and luxuriance of genius which centers in the Elizabethan age."[120]

The more unlike two mating groups are genetically, the more likely it is that for many traits the hybrid offspring will be superior to either of the parental groups and will be a mosaic of their characters for the rest. It is far less likely that the offspring of such matings will exhibit anything like the frequency of defective traits which occurs in matings between members of the same ethnic group. This is due to the fact that most defective genes are carried in the recessive state and are more likely to be matched within the carrier's own ethnic group than in some other. Furthermore, genes for certain desirable traits unique to different ethnic groups are, of course, carried in the dominant state, and the offspring of such mixtures will show the effects of the combination of these genes not only in the expression of certain traits of the parental stock but also in others which are themselves unique.

While it may be true of plants that in some cases hybrids will combine some of the undesirable traits of both parental stocks, the traits of human beings over a large area of the globe are such that, when under hybridization they do combine, there appears to be a gain on the whole rather than a loss of biological fitness. This is a fact which has not been sufficiently stressed, and it is one of the first importance. It would seem that all the ethnic groups possess qualities which under hybridization result, on the whole, in the emergence of novel and biologically fit types, not in reversionary unfit ones. The latter types are definitely the rare exceptions, which in the course of time are naturally eliminated; the former survive and reproduce not only their kind but also, again under conditions of hybridization, new kinds. It will be seen, then, that the beliefs relating to the alleged harmfulness of hybridization are quite erroneous and that they constitute a part of the great mythology of race. The truth is that ethnic group mixture constitutes one of the greatest creative events in the progress of humankind.

Long ago Professor F. H. Hankins, in his book *The Racial Basis of Civilization* (1931) wrote that "in the everchanging texture of racial qualities and in the infinite combinations still to be made there may in the future arise race blends quite as excellent as those which produced the Age of Pericles, the wonderful thirteenth century, the Renaissance, or the present era in European civilization."[121] It is possible to go even further and say that should reason and humanity prevail, that there will be no strangers, only friends we have not yet met, where conciliation and cooperation prevail between peoples, rather than confrontation and competition, the future will see blends of humankind not only "quite as excellent," but more fully fulfilled than humankind is today. As Professor F. J. Trembley has said:

> For a million years man has been fusing, with consequent great increase in form and structure and in cultural heritage. He has produced an incomplete civilization along the way, but it is a civilization which possesses the potential seeds of a heaven on earth. Should we erect any artificial barriers to this fusion which seems to have done so much for man?[122]

To this we may, in conclusion, add the words of a great American scientist, William E. Castle: "So far as the biologist can see, human race problems are not biological problems any more than rabbit crosses are social problems. The rabbit breeder does not cross his selected races of rabbits unless he desires to improve upon what he has. The sociologist who is satisfied with human society as now constituted may reasonably decry race crossing. But let him do so on social grounds only. He will wait in vain, if he waits to see mixed races vanish from any biological unfitness."[123]

Notes

1. For a discussion of the origin and misuse of this term, see Appendix C.

2. Joseph P. Widney, *Mankind: Racial Values and the Racial Prospects* 1 (Los Angeles: Pacific Publishing, 1917), 167; H. H. Goddard, *The Kallikak Family: A Study in the Heredity of Feeblemindedness* (New York: Macmillan, 1912); H. H. Goddard, "Mental Tests and the Immigrant" *Journal of Delinquency* 2 (1917): 243–277; Madison Grant, *The Passing of the Great Race* (New York: Scribner's Sons, 1916; 2nd ed., 1919); Lothrop Stoddard, *The Rising Tide of Color* (New York: Scribner's Sons, 1920); Lothrop Stoddard, *The Revolt Against Civilization: The Menace of the Under Man* (New York: Scribner's Sons, 1922); Albert E. Wiggam, *The New Decalogue of Science*

(Garden City, NY: Garden City Publishing, 1925); Albert E. Wiggam, *The Fruits of the Family Tree* (Garden City, NY: Garden City Publishing, 1926). For a devastating critique of these and related works see Stephen Jay Gould, *The Mismeasure of Man* (New York: W. W. Norton, 1981).

3. See, for example, Alfred Rosenberg, "Der Mythus des 20," *Jahrhunderts* (Munich: Hoeneichen-Verlag, 1930): 85–86; Albert Chandler, *Rosenberg's Nazi Myth* (Ithaca: Cornell University Press, 1945), 71; Alfred Rosenberg, *Race and History* (New York: Harper & Row, 1970); Robert Cecil, *The Myth of the Master Race: Alfred Rosenberg and Nazi Ideology* (New York: Dodd, Mead, 1972).

4. Grant, *Passing of the Great Race,* 1st ed., 80–81.

5. Aleš Hrdlička, *The Old Americans* (Baltimore: Williams and Wilkins, 1925), 54.

6. John Koumaris, "On the Morphological Variety of Modern Greeks," *Man* 48 (1948): 127.

7. For a discussion of the half-caste in Western society, see Cedric Dover, *Half-Caste* (London: Secker & Warburg, 1937); also Everett V. Stonequist, *The Marginal Man: A Study in Personality and Culture Conflict* (New York: Scribner, 1937); J. O. Reinemann, "The Mulatto Children in Germany," *Mental Hygiene* 37 (1953): 365–76. For a moving example of the history of American Indian ancestry see Sidner J. Larson, *Catch Colt* (Lincoln: University of Nebraska Press, 1955).

8. William E. Castle, "Biological and Social Consequences of Race Crossing," *American Journal of Physical Anthropology* 9 (1926): 147.

9. Ralph Waldo Emerson, "Race," in *English Traits* (Boston: Phillips, Sampson & Co., 1856), 62.

10. John W. Gowen, *Heterosis* (New York: Hafner Publishing, 1964); David Rife, *Hybrids* (Washington, D.C.: Public Affairs Press, 1965).

11. It was probably Darwin who first suggested that it was the bringing together of dissimilar germinal substances rather than the mere act of crossing, which produced an increase in size and vigor in hybrid plants and animals. See Charles Darwin, *Variation of Animals and Plants Under Domestication* (London: Murray, 1867).

12. As early as 1859 Darwin wrote: "Hence it seems that, on the one hand, slight changes in the condition of life benefit all organic beings, and on the other hand, that slight crosses, that is, crosses between the males and females of the same species, which have been subjected to slightly different conditions, or which have slightly varied give vigor and fertility to the offspring." *The Origin of Species* (London: Murray, 1859), chap. 9.

13. Genetically this is stated as follows: Each inbred line is homozygous or nearly so for its genes or certain ones, but each different inbred line is homozygous for different alleles of many genes, with consequent heterozygosity in the F_{1s} between them.

14. Amram Scheinfeld, *The New You and Heredity* (Philadelphia: Lippincott, 1950), 516.

15. Lionel S. Penrose, "Evidence of Heterosis in Man," *Proceedings of the Royal Society,* B, 144 (1955), 203–13.

16. E. Lucas Bridges, *Uttermost Part of the Earth* (London: Hodder & Stoughton, 1948), 520.

17. Ashley Montagu, *Prenatal Influences* (Springfield, IL: Thomas, 1962), 287.

18. Ashley Montagu, *An Introduction to Physical Anthropology,* 3rd ed. (Springfield, IL: Thomas, 1960), 72–77.

19. R. Ruggles Gates, "Disadvantages of Race Mixture," *Nature* 170 (1952): 896.

20. Penrose, "Heterosis."

21. Douglas Murphy, *Congenital Malformations,* 2nd ed. (Philadelphia: Lippincott, 1947), 15; P. H. Saldanha, "The Genetic Effects of Immigration in a Rural Community of Saõ Paõlo, Brazil," *Acta Geneticae Medicae et Gemellologiae* 11 (1962: 158–224.

22. Frederick S. Hulse, "Exoganie et Heterosis," *Archives Suisse d'Anthropologie Generale* 22 (1957): 103—25, translated as "Exogamy and Heterosis," *Yearbook of Anthropology,* 9 (1964), 241—57.

23. Jean Hiernaux and Heintz N. Hiernaux, "Croissance biométrique des Franco-Vietnamiens," *Bullétins et Mémoires de la Société Anthropologiques de Paris* 1, Serie XIIe (1967): 55–89.

24. Jean Benoist, "Les Martiniquais: Anthropologie d'Une Population Metisee." *Bullétin et Mémoires de la Société d'Anthropologie Paris* 11 (1963), 241–432.

25. W. J. Schull, "Inbreeding and Maternal Effects in the Japanese," *Eugenics Quarterly* 5 (1962): 14–22.

26. Eugene Strouhal, "Anthropometric and Functional Evidence of Heterosis From Egyptian Nubia," *Human Biology* 43(1971): 271–87.

27. James C. King, "Inbreeding, Heterosis and Information Theory," *American Naturalist* 95 (1962): 345–64.

28. *Report of the Commission on Mixed Marriages in South Africa* (1939) in *Nature* (14 September 1940): 357.

29. William Crocker, "Botany of the Future," *Science* 88 (1938): 391; David Tilman, and Johannes Knops, "Productivity and Sustainability Influenced by Biodiversity in Grassland Ecosystems," *Nature* 379 (1966): 718–20.

30. For a discussion of such interspecific and intergeneric crosses in the non-human primates see Ashley Montagu, "A Hybrid Gibbon," *Journal of Mammalogy* 31 (1950): 150–53.

31. For a description of these remains see Theodore McCown and Arthur Keith, *The Stone Age of Mount Carmel,* vol. 2 (Oxford: Clarendon Press, 1939). For a discussion of the hybridization hypothesis explanatory of the variability of these remains see Montagu's review of the above work under the section "Prehistory" in the *American Anthropologist* 42 (1940): 518–22.

32. Ashley Montagu, "Prehistoric Hybridization," *Man* 62 (1962): 25; Jonathan Marks, *Human Biodiversity: Genes, Race, and History* (New York: Aldine de Gruyter, 1995).

33. Sewall Wright, *Principles of Live Stock Breeding,* U.S. Department of Agriculture Bulletin 905 (Washington, D.C.: Government Printing Office, 1920).

34. Julian Huxley, *Evolution in Action* (New York: Harper, 1953): 173–74.

35. James Viscount Bryce, *The Relations of the Advanced and the Backward Races of Mankind* (Oxford: Clarendon Press, 1902), 17–18.

36. In a well-known textbook of psychology an account is given of a young girl who belongs in the genius class, without any mention being made of the fact that she is the daughter of a Black father and a white mother. In Los Angeles, in nonsegregated public schools attended by Black and white children, it was found that 500 Black children ranked slightly higher in intelligence than the white group in the same

schools with whom they were compared. References to such findings are seldom seen or heard. See W. W. Clark, *Los Angeles Negro Children* (Educational Research Bulletin, Los Angeles, 1923). An outstanding example of distortion of the facts during World War II was provided by Representative Andrew J. May of Kentucky, chairman of the House Military Affairs Committee, who caused the suppression for use by the United States Army of a pamphlet, *The Races of Mankind,* written by two anthropologists, Professor Ruth Benedict and Dr. Gene Weltfish, of the Department of Anthropology, Columbia University. In July, 1947, Mr. May was unlucky enough to be convicted and sentenced to prison for bribery and conspiracy while in office., and for the services to his country was rewarded with a pension. *The New York Times* (4 December 1949), 64.

37. Harry Shapiro, *Descendants of the Mutineers of the Bounty* (Memoirs of the Bernice P. Bishop Museum, Honolulu, 1929, vol. 11, no. 1), and H. Shapiro, *The Heritage of the Bounty* (New York: Simon & Schuster, 1936); Ian Ball, *Pitcairn: Children of Mutiny* (Boston: Little, Brown, 1973).

38. Harry Shapiro, *Descendants of the Mutineers,* 69.

39. Harry Shapiro, *Race Mixture* (Paris: UNESCO, 1953), 44.

40. J. B. Condliffe, *New Zealand in the Making* (London: Allen & Unwin, 1930); Felix M. Keesing, *The Changing Maori* (New Plymouth, NZ: Avery & Sons, 1928).

41. Foreword, in Ernest Beaglehold and Pearl Beaglehole, *Some Modern Maoris* (Wellington: New Zealand Council for Education Research, 1946), xvi.

42. Ibid., 298–328; Walter Nash, "Democracy's Goal in Race Relationships–with Special Reference to New Zealand," in *The Role of the Races in Our Future Civilization,* ed. Harry W. Laidler (New York: League for Industrial Democracy), 12–16.

43. The evidence for these statements is to be found in a large number of scattered books, periodicals, and newspapers. Among these I would particularly draw attention to the following: George Wilkins, *Undiscovered Australia* (London: Benn, 1928), 242–62 and the plate opposite p. 256 showing half-caste girls; Jack McLaren, *My Crowded Solitude* (London: Newnes, 1926); Cecil Cook, *Report of the 27th of June, 1933, by the Chief Protector of Aboriginals in the Northern Territory of Australia,* reprinted in the Report of the Commission on Mixed Marriages in South Africa (1939), 52; Michael Terry, *Hidden Wealth and Hiding People* (New York: Putnam, 1934); Ion L. Idriess, *Over the Range* (Sydney: Angus & Robertson, 1937); Daisy Bates, *The Passing of the Aborigines* (London: Murray, 1938); J. R. B. Love, *Stone Age Bushmen of To-Day* (London: Blackie, 1936); S. D. Porteous, *The Psychology of a Primitive People* (New York: Longmans, 1931); Ashley Montagu, *Coming into Being among the Australian Aborigines,* 2nd ed. (London & Boston: George Routledge, 1974); C. E. C. Lefroy, "Australian Aborigines: a Noble-Hearted Race," *Contemporary Review* 135 (1929): 22; Cedric Dover, *Half-Caste* (London: Secker & Warburg, 1937); Eleanor Dark, *The Timeless Land* (New York: Macmillan, 1941); Xavier Herbert, *Capricornia* (New York: Appleton-Century, 1943); A. O. Neville, *Australia's Coloured Minority* (Sydney: Currawong Press, 1947); Anthony Barnett, *The Human Species* (New York: Norton, 1950), and plate 12 opposite p. 117; R. Ruggles Gates, "Studies in Race Crossing," *Zeitschrift für Morphologie und Anthropologie,* 47 (1956): 233–315; R. Ruggles Gates, "The Genetics of the Australian Aborigines," *Acta Geneticae Medicae et Gemellologiae* 9 (1960): 7–50; Charles Chewings, *Back in the Stone Age* (Sydney: Angus & Robertson, 1936); Mary D. Miller and

Florence Rutter, *Child Artists of the Australian Bush* (London: Harrap, 1952); Charles P. Mountford, *Brown Men and Red Sand* (London: Phoenix House, 1950); Ronald Berndt and Catherine Berndt, *From Black to White in South Australia* (Chicago: University of Chicago Press, 1952); Donald Stuart, *Yandy* (Melbourne: Georgian House, 1959); R. Berndt and C. Berndt, *The World of the First Australians;* A. P. Elkin, *The Australian Aborigines,* 2nd ed. (Sydney: Angus & Robertson, 1954); Frederick D. McCarthy, *Australia's Aborigines* (Melbourne: Colorgravure Publications, 1959); A. A. Abbie, *The Original Australians* (London: Frederick Muller, 1969); F. S. Stevens, ed., *Racism: The Australian Experience,* 3 vols. (Sydney: Australian and New Zealand Book Co., 1971–72); Charles Duguid, *No Dying Race* (Sydney: Angus and Robertson, 1964).

44. Cecil Cook, *Report on the 27th of June, 1933, by the Chief Protector of Aboriginals in the Northern Territory of Australia.* Darwin: 1933. Reprinted in *the Report of the Commission on Mixed Marriages in South Africa* (Pretoria, 1939)

45. Norman Tindale, "Survey of the Half-Caste Problem in South Australia," *Proceedings of the Royal Geographical Society,* South Australian Branch, session 1940–41, 66–161.

46. J. Mathew, *Eaglehawk and Crow* (London: Nutt, 1899), 78. Commenting on Mathew's report, Professor S. D. Porteous, in one of the most wrong-headed and condescending works ever published on the subject (and, of course, supported and made possible by one of our Foundations), says, "Whatever the explanation of the situation, the inference that the aboriginal children excelled the white children of the rest of Victoria in scholarship is, of course, ridiculous." *The Psychology of a Primitive People* (New York: Longmans, 1931), 380.

47. Elsbeth Huxley, "Australia's Aborigines Step Out of the Stone Age," *New York Times Magazine,* 20 June 1965, 50. For some idea of the difficulties the aboriginal child faces in the white school environment see Gloria Phelan, "Aboriginal Children in New South Wales Schools," *Integrated Education* 3 (1965), 36–41.

48. Reported in the *London Daily Express,* 27 May 1926; also see p. 11, note 4, in Ashley Montagu, *Coming into Being among the Australian Aborigines* (London and Boston: George Routledge, 1974).

49. Mary D. Miller and Florence Rutter, *Child Artists of the Australian Bush* (London: Harrap, 1952. See also W. A. McElroy, "Aesthetic Appreciation in Aborigines of Arnhemland. A Comparative Experimental Study," *Oceania* 23 (1952): 81–94; Herbert Read and Charles P. Mountford, "Australia: Aboriginal Painting from Arnhemland," *UNESCO World Art Series* (New York: Columbia University Press 1955).

50. For authoritative and appreciative studies of Australian aboriginal art see Ronald Berndt, ed., *Australian Aboriginal Art* (New York: Macmillan, 1965).

51. Charles P. Mountford, *The Art of Albert Namatjira* (Melbourne: Bread and Cheese Club, 1944).

52. Norman Tindale, "Survey of the Half-Caste Problem in South Australia," *Proceedings of the Royal Geographical Society, South Australian Branch,* session 1940–41, 124; Ronald M. Berndt, ed., *Australian Aboriginal Art* (New York: Macmillan, 1964); Peter Sutton et al., *The Art of Aboriginal Australia* (New York: Braziller, 1988).

53. William Krauss, "Race Relations in the Islands of the Pacific," *Journal of Heredity* 32 (1941) 371–78.

54. William Krauss, "Race Crossing in Hawaii," *Journal of Heredity* 32 (1941): 371–78; Romanzo C. Adams, *Interracial Marriage in Hawaii* (New York: Macmillan, 1937), 232–35; Newton E. Morton et al., "Genetics of Interracial Crosses in Hawaii," *Eugenics Quarterly* 9 (1962): 23–24.

55. Krauss, "Race Crossing." Consult further E. Finch, "The Effects of Racial Miscegenation," in *Papers on Inter-Racial Problems,* (Universal Race Congress, 1911), 108–12; Frederick L. Hoffman, "Miscegenation in Hawaii," *Journal of Heredity* 8 (1917): 12; Leslie Dunn and A. M. Tozzer, "An Anthropometric Study of Hawaiians of Pure and Mixed Blood," *Papers of the Peabody Museum of American Archaeology and Ethnology, Harvard University,* 11 (1928), 90–211; Clark Wissler, "Growth of Children in Hawaii: Based on Observations by Louis R. Sullivan," *Bernice P. Bishop Museum Memoirs,* (Honolulu, 1930), 105–207; Thomas Blake Clark, "One World on an Island," *Research in Race Relations* 47, 1 (1947): 14–21; Edwin G. Burrows, *Hawaiian Americans* (New Haven: Yale University Press); and for a discordant view, V. Mac-Caughey, "Race Mixture in Hawaii," *Journal of Heredity* 10 (1919): 41–47, 90–95; Morton et al., "Genetics of Interracial Crosses."

56. Morton et al., op. cit.

57. For an account of some of these cases see Dover, *Half-Caste,* 176–87; see also Douglas Oliver, *The Pacific Islands* (Cambridge: Harvard University Press, 1951).

58. Handy, quoted by Keesing, *The Changing Maori;* Jane Ritchie and James Ritchie, *Growing Up in Polynesia* (Sydney: Allen & Unwin, 1979).

59. S. Harrington Littell, "All Races Necessary," *New York Times,* 3 September 1944.

60. Franz Boas, "The Half-Blood Indian: an Anthropometric Study," *Popular Science Monthly* 14 (1894), 761–70; reprinted in Boas, *Race, Language and Culture,* (New York: Macmillan, 1940), 138–48.

61. Louis Sullivan, "Anthropometry of Siouan Tribes," *Proceedings of the National Academy of Sciences* 6 (1920): 131–34; Wilson D. Wallis, "Variability in Race Hybrids," *American Anthropologist* 40 (1938): 680–97.

62. R. Ruggles Gates, "A Pedigree Study of Amerindian Crosses in Canada," *Journal of the Royal Anthropological Institute* 58 (1928): 530. See also the magnificent work of Marcel Girant, *Le Métis Canadien* (Paris: Institut d'Ethnologie, 1950).

63. G. D. Williams, "Maya-Spanish Crosses in Yucatan," *Papers of the Peabody Museum of American Archaeology and Ethnology, Harvard University* 13 (1931), 1–256.

64. Marcus S. Goldstein, *Demographic and Bodily Changes in Descendants of Mexican Immigrants* (Austin: Institute of Latin-American Studies, 1943).

65. Milton Krogman, *The Physical Anthropology of the Seminole Indians* (Comitato Italiano per lo studio dei problemi della populazione, serie 3 II, ix–199, Rome, 1935).

66. Clinton A. Weslager, *Delaware's Forgotten Folk* (New Brunswick: Rutgers University Press, 1972).

67. Melville Herskovits, *The American Negro* (New York: Alfred A. Knopf, 1928) and *The Anthropometry of the American Negro* (New York: Columbia University Press, 1930).

68. Charles Davenport and Morris Steggerda, *Race Crossing in Jamaica* (Washington, D.C.: Carnegie Institution, 1929).

69. Kenneth L. Little, "Some Anthropological Characteristics of Anglo-Negro Children," *Journal of the Royal Anthropological Institute* 73 (1943): 57–73, K. L. Little, *Negroes in Britain* (London: Kegan Paul, 1948).

70. Andrew Hacker, *The Persistence of Inequality: Black and White, Separate, Hostile, Unequal* (New York: Scribner's [Macmillan], 1992); Bob Blauner: *Racial Oppression in America* (Berkeley: University of California Press, 1972); Bob Blauner, *Black Lives, White Lives: Three Decades of Race Relations in America* (Berkeley: University of California Press, 1989); Alphonso Pinkney, *The Myth of Black Progress* (New York: Cambridge University Press, 1984); Steven Shulman and William Darity, Jr., eds., *The Question of Discrimination: Racial Inequality in the U.S. Labor Market* (Middletown, CT: Wesleyan University Press, 1989); John F. Dovidio and Samuel L. Gaertner, eds., *Prejudice, Discrimination, and Racism* (Orlando: Academic Press, 1986); Walter E. Williams: *The State Against Blacks* (New York: McGraw-Hill, 1982); Richard Polenberg, *One Nation Divisible: Class, Race, and Ethnicity in the United States Since 1938* (New York: Viking Press, 1980); Colin Greer, *Divided Society: The Ethnic Experience in America* (New York: Basic Books 1974); Richard L. Zweigenhaft and G. William Domhoff, *Blacks in the White Establishment? A Study of Race and Class in America* (New Haven: Yale University Press, 1991).

71. Davenport and Steggerda, *Race Crossing in Jamaica,* 469.

72. Ibid., 471.

73. Herbert S. Jennings, *The Biological Basis of Human Nature* (New York: Norton, 1930), 280. Jennings somewhat modified this in his *Genetics* (New York: Norton, 1935), 280. The same comment may be made on Jennings's "The Laws of Heredity and Our Present Knowledge of Human Genetics on the Material Side," in J. W. Corrigan, ed., *Scientific Aspects of the Race Problem* (New York: Longmans, 1941): 71–72.

74. William Castle, "Race Mixture and Physical Disharmonies," *Science* 71 (1930): 603–06. Davenport replied to this: "We certainly never drew the conclusion that the Negro-white cross is inferior to the Negro or the whites; but we did find some cases of browns that seemed to present greater extremes—and sometimes less well-adjusted extremes—than either of the parental races. Our conclusion is not as Castle suggests it is, that the browns are a degradation of the white race.' Our conclusion is given at p. 477: 'While on the average, the Browns are intermediate in proportions and mental capacities between Whites and blacks and although some of the Browns are equal to the best of the blacks in one or more traits, still among the Browns there appear to be an excessive percent over random expectation who seem not to be able to utilize their native endowment.'" "Some Criticisms of 'Race Crossing in Jamaica,'" *Science* 72 (1930): 501–02. In another paper written in the same year Davenport expressed himself unequivocally in the matter of Negro-white crosses. These, he wrote, seem to be "of a type that should be avoided." "The Mingling of Races," in Edmund Cowdry, ed., *Human Biology and Racial Welfare* (New York: Hoeber, 1930), 565.

75. R. M. Fleming, "Physical Heredity in Human Hybrids," *Annals of Eugenics* 9 (1939): 68.

76. Kenneth L. Little, "Some Anthropological Characteristics of Anglo-Negro Children," *Journal of the Royal Anthropological Institute* 73 (1943): 66.

77. Ibid., 72.

78. Charles R. Stockard, *The Genetic and Endocrine Basis for Differences in Form and Behavior* (Philadelphia: Wistar Institute of Anatomy and Biology, 1941), 37–38. For an excellent independent criticism of Stockard's views see Alejandro Lipschütz, *El indoamericanismo y el problema racial en las Américas* (Santiago: Editorial Nascimento, 1944), 268–79. For a racist account of the decline of Portugal as a result of intermixture see Stuart O. Landry, *The Cults of Equality* (New Orleans: Pelican Publishing, 1945), 92–96. Landry thinks more highly of Spain, hence, her people "never committed race suicide by marrying with inferior races" (p. 95).

79. Stockard, ibid., 491.

80. William Castle, "Dog Crosses and Human Crosses," *Journal of Heredity* 23 (1942): 249–52.

81. Ibid., 252.

82. H. Kalmus, *Genetics* (London: Pelican Books: 1948), 158.

83. For an illuminating discussion of this see Gerald Brenan, *The Spanish Labyrinth* (New York: Macmillan, 1943).

84. T. L. Woo and G. M. Morant, "A Biometric Study of the 'Flatness' of the Facial Skeleton in Man," *Biometrika* 36 (1934) 196–250; J. M. Crichton, "A Multiple Discriminant Analysis of Egyptian and African Negro Crania," *Papers of the Peabody Museum of Archaeology and Ethnology Harvard University* 57 (1966): 46–67.

85. Carleton Putnam, *Race and Reason* (Washington, D.C.: Public Affairs Press, 1961), 37; Chehik A. Diop, T*he African Origin of Civilization* (New York: Lawrence Hill, 1974); Martin Bernal, *Black Athena, The Afroasiatic Roots of Classical Civilization*, vol. 1 (New Brunswick: Rutgers University Press, 1987); F. M. Snowden, Jr., *Blacks in Antiquity* (Cambridge: Harvard University Press, 1970); The Menil Foundation, *The Image of the Black in Western Art*, 7 vols. (Cambridge: Harvard University Press, 1976); Frank H. Hankins, *The Racial Basis of Civilization* (New York: Alfred A. Knopf, 1971).

86. R. W. Livingstone, *The Greek Genius and its Meaning to Us* (Oxford University Press, 1924).

87. Carey, M. D., and R. H. Warmington, *The Ancient Explorers* (London: Meuthen, 1929).

88. John Angel, "Social Biology of Greek Culture Growth," *American Anthropologist*, n.s., 48 (1946): 493–533; John Angel, "Report on the Skeletons Excavated at Olynthus," in David Robinson, *Excavations at Olynthus;* Angel, "A Racial Analysis of the Ancient Greeks," *American Journal of Physical Anthropology*, n.s., 2 (1944): 329–76. See also John L. Myres, *Who Were the Greeks?* (Berkeley: University of California Press, 1930); Matthew Thompson McClure, "Greek Genius and Race Mixture," in *Studies in the History of Ideas*, vol. 3 (New York: Columbia University Press, 1935), 25–33; John Baldry, *The Unity of Mankind in Greek Thought* (New York: Cambridge University Press, 1965); Aubrey Diller, *Race Mixture Among the Greeks Before Alexander,* Illinois Studies in Language and Literature, University of Illinois, vol. 20 (Urbana, 1937); John W. Gowen, *Heterosis* (New York: Hafner Publishing, 1964); M. S. F. Hood, "The Aegean Before the Greeks," in *The Dawn of Civilization,* ed. Stuart Piggott (New York: McGraw Hill, 1961), 219–28; George Huxley, "The Genesis of Greece," in Michael Grant, ed., *The Birth of Western Civilization* (New York: McGraw-Hill, 1965), 27–50; Andrew Lintott, *Violence, Civil Strife, and Revolution in the Celestial City,* 2nd ed. (London:

Croom-Helm, 1987); Peter Green, "Downtreading the *Demos,*" *The Times Literary Supplement* (London), 11 February 1983.

89. Henry E. Garrett, "The Egalitarian Dogma," *Perspectives in Biology and Medicine 4* (1961): 480–84. For the criticism of this article see the same journal, volume 5 (1961), 122–43, and later issues. See also Juan Comas, "'Scientific' Racism Again?" *Current Anthropology* 2 (1961): 303–40; Henry E. Garrett, "The Scientific Racism of Juan Comas," *The Mankind Quarterly* 2 (1961): 100–106; Henry E. Garrett and W. C. George, "Findings on Race Cited," *New York Times,* 10 October 1962, p. 46.

90. Castle, "Race Mixture" 604.

91. Alan Goodman, "Bred in the Bone?" *The Sciences* March/April 1997: 20–25); Norman J. Sauer, "Forensic Anthropology and the Concept of Race." *Social Science and Medicine* 34(2)(1992): 107–11); Ismael Reed, ed., *MultiAmerica: Essays on Cultural Wars and Cultural Peace* (New York: Viking, 1997).

92. Julilan Lewis, *The Biology of the Negro* (Chicago: University of Chicago Press, 1942); William M. Cobb, "The Physical Constitution of the American Negro," *Journal of Negro Education* 3 (1934), 340–88; Gunnar Myrdal, *An American Dilemma: The Negro Problem and Modern Democracy* (New York: Harper, 1944), 137–53; UNESCO, The General History of Africa. 8 vols. (Berkeley: University of California Press, 1981); Robert P. Stuckert, " African Ancestry of the White American Populatiopn," Ohio Journal of Science 58 (1959), 155–60.

93. S. J. Holmes, *The Negro's Struggle for Survival* (Berkeley: University of California Press, 1937); Lewis, *Biology of the Negro;* Myrdal, *An American Dilemma,* 15–81.

94. Eugen Fischer, "Die Rehobother Bastards und das Bastardierungsproblem heim Menschen," *Jena* 1913; Phillip V. Tobias, "On a Bushman-European Hybrid Family," *Man* 54 (1955), 179–82; Phillip V. Tobias, ed., *The Bushmen* (Cape Town: Human & Rousseau, 1978); Margo & Martin Russell, *Afrikaners of the Kalahari: White Minority in a Black State* (Cambridge: Cambridge University Press, 1979); Richard B. Leer, *The !Kung San: Men, Women and Work in a Foraging Society* (Cambridge: Cambridge University Press, 1979); Richard B. Lee and Irven De Vore, eds., *Kalahari Hunter-Gatherers* (Cambridge: Harvard University Press, 1976); Lorna Marshall, *The !Kung of Nyae Nyae* (Cambridge: Harvard University Press, 1976).

95. S. J. O'Brien, D. E. Wildt, and M. Bush, "The Cheetah in Genetic Peril," *Scientific Monthly* 254 (1986): 84–92.

96. David F. Bowers, ed., *Foreign Influences in American Life* (Princeton: Princeton University Press, 1944).

97. J. P. Lotsy and W. A. Goddijn, "Voyages of Exploration to Judge of the Bearing of Hybridization upon Evolution, vol. 1: South Africa," *Genetica* 10 (1928), viii–315.

98. Watts, *In the Mission Field,* quoted by W. A. Cotton in *The Race Problem in South Africa* (London: Student Christian Movement, 1926).

99. Roger Bastide, *The African Religions of Brazil: Towards a Sociology of the Interpretation of Civilizations* (Baltimore & London: Johns Hopkins University Press, 1978), 222; Edgardo Roquette–Pinto, "Contribuiçaõ antropologia do Brasil," *Revista de Imigraçaõ y Colonizaçaõ* 3 (1940); Donald Pierson, *Negroes in Brazil* (Chicago: University of Chicago Press, 1942); Ruediger Bilden, "Racial Mixture in Latin America—With Special Reference to Brazil," in Harry W. Laidler, ed., *The Role of the*

Races in Our Future Civilization (New York: League for Industrial Democracy 1942), 49–54; Rene Ribeiro, "Situaçaõ Ethnica do Nordeste," *Sociologia* 15 (1953): 210–59; Lorenzo D. Turner, "The Negro in Brazil," *Chicago Jewish Forum* 15 (1957): 232–36; Arthur Ramos, *The Negro in Brazil* (manuscript) (Washington, D.C., 1939); Willard Price, "Race Barriers Broken," *The Spectator,* 5 September 1952, 291–92; Florestan Fernandes, *The Negro in Brazilian Society* (New York: Columbia University Press, 1969); Magnus Mörner, ed., *Race and Class in Latin America* (New York: Columbia University Press, 1971); Charles Wagley, *An Introduction to Brazil* (New York: Columbia University Press, 1971); Marvin Harris, *Town and Country in Brazil* (New York: Columbia University Press, 1956); Gilberto Freyre, *The 'Mansions' and the 'Shanties'* (New York: Alfred A. Knopf, 1963); G. Freyre, *Order and Progress* (New York: Alfred A. Knopf, 1970); see also Douglass G. Glasgow, "Brazil's Black Underclass," *The New York Times* 30 November 1984, p. A30; Robert P. Stuckert, " African Ancestry of the White American Population," *Ohio Journal of Science* 58 (1958), 155–60.

100. Arthur A. Ramos, *Introduçaõ à antropologia Brasileira* (Rio de Janeiro: Civilizaçaõ Brasileira, 1951); Claudio Esteva Fabregat, *Mestizaje in Ibero-America* (Tucson: University of Arizona Press, 1994).

101. Maria Pourchet, "Brazilian Mestizo Types," in *Handbook of South American Indians,* ed. Julian Steward, vol. 5 (Washington, D.C.: Smithsonian Institution, 1950), 119.

102. Gilberto Freyre, *The Masters and the Slaves* (New York: Alfred A. Knopf, 1948), 74.

103. Personal communication of Professor Armand Angulo.

104. Ernst Rodenwaldt, *Die Mestizen auf Kisar,* 2 vols. (The Hague: Martinus Nijhoff, 1927).

105. A. Bonifacy, "Les Métis Franco-Tonkinois," *Revue Anthropologique* 21 (1911): 259–66.

106. T. V. Holbé, "Métis de Cochinchine," *Revue Anthropologique* 24 (1914): 281–93, 26 (1916): 449–66.

107. Wolfgang Abel, Über Europäer-Marokkaner und Europäer-Annamiten-Kreuzungen," *Zeitschrift für Morphologie und Anthropologie* 36 (1937): 311–29.

108. P. Huard and A. Bigot, "Recherches sur Quelques Groupes Ethniques Observés en Indochine," *Travaux de l'Institut Anatomique de L'École Supérieure de Médicine de l'Indochine* (Hanoi) 6 (1939).

109. Yun-Juei Tao, "Chinesen-Europäerinnen-Kreuzung," *Zeitschrift für Morphologie und Anthropologie,* 33 (1935): 349–408.

110. Jean Hiernaux and Heintz N. Hiernaux, "Croissance Biométrique des Franco-Vietnamiens," *Bulletins et Mémoires de la Société d'Anthropologie de Paris* I, Serie XII (1967): 55–89.

111. R. M. Fleming, "Physical Heredity in Human Hybrids," *Annals of Eugenics* 9 (1939): 68.

112. Davenport and Steggerda, *Race Crossing in Jamaica,* 423–24.

113. C. W. Sargent, C. H. Westfall, and F. M. Adams, "The Obstetric Risk of the Japanese Woman with a Caucasoid Husband," *American Journal of Obstetrics and Gynecology* 76 (1958): 137–40. See also Morton, et al. "Genetics of Interracial Crosses," 23–24; Newton E. Morton, Chin S.Chung, and Ming-Pi Mi et al. *Genetics of Interracial Crosses in Hawaii* (New York: Karger, 1967).

114. Cedric Dover, *Half-Caste;* Prasanta Mahalanobis, "Anthropological Observations on the Anglo-Indians of Calcutta," *Records of the Indian Museum* 23 (1922–40), 1–187; P. Mahalanobis, "Analysis of Race Mixture in Bengal," *Journal of the Asiatic Society of Bengal* 23 (1927): 301–33; Elliot Smith, "The Influence of Racial Admixture in Egypt," *Eugenics Review* 7 (1915): 163–83; D. Frenchman, "Mixing of Races," *Eugenics Review* 41 (1949): 98; Jack C. Trevor, "Race Crossing in Man," *Eugenics Laboratory Memoirs* 36 (1953): iv–45; R. Ruggles Gates, "Studies in Race Crossing: The Japanese War Children," *Zeitschrift für Morphologie und Anthropologie* 49 (1958): 129–47; Raffaello Battaglia, "La Genetica Umana e l'Incrocio Razziale," in, *Le Razze e i Popoli della Terra* 1, ed. Renato Biasutti (1959): 323–54.

115. R. K. Nabours, "Emergent Evolution and Hybridism," *Science* 71 (1930): 374.

116. Herbert Jennings, *The Biological Basis of Human Nature* (New York: Norton, 1930), 280.

117. Herbert Jennings, "The Laws of Heredity and Our Present Knowledge of Human Genetics on the Material Side," in *Scientific Aspects of the Race Problem,* ed. J. W. Corrigan (New York: Longmans, 1941), 71. As "probable" disadvantages of race crossing Jennings refers to Davenport and Steggerda's inferences from their observations on Jamaican white and Negro crosses. Jennings, however, admits that "critical and unambiguous data on this matter are difficult to obtain for man," p. 72.

118. Before this, two geneticists, East and Jones, had stated that "the great individuals of Europe, the leaders in thought, have come in great numbers from peoples having very large amounts of ethnic mixture." E. M. East and D. F. Jones, *Inbreeding and Outbreeding* (Philadelphia: Lippincott, 1919), 99.

119. Ernst Kretschmer, *The Psychology of Men of Genius* (New York: Harcourt, Brace, 1931), 99.

120. John Murphy, "Racial Crossing and Cultural Efflorescence," in J. Murphy, *Lamps of Anthropology* (Manchester: Manchester University Press, 1943), 138.

121. Frank H. Hankins, *The Racial Basis of Civilization* (New York: Alfred A. Knopf, 1931), 351. This work contains an excellent discussion of "race" mixture.

122. Francis J. Trembley, "Evolution and Human Affairs," *Proceedings of the Pennsylvania Academy of Science* 23 (1949): 192.

123. Castle, "Biological and Social Consequences of Race Crossing," 156. See also E. W. Barnes, "The Mixing of Races and Social Decay," *Eugenics Review* 41 (1949): 11–16; and A. Dickinson, "Race Mixture: A Social or a Biological Problem?" *Eugenics Review* 41 (1949): 81–85; George D. Snell, "Hybrids and History: The Role of Race and Ethnic Crossing in Individual and National Achievement," *Quarterly Review of Biology* 26 (1951): 331–47; William B. Provine, "Geneticists and the Biology of Race Crossing," *Science* 182 (1973): 790–96.

11

Eugenics, Genetics, and Race

Human beings are complex organisms, and it is never an easy thing to analyze the motives involved in their behavior. The fact is that the individual himself is rarely able to give a satisfactory account of the motives for his conduct, since the elements entering into it are numerous, obscure, and complicated. One should therefore be wary in attempting to interpret the behavior of others. This applies with especial force to eugenists. Eugenists are persons who believe that the human race, or their particular branch of it, is rapidly decaying and that, if the race is to be made safe for the future, steps must be taken to eliminate the undesirable decay-producing elements and to secure a general improvement in the physical and mental constitution of their race by selective breeding.

Eugenics means good breeding. Francis Galton (1822–1911), its founder, defined it as

> the science of improving stock, which is by no means confined to questions of judicious mating but which, especially in the case of man, takes cognizance of all influences that tend in however remote a degree to give to the more suitable races or stains of blood a better chance of prevailing speedily over the less suitable than they otherwise would have had.[1]

It is quite clear from this definition that the founder of eugenics was convinced of the existence of "higher" and "lower," "superior" and "inferior," races, and that he considered it a desirable thing that the "superior" races should prevail over the "inferior" races, and that as speedily as possible. Thus, we perceive that implicit in the eugenic movement from the outset lurked the doctrine of racism.

Indeed, early in his career, Galton, in giving an account of his experiences among the Damara of South Africa, comparing the mental traits of the Damara with his dog, wrote that "the comparison reflected no great honour on the man."[2] Throughout his writings the strong influence of the idea of inborn determinants of behavior is clearly evident.

Eugenists are, in general, sincerely enthusiastic persons who are anxious to be of service to their fellows, not to mention future generations, but they are also, in many instances, dangerous persons. A little knowledge is a dangerous thing, and a great deal of the world's unhappiness is due to well-meaning persons, including scientists, who, possessing a little knowledge, attempt on the basis of it to make decisions for others whose true condition they do not understand and whose future it would be impossible for anyone to predict. It is to be feared that a large number of the most vocal eugenists fall into this category. Furthermore, it is known that the sins of some eugenists are less venal than the sins of those who have merely acted on the basis of half-baked knowledge. In the United States, and elsewhere, eugenics was early converted into a movement in the service of class interests. This is well seen in the writings of such men, to name but two, as the late Madison Grant and Henry Fairfield Osborn. In this connection Professor E. G. Conklin wrote:

> Nowadays one hears a lot of high sounding talk about 'human thoroughbreds,' which usually means that those who use this phrase desire to see certain narrow and exclusive social classes perpetuated by close inbreeding; it usually has no reference to good hereditary traits wherever found, indeed such traits would not be recognized if they appeared outside of the elite 'four hundred.' Such talk probably does neither harm nor good; the 'social thoroughbreds' are so few in number and so nearly sterile that the mass of the population is not affected by these exclusive classes.[3]

So long as no attempt is made to impose such views upon the population, no great harm can be done. All of us, however, have some knowledge of the tragic effects of the teaching of mythological race doctrines and of the practice of race hygiene in Germany. Similar attempts have frequently been made in the United States, including bills introduced into state legislatures, and passed in thirty of them, making it either a criminal offense or unlawful for persons of different colors or races to intermarry, as well as in any way to assist such a union. Such activities, among others, caused eugenics to fall into disrepute among scientific students of eugenics and genetics, genetics being the science of heredity upon which eugenics is allegedly based. The clear stream of science must not be polluted by the murky visions of politicians and the prescriptions of effete castes distinguished by a hypertrophied sense of their own importance.

While it is praiseworthy to look forward to, and to work for, a more humane humanity and a world with fewer genetically-originated diseases and disorders of the body and the mind, and perhaps greater numbers of highly intelligent and healthy persons, it is quite certain that such a state could never be achieved by such practices as the eugenists have in the past recommended. During the heyday of the eugenics movement more than 60,000 American citizens were eugenically sterilized.[4] Certain genetically inherited disorders may raise the question of sterilization, but one is deceived if one believes that by such measures these conditions would be appreciably reduced. Were every individual predisposed to such disorders sterilized for the next two thousand years, the reduction in the number of afflicted individuals in the population at the end of that time would not exceed 50 percent. Superior methods are available, but they do not appeal to eugenists, who fail to understand that eugenics should be a social science, not a biological one.

The objections to negative eugenics are clear, unequivocal, and unanswerable. The recommendations of negative eugenics are: (1) theoretically unsound, and therefore (2) practically unjustifiable, not to mention the dangers of the political misapplication of such unsound ideas, as was the case in Nazi Germany; (3) fertility is generally reduced in those affected by recessively determined abnormalities; (4) even when such individuals breed, their offspring in most cases are healthy; (5) even if it were possible, sterilization of the heterozygous carriers would waste an enormous potential of normal births; (6) conditions due to rare dominant genes usually result in infertile individuals; and in (7) other conditions due to unfavorable dominant genes the fertility is usually low, hence, (8) most conditions due to defective genes are self-limiting since their bearers do not propagate; (9) carriers of defective genes also carry a large number of normal genes which in homozygous state often give rise to above-average traits; (10) many hereditary disorders are amenable to environmental alleviation; (11) the increase in population mobility and the collapse of innumerable barriers to intermixture between large numbers of people who were hitherto separated reduces the chances of deleterious genes coming together; (12) sterilizing homozygotes who show a defective trait due to recessive genes still leaves by far the greater number of individuals carrying the gene in heterozygous state to circulate freely throughout the population. If, for example, the frequency of a recessive gene in the general population were 1 in 1,000, that would mean that the homozygote in whom the defective trait was expressed would occur in 1 out of 1,000,000 individuals. Supposing the homozygous individual were sterilized, that would still leave 999 heterozygotes to distribute the gene. Clearly, a rather inefficient and ineffectual way of dealing with the problem; (13) since the number of genes of any given sort in the human species is usually very large, any artificially induced changes in their number in any local portion of the species is likely to have very little if any effect upon the total frequency; and finally (14) because negative eugenics overlooks such facts it would certainly do more harm to the human species than defective genes are capable of doing.

The very condition of "feeble-mindedness," for example, one of the most popular of the biological bogeys of the eugenist, is often the expression of inadequate socialization or education in the process of becoming a social human being. In offering their dubious cures for our alleged ills the extremists among eugenists go even further and pretend to perceive biological differences between races. They arbitrarily designate as "superior" the race or stock to which they happen to belong and as "inferior" all or most of the others. The corollary to this is that race mixture should be prevented if racial degeneration, according to their definition, is not to ensue. It is with this aspect of eugenics that we are concerned here.

The term "race," as we have seen, is an unscientific one. Science knows of nothing in the real world relating to human beings which in any way corresponds to what this term is usually assumed to mean, that is, a group of individuals marked off from all others by a distinctive heredity and the possession of particular physical and mental traits. In this sense there is actually only one race, or one thing which corresponds to it, and that is the human race, embracing every human being. It is, of course, clear that there exist certain groups within the human race which are characterized by differences in pigmentation, hair form, nose form, and other traits. These we have already called "ethnic groups."

If, as seems clear, all human groups are derived from a common ancestry, then it is also clear that such differences represent the expression of the combined action of mutant genes, genetic drift, hybridization, natural and social selection. In any event, such ethnic groups would by the very fact of their existence prove, in the scale of natural values, biologically fit. There can, therefore, be no argument on the score of the physical or biological structure of any ethnic group—unless an appeal be made to purely arbitrary and irrelevant aesthetic standards.

Actually, the argument is always based on the existence of alleged mental and cultural differences; these are invariably assumed to be biologically determined. For such an assumption there is not, as we have seen, a scrap of evidence. On the contrary, the substantial body of evidence now available proves that when the members of any ethnic group are given for the first time adequate opportunities, they do, on the average, quite as well as any who have long enjoyed the advantages of such opportunities. And as Boas has said, "if we were to select the most intelligent, imaginative, energetic and emotionally stable third of mankind, all races would be represented."[5]

As we have seen, there exists no evidence whatever that mental ability and cultural achievement are functions which are in any way associated with genes linked with those for skin color, hair form, nose shape, or any other physical character. It is, therefore, from the genetic standpoint, impossible to say anything about a person's mental ability or cultural achievement on the basis of such physical traits alone.

The core belief, the very essence, of racism and race is that there exists a biological linkage between physical appearance, mental ability, and the competence to achieve a high civilization. The facts of science make it unequivocally clear that there exists no genetic linkages whatever between those three conditions, that they are quite independent of one another, and that the potentialities for the achievement of mental ability are, under similar circumstances, alike in all ethnic groups.

Cultural differences between peoples are due to a multiplicity of historical causes that have nothing whatever to do with genes and that are essentially and fundamentally of a social nature. To the same causes are due the differences in cultural conduct, the behavior, of the members of those different cultures. Hence, on biological grounds and as a consequence of the common ancestry of all peoples—however much they may differ from one another in their physical characters—there is every reason to believe that innate mental capacity is more or less equally distributed in all its phases in all human groups. If this is so, and this is a matter which can be tested, there can be not the slightest justification for the assertion that ethnic mixture would lead to the intellectual deterioration of any people. The evidence is all to the contrary, as the facts of hybridization among human beings prove. In this connection Julian Huxley has written that he regards it as "wholly probable that true Negroes have a slightly lower average intelligence than the whites or yellows."[6] But neither this nor any other eugenically significant point of racial difference has yet been scientifically established.[7] "Further, even were the probability to be established that some 'races' and some classes are genetically inferior to others as a fact, it seems certain, on the basis of our present knowledge, that the differences would be small differences in average level, and that the ranges would overlap most of their extent—in other words, that a considerable proportion of the 'inferior' group would be actually superior to the lower half of the 'superior' group. Thus no really rapid eugenic progress would come of encouraging the reproduction of one class or race against another."[8]

Huxley committed a rather common methodological error when he opined that true blacks probably have a slightly lower average intelligence than whites or yellows. The question must be asked: "Average intelligence measured by what standard?" Surely, it should at this late date be evident that intelligence, by whatever standard it is measured, is always largely a function of cultural experience as well as of inherent potentialities.[9] The fact that this is so is strikingly brought out with reference to the blacks themselves and in relation to whites by the results obtained in the Army intelligence tests carried out on black and white recruits during World War I. These tests showed that Northern black recruits on the average did better on the tests than Southern black recruits. The tests also showed that blacks from certain Northern states on the whole did better in the tests than white

TABLE 11.1

ARMY COMPREHENSIVE ALPHA TESTS: WHITE RECRUITS FROM ELEVEN
SOUTHERN STATES COMPARED WITH BLACK RECRUITS FROM FOUR NORTHERN STATES[a]

WHITES		BLACKS	
State	*Median Score*	*State*	*Median Score*
Arkansas	35.60	Ohio	45.35
Mississippi	37.65	Illinois	42.25
North Carolina	38.20	Indiana	41.55
Georgia	39.35	New York	38.60
Louisiana	41.10		
Alabama	41.35		
Kentucky	41.50		
Oklahoma	43.00		
Texas	43.45		
Tennessee	44.00		
South Carolina	45.05		

[a]Computed from the data in Yerkes (ed.), "Psychological Examining in the United States Army," *Memoirs of the National Academy of Sciences*, XV (1921), 690 and 691, tables 205–06. Data for the Negro recruits was available for only twenty-four out of the forty-eight states and the District of Columbia. Had data been available for all areas of the United States, it is quite probable that several more states would have shown higher median scores for blacks than for whites of some other states. See Ashley Montagu, "Intelligence of Northern Negroes and Southern Whites in the First World War," *American Journal of Psychology*, LXVIII (1945), 161–88.

recruits from almost all the Southern states. The median scores of the groups concerned can be seen in Table 11.1.

From Table 11.1 it will be seen that the blacks from Ohio with a median score of 45.35 did better than the whites of eleven states, all of which happen to be Southern. blacks of Illinois with a score of 42.25 and the blacks of Indiana with a score of 41.55 did better than the whites from seven Southern states, while the blacks from New York with a score of 38.60 did better than the whites from three Southern states. All the evidence indicates that the blacks from the Northern states who did better than the blacks and whites from the Southern states listed did so not because of any inborn differences between them but because the social and economic opportunities of the Northern blacks had been superior to those enjoyed by Southern blacks and whites. The results of these tests have been fully corroborated by tests made on Northern and Southern black children.[10]

Marcuse and Bitterman have shown that the scores made on these tests are highly correlated with the yearly educational expenditures of the states

TABLE 11.2

BANK-ORDER CORRELATIONS BETWEEN MEDIAN BETA SCORES FOR
THE VARIOUS STATES AND MEDIAN ALPHA SCORES,
ANNUAL EDUCATIONAL EXPENDITURES (1910) AND PER CAPITA INCOMES (1919)[a]

	Educational Expenditures Per Capita Population 5–17 Years	*Per Capita Income*	*Alpha[b] (White)*	*Alpha[b] (Black)*
Beta (white)[c]	.64 (.81)[d]	.50 (.64)[d]	.67	
Beta (black)[c]	.72 (.76)[d]	.67 (.72)[d]		.65

[a]From Marcuse and Bitterman, "Notes on the Results of Army Intelligence Testing in World War I," *Science*, 104 (1946), 231–32.
[b]Alpha tests were given to literates.
[c]Beta tests were designed for illiterates and foreigners.
[d]Figures in parentheses are comparable correlations with median Alpha scores.

from which the testees were drawn as well as with the per capita income prevailing in those states. These facts are well brought out in Table 11.2, and, as Marcuse and Bitterman remark, "It is probably most warranted to conclude from the correlations presented here that Beta scores, like Alpha scores, are strongly influenced by cultural factors concomitant with the socioeconomic levels of the states."[11]

It is not impossible that there exist differences in the distribution of the kinds of temperament, intelligence, and other behavioral traits in different ethnic groups, but if such differences exist, they must, as Huxley has pointed out, be very small. The important fact is, surely, that every living ethnic group has survived to the present time because it has been able to meet the demands of its particular environment or environments with a high order of intelligence, of mental plasticity, flexibility, adaptability, and the necessary physical vigor. This is a truth which holds for the most isolated group of aborigines as for the most technologically advanced peoples. Measured by such standards, it seems probable that there are no significant differences in the intelligence potentials of different ethnic groups.

When eugenists have asserted that there has been a great increase in degeneracy, criminality,[12] and "feeble-mindedness," and that the race is rapidly deteriorating, they do so generally without benefit of a full knowledge of the facts whereof they speak, for the truth is that except for the *ex cathedra* manner in which such statements are usually delivered, no real evidence is ever forthcoming in support of their jeremiads. The good will to help is blind and often cruel if it is not guided by true insight based on knowledge. A physician can be of use only when he has first carefully investigated the cause of disease and when it is quite clear what his remedies can effect; otherwise he is a positive danger.

Dr. Irving Langmuir, in his presidential address to the American Association for the Advancement of Science in 1943, uttered a pertinent criticism in this connection. "We often hear realists," he said,

> deplore the effects of charity which tend to keep the unfit alive. We are even told that the whole course of evolution may be revised in this way. Similar arguments could be used against the surgeon who removes an appendix or a doctor who uses a sulfa drug to cure pneumonia.
>
> But what is the need of developing a race immune to appendicitis if we possess means of preventing their ill-effects? The characteristics that determine fitness merely change from those of immunity to those which determine whether a race is able to provide good medical treatment.[13]

Today our many varieties of recording facilities are immeasurably superior to those in existence a hundred years ago, and our hospitals, physicians, resident care facilities, police, and incentives to crime are vastly more numerous. Yet, in spite of all these tokens of "decline," the expectation of life of the average individual at birth has in modern times practically doubled, while some of the worst scourges of humankind, such as the vitamin-deficiency diseases, the venereal diseases, typhoid, typhus, yellow fever, diphtheria, tuberculosis, and many others, have been brought under control. Recently a new strain of tuberculosis has developed, but this too will likely be brought under control with new discoveries. During this century there has been such a burgeoning of invention and discovery, such a flowering of intellectual development, as the world has never before witnessed, and all this, presumably, as a sort of efflorescence of the process of deterioration. The swan song of a world the eugenist never made. Or have the great achievements of the past hundred years, perhaps, been due to the genius of a few individuals who have managed to carry the burden of the mediocrities along with them? This is a view which is frequently urged by "superior" persons. It is a sad commentary upon the understanding and the charity of those who hold it and it does scant justice to untold millions of individuals who were never given a chance, who made good as best they knew how—which was more often than not as best they were permitted—and who died unmourned and unremembered.

Let us give human beings equal social, cultural, and economic opportunities, and then we shall be able to judge how many, if any, genetically "inadequate" individuals we have among us. We shall then be in a position to judge the nature of the biological measures that ought to be instituted to ensure the welfare of our species. Surely it should be clear that these measures would not really be biological, but social, and that in their effects the social advantages would always be greater than the biological ones. This would, surely, be the most reasonable procedure, in view of the fact that in most cases it would take many hundreds of years to eliminate, even partially, a single defective trait.[14] Only a few generations would be required for a purely social endeavor to determine whether or not many of the alleged deteriorative factors said to be undermining the health of the race could be eliminated by improving the social environment. Our present social ills are, for the most part, produced not by genetically "inadequate" persons, but by socially inadequate ones, and the remedy for those ills therefore lies first in the improvement of the social environments of our species. Our troubles, it must be repeated, emanate not from biological defectives but from social defectives; and, in general, social defectives are produced by society, not by genes. It is social, not biological, therapy that is indicated.

The great fallacy committed by eugenists and by numerous others is that, having to some extent followed the work of geneticists in breeding certain characters in other animals within the walls of a laboratory, they have extrapolated from the laboratory findings on such lower animals to conditions vastly more complex and obscure, and which have, moreover, never formed the subject of experimental investigation. Human beings are not representative of strains similar to the selected pure strains of mice and rabbits which form the geneticist's material. Naive and uninformed persons believe that if in the geneticist's breeding laboratory the genetics of a certain trait is studied and the experimenter can at will breed his animals for that trait, the same thing can be done for human beings. Theoretically and under certain ideal conditions and given scores of generations of selected human beings this could be done for some, but not for all, traits. Obviously this is impractical; if it were practical it would still be open to question whether it would be desirable.[15]

Geneticists, to whose work the eugenist frequently appeals, have in some cases not been altogether guiltless in assisting the purposes of the eugenist, and some of them have been scientifically almost as badly deluded as the most uncritical of eugenists.[16] Much of the research of geneticists has been on breeds of domesticated plants and animals that have been rendered highly uniform by intense inbreeding and selection. Geneticists have also studied traits produced by mutant genes, and certain human congenital abnormalities. Others studied the effects of crossing between species. From these researches a great body of facts have emerged which, by some geneticists, were at once extrapolated to humans and uncritically applied to the differences existing between human populations. The error committed lies in the assumption that human populations are genetically as simple as domestic races of plants or animals. They are not. As Haldane has pointed out, the attempt to build a human genetics on the basis of results obtained from domestic races, laboratory mutants, and species crosses is as erroneous as would be the attempt to build biochemistry on a study of the reaction of simple crystalloids. This does not mean that much needed and invaluable information for the better understanding of the human genetics cannot be obtained from researches on natural and artificial populations of animals, but it does mean that one must be extremely cautious in making use of such data.

A special duty therefore devolves upon geneticists to take special pains to correct the possible misinterpretations which their findings may be given, for such misinterpretations can be socially extremely dangerous. Geneticists should be clear and make it clear that their findings are misleading when applied to human populations or groups. Unlike many eugenists, scientists frankly confess that they do not know all the answers. The truth is that we do not yet know enough about human heredity to meddle with human beings in order to improve the stock. Two mediocrities may produce a genius; two geniuses may produce a mediocrity. In view of the fact that the genes for defective traits are frequently carried in the recessive condition, it is generally impossible to spot them in apparently otherwise normal individuals, and it is in most cases therefore impossible to predict when they are likely to crop out. Selective breeding, as understood by the eugenist, is inbreeding, and that is a notoriously dangerous process, for by such means the chances are greatly increased of bringing together recessives of a character detrimental to the organism. By outbreeding such recessives become associated with dominants and therefore remain unexpressed.

When selection is practiced on animals, we keep only those animals that exhibit a particular trait; the others, showing undesired traits, are killed. Humankind, it is very much to be feared, is not to be saved by being treated like a lot of race horses or a strain of dogs, at the fancier's discretion. Human beings require to be treated as human beings, as something rather more than animals; for the ills from which our particular sample of humankind suffers result from the misuse of humankind's capacities for being human. Those ills are not due to the totally irrelevant fact that people are members of the animal kingdom subject to the laws of genetics as are all other animals.

In effect, eugenists tell us that by random mating defective traits are accumulated in the recessive state until the whole population becomes affected. The defects so carried will then become expressed and will wreak havoc upon such a population. Upon this kind of fantastic reasoning Dobzhansky has made the following adequate comment:

> It is not an easy matter to evaluate the significance of the accumulation of germinal changes in the population genotypes. Judged superficially, a

progressive saturation of the germ plasm of a species with mutant genes a majority of which are deleterious in their effects is a destructive process, a sort of deterioration of the genotype which threatens the very existence of the species and can finally lead only to its extinction. The eugenical Jeremiahs keep constantly before our eyes the nightmare of human populations accumulating recessive genes that produce pathological effects when homozygous. These prophets of doom seem to be unaware of the fact that wild species in the state of nature fare in this respect no better than man does with all the artificiality of his surroundings, and yet life has not come to an end on this planet. The eschatological cries proclaiming the failure of natural selection to operate in human populations have more to do with political beliefs than with scientific findings.[17]

Certainly we could do a great deal to reduce genetic disorders among us. It is also important to realize that many individuals with conditions determined by their genes are today alive who in the past would not have survived long. It should, however, be clear that wherever in an ethnic group or nation such individuals exist they constitute a problem which can be dealt with by social means alone—social means based upon humane social principles and sound scientific knowledge. To proceed on the basis of the one without the other would be dangerous and undesirable.[18]

At present the healthy person is in all ethnic groups far more numerous than the person who is not, and the chances are excellent that cross-breeding between such groups will decrease rather than increase the incidence of genetic disorders. Hence, we may conclude that there is nothing in the nature of any ethnic group, taken as a whole, that could upon either genetic or eugenic grounds be construed as leading to any ill effects under crossing. In conclusion, then, until humans have put their social house in order, it would be unwise to indulge in any strenuous biological exercises, for a rickety house standing on shaky foundations is not the proper place for such performances.

Notes

1. Francis Galton, *Inquiries into the Human Faculty and Its Development* (London: Macmillan, 1883).

2. Francis Galton, *The Narrative of an Explorer in Tropical South Africa* (London: John Murray, 1853), 134.

3. Edwin G. Conklin, *Heredity and Environment* (Princeton: Princeton University Press, 1939), 306. For a brilliant "anatomy" of some of the English eugenists see Lancelot Hogben, *Dangerous Thoughts* (New York: Norton, 1940), 44–58. For good critical historical discussions of the eugenics movement see Mark H. Haller, *Eugenics: Hereditarian Attitudes in American Thought* (New Brunswick: Rutgers University Press, 1963); Stefan Kuhl, *The Nazi Connection: Eugenics, American Racism,*

and German Nationalism (New York: Oxford University Press, 1944); Kenneth Ludmerer, *Genetics and American Society* (Baltimore: Johns Hopkins University Press, 1972); Donald K. Pickens, *Eugenics and the Progressives* (Nashville: Vanderbilt University Press, 1968); William B. Provine, "Geneticists and the Biology of Race Crossing," *Science* 182 (1973): 790–96; Daniel J. Kevles, *In the Name of Genetics* (New York: Knopf, 1985).

4. I say "past" because there have been happy evidences of a return to sanity among some eugenicists. See, for example, Frederick Osborn's *A Preface to Eugenics* (New York: Harper, 1940). See also Julian Huxley, "Eugenics and Society," in his *Man Stands Alone* (New York: Harper, 1941).

5. Franz Boas, *Anthropology and Modern Life* (New York: Norton, 1928), 75.

6. It is of interest to note that Huxley's grandfather, Thomas H. Huxley, wrote in 1865: "It may be quite true that some negroes are better than some white men; but no rational man, cognizant of the facts, believes that the average negro is the equal, still less the superior, of the average white man. . . . The highest places in the hierarchy of civilization will assuredly not be within the reach of our dusky cousins." "Emancipation—Black and White," in his *Science and Education* (New York: Collier, 1901), 64–65.

7. Elsewhere J. Huxley states that "the genetic variability of the human species is so well distributed that the average genetic difference between classes or social groups and different nations or ethnic groups is negligible or small in its effects compared with the improvements which can be effected through better living conditions and education." *Heredity East and West* (New York: Schuman, 1949), 185.

8. J. Huxley, *Man Stands Alone,* 53.

9. Not to mention numerous other environmental factors, prenatal, nutritional, neuro-humoral influences depending upon the mother's psychological state, and the like. See A. Montagu, *Prenatal Influences* (Springfield, IL: Thomas, 1962); A. Montagu, *Life Before Birth* (New York: New American Library, 1964).

10. Otto Klineberg, *Negro Intelligence and Selective Migration* (New York: Columbia University Press, 1935).

11. F. L. Marcuse and M. E. Bitterman, "Notes on the Results of Army Intelligence Testing in World War I," *Science* 104 (1946): 231–32.

12. For an examination of the problem of crime in our society see A. Montagu, "The Biologist Looks at Crime," *Annals of the Academy of Political and Social Science* 217 (1941): 46–57; Robert K. Merton and M. F. Ashley Montagu, "Crime and the Anthropologist," *American Anthropologist* 52 (1940): 384–408; Willem A. Bonger, *Race and Crime* (New York: Columbia University Press, 1943); Harry E. Barnes and Negley K. Teeters, *New Horizons in Criminology* (New York: Prentice-Hall, 1943.

13. Irving Langmuir, "Science, Common Sense and Decency," *Science* 97 (1943): 6.

14. Informed eugenists are well aware of this fact, but the informed eugenist in practice has often been indistinguishable from the extreme eugenist. Whatever the informed eugenist may say, we must judge him, as we must everyone else, by what he does or proposes to do.

15. While breeding for certain desirable characters in plants or lower animals, it frequently happens that certain undesirable characters are developed. The genes for these, carried as recessives, under normal conditions remain unex-

pressed, but under controlled breeding find expression because of their unsuspected linkage with the genes physiologically associated with the trait considered desirable. For example, Asdell has observed that "all the intersexual goats he had seen (about 200) were hornless. Hornlessness is inherited as a simple dominant trait. Since then much inquiry and observation have failed to unearth a single intersex. If they exist, they must be very rare. This suggests that there is a close linkage between the two genes, an important point economically, since selection for hornlessness has been practiced by pedigree goat breeders for some time. The goat breeders have evidently been increasing the gene frequency for intersex by selecting for hornlessness and are thus doing themselves harm." S. A. Asdell, "The Genetic Sex of Intersexual Goats and a Probable Linkage with the Gene for Hornlessness," *Science* 99 (1944): 124.

16. See, for example, the article by the distinguished geneticist Cyril D. Darlington, "The Genetic Understanding of Race in Man," *International Social Science Bulletin* (UNESCO) 2 (1950): 479–88. See also the reply to this by A. Montagu, "Answer by an Anthropologist to a Geneticist about the Understanding of Race in Man," *International Social Science Bulletin* (UNESCO) 3 (1951): 1007–10. See also Cyril D. Darlington, *The Evolution of Man and Society* (New York: Simon and Schuster, 1969), and for a devastating review see Carroll Quigley, "Review of Darlington's 'The Evolution of Man and Society,'" *American Anthropologist* 73 (1971): 434–39.

17. Theodisius Dobzhansky, *Genetics and the Origin of Species,* 1st ed. (New York: Columbia University Press, 1937), 126.

18. J. E. Mead and A. S. Parkes, eds., *Biological Aspects of Social Problems* (New York: Plenum Press, 1955); J. E. Mead and A. S. Parkes, *Genetic and Environmental Factors in Human Ability* (New York: Plenum Press, 1966); Lord Platt and A. S. Parkes, *Social and Genetic Influences on Life and Death* (New York: Plenum Press, 1967).

12

Race and Culture

The questions are often asked: "Why is it that the cultures of different races differ so much from one another? Is this because race and culture are inseparable?" "Do differences in race have anything to do with the differences in cultural development as between the races?" The answer to these questions is really simple. Cultures differ from one another to the extent to which the history, the experience, of each of the interacting groups has differed. By "history," by "experience" we mean anything that a person or group of persons has undergone or lived, perceived, or sensed. No matter with what groups of humans we may be concerned, culture is in its broadest and fundamental sense not merely an aspect but a function of experience. Cultures are created by human beings. The definition of culture itself constitutes the answer to our question: culture is the humanmade part of the environment. It is human beings, not supernaturals or genes that create the ways in which they live. The way of life of a people is its culture. The visitor to an indigenous tribe who wrote of its manners and customs, "Customs beastly: manners none," was not likely to make much progress in the understanding of these matters. Race and culture do not appear to be in any way connected. As Klineberg has pointed out:

> The argument from the cultural contributions of a particular ethnic group to the inborn racial characteristics of that group falls down for many reasons: cultures may vary while race remains unchanged, the same culture may be found in groups of different race, what looks like a superior cultural contribution from one point of view may seem much less significant when another criterion is applied, etc. Studies of race mixture are similarly inconclusive, since individuals of mixed racial heredity cannot be shown to be different in their inborn psychological characteristics from those of 'pure' race. Finally, there is no evidence that some racial groups are biologically more 'primitive' or undeveloped than others.
>
> This does not mean that heredity plays no part in the determination of behavior. On the contrary, there is good evidence that 'individuals' and 'families' may be distinguished from others in terms of hereditary as well

as acquired characteristics. As regards large racial groups, however, there appears to be about the same range of hereditary capacities in one group as in another. The fact that differences in behavior between such groups obviously exist, is no proof that they exist because they are inborn.[1]

The reason the cultures of other ethnic groups are so often different from our own is that they have been exposed to experiences which differ as considerably from our own as do the cultures in question. If you or I, with our present genetic background, had been born and brought up among a group of Australian aborigines, we would be, culturally, behaviorally, Australian aborigines, though physically we would retain the appearance of our own background; although facial expression is likely to be strongly influenced by the unconcious influences of the aboriginal culture, even to the matter of gestures and gait. Experience is determined by the place and the culture in which groups and individuals live and have their being, and for this reason groups and persons belonging to different cultures will differ mentally from one another. Our physical structures would not have varied significantly, because they were for the most part genetically determined by our biological parents, but our physical expression would almost certainly have been modified, and our cultural equipment would be that of an Australian aboriginal. Why? Because culture is learned—and by "culture" is to be understood the way of life of a people; its ideas, sentiments, religious and secular beliefs, its language, tools and other material products, its institutions, customs, values, and ideals. Culture begins with socialization virtually at birth, if not before, with learning, and terminates only with death. Because culture is something that one acquires by experience, unlike one's physical appearance, which one acquires through the action, for the most part, of inherited genes, but which under the influence of socializing and culturalizing factors is subject to considerable modification. The culture of persons, as of groups, will differ according to the kinds of experience they have undergone. That socializing experience is *culturally, not biologically* transmitted.[2]

Illuminating in this connection is a study by Professor Erwin H. Ackerknecht, who has brought together the facts concerning white children who had been abducted from their parents by North American Indians during the eighteenth and nineteenth centuries. Professor Ackerknecht gives us the accounts of eight fairly well-recorded life histories of such children.

All these children were taken by the Indians when they were between the ages of four and nine years, with the exception of a girl who was taken in adolescence. All of them forgot their native culture, and even the girl who had been captured when she was 15 years of age became completely Indianized. In every case these "white Indians" resisted all attempts to persuade them to return to their white relatives and to the culture of their birth. As Ackerknecht says, the "white Indians" seemed to have found "a kind of unity of thought and action and a kind of social cohesion which deeply appealed to them, and which they did not find with the whites, especially not with the pioneers. There is no doubt that this fact largely contributed to their staying with the Indians."[3]

The remarkable fact about these "white Indians" is that they not only became completely Indianized culturally in the sense of manifesting purely Indian forms of social behavior, but they also developed all the physical powers of resistance said to be peculiar to Indians. Furthermore, most of them lived to be extremely old. Finally, all of them had acquired the facial expression and outward impassability characteristic of the Indian. Samuel Stanhope Smith was among the first, if not the first, to comment upon this fact. In 1810 he wrote,

> Another example of the power of society in forming the countenance is well known to all those who are acquainted with the savage tribes spread along the frontiers of these states. Among them you frequently meet with persons who have been taken captive in infancy from Anglo-American families, and grown up in the habits of savage life. These descendants of the fairest Europeans universally contract such a resemblance of the natives, in their countenance, and even in their complexion, as not to be easily distinguished from them; and afford a striking proof that the differences in physiognomy, between the Anglo-American, and the Indian depend principally on the state of society.[4]

Of many of these "white Indians" it is expressly recorded that, having been accustomed to Indian ways they could no longer sleep in a house or in a bed.[5]

Such facts should go a long way toward disproving the view that culture is something that will express itself in genetically determined form no matter what the environmental influences to which the person is exposed.

It should always be remembered that the organism does not inherit traits, but only genes, and that genes do not determine traits, but in interaction with the environment and the effects of its own idiosyncratic history, influence their physiological and behavioral development.[6]

The culture of different peoples, as of different individuals, is to a large extent a reflection of their past history or experience. This is a point worth more than laboring. If the cultural status of any variety of human is determined merely by its experience, then it is evident that by giving all people the opportunity to enjoy a common experience—supposing for the moment that this was desirable—all varieties would become culturally and mentally equal. That is, they would become equal in the sense that they would have benefited from exposure to the same kind of experience, the individual's own contribution to his or her development, always allowing, of course, for the idiosyncratic history of the individual, the fact that no two persons can ever be alike in their reception of and response to the same experience. There will always, fortunately, continue to exist great differences between persons.[7]

There can be little doubt that genetic differences in temperament and intellectual capacity exist between the individuals comprising every variety of human, no two individuals in this respect ever being alike; but it takes the stimulus of a common experience to bring them out and to render them comparable. It is because of differences in their history, in cultural experience, that individuals and groups differ from one another culturally, and it is for this reason that cultural achievement is an exceedingly poor measure of the cultural potentialities of a person or a group.[8]

This is not a novel idea. It was stated by the great French statesman and economist Robert Jacques Turgot (1727–1781) two centuries ago, when he wrote that "The human mind contains everywhere the germs of the same progress; but nature, partial in her gifts, has endowed certain minds with an abundance of talents which she has refused to others; circumstances develop these talents or relegate them to obscurity; and to the infinite variety of these circumstances is due the inequality in the progress of nations."[9]

For all practical purposes, and until further evidence to the contrary be forthcoming, we can safely take the culture of a people to be the expression principally of a particular history of cultural experience. Obviously, all learned activities are culturally, not biologically, determined, whether those activities are based upon physiological urges or traditional practices. The generalized needs which all human beings inherit in common continue to be present in all human beings in all cultures; but how these needs are permitted to express themselves and how they are satisfied is something determined by custom and tradition and varies not only in different cultures but within different groups within the same culture. For example, one of the fundamental needs which we all inherit is the need to eat. Different human groups, to whom the same foodstuffs may or may not be available; not only eat different foods but prepare them in different ways, and consume them, with or without implements, in various ways, usually established only by custom.

The potentiality for speech is biologically determined, but whether we speak, what we speak, and how we speak, is determined by what we hear in the culture in which we have been culturalized. Human beings everywhere experience, when they are tired, the desire to rest, to sit down, to lie down, or to sleep; but the manner in which they do all these things is culturally determined by the customs of the group in which they live. Many other instances will doubtless occur to the reader. The point to grasp here is that even our fundamental biological needs are more or less culturally controlled and regulated or culturalized and that their very form and expression, not to mention satisfactions, are molded according to the dictates of tradition. Culture, tradition, channels our biological processes.

In view of the immense number of different cultural influences that enter into the structure and functioning of different groups and the individuals composing them, it is surely the most gratuitous, as it is the most unscientific procedure to assert anything concerning assumed genetic conditions without first attempting to discover what part these cultural influences play in the production of what is predicated. Obviously, no statement concerning the mentality of a person is of any value without a specification of the conditions of the environment in which that mentality developed. The introduction of genes or heredity as the *deus ex machina* to account for cultural differences between people may be a convenient device for those who must do everything in their power, except study the actual facts, to find some sort of support for their prejudices, but it is a device which will hardly satisfy the requirements of an acceptable scientific method. Such devices must be accepted in a charitable spirit as the perverse efforts of some of our misguided fellows to maintain their own shaky feelings of superiority by depreciating the capacities of others. John Stuart Mill, more than a hundred years ago, in his *Principles of Political Economy* (1848), put the stamp upon this type of conduct. He wrote: "Of all the vulgar modes of escaping from the consideration of the effect of social and moral influence on the human mind, the most vulgar is that of attributing the diversities of conduct and character to inherent natural differences."[10] In his *Physics and Politics* (1869) Walter Bagehot said much the same thing: "When a philosopher cannot account for anything in any other manner, he boldly ascribes it to an occult quality in some race." While the number of people who do this sort of thing has greatly increased since the days of Mill and Bagehot, the number who realize the absurdity of such practices has also grown considerably, so that on this count there is no need to despair of the future. The situation often gets qualitatively better as it looks quantitatively worse. The facts now available concerning the peoples of the earth render it quite clear that they are all very definitely brothers under the skin.

It is, perhaps, too much to expect those who have been educated in the contrary belief to accept such a view; the least, therefore, that we can do is to provide the children in our schools with a straightforward account of the facts instead of filling their guiltless heads with the kinds of prejudice that we find distributed through so many of the books and so much of the teaching with which they are provided. Surely, a sympathetic understanding of people who behave "differently," look "differently," cannot

help but broaden one's horizons and lead to better human relationships
all around. Socially this is, of course, greatly to be desired, and in the
United States a beginning has already been made in this direction in several cities. Such enterprises, however, must be multiplied several thousand
times. Here, obviously, there is much work to be done.

But let us return to our main discussion, for though school children
and others have frequently heard of physical relativity, few, if any, children,
and hardly anyone else (apart from anthropologists), ever encounter the
concept of "cultural relativity." From the standpoint of the well-being and
happiness of humankind the latter is a vastly more important conception
to grasp than the former.

Cultural relativity implies that all cultures must be evaluated in relation to their own history, and carefully, not by the arbitrary standard of
any single culture such, for example, as our own. Judged in relation to its
own history, each culture is seen as the resultant of the responses to the
challenges which that history may or may not record. If those challenges
have been limited in nature, so will the culture reflecting their effects. If
the challenges have been many and complex in character, then the culture will reflect that complexity. Culture is essentially a relation that is the
product of the interaction between several correlates—flexibility, forma-
bility sensitivity and experience, a biological being, who responds to the
challenges of his environments, the other simply experience. If we agree
that humankind is everywhere plastic, adaptable, and sensitive, then we
can most satisfactorily account for the mental and cultural differences between the varieties of humans on the basis of different experiences. And
this, when everything is taken into consideration, seems to be the principal explanation of the mental and cultural differences that exist between
ethnic groups.

Let me give one or two examples of cultural relativity, as it were, in action. Five thousand years ago the ancestors of the present highly cultured
peoples of Europe were "backward barbarians" settled in the wilds of Europe. The ancestors of the modern Englishman were living in a Stone Age
phase of culture, being culturally not much more advanced than many
peoples whom we today call primitive or non-literate. When in 54 B.C. Caesar conquered the Britons he found them to be in a Bronze Age phase of
cultural development. Five thousand years ago Europe was inhabited by
hordes of "barbarians," at a time when the kingdoms of Upper and Lower
Egypt were at their height.[11] These have long since passed into history, but
five thousand years ago and less the peoples of these great cultures could
have looked upon the Europeans as barbarians who by nature were completely incapable of civilization—and hence better exterminated lest they
pollute the "blood" of their superiors. Whatever sins the Europeans have
since committed, they have at least shown that given a sufficient amount of

time and experience they were capable of civilization to a degree not less than that to which the peoples of Egypt of the First and Second Dynasties (3200–2780 B.C.) attained.

It should be a sobering thought to learn that the great basic discoveries on which modern civilization rests—writing, and later the alphabet, the wheel, the astronomical calendar, metallurgy, and so on—were made in the Middle East, at a time when most of the peoples of Northwestern Europe were "backward barbarians."

Here we have an example of cultural relativity. If we use time as our frame of reference, we might ask: "Since the Egyptians have had a much longer time than we to develop culturally, why haven't they developed as far as we have?" Disregarding the dubious notion that any human group has enjoyed a longer time in which to develop than any other, the answer is that time is not a proper measure to apply to the development of culture or cultural events. Time is only a convenient framework from which to observe their development. Cultural changes that among some peoples it has taken centuries to produce are among other peoples often effected within a few years.[12]

The rate of cultural change is dependent upon many different factors, but the indispensable condition for the production of cultural change is the irritability produced by the stimulus of such new experiences; cultural change is exceedingly slow. Hence, if new experience is the chief determinant of cultural change, then the dimension by which we may most efficiently judge cultures is that of the history of the experience which has fallen to the lot of the cultures observed. In other words, to evaluate cultural events properly one must judge them by the measure of experience viewed through the framework of time.[13] We of the Western world have packed more experience into the past two thousand years than have the Australian aborigines, during their 60,000 years of continuous settlement of Australia.

Experience, or variety of cultural contacts, not time, is the all-important factor. It would obviously be wrong to expect an Australian aboriginal to behave like an Eton and Oxford graduate; but that is not to say that, with similar experience, he would not do at least as well at either institution. Until the very recent period the Australian aborigines were even more cut off from almost all cultural contact than the Britons were during the Upper Paleolithic and the Mesolithic. Britain was situated well within the periphery of the eddying streams of European cultural development— from Neolithic times onward. Britons experienced the influx of many different cultures, such as the Celtic, Scandanavian, Saxon and other cultures, and enjoyed the advantages of increasingly frequent and close contacts with the peoples of Europe. The fructifying influence of such contacts enabled them to acheive a comparatively appreciable measure of social development by the time Caesar landed on their shores. The Australian aborigines, on the other hand, had been almost completely isolated upon their continent for countless generations without such contacts with the cultures of other peoples; their culture is therefore quite different.

Race and culture are not inseparably connected. The basic biological needs and the potentialities for behavior associated with them probably do not vary significantly from one ethnic group to another. What varies is the social stimulation to which these needs and potentialities are exposed and subsequently organized. The diversity of cultures we encounter represent the adjustment different human groups have made to the experiences and the problems they have been called upon to meet and solve. As Haldane has put it,

> There are presumably differences in the median innate capacities of human groups for various forms of achievement. But the differences between members of a group are much greater than the differences between group medians. Hence, environment, and particularly tradition, are more important than innate differences between human cultures.[14]

Any judgments of value we may attempt to make between our own culture, whatever that may be, and that of other peoples will be invalid unless they are made in terms of history, of experience. Bearing this cardinal principle in mind, we shall be able to steer a clear course. It cannot be too strongly emphasized, as the distinguished historian Erich Kahler has said, that the

> historical evidence proves beyond doubt that the exact opposite of what the so-called race theory pretends is true; any desired advance in human evolution has been accomplished not by breeds that are pure either mentally or physically, not by any cultural inbreeding, but by intermixture, by mutual impregnation of different stocks and cultures.[15]

It is, indeed, from the mixtures of cultural traditions that many of the major triumphs of civilization have come. If the essential physical differences, then, between the varieties of humans are limited to superficial characters, such as color of skin, form of hair, and form of nose, and the cultural and mental differences are due merely to differences in experience, then from the social-biological standpoint all humans must be adjudged fundamentally equal; that is to say, equally good in a biological sense and in cultural potentiality.

All normal human beings are born as culturally undifferentiated organisms; they become culturally differentiated according to the social group into which they happen to be born. Some of the culturally differentiating media are neither so complex nor so advanced as others; the individuals developed within them will be culturally the products of their group. As individuals, they can no more be blamed or praised for belonging to their particular group than a fish can be either blamed or praised for belonging to its particular class in the vertebrate series. Culture, the culture of any group, is more or less determined by adventitious factors, which the group, as a group, has usually done little to bring about. Members of the more technologically advanced cultures have simply enjoyed the benefits of a broader experience and more varied contacts than members of the less technologically advanced cultures.[16] As Boas has said:

> The history of mankind proves that advances of culture depend upon the opportunities presented to a social group to learn from the experience of their neighbors. The discoveries of the group spread to others, and, the more varied the contacts, the greater are the opportunities to learn. The tribes of simplest culture are on the whole those that have been isolated for very long periods and hence could not profit from the cultural achievements of their neighbors.[17]

In short, history teaches us that there is no inherent tendency in any human group that distinguishes it from any other to develop from a state of "barbarism" to one of "high culture." It is only under certain culturally stimulating conditions, which are for the most part accidentally determined, that any group will ever progress to a state of technological advance, for human beings beyond all other creatures are gifted with the capacity to turn accidents into opportunities. In the absence of such conditions no human group will ever move beyond the state of culture determined by the totality of conditions operative upon it. That should be obvious.

With respect to the alleged unchangingness of human nature, which racists almost always proclaim, consider, for example, the case of the Greeks. In spite of a remarkable biological continuity with their ancestors of classical times,[18] the people of modern Greece have been unable to match the innumerable acheivements in the arts and sciences of their ancestors more than two thousand years ago. To what, then, is due this striking difference between the Greeks of the fifth century before Christ and those of the twentieth century? A study of the tragic history of political anarchy, war, massacre, social disorganization, conquest, and oppression which has been the lot of the Greek people during the past two thousand years suggests the direction, at least, in which we should look for an answer.[19]

As Professor Wilder Penfield, one of the world's great neurologists, has written,

The brains of the Greek patricians who rose to such superiority of intellectual achievement during the golden age of Classical Greece were no different structurally from the brains of Greeks in the so-called dark ages that followed. The subsequent low level of intellectual output was the result of changing environment, and the disappearance of fair competition, freedom and public rewards for excellence.[20]

What were the Greeks in the second millennium B.C.? A few scattered peoples of peasant status. Who were the Romans in the sixth century B.C.? Some thousand farmers dispersed over the seven hills by the Tiber. What warrant was there for the promise they so richly realized subsequently in these Mediterranean lands? And yet from these lowly peasants came two of the most highly developed civilizations the world has known, the civilizations to which the western world owes so much it calls its own.

The seafaring Scandinavians of the Bronze Age were undoubtedly the ancestors of the modern Scandinavians, yet how different is the cultural behavior of the modern relatively sedentary Scandinavians from that of their raiding forebears!

The boisterous joy of life of the English of Elizabeth I's time and the lusty libertinism of the Restoration contrast sharply with the prudery of the Victorian Age. The Englishman's "nature" was different in the sixteenth century as compared with that in the seventeenth century, and still more different in the nineteenth century.[21]

With respect to the Germans it would be difficult to do better than cite the comments of an eighteenth-century Scotsman, William Guthrie, who wrote: "The Germans are brave, and when led by able generals, particularly by Italians, have often performed great deeds."[22] "Being led by able generals, particularly Italians" is a remark which in the light of later German-Italian military relations is quite too piquant, and should provide an interesting commentary in itself upon the mutability of human nature.

And what shall we say of the differences in cultural behavior of such biologically near kin as the New Mexican sedentary Pueblo and the nomadic Navaho Indians, or the behavior of those inhabitants of Mexican Indian villages that are completely Hispanicized? And what can have happened to the alleged "warlike nature" of the American Indians who today live at peace?[23]

Is the cultural behavior of the Island Japanese the same as it was a century and a half ago? Compare the great Polynesian maritime peoples with their descendants today in Hawaii and New Zealand. Biologically they are mostly the same people, but so far as the expression of their "nature" is concerned they are virtually completely Westernized.

What did white Americans achieve culturally or by way of invention up to the time of the War of Independence? Very little, indeed. "Who reads an

American novel?" asked Sidney Smith early in the nineteenth century. Who, indeed, if not the whole world? And who doesn't acclaim the inventiveness, the science, and the scholarship of Americans? Why, then, was it that Americans appeared to be so backward in comparison with Europeans? May not the fact that the conditions of life under which most Americans were forced to live by rulers primarily interested in exploiting the American colonies, have had something to do with this lack of achievement? The evidence points strongly in that direction.[24] The nature of Americans has changed with the changing conditions of life. The one thing characteristic of human nature is, surely, its changeability under changing conditions.

The outstanding characteristic of humans is the ability to make all the necessary changes within themselves to meet the demands of a changing environment. This trait, flexibility, plasticity, educability or adaptability, is the one which, in the human species as a whole, has had the greatest demands made upon it by natural selection. Survival of the human species and its progress has depended upon this ability of human nature to change in adaptation to changed conditions.

What most people take to be human nature is really second nature, a nature which has been acquired within the limits of the potentialities of being human within a specific culture. Human nature is a pattern of behavior, and this pattern of behavior is known to be capable of change not only from generation to generation but in the same individual within a single generation. As the second President of the United States, John Adams, wrote, "Education has made a greater difference between man and man than nature has made between man and brute."[25]

It has often been argued that racial enmities between people will disappear only when all physical racial differences between them have been obliterated. That is a fallacious argument for the simple reason that the real source of racial hostilities is not biological, but cultural. It would be equally erroneous to argue from this that such hostilities will therefore disappear only with the obliteration of all cultural differences between men.

The world would be immensely the poorer for such a cultural leveling, and such a process would not, in any event, bring about the desired effect. Perfection of human nature and achievements, it cannot be too often emphasized, is not obtained by the ascendancy of one form of excellence, but by the blending of what is best in many different forms; by harmonizing differences, not by rendering them more discordant. The deep peril and disease of our age is that the cultural differences that exist between ethnic groups tend to become attenuated too soon. In this attenuative process are often lost the unique virtues of a culture even before the dominant culture has grasped their meaning. And as often as this happens is humankind impoverished. As John Collier, a former commissioner of Indian Affairs, pointed out, the history of our species tells us that cultural diversity is the creative force in history. The ideal of a way of life which, in the Western world, the religion we call Christianity, for example, represents the blending of the elements of many different traditions. Hebrew monotheism and morality, Greek philosophy, Oriental mysticism, Roman law, all entered into its shaping. Christianity is only one of countless examples of the profound truth that cultural "diversity is the essential nurture of the spirit of man, the seed-bed of our human future. The cross-fertilization of contrasting cultures is the maker of our human power."[26]

Stressing superficial differences between people only helps to foster the illusion that there may be more fundamental differences behind them. What in truth and in justice requires to be done is to stress the fundamental kinship of humankind: to stress the likenesses which we all bear to one another, and to recognize the essential unity in all humankind in the very differences which individuals of all ethnic groups display. Unity neither implies nor necessitates uniformity. It is important that human beings shall be united, but not that they shall be uniform. We must learn to recognize the all-importance of our common humanity and the triviality of the things that divide us. The world must be re-established as a vast community in which every ethnic group is freely permitted to give as well as to receive. Such an ideal will never be achieved by the ignorant, the sinful, and the malicious stressing of differences, but by the broader, saner, and more humane sympathetic recognition of the fundamental likenesses, rejoicing in the significance of the differences, the preciousness, indeed of the differences, and, finally, by the utilization and interchange of the differences to strengthen each other in living a fuller, a more varied, a more gratifying, and a more peaceful life.

Notes

1. Otto Klineberg, "Race Differences: The Present Position of the Problem," *International Social Science Bulletin* (UNESCO) 2 (1950): 465.

2. Carl J. Warden, *The Emergence of Human Culture* (New York: Macmillan, 1936); Carl J. Warden, *The Evolution of Human Behavior* (New York: Macmillan, 1932); A. Irving Hallowell, *Culture and Experience* (Philadelphia: University of Pennsylvania Press, 1955); A. L. Kroeber, *The Nature of Culture* (Chicago: University of Chicago Press, 1952); Leslie L. White, *The Evolution of Culture* (New York: McGraw-Hill, 1949); Leslie L. White, *The Science of Culture* (New York: Farrar, Straus, & Co, 1949); Clyde Kluckhohn, *Culture and Behavior* (New York: Free Press, 1962); Clyde Kluckhohn, *Mirror For Man* (Tucson: University of Arizona Press, 1985); Ashley Montagu, *Man: His First Two Million Years* (New York: Columbia University Press, 1962); John Middleton, ed., *From Child to Adult* (New York: American Museum of Natural History, 1970); Andrew P. Vayda, ed., *Environment and Cultural Behavior* (New York: American Museum of Natural History, 1969); Robert Hunt, ed., *Personalities and Cul-*

tures (New York: American Museum of Natural History, 1967); Ashley Montagu, ed., *Culture: Man's Adaptive Dimension* (New York: Oxford University Press, 1968); Ashley Montagu, ed., *Culture and the Evolution of Man* (New York: Oxford University Press, 1970); George D. Spindler, ed., *Education and Culture: Anthropological Approaches* (New York: Holt, Rinehart & Winston, 1963); W. D. Hambly, *The Origins of Education Among Primitive People* (London: Macmillan, 1926); Michael Cole et al., eds., *The Cultural Context of Learning and Thinking* (New York: Basic Books, 1971).

3. Erwin Ackerknecht, "White Indians," *Bulletin of the History of Medicine* 15 (1944): 15–36, 34.

4. Samuel Smith, *An Essay on the Causes of the Variety of Complexion and Figure in the Human Species,* 2nd ed., (New Brunswick, NJ: Simpson, 1810), 171–72.

5. Howard H. Peckham, *Captured by Indians* (New Brunswick, NJ: Rutgers University Press, 1954); June Namais, *White Captives! Gender and Ethnicity on the American Frontier* (Chapel Hill: University of North Carolina Press, 1993).

6. For a discussion of the moral and international consequences of these facts see Barbara Wootton, *Testament for Social Science* (New York: Norton, 1951), 146–52.

7. Richard C. Lewontin, Steven Rose, and Leon J. Kamin, *Not In Our Genes* (New York: Pantheon, 1984).

8. For an illuminating exposition of cultural relativity see Ruth Benedict, *Patterns of Culture* (Boston: Houghton Mifflin, 1934).

9. Robert J. Turgot, *Tableaux Philosophique des Progrès Successifs de l'Esprit Humain,* in *Œuvres de Turgot,* ed. Gustave Schelle (Paris: Alcan), 214.

10. John Stuart Mill, *Principles of Political Economy* I (London: Longmans, 1848), 340.

11. It has been stated that Cicero had an extremely low opinion of the mental capacities of the Britons. Thus, he is alleged to have written in a letter to his friend Atticus, "Do not obtain your slaves from Britain, because they are so stupid and so utterly incapable of being taught that they are not fit to form part of the household of Athens." See Benedict, *Race: Science and Politics* (New York: Viking, 1943), 10. The truth is that Cicero made no such derogatory remark. What he wrote was " . . . there is not a scrap of silver in the island, nor any hope of booty except from slaves; but I don't fancy you will find any with literary or musical talent among them." Ep. ad Att. 4.16.13. Loeb Library, vol. 1, p. 324. Cicero was wrong. The talents were there, but it took some 1,500 years of development before they could find expression. This long period of cultural lag, in spite of the presence of the Romans in Britain for some four centuries is worth noting. It would be interesting to know who started the Cicero hare. It keeps recurring in the literature.

12. Pitirim A. Sorokin and Robert K. Merton, "Social Time: A Methodological and Functional Analysis," *American Journal of Sociology* 42 (1937), 615–29; P. Sorokin, *Sociocultural Causality, Space, Time* (Durham: Duke University Press, 1943) 158–225.

13. A. Montagu, "Social Time: A Methodological and Functional Analysis," *American Journal of Sociology* 44 (1938): 282–84.

14. J. B. S. Haldane, "The Argument from Animals to Men: An Examination of its Validity for Anthropology," *Journal of the Royal Anthropological Institute of Great Britain and Ireland* 36 (1956): 1–14.

15. Erich Kahler, *Man the Measure* (New York: Brazillier, 1943), 30.

16. It is of interest to note here that the eighteenth-century students of man, such as Ferguson, Reid, Hume, Stewart, and Adam Smith, solved the problem of the cultural diversity of man in much the same way. "They were struck with the vast differences in culture, as well as with accounts of men of different physical features, but, on the basis of their major presupposition that human nature is fundamentally the same, they solved the problem of differences in achievement by judging the different peoples to be at different stages of maturity." Gladys Bryson, *Man and Society* (Princeton: Princeton University Press, 1945), 53.

17. Franz Boas, "Racial Purity," *Asia* 40 (1940): 231–34.

18. See Chapter 10.

19. Georg Brandes, *Hellas: Travels in Greece,* translated by Jacob W. Hartmann (New York: Adelphi, 1926).

20. Wilder Penfield, "Letter to the Editor," *Perspectives in Biology and Medicine* 6 (1963): 540–41.

21. For some interesting comments bearing on these points see William D. Babington, *Fallacies of Race Theories* (London: Longmans, 1895), 235 ff.; also Geoffrey Gorer, "Some Notes on the British Character," *Horizon* 29 (1949–50): 369–79.

22. Quoted in Johann G. Kohl, *England, Wales, and Scotland* (London: Chapman & Hall, 1844), 79. It is necessary to add that Kohl did not quite approve these statements.

23. During the making of a film on location in Florida which required the firing by Indians at whites, the Seminole Indians who had been hired for the occasion balked on the ground that they had made a treaty with the United States that prohibited taking up arms against the white man. See *New Yorker* 27 (12 May 1951), 23.

24. For a good discussion of this subject see Mitchell Wilson, *American Science and Invention* (New York: Simon & Schuster, 1954).

25. Page Smith, *John Adams*, I (New York: Doubleday, 1963), 220.

26. John Collier, "The Creative Value of Cultural Diversity," *Trends & Tides* 2 (1946): 5–6.

13

Race and War

More than a hundred years have passed since that fateful morning when a dust-laden Prussian officer cantered into Paris at the head of a small advance party of Uhlans, thus signalizing the capitulation of the French and the unequivocal victory of the Germans in the Franco-Prussian War of 1870. Forty years later this selfsame Prussian officer, now a general, did something he had never done before: he wrote a book. It was entitled *Germany and the Next War*. Published early in 1912, few books before or since have been so fervidly and widely discussed. In this book the author, General Friedrich von Bernhardi, then in charge of the military history department of the German general staff, boldly threw down the gauntlet to the world and, virtually with saber in hand, called upon the German people to protest against the "aspirations for peace which seem to dominate our age and threaten to poison the soul of the German people."

It is understandably hard for an iron-headed soldier, after some forty years of comparative inactivity, to recall an event so stirring as the entry at the head of a victorious army into a defeated enemy's capital, without feeling that if things were not actually going to the dogs, at least it was high time that something was done by way of preventing the contingency. And so, in order to convince the German people of the "unnaturalness" of that "inactivity which saps the blood from a nation's sinews," von Bernhardi wrote his call to arms. His blast, aimed mainly against England, at once became an international bestseller, and went into many printings in the many lands in which it was published. Making the pen temporarily do service for the sword, with ink for blood, "War," declared von Bernhardi, "is a biological necessity"; it "is as necessary as the struggle of the elements in Nature"; "it gives a biologically just decision, since its decisions rest on the very nature of things. . . . The whole idea of arbitration represents a presumptuous encroachment on the natural laws of development," for "what is right is decided by the arbitrament of War."[1] In proof whereof the abuse of such Darwinian notions as "the struggle for existence," "natural selection," and "survival of the fittest" are invoked with a loud fanfare of trumpets. According to von Bernhardi, it is plainly evident to anyone who makes a study of plant and animal life that "war is a universal law of nature."[2]

Darwin himself regarded the biological influence of modern war as distinctly bad. In *The Descent of Man* he wrote: "In every country in which a large standing army is kept, the finest young men are taken by the conscription or are enlisted. They are thus exposed to early death during war, are often tempted into vice, and are prevented from marrying during the prime of life. On the other hand, the shorter and feeble men, with poor constitutions are left at home and consequently have a much better chance of marrying and propagating their kind."

As Professor S. J. Holmes, the eminent social biologist, put it: "One may be a strict orthodox Darwinian and maintain with entire consistency that, under present conditions, war is an evil of the very first magnitude."[3]

Von Bernhardi's declaration and fortification of Germany's will-to-war—for it had the highest official sanction and approval—was published in 1912. Two years later the greatest holocaust the world had yet known was launched upon its ghastly way by those

> vultures sick for battle
> Those bloodless wolves whose dry throats rattle,
> Those crows perched on the murrained cattle,
> Those vipers tangled into one."
> —*After Shelley, "To Sidmouth and Castlereagh*

—the befuddled, inhuman, militaristic nationalistic von Bernhardis and the other legislators of a victimized Europe.

World War I came to a provisional end in 1918, having cost the lives of eighteen million men. Eight million were slaughtered upon the fields of battle and ten million civilians died either directly or indirectly as a result of the war. As for the maimed and wounded combatants, these amounted to a mere twenty million. The cost to the United States of running this fracas amounted to $125,000,000 a day during the first three years and $224,000,000 a day, or $10,000,000 an hour, during 1918, the total cost of the killing amounting to some four hundred billion dollars.[4]

During World War II the United States was spending $250,000,000 a day on the war, and by 1945 the total cost had run up to one thousand and thirty billion dollars. The number of military personnel who were killed in action for all combatants was about twenty million, civilian dead numbered about twenty-five million, in addition some six million Jews were put to death by the Nazis. The damage to material property, not to mention the tragedies that were suffered by those who were left alive, was and continues to be incalcuable.[5]

Although most human beings now living, with the exception of some militarists and politicians, can see neither sense, good, nor anything but misery in war, there are many who, like von Bernhardi, continue to aver that war has its biological justification. Among these was my old teacher and friend, Sir Arthur Keith (1866–1955), anatomist, physical anthropologist, and Conservator of the Hunter Museum at the Royal College of Surgeons in London. In many articles beginning in 1915 and in later books he maintained that the impulses which lead men to aggressive and defensive wars are "nature's mechanisms for preserving the individual and the tribe or nation" and "make individuals and nations willing to risk life itself to further the means and opportunities of life."[6] In all theories of this kind race and race prejudice are conceived by their proponents to play a basic and natural role.

Sir Arthur Keith's opinions on this subject first received wide attention with the publication of his rectorial address to the students of Aberdeen University in 1931.[7] In the present chapter I propose to take Sir Arthur Keith's views on the nature of war and its relation to race prejudice and, treating them as representative of the "race-prejudice—biological-nature-of-war" school, subject them to a brief critical examination.

Keith begins by declaring his firm conviction that "prejudices are inborn; are part of the birthright of every child." These prejudices "have been grafted in our natures for a special purpose—an evolutionary purpose. They are essential parts of the evolutionary machinery which Nature employed throughout eons of time to secure the separation of man into permanent groups and thus to attain production of new and improved races of Mankind." "Nature endowed her tribal teams with this spirit of antagonism for her own purposes. It has come down to us and creeps out from our modern life in many shapes, as national rivalries and jealousies and as racial hatreds. The modern name for this spirit of antagonism is race-prejudice." "Race-prejudice, I believe," continues Keith, "works for the ultimate good of Mankind and must be given a recognized place in all our efforts to obtain natural justice in the world."[8] Here, sadly, we may recall von Bernhardi's "war renders a biologically just decision, since its decisions rest on the very nature of things." It is the same argument, endlessly repeated, in almost the same words.

And now for the passage for which Keith gained widespread notoriety:

Without competition Mankind can never progress; the price of progress is competition. Nay, race-prejudice and, what is the same thing, national antagonism, have to be purchased, not with gold, but with life. Nature throughout the past has demanded that a people who seeks independence as well as peace can obtain these privileges only in one way—by being prepared to sacrifice their blood to secure them. Nature keeps her

orchard healthy by pruning; war is her pruning-hook. We cannot dispense
with her services. This harsh and repugnant forecast of man's future is
wrung from me. The future of my dreams is a warless world.[9]

As for war being Nature's "pruning hook," entirely aside from the egregious acceptance of war as a law of nature, Sir Arthur here was guilty of the
error of many other authorities, of false analogy, his statements demonstrating the dangers of untidy thinking. Society is not an *orchard;* nature is
not a conscious force choosing some to live and some to die; and in any
case, the metaphor is ill chosen because pruning removes old canes, weak
canes, and canes that will no longer bear, so that the young and the strong
may have more air and more nourishment to live. The analogy with war,
where the young and the strong are always killed first, would be so inept as
to be ridiculous, were it not so tragic.

Essentially similar views had been expressed by Keith in his 1919
Robert Boyle Lecture *Nationality and Race.*[10]

Unlike von Bernhardi, Keith was a scientist and, as all who knew him
well agreed, a man of the noblest and most generous character who was
himself as free of anything resembling race prejudice as a person could be.
Nevertheless, in his treatment of the subject of race prejudice and war the
fact was unfortunately betrayed that he had overstepped the boundaries of
his own particular field, physical anthripology, a field to which he made interesting contributions. Another teacher of mine, Charles Singer, the historian of science, has well said, that "even professional men of science, when
they pass beyond the frontiers of their own special studies, usually exhibit
no more balanced judgment or unprejudiced outlook than do non-scien-
tific men of comparable social and educational standing." Sir Arthur Keith
was a case in point.

During the period of Keith's heyday, anthropologists, on the whole,
while disagreeing with his views, nevertheless failed to speak out in criticism of them. The combined effect of centuries of original sin, decades of
social Darwinism, and years of conflict between nations in an age of violence, of burgeoning psychoanalysis with its challenging postulation of a
drive toward destruction, the "death instinct," added to a certain reluctance to engage in controversy, and was too much to confront. Thus, Sir
Arthur's views remained unchallenged, and widely discussed in the press
gave much comfort to politicians, theologians, writers of various sorts, and
countless ordinary people.

Among the many scientists who were greatly influenced by Sir
Arthur's views was Raymond Dart, professor of anatomy at the University
of the Witwatersrand Medical School, in Johannesburg, South Africa.
Here, as an anatomist, Dart was called upon to investigate a fossil skull,
which had been discovered by a miner in 1923. In 1925, after a thorough

study of the skull, Dart published an article describing it as "the missing link," between ape and man, and named it *Australopithecus africanus*. His work with the skull together with later discovery of some fragmentary fossil animal bones, which Dart saw as "weapons," turned Dart into a paleoanthropologist as well as an "authority" on the behavioral characteristics of the australopithecines.

This led Dart to publish an article entitled "The Predatory Transition from Ape to Man," for which he experienced some difficulty in finding a place, until he was offered one in a newly founded, short-lived journal, called the *International Anthropological and Linguistic Review.* It was published in its first volume in 1953–54. In this "tooth and nail" sally Dart argued that our prehistoric ancestors were carnivorous, predatory, and cannibalistic. This article is summarized in Chapter 15 of this volume.

The direct influence of Dart on writers such as Robert Ardrey, whose best-selling books, beginning with *African Genesis,* continue to be read to the present day, as are the similar works of many other writers of various professions, and too numerous to mention here. For more on Ardrey, see Chapter 15, this volume.

The Nature of "Nature"

What all these writers have in common is the belief that prejudice, aggression, hostility, and war, are the expression of a natural drive which is common to all living creatures. Earlier writers personified the idea and generally endowed the word nature with a capital "N." Keith's "Nature" is apparently a very intelligent being, working things out purposefully with much premeditation. I use the term "intelligent" here in a generic sense to cover the operations of what is conventionally understood as the intellect; I make no comment on the quality of that putative intelligence, beyond saying that an intellect which can conceive of no better device to improve its breed than by warfare is in dire need of a rigorous resurvey of the evidence. For surely the biological vitality of a species can be preserved and improved by many immeasurably more effective means than this—means which do not necessitate or require the annihilation of a single individual. But what, in fact, is this Nature of von Bernhardi and of Keith which, according to them, justifies race prejudice and renders war a biologically inescapable necessity?

Apparently it is an anthropomorphism akin to the élan-vital of Bergson or the "life-force" of Bernard Shaw. In other words, it would appear to be some form of directing Godhead with the capital "G" in very much the old style, divested here and there of a few sacraments and perfectly clean shaven, but otherwise much the same. Voltaire's gibe that if God had made men after his own image they had returned the compliment, is as appropriate a truth today as it ever was. Nature or God today is a psychiatrist or an anthropologist perhaps even a mathematical physicist—sometimes an entelechist, and often enough merely a set of differential equations, unlimitedly limited and with an infinite number of functions at one and the same time, but if the truth were really known, merely a set of conditioned reflexes in the cosmic movement continuum. In fact, Nature may mean anything, according to the whim of the user.[11] Nature, says Aristotle, makes some men slaves and others free. In Nature, says Hobbes, "the life of man is solitary, poor, nasty, brutish, and short"; it is a condition of "war of every man against every man," in which "the notions of right and wrong, justice and injustice have no place" and "force and fraud are the two cardinal virtues." "The state all men are naturally in," replies Locke, is "a state of perfect freedom to order their actions . . . as they think fit, within the bounds of the law of nature . . . a state also of equality." "Nature," writes Wordsworth, "to me all in all, she never did betray the heart that loved her." "Nature," rejoins Tennyson, "red in tooth and claw, shrieks against the creed of man." And as Professor A. F. Pollard, the historian, has remarked of these antinomies, "Some see red, others see God; it all depends upon the kingdom that is within them."

In fact Nature is the name we give to the projection of the totality of our ignorance concerning the forces which are conceived to be involved in, or responsible for, the generation of life and its maintenance. Nature is not a "thing-in-itself" that operates upon other things. The term denotes, rather, if it denotes anything at all, an artificial construct whose function is to serve as a general stereotype for our ignorance, in addition to serving as a *deus ex machina* to which, in a quandary, we may appeal in order to be comfortably relieved of our perplexities. For most people to say that a thing is "natural" explains it. But does it? What do we mean by "natural"?

Prejudices are natural according to Keith and others, Monsieur Jourdain was amazed to learn that while some men naturally write poetry, he had been speaking prose all his life, warfare was natural according to von Bernhardi, and "the golden lie" according to Plato, and some of his modern successors. Nature, it is further added, operates according to definite laws. All, in fact, is determined by law. The movements of the planets are determined by laws as immutable as those which determine the behavior of a dog or a man.

But all this is mythical. The universe, as far as we know, is composed of a system of ever changing relations, in the form, for example, of electromagnetic fields, gases, stresses, forces, strains, velocities, dimensions, substances, and so forth, truly *ad infinitum*.

Nothing in it is fixed; all is flux.[12] Between certain limits of infinity or finity, that is, in a given space-time continuum, the relations of certain planetary velocities, for example, may remain (relatively) constant. The recurring averages in which these relations manifest themselves may be calculated to a high degree of probability, and when so calculated they may be stated as laws. These laws are always probability laws, and are valid only as long as the relations of the planetary velocities, as well as numerous other factors, remain (relatively) constant. Should any of these relations change, the old laws will have to be modified, or entirely new ones will have to be elaborated.

With this in mind we may proceed further, and for the purpose in view let us be deliberately brief and therefore oversimple. A unicellular organism living at the bottom of a stagnant pool and environed by a stable universe of internal and external stimuli will tend to undergo little change as long as the constancy of these stimuli persists; but modify its relations, the form and nature of the stimuli acting upon it, alter its internal and external environments, and if you go on long enough—let us say for a few thousand million years—sufficiently and adequately varying the nature of the environmental stimuli, and allowing for the important part played by the inherent tendency of the organism to vary, you will, let us suppose, produce a human. And your human, as an organism, will obviously represent the sum of the effects of the responses to the totality of the environments organically made by your human's ancestors. Organically, your human will be the product of an innumerable variety of conditions—the changing relations collectively called "heredity" and "environment."

So will be, and so indeed is, any plant or any other form of animal life. Thus, all plant and animal life is not produced according to definite laws, but in response to a series of arbitrary or chance alterations in the relations of the conditions affecting it. Nature is thus not an intelligent, teleologically directed process which acts according to predetermined law, but is a composite of chance relations which may be arbitrarily observed as unit groups of recurring averages of relations, the behavior of the independent variables, or the quanta[13] of which both are indeterminable and unpredictable, whence *the principle of indeterminacy* or, perhaps, *limited meaningful measurability*. Humankind may, indeed, owe its present supremacy to just such a series of undetermined chance relations, which may be more briefly described as an accident, the accident referred to having been initiated some five million or more years ago, when owing to the denudation of the forests, due to climate and tectonic plate changes, a group of unspecialized anthropoidlike creatures, resembling the extinct apes known to paleontologists as the australopithecines, were constrained to assume a life upon open savanna. This revolutionary change in their environment must be considered an important factor in contributing to the ultimate development of all those physical traits which we have learned to recognize as distinctively human. Those apes who lived in the unaffected regions stayed in the forest and remained apes.

Was there any directive, purposeful, intelligent, natural force at work here? None at all. A series of accidentally precipitated environmental changes may have been responsible for the adaptation of life on the savanna, along with the changes produced by mutation—and all mutation is random. The colossal number of varied forms of life, extinct and living, which are to be found upon this earth today have arisen because of the operation of very similar causes. Every form of life with which we are acquainted owes its peculiar form to the enormous number of changes which have been and are in process of taking place both in the materials of its inherent structure and in the environment peculiar to each—the internal as well as the external environment. These changes are not regulated by law, but by chance. The processes of the universe of life are discontinuous and practically infinitely variable. The universe consists of an infinitely changeable and changing series of relations. Action and reaction, stimulus or challenge and response, take place always relatively, never absolutely. Nature, in short, in the determined immutable sense of the traditionalists, does not exist save as a procrustean socially invented fiction.

The law and order that humans see in nature they introduce there, a fact of which most of us seem to have grown quite unconscious. Natural systems of classification fit so well into presuppositional theories that, following an unconscious pragmatic principle, they are assumed to be true, or at least representative of the truth, the latter being conveniently defined as correspondence with the reality of whatsoever it may be; in this way the tacit assumption is made that one has but to seek and one will find the law and order that undoubtedly exists in nature. This process is termed "discovery."

However, while systems of classification are of value in aiding the process of discovery and understanding, such systems are nonetheless quite artificial and do not in any way reflect a law and order which characterizes the operation of the processes we commonly ascribe to nature itself. Nature is a fiction that uses neither measuring rod nor timetable. It is humans alone who use such instruments in order that they may the more fittingly orient themselves to this self-created fiction. The classificatory systems of man are interpretative devices and merely represent the attempt—and it is a grand attempt—to unravel the tangled skein of some of the relations of the various forms of life to one another, but no more, a compromise between the complexity of biological fact and the logic of practical convenience. Of this some among us lose sight, and confuse ourselves in the belief that the law and order which they have worked out into an adequate scheme is the law and order according to which nature "works." "Homo additus Naturae," remarked Bacon, long ago.

Nature, if it consists of anything, represents a discontinuous complex of interactive processes, a network of entangled gossamer strands, which humans attempt to gather together and spin into a web which is then naively imagined to be the real thing, the "real thing" being merely as one sees it, and human see "the real thing" in an infinite number of ways, according to the kingdom that is within them. Nature comes in this way to mean anything, and what may mean anything, in fact means nothing. It is a personification of purely imagined purposes. As an explanatory principle the idea of nature is without the slightest value; psychologically, perhaps, the term may not be without some significance in the sense of Nietzsche's words in *The Joyful Wisdom:* "Laws and laws of nature are the remains of mythological dreaming." Such "laws of nature" can be a menace. If one thing is natural to humans it is to be artificial. And the artificial, it has been said, is the highest form of the natural.

Julian Huxley, I think, adequately disposed of the type of purposive personification in which Sir Arthur Keith indulged. "The ordinary man," he wrote,

> or at least the ordinary poet, philosopher, and theologian, is always asking himself what is the purpose of human life, and is anxious to discover some extraneous purpose to which he and humanity may conform. Some find such a purpose exhibited directly in revealed religion; others think they can uncover it from the facts of nature. One of the commonest methods of this form of natural religion is to point to evolution as manifesting such a purpose. The history of life, it is asserted, manifests guidance on the part of some external power; and the usual deduction is that we can safely trust that same power for further guidance in the future.
>
> I believe this reasoning to be wholly false. The purpose manifested in evolution, whether in adaptation, specialization, or biological progress, is only an apparent purpose. It is just as much a product of blind forces as is the falling of a stone to earth or the ebb and flow of the tides. It is we who have read purpose into evolution, as earlier men projected will and emotion into inorganic phenomena like storm or earthquake. If we wish to work towards a purpose for the future of man, we must formulate that purpose ourselves. Purposes in life are made, not found.[14]

Professor A. P. Pollard has said: "The statement that 'war is natural' has no meaning, and any comment on it must be mainly speculation as to what those who make it imagine they mean when they repeat the words. 'Natural' to whom, when, and under what conditions? 'Let dogs delight to bark and bite, it is their nature to.' Is it the nature, too, of men of science?"[15] About as natural as the alleged "universal law of Nature" which makes the whole of nature "fight" and some scientists "bark and bite." We are told that even trees and flowers "fight." Do they? There is not the slightest evidence that they do. And if they do, what connection has this "fighting" with the warfare practiced by humans? Some flowers digest insects; some plants "strangle" others. Does this constitute war between the flowers and the insects concerned? Do the plants that strangle others have to plead guilty to murder? Are these "warlike" actions of plants and flowers advance or rearguard actions?

Apropos of plants, Professor Frits Went writes,

> In our minds the struggle for existence is usually associated with a ruthless extermination of the less well adapted by those better adapted. There is no cold war or even aggression in the desert or jungle. Most plants are not equipped with mechanisms to combat others. All plants grow up together and share whatever light or water or nutrients are available. It is only when the supply of one of these factors becomes critical that competition starts. But it appears likely that in the jungle, as in the desert, survival is taken care of by the control of germination . . . As a general moral we conclude that war as man wages it finds no counterpart in nature, and it has no justification on the basis of evolution or natural selection.[16]

It would be extremely helpful to know whether it is defensive or offensive war that is natural. Sir Arthur Keith believed that both are. The illegitimate use of such terms as "struggle," "fighting," "force," or so forth, when applied to plant and animal life, and the deliberate confusion of these terms with "war" occur too often, and too frequently are allowed to pass unchallenged.[17]

Professor Pollard has amusingly remarked of this confusion:

> The sun and the moon, we suppose, declare war with great regularity because they get into opposition every month. Parties in the House of Commons are perpetually at war because they are opposed. The police wage war because they are a force; for 'naturally' if we use force against a criminal, we must needs make war upon other communities. War, indeed will last for ever, because men will never 'cease to struggle.' So the League of Nations has obviously failed whenever a stern parent is caught in the act of chastising a peccant child; and 'fighting' will go on without end because drowning men will fight for life, doctors will fight disease, and women will fight for places at drapery sales. And this is war![18]

The semantic fallacy could not be pointed more neatly.

Man kills a variety of animals for the purposes of food and various other uses, but he does so as a husbandman, a domesticator of animals, not as a maker of war upon animals. He breeds animals in order to eat them. Does this constitute war? In any event, is the domestication and slaughtering of these animals natural? It is certainly not natural to humans, who initiated the domestication of animals not more than ten thousand years ago. Moreover, it is more unnatural for the vast majority of the animals who are members of the same order of mammals as man, namely, the primates, to attack other animal groups or, except on rare occasions, consume any part of them. The anthropoid apes are vegetarian. The fact is that humans possess the gastrointestinal tract of a herbivore, like the anthropoids. Humans' meat eating is probably a taste acquired under conditions of scarcity. But it is neither innate in the psychophysical disposition of humans nor necessary that they may live, to kill any animal whatever, or plant, for that matter, at least not for humans living in the highly civilized centers of the Western world. Humans' taste in food is culturally determined, like the taste for tobacco or alcohol. Under indigenous conditions of life he is forced to kill animals for food and apparel, just as it was considered "natural" for some nations, not so long ago, to kill prisoners of war in order that the food supply might not unnecessarily be depleted. Animals in the wild state kill digestible numbers and varieties of other animals, where they are available, not because they are aggressive, but in order to satisfy their hunger, for the very good reason that they have no other means of remaining alive—but humans do.

In medieval England it was considered natural and legal for all claims to real property to be settled and tried by battle. Since those days humans have elaborated more peaceful means of settling such disputes, not by blood but by reason, because of an understanding and sympathy made possible by a more enlightened form of culture. For culture, if it means anything, represents our ability to elaborate and improve upon the normal processes of the universe, commonly called "Nature." It is through the agency of culture that humans are able to develop and improve upon original endowment, to turn whatever may be left first, into second, nature. It is not so much that culture is an extension of people as that people are an extension of culture. Indeed, today, by means purely cultural, humans are in a position to control and regulate, in almost every possible respect, their own future evolution. Humans hold the power within themselves of total self-extermination or alternatively more complete development, and it will be by the weakness or strength of our humanity alone that either the one or the other effect will eventually be brought about.

The Nurture of Nationalism

Fundamentally, humans are quite intelligent creatures, but most, alas, are victims of the two-handed engine of their culture, which deforms their minds and renders them unintelligent. Outworn traditional teachings have made of Western humans shockingly unintelligent creatures who live under the continuous and unrelieved domination of a chaos of ideas more degrading, more stupid, more idiotic, and more saddening than it may ever be possible to describe. This confused morality has without question been substantially responsible for humankind's present deplorable state, for the basic behavioral needs and patterns of thought of every child born into the contemporary world today have been conditioned according to the prescriptions of these outworn teachings, so that culturally humankind has come to be a function almost entirely of the reigning spirit of confusion and prejudice. And since humans function without effort as victims of confusion and prejudice, they arrive at the belief that it is natural to act and think thus. In this way is produced the mentally and spiritually bludgeoned individual who gropes his way confusedly through life—and whose number is legion. The frustrations which he has suffered seek an outlet in aggressiveness, and it is in his world alone that force and war still remain a legitimate and defensible means of settling a difference.[19]

With regard to Keith's "race prejudice," that, of course, is an acquired sentiment, a constellation of socially acquired emotions, as Sir Arthur Keith would undoubtedly have known had he made as deep a study of cultural anthropology as he had of anatomy. Nature, according to him, secures the separation of humankind into permanent groups by means of the operation of race prejudices, which express themselves as national rivalries and jealousies, in order to produce "new and improved races of mankind."

The truth is that national rivalries and jealousies have no necessary connection with race, and that so far from producing "new and improved races of mankind," they are the principal causes of the impoverishment and destruction of peoples. Race, as we have seen has often been made the pretext for war, but race is a myth, just as the nationalism of which Keith had in mind when he spoke of "national rivals and jealousies."

A nation is a stable, historically developed community of people with a territory, economic life, distinctive culture, and common language. Nationalism is another thing. Evolved independently by the nations of Europe as early as the twelfth century, in its modern virulent form nationalism dates back to the beginning of the nineteenth century. Nationalism is a state of mind, in which the supreme loyalty of the individual is felt to be due to the nation-state. Bound together by consciousness of kind, usually by assumed "blood-ties," nationalism is a learned emotion, conditioned by parents, teachers, school, religion, song, poetry, pageantry, prose, and a ruling class or ruler. Nationalism has no biological roots whatever. It is a myth and an illusion of great power and emotional force.[20] As the Nobel prizewinning Norman Angell (1876–1932), economist and internationalist, said in his famous book *The Great Illusion*, published in 1910, "Political nationalism has become, for the European of our age, the most important thing in the world, more important than civilization, humanity, decency, kindness, oity; more important than life itself."

The truth of those words has been hideously confirmed by the wars and massacres that have destroyed the last vestiges of what was once understood by civilization.

In his admirable book *The Illusion of National Character,* Hamilton Fyfe summarized the evils of nationalism thus:

> The result of inventing national blood-ties has been disastrous. From the mistaken belief that there exists root-differences, due to different ancestry, between peoples of different nations spring: (1) the ignorant conceit cherished by almost all of them that their country is superior to other countries; (2) the dangerous delusions of patriotism; (3) the chimera of national honor. These, pressed into the service of economic rivalry, are the most potent causes of war.[21]

Keith as a Lowland Scot came from a background with a long past history of conflict with the Highland Scots, as well as with the English, which, combined with the age of conflict in which he lived, exerted a considerable influence in forming his views concerning the place of prejudice in civilization.

Keith regarded nationalism as due to a form of natural selection operating from inherited psychological bases. Were this to be true it would be a form of selection peculiar to humans alone, for no other animal, as far as we know, exhibits the slightest symptom of anything akin to what Keith called "race prejudice." So-called race prejudices among different animals, like their so-called "natural" fears and terrors, are acquired, not inborn. This is probably true of the psychological barriers that exist between different groups of birds and in various other creatures. Experiments on young animals first carried out by Benjamin Kidd many years ago, and by numerous investigators since, conclusively prove that the so-called "instinctive" fear and terror, exhibited in the presence of their allegedly natural enemies by the adult members of the species, are reactions which are generally completely absent in the young and that such reactions are learned from other members of the species or by individual experience.[22] A lamb or any other animal, for example, which has had no long association with members of its own species from whom it could have acquired the fear—or past experience with lions—will exhibit not the slightest fear of a lion when confronted with one. On the other hand, when chickens raised in complete isolation are first brought into association with other chickens they sometimes exhibit both fear and aggressive reactions.[23] A certain amount of social, of cooperative, experience would seem to be necessary if the fears nurtured by isolation or any other factors are to be overcome.

No animal or human being is born with any prejudice or specific fear whatever, either of snakes, mice, or the dark, to mention a few of the most familiar common fears usually considered of "instinctive" origin; all these fears or prejudices are acquired by learning and may, and usually do, act very like conditioned reflexes, simulating physical reflexes which are innate, but which in these cases are conditioned to react culturally, not biologically or instinctively.

Upon the theory that race prejudice is innate, how are we to account for the well-authenticated fact, familiar to most people of experience, that children of one nation, brought up in the milieu of a "foreign" nation, feel no prejudices whatever, in wartime or in peacetime, against the nation of their adoption but, on the contrary, are generally to be found in the ranks of their adopted land fighting against the motherland of their ancestors, whether it be with ideas or with powder? No more impressive demonstration of this is to be found than in the case of the thousands of Japanese Americans who in World War II bravely fought on all fronts as American citizens and soldiers against the Axis forces. Japanese Americans especially distinguished themselves in action against Japanese forces.[24] In fact, the Japanese American 442nd Regimental Combat Team was the most decorated unit in United States history.[25]

A notorious example of transmutation is the case of Houston Stewart Chamberlain, the author of that stupendous miracle of racist nonsense *The Foundations of the Nineteenth Century* (1910) in which the spectacle is witnessed of an apostate Englishman glorifying the Teutonic spirit, the German brand in particular, at the expense, among others, of his ancestral land and heritage. One may well wonder what happened to Chamberlain's "birthright" of prejudice when as an adult he became a champion of German prejudices.[26] Possibly William James's law of transitoriness of instinct may be invoked here. And what shall we say of Sir Thomas Browne (1605–82), the author of *Religio Medici*, who wrote: "I am of a constitution so general, that it consorts and sympathiseth with all things; I have no antipathy, or rather idiosyncrasy, in any thing. Those national repugnances do not touch me, nor do I behold with prejudice the French, Italian, Spanish or Dutch?"

Or of Oliver Goldsmith (1728–74) who wrote,

Among all the famous sayings of antiquity, there is none that does greater honor to the author, or affords greater pleasure to the reader, (at least if he be a person of a generous and benevolent heart), than that of the philosopher, who being asked what countryman he was, replied that he was a citizen of the world. How few are there to be found in modern times who can say the same, or whose conduct is consistent with such a profession! We are now become so much Englishmen, Frenchmen, Dutchmen, Spaniards, or Germans, that we are no longer citizens of the world; so much the natives of one particular spot, or members of one petty society, that we no longer consider ourselves as the general inhabitants of the globe, or members of that grand society which comprehends the whole human kind . . . Let a man's birth be ever so high, his station ever so exalted, or his fortune ever so large, yet, if he is not free from the national and all other prejudices, I should make bold to tell him, that he had a low and vulgar mind, and had no just claim to the character of a gentleman. And, in fact, you will always find, that those are most apt to boast of national merit, who have little or no merit of their own to depend on, that which to be sure, nothing is more natural: the slender vine twists around the sturdy oak for no other reason in the world, but because it has not strength sufficient to support itself.[27]

Or of that great and universal genius Thomas Young (1773–1829), who, as a young man, wrote:

A man who has formed intimacies and friendships with inhabitants of different parts of the globe will find enough to love and to disapprove among every people; and perhaps one who has acquired the faculty of communicating his thoughts with equal ease and pleasure to the individuals of several nations, will find himself as much at home in the one as in the other. Certainly one who is totally destitute of this attainment can never be admitted to judge with impartiality of the character of any country.[28]

As David Hume, the eighteenth century Scottish philosopher (1711–76); author of the great *A Treatise of Human Nature*, 1739–40, wrote,

The vulgar are apt to carry all national characters to extremes; and, having once established it as a principle that any people are knavish, or cowardly, or ignorant, they will admit of no exception, but comprehend every individual under the same censure. Men of sense condemn these undistinguishing judgments; though, at the same time, they allow that each nation has a peculiar set of manners, and that some particular qualities are more frequently to be met with among one people than among their neighbours.[29]

It has often been said that the differences between one race and another are only skin deep. The truth apparently is that it isn't even that, for it is a common experience that when we get to know others well, however they may differ from us physically, even the consciousness of obvious physical differences tends to vanish. In the xenophobic or racist world the physical differences existing between the members of different races are often claimed to constitute a natural social barrier to co-mixture. The following observations—which can be easily checked in groups in which members of different races have lived intimately together—suggest that such claims represent nothing more than a pigment of the imagination.

During the course of the last forty years I have been consulted by various adoption agencies, families, and individuals as to the race of a particular child. The adoption agencies have been anxious to place children with families in which there would be no disparity between the race of the child and that of the adopting parents. Families and individuals have generally had the same interest in selling expert advice: They have simply wanted the question answered that others had raised concerning the racial identity of a child (and, in one case, of an adult) with whom they had long been intimately familiar.

What has been most striking and illuminating to me is that, in every case in which I was consulted (by an individual, husband or wife, a group of brothers and sisters, or a grandmother), the child—always of a white mother—clearly was the offspring of a black father. One did not have to be an expert to perceive this. And yet none of my clients, all of whom were white, could see it. Indeed, what led to my being consulted at all in all but one of the cases were the mounting comments of neighbors and others on the obvious black features of the child and the incongruity and awkwardness of this in a white family and a white neighborhood.

I speak here of five unrelated children, four under two years of age and one over 21 years of age at the time of the consultations. In a typical case, the child had been adopted about six weeks after birth. The parents were an educated middle-class couple in their mid-20s, and the child at the time of consultation was some 13 months of age. The adoptive parents were upset because friends and neighbors were saying that the child was clearly black. The child, in fact, was a hybrid, and when I informed the parents of this they simply found it unbelievable. It was not that it was going to make the slightest difference in their love for the child, but they just could not see the child in any way physically different from themselves or from white children of the same age. In all four other cases as well, those consulting me could not see that the individual in question was in any way racially different.

In each case we talked about the situation for some time. I pointed out that what really mattered was what had in fact occurred: that their love for the child transcended all racial prejudices; that through their love they had invested the physical appearance of the child with the kind of individuality with which one perceives the differences between members of the same family; and that this was exactly as it should be. They fully agreed, and in each case their attachment to the child was, if anything, intensified.

Perhaps the most astonishing of these cases involved a 21-year-old woman and her six brothers and sisters. Let us call her Mary. Brought up together in the same household with Mary, the six siblings who came to see me simply wanted to satisfy a long-standing curiosity. They were whites of European background, their parents were white, Mary was white, all were of a lower-middle-class socioeconomic status. All through their lives, Mary had been treated by others as black. In school they had become involved in many a fight because she had been so treated by other children; there had been later discriminations against her. The brothers and sisters wanted to know whether there could be the least truth in such an imputation. They brought with them good black-and-white photographs of Mary from childhood to her then present age. From these photographs, one could not draw any other conclusion than that one of her parents must have been black. Yet these six people had lived with Mary for 21 years and had not seen her as physically in any significant way different from themselves.

In all these instances, it was clear to me that what these people perceived in the other was someone whom they loved, and that the physical differences to which they had been habituated were seen as no more significant than those existing between members of any family. I have had much the same experience myself with people among whom I was not brought up and with whom I spent only a few days once a year. Years ago I used to attend an annual race institute in a Southern community. Here I spent virtually all my time with blacks, and I vividly recall how, after the first few days, I literally had to shake myself in order to make myself aware that I was supposed to be among people of a different race. Within a few days I had lost all sense that there was any difference between these people and myself. Each year I returned I had the same experience all over again.

It seems evident that the readiness with which we are prepared to accept others as human beings determines how we perceive them. It would appear that, with familiarity, even marked differences, such as skin color, hair form, and nose shape, may cease to be perceived as such. Racists who perceive such differences as barriers to race mixture will find no support for their beliefs in the facts.[30]

National and racial stereotypes mostly serve ill purposes, since they conceal complexities and embody irrational hatreds, fear, and hopes.

As we have seen, there is every reason to believe that race sentiment and antipathies are comparatively recent developments in the societies of the West.

In America, where white and black populations frequently live side by side, it is an indisputable fact that white children do not learn to believe themselves superior to black children until they are told that they are so[31] a fact revealingly illustrated by the words of a white American farmer from the South who, in answer to the query as to what he thought of blacks, replied, "I ain't got anything against niggers; I was 14 years old before I know'd I was better than a nigger." Numerous other examples could be cited of the cultural acquisitions of prejudices, but we have already dealt with the mechanism of race prejudice upon an earlier page, where we have seen that all ideas of race prejudice are inherited in just the same manner as are our clothes, not innately but culturally. Each person as a social being is custom made, whose own ideas are tailored according to the prevailing fashion.

The statement so frequently heard that "war is a universal and everlasting law of Nature" is at best a shallow judgment, for it seems never to occur to those who make it that the conflicts which they are pleased to term "war" and which are alleged to take place between animals in the wild state are pertinent only in referring to conflicts between animals of widely separated species, genera, orders, and, almost universally, classes. Under certain conditions lions will attack almost anything that moves; so will, to a lesser extent, wolves and hyenas; domestic cats will kill small rodents and birds; monkeys will kill birds and insects; baboons and chimpanzees will sometimes kill and eat a small monkey; but in all these examples, selected at random, it is *inter*specific killing that occurs, not *intra*specific. Under natural conditions it is not usual for animals of one species to prey upon, or to fight with, each other, but rather to attack only animals of different breeds. To this rule there are few exceptions. Of course, hungry animals will devour, upon occasion, members of their own species, but this is a form of conduct which is normally resorted to only under extreme conditions. In serious conflicts between wild or domesticated animals of the same species the fight is rarely between more than two animals, and usually the causes and the motives which have provoked the fight are similar to those which influence humans, namely, the will to possess a sexually desirable mate or an object of physical value such as food. Gibbons feed contentedly in the same tree with monkeys such as macaques and langurs, but will not tolerate the presence of another gibbon group of the same species or any other. However, chimpanzees will attack a recently developed splinter group that is regarded as competition in the struggle for existence, but generally live peacefully.[32] Practically all vertebrates defend themselves against attack by members of other groups of their own species. But this sort of defensive fighting is quite different from war. War is an organized attack of one community upon another community, and as such is never fought by animals other than those of the "human" variety. It is impossible to produce more than one or two instances from the animal kingdom to show that a form of behavior resembling warfare is waged by one group of its members upon any other group of the same species—as a means of improving the species or what not.

Pliny the Elder (A.D. 23–79) is perhaps the earliest writer to have pointed out that man is the only creature that makes war upon his own kind.

> In fine, all other living creatures pass their time worthily among their own species: we see them herd together and stand firm against other kinds of

animals—fierce lions do not fight among themselves, the serpent's bite attacks not serpents, even the monsters of the sea are only cruel against different species; whereas to man, I vow, most of his evils come from his fellow man.[33]

It was Leonardo da Vinci who defined man as the creature that persecutes its own as well as other living species.

The Unnaturalness of War

If one thing is certain, it is that it is not natural for members either of the same species or of any other to wage "war" upon one another. "One species of animal may destroy another and individuals may kill other individuals, but group struggles to the death between members of he same species, such as occur in human warfare, can hardly be found among non-human animals."[34] As Dr. L. P. Jacks wrote, while World War I was raging, "there is nothing in the life of the lowest beasts which can be compared for utter senselessness with the mutual rending to pieces of the Nations." War, let it be said at once, is the most unnatural, the most artificial, of all human activities, for it originates in artificial causes, is waged by artificial entities called "states," and is fought from artificial motives, with artificial weapons, for artificial ends. Like our civilization, war is an artificial product of that civilization itself, the civilization that has been achieved by the repeal and the repudiation of those very processes of so-called "Nature" which our von Bernhardis are pleased to regard as an everlasting universal law.[35] As Julian Huxley has pointed out, "War, far from being a universal law of nature, or even a common occurrence, is a very rare exception among living creatures."[36]

First among ten pertinent and basic principles subscribed to by over 2000 American psychologists is the following:

> *War can be avoided: War is not born in men; it is built into men.* No race, nation, or social group is inevitably warlike. The frustrations and conflicting interests which lie at the root of aggressive wars can be reduced and re-directed by social engineering. Men can realize their ambitions within the framework of human cooperation and can direct their aggressions against those natural obstacles that thwart them in the attainment of their goals.[37]

We have seen that there is good reason to believe that aggressive race sentiment and prejudice are comparatively recent developments of civilized people. So too, there is good reason to believe that warfare is but a recent development resulting from the artificial and perverted activities of people living in highly civilized populations. Among our prehistoric ancestors of anything resembling warfare has ever been found. Plenty of implements of a rather simple nature have been discovered in association with the remains of ancient humans, but they appear to have been made for use against animals, not against one another. Throughout the Old Stone Age (Paleolithic), a period which occupies 96 percent of humankind's entire history, all known human groups lived by foraging, food-gathering, and hunting, as did the Middle Stone Age (Mesolithic) groups who succeeded them.

Adam Smith long ago pointed out that a hunting population is always thinly spread over a large area and possesses but little accumulated property. From their earliest days humans were generalists in their adaptive exploitation of the environment, as are most existing gatherer-hunting people today. Among indigenous peoples their hunting grounds were generally marked off by definite boundaries, boundaries separating different communities; "these boundaries were sacred, and as no one would think of violating them they could not form a cause of war." "Savages," writes Ellis,

> are on the whole not warlike, although they often try to make out that they are terribly bloodthirsty fellows; it is only with difficulty that they work themselves up to a fighting pitch and even then all sorts of religious beliefs and magical practices restrain warfare and limit its effects. Even among the fiercest peoples of East Africa the bloodshed is usually small. Speke mentions a war that lasted three years; the total losses were three men on each side. In all parts of the world there are people who rarely or never fight; and if, indeed . . . the old notion that primitive people are in chronic warfare of the most ferocious character were really correct, humanity could not have survived. Primitive man had far more formidable enemies than his own species to fight against, and it was in protection against these, and not against his fellows, that the beginnings of cooperation and the foundation of the State were laid.[38]

Verrier Elwin, writing of the Gonds and Baigas of Central India, tells a charming story which throws some light on the attitude of indigenous peoples to war.

> An old woman put it very well. 'This,' she said, 'is how God equalizes things. Our sons and daughters die young, of hunger or disease or the attacks of wild beasts. The sons and daughters of the English could grow old in comfort and happiness. But God sends madness upon them, and they destroy each other, and so in the end their great knowledge and their religion is useless and we are all the same.'[39]

"Some of the tribesmen," writes Elwin,

always excited by a quarrel, were anxious to help. A party of Baigas came one day with a bundle of bows and arrows which they wanted me to forward to the Government to aid in the war. When I told them that modern battles were no longer fought with these weapons they were much concerned. 'But if they use guns people will really get killed,' they said.[40]

The anthropologist W. J. Perry wrote: "Civilized people are far more ferocious than the majority of 'savages,' and whenever 'savages' are uncommonly ferocious, it is usually possible to detect the influence of civilized men. It is the civilized man who is the savage."[41]

Dr. Ragner Numelin, having made a thoroughgoing study of the subject, concludes that:

> Warfare as such, i.e., organized warfare, is . . . not customary among primitive peoples. When war occurs it is obviously more of the nature of robbery and plundering raids. The simplest communities do not organize war, and war for expansion is relatively rare in the primitive world . . . Further, we have found that peaceable relations dominate among the primitive, wandering peoples, the food-gatherers, the fishing and hunting tribes. The rather peaceful character of such peoples is usually confirmed by their traditions and legends which often form a rich ethological treasure house. Instead of spending their days in fighting they lead peaceful lives when left undisturbed. They seldom use violence in their personal relations and they do not fight as communities. Savages do not usually live at odds with their neighbors.[42]

War came into being only after men had begun to cultivate the land upon which they were then able to settle permanently. Such an agricultural stage of development, we know, first appeared among men about ten thousand years ago, in Upper Neolithic times.[43] The agricultural life results in the accumulation of property, the accumulation of property eventually results in more or less organized industry, industry in wealth, wealth in power, power in expansive ambitions, and the desire to acquire additional property—the source of additional power—necessary to gratify those ambitions, and thus, by no very complicated process, in war. Such conditions, which are peculiar to the industrial civilizations of today, are, of course, highly artificial, as are the prejudices and the race sentiment which they serve to generate.

In the modern world undoubtedly the most potent cause of war is economic rivalry, sheer greed for the advantages of more territory, as it was in the days of kleptomaniac imperialism, and today in the form of "ethnic cleansing." These are social phenomena having no biological basis whatever. The desire for foreign concessions and markets, an expanding population, the lust for *Lebensraum*—such things will upon little provocation set nations in opposition and at each other's throats.[44]

It is from such economic causes that patriotism, chauvinism, and the widespread fear of aggression arise, which more than anything else serves to consolidate the group and the generation of race prejudice.[45] As Malinowski put it, "human beings fight not because they are biologically impelled but because they are culturally induced, by trophies, as in headhunting, by wealth as in looting, by revenge as in punitive wars, by propaganda as it occurs under modern conditions."[46]

If all this is true, then it is apparent that war arises not as a consequence of natural or biological conditions but from purely contrived artificial social conditions created by highly "civilized" modes of interaction between human groups.

The Naturalness of Cooperation and Altruism

With respect to the "natural antagonisms" with which humankind is supposed to be endowed, it may be said at once that these are pure creations of the imagination, for certainly there exists no evidence that humans are born with any antagonisms whatever.[47] The evidence is, on the other hand, quite contrary to such a suggestion. Sir Charles Sherrington has set out some of this evidence in his masterly book *Man on His Nature*, while Professor W. C. Allee long ago set out the reasons together with the evidence, observational, inductive, and experimental, which indicates that the spirit of altruism, of cooperation, is very much more natural to humans than is that of egoism or antagonism. "After much consideration," wrote Professor Allee,

> It is my mature conclusion, contrary to Herbert Spencer, that the cooperative forces are biologically the more important and vital. The balance between the cooperative, altruistic tendencies and those which are disoperative and egoistic is relatively close. Under many conditions the cooperative forces lose. In the long run, however, the group-centered, more altruistic drives are slightly stronger. "If cooperation had not been the stronger force, the more complicated animals, whether arthropods or vertebrates, could not have evolved from the simpler ones, and there would have been no men to worry each other with their distressing biologically foolish wars. While I know of no laboratory experiments that make a direct test of this problem, I have come to this conclusion by studying the implications of many experiments which bear on both sides of the problem, and from considering the trends of organic evolution in nature. Despite many known appearances to the contrary, human altruistic drives are as firmly based on an animal ancestry as is man himself. Our tendencies towards goodness, such as they are, are as innate as our tendencies toward intelligence; we could do well with more of both.[48]

Prince Petr Kropotkin arrived at similar conclusions at a time when such ideas were scarcely mentioned; these he set out in a remarkable book, *Mutual Aid.* "If," wrote Kropotkin,

> we resort to an indirect test, and ask Nature: 'Who are the fittest: those who are continually at war with each other, or those who support one another?' we at once see that those animals which acquire habits of mutual aid are undoubtedly the fittest. They have more chances to survive, and they attain, in their respective classes, the highest development of intelligence and bodily organization.[49]

J. B. S. Haldane concluded that "in so far as it makes for the survival of one's descendants and near relations, altruistic behaviour is a kind of Darwinian fitness, and may be expected to spread as the result of natural selection."[50] And this, indeed, is what Darwin believed. "As man advanced in civilization," he wrote, "and small tribes are united into larger communities, the simplest reason would tell each individual that he ought to extend his social instincts and sympathies to all members of the same nation, though personally unknown to him. This point being once reached, there is only an artificial barrier to prevent his sympathies extending to the men of all nations and races."[51]

The biologist William Patten as long ago as 1920 devoted a highly original book to the consideration of cooperation as a factor in evolution.[52] Indeed, many distinguished students of evolutionary process have dealt with the evidence pointing to the cardinal importance of the role which cooperation has played in evolution, but their work was not congenial to the Age of Social Darwinism, and is only now being rescued from the neglect into which it has fallen.[53]

Professor A. E. Emerson's views on the biological basis of social cooperation are identical with those of Allee. Emerson points out that: "Just as the cell in the body functions for the benefit of the whole organism, so does the individual organism become subordinate to the population. It is in harmony with natural law to have an individual function for the benefit of other contemporary individuals and also for future generations. This principle gives us a scientific basis for ethics."[54]

Professor Emerson goes on to say:

> Cooperation is probably not an end in itself, but is rather a means to an end. The all-over directional trend in organic evolution seems to have been toward optimum conditions for existence. What was the uncontrolled external environment of the cell became the balanced internal environment of the multicellular organism. Selection of variations leads toward more efficient division of labor and more integration and cooperation between the parts. Differentiation would be useless without

integration, and integration would be useless without differentiation. Natural selection has constantly guided organic evolution in the direction of increasing complexity and increasing cooperation. This trend is easily seen in the study of the evolution of intraspecific populations and reaches it culmination in the social insects and in man.[55]

Certainly aggressiveness exists in nature,[56] but there is also a healthy nonruthless competition and strong basic drives toward social and cooperative behavior. These forces do not operate independently, but together, as a whole, and the evidence strongly indicates that of all these drives the principle of cooperation is dominant and biologically the most important. The coexistence of so many different species of animals throughout the world is sufficient testimony to the importance of that principle. It is probable that humans owe more to the development of their cooperative drives than to any other in their biological and social evolution.[57] The future of humankind lies with the further development of these cooperative drives, not with their abrogation.

In 1939 a group of leading scientists formulated the principle naturally operative in governing human conduct as follows: "The probability of survival of a relationship between individual humans or groups of humans increases with the extent to which that relationship is mutually satisfying." This principle being but a special case of the more general principle that "the probability of survival of individual, or groups of, living things increases with the degree with which they harmoniously adjust themselves to each other and their environment."[58] This, essentially, is the principle of cooperation, of mutual aid, the conscious recognition of which has been the basis of most religious and ethical systems. The biological corroboration of the soundness of that ethical principle must be counted one of the greatest discoveries in human history. That principle has played a great part in the development of humankind. It must be made to play an even greater role in the future. Our efforts to obtain natural justice in the world will be rewarded only when we have eliminated such pathological phenomena as race prejudice and the causes which give rise to it from our sick societies.

The original conception of natural justice which was held by people down to the nineteenth century was one that was valid for the whole community of humans. It was in principle an explicit recognition of the intrinsic worth of human personality, implying universal equality and brotherhood. The shift in meaning, in the nineteenth century, from nature as harmony and design to nature as struggle largely contributed to the eclipse of the concept of justice as an ideal of human relations, and to the emergence of the idea that what is just is determined by the arbitrament of force, the survival of the fittest.[59]

Without strong drives to cooperation, sociability, and mutual aid, the progress of organic life, the improvement of the organism, and the strengthening of the species becomes utterly incomprehensible. Indeed, Haldane and Huxley independently suggest that competition between adults of the same species is on the whole a biological evil. The biological effects of such competition, it seems likely, writes Haldane,

> render the species as a whole less successful in coping with its environment. No doubt weaklings are weeded out, but so would they be in competition with the environment. And the special adaptations favoured by interspecific competition divert a certain amount of energy from other functions, just as armaments, subsidies, and tariffs, the organs of international competition, absorb a proportion of the natural wealth which many believe might be better employed.[60]

Not "nature red in tooth and claw" but cooperation is the primary law of natural conduct. As we have seen, the widespread belief so effectively expressed by Sir Arthur Keith of the "pruning-hook" theory of war is an idea which on the face of it is absurd; for, as everyone knows, the manner in which modern war acts is to kill off the "fittest" combatants, jealously preserving the weakest, such as the mentally and bodily diseased, disordered, or generally unfit. And in any case, as World War I fully proved, the nation superior to all others in the processes of waging war, the most ingenious and fertile in the invention and use of the instruments of destruction, may in spite of this lose the war by the selectively irrelevant fact of being overwhelmingly outnumbered.

Referring to World War I, Professor Alfred Pollard aptly remarked that

> if the result had depended on scientific invention the Germans would have won. As it was, the neutralized enormous odds in numbers to such an extent that for four years the principal front hardly shifted on an average more than half a dozen miles in either direction. The Allied victory was due not to scientific superiority but to the economic exhaustion of the foe, and to the fact that in Foch's decisive campaign America was pouring more fresh troops into the line of battle in a month that the Germans could raise in a year.[61]

In any event, under any conditions, it is not the "fittest" who are likely to survive but the "fit," the more adaptable.

From the standpoint of natural selection it is apparent to all those who lived through it that the Germans, who proved themselves the most resourceful and certainly not the least valorous of all the combatants, should, on the basis of "brains" alone, have won the war of 1914–18. Instead, they lost it. Something clearly had gone wrong with "natural selection," or, rather, with war as an agency of it. It was, indeed, the confidence in "reek-ing tube and iron shard" which led the Germans from an even and peace-ful development into the disaster of war and humiliation, and eventually made Hitler possible.

As a matter of fact, the whole concept of war as an agency of natural se-lection in the case of humans breaks down when we consider that through-out the historic period there were numerous instances of victories in war gained by peoples who were culturally less developed than those whom they conquered. It must, however, be freely acknowledged that on the whole up to the modern era the peoples victorious in war were generally superior to the people whom they conquered—superior in the strict sense of the *military* superiority of the combatant *individuals*. In former times men actually fought with one another, the superior warrior (who may have been superior simply because he had been better fed) generally killing the inferior in hand-to-hand combat. But in modern warfare the combatants scarcely ever see each other, and when they do it is not military skill or na-tive superiority which decides who shall die, but a shell fired from a battery some miles away or a machine gun hundreds of yards distant, or a bomb dropped from an airplane thousands of feet above them. In actual battle the superior men are the first to go over the top; in dangerous and gener-ally useless raids they are the first to be chosen—and killed. Where, in all this mindless slaughter, is there to be detected any evidence of natural se-lection? Selection, certainly, in that the superior are selected for death and the inferior are protected against it—in this way does modern warfare act as an agency of unnatural selection, for the worst.[62] Modern wars are harm-ful to humanity, they are dysgenic, not eugenic.

Julian Huxley has stated the point clearly.

> The more total war becomes, both intensively, as diverting more of the en-ergies of the population from construction to destruction, and exten-sively, as involving more and more of the countries of the globe, the more of a threat does it become to the progress of the human species. As H. G. Wells and many others have urged it might even turn back the clock of civ-ilization and force the world into another Dark Age. War of this type is an intra-specific struggle from which nobody, neither humanity at large nor any of the groups engaged in the conflict, can really reap any balance of advantage, though of course we may snatch particular advantages out of the results of war.[63]

Humanity has reached its present state of civilization through its re-markable powers of creativity, a creativity, however, which, with the devel-opment of what has been called "progress," has been increasingly devoted to destructive ends; not because of any inborn tendency to do so, but because of a socialization that leads its members into a morass of insecurities and unresolved problems, which find pathological resolution in socially sanctioned reactions to frustration. Babies are not born evil or brutal, they may grow to be so by the denial of love and the encouragements they need for healthy growth and development. And until we fully realize the implication of those words, there is no solution to either the race problem, or for the matter of that, to the long term survival of humanity.[64]

All that is fine, noble, beautiful, and desirable in our civilization has been achieved through the resolute determination of individual minds not so much to conquer and to vanquish what Tennyson, reflecting the temper of his time, called "Nature, red in tooth and claw," but to enlist the aid of "Nature" in the service of the whole of animated as well as inanimate nature, for what we are doing to the world in which we live is merely a reflection of what we are doing to ourselves and to our fellow human beings.

It may be an oversimplification, but it is not far from the truth to say that so much that is ugly, inhuman, and destructive in our civilization is largely due to the activities of those who are anxious to exploit people for their own advantage and who use various measures of control only toward that end. To them war is a profitable activity, for it increases their power as well as their fortunes. It is individuals of this order, in all countries and from the earliest historical times, who help to make wars, not nature. Others who assist have the *status quo* to maintain.[65] "The fault, dear Brutus, lies not in our stars, but in ourselves."

Humanity has too long been deceived by a chaos of ideas for which there is not the slightest basis in fact, ideas which represent, as Spinoza said, the errors of the ages grown hoary with the centuries. The flowers that bloom in the verbal spring of such writers as von Bernhardi and Sir Arthur Keith, not to mention the Hitlers of this world, have nothing whatever to do with either the logical case or the factual reality. Nay, in spite of Kant and others, there is no instinct toward peace in man just as there is none toward war. The early Egyptians, the Minoans of Crete, and the people of Mohenjo-Daro, in India, did not wage war, for the good reason that it was totally unnecessary for them to do so, since socially and economically they were entirely sufficient unto themselves. Aboriginal Australians, however, have on occasion fought with one another, because for reasons—such as a dog or a wife—it seemed desirable for them to do so. Humans, it seems, fight only when and if they want to; and under indigenous conditions that appears to be very seldom indeed. There is nothing within the nature of humans, no *primum mobile*, no innate prejudice, save for such prejudices as have been cultivated in them by their social experience, which causes them to develop such emotional attitudes.[66]

I conclude this chapter with two paragraphs, one from Michael Lewis' book *The Culture of Inequality*, because it says so well what the race problem really is in America, and the other from an article by the historian, Albert F. Pollard, which I read in the 1925 student publication, *Vincula,* and which left an indelible impression upon me, as I expect it will upon the reader. Michael Lewis writes:

> The American culture of inequality is a tragic paradox writ large. It justifies the persistence of inequality in a society which stands firmly upon a foundation of equalitarian principle. It explains the persistence of inequality in terms consonant with equalitarian belief. It honors individual capacity, freedom, and dignity, while at the same time it is a source of profound personal discontent and, for some, of despair. It celebrates equal opportunity as a reality while it makes a fact of unequal opportunity. It troubles us, but we regard any criticism of its premises as heresy and those who engage in such criticisms as eccentrics or worse. And while it is a source of contemporary social stability, the trouble which is its issue can portend, as we shall see, a destabilized American future.
>
> The culture of inequality is the dialectic of our time. It contains the polarities of belief and intent which will probably shape the foreseeable future of American society—unless, of course, we are able to see it for what it is.[67]

Professor Pollard, in 1925, with World War I still in mind, warned for the future of humanity that,

> There looms a day of judgment, a day of judgment pronounced by man upon himself as having committed suicide because he was not fit to live. For we come to a common issue between a common mind to live and common 'nature' to kill. If there is Armageddon all will be taken, none will be left, and Fate will be common to victors and vanquished, rich and poor, all the nations, and both the hemispheres. To learn lest we perish is the logic of the League of Nations; learn to destroy is the teaching of 'natural' war. Whether mankind survives depends less on its science than on its humanity, upon whether we trust an increasing control over physical forces to men with a decreasing sense of responsibility for their use, and whether we regard as more 'natural' the war we think rooted in Nature or the peace we owe to our mind.[68]

Notes

1. It would seem that this idea is at least as old as the sixth century before Christ. We find it clearly stated in a fragment left us by Heracleitus of Ephesus (ca. 500 B.C.). "We must know," he writes, "that war is common to all and that strife is justice, and that everything comes into being by strife." Heracleitus, fragment LXII, trans. by W. H. S. Jones, p. 491.

2. Friedrich von Bernhardi, *Germany and the Next War* (New York: Longmans, 1912), 16–37. Compare with this the following passage written in 1942 by Lord Elton: "War, however we may hate it, is still the supreme agent of the evolutionary process. Blind, brutal and destructive, it remains the final arbiter, the one test mankind has yet contrived of a nation's fitness to survive." *Saint George or the Dragon* (London: Collins, 1942).

3. S. J. Holmes, *Life and Morals* (New York: Macmillan, 1948), 198. For a more extended discussion of Darwinism applied to man see Ashley Montagu, *Darwin, Competition, and Cooperation* (New York: Schuman, 1952).

4. Ernest Bogart, *Direct and Indirect Costs of the Great World War* (New York: Oxford University Press, 1919), 265–68.

5. Henry P. Fairchild, *The Prodigal Century* (New York: Philosophical Library, 1950), 244; *Academic American Encyclopedia*, vol. 20 (1993), 280.

6. Arthur Keith, *Essays on Human Evolution* (New York: Putnam, 1947), and *A New Theory of Human Evolution* (New York: Philosophical Library, 1950); for the views of the American warmongers see Richard Hofstadter's brilliant account in his *Social Darwinism in American Thought, 1860–1915* (Philadelphia: University of Pennsylvania Press, 1944). See also George Nasmyth, *Social Progress and the Darwinian Theory* (New York: Putnam, 1916).

7. Arthur Keith, *The Place of Prejudice in Modern Civilization* (New York: John Day, 1931).

8. In a book published in 1945 its author, echoing Keith, writes: "Whatever may be said against it, in so far as it keeps the race pure, race prejudice is admirable and even necessary." Stuart O. Landry, *The Cult of Equality* (New Orleans: Pelican Publishing), 257. The nonsense of such statement is sufficiently refuted by the fact that whenever and whatever ethnic groups meet they have mixed, and by the very consequential fact that no human being alive today is of unmixed origin.

9. Keith, *Place of Prejudice*, 50. In *An Autobiography* (New York: Philosophical Library, 1950), Keith writes of this address: "I was soon to be aware of the disturbance to which may rectorial address had given rise. My good friend, Dr. Katherine Trail, widow of my venerated mentor of early days, wrote me a most indignant letter accusing me of fanning the embers of war. Other critics laid hold of an unfortunate metaphor I had used—the 'pruning—hook of war' . . . My little booklet met with no demand. And all the time Hitler was demonstrating to the world the truth of my thesis." On the contrary, Hitler was demonstrating the evils to which such views as Keith's could lead.

10. Keith, *Autobiography*. For a critical examination of these views see Ashley Montagu, *The Nature of Human Aggression* (New York: Oxford University Press, 1976).

11. "Nature is a word, always very loosely used, to which time has brought increasingly sentimental connotations. The decline of one superstition has encouraged the growth of another. God the Father has been dethroned from many simple hearts only to be replaced by Nature the Mother, an entity of strikingly similar characteristics, mingling benevolence and vindictiveness in quite the old familiar proportions. Nature has consciousness and makes rules and plans, and takes revenge. She is jealous and cannot bear interference. Her workmanship is perfect. Her desire for mastery is always overwhelming, and no one ever gets the upper hand of her for long." Doris L. Moore, *The Vulgar Heart* (London: Cassell, 1945), 126.

12. Fred Hoyle, *The Nature of the Universe* (New York: Harper, 1951); C. F. von Weizsäcker, *The History of Nature* (Chicago: University of Chicago Press, 1950).

13. On quanta and genes see Erwin Schrödinger, *What is Life?* (New York: Macmillan, 1945).

14. Julian Huxley, *Evolution: The Modern Synthesis* (New York: Harper, 1946), 576.

15. Albert F. Pollard, "The War of Nature and a Peace of Mind," *Vincula* (University of London Students Journal), (14 December 1925), 60.

16. F. W. Went, "The Ecology of Desert Plants," *Scientific American* 192 (1955): 75.

17. This confusion could not be better illustrated that by Hitler's remark that "war is the most natural, the most every-day matter. War is eternal, war is universal. There is no beginning and there is no peace. Any struggle is war." Hermann Rauschning, *The Voice of Destruction* (New York: Putnam, 1940), 7–8.

18. Pollard, "The War of Nature," 61.

19. Montagu, *Nature of Human Aggression.*

20. Ernest Barker, *National Character,* 4th ed. (London: Methuen & Co. 1948); Bill Ashcroft, Gareth Griffiths, and Helen Tiffin, eds., *The Post-Colonial Studies Reader* (New York: Routledge, 1995); Paul R. Brass, *Ethnicity and Nationalism: Theory and Comparison* (Thousand Oaks, CA: Sage, 1996); H. C. Brookfield, *Colonism, Development, and Independence: The Case of the Melanesian Islands in the South Pacific* (Cambridge: Cambridge University Press, 1992); Frank P. Chambers, Christina Phelps Grant, and Charles C. Bayley, *This Age of Conflict: A Contemporary World History 1914–1943* (New York: Harcourt Brace, 1943); Michael Demiaskevich, *The National Mind: English, French, and Germans* (New York: American Book Company, 1938); Bogdan Denitch, *Ethnic Nationalism: The Tragic Death of Yugoslavia* (Minneapolis: University of Minnesota Press, 1994); Jack P. Greene and J. R. Pole, eds., *Colonial British America: Essays in the New History of the Modern Era* (Baltimore: Johns Hopkins University Press, 1984); Liah Greenfeld, *Nationalism: Five Roads to Modernity* (Cambridge: Harvard University Press, 1992); J. A. Hobson, *Imperialism: A Study* (Ann Arbor: University of Michigan Press, 1965); Richard Hofstadter, *Social Darwinism in American Thought 1860–1915* (Philadelphia: University of Pennsylvania Press, 1944); O. Mannoni, *Prospero and Caliban: A Study of the Psychology of Colonization* (New York: Praeger, 1956); George Nasmyth, *Social Progress and the Darwinian Theory* (New York: G. H. Putnam's, 1916); John Oakesmith, *Race and Nationality* (New York: Frederick A. Stokes, 1919); Edward W. Said, *Culture and Imperialism* (New York: Vintage Books, 1994); Charles L. Sanford, ed., *Manifest Destiny and the Imperialism Question* (New York: Wiley, 1974)—this contains an excellent bibliographical essay; L. L. Snyder, *Varieties of Nationalism: A Comparative Study* (New York: Holt, Rinehart & Winston, 1976); Louis L. Snyder, ed., *The Dynamics of Nationalism: Readings In Its Meaning and Development* (Princeton: Van Nostrand, 1964)—among other virtues Snyder's *Readings* contains a full bibliography of books on nationalism; L. L. Snyder, ed., *The Imperialism Reader* (Princeton: Van Nostrand, 1962); L. L. Snyder, *Encyclopedia of Nationalism* (New York: Paragon House, 1990); L. L. Snyder, *German Nationalism: The Tragedy of a People* (Harrisburg: Stackpole, 1952); L. L. Snyder, *The Roots of German Nationalism* (Bloomington: University of Indiana Press, 1978); Albert K. Weinberg, *Manifest Destiny: A Study of Na-*

tionalist Expansion in American History (Baltimore: Johns Hopkins University Press, 1935); Herbert Ziegler, *Nazi Germany's New Aristocracy* (Princeton: Princeton University Press, 1938).

21. W. Hamilton Fyfe, *The Illusion of National Character* (London: Watts, 1946).

22. Daniel S. Lehrman, "Semantic and Conceptual Issues in the Nature-Nurture Problem," in *Development and Evolution of Behavior*, eds. Lester R. Aronson, Ethel Tobach, Daniel S. Lehrman and Jay S. Rosenblatt (San Francisco: Freeman & Co., 1970), 17–52; Lester R. Aronson et al., eds., *Selected Writings of T. C. Schneirla* (San Francisco: Freeman & Co., 1972); W. H. Thorpe, *Animal Nature and Human Nature* (New York: Anchor-Press/Doubleday, 1974); Peter H. Klopfer, *Behavioral Aspects of Ecology*, 2nd ed. (Englewood Cliffs: Prentice-Hall, 1973); J. L. Cloudsely-Thompson, *Animal Conflict and Adaptation* (London: Foulis, 1965); W. C. Allee, *The Social Life of Animals* (Boston: Beacon Press, 1958).

23. Brückner, "Untersuchungen zur Tiersoziologie, insbesondere zur Auflösung der Familie," *Zeitschrift für Psychologie* 128 (1933): 1–110.

24. Full accounts of the activities of Japanese American members of the forces of the United States may be read in the files of the Japanese American newspaper Pacific Citizen, published at Salt Lake City, Utah.

25. Ibid., 21 (6 October 1945), I; T. D. Murphy, *Ambassadors in Arms* (Honolulu: University of Hawaii Press, 1954).

26. Houston Stewart Chamberlain, *The Foundations of the Nineteenth Century* (London, New York: Lane, 1910).

27. Oliver Goldsmith, *On National Prejudices. The Miscellaneous Works* (New York: Putnam, 1850).

28. George Peacock, *Life of Thomas Young* (London: Murray, 1855), 107.

29. David Hume, *A Treatise of Human Nature.*

30. A. Montagu, "On the Nonperception of 'Race' Differences," *Current Anthropology* 18 (1977):743–44.

31. E. Horowitz, "The Development of Attitudes toward the Negro," *Archives of Psychology* 194 (1936); Marian Radke and Helen Trager, "Children's Perceptions of the Social Roles of Negroes and Whites," *Journal of Psychology* 29 (1950): 3–33; H. Trager and M. R. Yarrow, *They Learn What They Live: Prejudice in Young Children* (New York: Harper, 1952).

32. Frans de Waal, *Peacemaking Among Primates* (Cambridge: Harvard University Press, 1989); F. de Waal, *Good-Natured: The Origins of Right and Wrong in Humans and Other Animals* (Cambridge: Harvard University Press, 1996); F. B. M. de Waal, *Chimpanzee Politics: Power and Sex Among Apes* (New York: Harper and Row, 1982); Margaret Power, *The Egalitarians: Human and Chimpanzee* (New York: Cambridge University Press, 1991).

33. Pliny, *Natural History*, 7.1.5.

34. Warder Allee, *Cooperation Among Animals* (New York: Schuman, 1950), 200. It is even likely that the ants who are in any event too far removed from man to have any relevance for his behavior, form no exception to this rule. See Norman R. F. Maier and Theodore C. Schneirla, *Principles of Animal Psychology* (New York: McGraw-Hill, 1935), 164 ff.; and T. Schneirla, "'Cruel' Ants-and Occam's Razor," *Journal of Comparative Psychology* 34 (1942): 79–83.

35. For an interesting discussion of "animal warfare," in which the author extends the meaning of "warfare" to embrace attacks upon animals of widely separated species, see Quincy Wright, *A Study of War*, 2 vols. (Chicago: University of Chicago Press, 1942), 24–52, 479–518.

36. Julian Huxley, *On Living in a Revolution* (London: Chatto & Windus, 1944), 61.

37. Gordon Allport, "Human Nature and the Peace," *Psychological Bulletin*, 42 (1945): 37–68.

38. Havelock Ellis, *The Philosophy of Conflict* (London: Constable, 1919), 51–52. Ellis was here summarizing the work of Rudolf Holsti, *The Relation of War to the Origin of the State* (Helsingfors: New Printing Co., 1913). For confirmatory views see Quincy Wright's chapter "Primitive Warfare," in *A Study of War* (Chicago: University of Chicago Press, 1942), 53–100, and Wilfrid D. Hambly, "Primitive Warfare," *Chicago Natural History Museum Bulletin* 17 (1946): 4–5; Ashley Montagu, "The Nature of War and the Myth of Nature," *The Scientific Monthly* 54 (1942): 342–53.

39. Verrier Elwin, *The Tribal World of Verrier Elwin* (New York: Oxford University Press, 1964), 121.

40. Ibid., 121–22.

41. W. J. Perry, "Man the Primeval Pacifist," *Vincula* (14 December 1925): 64.

42. Ragnar Numelin, *The Beginnings of Diplomacy* (New York: Philosophical Library, 1950), 104.

43. V. Gordon Childe, *The Dawn of European Civilization*, 4th ed (New York: Alfred A. Knopf, 1947); *Man Makes Himself* (New York: Oxford University Press, 1940); "War in Prehistoric Societies," *Sociological Review* 33 (1941), 126–38.

44. See Bernhardi, *Germany and the Next War*, for a most illuminating exemplification of this view. See also John U. Nef, *War and Human Progress* (Cambridge: Harvard University Press, 1950); L. L. Bernard, *War and its Causes* (New York: 1944).

45. Richard J. Barnet, *The Roots of War* (Baltimore: Penguin Books, 1972).

46. Bronislaw Malinowski, "War-Past, Present, and Future," in *War as a Social Institution*, eds. J. D. Clarkson and T. C. Cochran (New York: Columbia University Press, 1941), 23–24.

47. Lauretta Bender, "Genesis of Hostility in Children," *American Journal of Psychiatry* 105 (1948): 241–45; A. Montagu, *On Being Human*, 2nd ed. (New York: Hawthorn Books, 1969); A. Montagu, *The Direction of Human Development* (New York: Hawthorn Books, 1970); David P. Ausubel, *Theory and Problems of Child Development* (New York: Grune and Stratton, 1958); Leonard Eron, Leopold O. Walder, and Monroe M. Lefkowitz, *Learning of Aggression in Children* (Boston: Little, Brown & Co., 1971); A. Montagu, *Growing Young* (Westport, CT: Bergin & Garvey, 1989).

48. Warder C. Allee, "Where Angels Fear to Tread: A Contribution for General Sociology to Human Ethics," *Science* 97 (1943): 521. See also the same author's *Cooperation among Animals* and his *Animal Aggregations* (Chicago: University of Chicago Press, 1931). Along similar lines see Montagu, *On Being Human; Darwin, Competition and Cooperation;* and *Direction of Human Development.*

49. Petr Kropotkin, *Mutual Aid: A Factor in Evolution* rev. ed. (Boston: Porter Sargent, 1955). For an excellent resume on modern research findings on cooperation see Robert Augros and George Stanciu, *The New Biology* (Boston: Shambhala, 1987); Vladimir J. Novák, *The Principles of Sociogenesis* (Prague: Academia Czechoslo-

vak Academemy of Sciences, 1982); J. Milikovsky and J. A. Novák, eds., *Evolution and Morphogenesis,* 2 vols. (Proceedings of the International Symposium, Plezen, Czochoslovak Academy of Sciences, Prague, 1985).

50. J. B. S. Haldane, *The Causes of Evolution* (New York: Longmans, 1932), 130; J. B. S. Haldane, *Heredity and Poltics* (New York: Norton, 1938), 88.

51. Charles Darwin, *The Descent of Man* (London: Murray, 1871), chap. 4, 187–88.

52. William Patten, *The Grand Strategy of Evolution* (Boston: Badger, 1920).

53. Patrick Geddes and J. Arthur Thomson, *Evolution* (New York: Holt, 1911); P. Geddes and J. A. Thomson, *Sex* (London: William & Norgate, 1911); L. L. Bernard, *Some Neglected Factors in Evolution* (New York: Putnam, 1911); Hermann Reinheimer, *Evolution by Cooperation: a Study in Bio-economics* (London: Kegan Paul, 1913); H. Reinheimer, *Symbiosis: A Socio-physiological Study of Evolution* (London: Headley, 1920); Leo S. Berg, *Nomogenesis, or Evolution Determines by Law* (London: Constable, 1926); R. W. Gibson, *The Morality of Nature* (New York: Putnam, 1923); Yves Delage and Marie Goldsmith, *The Theories of Evolution* (London: Palmer, 1912); W. C. Allee et al., *Principles of Animal Ecology* (Philadelphia: Saunders, 1949); and numerous other works. For a discussion of these works see Montagu, *Darwin, Competition and Cooperation;* Montagu, *Direction of Human Development.*

54. Alfred E. Emerson, "The Biological Basis of Social Cooperation," *Illinois Academy of Science Transactions* 39 (1946): 9–18.

55. Ibid., 15.

56. Nicholas Collias, "Aggressive Behaviour among Vertebrate Animals," *Physiological Zoology* 17 (1944), 83–123; J. P. Scott, *Aggression* (Chicago: University of Chicago Press, 1958); Roger Johnson, *Aggression in Man and Animals* (Philadelphia: Saunders, 1972).

57. Allee speaks of the "great drive toward natural altruism that extends throughout the whole animal kingdom." "Biology and International Relations," *New Republic* 112 (1945): 817; see also Montagu, ed., *Culture and the Evolution of Man* (New York: Oxford University Press, 1962); Sherwood L. Washburn, ed., *Social Life of Early Man* (Chicago: Quadrangle Books, 1961).

58. Chauncey D. Leake, "Ethicogenesis," *Proceedings of the Philosophical Society of Texas* (1944), 32–33; Augros and Stanciu, *New Biology.*

59. For an excellent discussion of this subject see Laurence Stapleton, *Justice and World Society* (Chapel Hill: University of North Carolina Press, 1944). See also Gladys Bryson, *Man and Society* (Princeton: Princeton University Press, 1945); Herschel Baker, *The Dignity of Man* (Cambridge: Harvard University Press, 1974); Hugh Miller, *The Community of Man* (New York: Macmillan, 1949), and *Progress and Decline* (Los Angeles: Ward Ritchie Press, 1963).

60. Haldane, *The Causes of Evolution,* 125–26.

61. Pollard, "The War of Nature," 61. Liddell Hart, *Through the Fog of War* (New York: Random House, 1938); George A. Panichas, ed., *Promise of Greatness: The War of 1914–1918* (New York: John Day, 1968); Michael Walzer, *Just and Unjust Wars: A Moral Argument with Historical Illustrations* (New York: Basic Books, 1977); Notrman E. Dixon, *On the Psychology of Military Incompetence* (London: Jonathan Cape, 1988); David L. Bender and Bruno Leone, eds., *War and Human Nature: Opposing Viewpoints* (St. Paul: Greenhaven Press, 1983); Joseph J. Fahey and Richard

Armstrong, *A Peace Reader: Essential Readings on War, Justice, Non-Violence and World Order* (New York/Mahah: Paulist Press, 1992); Signe Howell and Roy Willis, *Societies at Peace: Anthropological Perspectives* (London and New York: Routledge, 1989); Ashley Montagu, ed., *Learning Non-Aggression: The Experience of Non-Literate Societies* (New York: Oxford University Press, 1978); Ashley Montagu, *One World or None* [a film] (New York: The American Federation of Scientific Workers/Washington: The National Committee on Atomic Information, 1946); Michael N. Nagler, *America Without Violence: Why Violence Persists and How You Can Stop It* (Covelo, CA: Island Press, 1982); Ralph Pettman, *Biopolitics and International Values: Investigating Liberal Norms* (New York: Pergamon Press, 1981); Leslie E. Sponsel and Thomas Gregor, eds., *The Anthropology of Peace and Nonviolence* (Boulder: Rienner, 1994); Aline M. Stomfay-Stitz, *Peace Education in America, 1828–1990: Sourcebook for Education and Research* (Metuchen, NJ: Scarecrow Press, 1993); Paul R. Turner and David Pitt, *The Anthropology of War and Peace* (Granby, MA: Bergin & Garvy, 1989); UNESCO, *The Nature of Conflict: Studies on the Sociological Aspects of International Relations* (Paris: UNESCO, 1957).

62. Vernon L. Kellogg, *Military Selection and Race Deterioration* (New York: Oxford University Press, 1916), 178.

63. Huxley, *On Living in a Revolution*, 66.

64. Montagu, *On Being Human;* Montagu and Matson, *The Human Connection* (New York: McGraw-Hill, 1979); A. Montagu, *Education and Human Relations*, 3rd ed.(Westport, CT: Greenwood Press, 1997).

65. A. L. Rowse, *Appeasement: A Study in Political Decline, 1933–39* (New York: Norton: 1961).

66. For an admirable discussion of race relations and war see Charles Andrews, "Racial Influences," in *The Causes of War,* ed. Arthur Porritt (New York: Macmillan, 1932), 63–113.

67. Michael Lewis, *The Culture of Inequality* (Amherst: University of Massachusetts Press, 1978), 48.

68. Albert F. Pollard, "The War of Nature," 61.

14

Race and Blood

In his inspiring and provocative book *Man: Real and Ideal,* Professor E. G. Conklin writes: "Ashley Montagu would discard wholly the word 'race' in the case of man because of social prejudices associated with that word and substitute for it 'ethnic group' or 'caste.' I wholly sympathize with his desire to get rid of race prejudice, but not by denying the existence of races or by giving them another name, for 'What's in a name?'"[1] Apparently I have been unclear in my proposals, for these statements do not correctly represent my viewpoint,[2] but it is not with these statements that I am here concerned, but with Professor Conklin's question, "What's in a name?"

What, indeed? I suggest, with most students of language, that names are words and that words rule our lives; that in this sense words are among the most important things we have to deal with in the course of our lives. I suggest that the meaning of most, if not all, words are to some extent emotionally determined and that humans, are, in large part, creatures of emotion. And because emotions attach to words rather than to ideas, it is important to be aware of the fact that words frequently have an emotional rather than a factual basis. It is Freud who said:

> Words and magic were in the beginning one and the same thing, and even today words retain much of their magical power. By words one of us can give to another the greatest happiness or bring about utter despair; by words the teacher imparts his knowledge to the student; by words the orator sweeps his audience with him and determines its judgments and decisions. Words call for the emotions and are universally the means by which we influence our fellow creatures.[3]

Henry James remarked, "All life comes back to the question of our speech—the medium through which we communicate." And as Francis Bacon said before him, "Men believe that their reason is lord over their words, but it happens, too, that words exercise a reciprocal and reactionary power over our intellect. Words, as a Tartar's bow, shoot back upon the understanding of the wisest, and mightily entangle and pervert the judgment."

Finally, names, words, not only serve to describe, but also often serve to create ideas and stereotypes, which become our personal reality. Or to paraphrase Goethe, where an idea is wanting a word can always be found to take its place. Furthermore, to repeat, it should be clear that emotions constitute a fertile soil for ideas, and that emotions are often in the first place attached to words rather than to ideas; by that route emotional ideas are often generated. The word and the emotion are often conflated, so that when the idea, word, or perception of race is presented, the emotion associated with it, especially in a racist society, is simultaneously aroused. This phenomenon, or *cathexis*—that is, concentration of psychic energy upon a given object—is, in other words, the investment of the psychic energy of a drive in a conscious or unconscious mental representation such as a concept, idea, image, fantasy, symbol or conduct. The emotional identification with a group often energizes enmity towards others, and results in rationalization to defend it. The space between an idea and the reality can be very great indeed, and misleading. The modern movement of semantics and semantogenetics is devoted to the analysis of this form of human behavior and the tracing of its consequences.[4]

Words fashion the thoughts of humankind, and most people become the prisoners of their vocabularies. Where words are concerned there are two classes of people—those who habitually control their words by critical analysis, they are in the minority; and those whose words, whose verbal habits, control and determine their thoughts—they are in the great majority. The latter are the "word patriots," the "word sentimentalists," the racists, unconscious or declared. With them, to whom, a name, a word, a very little word, often means the difference between life and death, we are here concerned. A first step toward clear thinking is the declaration of a moratorium on words that create muddled thinking.

There are many words in our vocabulary that are characterized by an exaggerated emotional content; words distinguished by a high emotional and low rational quality. "Race" is such a word; "blood" is another. The word "race" has assumed a high emotional content in relatively recent times; "blood," on the other hand, is a word which, from the beginning of recorded history, and certainly long before that, has possessed a high emotional content.

That blood is the most immediately important constituent of the human body must have been remarked by humans early in their history. The weakening effect or actual death produced by an appreciable loss of blood can hardly have escaped their attention. Hence, the identification of blood as vital to life, and its investment with special life-giving qualities, must have been almost inevitable steps in the process of endowing this essence with meaning. Among all indigenous peoples blood is regarded as a most powerful element possessed of many varied and potent qualities. To enumerate these and the functions they are believed to perform would alone fill a volume. In the cultural dynamics of Western civilization the concept of "blood" has played a highly significant role. From the earliest times it has been regarded as that most quintessential element of the body which carries, and through which is transmitted, our hereditary qualities. Thus, all persons of the same family stock were regarded as of the same "blood." In a community that mostly consisted of family lines whose members had, over many generations, intermarried, it is easy to understand how, with such a concept of "blood," the community or nation would come to regard itself as of one "blood," distinct, *by blood,* from all other communities or nations. This, indeed, is the popular conception of "blood" which prevails at the present time. Thus, for example, if one turns to the *Oxford English Dictionary* and looks under "blood," the following statement is found: "Blood is popularly treated as the typical part of the body which children inherit from their parents and ancestors; hence that of parents and children, and of the members of a family or race, is spoken of as identical, and as being distinct from that of other families or races."

As Dobzhansky put it:

Before the rediscovery of Mendel's work the transmission of heredity was thought of in terms of inheritance of 'blood.' Parental 'bloods' mix and give rise to the 'blood' of the child which is a compromise between those of the parents. In a sexually reproducing population the available variety of 'bloods' mingle owing to intermarriage. If such a population is left undisturbed, the continuous mixing process will result in an uniform solution which will represent the 'blood' of a race or a variety. When a complete or near complete uniformity is reached you will have a 'pure race'—a group of individuals with identical germ plasms. If two races mingle, a mixed race arises; if race miscegenation ceases, a new 'pure race' will eventually result.

"It is most unfortunate," Dobzhansky adds, "that the theory of 'blood' though invalidated decades ago, still colors not merely the thinking of laymen but finds its way, explicitly or implicitly, into textbooks."[5]

It is this conception of "blood" as the carrier of the heritable qualities of the family, race, or nation which has led to its application in such extended meanings as are implied in terms such as "blue blood," "bad blood," "blood royal," "pureblood," "full blood," "half blood," "good blood," "blood tie," or "blood relationship," and "consanguinity." Supposed racial and national differences are, of course, recognized in such terms as "German blood," "English blood," "Jewish blood," and "black blood"; so that today the words "race" and "blood" are still used by many as synonyms, or equivalent terms.

When the meaning of these terms is examined, the manner in which the general conception of "blood" operates may be more clearly perceived. Thus, the term "blue blood," which refers to a presumed special kind of blood supposed to flow in the veins of ancient and aristocratic families, actually represents a translation from the Spanish *sangre azul*, the "blue blood" attributed to some of the oldest and proudest families of Castile, who claimed never to have been contaminated by "foreign blood."[6] Many of these families were of fair complexion, hence in members of these families the veins would, in comparison with those of the members of the predominantly dark-complexioned population, appear strikingly blue. Hence, the difference between an aristocrat and a commoner could easily be recognized as a difference in "blood"; one was a "blue blood," and the other was not. It is of interest to note that members of the "upper crust" of sociogenetically established "upper class" in America are often referred to as "bluebloods."

The expression "blood royal" refers to the generally accepted notion that only persons of royal ancestry have the "blood of kings" flowing in their veins. No person, however noble his ancestry, can be of the "blood royal" unless he has the blood of kingly ancestors circulating in his veins. Thus, kings have usually been held to belong to a special class of humankind, principally by virtue of the supposed unique character of their blood. In order to keep the "blood" of the royal house pure, marriages were arranged exclusively between those who were of "royal blood."

In common parlance and in the loose usage of many who should know better, terms like "full blood," or "pure blood," and "half blood" clearly illustrate the supposed hereditary character of the blood and the manner in which, by simple arithmetical division, it may be diluted. Thus, "full blood" and "pure blood" are expressions which are alleged to define the supposed fact that a person is of unadulterated blood; that is, he is a person whose ancestors have undergone no admixture of blood with a commoner or members of another race. Within the last century these terms have come to be applied almost exclusively to persons who are not of the "white race," to persons, in short, whose place is considered to be on the presupposed inferior rungs of the racial ladder. It is possible that this restricted usage has been determined by the fact that these expressions have generally done most service in the description of indigenous peoples or of slaves, as in "full-blooded Negro," "pureblood Indian," or merely "full blood," or "pureblood." Such an imputed lowly association would be sufficient to secure the nonapplication of the term to any member of the self-styled superior races.

A "half blood," in contradistinction to a "full blood," or "pure-blood," is supposed to be half of one race and half of another—for example, the offspring of an Indian and a white. What is actually implied is that while a full blood or pureblood may claim relationship through both parents, a half blood may claim relationship through one parent only. For example, the offspring of a white and a black, is for all practical purposes classed with the group to which the black parent belongs, and his white ancestry is, for the same purposes, ignored. In practice, it often works out that the half blood is not fully accepted by either of the parental groups, because of his or her "adulterated blood," and they become in the true sense of the expression "half caste," belonging to neither caste; for in Western society, as we have seen in an earlier chapter, the so-called different races are, in reality, treated as if they belonged to different castes.

A person is said to be of "good" or "gentle" blood if he or she is of "noble" birth or of "good" family. Here the assumed biological determinance of social status by blood is clearly exhibited; that is to say, a person's rank in society is assumed to be determined by his "blood," when, in fact, it is in reality the other way around, "blood" is actually determined by rank. The ancestors of all noblemen were once common people, plebeians. It was not a sudden metamorphosis in the composition of their blood which transformed them into nobles; it was rather an elevation in social status, which endowed them with supposedly superior qualities that were not biological in any sense whatever and belonged purely to the ascriptive variety of things. That is to say, they had no real, but a purely imagined, existence.

The statement that a person is of "bad blood," in the sense that he is of common or inferior character or status, is rarely encountered, for the reason, presumably, that those who use such terms have not considered the "blood" of such persons worth mentioning at all. Thus, for example, while there is an entry in the *Oxford English Dictionary* for "blood worth mention," there is none for blood not worth mention. In the sense in which "blood" is considered as the seat of the emotions, "bad blood" is taken to be the physiological or serological equivalent of ill feeling. In this sense, of course, "bad blood" may be created between persons of "good blood." The term "blood relationship" and its Anglicized Latin equivalent "consanguinity," meaning the condition of being of the same "blood" or relationship, by descent from a common ancestor, enshrine the belief that all biological relationships are reflected in, and are to a large extent determined by, the character of the blood. This venerable error, along with others, requires correction.

The brief analysis of the variety of ways in which "blood" is used and understood in the English language and in Western civilization in general renders it sufficiently clear that most people believe that blood is equivalent to heredity and that blood, therefore, is that part of the organism that determines the quality of the person. By extension, it is also generally believed that the social as well as the biological status of the person is determined by the kind of blood he or she has inherited. These beliefs concerning blood are probably among the oldest surviving from the earliest days of humankind. Certainly they are found to be almost universally distributed among the peoples of the earth in much the same forms, and their antiquity is sufficiently attested by the fact that in the graves of prehistoric men red pigments are frequently found in association with the remains. These pigments were, probably, used to represent the blood as the symbol of life and humanity, a belief enshrined in the expression, "he is flesh and blood," to signify humanity as opposed to deity or disembodied spirit. There in the grave was the flesh, and the pigment was introduced to represent the blood.

As an example of a myth grown hoary with the ages and for which there is not the slightest justification in scientific fact, the popular conception of "blood" is conspicuous. Were it not for the fact that it is a bad myth, harmful in its effects and dangerous in its possible consequences, it might well be allowed to persist; but since great harm has already been done, and will continue to be done unless this myth is exposed for what it is—an understandable misinterpretation of the function of blood—it is today more than ever necessary to set out the facts about blood as science has come to know them.

In the first place, blood is in no way connected with the transmission of hereditary traits. The transmitters of hereditary traits are the genes which lie in the chromosomes of the germ cells represented by the spermatozoa of the father and the ova of the mother, and nothing else. These genes, carried in the chromosomes and cell substance of a single spermatozoon and a single ovum, are the only parts of the organism concerned with the transmission of heredity.[7] Blood has nothing whatever to do with heredity, either biologically, sociologically, or in any other manner.

As Dobzhansky says:

> Germ plasms are not miscible 'bloods.' They are sums of discrete genes which, if unlike but present in the same individual, do not mix by segregate according to the rules established by Mendel. In sexually reproducing organisms, an individual inherits only one-half, not all of the genes each parent possesses; and it transmits to its children one-half of its genes. Every sex cell produced by an individual is likely to contain a somewhat different complement of genes from every other sex cell of the same individual. Brothers and sisters have different hereditary endowments. The variety of genes present in populations of many sexually reproducing species, including man, is so great, and the number of combinations which they are capable of producing is so colossal, that it is unlikely that any two individuals (identical twins excepted) ever have exactly the same germ plasms.[8]

The belief that the blood of the pregnant mother is transmitted to the child in the womb, and hence becomes a part of the child, is ancient but erroneous. Scientific knowledge of the processes of pregnancy have long ago made it clear that there is *normally* no actual intermingling of the blood of the mother with that of the fetus. Blood cells are far too large to pass through the placental barrier to the fetus.[9] The developing fetus manufactures its own blood, and the character of its various blood cells, both morphologically and physiologically, is demonstrably different from that of either of its parents. These facts should forever dispose of the ancient notion, which is so characteristically found among indigenous peoples, that the blood of the mother is continuous with that of the child. This same ancient belief is to be found in the works of Aristotle on generation.[10] Aristotle held that the monthly periods, which fail to appear during pregnancy, contribute to the formation of the child's body. Modern scientific investigation demonstrates that this and similar notions are quite false, and thus completely disposes of the idea of a blood tie between any two persons, even when they are identical twins. Hence, any claims to kinship based on the tie of blood can have no scientific foundation of any kind. Nor can claims of group consciousness based on blood be anything but fictitious, since the character of the blood of all human beings is determined not by their membership in any group or nation but by the fact that they are human beings.

The blood of all human beings is in every respect the same, that is, in the agglutinating properties of the blood which yields the blood groups and in the Rh factor. But these agglutinating properties of the blood groups and the many serologically distinguishable Rh groups are present in all humans, and in various populations of humanity they differ only in their frequencies. This distribution is a matter not of quality but of quantity. There are no known or demonstrable differences in the character of the blood of different peoples, except that some traits of the blood, like sickle-cell anemia and thellasemia are possessed in greater frequency by some than by others. In that sense St. Paul's *obiter dictum* "[that God] hath made of one blood all nations of men for to dwell on all the face of the earth"[11] is literally true.

Scientists have for many years attempted to discover whether or not any differences exist in the blood of different peoples, but the results of such investigations have always been the same—*no difference has been discovered*, except in the statistical distribution of the traits that all human beings possess in common and the absence or presence of a blood type compared with other populations present in other populations.[12] In short, it cannot be too emphatically or too often repeated that in every respect the blood of all human groups is the same, varying only in the frequency with which certain of its many components are encountered in different populations. This similarity cuts across all lines of caste, class, group, nation, or ethnic group. Obviously, then, since all people are of one blood, such difference as may exist between them can have absolutely no connection with blood.

Such facts, however, did not in the least deter Nazi propagandists from using the "blood" myths to set human beings against each other. The official Nazi view of the matter was presented to Congress of the Nazi Party at Nuremberg, exactly six years before the invasion of Poland, by the official Nazi distorter of the truth, Alfred Rosenberg—who was subsequently hanged as a war criminal at Nuremberg. "A nation," said Rosenberg,

> is constituted by the predominance of a definite character formed by its blood, language, geographical environment, and the sense of a united political destiny. These last constituents are not, however, definitive; the decisive element in a nation is its blood. In the first awakening of a people, great poets and heroes disclose themselves to us as the incorporation of the eternal values of a particular blood soul. I believe that this recognition of the profound significance of blood is now mysteriously encircling our planet, irresistibly gripping one nation after another.[13]

The concept of race which equates the inheritance of the individual or of the group with the transmission of hereditary traits or qualities through the blood dates from a period when the nature of heredity was not understood and the existence of such things as genes was unknown. During that period, the eighteenth and nineteenth centuries, the race concept was developed. It has been seen that this concept is false and misleading, producing atrocious absurdities of thought and conduct.

The extravagant and preposterous claims the Nazis made on the basis of the blood myth, are matched only by those supernationalists who declared that through "ethnic cleansing" they could prevent the adulteration of their nation's blood. During World War II such claims were underscored and given much publicity when the American Red Cross segregated the blood of blacks for the purposes of transfusion.

In July 1958 a law was passed in the State of Louisiana requiring the segregation of the blood obtained from blacks. The blood segregation bill was the result of the efforts of Louisiana's Joint Legislative Committee on Segregation. In other words, the myth of "blood" was almost as strongly entrenched in America as it was among the Nazis.[14] This was an undesirable and dangerous situation, and though the facts concerning blood are much better known, superstitions for which there are no bases in fact continue. The reality, of course, is that the blood of any individual is potentially compatible with the blood of any other individual.

It is a sad reflection on civilized Americans that it was a black scientist, Dr. Charles Drew, who originated the blood bank and the improvement of blood hemoglobin techniques, which have been the means of saving million of lives, and will continue to do so forever.[15]

The archaic concerns about the ethnic make-up of blood donors are, of course, based on the antique misconception that blood is the carrier of hereditary traits.[16] Any group regarded as possessing racially inferior traits, could potentially transmit these traits to the receiver of the transfusion. Both prejudices are groundless. But observe how real unreal ideas, names, and words may become if only they are believed to be real. If I say that certain persons belong to certain "aburals" and their "nottals" differ from my nottals because I belong to a different abural, I may be talking utter nonsense; but if I believe that what I am saying is actually meaningful and true, it may be nonsense to others, but it is truth to me. When, however, most people believe in the existence of aburals and call them races and in nottals, which they call "blood," these words become meaningful counters of their lives, the means by which they handle "reality." But what we take for reality is often only appearance, hence, we must be on our guard against words which pass for representatives of reality, but are, in fact, nothing but desperate inventions—bags into which we have breathed our own hot air. "Words," said Thomas Hobbes, "are wise men's counters, they do but reckon by them. But they are the money of fools."

What modern science has revealed about blood, then, renders all such words as "blood royal," "half blood," "full blood," "blood relationship," and the other terms to which reference has been made meaningless in point of fact and dangerously meaningful in the superstitious social sense.

Is it too much to expect that this false belief, the myth of "blood," will soon make way for the scientifically established universal truth that all human beings, no matter of what creed or complexion they may be, and allowing for all the interesting variations in the frequencies of certain blood types, are fundamentally of one and the same blood?

Notes

1. Edwin Conklin, *Man: Real and Ideal* (New York: Schribner, 1943), 20.
2. See Appendix A.
3. Sigmund Freud, *Introductory Lectures on Psycho-Analysis* (London: Allen & Unwin, 1922), 13.
4. See Alfred Korzybski, *Science and Sanity*, 2nd ed (Lancaster: Science Press, 1941); S. I. Hayakawa, *Language in Action* (New York: Harcourt, Brace, 1941); Stuart Chase, *The Tyranny of Words* (New York: Harcourt, Brace, 1938); C. K. Ogden and I. A. Richards, *The Meaning of Meaning* (New York: Harcourt, Brace, 1923); Hugh Walpole, *Semantics: The Nature of Words and Their Meanings* (New York: Norton, 1953); J. Dan Rothwell, *Telling It Like It Isn't* (Englewood Cliffs: Prentice-Hall, 1982); Ashley Montagu, "The Language of Self-Deception" in *Language in America* eds. Postman et al. (New York: Pegasus Press, 1969), 82–95; Ossie Davis, "The Language of Racism" in *Language in America*, eds. Neil Postman, Charles Weingartner, and Terence P. Moran (New York: Pegasus, 1969).

5. Theodosius Dobzhansky, "Genetics and Human Affairs," *Teaching Biologist* 12 (1943): 97–104.

6. The blood in the veins is dark red in color, while the veins themselves are creamy white. The blue appearance of the veins through the skin is due to the refractive properties of the tissues through which they are observed.

7. Ashley Montagu, *Human Heredity,* 3rd ed. (New York: New American Library, 1963); Max Levitan and Ashley Montagu, *Textbook of Human Genetics* (New York: Oxford University Press, 1971); W. F. Bodmer and L. L. Cavalli-Sforza, *Genetics, Evolution, and Man* (San Francisco: Freeman, 1976).

8. Dobzhansky, "Genetics and Human Affairs," 102.

9. A. Montagu, *Prenatal Influences* (Springfield, IL: Thomas, 1962).

10. Aristotle, *De generations animalum,* I. 20.

11. *Acts* 17:26

12. A. E. Mourant, *The Distribution of the Human Blood Groups* (Springfield. IL: Thomas, 1962); R. R. Race and Ruth Sanger, *Blood Groups in Man* (Springfield, IL: Thomas, 1958); A Montagu, *An Introduction to Physical Anthropology* 3rd ed. (Springfield, IL: Thomas, 1960); William C. Boyd, *Genetics and the Races of Man* (Boston: Little, Brown, 1950).

13. *Vossische Zeitung,* 3 September 1933. Rosenberg himself was a Baltic Russian, and did not become a "German" until 1923 when the Russians refused to allow him to return to Reval, where he was born. See *Memoirs of Alfred Rosenberg* (New York: Ziff-Davis, 1949). Rosenberg's chief collection of essays is entitled *Blood and Honor (Blut und Ehre).* See also Albert R. Chandler, *Rosenberg's Nazi Myth: Race and History* (Ithaca: Cornell University Press, 1945); Robert Cecil, *The Myth of the Master Race: Alfred Rosenberg and Nazi Ideology* (New York: Dodd, Mead, 1972).

14. For an able analysis and discussion of the character of the blood in the varieties of man see Julian H. Lewis, *The Biology of the Negro* (Chicago: University of Chicago Press, 1942), 82 ff.

15. Miles Shapiro, *Charles Drew: Founder of the Blood Bank* (Austin: Raintree Steck-Vaughan, 1997); Spencie Love, *One Blood: The Death and Resurrection of Charles R. Drew* (Chapel Hill: University of North Carolina Press, 1996).

16. It was the ancient belief that the seed comes from all parts of the body and is carried in or is merely a specialized portion of the blood. For a clear expression of this view, which has persisted down to modern times, see Hippocrates, *Airs, Waters, and Places,* xiii 14. Such views, it may here be mentioned in passing, formed the basis of the erroneous belief in the inheritance of acquired characters, for if the blood gathered the seed from every part of the body, any modification of the body would be reflected in the seed, and hence would be transmitted to the offspring.

15

Innate Aggression and Race

"Original sin," or what our Victorian ancestors so charmingly called "Innate Depravity"—which somehow made it wrong to take a walk in the park or listen to anything but divine music on Sundays and made Sundays, as Rupert Brooke put it, so full of impalpable restraints—has really never died. It has simply suffered a generational secular change.

For several decades, one of the most popular novels on college campuses has been William Golding's *Lord of the Flies*.[1] Why should this novel, which tells the story of a group of schoolboys stranded on a desert island who turn into archetypal savages and begin to hunt each other, have so wide an appeal? Golding has himself been quoted as saying that the book "is an attempt to trace the defects of society back to the defects of human nature." This novel has enjoyed a wide readership on American college campuses, and it was made into a film. Its appeal to young people is not strange, for in the world of violence in which they live Golding's novel supplies them with an easy answer for it "explanation." The novel in some courses in sociology has been used as a vivid evidence of "innate depravity," of the alleged natural nastiness of man. It could hardly be expected to be otherwise.[2] Margaret Mead described the novel as "one of the most insightful treatises on the possibilities of human aggression." She also highly praised Konrad Lorenz's book *On Aggression*,[3] in which the Nobel Prize laureate, recognized for his work on animal behavior, endeavored to show that man's "fighting instinct," which is directed against his fellow man is the major cause of his troubles. The journalist Robert Ardrey in several books argued the same thesis, and later Desmond Morris, who created a worldwide best-seller in *The Naked Ape*,[4] went even further. For while those authors believed that there remained some hope if we would but take the trouble to understand our own nature and exercise some measure of control over it, Morris literally said that it is "rubbish" to believe that "we shall control our aggressive and territorial feelings. Our raw animal nature," he added, "will never permit it." As an anthropologist, part of whose interests embrace the science of rubbish, namely, archaeology, there is this to say

369

with regard to the findings of science which are so confidently dismissed by Morris and his colleagues as "rubbish."

In this chapter I inquire into the validity of the views on human nature expressed principally in the widely read and influential books of Robert Ardrey and Konrad Lorenz, namely Ardrey's *African Genesis,*[5] and *The Territorial Imperative,*[6] and Lorenz's *On Aggression.* In these books the authors argue that man is by instinct an aggressive creature, and it is this innate propensity to violence that accounts for individual and group aggression in man. This Hobbesian view of human nature is not new; it is probably older than the doctrine of Original Sin, and was widely prevalent during the reign of muscular Darwinism and its subsequent off-spring Social Darwinism.[7] It was a view that was embraced by Freud who, writing at the end of World War I, concluded that "a powerful measure of desire for aggression has to be reckoned as part of man's instinctual endowment. . . . *Homo homini lupus;* who has the courage to dispute it in the face of all the evidence in his own life and in history?"[8] Freud's postulation of a drive toward death, *thanatos,* as an intrinsic part of human nature is well known.[9]

The death instinct, as it came to be known, has been largely repudiated by psychoanalysts, but the conception of such an instinct or drive toward destruction has lost none of its force in the minds of many people. Its revival, in the new garb given it in the writings of Ardrey and Lorenz, came at a period in history that rendered the views expressed by such writers most congenial to their lay readers. The layman was bewildered and still is. Two world wars, the breakdown in political, public, and private morality, the ever-increasing crime rates, the development of a climate and culture of violence, together with the consciousness of an apocalyptic realization of irreversible disaster, are quandaries enough to cause many to look desperately for some sort of an answer, for some explanation of the meaning, of the causes which seem to be leading humankind to destruction. Or is it possible that civilization has a natural resistance against improving itself?

It is understandable that under such circumstances people will readily embrace an explanation having the appearance of plausibility, especially when that explanation is offered pretentiously, with at least the appearance of support from the armamentarium of scientific learning, observation, discoveries, experiments, facts, and authorities. In addition, when the exponents of that explanation are able and eloquent writters, it is all the more easy for those who are not themselves authorities to be carried away by the arguments. What is almost certain to escape many readers, including some scientists, is that the apparatus of scientific learning, observations, experiments, and facts, however authoritative, do not speak for themselves but are always at the mercy of their interpreters. However thoroughly established the facts, their interpretation is always subject to human error, tendentiousness, and prejudice. Hence, the checks and controls that scientists from the relevant fields bring to bear upon the interpretation of the facts on which they are the experts, constitute the means and the measure by which such interpretations are judged. By such measures the theories of Ardrey and Lorenz have been found to be unsound.[10]

What is most serious is that Ardrey and Lorenz show themselves to be so enamored of their own theories that they became quite insensible to facts that did not support them, and seemed to be unaware of the facts that would disprove them. It is therefore not surprising that they often got the facts they chose to offer as support for their theories twisted, or just plain wrong. We must endeavor once again to set the record straight, to correct what still threatens to become an epidemic error concerning the causes of human aggression, by drawing attention to the real causes of such behavior.

It is very easy to accept the idea of an instinctive cause for man's aggression, for that explains everything. But what explains everything in fact explains nothing. There is an old English proverb, at least as old as the seventeenth century, that says, "Let him make use of instinct, who cannot make use of reason." I am not sure that it has quite the meaning intended here, but it will serve to make the point in much the same sense that John Stuart Mill intended when he observed, in 1848, that "Of all the vulgar modes of escaping from the consideration of the effect of social and moral influence on the human mind, the most vulgar is that of attributing the diversities of conduct and character to inherent natural differences."[11] If no other rational explanation appeals, or even when it does, instinct is likely to trump every card in the pack because it appears to be so fundamental, so recondite, so all-embracing, and so simple. For these reasons, among others, the notion of "instinct" as an explanation of human aggression has so much greater an appeal than any other exegesis. To those who find such an explanation acceptable, it makes little difference that for many years scientists have entertained such grave doubts concerning the existence of instincts in humans, that for almost half a century fewer and fewer scientists have used the term in connection with humankind.

The critical examination of the concept of instinct in humankind began in 1919 with the appearance of Knight Dunlap's article, "Are There any Instincts?"[12] and was thoroughly discredited with the publication in 1924 of L. L. Bernard's classic work, *Instinct: A Study of Social Psychology*.[13] In spite of sporadic attempts to revive the idea of the existence of instincts in humans[14] the notion has no scientific validity whatever, nevertheless it is widely embraced by psychoanalysts and some psychiatrists. The best known and most widely quoted definition of an instinct was that given by William McDougall in *An Introduction to Social Psychology*, first published in 1908, and which by 1960 had gone into thirty editions. In this widely influential book an instinct was defined as:

an inherited or innate psycho-physical disposition which determines its possessor to perceive, and to pay attention to, objects of a certain class, to experience an emotional excitement of a particular quality upon perceiving such an object, and to act in regard to it in a particular manner, or, at least, to experience an impulse to such action.[15]

Definitions of instinct, whatever form they may have taken, have, in fewer words, tended to follow the essentials of McDougall's version. Tinbergen's rather elaborate ethological definition, for example, constitutes only one of many variations on the McDougallian theme. An instinct, according to Tinbergen, is "a hierarchically organized nervous mechanism which is susceptible to certain priming, releasing and directing impulses of internal as well as of external origin, and which responds to these impulses by coordinated movements that contribute to the maintenance of the individual and the species."[16]

Essentially, we find that most definitions of instinct embody the same assumptions. The most common of these appear to be: (1) innate determiners of some sort which, (2) when affected by particular stimuli, (3) call into function certain neural, glandular, and muscular mechanisms, (4) that underlie particular patterns of behavior or even "psychological states." Such definitions of instinct are invariably based upon the study of behavior in "lower" animals, and not the behavior of humans. Tinbergen, for example, is properly cautious when he comes to touch upon the possibility of instincts in humans. What has been proved in other animals, he writes, has not been proved in humans. "Further, different species have different instincts. For instance, while many species have a parental instinct, others never take care of their offspring and hence probably do not have the corresponding neurophysiological mechanisms. . . ." Furthermore, "a species might lack a certain instinct because, having lost it relatively recently, it retained the nervous mechanism but not the required motivational mechanism. So long as we know nothing about such things, it would be as well to refrain from generalizations."[17] That sounds a proper note of caution. But even Tinbergen's assumption that his interpretation of "instinct" holds for other animals, calls for the most careful, skeptical examination. The truth is that the concept of "instinct" has assumed the form of a doctrine, and perhaps represents the outstanding example of reification in the whole realm of science, the employment of an abstraction as if it had a real existence. The revival of the abstraction "instinct" by Lorenz and Tinbergen in their studies of animal behavior has been thoroughly examined and their interpretation of the term rejected on the strongest grounds of evidence and theory.[18]

Rationalizing on the basis of insufficiently analyzed evidence is a practice probably as old as humanity itself. That is a dangerous exercise, which is liable to produce pseudological arguments. Even scientists are not immune to such exercises, especially when they become enamored of theories that tend to make them insensible to alternative interpretations of the facts. The trouble is that many people confuse fact with theory. Facts are evidence; theory is interpretation of that evidence. Facts are reliable if they hold up in repetitions of investigations of their reality; a theory is valid if it offers the best possible interpretation of the facts—that is, the soundest and most logical. For example, with respect to the problem of aggression we face two major questions. The first concerns Lorenz's evidence for an "instinct" of aggression in animals. We ask: Is the evidence he offers reliable; does it include all of the important facts now available and relevant to behavior in other animals; and how validly does he interpret this evidence—for example, without appealing to authority or to personal prejudices, and so on? The second question is: How well do the evidence and the argument that Lorenz offers for other animals apply to humans? Readers must accept the possibility that Lorenz's proffered answer to the first is not valid; for example, that it is so misleading that his theory of aggression as innate is not really supported even for nonhuman animals. If this is the case, and we think it is the case, anyone (e.g., Ardrey) who relied on Lorenz for an answer to the first would have done well to reconsider any arguments based on Lorenz. Lorenz himself took for granted (and elaborately rationalized) his conclusion that he has answered this correctly. That is, he considered he had demonstrated the soundness of his belief that "instinctive aggression" exists in nonhuman animals. It is doubtful that he had done so, for reasons made clear elsewhere. Moreover, we hold that Lorenz has not demonstrated how any answer to this first question may bear on the second. This is not to say that a really valid answer to the first question could have some important bearing on the second. We agree with those writers who have stated that Lorenz's procedure of applying his doctrine of innate aggression in "lower animals" directly to humans was naive. In the case of humans it is possible to say that in spite of all attempts to saddle humans with instincts, all such attempts have thus far failed. The only instinctlike traits in humans are the reaction to a sudden withdrawal of support, and the reaction to a sudden loud noise. It has been reasonably suggested that these reactions are learned during the birth process.[19]

The notable thing about human behavior is that it is learned. Every form of human behavior is learned from other human beings. From any dominance of biologically or inherited predetermined reactions that may prevail in the behavior of other animals, humans have moved into a new zone of adaptation in which their behavior is dominated by learned responses. It is within the dimension of culture, the learned, the human-made part of the environment that humans grow, develop, and have their being as behaving organisms.[20]

Whatever other recondite elements may be involved in human behavior, and whatever the limits that our genetic constitution may set upon our learning capacities, this is the conclusion of the behavioral sciences—the sciences concerned with the study of the origins and causes of human behavior. If anyone has any evidence to the contrary, please let them bring it forth. That genes play some part in the development of some human behavior is probable, but that is very different from saying that human behavior is biologically determined.[21]

For an account of the manner in which humans probably came to lose such remnants of any instincts they may originally have had, the reader may refer to my book, *The Human Revolution.*[22] I have already discussed some of the probable reasons for the popularity of Ardrey's and Lorenz's explanation of the supposed causes of human aggression. There is yet another, perhaps the principal, reason for the popularity of works of this kind, including novels such as *Lord of the Flies* and *The Naked Ape,* which all serve to underscore that putative trait of human nature, "innate depravity."

In a world in which hostility and aggression seem to be a part of human nature, in which individual and group violence would seem to constitute the incontrovertible evidence of the mark of Cain that virtually every human carries, it is very gratifying to be told that this is indeed so; for those who are ready to grasp at such an explanation of human aggression it provides relief for that heavy burden of guilt many persons carry for being as they are. If one is born innately aggressive, then one cannot be blamed for being so. Hence when books such as those by Ardrey and Lorenz appeared, they were welcomed with all the fervor of a sinner seeking absolution. Ardrey and Lorenz stand in a sort of apostolic succession to those who with millennial ardor have sought to restore the wicked and the unregenerate to the true faith. For is it not written in Romans 7:18–24:

> For I know that in me (that is, in my flesh,) dwelleth no good thing: for to will is present with me; but how to perform that which is good I find not. For the good that I would I do not: but the evil that I would not, that I do. Now if I do that I would not, it is no more I that do it, but sin that dwelleth in me. I find then a law, that, when I would do good, evil is present with me. For I delight in the law of God after the inward man: But I see another law in my members, warring against the law of my mind, and bringing me into captivity to the law of sin which is in my members. O wretched man that I am! who shall deliver me from the body of this death?

Never was the question more eloquently and poignantly put. But most people, like Pontius Pilate in a similar situation, would not stay for an answer, but continued to seek an answer that was more congenial to them, one that promised absolution from the sin that held them captive. But for emancipation from that sin they would not look, for is it not written into our very flesh that can never be? It is this sort of thinking, so damaging, so pessimistic, so fettering of the human spirit, that is so dangerous because it diverts the focus of attention from the real causes of the "sin," of aggression, and encourages a Jansenist view of the nature of the human condition. The evidence of scientific inquiry does not support this dismal view of human nature; still less does it provide any support for the idea of "innate depravity," whatever form that doctrine may take. Certainly the views of Ardrey, Morris, and Lorenz concerning human nature have no scientific validity whatever.[23]

It would seem that the last 40 years of anthropological research and discovery in the field and in the laboratory, taken together with the findings of the behavioral sciences, have done little to impact the thinking of the masses. While the findings of these disciplines are wholly opposed to the deeply entrenched view that humankind is an innately aggressive lot, most people tend to dismiss these findings out of hand or ridicule them as a rather eccentric idealistic heterodoxies, which do not deserve to become generally known. In preference to examining the scientific findings they choose to cast their lot with such "authorities" as Golding whose *Lord of the Flies* offers a colorful account of the allegedly innate nastiness of human nature, and Ardrey who in *African Genesis* and *The Territorial Imperative* similarly seeks to show that humans are innately aggressive creatures.

The first part of *African Genesis* is devoted to a discussion in favor of the validity of Professor Raymond Dart's claims for an osteodontokeratic culture[24] among the australopithecines. In the second part Ardrey argues that since the australopithecines made use of tools, and employed some of them as weapons with which to bash in the skulls of baboons, the australopithecines were therefore "killers," and that therefore human beings are "killers" by nature! Ardrey's book constitutes, perhaps, the most illuminating example of the manner in which a man's enthusiasms may prejudice his judgment.

Ardrey refers to some of his early personal experiences of violence which convinced him of the murderousness of human nature. Hence, when through the distorting glass of his prejudgments he looks at a tool it becomes not simply a scraper but a weapon, a knife becomes a dagger, and even a large canine tooth becomes "the natural dagger that is the hallmark of all hunting mammals," while in "the armed hunting primate" it becomes "a redundant instrument." "With the advent of the lethal weapon natural selection turned from the armament of the jaw to the armament of the hand."[25]

But the teeth are no more an armament than is the hand, and it is entirely to beg the question to call them so. Virtually all the members of the order of primates, other than man, have large canine teeth, and these animals, with the exception of the baboons, are predominantly vegetarians, and it is principally because they are vegetarians that they require large canine teeth; that such teeth may, on occasion, serve a protective purpose is entirely secondary to their main function, which is to rip and shred the hard outer coverings of plant foods.

Primates are not usually belligerent unless provoked, and the more carefully they are observed the more remarkably revealing do their unquarrelsomeness and cooperativeness become.[26] The myth of the ferocity of "wild animals" constitutes one of Western man's supreme rationalizations, for it not only has served to "explain" the origins of our aggressiveness, but also to relieve us of the responsibility for it—for since it is "innate," derived from our early apelike ancestors, we can hardly, so we rationalize, be blamed for it! And some have gone so far as to add that nothing can be done about it, and that therefore wars and juvenile delinquents, as Ardrey among others tells us, will always be with us! From one not-so-minor fallacy to another Ardrey swept on to the grand generalization. At this point it needs to be said that Ardrey's views are firmly based on and derived from those of Professor Raymond Dart, who in an article entitled "The Predatory Transition from Ape to Man,"[27] published in 1953–1954, argued that man's animal ancestry was carnivorous, predatory, and cannibalistic in origin, and went on to add that

> The blood-bespattered, slaughter-gutted archives of human history from the earliest Egyptian and Sumerian records to the most recent atrocities of the second World War accord with early universal cannibalism, with animal and human sacrificial practices or their substitutes in formalized religions and with the worldwide scalping, head-hunting, body-mutilating and necrophiliac practices of mankind in proclaiming this common bloodlust differentiator, this predaceous habit, this mark of Cain that separates man dietetically from his anthropoidal relatives and allies him rather with the deadliest of Carnivora.

Ardrey put this in the following words: "The human being in the most fundamental aspects of his soul and body is nature's last if temporary word on the subject of the armed predator. And human history must be read in these terms." In furtherance of this argument "tools" for Ardrey are not only identified as "weapons," but, he goes on to imply, nay, indeed, he states, "that when any scientist writes the word 'tool,' as a rule he refers to weapons. This is a euphemism."[28]

Perhaps this opportunity should be taken to assure the reader that when scientists write the word "tool" they mean exactly what they say, and that euphemisms are not, as Ardrey says, "normal to all natural science."[29] Some tools may be used as weapons and even manufactured as such, but most tools of prehistoric humans, from their earliest days, were most certainly not designed primarily to serve as weapons. Knives were designed to cut, scrapers to scrape, choppers to chop, and hammers to hammer. That such tools could be used as weapons is true, but to serve as weapons was not their primary purpose nor the reason for which they were devised. "Man," Ardrey tells us, "is a predator whose natural instinct is to kill with a weapon."[30] But humans have no instincts, and if they had, they could hardly include the use of weapons in their psychophysical structure. Early man's hunting, according to Ardrey, was due to instinctive belligerence, not to the hunger for food. "When the necessities of the hunting life encountered the basic primate instincts, then all were intensified. Conflicts became lethal, territorial arguments minor wars. . . . The creature who had once killed only through circumstance now killed for a living."[31] This was "the aggressive imperative."

The evidence did not and does not support Ardrey's theories. Whatever "the basic primate instincts" may be, they are not what Ardrey implies. Indeed, when he forgets himself, he writes of "the non-aggressive vegetarian primate," which is precisely what all primates tend to be. But Ardrey would have us believe the contrary: The basic primate instincts, according to him, are aggressive. And, of course, with the assumption of hunting as a way of life, these, according to him, would become intensified. But in previous pages, and at greater length elsewhere,[32] I have already given the evidence for the contrary view. This evidence renders Ardrey's interpretations quite unacceptable. Everything convincingly points to the nonviolence of the greater part of the life of early humans, to the contribution made by the increasing development of cooperative activities, the very social process of hunting itself, the invention of speech, the development of food-getting and food-preparing tools, and the like.

Ardrey did not mention these facts, except perhaps obliquely as a doctrine scheming scientists foisted upon an unsuspecting world. The truth is that Ardrey was arguing a thesis, the thesis of "innate depravity." It is an unsound and dangerous thesis, because it perpetuates unsound views which justify, and even tend to sanction, the violence humans are capable of learning, but which Ardrey erroneously believed to be inherited from our australopithecine ancestors. When humans hunt they are the predators and the hunted animal is the prey. But prehistoric humans did not hunt for pleasure, in order to satisfy their "predatory instincts." They hunted for food, to satisfy their hunger, and the hunger of those dependent upon them. They did not hunt because they were "killers," any more than people who today are involved in the processing of animals for food at our modern table.

Prehistoric humans hunted because they desired to live—that hardly makes them killers, no more than, for those who do so, continuing in the habit of eating meat makes them killers. When Ardrey admiringly presents us with *West Side Story* as a "vivid portrait of natural man," in which "we watch our animal legacy unfold its awful power," in the form of juvenile delinquents in their "timeless struggle over territory, as lunatic in the New York streets as it is logical in our animal heritage," we can only say, "in police parlance," that it is worthy of Golding's *Lord of the Flies,* in which a similar view of the depravity of human nature is unfolded.

Ardrey has further elaborated his views in a book entitled *The Territorial Imperative.* Here, Ardrey endeavored to show that human aggressiveness is based on an allegedly innate territorial nature. Humans, he argues, have an innate compulsion to gain and defend exclusive territory, preserve or property. Their territorial nature, he says, is genetic and ineradicable. Ardrey devotes the greater part of his book to a discussion of territoriality in many different kinds of animals. He attempts to show that territoriality in animals is innately determined. The informed student of these matters would be interested in knowing why the evidence that leads to the opposite conclusion was not considered. Ardrey wrote that "The disposition to possess a territory is innate. . . . But its position and borders will be learned."[33] Certainly it is biologically and socially valuable for many animals to possess their own special territory, and certainly there are strong drives in most animals to defend their territory against trespassers, but such drives are not necessarily innate. They may be learned in just the same way in which animals learn the position and borders of their territory. Territory is defined as an area defended by its occupants against competing members of the same species. But there are many animals that do not exhibit such behavior. The California ground squirrel, adult male long-tailed field mice, she-wolves, the red fox, the Iowan prairie spotted skunk, the northern plains red fox, and in the superfamily to which man belongs, the Hominoidea, the orangutan, the chimpanzee, and the gorilla, as well as many other animals. As Bourlière observed in his admirable book, *The Natural History of Animals,* "It would seem that territorial behavior is far from being as important in mammals as in birds."[34]

Ardrey fails to consider the significance of these many exceptional cases. And while he does mention the chimpanzee, he omits any reference to the orangutan[35] and the gorilla.[36] On the naturally not unamiable chimpanzee's non-territoriality he comments, "The chimpanzee has demonstrated, I presume, that we must reckon on some degree of innate amity in the primate potential; but as I have indicated, it is a very small candle on a very dark night."[37]

On the contrary, the non-territoriality of the great apes constitutes, one would have thought, a very bright beacon in a cloudless sky, for if, as is evident, our nearest collateral relatives are wanting in anything resembling an inborn territorial drive, it is highly improbable that any form of human was ever characterized by such a drive. Arguments based on fish, birds, and other animals have no relevance for humans. "The otherwise admirable animal," the chimpanzee, is for Ardrey, "an evolutionary failure,"[38] while the aggressive baboon is "an outrageous evolutionary success."[39] But baboons are not agressive.[40] Apparently evolutionary failure or success is to be measured by the yardstick of population number.

The baboons are many, the great apes are few and are threatened with extinction. There is little evidence that the great apes were ever numerous, but that they are today few in number and threatened with extinction is all too tragically true. The diminishing numbers of these primates is due not to their lack of territoriality, but to the encroachments upon both their habitats and their lives by people with weapons against whom they are utterly defenseless. No matter how highly developed their territorial sense might have been, they could never have withstood these onslaughts.

What Ardrey's "territorial imperative" represents is a revival in modern dress of the stout old "instinct of property," an interest in real estate, which, together with such oddities as the "instinct of philoprogenitiveness" and others were repudiated by scientists half a century ago.[41] Ardrey deplores the rejection of "instinct" in man, and actually goes so far as to suggest that "a party line" has appeared in American science designed to perpetuate the "falsehood" that instincts do not exist in humans. These political subtleties do not belong in a serious work, but serve to indicate Ardrey's prejudices. Ardrey needs the concept of "open instincts," of innate factors, to support his argument, it is fundamental to his thesis, and without "instincts" his whole superstruture collapses, the fatal flaw in his theory, the rift in the playwright's lute, is that humans are human because they have no instincts, because all that they are is they have learned, acquired, from their culture, from the human-made part of the environment, from other human beings. Ardrey declined to accept that truth, more enamored, as he was, of his theories than he was of the facts. This is rather a pity because he would have served himself, and us all, a great deal more worthily had he only realized that a scientist is not interested in proving or in disproving theories, in believing or in disbelieving, but in discovering what is and stating it. Perhaps that is what he thought he was doing.

Thomas Henry Huxley once remarked of Herbert Spencer that his idea of a tragedy was a beautiful theory killed by an ugly fact. In Ardrey's case the beautiful facts render his ugly theories otiose. What is the explanation of the appeal such books have for so many people? Golding's novel is a rattling good story. Ardrey's books are excitingly written and hold the reader spellbound. But these qualities are not the secret of their appeal. What, then, is? Such books are both congenial to the temper of the times and comforting to the reader, gratified to find father confessors who will relieve one of the burdensome load of guilt we bear by shifting the responsibility for it to our "natural inheritance," our "innate aggressiveness." If it is our "nature" to be what we are, if we are the lineal descendants of our "murderous" ancestors, we can hardly be blamed or blame ourselves for the sin of being little more than made-over apes. Our orneriness is explained, and so is the peccant behavior of children, juvenile delinquency, crime, rape, murder, arson, and war, not to mention every other form of violence. It is all simply explained: it is due to our innate aggressiveness. There is nothing new in all this. We have heard it before.

During the latter half of the nineteenth century, and during the early part of the twentieth century, this viewpoint formed the foundation for the doctrine of "Social Darwinism." It was implied in such ideas as "The Survival of the Fittest" and "The Struggle for Existence," and in such phrases as "The weakest go to the wall," "Competition is the lifeblood of a nation," and the like. Such ideas were not merely taken to explain, but were actually used to justify, violence and war. As General von Bernhardi put it in 1912, "War is a biological necessity . . . it is as necessary as the struggle of the elements in Nature . . . it gives a biologically just decision, since its decisions rest on the very nature of things."[42] One wonders what von Bernhardi would have said after the "biologically just" defeat of Germany in two world wars? No doubt, the general would have had little difficulty in finding an "explanation." The new liturgy of "innate aggression," as an explanation of man's proclivities to violent behavior, does not seek to justify that behavior, but by thus "explaining" it to point the direction in which we must proceed if we are to exercise some measure of control over it.

Toward this end, Dr. Konrad Lorenz, one of the founders of the modern science of ethology—the study of behavior under natural conditions of life—dedicated himself in his book, *On Aggression,* published in April 1966.

In *On Aggression* Lorenz set out his views at length. In many respects they parallel those of Ardrey. Ardrey's and Lorenz's views suffer from the same fatal defect, namely, extrapolation from other animals to man. Why do reasonable beings behave so unreasonably, asks Lorenz. And he answers,

> Undeniably, there must be superlatively strong factors which are able to overcome the commands of individual reason so completely and which are so obviously impervious to experience and learning . . . All these amazing paradoxes, however, find an unconstrained explanation, falling into place like the pieces of a jigsaw puzzle, if one assumes that human behavior, far from being determined by reason and cultural tradition alone, is still subject to all the laws prevailing in all phylogenetically adapted instinctive behavior. Of these laws we possess a fair amount of knowledge from studying the instincts of animals.[43]

It is in these sentences that the flaws in Lorenz's argument are exhibited. First he assumes that the frequent irrational behavior of humans is phylogenetically based. Second, this enables him to conclude that the "laws" derived from the "study of the instincts of animals" are applicable to humans. There is, in fact, not the slightest evidence or ground for assuming that the alleged "phylogenetically adapted instinctive" behavior of other animals is in any way relevant to the discussion of the motive-forces of human behavior. The fact is, as we have already stated, that with the exception of the instinctoid reactions in infants to sudden withdrawals of support and to sudden loud noises, the human being is entirely instinctless. Those who speak of "innate aggression" in man appear to be lacking in any understanding of the uniqueness of human evolutionary history. Unacquainted with the facts, or perhaps undeterred by them, they insist on fitting whatever facts with which they are acquainted into their theories. In so doing they commit the most awful excesses. But, as is well known, nothing succeeds like excess.

Lorenz's assumptions and interpretations are typical. "There is evidence," he wrote, "that the first inventors of pebble tools—the African Australopithecines—promptly used their new weapon to kill not only game, but fellow members of their species as well."[44] In fact there is not the slightest evidence for such a statement. Lorenz continued, "Peking Man, the Prometheus who learned to preserve fire, used it to roast his brothers: beside the first traces of the regular use of fire lie the mutilated and roasted bones of *Sinanthropus pekinensis* himself."[45]

Lorenz's interpretation of the "evidence" is one he shares with many others, but it is gravely doubted whether it is sound. The cracked bones of Peking man may represent the remains of individuals who died during a famine and who may have been eaten by their surviving companions. This sort of thing has been known to occur among most peoples of whom we have any knowledge. There is little reason to extrapolate the rare instances of cannibalism in human history to prehistoric humans in general. It is absurd to suggest that Peking man used fire "to roast his brothers." Did Lorenz seriously believe that Peking man made a practice of "roast brother"? As another possibility it does not appear to have occurred to Lorenz that, like some contemporary peoples, burning the corpse may have been Peking man's way of disposing of the dead. Lorenz writes, "One shudders at the thought of a creature as irascible as all pre-human primates are, swinging a well-sharpened hand-ax."[46] For a serious student of animal behavior Dr. Lorenz appears to be singularly ill-informed on the temperaments of prehuman primates. It is not "irascibility" which is the term most frequently used to describe the temperaments of "pre-human primates" by those who know them best, their descendents, but "amiability." The field studies of Fossey and Schaller on the gorilla; of Goodall on the chimpanzee; of Harrisson and De Waal on the orangutan; of Strum on baboons, as well as those of others,[47] show these creatures to be anything but irascible. All the field observers agree that these primates, under ordinary circumstances, are amiable and quite unaggressive, and there is not the least reason to suppose that man's pre-human primate ancestors were in any way different. Captured monkeys and apes in zoos and circuses are not the best examples from which to deduce the behavior of such primates under natural conditions. Lorenz writes of early man faced with "the counter-pressures of hostile and neighboring hordes."[48] Again, there exists not the slightest evidence of hostility between neighboring hordes of early humans. The populations of early humans were very small, a few score or more at most. "Neighboring hordes" would have been few and far between, and when they met it is extremely unlikely that they would have been any less friendly than food-gathering hunting peoples are today.

"The hostile neighboring tribe," writes Lorenz, "once the target at which to discharge phylogenetically programmed aggression, has now withdrawn to an ideal distance, hidden behind a curtain, if possible of iron. Among the many phylogenetically adopted norms of human social behavior, there is hardly one that does not need to be controlled and kept on a leash by responsible morality."[49] And there we have it: man's aggressiveness is "phylogenetically programmed," and can be kept within bounds only by moral controls. Lorenz knew a great deal about the behavior of animals, but with respect to humans he apparently knew very little else that is not in the realm of nineteenth-century desk anthropology. Like Ardrey, he extrapolated his dubious interpretations concerning animal behavior to still more dubious conclusions concerning humans. Since all instincts, according to Lorenz, are characterized by "spontaneity," and it is this spontaneity which makes "the aggression drive" so dangerous, it is unfortunate that he was unable to provide the reader with some convincing examples of such human spontaneous aggression. But all that Lorenz could do was to cite the "very exact psychoanalytical and psycho-sociological studies on Prairie Indians, particularly the Utes" of Sydney Margolin.[50]

According to these "very exact" studies, the Prairie Indians "led a wild life consisting almost entirely of war and raids," and that therefore, "there must have been an extreme selection pressure at work, breeding extreme aggressiveness." Since Doctors Omer Stewart and John Beatty have independently shown how utterly erroneous this account is of the Prairie Indians in general and of the Utes in particular,[51] it only needs to be remarked that Lorenz's example of spontaneous aggression in humans has not a leg to stand upon, and that the alleged "excess of aggression drive" "may have produced changes in the hereditary pattern"[52] of the Utes are statements which derive no support whatever from the facts. However Lorenz chose to see aggression his way. Nowhere, for example, did he consider how other scientists have looked at aggression. He neglected for example, to discuss the possibility that a considerable proportion of aggressive behavior represents a reaction to frustration.[53] Nor did he address the view that in many instances aggressive behavior is situational, provoked by situations and conditions having nothing whatever to do with anything "phylogenetically" or otherwise "programmed" in the individual. As a general and outstanding example of the spontaneity of instinctive aggression in humans, Lorenz cites "militant enthusiasm" which can be "elicited with the predictability of a reflex" when the proper environmental stimuli are available.[54] The possibility that "militant enthusiasm" may be learned behavior was not considered by Lorenz. His *ex cathedra* statements are no substitute for the hard evidence that militant enthusiasm, like every other kind of enthusiasm, is learned.

Lorenz largely ignored the roles of learning and experience in influencing the development and expression of aggression. Yet we now have abundant and clear evidence, for both animals and humans, that learning and experience play substantive roles in the development of individual or group aggression. Where aggressive behavior is unrewarded and unrewarding, it is minimally if at all evident.

"Let dogs delight to bark and bite, it is their nature to." Lorenz, who wrote a charming book on dogs,[55] felt it is the nature, too, of man. Is it? What is human nature? What is most important to understand in relation to that question is the unique evolutionary history of humans—the manner in which apes were gradually transformed into humans as they moved from a dimension of limited capacity for learning into an increasingly enlarging zone of adaptation. In this zone of adaptation humans became entirely dependent upon learning from the humanmade part of the environment, that is culture, for their development as functioning human beings. The human brain, far from containing any "phylogenetically programmed" determinants for behavior, is characterized by a supremely highly developed generalized capacity for learning; this principally constitutes our innate hominid nature, and humans must learn their human nature from the human environment, from the culture that humanizes them.

As we trace the details of human evolutionary history we see that it is with the development of culture that the brain began to grow and develop in a feedback interaction with culture as an organ of learning, retrieval, and intelligence. Under the selection pressures exerted by the necessity to function in the dimension of culture, instinctive behavior would have been worse than useless, and hence would have been negatively selected, assuming that any remnant of it remained in humankind's progenitors. In fact, I also think it doubtful that any of the great apes have any instincts. On the contrary, it seems that as social animals they must learn from others every form of behavior they come to know and do. Their capacities for learning are simply more limited than those of *Homo sapiens*. As Clifford Geertz has put it:

Recent research in anthropology suggests that the prevailing view that the mental dispositions of man are genetically prior to culture and that his actual capabilities represent the amplification or extension of these pre-existent dispositions by cultural means is incorrect. The apparent fact that the final stages of the biological evolution of man occurred after the initial stages of the growth of culture implies that 'basic,' 'pure,' or 'unconditioned,' human nature, in the sense of the innate constitution of man, is so functionally incomplete as to be unworkable. Tools, hunting, family organization, and, later, art, religion, and 'science' molded man somatically; and they are, therefore, necessary not merely to his survival but to his existential realization. It is true that without men there would be no cultural forms; but it is also true that without cultural forms there would be no men.[56]

Given the highly flexible genetic potentialities of humans, whatever the individual becomes is what that individual learns to be. Throughout the two or three million years of human' evolution the highest premium has been placed on cooperation, not merely intragroup cooperation, but also upon intergroup cooperation; had this not been so there would be no human beings today.[57] Intra- or intergroup hostilities, in small populations, would have endangered the very existence of such populations, for any serious reduction in numbers would have made the continuance and maintenance of such populations difficult. There is not the slightest evidence, nor is there the least reason to suppose, that such conflicts ever occurred in human populations before the development of agricultural-pastoral communities, not much more than 12,000 years ago.

The myth of the aggressiveness of early humans belongs in the same class as the myth of "the beast," that is, the belief that most if not all "wild" animals are ferocious killers. In the same class belongs the myth of "the jungle," "the wild," "the warfare of Nature," and, of course, the myth of "innate depravity" or "original sin." These socially inherited myths represent the projection of our acquired deplorabilities upon the screen of "Nature." What we are unwilling to acknowledge as essentially of our own making, the consequence of our own disordering in the human-made environment, we saddle upon "Nature," upon "phylogenetically programmed" or "innate" factors. It is very comforting, and if, somehow, one can connect it all with findings on greylag goslings, studied for their "releaser mechanisms," and relate the findings on fish, birds, and other animals to humans, it makes everything all the easier to understand and to accept.

What, in fact, such writers do, in addition to perpetrating their wholly erroneous interpretation of human nature upon an only too willing multitude, is to divert attention from the real sources of human aggression and destructiveness, namely, the many false and contradictory values by which, in an overcrowded, highly competitive, threatening world, we so disoperatively attempt to live. It is not human nature, but nurture, in such a world, that requires our attention.

If one spends years in a zoo, as Desmond Morris did, observing and studying the animals, both inside and outside the cages of the London Zoo, it is not surprising that one comes to see the rest of the world as something of a zoo, and that he should write a book entitled *The Human Zoo*.[58] Under such circumstances, unless one is very careful, one is in danger of falling into an extreme biologistic bias in which not only the nakedness of the made-over ape's body but the rawness of its animal nature become the major features that impress the observer. One perceives, or rather apperceives, not only according to the kingdom that is within one, but not altogether surprisingly according to the kingdom that one is within. It is a great pity that in *The Naked Ape* Morris deliberately chose to write a zoo story, instead of writing the story of human evolution to its present state. "We must take a long, hard look at ourselves as biological specimens and gain some understanding of our limitations. That our intelligence can dominate all our biological urges," Morris believes is impossible. "Our raw animal nature will never permit it." And of "our raw animal nature" Morris gives a fascinating account in this readably written and knowledgeable book. The only trouble with Morris's account of human nature is that it hasn't a leg to stand on. He presents his assumptions as if they were facts. This is a particularly serious fault in a book designed for the lay reader, who will be bound to regard the work as authoritative. An authority is one who *should* know. Many of Morris' colleagues felt that he should have known better. It is not enough to be a zoologist if one is to speak with authority on the human animal. The zoologist can speak of the animal but not of the human. Morris has subtitled his book "A zoologist's study of the human animal." If he had, indeed, written as a zoologist this might have been a splendid work, for Morris has written an excellent account of the evolution and significance of human physical traits, but was not been content with that, but wandered into a dimension in which many a writer before him has become confused and lost. That dimension is the world of humanity, of the human-made part of the environment, or what the anthropologist calls culture. On physical matters Morris makes a good enough physical anthropologist, but on human behavioral traits and artificial ways of adapting to the environment Morris still speaks as a zoologist or old-time physical anthropologist, and that simply isn't good enough, for in the dimension in which humans functions as human beings one must be a cultural anthropologist in order to make any sense of the great big buzzing confusion of conduct, and a cultural anthropologist Morris simply is not.

Morris seemed to be wholly unaware of the fact that both genetically and culturally humans have shifted their principal means of adaptation, namely, to the learned part of the environment: culture. Morris believed that it is nonsense to think "that we shall control our aggressive and territorial feelings." Here Morris aligns himself with Ardrey and Lorenz. The fundamental errors committed by these authors are repeated by Morris. He plumbs for innate aggression. As for territoriality, "Unhappily, where matters as basic as territorial defence are concerned, our higher brain centers are all too susceptible to the urgings of our lower ones."[59] This goes one better than Plato and endows the emotions with a strong ascendancy over the reason. This dichotomy has always been an artificial one, and has done a great deal of harm in the western world. The early church fathers found it most useful to identify the "base" emotions with all that they considered sinful and evil in the flesh, over which the "reason," with the help of the church, could administer some sort of control. It is a simple doctrine and it has had a very wide appeal.

In the works of Ardrey, Lorenz, and Morris, the view presented of human nature, in the guise of "science," assumes a new form, holding that humans are innately aggressive creatures whose aggressiveness cannot be adequately controlled by reason, and this being so we must look to other means by which that aggressiveness may be mitigated or at the very least channeled. This is, of course, in the direct line of descent of the doctrine of "Original Sin." "Innate depravity," it says, cannot be eliminated, it can only be ameliorated. Hence, that dismal fact must be recognized, in order that we may the more intelligently be able to do what is indicated. But what that might be we are never directly told, though it would not be difficult to guess what these authors have in mind.

Morris is very properly concerned about the effects of overcrowding in the genesis of aggressive behavior, and recommends population control. Here we can be at one with Morris. But when he asserts that overcrowding elicits aggressive reactions, we may demur. The aggression elicited is not reactive but responsive; not innate, but learned. There are innumerable examples of this in human populations in which the density of people living in the same area has been very high and in which the intra- and intergroup aggression has been minimal. For example, in China, India, Indochina, among the Hopi, the Navajo, the Swiss, and a good many others.[60] It may, of course, be argued that such peoples have learned to control their "innate" aggressiveness. Indeed, it may, but upon the null hypothesis it would be simpler to assume that there was no innate aggressiveness to begin with, and that these people have simply learned not to respond with aggressiveness when frustrated or under any other conditions. Aggression is elicited only when it is a learned way of responding to certain conditions. If Morris or anyone else has any evidence that human aggression is produced in any other way it would be interesting to see it. Thus far I know of no one who has been able to produce such evidence. If it exists it should surely not be difficult to produce it. The unfortunate thing about books such as those of the innate aggressionists is that they read plausibily, they do not fit the facts concerning the structure of human behavior, yet they will nevertheless fit the socially inherited prejudices of many readers.

Aggression is readily "explained" by attributing it to innate factors, especially when that "explanation" is buttressed with a colorful but largely erroneous account of human evolution together with the extrapolation of questionable and misinterpreted findings from animals to humans.

Is it rational to expect humans to behave rationally? Not when they are pleading a cause, whether it be themselves or a thesis, and certainly not when, as is true of most people, they are given to mistaking their prejudices for the laws of nature. The belief in instinct is such a prejudice, and the views of writers such as Ardrey, Lorenz and Morris that humankind's propensity for violence is due to an instinct is another. Far from being born with a disposition toward aggression, the evidence indicates, humans are born with a highly organized system of drives that are all oriented in the direction of growth and development in cooperation. The evidence indicates that humans are oriented toward growth and development in the ability to relate in such a manner toward others in behavior calculated to confer survival benefits upon others in a creatively enlarging manner. The evidence indicates that it is when these drives are frustrated that humans tend to become disordered and the victim of others who have been equally disordered.[61]

Health is the ability to love, to work, to play, and to think soundly. To be able to love one must learn to do so. Love is a basic need; it is the humanizing need. Failure to be so humanized during the first half dozen years of childhood results in a progressive dehumanization that leads to every kind of destructive behavior, all of it learned in a disordered and misguided attempt to adjust to a disordered and a disordering human-made world. The fault lies not in our nature, but in our second nature—our acquired nature—and it is in the latter that the remedy also lies.

The basic behavioral needs are part of the system of basic needs with which we are all born. These are the need for love, friendship, sensitivity, thinking, knowing, learning, organization, curiosity, wonder, imagination, creativity, openmindedness, flexibility, experimental-mindedness, resiliancy, enthusiam, touching, sense of humor, joyfulness, laughter, tears, optimism, honesty, trust, dance, song and compassionate intelligence. I have dealt with each of these needs in detail in my book, *Growing Young*, to which the reader should refer.[62]

Notes

1. William Golding, *Lord of the Flies* (New York: Harcourt, Brace & Co., 1954).
2. For a critical examination by various authors of Golding's thesis, see William Nelson, ed., *William Golding's Lord of the Flies: A Source Book* (New York: Odyssey, 1963).

3. Konrad Lorenz, *On Aggression* (New York: Harcourt, Brace & World, 1966).

4. Desmond Morris, *The Naked Ape* (New York: McGraw-Hill, 1968).

5. Robert Ardrey, *African Genesis* (New York: Atheneum, 1961).

6. Robert Ardrey, *The Territorial Imperative* (New York: Atheneum, 1966).

7. Ashley Montagu, *Darwin, Competition, and Cooperation* (Westport, CT: Greenwood Press, 1973); Richard Hofstadter, *Social Darwinism in American Thought, 1860–1915* (Boston: Beacon Press, 1961).

8. Sigmund Freud, *Civilization and Its Discontents* (London: Hogarth Press, 1930).

9. Sigmund Freud, *Beyond the Pleasure Principle* (London: Hogarth Press, 1922).

10. Ashley Montagu, ed., *Man and Aggression,* 2nd ed. (New York: Oxford University Press, 1973).

11. John Stuart Mill, *Principles of Political Economy,* 2 vols. (London: Longmans, 1848).

12. Knight Dunlap, "Are There Any Instincts?" *Journal of Abnormal and Social Psychology,* 14: 307–11, 1919–20. See also L. L. Bernard, "The Misuse of Instinct in the Social Sciences," *Psychological Review* 28: 96–118, 1921; Ellsworth Faris, "Are Instincts Data or Hypotheses?" *American Journal of Sociology,* 27: 184–96, 1921–22; Zing Yang Kuo, "Giving Up Instincts in Psychology," *Journal of Philosophy* 18:645–64, 1921.

13. L. L. Bernard, *Instinct: A Study in Social Psychology* (New York: Holt, 1924).

14. Ronald Fletcher, *Instinct in Man* (New York: International Universities Press, 1957).

15. William McDougall, *An Introduction to Social Psychology,* 14th ed. (New York: Barnes & Noble, 1960), 25.

16. Niko Tinbergen, *The Study of Instinct* (Oxford: Clarendon Press, 1951), 112.

17. Ibid.

18. See especially D. S. Lehrman, "A Critique of Konrad Lorenz's Theory of Instinctive Behavior," *Quarterly Review of Biology* 28 (1953) 337–63; John Klama (pseudonym for the nine critical examiners of the notion of biological aggression who cojoined their views in a single text) *Aggression: The Myth of the Beast Within* (New York: John Wiley, 1988); Lester R. Aronson, Ethel Tobach, Jay S. Rosenblatt, and Daniel S. Lehrman, eds., *Selected Writings of T. C. Schneirla* (San Francisco: W. H. Freeman, 1972); Lester R. Aronson, Ethel Tobach, Jay S. Rosenblatt, and Daniel S. Lehrman, eds., *Development and Evolution of Behavior: Essays in Memory of T. C. Schneirla* (San Francisco: W. H. Freeman, 1970).

19. Nandor Fodor, *In Search of the Beloved: A Clinical Investigation of the Trauma of Birth and Pre-Natal Conditioning* (New York: Hermitage Press, 1949), 383.

20. Ashley Montagu, ed., *Culture: Man's Adaptive Dimension* (New York: Oxford University Press, 1968).

21. See, for example, the studies in Jerry Hirsch, ed., *Behavior-Genetic Analysis* (New York: McGraw-Hill, 1967).

22. Ashley Montagu, *The Human Revolution* (New York: Bantam Books, 1967).

23. Ashley Montagu, *The Nature of Human Aggression* (New York: Osford University Press, 1976); Ardrey, *African Genesis;* Morris, *The Naked Ape;* Lorenz, *On Aggression.*

24. That is a culture in which these earliest manlike creatures utilized bone, teeth, and horn as tools.

25. Ardrey, *African Genesis.*

26. Frans De Waal, *Good Natured: The Origins of Right and Wrong in Humans and Other Animals* (Cambridge: Harvard University Press, 1996); F. De Waal, *Peacemaking Among Primates* (Cambridge: Harvard University Press, 1989) F. De Waal, *Chimpanzee Politica: Power and Sex Among Apes* (New York: Harper & Row, 1982).

27. Raymond A. Dart, "The Predatory Transition from Ape to Man," *International Anthropological and Linguistic Review,* vol. 1, (1953–1954), 201–208, 207–208.

28. Ardrey, *African Genesis,* 306.

29. Ibid.

30. Ibid., 316.

31. Ibid., 317.

32. Ashley Montagu, *The Human Revolution* (New York: Bantam Books, 1967.

33. Ardrey, *African Genesis,* 25.

34. François Bourlière, *The Natural History of Animals* (New York: Alfred A. Knopf, 1954), 99–100.

35. Barbara Harrisson, *Orang-Utan* (New York: Doubleday, 1963).

36. George Schaller, *The Mountain Gorilla: Ecology and Behavior* (Chicago: University of Chicago Press, 1963), and the same author's *The Year of the Gorilla* (Chicago: University of Chicago Press, 1964).

37. Ardrey, *African Genesis,* 222.

38. Ibid., 223.

39. Ibid., 222.

40. Shirley C. Strum, *Almost Human* (New York: Random House, 1987); on the gorilla see Dian Fossey, *Gorillas in the Mist* (New York: Houghton Mifflin, 1983).

41. L. L. Bernard, *Instinct: A Study in Social Philosophy* (New York: Holt, 1924); Otto Klineberg, *Social Psychology,* revised (New York: Holt, Rinehart & Winston, 1954), 63–75; David Krech and Richard S. Crutchfield, *Theory and Problems of Social Psychology* (New York: McGraw-Hill, 1948).

42. Friedrich von Bernhardi, *Germany and the Next War* (New York: Longmans, 1912).

43. Lorenz, *On Aggression,* 237.

44. Ibid., 239.

45. Ibid.

46. Ibid., 241–42.

47. Jane Goodall, "My Life among Wild Chimpanzees," *National Geographic* 124 (1963): 272–308; Dian Fossey, *Gorillas in the Mist* (Boston: Houghton Mifflin, 1983); Schaller, *The Mountain Gorilla;* Harrisson, *Orang-Utan;* Southwick, ed., *Primate Social Behavior* (Princeton: Van Nostrand, 1963); Irven DeVore, ed., *Primate Behavior* (New York: Holt, Rinehart & Winston, 1965); Allan M. Schrier, Harry F. Harlow & Fred Stollnitz, eds., *Behavior of Nonhuman Primates,* 2 vols. (New York: Academic Press, 1965); De Waal, *Good Natured, Peacemaking, Chimpanzee Politica.*

48. Ibid., 243.

49. Ibid., 253.

50. Ibid., 244.

51. See their articles in Ashley Montagu, ed., *Man and Aggression* (New York: Oxford University Press, 1968), 103–115.

52. Lorenz, *On Aggression,* 244.

53. John Dollard et al., *Frustration and Aggression* (New Haven: Yale University Press, 1935).

54. Lorenz, *On Aggression,* 272.

55. Konrad Lorenz, *Man Meets Dog* (Boston: Houghton Mifflin, 1955).

56. Clifford Geertz, "The Growth of Culture and the Evolution of Mind," in *Theories of the Mind,* ed. Jordan Scher (New York: Free Press, 1962), 736.

57. Ashley Montagu, *Darwin, Competition and Cooperation* (New York: Schuman, 1952; Westport CT, Greenwood Press, 1973); A. Montagu, *The Human Revolution* (New York: Bantam Books, 1967); Robert Augros and George Stanciu, *The New Biology* (Boston: Shambada, 1987).

58. Desmond Morris, *The Human Zoo* (London: Cape, 1969).

59. Ibid., 177.

60. Ashley Montagu, ed., *Learning Non-Aggression: The Experience of Non-Literate Societies* (New York: Oxford University Press, 1978).

61. Ashley Montagu, *The Direction of Human Development,* (New York: Harper & Bros., 1955; revised edition New York: Hawthorn Books, 1970.

62. Ashley Montagu, *Growing Young,* 2nd ed. (Westport, CT: Bergin & Garvey, 1989).

16

Myths Relating to the Physical Traits of Blacks

Among the many myths concerning race, those that relate to the physical characters of American blacks are of special interest. These myths illustrate rather clearly the manner in which any trait may be seized upon and transformed into an "inferior trait" by the simple device of asserting it to be so.

The chief visible characters popularly held to distinguish the blacks from whites are skin color and hair form. Other characteristics in which blacks have been, and to some extent still are, held to differ from whites are brain size; facial features, including form of nose; bone measurements, including length of arms and hands; genitalia and pelvis size; skin color and hair type; body odor; and the like.

Before we proceed to examine physical traits it should be stated that the American black must be regarded as one of the newest admixtures or varieties of human. By "variety" I do not mean race, in any sense of that misused word, but as Americans, with a variegated ethnic history, who happen to display physical traits that are associated with various shades of black skin, in the same sense as whites are called "whites."

Like whites, American blacks exhibit evidence of considerable admixture with other ethnic groups, representing, in America, the end effect of mixture between different African peoples, some American Indians, and whites of every description—principally whites of British origin. Out of this mixture has emerged a unique type of great variability, or ethnic group-in-the-making represented by American blacks. The type is even yet not fully consolidated, but is still in process of formation. All the evidence indicated that while at the present time American blacks occupy, so far as their physical traits are concerned, a position somewhere between the multi-varied blacks of African, on one hand, and whites and a relatively small proportion of American Indians, on the other. Should the social barriers against intermarriage be maintained, there would be a tendency to stabilize around a type which is rather more black than otherwise. Even so, the

391

physical traits of blacks will continue to be characterized by many elements bearing the evidences of ethnic intermixture.[1]

The results of investigations thus far carried out make the following summary of the physical traits of the "typical American black" possible.[2] It is to be understood that the findings on the traits here mentioned have been repeatedly substantiated and confirmed by different investigators working independently. The traits described here are to be read as conditions in blacks as compared with Old American whites,[3] or mixed Europeans.

A large number of traits have been omitted from this summary for several reasons; some because black and whites do not differ in many traits, others because information is lacking, and still others because for blacks the available evidence is unsatisfactory and requires separate discussion. We may now briefly consider the summarized differences.

The Non-Significance of Anthropometric Differences

Brain Size

On average, the heads of blacks have in the past been stated to be about 2 mm longer and about 1 mm narrower than the heads of whites. In accordance with this form the black head height would be lower than the head heights of whites by about 5 mm. The mean cubic capacity of the interior of the black skull—as compared with that of the white, as determined by Wingate Todd at Cleveland on a dissecting-room population—was 1350.25 cc for 87 black males, and 1391.08 cc for 167 white males.[4] The difference, in the male, is here a matter of 41 cc more in whites. Cranial capacity and brain weight are variable traits, and there are few observations into which the personal factor of the investigator enters so much as in the determination of these traits. But when all is said and done, more will have to be said than done, for it has been shown long ago by Peterson in his classic examination of the data on the subject that there is no correlation whatever between head size, whether of skull, brain, or height of forehead, and intelligence; nor does intelligence bear any significant relationship to slight or even large variations in brain volume.[5]

Todd's difference of 41 cc may have been as reliable an estimate on small samples of American blacks and whites of similar social status as it is possible to obtain. In a later report of work done under Todd's direction, Simmons gives the average cranial capacities of groups of black and white American skulls obtained by water measurement of large samples. Capacities were 1467 cc for black males and 1517 cc for white males, a difference of 50 cc greater in white males.[6]

In discussing head size and brain size it is necessary to bear in mind that those of American blacks are some 2 mm shorter in total stature than those of whites. While this difference may not be related, it should be noted there that all the recorded differences were found on dissecting room populations, so that this difference in brain size may reflect nothing more than may be expected in an impoverished population.

The heads of blacks tend to be long as compared to the tendency toward reduction in length and a compensatory increase in breadth and height in whites. Reliable evidence is lacking on the relative thickness of the bones of blacks as compared with the white skull, but if there is any real difference, it must be slight and would make, except in aged individuals, little difference in cranial capacity. In short, the size of the black head is slightly smaller than that of the white, and different in shape, being long rather than broad, but the difference of some 41 to 50 cc in cranial capacity suggesting a slightly smaller brain volume in blacks as compared with whites, is, in point of fact, only one-and-a-half-ounces, and falls well within the normal range of variation of white cranial capacities. This difference is so minuscule that it can hardly be regarded as significant from any point of view. Furthermore, it cannot be too often emphasized that brain size within its normal range from 750 cc to 1500 cc or more has no relation whatsoever to learning ability or intelligence. But since a difference in brain size, which is not quite the same thing as cranial capacity, has formed one of the chief subjects of general discussions concerning differences between blacks and whites, it is necessary to discuss this matter some what more in detail here.[7] A few examples may be given illustrating the kind of pseudo-scientific and popular beliefs which have been held in the past, and which reappear occasionally in our own time.

An early work typical of American anti-black literature, entitled *The Negro A Menace to Civilization* (1907), by R. W. Shufeldt, M.D., "Major, Medical Department, United States Army (Retired)"[8] and the work of a clergyman, A. H. Shannon, on *The Negro in Washington* (1930)"[9] found support in the writings of the "older anthropologists." Until recently there were several writers on these matters, who could hardly have been described as anthropologists, who subscribed to such statements. To what lengths certain writers can go in these matters may be illustrated by the case of Dr. Lidio Cipriani, an associate of the National Museum and the University of Florence, Italy. During the progress of the Italian campaign in Ethiopia Dr. Cipriani published a book for the purpose of justifying that campaign, and here we have my translation of Dr. Cipriani's own summary of Chapter 5 of that remarkable work:

> Researches conducted on the brain of the African and on its physiological and psychological functions reveal the existence of a mental inferiority

which it is impossible to modify and which excludes the possibility of its development in our own manner. The Africans are particularly unadapted to assimilate European civilization. Since this depends upon the characters of the race, which are transmissible, with crossing, it is necessary to develop certain eugenical norms, above all for Europeans living in contact with the Africans. In this connection the important observations which have been made on Negroes imported into America since the seventeenth century have the greatest value.[10]

The subjective determination and pretentious evaluation of the evidence are apparent here. One of the revealing classical examples of bias in this field is represented by the late Professor R. Bennett Bean's study (1906) of the black brain.[11]

Professor Franklin P. Mall, in whose laboratory at Johns Hopkins University this research was conducted, was so dissatisfied with Bean's interpretation of the evidence that he was led to investigate the problem for himself. It should be stated here that Mall was the outstanding American anatomist of his time and that he was responsible for training a large majority of America's most notable anatomists. Utilizing the racial criteria of Bean and others, Mall and his colleagues were quite unable to distinguish black from white brains, and after pointing out the technical, instrumental, personal, and other errors, as well as the contradictory results involved in Bean's work, Mall concluded:

> In this study of several anatomical characters said to vary according to race and sex, the evidence advanced has been tested and found wanting. It is found, however, that portions of the brain vary greatly in different brains and that a very large number of records must be observed before the norm will be found. For the present the crudeness of our method will not permit us to determine anatomical characters due to race, sex or genius and which if they exist, are completely masked by the large number of marked individual variations. The study has been still further complicated by the personal equation of the investigator. Arguments for difference due to race, sex and genius will henceforward need to be based upon new data, really scientifically treated and not on the older statements.[12]

Certain differences said to exist in the character of the sulci of the black brain compared with the white are unfounded. Except for the difference in "a general way" of the fissural pattern of the frontal lobes, no differences whatever are perceptible, and "one could not distinguish a particular brain as belonging to a particular race on the basis of a difference in fissuration of the frontal lobes."[13]

Poynter and Keegan noted that the black brain generally displays "a prominent parietal lobe in contrast to the 'ill filled' frontal region." But quite clearly this so-called "characteristic" merely represents an accommodation of the shape of the black head, which, it will be recalled, is on average longer, narrower, and lower than the head of the white. Poynter and Keegan wisely recognized that, since their findings demonstrate that the black brain displays traits that fall within the limits of variation of the white brain, "it is not possible to establish a single morphological feature which can be claimed as absolutely characteristic."[14] Similarly, Fischer concluded that "the convolutions and the furrows or sulci between them vary so much from individual to individual that no racial distinctions can be ascertained."[15]

Levin, of the Bechterew Institute for Brain Research at Leningrad, has shown that the available evidence afforded no grounds whatever for any belief in racial or "inferiority" signs in human brains, whether they be of great men or of "savages."[16]

Were the black brain actually somewhat smaller than that of the white, the difference would be found to be so small that it could hardly be considered significant for the mental functioning of blacks compared with that of whites. Within the limits of normal variation, differences in brain size have about as much relation to intelligence and cultural achievement as differences in body size, and as far as the available evidence goes, that is none.

Weidenreich, anatomist and physical anthropologist, has put the matter succinctly: "The length of the alimentary canal of man," he writes, "varies between 14 and 45 feet, but no physiologist has ever ventured that an individual with a long intestine has a more effective digestion than one with a short intestine. In principle, it is against all that we know of the relation between function and structure of the organs to suppose that greater size guarantees superior function."[17]

The black "Kaffirs" and Amahosa of Africa, the Japanese, the American Indians, the Eskimos, and the Mongols all have brains that are larger than those of the average white.[18] On the same grounds as some whites proclaim themselves superior to blacks they should proclaim these peoples superior to themselves—thus far, however, there is no indication that they are likely to do so. The fact is that the external morphology of the human brain, or the traits of size and weight, have nothing whatever to do with its functional capacities; these, on the other hand, must be considered as due to a complex of conditions, such as the genetically determined internal chemical structure of the cells and neurones and the organization to which these are subjected by experience, the abundance of the blood vessels, the character of their walls, and the efficiency of the drainage.[19]

Upon these matters we have no evidence adequate for a definitive judgment beyond the statement that at the present time there exists no evidence in support of the popular belief that significant differences exist between the brains of blacks and those of whites. So far as the brain itself is concerned we may conclude with the words of a distinguished neuroanatomist and physical anthropologist, Professor W. E. Le Gros Clark, that "in spite of statements which have been made to the contrary, there is no microscopic or macroscopic difference by which it is possible for the anatomist to distinguish the brain in single individuals of different races."[20]

When work on the electrical activity of the brain was first published, some differences in what were claimed to be racial patterns of activity were soon found to be untenable. The world's leading authority on electroencephalography ("brain waves"), Dr. W. Grey Walter, had this to say on the subject:

> Slight differences there seem to be, as Mundy-Castle has found in Africa, but scarcely more than can be accounted for by the varying traditions and standards of life and nourishment. And did not the brains of these people establish and elaborate these traditions, accept or modify these standards? Unluckily for our peace of mind, there do exist precipitous gradients of economic and political differences; but brain physiology detects no incompatibilities; indeed in regions where the shades and textures of the human race are freely blended, there is found the richest variety, the most lively growth.[21]

To conclude this sorry story of brain mythology:

Throughout the nineteenth century and well into the first third of the twentieth century anthropologists and biologists generally were understandably busy identifying brain size with intelligence and expressing themselves, if not with such asperity, much in the manner of Thomas Henry Huxley, one of the leading biologists of his day, who, writing in 1860 said,

> It may be quite true that some Negroes are better than some white men; but no rational man, cognizant of the facts, believes that the average Negro is the equal, still less the superior, of the average white man. And, if this be true, it is simply incredible that, when all his disabilities are removed, and our prognathous relative has a fair field and no favor, as well as no oppressor, he will be able to compete successfully with his bigger-brained and smaller-jawed rival, in a contest which is to be carried on by thoughts and not by bites.[22]

Huxley, a brilliant, humane, and witty man who, on occasion, could be bitter, was thoroughly caught up in the midst of the endemic racist world in which he and his colleagues lived, and as a "rational man, cognizant of facts," he was unable to break through the tyranny of what he believed were the "eternal verities." However, with his conditional "if this be true," he did leave himself an escape hatch, so that some thirty-six years later, Huxley could write that "Thoughtful men, once escaped from the blinding influences of traditional prejudice," would accept Darwin's evidence for man's "lowly" origins, but to the end of his life he seems to have been unable to escape from "the blinding prejudices" relating to the black's place in the family of humankind. Finally, the coup-de-grace to the brain hierarchy mythology may be administered by the following from my own experience:

As an anatomist in charge of teaching gross anatomy in the dissecting-room, to medical, dental, and graduate students, for almost twenty years, it was my custom to demonstrate how to remove the brain together with the three meninges (membranes) in which it is enclosed. This is not an easy task, and requires a fair amount of skill. The body from which the brain is removed has been preserved by the infusion of formaldehyde, and the blood vessels injected with red for the arteries and blue for the veins, the body hangs from the earholes for a week or so until the infusions are widely distributed. The body is then taken down and refrigerated in individual cubicles for varying periods of time, according to need. During this process every cadaver undergoes individual changes, such as shrinkage of the brain, or increase in size and/or weight owing to the accumulation of fluid, up to the level at which the brain was severed, and duration and manner of handling. Injected blood vessels harden so that the weight differences in the chalky material with which the vessels have been filled, would alone be sufficient to account for differences in brain weight; these various factors, in addition to the factor of aging, add up to the irrefutable conclusion that neither brain weight, nor brain size, nor its dimensions, are significantly different between blacks and whites.

With respect to the commonly repeated statement that the cranial sutures in blacks unite earlier than in other races "and thus cause a stunting of the Ethiopian intellect shortly after arriving at puberty," it has been well established, as a result of the fundamental studies of Todd and Lyon on suture closure in blacks and whites, that no significant differences in the character of suture closure exist between blacks and whites. The authors conclude their studies with the statement: "We repeat that there is one modal type of human suture closure upon outer and inner faces of the cranium, common to white and Negro stocks."[23] As far as the growth and development of the skull are concerned, there are no significant differences in the pattern and rate of growth in certain bones of the skull, and these differences are already apparent during fetal development; as Schultz has said, "These differences are essentially the same as those which distinguish adult Whites from adult Negroes."[24]

Thus, Limson found that in black fetuses the occiput was more prominent and convex and the external occipital protuberance more strongly formed than in white fetuses. Limson also found that the dental arch projects farther forward and that the anterior nasal spine is smaller in black than in white fetuses.[25] These are precisely the regions of differential growth that Todd and his coworkers have shown to distinguish the adult black cranium, namely, greater expansion of the occipital bone and the back of the head and greater forward growth of the upper jaw and dental arch.[26]

This difference in the detailed growth pattern of the jaw has been shown to hold good in black fetuses in respect to the premaxillary bone, which tends to lose its independence later than in the white. This fact is significantly correlated with the slightly greater projection of the upper jaw in blacks than in whites.[27] The projection of the upper jaw is not a true prognathism similar to that which occurs in the anthropoid apes, for in the latter the early arrest in the growth of the brain case and the continued growth of the jaws and dental arches is a concentration of events that does not occur in any form of human being. The projection of the upper jaw in blacks is accentuated as compared with the conditions in whites because in the latter there is an earlier arrest of growth in the upper jaw. This greater growth of the maxilla in blacks is also responsible for another apparent, though unreal, difference in the appearance of the head. This is the apparently greater projection of the white cranium beyond the face—this appearance does not reflect any real difference in the character of the cranium, but rather constitutes the reflection of the lesser projection of the jaws in whites—in whom the jaws have tended, as it were, to shrink under the top of the head rather more than in blacks.

From every point of view the reduction in the size of the upper jaw in whites must be considered unfortunate, for the resulting restriction in space is responsible for a larger number of disorders, such as failure of development of teeth, the impaction, noneruption, crowding, or rotation of teeth, deflection of the nasal septum, cleft palate and harelip, and other abnormalities.[28] The retention of the ability for continued growth of the maxilla in blacks as compared with the loss of this ability in whites would here, indubitably, confer a distinct advantage upon blacks.

Facial Features

With respect to the shape of the nose of blacks, this is extremely variable, but is stabilized around a rather shorter, flatter, and broader nose than that of the average white. It has been suggested that the broad nose and larger nasal passages of American blacks was originally adapted to meet the requirements of air breathed at relatively high temperatures, whereas the relatively long narrow nose of the white is adapted to the breathing of air at relatively low temperatures. A statistical investigation of this problem supports this suggestion with some degree of probability.[29]

Statements to the effect that the black nose is more primitive than that of the white are unsound. For example, Dr. Victor Heiser has stated that the fact that the Philippine Negritos "were true Negroes is shown by the one piece cartilage in their spreading noses; all other races have a split cartilage. Even the octoroons show this negroid test of Negro blood."[30] This statement was repeated and elaborated in November, 1936, in the now defunct Collier's magazine. In a more recent work we are told that "There is a great difference between whites and blacks in the structure of the nasal cartilages."[31]

Professor Montague Cobb has thoroughly disposed of these myths by citing the facts which prove that no split cartilage occurs in any monkey, ape, or human, and that there are no significant features of the nasal cartilages, except those of size, which distinguish the black nose from the white nose.[32]

Actually, the black nose merely exhibits a difference in form, and there is every reason to believe that the original form of the African black nose persisted in Africa as an adaptively valuable trait and that in the American black the form of the nose, while still variable, presents a form intermediate between African black, white, and American Indian. The greater the admixture of white ancestry the more white does the form of the nose appear. Even so, there is a marked tendency toward persistence of the broad nose. This, among other characters, has been termed an "entrenched Negro character,"[33] but with admixture shows significant change.

Other such features are lip thickness, mouth width, interpupillary distance, and ear height. As for the apparently larger eye of blacks, this is an illusion resulting from the comparatively less angular orbit of blacks. On the other hand, Caroline Day's careful observations[34] clearly show that two of Todd's most "dominantly entrenched Negro traits," namely, lip thickness and breadth of nose, readily undergo change toward the white lip and nose under hybridization.

The slope of the forehead in blacks, as Day has shown, is not significantly different from that in whites, and we have already seen that this apparent "difference" is an illusion due to the slightly greater "prognathism" of blacks. A still more significant contribution to the alleged low-foreheadedness of blacks is the fact that the level at which the hair grows on his head is lower upon the forehead than it is in whites. With admixture this low level of the hairline appears to be one of the first features to yield—as a glance through Day's photographs of black-white individuals will show.

In African blacks the chin is not as prominent as it is in whites. In American blacks the chin prominence is intermediate between the condition in

Africans and that in whites, as may be seen from Day's figures, which it is generally agreed show an exaggeratedly high proportion of lack of chin protrusion, 38.9 percent in females and 50.5 percent in males. It is clear, however, that chin protrusion increases with increase in the proportion of white admixture.

Bone Measurements

References made to the larger hands and longer legs and arms of blacks, are entirely unsound. The black torso is slightly less than an inch and a quarter shorter than that of the white, the black leg a little less than an inch and a quarter longer.[35] The black upper extremity is about an inch longer, the upper arm being relatively shorter and the forearm relatively longer than in the white. As for breadth and length of hands, Todd and Lindala found no significant differences in these dimensions, a fact which led these investigators to remark: "It is rather astonishing to find that the 'long narrow hand' of the Negro vanishes on the average."[36] It was considered by these authors that this finding could not be imputed to the admixture of white ancestry, since their series gave many evidences of relative purity of strain. Herskovits also failed to find any significant difference in the width of the black hand.[37] While the black hand as a whole is not longer than the hand of the whites, the fingers are, on the whole, longer, for Herskovits found that the middle finger is longer in blacks than in whites. This would then make that portion of the hand in the black which extends from the wrist to the base of the fingers shorter than in the white, but this supposition requires confirmation.

With respect to the length of the thumb there exist some observations on the skeletal thumb in nine African blacks and fifteen whites which indicate that the African black thumb is about 1.7 mm shorter in relation to the length of the middle finger than the relative thumb length of the average Englishman.[38] These findings corroborate in a striking manner the earlier findings of Schultz, who found the length of the thumb in relation to the middle finger in eighteen adult blacks to be 1.8 mm less than in fourteen adult whites.[39] In relation to the length of the hand, Schultz found that in both black fetuses and black adults the thumb was relatively shorter than in whites.[40]

Hence, as far as the upper extremity is concerned it would appear that every part of it is perfectly proportionate to the other, and that its greater length is actually due to a compensatory adjustment in relation to the shorter torso.

The black lower limb is 26 mm, that is, a little less than an inch, longer than in the white and, unlike the case of the upper extremity, there is no difference in the proportions of the length of the thigh or lower leg. "The long shin of the Negro is an illusion of its circumference, as his long foot is an illusion of its flatness."[41] The length and breadth of the black foot show no significant differences from those features of the foot of whites and are entirely proportional to leg length.[42]

Since the 1930s, when black athletes were admitted into sports such as races of every distance, broad jumpers, hurdlers, and the like, attempts to show that black athletes enjoy an unfair advantage owing to their alleged possession of a longer heel bone and longer calf muscles. These claims have been examined by Professor Montague Cobb who, as a human anatomist and physical anthropologist was in an excellent position to do so. He made a careful study of the feet and heel bones of the most famous athletes of the time, including Jesse Owens, who had run faster and jumped further than anyone had done before. At the same time Cobb made a similar study of the same structures in whites. Comparing the measurements for blacks and whites he could find no difference between them, has furthermore shown that many of the outstanding black athletes have legs and feet which are predominantly white in character, and concluded that black lower extremity traits are not in any way significantly associated with black athletic ability. "There is not a single characteristic, Cobb wrote, "which all the Negro stars in question have in common which would definitely identify them as Negroes."[43]

In this connection it may be noted that Malafa, in an investigation of the bodily traits of sprinters and non-athletes, carried out on 100 white students from the grammar schools of Brno, Czechoslovakia, found that long legs were one of the principal trait which distinguished the athletes from the nonathletes.[44] This trait constitutes, of course, a selective factor—and is not correlated with ethnic traits.

One more fact concerning the black foot: The alleged longer heel bone is nonexistent, but in both fetuses and adults the appearance of greater length is "caused entirely by a thick layer of subcutaneous fat."[45]

Studies made by Tanner and his team on Olympic athletes may possibly throw some light on the outstanding successes of black athletes. Tanner found that black sprinters averaged 86.2 cm in leg length while white sprinters average 83 cm. Similar differences were noted in arm length. In blacks, sitting height was 92.5 compared with 93.5 in the whites. Hip width averaged 26.8 centimeters in blacks, and 28.5 cm in whites. "The ratio of length to sitting height for sprinters, 400-meter runners and high jumpers averaged 0.88, 0.92 and 0.93 in whites, and 0.93, 0.97 and 1.01 in Negroes." "Evidently the Negroes have longer limbs and narrower hips than the whites, even at approximately the same overall size. In the comparison of Negro and white weight lifters exactly the same differences occurred."[46]

Tanner's group also found a distinct difference in the composition of the Negro calf compared with that of the white in bother sprinters and

400-meter men. The Negroes have wider bones and narrower muscles. In the 400-meter competitors, for example, the Negro tibia breadth averages 4.5 centimeters compared with the white's 4.2 cm; in calf muscle breadth the Negroes average 7.4 cm. and the whites 7.9 cm. In fat also the Negroes are lower.[47]

An advantage of 3.2 cm, the equivalent of an inch and a quarter in leg length, may account for the black's superiority as a sprinter. In long distance running, however, regardless of ethnicity, the advantage is with the shorter-legged individual. Short legs can be moved more rapidly than long ones, and seem to confer some physiological as well as mechanical advantage.

Pelvis and Male Genitalia

It is frequently stated that the black pelvis differs from that of the white in being longer and narrower. This statement is not quite true. The black pelvis is smaller in all its dimensions. Todd and Lindala write:

> The male Negro pelvis is small in all its dimensions compared with the male White and its true pelvic component is long compared with the height of the iliac crest over perineum or over tuber ischii. Superposed on a common bodily size the female White pelvis is relatively some 10 mm longer and broader than the male though its absolute dimensions are less. The female Negro pelvis is relatively only 6 mm longer than the male but 21 mm broader.[48]

It is to be doubted whether there is any truth in the statement sometimes made that because the black female has a narrower pelvis than the white female she is less likely to experience a satisfactory outcome to a pregnancy produced by a white male than to one produced by a black male. The implied suggestion here is that the rounder-headed white is likely to produce a fetus that will have a head larger and rounder than can be safely delivered through a small, narrow pelvis "designed" for the delivery of black-fathered children. We have already seen that in the only investigation made of this subject, in the case of Japanese-white unions, there is not the slightest support for such beliefs.[49]

Caldwell and Moloy have, from the obstetrical point of view, investigated the anthropometric characters of the pelvis of black and white females.[50] These investigators find that female pelves may be classified into three types: (1) the gynecoid, or average female type, which occurs in 42 percent of all females; (2) the android type, more closely approximating the male form than the female pelvis, which occurs in 15.7 percent of black females and in 32.5 percent of white females; and (3) the anthropoid type, with along antero-posterior diameter and a relatively narrow transverse diameter, occurring in 40.5 percent of black females and in slightly less than half that percentage of white females.

Obstetrically, the most dangerous form of the pelvis is the android type, which occurs among white females with double the frequency than among black females. The other two types of pelvis present no especial obstetrical difficulties. It therefore seems improbable that the form of the black female pelvis plays any more significant role in difficult labor and delivery than in the case of white females.

Davenport and Steggerda "entertained the hypothesis that, in the case of the black woman who carried a mulatto child in utero, her narrow pelvic outlet and the child's large head might offer an important disharmony."[51] In order to test this hypothesis, Steggerda, who did the actual measuring, proceeded to examine the heads of newborn children of both groups. He found that the heads of the newborn black infants were slightly smaller at birth than those of white newborn infants, and it is evident from their findings that no disharmonies between pelvic outlet and shape of the head occurred in the Jamaica series examined by these authors. Data on the pelves were not available to Davenport and Steggerda, but the data that have since appeared render the suggestion of a significant disharmony of the kind hypothesized highly improbable.

It is a common belief that the penis of the black is appreciably larger than that of the white. The view is an old one. Blumenbach (1752–1840), the founder of the science of physical anthropology, referred to this as long ago as 1775. He states: "This assertion is so far borne out by the remarkable genitory apparatus of an Aethiopian which I have in my anatomical collection. Whether this prerogative be constant and peculiar to the nation I do not know."[52] Upon this subject there exists no scientific evidence whatever. To my knowledge, only one acute observer, Geoffrey Gorer, who visited many peoples in a good part of West Africa, in conversation with John Dollard, as the latter reports in his book *Class and Caste in a Southern Town*, stated that the black genitals were not disproportionately larger than those of whites.[53]

Dollard, commenting upon his inquiries into the sexual mores of "Southerntown," writes:

> There is a widespread belief that the genitalia of Negro males are larger than those of whites; this was repeatedly stated by white informants. One planter, for example, said he had visual opportunity to confirm the fact; he had gone to one of his cabins, and on entering without warning, found a Negro man preparing for intercourse. Informant expressed surprise at the size of his penis and gave an indication by his arm and clenched fist of its great length and diameter. It was further said that this

impression was confirmed at the time of the draft examination of Negroes at the Southerntown Courthouse in 1917. Two physicians from other states have verified this report on the basis of draft-board experience.[54] A Negro professional, on the other hand, did not believe that Negroes have larger genitalia than whites. He had worked in military camps where he had a chance to see recruits of both races naked, and said there was the usual variation within races, but no uniform difference as between races.[55]

Commenting upon these statements Dollard writes: "One thing seems certain—that the actual difference between Negro and white genitalia cannot be as great as they seem to be to the whites; it is a question of the psychological size being greater than any actual difference could be ... the notion is heavily functional in reference to the supposed dangers of sexual contact of Negroes with white women."[56]

It is probable that Dollard has here given the correct explanation of the facts, namely, that any difference in size that may exist has, like body odor (see below), been exaggerated, the alleged larger size of the genitalia of blacks being for the most part a function of the whites' belief in the undesirability of contact with blacks.

My experience as an anatomist working for many years in American dissecting laboratories bears this out. If there is any difference is size, it is probably so small that the exaggerated belief may be dismissed as but another one of the legends that have been built up about the anatomy of the American black.

Skin Color and Hair Type

Skin color is a complex trait and depends upon a multiplicity of factors for its expression. As is well known, every gradation from black to white occurs among American blacks. The greater the admixture of white ancestry the more white, as a rule, does the skin appear. Barnes has shown "that the percentage of Negro pigmentation of the American Negro increases quire rapidly until puberty, with a maximum at the age of 15; decreases rapidly until about the age of 35; and then decreases very slowly the remainder of life."[57] This finding is in essential agreement with the independent findings of Steggerda, and of Todd and van Gorder.[58]

The inheritance of skin color is a cumulative process involving the operation of multiple factors, the individual having the largest number of factors usually showing the character developed to the highest degree. In black-white crosses the genes for black pigment are not completely dominant over those for lighter color; the first generation is mulatto, or intermediate, in shade. Their offspring, however, exhibit great variability of skin color, grading from black to white; and it is apparent that in the second generation variability is higher than in the first. This is an effect of multiple-factor inheritance, for, owing to the large number of factors now present, they are segregated in combinations more distributively variable than those in the original ancestors. This form of blending inheritance is essentially Mendelian. The evidence thus far suggests that there are at least six pairs of genes conditioning skin color, yielding 26 or 64 possible gene combinations, and at least as many black and white phenotypes combined—assuming that the gene pairs have approximately the same effect. In reality a far wider range of phenotypes is observed, suggesting the existence of other modifying genes affecting skin color. Further investigation of a most refined laborious nature remains to be carried out before the exact mechanism of the inheritance of skin color is fully understood.

Black children cannot be born to parents one of whom is, hypothetically of course, "pure" white and the other "pure" black. The children of such unions are mulattos. When a infant of color is born to "white" parents it is proof that both the parents carry genes for these traits.

Black is the dominant hair color among blacks, although red, dark brown, light brown, and gray-brown occur occasionally; the lighter hair colors are more common among those with half or more white ancestry. Black hair color is one of the most dominantly entrenched black features. On the other hand, hair form is, interestingly enough, one of the most easily modifiable of traits. While among American blacks every kind of hair from tightly curled to straight is to be found, it is clear that under hybridization hair form yields most readily to the influence of new genes. This fact was strikingly brought out in the classic study of Fischer on the hybrids of Hottentot-Dutch ancestry in South Africa—one group with dominantly woolly hair, the other with dominantly straight hair. Fischer found that among the group tightly curled hair occurred in 29 percent, wavy hair in 49 percent, and straight in 22 percent.[59]

Davenport and Steggerda found that among Jamaicans tightly curled hair occurred in 100 percent of blacks, in 86.7 percent of browns, and in 1 percent of whites. Curly hair occurred in none of the blacks, in 11.4 percent of browns, and in 30 percent of whites. Wavy hair did not occur in blacks, but was found in 2 percent of browns and in 30 percent of whites; 39.2 percent of the whites had straight hair. In Caroline Day's series of black-white families, hair form varied with degree of admixture. Hooton, summarizing Day's findings, writes:

As far as our data carry us we may conclude that 1/2 N males, 1/2 N females, and even 3/4 N females may exhibit the entire range of hair curvatures generally recognized, but that, if Day's information is valid, distinctively Negroid forms of hair, such as frizzly and woolly, do not appear unless there is at least 3/8 of Negro blood in the individual.[60]

The inheritance of hair form in black-white crosses has been studied by Davenport,[61] who found straight hair to be a recessive condition. Wavy or curly hair is a heterogeneous condition, so that wavy plus wavy yields off-spring that are straight, wavy, and curly in the proportion 1:2:1. Curly plus curly yields mostly curly; yet 14 percent of the offspring show straight hair, so that it is apparent that some curly-haired parents carry the gene for straight hair as a recessive.

Straight plus curly produces a good many curly-haired offspring. Post, analyzing Day's data, writes:

> Of the total number of 428 offspring, seventy-five have curlier hair than the more curly parent, while only forty-three have straighter hair than the straighter parent. This is all negative evidence for a general domi-nance of the curlier condition ... The six forms merge into each other. .... There is no evidence for the emergence of a New American Negro type, in regard to hair form, such as Herskovits has lately de-scribed for skeletal proportions.[62]

It may, of course, be argued that the intermediate types of hair form, as well as hair color, exhibited by American blacks do constitute at least an ap-proach to a new type, for the genetic behavior of hair form is, in the char-acter of its blending, not unlike that of skin color and quite clearly shows many gradation of form, intermediate between the hair forms exhibited by African black and white ancestors. Thus, it would seem that Herskovits' general finding concerning the emergence of a new American black type holds good also for the character of the hair form.

It is a common belief that the black is more glabrous (i.e., less hairy) than whites. This belief is well founded; for, although it is still uncertain whether blacks possess fewer hair follicles, it is clear that the development of body hair, in both thickness and distribution, is considerably less than in whites. Danforth's investigations lead him to believe that a reduction in the number of hair follicles has occurred in blacks and that there is also a re-duction in the growth of individual hairs.[63] This would appear to be the most plausible explanation of the relative glabrousness of blacks. In an in-vestigation of the facial hair of blacks and whites Trotter found that there was no difference in the actual number of hairs, but that the average thick-ness of the facial hairs of blacks was less than that of the whites; also, the hairs of black women were somewhat shorter than those of white women.[64]

In blacks, as compared with whites, the general tendency toward re-duction in the amount of hair and the character of its distribution have proceeded farther, as is evidenced by the reduction in the number of hair follicles on the fingers, toes,[65] arms, and hands of blacks.[66]

In American blacks, as is to be expected, every form of hair distribution and development maybe observed; the greater the amount of white admixture the greater the distribution and thickness of hair. These facts are well brought out in Day's observations on black-white families. From these observations it would appear that facial hair reaches a medium degree of thickness in individuals with 3/8 and less of white ancestry.[67] It is highly probable that the genetic mechanisms here operative are much the same for hair distribution and thickness as for skin color and hair form, with the presence of multiple factors and the consequent segregation of intermediate forms.

On the whole, American blacks show a distribution of body hair and an intensity of hair growth intermediate between the condition in African blacks and American whites.

Body Odor

One of the most popular entrenched beliefs, which in some areas persists to this day, is that blacks possess a unique and objectionable body odor. During Dollard's investigations in "Southerntown" he encountered this belief, and his references to it are worth reproducing here:

> Among beliefs which profess to show that Negro and white cannot intimately participate in the same civilization is the perennial one that Negroes have a smell extremely disagreeable to white people. This belief is very widely held both in the South and in the North. A local white informant said that Negroes smell, even the cleanest of them. It might not be worse than other human smells, but it was certainly different. It was asserted to be as true of middle-class Negroes as of others, at least upon occasion. Another informant swore that Negroes have such an odor that sometimes white people can hardly stand it. He described it as a 'rusty' smell. This odor was said to be present even though they bathe, but to be somewhat worse in summer. Another white informant described the smell as 'acrid.'

Dollard, however, stated that he could detect no difference in odor between the groups.[68]

Shufeldt remarks that the body order of blacks is "sometimes so strong that I have known ladies of our own race brought almost to the stage of emesis when compelled to inhale it for any length of time."[69] Perhaps. But the fact is that many whites have been almost equally nauseated by the odor of some of their fellow whites. Members of other ethnic groups find the body odor of whites most objectionable. Thus, the great Japanese anatomist Buntaro Adachi wrote that when he first settled in Europe he found the body odor of Europeans repellent—strong, rancid, sometimes sweetish, sometimes bitter. As time drew on he became accustomed to it, and still later found it sexually stimulating.[70] Similar reactions will be found recounted elsewhere.[71]

Body odor depends upon a large number of factors. Human sweat is of complex structure and is a compound of the secretion of the sebaceous glands (the fat-secreting glands opening usually in relation to the hair follicles) and the sweat glands proper. Among the known constituents of sweat are water, sodium chloride, phosphates, uric acid, glucose, creatinine, aromatic acids, ethereal sulphates of phenol and skatoxyl, neutral fat, fatty acids, cholesterol, albumin, and iron. Depending upon the amount of these substances present at anyone time, the odor of the sweat will vary in the same individual from time to time and under different environmental and dietary conditions.

Upon this subject there have been no really adequate studies. All that we at present know is that body odor varies from individual to individual within the same ethnic group and that members of different ethnic groups, and even classes, find the odor of members of other ethnic groups and classes distinctly different and frequently objectionable. Klineberg refers to

> an experimental attempt to throw a littler further light on this question . . . in an unpublished study by Lawrence, who collected in test tubes a little of the perspiration of white and black students who had just been exercising in the gymnasium. These test tubes were then given to a number of white subjects with instruction to rank them in order of pleasantness. The results showed no consistent preference for the white samples; the test tube considered the most pleasant and the one considered the most unpleasant were both taken from whites.

Klineberg concludes:

> There may be racial difference in body odors, but it is important first to rule out the factors referred to above, particularly the factor of diet, before a final conclusion is reached. It is obvious that cleanliness is also a factor of importance. In any case the phenomenon of adaptation enters to remove any special unpleasantness arising from the presence of a strange group.[72]

The subject of ethnic differences in the odor of sweat was fully discussed and documented by Professor Julian Lewis in 1942 in his classic book *The Biology of the Negro,* all the evidence pointing to environmental factors in the production of the odor of sweat, such as cleanliness, diet, and endemic bacteria in the decomposition of the various contents of sweat.[73]

The fact is that sweat in itself is odorless. Shelley, Hurley, and Nichols have investigated this matter, and shown that pure apocrine sweat as it initially appears on the skin is both sterile and odorless, and that the odor is due to the decomposition effects produced by the action of bacteria.[74]

Morlan conducted an experiment on the perception of body odor in which two blacks and two whites were the subjects. The judgment of 59 persons in 715 experiments were recorded. The experiment was so set up as to eliminate any possibility of accidental factors or recognition of the subjects. In all there were 157 incorrect answers, and in 368 instances the persons tested stated that they could not tell, while in 190 instances the attribution was incorrect. In short, 51.4 percent out of a total of 715 experiments the persons tested were unable to recognize body odor as in anyway distinctive, while in 21.9 percent of instances the attribution was incorrect. In other words, the total number of failures was 73.3 percent as compared with 26.7 percent correct attributions. Those who considered themselves good judges did no better than the others.[75]

While comparative studies in the physiology and chemistry of black and of white sweat do not exist, there do exist several studies of the sweat glands in blacks and whites from the anatomical standpoint.

Clark and Lhamon, in a study of the sweat glands of the hands and feet of blacks, found that there were more abundantly supplied with exocrine glands[76] than were those of whites.[77] Glaser, in an investigation of sweat glands in one Bantu black and in one European, found that "the regional distribution of the sweat glands in the Negro agrees closely with that usually given for the European. . . . In the great majority of regions compared, however, the Bantu has more sweat glands than the European, and this is probably of considerable value to him in resisting extremes of heat."[78]

Homma, in a study of the apocrine glands of 10 blacks and 12 whites, found that such glands occurred three times more abundantly in blacks than in whites, and that, while such glands did not occur in the breasts of whites, they were sometimes to be found in the breasts of blacks.[79]

It is evident, then, that if blacks possess a greater number of sweat glands than whites, heat regulation under high temperatures would be more efficiently performed in them than in whites, and it is also possible that, if there is any difference in the odor of their sweat, it is probably not a difference in kind, but in degree or intensity, due to the cumulative action of the number of glands involved. As in the majority of traits in American blacks, their sweat glands are probably intermediate in number between those of African blacks and those of whites.

Conclusion

We may conclude this survey, then, with the statement that the American black represents an amalgam into which have entered the genes of

African blacks, whites of many nations and social classes, and some American Indians, and that so far as their physical characteristics are concerned, American blacks represent the successful blending of these three principal elements into a unique biological type. All their characteristics are perfectly harmonic, and all the evidence supports the fact that they represent a perfectly adapted biological type. Their biological future is definitely bright.

Myths are created to fill psychological needs. The need to make blacks inferior has given rise to the mythology of his alleged inferior physical status. The genetic differences between blacks and whites are very small indeed. Professor Bentley Glass has pointed out:

> In all, it is unlikely that there are many more than six pairs of genes in which the white race differs characteristically, in the lay sense, from black. Whites or blacks, however, unquestionably often differ among themselves by a larger number than this, a fact which reveals our racial prejudices as biologically absurd. It is only the consistency of the difference, not its magnitude, which looms so large in our eyes. Differences between other races are probably even less, and those between such sub-racial groups as 'Nordics' and 'Mediterraneans' are negligible. *The chasm between human ethnic groups and peoples, where it exists, is psychological and sociological; it is not genetic!*[80]

Notes

1. See Melville J. Herskovits, *The American Negro* (New York: Alfred A. Knopf, 1928); William M. Cobb, "The Physical Constitution of the American Negro," *Journal of Negro Education* 3 (1934): 340–88; W. Cobb, "Physical Anthropology of the American Negro," *American Journal of Physical Anthropology* 29 (1942): 113–223.

2. This summary is based on the work of Charles B. Davenport and A. G. Love, *Army Anthropology: Based on Observations Made on Draft Recruits 1917–1918 and on Veterans at Demobilization, 1919* (Medical Department of the U.S. Army in the World War, vol. 15, pt. 1) (Washington, D.C.; GPO, 1921); Wingate Todd and Anna Lindala, "Dimensions of the Body, Whites and American Negroes in Both Sexes," *American Journal of Physical Anthropology* 12 (1928): 35–119; Charles Davenport and Morris Steggerda, *Race Crossing in Jamaica* (Washington: Carnegie Institution); Melville J. Herskovits, *The Anthropometry of the American Negro* (New York: Columbia University Press, 1930); V. K. Cameron and H. Smith, "The Physical form of Mississippi Negroes," *American Journal of Physical Anthropology* 17 (1931): 193–201; Caroline Day, *A Study of Some Negro-White Families in the United States* (Cambridge: Peabody Museum, Harvard University, 1932).

3. The comparisons are made with the Old American series of Hrdlicka because these represent the type of the ancestral white stock of the American black. See Aleš Hrdlička, *The Old Americans* (Baltimore: Williams and Wilkins, 1925).

4. T. Wingate Todd, "Cranial Capacity and Linear Dimensions," *American Journal of Physical Anthropology* 6 (1923): 97–194. The water method of determining cranial capacity was used.

5. Donald G. Paterson, *Physique and Intellect* (New York: Century, 1930); Stephen Jay Gould, *The Mismeasure of Man* (New York: Norton. 1981).

6. Katherine Simmons, "Cranial Capacities by Both Plastic and Water Techniques with Cranial Linear Measurements of the Reserve Collection, White and Negro," *Human Biology* 14 (1942) 473–98.

7. Paterson, *Physique and Intellect;* Gould, *Mismeasure of Man;* Havelock Ellis, *Man & Woman,* 8th ed. (London A. & C. Black, 1934).

8. R. W. Shufeldt, *The Negro: A Menace to American Civilization* (Boston: Badger, 1907), 35. This book, which is dedicated to the great paleontologist Edward Drinker Cope, constitutes one of the most virulent attacks—under a pseudo-scientific guise—upon the American Negro ever perpetrated. The statement pertaining to cranial capacity is as follows: "In the skull of the negro the cranial capacity of the brain itself is much undersized. On the average, the former will hold thirty-five fluid ounces, as against forty-five for the Caucasian skull. In the negro the cranial bones are dense and unusually thick, converting his head into a veritable battering-ram. Moreover, the cranial sutures unite very early in life. This checks the development of the brain long before that takes place in other races, and this fact accounts to some extent for the more or less sudden stunting of the Ethiopian intellect shortly after arriving at puberty."

9. "The older schools of anthropologists agreed among themselves in assigning to the Negro branch of humanity a smaller and a less highly developed brain than is exhibited by other races. By charts and otherwise, some of them sought to show the areas of the Negro brain not yet developed to the standard of the Caucasian. The logical results of the findings of these men, with their prodigious industry and patience, are distinctly discouraging to the Negro. Accepting their findings, there is provided an unanswerable argument against the degradation of the white group through the absorption of the Negro group." A. H. Shannon, *The Negro in Washington* (New York: Webb, 1930), 320.

10. Lidio Cipriani, *Un assurdo etnico: L'Impero Etiopico* (Firenze: R. Bamporad & F.O., 1936), 177.

11. R. Bennett Bean, "Some Racial Peculiarities of the Negro Brain," *American Journal of Anatomy* 5 (1906): 353–415. Bean (who was a Southerner) claimed to have detected certain racial differences in the brain of the black, such as its relatively small size, the reduction in the volume of the frontal and temporal lobes, and the anterior part of the corpus callosum—the great association tract connecting the two hemispheres—of the brain.

12. Franklin P. Mall, "On Several Anatomical Characters of the Human Brain, Said to Vary According to Race and Sex," *American Journal of Anatomy* 9 (1909): 1–32.

13. Cornelius J. Connolly, *External Morphology of the Primate Brain* (Springfield IL: Thomas, 1950), 203; see also G. Levin, "Racial and 'Inferiority' Characters in the Human Brain," *American Journal of Physical Anthropology* 22 (1937) 345–80; Phillip V. Tobias, "Brain Size, Grey Matter and Race—Fact or Fiction?" *American Journal of Physical Anthropology* 32 (1970): 3–26.

14. C. W. M. Poynter and J. J. Keegan, "A Study of the American Negro Brain," *Journal of Comparative Neurology* 25 (1915): 183–202; see also Gould, *The Mismeasure of Man,* 77–82.

15. Eugen Fischer, "Variable Characters in Human Beings," in *Human Heredity,* eds. E. Baur, E. Fischer, and F. Lenz (New York: Macmillan, 1931), 114–66.

16. Levin, *"Racial and 'Inferiority' Characters."*

17. Franz Weidenreich, *Apes, Giants, and Man* (Chicago: University of Chicago Press, 1946), 100.

18. For a table of brain or cranial capacities see Ashley Montagu, *An Introduction to Physical Anthropology,* 3rd ed. (Springfield, IL: Thomas, 1960), 458–59.

19. Henry H. Donaldson, "The Significance of Brain Weight," *Archives of Neurology and Psychiatry* 13 (1925): 385–86; Gerhardt Bonin, "On the Size of Man's Brain as Indicated by Skull Capacity," *Journal of Comparative Neurology* 59 (1934): 1–28; Otto Klineberg, *Race Differences* (New York: Harper, 1935), 77–92.

20. W. E. Le Gros Clark, *Fitting Man to His Environment* (Newcastle-upon-Tyne: King's College, 1949), 19.

21. W. Grey Walter, *The Living Brain,* (New York: Norton, 1953), 77–92; Richard Bergland, *The Fabric of Mind: A Radical New Understanding of the Brain and How it Works* (New York: Viking, 1985).

22. T. H. Huxley, "Emancipation in Black and White," *The Reader,* 20 May 1865, 561–62.

23. T. Wingate Todd and D. W. Lyon, "Cranial Suture Closure; Its Progress and Age Relationship. Part IV, Ectocranial Closure in Adult Males of Negro Stock," *American Journal of Physical Anthropology* 8 (1925): 149–68. Parts I–III of these studies were published in preceding numbers of the same journal.

24. Adolph Schultz, "Fetal Growth in Man," *American Journal of Physical Anthropology* 6 (1923): 389–400.

25. Marciano Limson, "Observations on the Bones of the Skull in White and Negro Fetuses and Infants," *Contributions to Embryology* 136 (1932): 204–22.

26. T. Wingate Todd, "The Skeleton," in *Growth and Development of the Child,* Part II (White House Conference on Child Health and Protection) (New York: Century, 1933): 26–130.

27. Ashley Montagu, "The Premaxilla in the Primates," *Quarterly Review of Biology* 10 (1935), 182–84; A. Montagu, "The Premaxilla in Man," *Journal of the American Dental Association* 23 (1936): 2043–57.

28. For a discussion of these matters see Montagu. "The Premaxilla in Man," and "The Significance of the Variability of the Upper Lateral Incisor Teeth in Man," *Human Biology* 12 (1940): 323–58.

29. Arthur Thomson and L. H. Dudley Buxton, "Man's Nasal Index in Relation to Certain Climatic Conditions," *Journal of the Royal Anthropological Institute of Great Britain and Ireland* 53 (1923): 920–22.

30. Victor Heiser, *An American Doctor's Odessy* (New York: Norton, 1936), 146.

31. Stuart O. Landry, *The Cult of Equality* (New Orleans: Pelican Publishing, 1945), 175.

32. William M. Cobb, "Your Nose Won't Tell," *Crisis* 65 (1938): 332–36.

33. T. Wingate Todd, "Entrenched Negro Physical Features," *Human Biology* 1 (1929): 57–69.

34. Day, *Negro-White Families*, 96–9.

35. Davenport and Love, *Army Anthropology;* Todd and Lindala, "Dimensions of the Body" 35–119.

36. Todd and Lindala, ibid., 73.

37. Herskovits, *Anthropometry*, 67–68.

38. Ashley Montagu, "On the Primate Thumb," *American Journal of Physical Anthropology* 15 (1931): 291–314.

39. Adolph Schultz, "The Skeleton of the Trunk and Limbs of Higher Primates," *Human Biology* 2 (1930): 381–83.

40. Adolph Schultz, "Fetal Growth of Man and Other Primates," *Quarterly Review of Biology* 1 (1926): 493–95.

41. Todd, "Entrenched Negro Physical Features," 57–69.

42. Todd and Lindala, "Dimensions of the Body," 74–75.

43. William M. Cobb, "Race and Runners," *Journal of Health and Physical Education* 7 (1936): 1–8.

44. R. Malafa, *On the Bodily Differences Between Sprinters and Non-Sportsmen* (Brno: Publications de la Faculté des Sciences de la Université Masaryk, 1933), 1–11.

45. Schultz, "Fetal Growth of Man and Other Primates," 499.

46. J. M. Tanner, *The Physique of the Olympic Athlete* (London: Allen & Unwin, 1964). For a good discussion of the subject see Martin Kane, "An Assessment of 'Black is Best,'" *Sports Illustrated*, 18 January 1971, 72–83.

47. Tanner, *Physique of the Olympic Athelete.*

48. Todd and Lindala, "Dimensions of the Body," 97–98.

49. See Chapter 10, this volume.

50. W. E. Caldwell and H. C. Moloy, "Anatomical Variations in the Female Pelvis and Their Effects in Labor, with a Suggested Classification," *American Journal of Obstetrics and Gynecology* 26 (1933): 479–15; Philip V. Tobias "On a Bushman-European Hybrid Family," *Man* 287 (1954): 1–4.

51. Davenport and Steggerda, *Race Crossing in Jamaica*, 423–24.

52. Johann F. Blumenbach, *De Generis Humani Varietate Nativa*, trans. by T. Bendyshe, "On the Natural Variety of Mankind," in *The Anthropological Treatises of Johann Friedrich Blumenbach* (London: Anthropological Society, 68, 1865).

53. Geoffrey Gorer, quoted by John Dollard, *Caste and Class in a Southern Town* (New Haven: Yale University Press, 1937), 161. See G. Gorer, *African Dances* (New York: Alfred A. Knopf, 1935).

54. During World War II an officer in the Medical Corps of the United States Naval Reserve, who for some five months worked in the main induction center in Mississippi, wrote me [Ashley Montagu] as follows: "I know nothing directly as to the size of the American Negro penis in erection. I have been told that it does not elongate much, but as far as the comparative size of the Mississippi Negro's flaccid penis when judged in relation to Mississippi whites I consider myself an expert. If size is a measure of superiority, and obviously psychologically, at least in Western culture it is, the white in the noble state of Mississippi is definitely inferior to the colored adult male in the general run of that population. To deny this fact is silly. Every physician there remarked about it and was jealous. For my own part I was finally compelled to modify my theories on the overwhelming importance of

economics as the basis for the peculiar hostility of the Southern white for the Negro and was led to believe that the roots of it were more probably to be located in the effort on their part to compensate for their sense of inadequacy in that direction." I quote these observations for what they may be considered to be worth.

55. Dollard, *Caste and Class,* 160–61. The morbid and revealing interest of many Southern white males in this subject is dramatically described by John H. Griffin in his book *Black Like Me* (Boston: Houghton Mifflin, 1961), 91–99.

56. Dollard, *Caste and Class,* 161.

57. I Barnes, "The Inheritance of Pigmentation in the Skin of the American Negro," *Human Biology* 1 (1929): 321–28.

58. Charles Davenport, *Heredity of Skin Color in Negro-White Crosses* (Washington, D.C.: Carnegie Institution, 1913); T. Wingate Todd and L. van Gorder, "The Quantitative Determination of Black Pigmentation in the Skin of the American Negro," *American Journal of Physical Anthropology* 4 (1921): 239–60.

59. Eugen Fischer, "Die Rehobother Bastards und das Bastardierungsproblem beim Menschen" *Jena* (1913).

60. E. A. Hooton, in Day, *Negro-White Families,* 85.

61. C. B. Davenport, "Heredity of Hair Form in Man," *American Naturalist* 52 (1908): 341.

62. Five types of hair form are distinguished here: straight, low waves, curly, frizzy, and tightly-curled (woolly).

63. C. H. Danforth, "Distribution of Hair on the Digits in Man," *American Journal of Physical Anthropology* 4 (1921): 189–204. See also Julian H. Lewis, *The Biology of the Negro* (Chicago: University of Chicago Press, 1942), 61–68.

64. Mildred Trotter, "A Study of Facial Hair in White and Negro Races," *Washington University Studies (Scientific Studies)* 9 (1922): 273–89.

65. Danforth, "Distribution of Hair."

66. Davenport and Steggerda, *Race Crossing in Jamaica,* 264–67.

67. Day, *Negro-White Families,* 86.

68. Dollard, *Caste and Class,* 378–79.

69. Shufeldt, *The Negro,* 33.

70. Buntaro Adachi, "Der Geruch der Europaër," *Globus* 83 (1903): 14–115.

71. William Plomer, the English writer, when a young man in the late 1920s, lived in Tokyo for some three years, and although not "going native," seldom spoke with a European; virtuallly all his friends were Japanese, and it was not long when catching the sight of stray Europeans, they looked odd or even grotesque. He had grown used to the Japanese face, while the mongrel features of Europeans, as he puts it, by contrast looked irregular. "Their complexions were not clear, their gait was ungainly, their manners were casual and uncouth, their voices too loud, their opinions too outspoken. Once or twice, too, at close quarters, one noticed their peculiar smell." Willliam Plomer, *Double Lives* (London: Jonathan Cape, 1943; New York: Noonday Press, 1956), p. 257. See also Klineberg, *Race Differences,* 128–31.

72. Ibid., 131.

73. Lewis, *Biology of the Negro,* 92–94.

74. Shelley, Harry J. Hurley, and Anna Nichols, "Axillar Odor," *Archives of Dermatology and Syphilology* 68 (1953): 430.

75. G. K. Morlan, "An Experiment on the Identification of Body Odor," *Journal of Genetic Psychology* 77 (1950): 257–65.

76. Exocrine or eccrine glads are distributed over the entire body, emptying their secretions through small ducts through the pores directly onto the skin surface. See Yas Kuno, *Human Perspiration* (Springfield, IL: Thomas, 1956).

77. E. Clark and R. H. Lhamon, "Observations on the Sweat Glands of Tropical and Northern Races," *Anatomical Record* 12 (1917): 139–47.

78. S. Glaser, "Sweat Glands in the Negro and the European," *American Journal of Physical Anthropology* 17 (1934): 371–76.

79. H. Homma, "On Apocrine Sweat Glands in White and Negro Men and Women," *Johns Hopkins Hospital Bulletin* 38 (1926): 367–71.

80. Bentley Glass, *Genes and the Man* (New York: Teachers College, Columbia University, 1943), 173–74.

17

Are the Jews a Race?

Jews for countless years have been referred to as members of a race. This has been done not only by the so-called man on the street but also by many scientists, doctors, philosophers, politicians, historians,[1] and the members of many other professions. When reference is made to the Jewish race, what is implied is that there exists a clearly defined, though widely scattered, people who are physically and behaviorally distinguishable from all other races—the Jewish race. It is worth noting that referenece is almost always to "the Jews," as if they were a distinctive entity, for that is what the definite article "the" does in particularizing the noun. That practice immediately prejudices the issue.

The so-called Jewish race is generally held to be characterized by a combination of physical and behavioral traits that renders any of its member recognizable anywhere on earth. The characteristic behavioral traits are alleged to consist in a quality of looking Jewish and behaving in a Jewish manner, hard to define but nevertheless real.

There are many persons who claim to be able to distinguish a Jew from all other people simply by the total appearance which he or she presents, even though the back is all that is visible to the observer.

It is not only non-Jews who assert these things and who make such claims, but Jews as a whole have prided themselves on being God's "chosen people" and hence distinguished from all other people. Many Jews insist that they belong to a distinct race, the Jewish race.

Whatever may be generally believed about Jews, and whatever they believe of themselves, the facts deserve to be dispassionately presented, together with an interpretation of their significance. Assertions and denials are of little value when based on emotion, or founded on misinterpreted observations, or both. It is only when the actual facts are clearly presented in the light of scientific investigation and correctly interpreted that assertions and denials are in order. Such statements differ from those which are usually made, and are therefore unlikely to appeal to persons who prefer to accept what their emotions or prejudices dictate, rather than be persuaded by scientific demonstration.

What, then, has the anthropologist to say in answer to the question "Are the Jews a 'race' or any other kind of entity?" Do they possess distinctive physical and behavioral traits? If they do, how do they come to be so characterized? To what extent are any of these putative traits real or inborn, and to what extent, if any, are they acquired?

These are some of the questions to be dealt with in the present chapter. Do the Jews possess a community of physical characteristics that distinguishes them as a distinct ethnic group among the peoples of humankind? To this question the answer of science is an unequivocal "No. They do not." This does not mean that some Jews are not recognized as such under certain circumstances, but it does mean that they are not distinguishable as a group or population upon the basis of physical traits. If they are not distinguishable as a distinct group upon physical grounds, upon what basis then, are they distinguishable, if at all, as an ethnic group, population, or what?

The answer to that question is that "the" Jews are neither a race, an ethnic group, nor a population. Individuals who identify themselves as Jews may vary in color from white to black and every intermediate shade, with hair that varies all the way from blond to black, every kind of eye color, every kind of nose and head shape, and the like. Jews have lived in many parts of the world, and wherever they have lived many of them have intermixed with members of the indigenous populations, that were often quite mixed themselves, hence the variability of Jews physically is quite probably greater than one is likely to encounter in any other population.

Let us now proceed to discuss the evidence for these statements.

Our sole authority for the early physical history of the Jews as an historic entity, which they once were, is, at present, the Old Testament. The physical anthropology of this work is far from consistent, but from it the following facts may be pieced together: The ancestors of the early Jews lived on the stretch of land skirting the western bank of the Euphrates. The home of Terah, Abraham's father, was Ur of the Chaldees, close to the Persian Gulf; here and to the southwest lived numerous Arab tribes, all of whom spoke closely related languages which, after the "brownish" son of Noah, Shem, we customarily term Semitic (Shemitic). The original converts to the religion which Abraham had founded were drawn from several of these tribes. Their physical differences, if any, were probably negligible. But shortly after they had established themselves as a distinct religious group intermixture commenced, first with the Canaanites of the lowlands, with whom they had traded for some time, and then with the Amorites of the highlands of the southwest. The Amorites are supposed to have been distinguished by a high frequency of red hair. The Hivites, Amalekites, Kenites, Egyptians, and the Hittites all mixed with the Jews during the early period of their history, as did many other peoples mentioned in the Old Testament.[2]

There is a reason to believe that the peoples mentioned were characterized by somewhat different frequencies of one or more distinctive physical characters. Thus, it is said that the Amorites showed a high frequency of red hair, while the Hittites, who spoke an Indo-Germanic language, presented two types, a tall, heavy-bearded, hook-nose type and a moderately tall, beardless type, with thick lips, a straight nose with wide nostrils, and "sunken" eyes.

We perceive, then, that already in the earliest period of their development the people whom we now call "the Jews" were a much mixed group, and while for classificatory purposes they might all be designated as Mediterranean in type, there can be no question but that they were at this period far from being a people of "pure" ancestry. Owing to their geographic position and relations we can be fairly certain that the peoples of the East from whom the Jews originated and the many others with whom they subsequently mixed were themselves of much mixed ancestry.

During the period of the Exodus (1220 B.C.) there was further mixture with the peoples with whom they came into contact, principally the types embraced under the Egyptians, and probably, also, some Hamitic peoples. Some 622 crania recovered from a Jewish cemetery at Lachish, dating back to approximately 750 B.C., show marked resemblances to those of the Dynastic Egyptians.[3] This is not to suggest that all Jews at that period resembled Egyptians, but it does suggest something vastly more significant than that, namely, that already, as early at 750 B.C., there existed local groups of Jews who in their physical traits resembled, or were identical with, the population among whom they were living; such a group differed from other groups calling themselves Jews. This is, in fact, exactly the state of affairs we encounter today, and there is every reason to believe that this has been progressively so from the earliest times. In other words, the Jews were never at any time characterized by a community of physical traits, but generally varied according to the populations among whom they lived. This would mean either that they originated from these populations or that they had become physically identified with them as a result of intermixture. We shall see that the latter explanation is the one which most nearly agrees with the facts.

During the Diaspora the Jews were dispersed to practically every part of the earth and have intermixed with numerous peoples. In the sixth century B.C., during the Babylonian captivity, there was some intermixture with many Mesopotamian peoples. During the Hellenistic period, in the fourth century B.C., Jews followed Alexander the Great into the Hellenistic world, into Egypt, Syria, Asia Minor, Macedonia, to mention a few of the more important regions into which they penetrated and settled. The pattern followed by these Jews was identical with that which the Jews have always followed with such great success: They took over the language of the

Greek-speaking populations and in general identified themselves with Hellenistic culture.

In the second century B.C., at the time of the Maccabees, there commenced the movement of the Jews into the Roman world which carried them to the farthest corners of the Roman Empire, especially to Western Europe and particularly to Spain, Italy, France, and the Rhineland of Germany. A large number of Jews settled along the Rhine in the region of Frankfurt, Mainz, Worms, Cologne, and Trier, all of which before the eleventh century had become centers of Jewish learning. The Middle German language spoken in that region during the Middle Ages, mixed with Laaz, Slavic, and Hebrew, was adopted by the Jews and is preserved, with but little modification, to this day in the form of Yiddish. It is preserved in its purest form practically unchanged to the present time in certain cantons of Switzerland. In its Eastern European form it is spoken by many more Jews than speak Hebrew or any other single language.

During the eleventh century, at the time of the First Crusade, the plunder and massacre of Jews by Christian knights[4] started a Jewish migration eastward, which was accelerated into a mass migration after the thirteenth century. These Rhineland Jews settled in what in now Galicia, Bukovina, and the southern and western Ukraine. Here they met and merged with the earlier Jewish settlements and adopted as their common language the speech of the Rhineland group, Yiddish. These Jews came to be known as the Ashkenazim (so named after the grandson of Noah Ashkenaz, and the Hebrew name for Germany), as distinguished from the Jews of Spanish origin, the Sephardim (the name comes from Sepharad, a place of exile mentioned in *Obadiah* 20 and early identified with Iberia).

It has been claimed that the modern Sephardim are a much more homogeneous group physically than the Ashkenazim and that they "preserve with reasonable fidelity the racial character of their Palestinian ancestors."[5]

That the Sephardic Jews are less variable in their physical traits than the Ashkenazim is possible, since they may be slightly less mixed. It is, however, to be doubted that they preserve with any fidelity at all the racial character of their Palestinian ancestors. This is greatly to be doubted for the reason that "their Palestinian ancestors" were themselves of different origins. Indeed, it is doubtful whether anyone is today in a position to say exactly what that Palestinian ancestry was. Certainly, even less can be said concerning the anthropological traits of the groups which entered into that ancestry. At the present time it would be wisest to take the view that if there does exist a significant difference between the Sephardim and the Ashkenazim, then that difference is due to the somewhat different post-Palestinian biological history of the two groups. As we shall see, there is a much greater proportion of blond types among the Ashkenazim than among the Sephardim. It must be recalled that during their residence in

Spain, from the beginnings of the eleventh to the end of the fifteenth century, the Sephardim almost certainly underwent some admixture with the Moors and for some three centuries with the non-Moorish populations of Spain and Portugal.

A list of the peoples with whom Jews have at one time or another intermixed would include a large proportion of the populations of the world. This does not mean that Jews as a whole have undergone such mixture, but—and this is the important point—the different populations of Jews have undergone independent and different kinds and degrees of intermixture with various populations. The result of such varying biological experiences would be, even if the Jews had commenced as a homogeneous group—which they did not—that a certain amount of diversification in physical traits would eventually be produced between local groups of Jews. That this is actually what has occurred is proved by both the historical facts and the analysis of measurable anthropological traits.[67]

The census of Jewish school children in Germany taken in the 1880s, under the direction of Rudolf Virchow, revealed that among 75,000 children 32 percent had light hair and 46 percent light eyes.[8] In Austria these figures were 28 and 54 percent, respectively, and in England 26 and 41 percent. As Maurice Fishberg pointed out in his classic work *The Jews* (1911), these figures follow the population trends for blondness as a whole, exemplified by the figures for England, Germany, and Riga, whereas in Italy, where the population is predominantly brunet, less than 12 percent of the Jews were blond, and in the Caucasus, North Africa, and Turkestan the percentage was even less (see Table 17.1).[9]

Even with respect to that unreliable, but formerly much-beloved child of the anthropologist, the cephalic index[10] or form of the head, the variation between different local groups of Jews is considerable.[11]

If, as is customarily done, the mean or average shape of the head is given, an incorrect idea is obtained of the actual conditions prevailing among Jews so far as the shape of head is concerned. It is the percentage distribution of the various head shapes in such a population which gives us a true account of these conditions. These percentage distributions show that head shape, or cephalic index, like all other traits, is variable among Jews as a whole, the head shape of Jews in various countries varying substantially from one to another, as is demonstrated in the following table.

Table 17.2 shows that Caucasian Jews have predominantly round heads, while those in North Africa, particularly those in Arabia, are predominantly longheaded, and those in Europe are predominantly of intermediate type. Much more significant characters than those so far mentioned are the blood groups A, B, AB, and O. The blood groups remain constant throughout life, they appear to have a very low mutation rate, and they are inherited according to the laws of Mendel. The proportions in

TABLE 17.1

PERCENTAGE DISTRIBUTION OF EYE COLOR AND HAIR COLOR AMONG JEWS[a]
(*The figures in parentheses refer to the females*)

REGION OR GROUP	EYES		HAIR			DARK TYPE	FAIR TYPE	MIXED TYPE
	Dark	Light	Dark	Fair	Red			
Poland	55.0	45.0	96.8	0.5	2.6	57.9	0.5	41.5
	(56.8)	(43.2)	(86.4)	(8.0)	(5.6)	(58.5)	(8.5)	(33.0)
Galicia	53.8	46.1	74.0	21.5	4.3	44.0	13.0	43.0
	(60.0)	(40.0)	(76.0)	(20.0)	(4.0)	(51.0)	(16.0)	(33.0)
Ukraine	56.7	43.3	76.4	19.3	4.3	51.3	16.2	31.0
	(61.8)	(38.1)	(83.1)	(14.0)	(2.9)	(68.6)	(6.9)	(24.3)
Southern Russia	64.8	35.2	81.7	14.8	2.4	58.1	10.5	27.9
	(75.6)	(24.4)	(83.0)	(14.6)	(3.5)	(68.3)	(4.9)	(24.4)
Lithuania	65.2	34.8	68.1	29.0	2.0	50.7	13.0	36.2
Rumania	48.7	51.3	83.3	14.7	2.8	47.0	11.0	42.2
Hungary	50.7	49.3	77.1	17.9	5.0	46.0	12.0	42.0
						(62.0)	(5.0)	(33.0)
Baden	48.8	51.2	84.9	12.8	2.3			
England	61.3	38.7	77.6	20.4	2.5			
	(66.8)	(33.2)	(88.1)	(11.9)	(0.0)			
Italy	67.6	32.3	88.2	11.8		60.2	14.7	25.0
Bosnia	69.1	30.9	80.0	18.2	1.8			
North Africa	83.1	16.9	92.2	5.2	2.6	76.4	4.6	19.0
Daghestan	93.0	7.0	97.0	0.5	2.5	97.0		3.0
Georgia	89.0	11.0	93.0	5.0	2.0	82.0	3.0	15.0
Turkestan	85.0	15.0	98.0	2.0		85.0	2.0	13.0
Samaritans	88.9	11.1	96.3	3.7	0.0			
	(88.9)	(11.1)	(92.6)	(0.0)	(7.4)			
Karaites	74.0	26.0	94.0	2.0	4.0	70.0	6.0	24.0
Yemen	100.0		100.0			100.0		

which these blood groups are found (actually the frequency of the genes) in different populations should tell us to what extent those populations resemble each other in respect, at least, to their gene frequencies for the blood groups. If, now, the blood groups of Jews from different regions are compared with one another, some interesting facts emerge. The distribution of these blood groups is shown in the following four tables (from Brutzkus). For the purposes of comparison the percentages for the surrounding Gentile populations (italicized) are also given.

The figures in Table 17.3 show that, with the exception of the Georgian and Persian Jews, and strangely enough the Jews from Yemen, in their blood group distributions the Jews of the Mediterranean region bear a

TABLE 17.2

PERCENTAGE DISTRIBUTION OF HEAD SHAPE (CEPHALIC INDEX) IN JEWS OF DIFFERENT REGIONS[a]

Cephalic Index	Daghestan Caucasus	Europe	North Africa	Yemen Arabia
Hyperdolichocephalic (−76)		2.89	25.97	71.80
Dolichocephalic (76–77)		7.36	24.67	14.10
Subdolichocephalic (78–79)	4.70	15.51	19.48	7.69
Mesocephalic (80–81)	6.10	25.78	13.00	2.56
Subbrachycephalic (82–83)	17.37	24.01	9.09	3.85
Brachycephalic (84–85)	23.94	15.97	6.49	
Hyperbrachycephalic (86–)	47.89	8.47	1.30	
Number of observations	2.3	2,641	77	78

[a]From Kautsky, *Are the Jews a Race?* The definitions of the cephalic index vary slightly from those generally accepted, but not sufficiently to affect the discussion.

TABLE 17.3

BLOOD GROUPS OF JEWS IN THE MEDITERRANEAN REGION

Town or Country	Number of Persons	A	B	AB	O
Monastir (Macedonia)	500	33.0	23.2	5.0	38.8
Morocco	642	35.9	19.9	7.3	36.9
Tunis	200	31.0	15.0	12.5	41.0
Aleppo (Syria)	173	34.0	20.0	8.0	38.0
Aleppo (Arabs)	*933*	*37.0*	*21.0*	*6.0*	*36.0*
Georgia	1,236	43.93	19.01	10.76	26.29
Persia	116	46.5	25.0	8.6	19.9
Georgians	*2,177*	*37.11*	*10.93*	*4.82*	*46.6*
Yemen	1,000	26.1	16.1	1.8	56.0
Palestine (Arabs)	*347*	*39.7*	*20.4*	*7.4*	*32.5*

close resemblance to the Arab populations. The Jews and Arabs of Aleppo are much alike in this respect, while Georgian Jews and non-Jews are much more unlike. Very different are the blood group distributions of the Jews in the Caucasus, the Crimea, and Turkestan.

From Table 17.4 it will be seen that the percentages for blood group B are significantly higher than they are for Jews of the Mediterranean region listed in table 17.3. The Jews of the Caucasus, Crimea, and Turkestan have apparently absorbed, sometime in their history, an appreciable number of persons possessing a substantial proportion of blood group B. It so hap-

TABLE 17.4

BLOOD GROUPS AMONG THE JEWS IN THE CAUCASUS, CRIMEA, AND TURKESTAN

Region or People	Number of Persons	A	B	AB	O
Daghestan	87	26.6	24.1	9.1	40.2
Samarkand	616	29.2	30.5	7.9	32.3
Crimea	500	34.4	32.6	12.2	20.8
Khirgiz	914	23.96	31.4	7.87	36.76

TABLE 17.5

BLOOD GROUPS AMONG THE JEWS OF WESTERN EUROPE

Town	Number of Persons	A	B	AB	O
Berlin	230	41.1	11.9	4.9	42.1
Berlin	2500	44.0	15.0	6.0	35.0
Amsterdam	705	39.4	13.4	4.5	42.6
Amsterdam	6679	41.7	8.6	3.0	46.8

pens that these regions were once inhabited by the Khazars, a Turco-Mongolian people, a large proportion of whom in the eighth century A.D., with the example set by the reigning family and nobility, adopted the Jewish faith and intermarried with Jews. It is believed that a large proportion of eastern European Jews were of Khazar ancestry. Since the Turco-Mongolian region exhibits high frequencies of blood group B, it is likely that the Khazars were similarly characterized, and that through them some, at least, of the Jews of these regions acquired some of their B genes.[12]

The high frequency of blood group A among the Jews from Berlin and Amsterdam (Table 18.5) is striking, as is the resemblance of the blood group distributions to those of the non-Jews, particularly in Berlin. The suggestion is that there has been an appreciable amount of admixture between Jews and non-Jews in these towns.

Muhsam, in a valuable study on the genetic origins of the Jews concludes that the case for "a highly diversified origin has much in its favor." Muhsam believes that some of the present Jewish communities, which he calls *eidoth* (plural of *eidah*, Hebrew for *community*), may be explained as the result

of secondary amalgamation of genetically different groups in the diaspora to form some of the present eidoth. There is some historical evidence that

TABLE 17.6

BLOOD GROUPS AMONG THE JEWS OF EASTERN EUROPE

Country	Number of Persons	A	B	AB	O
Russia	3,333	41.7	19.6	6.5	32.2
Russia	*10,151*	*31.7*	*21.9*	*7.5*	*33.9*
Poland	8.8	41.5	17.4	8.0	33.1
Poland	*11,488*	*37.8*	*20.8*	*8.9*	*32.5*
Rumania	1,135	39.0	17.5	5.3	38.2
Rumania	*1,521*	*43.3*	*15.6*	*7.4*	*33.7*

at the period of mass emigration of Jews from Palestine, from the destruction of the first temple, the Jews represented already a genetically fairly heterogeneous population. And although some emigrating groups must be assumed to have been large, on the scale of possible populations transfers of Antiquity, they formed, in the country in which they settled, isolates which may often have maintained their isolation for many generations. During this time the effect of the random genetic drift should be expected to have caused these isolates to differ considerably from the origin as well as from one another. Sooner or later one of these isolates may have merged with others to form, together with some foreign elements, an eidah as it appears today.[13]

This confirms what has been said above.

Sufficient, I hope, has been said concerning the origins of the Jews and of the variability of only a small selection of their physical traits to show how mixed and how variable Jews are in both their ancestry and their physical traits. As Siemens has concluded: "A study of the main characteristics of the indigenous stocks of various regions and the corresponding characteristics of the Jews that have lived among them in these regions indicates that the Jews are of heterogeneous types each of which conforms to a greater or smaller extent to the indigenous physical types."[14] From the standpoint of biological anthropology, and from the standpoint of zoology there is no such thing as a Jewish physical type, and there is not, nor was there ever, anything even remotely resembling a Jewish race or ethnic group.

Are Jews, then, constituted of a number of different ethnic groups distinguishable from other non-Jewish ethnic groups? The answer is No. There are certainly many different types of Jews, and among these there are certainly some who retain a physical resemblance to the Middle Eastern types whose genes they still carry, but the majority do not sufficiently differ from the populations among whom they live to justify being distinguished from those populations on physical grounds and classified as distinct ethnic groups. On physical grounds it is quite impossible to distinguish Jews from most of the native populations among whom they live in the Middle East, in the Orient, and in many other regions. Dr. Magnus Hirschfeld, an acute observer and himself a Jew, writes of his difficulty in distinguishing Jews from non-Jews in Palestine, "for in Palestine," he writes,

> there is no way of telling at first glance whether a person is a Christian, a Jew, or a Mohammedan.... Very seldom—much more seldom, anyway, than in Carlsbad or Marienbad—one sees the characteristic 'Struck'[15] heads or the Oriental beauties as they were painted in my youth by Sichel. The so-called 'Jewish nose' too, supposedly an Aramaic-Arab characteristic, is hardly more frequent than the pug nose. Noses of 'western' or 'northern' form predominate (to use Gunther's nomenclature), and the formation, too, of lips, hair, eyes and hands is hardly different from the average European types. One even sees, especially among the children, a surprisingly large number of blond and blue-eyed types. In a kindergarten I counted 32 blondes among 54 children, that is, more than 50 percent . . . not pure, but mixed, races are a matter of course biologically. How, then, should there be 'pure' races when we consider that every individual possesses and unites in himself a line of paternal and maternal ancestors embracing thousands, perhaps even hundreds of thousands of generations? How extraordinarily various must have been the mixture of genes over so long a period.[16]

And that has never been better said.

Writing of the Jews of Tunis, Sir Harry Johnston remarked upon the absence of strongly marked racial features among them, and the rarity with which one encountered a Jew who suggested a Semitic origin.[17]

Sir E. Dennison Ross, the distinguished orientalist, writing of his stay in Tiflis, Georgia, says, "In this town I was very much struck by the similarity, both in appearance and character, of the Greeks, Jews, and Armenians."[18]

Certainly anyone who has lived for any length of time in Italy will know that it is utterly impossible to distinguish a Jew from an Italian in that country. The same is not, however, true in all lands, for in England, in Germany, and in America it is certainly possible, with some degree of accuracy, to pick out many persons who are Jews as distinguished from non-Jews of all types. Is the fact that one can do so due to the physical traits of these persons, traits which distinguish them from the rest of the population?

Let us see. A number of Jews retain an aggregation of physical traits found in high frequencies in populations of the Middle East as well as those of the Mediterranean. In any population not exhibiting such an aggregate of physical traits some persons would be easily recognizable as Jews by virtue of this difference. But this does not mean that such physical traits are peculiar to all or most Jews, for, in fact, a large proportion of Jews do not possess such traits. Nor does it mean that some Jews alone possess the colligation of physical traits referred to, for many of the non-Jewish populations of the Near and Middle East as well as of the Mediterranean exhibit such traits in much higher frequencies than do Jews.

Furthermore, some Jews exhibit a certain quality of looking "Jewish," but again this quality is not peculiar to Jews, for it is the "look" which most of the peoples of the Near and Middle East possess. In the Occident persons of such origin are often taken to be Jews. This Jewish-looking quality occurring in any population not generally characterized by it renders it possible to recognize some persons as being Jews. Even so, one will often be wrong and mistakenly identify as Jews persons of non-Jewish origin, such as many Italians, Greeks, Turks, Arabs, Berbers, and related peoples. The quality of looking Jewish is not due so much to any biologically inherited traits of the persons in question as to certain culturally acquired habits of expression, facial, vocal, muscular, and mental. Such habits do, to an impressive extent, influence the appearance of the person and in large part determine the impression he makes upon others. Whether such persons will be identifiable as "Jews" will depend upon the character of the population among which they live. Such differences in facial expression are also seen as between different classes beginning at a very early age.

Without question a certain number of persons of Jewish cultural background exhibit a complex of physical traits which represent the residual expression of their remote Near Eastern ancestry. This is the type indistinguishable from that represented by millions of non-Jews of the Near and Middle East. In the Occident it is not difficult to recognize such persons as Jews when they do differ from the general population sufficiently to suggest their origin. That origin is not, in fact, Jewish but Eastern.

The fact is that the Jews are neither a race nor an ethnic group nor yet a number of ethnic groups—no more so, indeed than are Catholics, Protestants, or Moslems. It is, in fact, as incorrect to speak of a "Jewish race" or ethnic group as it would be to speak of a Catholic, Protestant, or Moslem race or ethnic group. What, then, does the term "Jew" mean? Strictly speaking, a person is a Jew by virtue of his adherence to the Jewish religion. If he is not a member of some organized form of Judaism, then he is not, strictly speaking, a Jew.

There is, however, another sense in which a person who does not subscribe to the tenets of the Jewish faith may nevertheless be correctly described as exhibiting Jewish traits, in just the same way as we say of a person that he looks or behaves like a Frenchman, or a German, or a member of any other national group. Jews do not constitute a national entity but, interestingly enough, many have preserved cultural traits, which we usually associate with differences in national culture; these traits, therefore, have a quasi-national character. Many Jews, wherever they have been, have clung tenaciously to their ancient beliefs and ways of life, more so than any other Western people of whom we have any knowledge, and they have generally preserved a certain community of cultural traits. These traits are cultural, not biological ones. Any person who is born into, or socialized in, a Jewish cultural environment will acquire the traits of behavior and certain personality traits peculiar to that culture. These are the traits which make many Jews socially "visible" in many of the communities in which they live. These traits, taken collectively, differ sufficiently from those which prevail in the communities in which Jews generally live to render them distinguishable from practically all other members of each of these communities.

It is extremely difficult to define the quality of "looking Jewish," even though it is doubtful whether anyone could be found who would deny that such a quality exists. This quality is exhibited not only in the facial expression but in the whole expression of the body—in its movements and in its gesticulations. Because the origin and nature of these traits have never been better described than by Fishberg I will give it in his words.

Although Fishberg's account is based largely on Jewish immigrants from eastern Europe to America it also holds true for many of their offspring.

> Centuries of confinement in the Ghetto, social ostracism, ceaseless suffering under the ban of abuse and persecution have been instrumental in producing a characteristic psychic type which manifests itself in his cast of countenance which is considered as peculiarly 'Jewish.' As a matter of fact, the Jews are not alone in having this peculiar expression. Physiognomies akin to that of the Ghetto face, as it may be called, are encountered among many other races and peoples who, as religious minorities, have been subjected to cruel treatment for many generations. The Armenians, whose lot has not been better than that of the Jews, are hardly to be distinguished from Jews by their facial features. The native Christians of Egypt, called the Kopts, and also the Basques in France and Spain, are said to 'look like Jews.' Many psychologists have spoken of a special psychology of religious minorities, but none have studied the effect of religious isolation, which often involves also social isolation on the facial features. But it is well known that the mental state has a great influence on the features of the individual. Emerson, in his *English Traits,* says 'Every religious sect has its physiognomy. The Methodists have acquired a face, the Quakers a face, the nuns a face. An Englishman will point out a dissenter by his manners. Trades and professions carve their own lines on faces and forms.' It is also well known that occupations have a remarkable influence on physiognomy. We often say one looks like a butcher, a carpenter, a tailor, a waiter, a coachman. Each one possesses a peculiar cast of countenance which easily betrays his vocation in life, and it by no means depends on the race stock to which he belongs. There are special varieties of facial

expression which at once tell the profession of a man. Who does not know the actor's face, the ecclesiastical, the musical, the artistic, the legal, the military face?

And Fishberg appropriately adds, "The 'Ghetto face' is not the result of the complexion, nor of stature, nor is it due to the size, prominence, or form of the nose, cheek-bones, lips or chin. It is purely psychic, just like the actor's, the soldier's, the minister's face."[19]

There can be little doubt that the quality of "looking Jewish" is completely lost by persons whose recent ancestors have abandoned Jewish culture for several generations. and who have themselves been raised in a non-Jewish culture. It is even lost, or is never developed, in Jews who have been socialized predominantly in a non-Jewish cultural environment.

What makes most persons or communities of persons visible or distinguishable as Jews is neither their physical appearance nor the fact of their adherence to the religion of Judaism, but certain cultural bodily traits which they have acquired in a Jewish cultural environment.

We have, then, a rather interesting situation: A person is never a Jew by virtue of belonging to some specific physical type, nor is a person necessarily recognizable as a Jew because he subscribes to the tenets of the Jewish faith; he is a Jew by religion, but in every other way he may be culturally non-Jewish. Finally, only those persons are recognizable as Jewish who exhibit certain behavioral traits commonly associated with Jews, yet such persons may not subscribe to the Jewish religion, but to some other religion or none at all.

We see, then, that actually it is membership in Jewish culture which makes a person a Jew, and nothing else, not even the adherence to Judaism.

One can distinguish many Jews from members of other cultural groups in the same way that it is possible to distinguish the English from such groups, or Americans, French, Italians, and Germans. Every cultural group differs in its way of life, from every other cultural group; and every cultural group shapes the behavior of each of its members according to its own ideas or pattern. Members of one cultural group do not readily fit into the pattern of another. Because of the complexities that characterize each separate pattern of culture, persons who have been brought up in one culture cannot and should not be expected to make a perfect adjustment to a different pattern of culture—however closely related the latter may be. Class differences are often very marked and recognizably so from an early age, and this goes not only for the way its members speak but also for the clothes they wear. In some societies to this day the combination of accent in speech and attire classifies a person beyond redemption. Even when individuals are anxious to free themselves from one culture and adopt, and become part of, another, such persons rarely, if ever, succeed in making a complete change; to some extent they may remain somewhat culturally disoriented. Once a cultural pattern has been woven, it is generally difficult to unravel it and weave a completely new one. The reason being that habits of behavior formed in early life become, in a real sense, part of one's second nature; it is notoriously difficult to disengage oneself from such habits in later life.

This, of course, explains why individuals of Jewish cultural background or persons of any other cultural background, try as they may, frequently fail to free themselves completely from the conditioning effects of that background.

What, in the case of individuals who are recognizable as Jews, are these conditioning effects that render them distinctive from other cultural groups? Before we attempt an answer to that question it must be emphasized that not all persons who have been brought up in a Jewish cultural environment exhibit Jewish cultural traits. There are many varieties and degrees of Jewish culture, some being much less complex than others, and a large proportion of them are modified by the culture in which the family or community happens to have lived for some generations. In addition, some individuals take rather more readily to the Gentile culture outside the home than they do to that within the home or local community, while others emancipate themselves early from the domestic cultural environment.

What distinguishes individuals who are recognizable as Jews from members of other groups is, of course, the addition of a certain cultural quality or flavor to their behavior. People habitually feel and think in certain culturally common ways, and such emotions and thoughts register themselves in the index which is provided by the sixteen muscles of expression of the face, not to mention the eyes.

Just as there is such a thing as an English, a German, a French, and Italian, and even an American cast of features, so there is such a thing as a Jewish cast of face. It is necessary to remember that the muscles of expression in the face are capable of producing an extraordinarily large number of different casts of countenance, in the same person as well as between the members of different cultures. This cast of face is often erroneously assumed to be biologically determined, but the fact is that it is culturally determined in precisely the manner which has been indicated.

Add to the culturally determined cast of face traditionally determined gesticulations of the face and body, character of speech, together with—in some parts of the world—certain similarly culturally determined preferences for color combinations, style, and total ensemble of clothes, and we have a powerful association of traits which can distinguish some Jews from non-Jews. That all these traits are culturally determined is readily proved by the fact that every last trace of them may be completely lost in a single generation following the adoption of a non-Jewish culture. That is, perhaps, most strikingly seen in many Anglo-Jewish and American-Jewish families.

There are few traits that are inherently objectionable, but certain differences in behavior exhibited by some Jews have been characterized by some who feel compelled to do so. Many of the traits which non-Jews find objectionable in Jews are the very traits upon which some of the latter pride themselves; resourcefulness, enterprise, and a certain audacity frequently labeled aggressiveness, as well as the habit of gesticulation, for example.

Centuries of dispossession, massacre, oppression, frustration, and discrimination forced upon many Jews the ineluctable development of a certain amount of enterprise or aggressiveness. Aggressiveness, under certain conditions, is a quality of considerable survival value, a form of adjustment. Oppression and frustration produce aggressiveness. It is a normal tendency of the human organism when it is frustrated, when it is made the object of aggression, to respond with counter aggression.[20] It may be pointed out that all drives or urges are in a sense aggressive, and in fact aggression has been described as that essential factor which provides a well-integrated personality with its necessary drive.

Arthur Koestler has one of his characters reflect, on the Jews, that they are

not an accident of race, but simply man's condition carried to its extreme—a branch of the species touched on the raw. Exiled in Egypt, in Babylon, and now over the whole globe, exposed to strange and hostile surroundings, they had to develop peculiar traits; they had no time or chance to grow that hide of complacency, of a specious security, which makes man insensitive to and forgetful of the tragic essence of his condition. They were the natural target of all malcontents, because they were so exasperatingly and abnormally human . . .

Made homeless in space, they had to expand into new dimensions, as the blind develop hearing and touch. The loss of the spatial dimension transformed this branch of the species as it would have transformed any other nation on earth, Jupiter or Mars. It turned their vision inwards. It made them cunning and grew them claws to cling on with as they were swept by the wind through the countries that were not theirs. It increased their spiritual arrogance: deprived of Space, they believed themselves chosen for eternity in Time. It increased the protective adaptability of their surface, and petrified their inner core. Constant friction polished their many facets: reduced to drift-sand, they had to glitter if they wanted to avoid being trodden on. Living in bondage, cringing became second nature to their pride. Their natural selector was the whip: it whipped the life out of the feeble and whipped the spasm of ambition into the fit. In all fields of living, to get an equal chance they had to start with a plus.

Condemned to live in extremes, they were in every respect like other people, only more so.[21]

Gesticulation is an Eastern trait, and no doubt a persisting cultural de-
rivative of the Eastern ancestry of much of Jewish culture. The gesticulations of many Jews are often seen as vulgar by peoples who are not given to
expressing themselves in any manner other than by speech "unadorned."
Such a judgment is, however, purely subjective. Many Jews regard their
habits of gesticulation as a kind of auxiliary language, without which they
are tongue-tied. Those who have studied these gestures find them very ex-
pressive indeed. Nevertheless, those who indulge in them are at once rendered identifiable as Jews, even though non-Jews may acquire the same
habits of gesticulation by association with Jews.

Interestingly enough, the gestures customarily used by many Jews have
been described as racially determined. Nothing could be further from the
truth. Scientific investigation of the gestural behavior of Eastern Jews and
Southern Italians living in New York City shows that the more members of
each of these groups becomes assimilated into the so-called "American-
ized" community the more do they lose the gestural traits associated with
the original group.[22] Gesture has no connection whatever with biological
factors, but merely represents a mode of expression conditioned by cultural conditions.

We see, then, that it is, indeed, not a difficult matter to distinguish
many Jews by means of certain traits which they exhibit; but it should also
be clear that those traits are all culturally determined and have no connection with inborn biological factors. Neither on physical nor on mental
grounds can Jews be distinguished as an ethnic group. With his usual
grace, in 1643, Sir Thomas Browne put the matter neatly some three and
one-half centuries ago. "Upon consult of reason," he wrote,

there will be found no easier assurance to fasten a material or temperamental propriety upon any nation; there being scarce any condition (but
what depends upon clime) which is not exhausted or obscured from the
commixture of introvenient nations either by commerce or conquest;
much more will it be difficult to make out this affection in the Jews; whose
race, however pretended to be pure, must needs have suffered inseparable commixture with nations of all sorts; not only in regard of their prose-
lytes, but their universal dispersion; some being posted from several parts
of the earth, others quite lost, and swallowed up in those nations where
they planted.[23]

How is it that there were men in the seventeenth century who were as
wise as Browne, and so few, comparatively, toward the end of the twentieth
century?

Reference may here be made to the oft-repeated assertion that Jews have a greater amount of brain power than other peoples. This assertion is not usually made in order to flatter Jews, but is rather urged as yet another count against them, because, it is held, owing to their superior brain power others are thereby placed at a disadvantage in competition with them.

Science knows of no evidence which would substantiate the claim that Jews or any other people have better brains than any other. This is not to say that such a difference may not exist; it may, but if it does, science has been unable to demonstrate it. The business acumen, the scholastic and the interpretative musical abilities of Jews have traditionally been encouraged in Jewish families. The life of the merchant has been forced upon Jews under the most unfavorable circumstances; under such conditions they have in each generation been forced to develop a sharpness of wit which would enable them to survive. Scholarship has been a revered tradition among Jews for many centuries; furthermore, it has, in the modern world, often been the one means the Jew had of raising himself socially or of escaping from the depressing conditions of life in the ghetto. It is a fact that in order to make his way in the world Jews had to offer a great deal more than anyone else. He had to be like other people, "only more so."[24]

It may be that owing to the great variety of intermixture that Jews have undergone, their considerable physical variability tends also to be exhibited in their mental capacities, that there may be a somewhat greater frequency of mentally well-endowed individuals among them. Whether this is so or not we cannot tell. In any event it would be of no great moment if we could, because it is not so much biological as cultural factors which, other things being more or less equal, determine the nature of a mind. As Boas has written:

> Our conclusion is that the claim to biologically determined mental qualities of races is not tenable. Much less have we a right to speak of biologically determined superiority of one race over another. Every race contains so many genetically distinct strains, and the social behavior is so entirely dependent upon the life experience to which every individual is exposed, that individuals of the same type when exposed to different surroundings will react quite differently, while individuals of different types when exposed to the same environment may react the same way.[25]

The facts, then, lead to the following conclusions: Owing to the original mixed ancestry of Jews and their subsequent history of intermixture with every people among whom they have lived and continue to live, Jews of different regions are neither genetically nor physically equivalent. In many countries in which they have lived for sometime, Jews closely resemble the general population in their physical traits, but many Jews may differ from that population in behavioral traits because they have been primarily socialized in a Jewish cultural environment rather than in that of the general population. As Huxley and Haddon have said: "The word Jew is valid more as a socio-religious or pseudo-national description than as an ethnic term in any genetic sense. Many 'Jewish' characteristics are without doubt much more the product of Jewish tradition and upbringing, and especially of reaction against external pressure and persecution, than of heredity."[26]

Jews would constitute a national group if they subscribed to the principle of Jewish nationality. Some Jews do, but these are the minority and not the majority. The majority are nationals of the country in which they were born or live. Some Jews, outside Israel, do subscribe to the principle of Jewish or Israeli nationality (not, in fact, the same things), but these are a minority, not the majority. Hearnshaw has spoken of nationality as "that principle compounded of past traditions, present interests and future aspirations which gives to a people a sense of organic unity and separates it from the rest of mankind." In this sense a proportion of Jews can be regarded as of Israeli nationality, namely, those who live in and regard themselves as citizens of Israel. But not all Israelis are Jews, and clearly the vast majority of Jews are not Israelis, although they may give support to an Israeli homeland for all Jews, quasi-Jews, and others, who wish to live in Israel.[27] It is by virtue of the traits of this quasi-Jewish national culture that a quasi-Jewish community may be said to exist, and that any person exhibiting these traits may be recognized as a Jew, whether he is an adherent of the Jewish religion or not. Such traits are not inborn, but acquired, and they have nothing whatever to do with biological or so-called racial factors. They are conditioned by culture alone. The Israeli people or nation should not be confused with the quasi-national Jews of the Diaspora. A large proportion of non-Jews of Arab-Islamic affiliation are citizens of the Israeli nation, while by far the majority of Jews are citizens, and will remain citizens, of other countries. Whether subscribers or not, Jews are identified with Judaism, nations by contrast are not identified with religion.[28]

There could, undoubtedly, be no better demonstration of the fact that the Jews are not a race or ethnic group than an inspection of the people of the Israeli nation. The variety of physical types represented among the Israeli Jews probably exceeds that to be found in almost any other land.

A Jewish physical type has been neither preserved nor transmitted down to the present day because such a "type" never existed; if such a type had existed it would long ago have been dissolved as a result of the subsequent intermixture of Jews with other peoples. What Jews have preserved and transmitted have been neither physical nor mental racial traits, but religious and cultural traditions and modes of conduct. The final conclusion is, then, that Jews are not and never have been a race or ethnic group, but that they are and always have been people of either Jewish faith or culture or both, widely dispersed among the nations of the earth and from the genetic point of view Jews are probably the most diverse of all known peoples.[29]

Notes

1. An historian writing in 1950 states that Disraeli "although Jewish by race was a practicing Christian." David Thomson, *England in the Nineteenth Century* (New York: Penguin Books, 1950), 107.

2. Samuel Kramer, *History Begins at Sumer* (New York: Doubleday, 1959); Gaalyahu Cornfield, *Archaeology of the Bible* (New York: Harper & Row, 1961); Leonard Cottrell, *The Anvil of Civilization* (New York: New American Library, 1957); G. Ernest Wright and David N. Freedman, eds., *The Biblical Archaeological Reader,* vol. 1 (New York: Anchor Books, 1961); David N. Freedman and Edward F. Campbell, Jr., *The Biblical Archaeological Reader,* vol. 2 (New York: Anchor Books, 1964); Sabatino Moscati, ed., *The Phoenecians* (New York: Abbeville Press, 1988).

3. D. L. Risdon, "A Study of the Cranial and Other Human Remains from Palestine Excavated at Tell Duweir (Lachish)," *Biometrika* 31 (1939): 99–166.

4. Malcolm Vivian Hay, *The Foot of Pride* (Boston: Beacon Press, 1950).

5. Carelton Coon, "Have the Jews a Racial Identity?" in *Jews in a Gentile World,* eds. I. Graeber and Steuart Britt (New York: Macmillan, 1942), 31.

6. Raphael Patai and Jennifer P. Wing, *The Myth of the Jewish Race* (New York: Scribner's, 1975); Paloma Diaz-mas, *Sephardim: The Jews from Spain* (Chicago: University of Chicago Press, 1992); Maurice Fishberg, *The Jews: A Study of Race and Environment* (New York: Schribner's, 1911); B[enzion] Netanyahu. *The Origins of the Inquisition in Fifteenth Century Spain* (New York: Random House, 1995).

7. Thus, in Daghestan in the Caucasus, only 7 percent of Jews showed light-colored eyes; among German Jews in Baden, however, this percentage rises to 51.2; in the city of Vienna the percentage was 30, in Poland 45 percent, but among the Samaritans of Jerusalem it is only 11.1 percent. It is the same with hair color. Among the Samaritans only 3.7 percent showed blond hair; in Italy the percentage rises to 11.8, in Romania to 14.7, to 17.9 in Hungary, 20.4 in England, and 29 in Lithuania. In the city of Riga, Latvia, the proportion was 36 percent. In Jerusalem Jewish Ashkenazi children showed 40 percent blonds and 30 percent blue eyes, while the Sephardim showed 10 percent blonds and even fewer blue eyes (see note 6 above).

8. Rudolf Virchow, "Gesammtbericht Über die von der deutschen anthropologischen Gesellschaft veranlassten Erhebungen Über die Farbe der Haut, der Haare und der Augen der Schulkinder in Deutschland," *Archiv für Anthropologie* 16 (1886): 275–475.

9. Fishberg, *The Jews,* 165–66.

10. The cephalic index numerically expresses the proportion of the breadth of the head in relation to its length; it is determined by multiplying the maximum breadth of the head by 100 and dividing that sum by the maximum length. The three indices thus yielded are: less than 76 points = longheaded (dolichocephalic),

76 to 80.9 points = medium-headed (mesocephalic), and over 81 points = broad-headed (brachycephalic).

11. Among London Ashkenazim one finds 25.3 percent of longheads (dolichocephals), 28.3 percent of moderately roundheads (mesocephals), and 47.4 percent of round- or broadheads (brachycephals); among South Russian Jews these figures are, respectively, 1, 18 and 81 percent; for London Sephardim these figures are 17 percent dolichocephalic and 34 percent brachycephalic; Galician and Lithuanian Jews yield a proportion of 85 percent brachycephals and only 3.8 percent dolichocephals. Patai and Wing, *Myth of the Jewish Race;* Diaz-mas, *Sephardim;* Fishberg, *The Jews.*

12. See A. E. Mourant, *The Distribution of the Human Blood Groups* (Springfield, IL: Thomas, 1954), 70–74; Patai and Wing, *Myth of the Jewish Race;* D. M. Dunlop, *The History of the Jewish Khazars* (New York: Schocken Books, 1967); Hugo von Kutschera, *Die Chazaren: Historische Studie,* 2nd ed. (Vienna: Adolf Holtzhausen, 1910).

13. H. V. Muhsam, "The Genetic Origin of the Jews," *Genus* 20 (1964): 53–54.

14. G. J. Siemens, "Anthropometric Effects of Recorded Cases of Miscegenation among Certain Caucasian Sub-Groups," *Ohio Journal of Science* 50 (1950): 45–52.

15. Hermann Struck, Jewish artist who specialized in rendering the heads of Jewish orthodox "types."

16. Magnus Hirschfeld, *Men and Women* (New York: Putnam, 1935), 277–78. Hirschfeld adds: "not pure, but mixed, races are a matter of course biologically. How, then, should there be 'pure' races among the whites when we consider that every individual possesses and united in himself a line of paternal and maternal ancestors embracing thousands, perhaps even hundreds of thousands of generations? How extraordinarily various must have been the mixture of genes over so long a period!"

17. Harry Johnston, *The Story of My Life* (Indianapolis: Bobbs-Merrill, 1943), 66–72.

18. E. Dennison Ross, *Both Ends of the Candle* (London: Faber & Faber, 1943), 72.

19. Fishberg, *The Jews,* 165–66.

20. See John Dollard et al., *Frustration and Aggression* (New Haven: Yale University Press, 1939).

21. Arthur Koestler, *Thieves in the Night* (New York: Macmillan, 1946), 355–56. Permission of The Macmillan Co.; Fishberg, *The Jews,* 163–67; P. Manteggazza, *Physiognomy and Expression* (New York: Scribner's, 1910).

22. David Efron, *Gesture, Race and Culture* (The Hague: Mouton, 1972); see also Weston La Barre, "The Cultural Basis of Emotions and Gestures," *Journal of Personality* 16 (1947), 49–68.

23. Thomas Browne, *Pseudodoxia Epidemica* 4.10 (London: Dod, 1646).

24. The American black, on the other hand, has, in the past, been forced to the opposite extreme. In order to succeed at all he must, as a rule, do worse than anyone else. He mustn't matter. See Abram Kardiner and Lionel Ovesey, *The Mark of Oppression* (New York: Norton, 1951).

25. Franz Boas, "Racial Purity," *Asia* 40 (1940): 234.

26. Julian Huxley and Alfred C. Haddon, *We Europeans* (New York: Harper & Bros., 1936), 73–74.

27. Milton Steinberg has suggested that the Jews may be recognized as a "minority nationality in Central and Eastern Europe, an emerging national in Palestine, and a religio-cultural group in Western democratic lands." *A Partisan Guide to the Jewish Problem* (New York: Bobbs-Merrill, 1945), 151. For other attempted definitions see Melville Herskovits, "Who are the Jews?" in *The Jews: Their History, Culture and Religion,* ed. Louis Finkelstein, 1151–71 (New York: Harper, 1949).

28. Erich Kahler, *The Jews Among the Nations* (New York: Ungar, 1967), 10.

29. These conclusions are fully supported by the definitive work on "The Myth of the Jewish Race" by Raphael Patai and Jennifer Wing, in their book of that title, published by Scribner's in 1975. Professor Patai is an anthropologist and Dr. Wing is a geneticist. Their conclusions were, in their own words, "(1) Jewish groups from different parts of the world are very different genetically; (2) Jews of a certain area tend to resemble the surrounding non-Jews more than they resemble Jews from other parts of the world; and (3) European Jews have a residue of non-European (Mediterranean) genes." Thus fully substantiating the conclusions drawn in this chapter.

18

The First Americans

Much of this chapter appeared as Chapter 16 of the 5th edition of *Man's Most Dangerous Myth*. Its focus was the social and economic problems faced by the American Indian as a direct result of the erroneous idea that the white European belonged to a "superior race," while the aboriginal peoples they encountered in America—Native Hawaiians, American Indians, and Alaskan Natives—were, as elsewhere, simply obstacles to be removed.

While living conditions of the American Indian, for example, have improved since the original writing, to quantify these changes has proved to be a difficult matter indeed, and far outside the scope of this present volume. In many cases the Native American[1] is a citizen of a nation within a nation, and therefore statistical data on various aspects of this group are frequently inadequate and inaccurate. The numbers proffered by agencies such as the U.S. Census, Bureau of Indian Affairs (BIA), and Indian Health Service (IHS) often do not reflect accurately the realities of this group of Americans.[2] Some of these statistics are included here, for they are illustrative of social and economic trends, but must be considered with caution. We have updated briefly some of the general themes of the original chapter, and encourage the interested reader to pursue a wide variety of the many contemporary sources.[3]

Native Americans represent the indigenous population of the United States. Yet for more than two centuries they have been aliens in their own land. Subjugated and ravaged by disease and force of arms, their homelands wrested from them, they have been dispossessed, displaced, and disparaged, and, in the case of the American Indian, confined to reservations. These tracts of land were useless to their conquerors—until oil or valuable minerals were discovered on them, at which point the inhabitants were again dispossessed and removed to still another unwholesome, federally-created ghetto.

Historical Perspective

The history of the American Indian presents a tragic picture of a mistreated, misunderstood, and misrepresented people. To speak of "the

American Indian's way of life" can be misleading, for there are many American Indian ways of life, each tribe having its own culture and usually its own distinctive language. Had the white man been prepared for it, he could have learned much that would have been of value to him from each of these cultures. Instead, he chose to take the view that, because these cultures were different and in other more material ways not as well developed as his own, they were inferior, and he had nothing whatever to learn from them; that, indeed, the sooner these cultures disappeared the better it would be for everyone.

This has been the view that the U.S. government and its officials have taken, in some respects even to the present day. The government's paralyzing paternalism has been psychologically and socially destructive to Native Americans, and created constant fear of the white man's authority, even in the form of the BIA.

In 1887 the Dawes Act, or General Allotment Act, was passed by the U.S. Congress to provide for the granting of individual landholdings to American Indians who would renounce their tribal holdings. Senator Teller in 1881 called Allotment, "a bill to despoil the Indians of their lands and make them vagabonds on the face of the earth." The act purportedly sought to absorb the Indians into the body politic of the nation, but what it led to was the widespread sale of lands to whites.

Barred from the best of their own world, Native Americans have been subjected to the worst of the white world, strangers in their own homeland—America's prisoners of war—a war of exploitation, massacre, and degradation. The shocking treatment of displaced American Indians by the federal government has constituted one of the most scandalous chapters in the history of the United States. Private and political greed were frequently the sole reason for this genocidal displacement of Indian tribes to unsuitable reservations, a practice that moved the great Sioux chief Spotted Tail to remark, with bitter irony, "Why does not the Great Father put his red children on wheels, so he can move them as he will?"

Displaced to land unfit for agriculture, forbidden to hunt, having had water rights stolen, having been exploited by Indian agents and traders, impoverished, restricted by lack of education and discouraged from leaving the reservation, the American Indians for many years truly were the "forgotten people" of America.

The wrongs and injustices committed against the American Indian stirred the conscience of many Americans, and Indian groups have not wanted for defenders.[4] Prominent among them have been, in many cases, the federally-appointed Indian commissioners. In 1879, Indian Commissioner G. W. Manypenny, in his book *Our Indian Wards* (1879), shocked the nation with his revelations. Shortly afterward Helen Hunt Jackson's book *A Century of Dishonor* (1881) created an even greater sensation with her excoriating account of the U.S. government's inhumane treatment of Indian tribes. Her famous novel on the same subject, *Ramona* (1884) (which became a play, a movie, and a song, all of them popular in their day and well into the twentieth century), presented even more dramatically the challenges faced by Indian People. But the public had a short memory, and while the lot of the Native American has improved, in some ways it is not much better than it was more than a century ago.

In 1924, with the passage of a citizenship act, the U.S. government affirmed the Native American's citizenship and right to full political equality. In 1934 Congress passed the Indian Reorganization Act, which laid the groundwork for democratic self-government on Indian reservations. Arizona and New Mexico were the last states to grant voting rights to American Indians until the right was confirmed in the courts in 1948. In 1946 Congress enacted the Indian Claims Commission Act, thus acknowledging the country's debt to the various Indian tribes for the lands from which they were dispossessed.[5] To this day many of those claims have not been paid. A Senate subcommittee on Indian education was created by Congress in 1967; additional measures were suggested by U.S. presidents Lyndon B. Johnson in 1968, and Richard Nixon in 1969, 1970, and 1971.

The Failure of an Education Program

The reservation constituted a federally created and perpetuated ghetto worsened by the government's failure to understand the elementary requirements of the people it so miserably contains. One of the ways in which the BIA's early efforts led to disaster is illustrated by the tragically misguided attempts at education. Perhaps in no other area was the federal government's failure more massive than in its utterly inappropriate educational programs. A closer look at this failure reveals a complete lack of comprehension of the meaning of cultural differences.[6]

For many years it was the practice of the federal government to take American Indian children, some as young as three years old, and commonly by the age of four and five, out of their homes and send them many miles away to boarding schools. When the children arrived at the government boarding schools, some as far away as 800 miles from home, their hair was cut, their clothing destroyed, and they were punished for speaking their native language. According to the figures of the BIA, in fiscal 1967 an estimated 51,234 Aleut, Eskimo, and Indian children attended bureau schools; of these, 34,804 were in boarding schools. An additional 4,268 children were living in dormitories while attending public schools. Neither the children nor the parents wanted to be separated, and these separations worked the worst kind of hardships on both. Even if the schools were excellent, which usually they were not, such separation was highly undesirable. We now know how very damaging these early separations were to the children, who came from a culture in which the family unit was and is traditionally very close. Each year Indian families would attempt to hide their children from the Indian agents and Army soldiers who were sent to "round them up." In one instance several Hopi men who refused to turn their children over were sent to Alcatraz Island.[7] The Indian family today remains a tightly knit unit, for example, 37 percent of American Indian households are married couples with children, versus 28 percent of non-Indian households.[8]

The damage of the separation was compounded when American Indian children were taught that their own culture and language were bad and that the dominant, white culture was superior. They were not allowed to carry out any religious or cultural ceremony or practice. Their most sacred institution, the family, was belittled, and Indian parents often lost the respect of their children. These long separations were barbaric and inhuman, and the kind of education the child was subjected to in the boarding schools—far from improving conditions for American Indians—only tended to worsen them, for that education tended to produce individuals who did not know who they were or where they were going.

The "Crossover Phenomenon"

The textbooks used in the schools contained no reference to the objects and things with which the Indian child was familiar, or to anything, indeed, with which they could identify; nothing about local geography or the traditions, myths, folklore, language, or history of their own people. The children were instructed in such a manner that they were made to feel not only that these things were unimportant, but also best treated as if they did not exist. The children were instructed in the "superior" culture, the white man's culture, and by implication made to feel that their own was something to be ashamed of. In short, the attempt was deliberately made to "de-Indianize" them, that is, "kill the Indian and save the child." And this, indeed, was long the policy of the BIA. It is a policy that never worked anything other than harm. It is a policy against which many American Indians, through their leaders, protested.

The academic failure pattern of the Indian student was so consistently uniform and well documented that it came to be known as the "crossover phenomenon." This is how it worked: For the first few grades in school the students kept pace with their white classmates. But between the fourth and seventh grades they began to fall behind, and by the time they were high school seniors they were, on the average, two and a half years behind their grade level, having made essentially no improvement from when they entered high school. The longer the Native American youth stayed in school the farther he or she fell behind in academic achievement. Only 1 percent of those who entered a federally run boarding school ever graduated from college.

The explanation of this crossover from relative performance to clearcut nonperformance is obviously not found in any differences in biological capacity for learning. The academic failure of Indian children in the adolescent years has been and, when schooling is inadequate, remains quite clearly due to the disorienting effects of the clash between the middle-class white values of the classroom and the values of the American Indian family.

When the values and attitudes the Indian child was taught at school bear no relation to those taught at home, the children were in effect suspended between two cultures. Confused and disoriented they become dissociated from both. Faced with the difficult task of choosing, many retreated altogether from their unbearable situation, falling into apathy, passivity, and depression. Without any aspiration toward achievement, many suffered the fate of the imageless individual—alienation from themselves and from a world they never made, a loss of identity and a resort to alcohol and drugs.

The refusal to accept the fact that Indian children had a right to their rich cultural heritage resulted in generations of miseducation and deepening debasement and depression of many lives. The net effect of the attempt to educate the Indian as a white man was a virtually complete cultural and personal disorientation, with profound effects on the individual and his or her culture.

The Present

The number of Native Americans recorded by the census of 1960 was reported to be 551,669. This figure, however, almost certainly represented a gross underestimate—in 1967 the National Congress of American Indians put the number at about one million. In 1980 it was about 1,200,000 and growing at the rate of 3.5% per year. The American Indian population has risen sixfold over the past four decades, to over two million in 1990, again an underestimate, 60 percent of whom live in tribal areas or in the surrounding counties.[9]

Today there are at least 557 federally-recognized American Indian tribes in the United States, including 230 Alaskan villages.[10] There are also about 135 American Indian groups consisting of more than 70,000 people without any Federal protection whatever. Professor of anthropology William A. Stearnes at Oneonta College, State University of New York, has eloquently described the conditions of these Americans in the following communication to the *New York Times* (5 September 1995),

In 1978 the Department of Interior pre-empted Congress's legislative prerogative and issued regulations by which Indian groups could petition for Federal tribal status.

A petitioning tribe is required to submit extensive documentation of its history, its social and political organization, and its ancestry. This information is evaluated by bureau staff members, who make a recommendation to the Assistant Secretary of Indian Affairs. Fewer than half of the petitioning tribes have successfully negotiated this process.

Tribes deserve a fair and competent evaluation of their petitions. Yet the most recent decisions on Federal Tribal status reflect a return to 19th century scientific racism, which promises dire consequences for many Indian people. In its evaluation of petitions, the Bureau of Indian Affairs has disparaged or ignored the work of social scientists and has rewritten standard histories.

The bureau argues instead that genealogy alone is the key to determining who is an Indian and what is an Indian tribe. And it unjustly rejects claims of Indian identity by demonstrating the presence of African or European ancestors in the family line of petitioning groups, information that is frequently derived from Jim Crow-era records.

The bureau remains insensible to the fact that Indians, especially in the south, had no control over how they were categorized racially. It would correct this oversight and spare us another form of cultural eradication by developing an understanding of what constitutes Indian-ness, something it has chosen not to do.

Many American Indian tribes with or without federal recognition, are still living in the direst poverty. Water rights, while upheld by the federal government though the U.S. Supreme Court, are still denied American Indians by individual states and organizations such as sportfishing groups. This problem is particularly acute in the west, where the issues of water being siphoned off the Colorado River—part of which belongs to Indian people—have yet to be resolved. And while voting about $3 billion dollars every year for meeting the government's treaty obligations with American Indian tribes, 90¢ of every dollar is siphoned off in bureaucratic waste of various sorts.[11]

Education

In 1934 the Indian Reorganization Act introduced the teaching of Indian History and culture into BIA schools, reversing the government's previous policy of "full assimilation and eradication of Indian culture."[12] The Indian Self-Determination and Education Act of 1975 gave tribes the authority to contract with the BIA in the operation of schools and to determine educational programs. The Educational Amendments Act mandated major changes in Indian schools, including empowering school boards, providing for local teachers, and direct school funding.

In 1995–96, the BIA reports having funded 187 various educational facilities. These included 116 day schools, 50 boarding schools on the reservations, 7 boarding schools off-reservation, and 14 dormitories. Most of the schools are operated by tribes or school boards and funded through the Education Amendments Act of 1978.[13] There were over 47,000 children enrolled in these schools and dormitories in the fiscal year ending 1996. The BIA also reports that more than 270,000 students in public schools were assisted by BIA funds provided by the Johnson-O'Malley Act of 1943.[14]

The BIA also estimates that more then 70,000 American Indian students attended colleges and universities in that year, 15,000 of whom received BIA grants for assistance with their fees.[15] There are also 24 tribally-controlled colleges, serving about 25,000 students and receiving about $28 million in BIA funds. The two BIA-operated post secondary schools, in Kansas and New Mexico, were funded at about $11 million and served 1,346 students for the same year.

The BIA provided financial support for the educational and other costs for 473 children in 24-hour institutional care, and served over nine thousand students under the Individuals with Disabilities Education (IDEA) Program.

The BIA's Family and Child Education (FACE) Program serves children 0–8 years old and their parents and caregivers. Since its inception in 1993 the BIA estimates that over 5,300 individuals have been served by this program, and that 200 adults received GED's or high school diplomas, and over 400 adults gained employment during their participation in FACE in 1995–96. That year the program received $7.5 million in funds for its operation.

Yet, even considering the many gains in the area of education for the American Indian, only 66 percent of Indian children graduate high school. And while more than 60 percent of these graduates enroll in some form of higher education, some estimate that only one in four complete their chosen program.[16] These numbers are well below the national average.

The "crossover phenomenon" described earlier in this chapter continues, though it is far better understood now than in the early days of the boarding schools. Studies of learning styles among American Indian and Alaskan Native children reveal that cultural values and early socialization experiences affect the way these children learn in the classroom. "The norms of their culture helped explain why the children were reluctant to speak in front of their classmates . . . for many Native children, a public display that violates community or group norms may be an uncomfortable experience. Perhaps it is this respect for norms that is responsible for the stereotypic 'silent Indian' child."[17] Further, many of these children come from a society in which, "the humility of the individual is a position to be respected and preserved. Advancing oneself above others or taking oneself too seriously violates this key value. If native children learn best cooperatively, they will experience discomfort and conflicts in classrooms that are too competitive or in which the competition is unfair."[18] This situation is being reversed, albeit slowly, as non-Indian teachers increase their awareness of these issues, and as more Indian teachers make their way into the schools and replace inappropriate teaching skills and methods with teaching style that are more in keeping with their students' needs.

American Indian elders, parents, and students must continue to have a strong voice in determining what shall go on in these schools. The damage wrought by years of institutionalized belittling of the American Indian experience will not soon be eradicated by the new schools, it will take time. But the time is long overdue for Native Americans to take their rightful place as individuals, as members of an ancient culture, and as U.S. citizens with a unique contribution to bring to the land of their birth.

Economic and Social Issues

American Indians remain the nation's poorest group, over 60 percent of reservation families and 31 percent of non-reservation families live below the poverty level, two to five times the national average. The Indian Health Service reports per capita income at $3–7000, one-third the national average. The unemployment rate is approximately 40 percent on the reservation; three to five times the national average. On many reservations the unemployment rate is 100 percent.

American Indians still have a higher unemployment rate (40 percent versus the national average of 6 percent), a smaller number of workers per thousand employed in "for profit" firms (255 versus 362), and a higher share of households with very low incomes (33 percent versus 24 percent). Fully forty percent of American Indians in tribal areas live in overcrowded or inadequate housing compared with 6 percent of the non-Indian population.[19]

The consequences of these conditions are not lost on those who provide health care on the reservation. The Indian Health Service reports that, while the birth rate is twice the U.S. average, the statistics for disease and death are also high.[20] Fetal Alcohol Syndrome is reported at 33 times the national average, alcohol-related deaths are up to 10 times the national average. The incidence of teen suicide and diabetes are 4 and 3 times the national average, respectively. Tuberculosis, which once ravaged the Indian population, is today somewhat under control, but still the Indian rate of incidence is at least eight times that of the general population.[21] Mortality due to influenza and pneumonia among Native Americans is still higher than reported for the general population.

In addition to these problems, there persists the problem of identity, not self-identity as in the past, but instead how to fit into the larger whole,

Many of the problems faced by Native Americans can be traced back to the conflicts between their desire to perpetuate their cultural heritage and the pressure to assimilate into the larger society. All ethnic groups wrestle with this conflict to some extent. A complicating factor for native Americans is that there is an incredible diversity of cultures that falls into the category of Native American. Rather than preserving one language and way of life, they must preserve hundreds of relatively complete cultures. The current generation of American Indian and Alaskan Native youth have a genuine choice between being proud to be an American and being proud to be a Native. . . . Or (and this is the more complex choice) they can lead lives that include productive elements of both. Given the pluralistic American tradition, many share the hope that Indian youth will find ways to do the latter, both for the sake of their fulfillment as individuals and for the enrichment of American society."[22]

Conclusion

There is no doubt that there have been improvements in many of the areas addressed in this chapter. In addition to the funding from Indian gaming, which has certainly alleviated conditions on many, but not all, reservations, there has also been an increase in Indian college graduates returning to the reservation to help their people. All this is taking place within the context of increased awareness on the part of both Indians and non-Indians.

Clearly more is required: education and constant reevaluation of the Native American situation and the design of ever better educational measures suited to their needs. It is the considered opinion of most of those who have worked with American Indians that what is needed is a well-funded curriculum that fits comfortably into the matrix of Indian culture, an educational experience that helps them adjust to their own changing culture, rather than exclusively to a culture that is alien to them. Native Americans need an experience in which education in their own culture constitutes a dominant motif, while at the same time they are prepared to meet the challenges of white American culture in a practical and harmonious manner.

For many years, Native Americans were, for the most part, silenced, the dominant culture being unwilling to take notice of their many problems, preferring instead to consider them taciturn—and preferring, in fact, to look the other way. But in recent years, under the pressure and unendurable weight of accumulated wrongs, they have begun to speak up. A new and unfamiliar voice continues to be heard in the land, gently, firmly, clearly, and increasingly louder. The voices continue to grow in number, volume, and influence. At the present time most of those speaking are young college-trained Native Americans who, looking back over the history of their people's relations with the government of the United States, and the consequences for all Americans, have resolved that the course of that history must be changed, and changed by the active involvement of Native Americans in the government of their own affairs. The prominent and admirably articulate representatives include Vine Deloria, Jr., a Lakota and former director of the National Congress of American Indians, whose forceful, eloquent, and witty books should be required reading—they are *Custer Died for Your Sins, The Trail of Broken Treaties, God is Red,* and *We Talk, You Listen;* Mel Thom of the Paiute tribe; Raymond Nakai, of the Navajo tribe, with over 250,000 members; and others. Indeed, the results are a widely discernible and continually rising Native American movement, a revolt against the white man's culture and its debasement of Native American culture.[23]

The Native American is becoming conscious of what many Americans have long forgotten—that government is the people, and therefore all individuals must make themselves responsible insofar as they are able for the government they desire. As U.S. citizens Native Hawaiians, Alaska Natives, and American Indians are beginning to appreciate the power of the vote and their right to be heard. They no longer considered themselves wards of the state,[24] and they are more than ever averse to every form of paternalism. The new leaders are resolved to see that justice is at long last given to their people and to enable Native Americans not only to take pride in their heritage, but also to bring the benefits of their life ways to all Americans.

As Vine Deloria, Jr., so eloquently put it many years ago, "It isn't important that there are only 500,000 of us Indians. What is important is that we have a superior way of life. We Indians have a more human philosophy of life. We Indians will show this country how to act human. Someday this country will revise it constitution, its laws, in terms of human beings, instead of property. If Red Power is to be a power in this country it is because it is ideological. The question is," he went on to say, "what is the nature of life? . . . What is the ultimate value of man's life? That is the question."[25]

Native Americans have made many adjustments and compromises, and rightly believe it is time that other Americans recognize their rights and respect their culture.

A Declaration with a Familiar Ring

These demands were clearly set out in the Declaration of the Five County Cherokee of Oklahoma. Those Americans who retain a decent consideration for the opinions of others will note with respect and admiration a close resemblance to the Declaration of Independence. The Cherokee declaration spoke for the Cherokee Indians, but speaks also for all Native Americans. The declarations says in part:

Now we shall not rest until we have regained our rightful place. We shall tell our young people what we know. We shall send them to the corners of the earth to learn more. They shall lead us. Now, we have much to do. When our task is done, we will be ready to rest. In these days, intruders, named without our consent, speak for the Cherokee. When the Cherokee government is the Cherokee people, we shall rest.

In these days, we are informed of the decisions other people have made about our destiny. When we control our destiny, we shall rest.

In these days, the High Courts of the United States listen to people who have been wronged. When our wrongs have been judged in these courts, and the illegalities of the past have been corrected, we shall rest.

In these days, there are countless ways by which people make their grievances known to all Americans. When we have learned these new ways that bring strength and power, and we have used them, we shall rest.

In these days, we are losing our homes and our children's homes. When our homeland is protected, for ourselves and for the generations to follow, we shall rest.

In the vision of our creator, we declare ourselves ready to stand proudly among the nationalities of these United States of America.

This is a beautiful and moving testament of a people's cry for justice. The leaders of the Native Americans no longer support institutions and practices that have proved so destructive. They will no longer subscribe to the fatalism of unrealistic alternatives in which the Native American has been so long imprisoned. Instead their goal is to teach their people how to confront directly the realities with which they are faced, and which they are capable of mastering. These young American leaders have just begun.

Notes

1. The term "Native American" is used in the context of this chapter to collectively refer to American Indians, Alaskan Natives, and Native Hawaiians. The reader is cautioned that these are not necessarily the terms chosen by these groups or their individual members to describe themselves, but are the convention at present and are used as such here.

2. For example, "there is no single definition of an Indian. The BIA considers a member of a recognized Indian tribe or an individual of one-quarter or more of Indian descent, as an Indian. The Department of Defense uses a more comprehensive term, *American Indian* or *Alaskan Native,* to describe a person who has origins in the original peoples of North America and who maintains cultural identification through tribal affiliation or community recognition. The Bureau of the Census uses self-identification." *A Review of Data on Native Americans,* Defense Equal Opportunity Management Institute (DOEMI) (Los Angeles Air force Station, September 1990).

3. Duane Champagne, *Native North American Almanac* (Detroit: Gale Research, Inc., 1994); Duane Champagne, *Native America—Portrait of the Peoples* (Detroit: Visible Ink Press, 1994); Duane Champagne, *Chronology of Native North American History* (Detroit: Gale Research, Inc., 1995); Ward Churchill, *Since Predator Came—Notes from the Struggle for American Indian Liberation* (Littleton, CO: Aigis Publications); Mary B. Davis, ed., *Native America in the Twentieth Century: An Encyclopedia* (New York: Garland, 1996); John Ehle, *Trail of Tears: The Rise and Fall of the Cherokee Nation* (New York: Doubleday, 1988); David H. Getches, Charles F. Wilkinson, and Robert A. Williams, Jr., *Federal Indian Law: Cases and Materials*, 3rd ed., (St. Paul, MN: West Publishing, 1993); Susan Guyette, *Planning for Balanced Development—A Guide for Native American Communities*, Sponsored by the Pueblo of Pojoaque (Santa Fe: Clear Light Publications, 1996); Brian M. Fagan, *The Great Journey: The Peopling of Ancient America* (New York: Thames & Hudson, 1987); M. Annette Jaimes, *The State of Native America: Genocide, Colonization, and Resistance* (Boston: South End Press, 1992); Alvin Josephy, *Now that the Buffalo's Gone* (Norman: University of Oklahoma Press, 1989); Barry T. Klein, *Reference Encyclopedia of the American Indian*, 7th ed. (West Nyak, NY: Todd, 1995); Sidner J. Larson, *Catch Colt* (Lincoln: University of Nebraska Press, 1995); Peter Nabakov, ed., *Native American Testimony* (New York: Viking Penguin, 1991); Joane Nagel, *American Indian Ethnic Renewal* (Cambridge: Oxford University Press, 1996); Richard J. Perry, *From Time Immemorial: Indigenous Peoples and State Systems* (Austin: University of Texas Press, 1996); George L. Russell, *American Indian Digest* (Phoenix: Thunderbird Enterprises, 1994); *Smoke Rising: The Native North American Literary Companion* (Detroit, MI: Visible Ink Press, 1995); David E. Stannart, *American Holocaust* (Cambridge: Oxford University Press, 1992); Jack Utter, *American Indians: Answers to Today's Questions* (Lake Ann, MI: National Woodlands Publishing, 1993); Reader's Digest, *Through Indian Eyes, The Untold Story of Native American Peoples* (Pleasantville, New York, 1995).

4. See Wilbur R. Jacobs, *Dispossessing the American Indian* (New York: Scribner's Sons, 1972); Dale Van Every, *Disinherited: The Lost Birthright of the American Indian* (New York: William Morrow, 1966); Jay David, ed., *The American Indian: The First Victim* (New York: William Morrow, 1972); Wayne Moquin and Charles van Doren, eds., *Great Documents in American Indian History* (New York: Praeger, 1973); Virginia Armstrong, ed., *I Have Spoken: American History Through the Voices of the Indians* (Chicago: Swallow Press, 1971); Virgil J. Vogel, ed., *This Country Was Ours* (New York: Harper & Row, 1972); Angie Debo, *And Still the Waters Run* (Princeton: Princeton University Press, 1972); George W. Manypenny, *Our Indian Wards* (Cincinnati: Robert Clarke & Co., 1880; reprinted New York: Praeger Publishers, 1973); William G. McLoughlin, *Champions of the Cherokees: Evan and John B. Jones* (Princeton: Princeton University Press, 1990); Robert F. Berkofer, Jr., *The White Man's Indian* (New York: Knopf, 1978); Roy W. Meyer, *History of the Santee Sioux: United States Indian Policy on Trial* (Lincoln: University of Nebraska Press, 1967); William Brandon, *The Last Americans: The Indian in American Culture* (New York: McGraw-Hill, 1974); Edgar S. Cahn and David W. Hearne, eds., *Our Brother's Keeper: The Indian in White America* (New York: New American Library, 1975); Vine Deloria, Jr., *God Is Red* (New York: Grosset & Dunlap, 1973); Vine Deloria, Jr., *Behind the Trail of Broken Treaties* (New York: Delacorte, 1974); Vine Deloria, Jr., *We Talk, You Listen* (New York:

Macmillan, 1970); Vine Deloria, Jr., *American Indian Policy in the Twentieth Century* (Norman: University of Oklahoma Press, 1995).

5. Office of Indian Education Programs. Bureau of Indian Affairs, U.S. Department of the Interior Annual Education Report 1993, Washington, D.C.

6. Washburn, Wilcomb E., *Red Man's Land—White Man's Law*.

7. Troy Johnson, personal communication. Dr. Johnson, Associate Professor of History and American Indian Studies at California State University, Long Beach, kindly reviewed this chapter and his extensive comments are most appreciated.

8. HUD, *Native American Housing: Challenges facing HUD's Indian Housing Program* (12 March 1997).

9. HUD, ibid.

10. BIA, 1997.

11. Rapid City: American Indian Relief Council, 1997.

12. BIA, *Title II: BIA Educational Programs* (Washington, DC: U.S. Department of the Interior, 1997).

13. BIA, ibid.

14. Ibid.

15. Ibid.

16. Robert Well, cited in *The Demographics of American Indians*, by Harold L. Hodgkinson, 24 (Washington, D.C.: Institute for Educational Leadership, 1990). *The American Indian College Annual Report* (1995) states that 90 percent of Native American students who leave the reservation for college drop out, while at the 29 Indian Colleges and Universities the reverse is the case; these institutions report a 90 percent success rate.

17. Karen Swisher, *American Indian/Alaskan Native Learning Styles: Research and Practice*, ERIC Digest 335175 (Charleston: ERIC Clearinghouse on Rural Education and Small Schools, 1991).

18. Ibid.

19. HUD, *Native American Housing*.

20. IHS statistics only consider those individuals who seek help from medical doctors rather than traditional healers.

21. Indian Health Service, *1997 Report*.

22. Harold Hodgkinson, *The Current Condition of Native Americans*, ERIC Digest 348202 (Charleston: ERIC Clearinghouse on Rural Education and Small Schools, 1992).

23. Stan Steiner, *The New Indians* (New York: Harper & Row, 1968).

24. In a strict legal sense, the ruling by John Marshall in the case of The Cherokee Nation *v.* Georgia, the relationship between the government and the Indian people is as government to ward. This ruling remains in effect, but self-determination is more becoming the reality.

25. Vine Deloria, Jr., *Custer Died for Your Sins* (New York: Macmillan, 1969); *God is Red; Behind the Trail of Broken Treaties; We Talk, You Listen*.

19

The Meaning of
Equal Opportunity

In a period when equality of opportunity, in a culture of inequality, is at long last coming to be accepted as a practical idea, it is more than ever necessary to be alerted to certain problems that are bound to develop and that are likely to be with us for some time. Black children, and children of Puerto Rican, Mexican, and Native American descent, as well as others, will increasingly continue to find themselves in schools and in other situations in which they will not, on the whole, do as well as white children. Nor, on the whole, will members of these ethnic groups continue to do as well in open competition in the marketplace as whites.

In schools and colleges the trend will continue for some time, among some of these non-establishment groups, to lag substantially behind in the deleterious IQ tests and in school performance, as well as in general achievement. In view of these probabilities, everyone concerned must understand what that lag almost certainly means, in order to guard against the danger of drawing the wrong conclusions.

Observe, it will be said by some, the non-establishment groups (especially blacks) now enjoy equal opportunities for education, and yet after years of exposure have not produced the great scientists, inventors, poets, painters, philosophers, as has the dominant, white, culture. Some will still ask: Does not this lack of achievement, under conditions of equal opportunity, fully and at long last, suggest genetic inferiority?

The answer is, that while it may seem so, the probabilities are that the so-called failure to achieve equally under conditions of "equal opportunity" is due to environmental rather than to genetic deficiencies. For this conclusion there exists a considerable amount of evidence, much of which we have already discussed in the preceding pages, and which we shall consider further in what follows.

It is easy to attribute differences in achievement, especially scholastic achievement, to differences in innate endowment, to heredity. But the heredity of the individual represents the expression of the interpenetration gene interactions, the environments in which those genes have undergone development, and the psychic environments resulting from the individual's own behavior.[1]

These interpentrations, the genetic, the social, and the organismic, are proceeding at one and the same time. Clearly, then, the sequences of environments must always be considered as a major factor when attempting to assess influences operative in the expression of any trait. The meaning of this statement does not always appear to have been understood by those who have drawn conclusions about "genetic inferiority." There is good reason to believe that what most of us have regarded as "equal opportunities," that is, the process of providing the young of different ethnic groups with the same conditions for learning and intellectual development have, in fact, never existed. Never existed for the simple reason that those opportunities are unequally afforded and received. The unequal reception, the evidence suggests, is due not to group genetic differences, but to group cultural differences, to culturally produced impediments to learning and thought at comparatively equal levels of abstraction.[2]

For high, even adequate, intellectual achievement certain prerequisite conditions are apparently necessary, quite unrelated to the quality of the genetic potentialities of the individual. The necessary conditions are complex, but may be briefly described as a stimulating cultural environment which encourages high aspiration levels. A black child from the inner city in the same classroom with a white child from a similar socioeconomic background is not enjoying equal opportunities in the classroom for the simple reason that the black child is not in a position to experience much of what he or she is being exposed to as relevant to himself, or herself. The school generally offers little that many non-white children can incorporate into the background of their own culture. Often, a non-white child's cultural group has differing perspectives on learning or abstract thought. The idea of achievement in the sciences, philosophy, and the humanities, not to mention ordinary school work may take a back seat to simple survival.[3]

Sadly, many black children come not only from a life of poverty, but from a poverty of hope, where inequality, stifled lives and dreams, broken homes, fatherlessness, and myriad other problems render them altogether lacking a framework within which to fit the ordinates to which they are being exposed. For many, much of what they learn is for the most part unachievable and meaningless, because they lack the means to put it together into a meaningful coordinate system. The individual, it seems, must be rooted in a three- or four-dimensional cultural matrix through the ordinates of which he or she can meaningfully incorporate, learn, what is being taught and ultimately become an integrated human being.

It is not pointed out often enough that every individual must learn to learn, and that a great part of this is accomplished by the kind of stimulation received in the home, in relationships with parents and siblings, long before the child gets to school. Children will learn in school in a manner largely influenced by the kind of learning they have experienced at home. Here many white children enjoy immense advantages over many non-white children. For example, by the time many poor black children arrive at school they have often suffered the kinds of deprivations that have resulted not only in a serious failure of development of their learning capacities, but also in their ability to assimilate what they do learn in anything like the meaningful context and manner in which the white child is able to learn.

The kind of changes that must occur before underprivileged children can enter the classroom on an equal footing with, and as prepared to learn as white children, are complex. These changes probably belong in the same category as those operative in many societies in which peoples of very different cultural backgrounds have come together without the more highly developed one, after many centuries, seeming to have any significant effect in stimulating the creativity of the acculturated group. I have already discussed this phenomenon in Chapter 10. Apparently certain specific conditions must be present in every culture before the latent potentialities for achievement in each population can be expressed.

What are these necessary conditions? They are no longer a matter of conjecture, but on the basis of increasing evidence may be dependably deduced and indicated. The conditions necessary for achievement in any society are: (1) a cultural background of respect for achievement in the family in which the child has been raised; (2) encouragements and rewards within the family and the culture that enable the individual to acquire whatever is necessary for achievement in an achieving society; (3) a society in which the conditions of individual development have not physically affected learning ability. Nutritional deficiencies during fetal development affect large numbers of brain cells, and thus similarly affect the child's ability to learn. During infancy or childhood, nutritional deficiencies may produce developmental delays, and thus seriously affect the child's ability to learn. Formerly, such developmental delays were viewed as "damage" to the brain, but it is now known that such delays are not due to an irreversible change, and that under the influence of improved conditions are no impediment to healthy development. Delayed development is qualitative, *not* quantitative or anatomical, and it is not irreversible.[4]

The effects of some diseases during the early stages of development, prenatal and postnatal, can be equally disturbing. Nutritional deficiencies, especially protein deficiencies, as well as deficiencies induced by disease, are widespread throughout the world. The combination of such factors as: (1) the continuous and demanding struggle for existence; (2) the debilitating effects of disease; and (3) the severity of malnutrition would limit the members of any population from achieving very much more than was necessary for bare survival. Add to this combination of factors those which continue to exist for many contemporary populations: (4) the absence of any cultural identity; and (5) lack of encouragements, rewards, incentives, motivations, and aspirations for extraordinary achievement, and we have the necessary and sufficient conditions for ensuring the nondevelopment of any and all potentialities for extraordinary or even ordinary accomplishment.

Potentialities require the proper nurturing environmental conditions if they are to grow and develop and find appropriate expression. The expression of any capacity requires opportunities which stimulate the capacities to develop into abilities. Human development is not simply a matter of the unfolding of genetic potentialities but principally a matter of the cumulative, active process of utilizing environmental inputs. The adequate utilization of those inputs depends upon the environmental opportunities afforded the utilizing mechanisms, that is, the genetic potentials. The joker in that pack is, of course, the word "opportunities."

What are "opportunities"? What most civilized peoples—comprising a great mass of socially undeveloped people living in their midst, who have been deprived of their birthright of development as mentally healthy human beings—have interpreted "opportunities" to mean is the hypocritically simplistic notion that political, legal, and educational rights somehow ensure the freedom to enjoy equal rights in everything else. This is, of course, untrue. The laws on the books assuring equal political, legal and educational rights to all citizens are, in practice, differentially applied and enforced. Equal laws do not in practice work out either as equality before the law or equality of opportunity. Prejudice and discrimination operate to maintain impassable barriers against the subclasses who, as I pointed out many years ago, are treated as members of a lower caste.[5]

In the deprived and depressed conditions under which members of such subclasses or castes are forced to live they are deprived of the greatest of all opportunities: *the opportunity to learn to respond with advantage to available opportunities.* The absence of this basic opportunity, by whatever means produced, seriously interferes with the *ability* to respond to the available opportunities.

The basic opportunity necessary for all human beings if they are to realize their potentialities is made up of the obverse of those factors I described as responsible for the lack of high achievement. The ingredients of basic opportunity, necessary for achievement, then, are: (1) freedom from the continuous pressure to survive, that is, the enjoyment of a certain amount of leisure; (2) good health or relative freedom from disease during fetal and childhood development; (3) freedom from the effects of malnutrition during fetal, childhood, and adult development; (4) growth and development in an environment whose cultural identity makes the world intelligible and meaningful. If the traditional roots are deep and extensive, and the cultural background rich and multidimensional, the child will have within him- or herself what used to be called "an apperceptive mass" which will enable him or her to respond with advantage to the larger environment. If, on the other hand, traditional roots are shallow or nonexistent and the cultural background arid or confusing, the child will be unable to take root and develop in what remains an essentially inhospitable environment. Finally, (5) for creativity and achievement: encouragement and nurturing of high aspiration levels, the fueling and development of incentives, and the promise and experience of rewards.

Genius or high achievement remains an unexpressed potentiality in the absence of these conditions. In order to start its motors running not only is the fuel necessary, the opportunities, but the fuel must be ignited, and that is accomplished not merely by turning the key, but by ensuring the presence of an adequately charged battery, the basic opportunity: that is, again, the opportunity to learn to respond with advantage to the available opportunities. And it matters not how otherwise well we attend to the design of the car, it will not run unless the basic requirements of its motor are met. So it is with human beings. Unless the basic requirements for achievement are met, no matter what external opportunities individuals are exposed to, they will largely be unable to respond. The process of achievement is a creative one, creating power by a complex of relations, which are only made possible in an environment of *basic opportunity*.

Most of us are not persons of great or extraordinary achievement, and it is desirable to recognize that in every human context it is not genius in some specific area that is of significance, but rather the generalized ability to make the appropriately successful responses to the ordinary challenges presented by the environment, to be plastic, flexible, and adaptable. And of such adaptive behavior all people everywhere, within the normal range of variation, are capable. Nevertheless, we tend to evaluate the status of societies by the measure of their extraordinary accomplishments.

This is fair enough, but it is quite unfair to draw the conclusion from the differences in accomplishment that societies having fewer accomplishments to their credit are therefore genetically inferior to the others. By this measure the Britons of 2,000 years ago would have been held genetically inferior to their Roman conquerors. But the truth is they were not genetically inferior, but only culturally different, and quite well adapted to the conditions of an Iron Age way of life. The Romans had become who they were because they had experienced for many years the influences of the many Mediterranean peoples to whom they were exposed; such fertilizing influences were absent in early Britain. It was not until an increasing invasion of foreigners introduced their lifeways that the Britons began to tick. But it was 500 years before that incredible burst of creativity in the sixteenth and seventeenth centuries allowed a Shakespeare to make his appearance, and an Isaac Newton.[6] It is premature as well as wholly unjustifiable to attribute differences in achievement between peoples to genetic factors.

It is, apparently, difficult to persuade those who are so ready to settle for a genetic explanation of differences in cultural achievement that it is only by equalizing basic opportunities for everyone that the conditions will be provided for any discussion of the role of genetic factors in social and individual differences in achievement. Until such basic opportunities are made available to everyone, all statements attributing differences in cultural achievement must be adjudged what they are: conjectures with no scientific basis or merit.

Ultimately, of course, the whole question of race is a pseudo one, a system of pseudological rationalizations based on insufficiently analyzed evidence designed, usually, to bolster prejudices and defend indefensible positions, which at once denies and rejects science, logic and humanity. However unsound and unreal such beliefs may be, we know only too well how very real the unsound and the unreal can become. Be that as it may, it cannot be too often repeated that the issue at stake is not one of science, but of ethics.

By virtue of the fact that he or she is a human being, every individual has a right to his or her birthright, which is development. The greatest riches of the person, of the community, of humanity, lies in the uniqueness of the contribution that each person has to make to others.

It is not a question of "superiority" or "inferiority" but the encouragement of individual fulfillment, whatever the individual's limitations, that society must consider among the first of the purposes for which it exists. The greatest of all talents, and the most important for the individual, is the talent for humanity. And what is talent? It is involvement. And the talent for being humane means the involvement in the welfare of one's fellow humans. All humans have the capacity for such involvement. Racists commit the greatest of all crimes because they block the development of this capacity and prevent its individual fulfillment. To the extent that these crimes are committed, to that extent is the individual, society, and humanity impoverished.

The deprivation of any person's right to fulfillment diminishes each of us; we have all been deprived, for we are all involved in each other. Whether we wish it to be or not, this involvement is inherent in the very nature of nature, and especially of human nature. The most basic of all opportunities is the right to growth and development as a humane being who has been deeply involved in the interaction of love with others, for the health and identity of each of us consists in the meaningfulness of our loving relationships.

Notes

1. For an excellent development of this statement see Richard Lewontin, Steven Rose, and Leon Kamin, *Not In Our Genes* (New York: Pantheon Books, 1984).

2. Ernest Baughman and Grant Dahlstrom, *Negro and White Children* (New York: Academic Press, 1968); Robert Crain and Carol S. Weisman, *Discrimination, Personality, and Achievement* (New York: Seminar Press, 1972); Christopher Jencks, *Inequality* (New York: Basic Books, 1972); Kent S. Miller and Ralph M. Dreger, eds., *Comparative Studies of Blacks and Whites in the United States* (New York: Seminar Press, 1973); Carl Senna, ed., *The Fallacy of IQ* (New York: The Third Press, 1973); Evelyn Sharp, *The IQ Cult* (New York: Coward, McCann & Geoghegan, 1972); Harry J. Crockett and Jerome L. Schulman, eds., *Achievement Among Minority Americans* (Cambridge, MA: Schenkman, 1973); O. D. Duncan, D. L. Featherman and B. Duncan, *Socioeconomic Background and Achievement* (New York: Seminar Press, 1972); Arthur Whimby with Linda Shaw Whimbey, *Intelligence Can Be Taught* (New York: Dutton, 1975); Paul Davis Chapman, *Schools as Sorters: Lewis M. Terman, Applied Psychology, and the Intelligence Testing Movement, 1890–1930* (New York: New York University Press, 1988); C. Liungman, *What Is IQ? Heredity, Intelligence, and Environment* (London: Gordon Cremonesi, 1970); Renee Fuller, *In Search of the IQ Correlation* (Stony Brook, NY: Ball-Sick-Bird Publications, 1975); Michael Lewis, ed., *Origins of Intelligence: Infancy and Early Childhood* (New York: Plenum, 1976); Gaston Viaud, *Intelligence: Its Evolution and Forms* (New York: Harper & Bros., 1960); Jack Fincher, *Human Intelligence* (New York: Putnam's Sons 1976); Ruth H. Munroe, Robert L. Munroe, and Beatrice B. Whiting, eds., *Handbook of Cross-Cultural Development* (New York: Garland, 1981); Gerald D. Berreman, ed., *Social Inequality: Comparative and Developmental Approaches* (New York: Academic Press, 1991).

3. Robert Coles, *Children of Crisis* (Boston: Little, Brown, 1967); Mary Greene and Orletta Ryan, *The Schoolchildren; Growing Up in the Slums* (New York: Pantheon, 1966); Nat Hentoff, *Our Children are Dying* (New York: Viking Press, 1967); Herbert R. Kohl, *36 Children* (New York: New American Library, 1967); Jonathan Kozol, *Death at an Early Age* (Boston: Houghton Mifflin, 1967); Bob Blauner, *Black Lives, White Lives* (Berkeley: University of California Press, 1989); Nicholas Lehman, *The Promised Land* (New York: Alfred A. Knopf, 1991); Gajendra K. Verma and Christopher Bagley, eds., *Race, Education and Identity* (New York: St. Martin's Press, 1979); Michael Lewis, *The Culture of Inequality* (Amherst: University of Massachusetts Press, 1992); David M. Fetterman, *Excellence & Equality* (Albany: State University of New York Press, 1988); Michael W. Homel, *Down From Equality* (Urbana: University of Illinois Press, 1984); Valerie Polakow Suransky, *The Erosion of Childhood* (Chicago: University of Chicago Press, 1982); Michael Mariott, "A World Defined by Dread," *The New York Times* (27 April 1992), B1, 4.

4. David A. Levitsky, ed., *Malnutrition, Environment, and Behavior* (Ithaca: Cornell University Press, 1979); Ashley Montagu, "Not By Bread Alone," *The Sciences*

(September 1979): 23–24; David E. Barrett and Deborah A. Frank, *The Effects of Undernutrition on Children's Behavior* (London: Gordon & Breach, 1987).

5. Ashley Montagu, "Race, Caste and Scientific Method," *Psychiatry* 4 (1941): 337–38.

6. Jacquetta Hawkes, *Early Britain* (London: William Collins, 1945); R. G. Collingwood and J. N. L. Myres, *Roman Britain and the English Settlements,* 2nd ed. (Oxford: The Clarendon Press, 1936).

20

Race and Democracy

In the present condition of domestic and world affairs we are, all of us, daily confronted with many conflicting, contradictory, and often novel viewpoints. It must be our task, seriously undertaken, to evaluate these ideas and viewpoints for ourselves, so that we may arrive at a just decision concerning them that will enable us to act effectively and for the best interest of everyone concerned. This chapter is written from the standpoint of those who believe that democracy is the best form of government for a free and intelligent people—a form of government in which every citizen has, or may have, an effective voice in regulating the manner in which he or she and his, or her, fellows shall be governed.

If it be agreed that democracy, messy as it is, is the form of government that prevails in this country and that among us live citizens who are members of different ethnic groups, it is a just and proper inquiry, and in the interests of us all, to ask whether there are any physical and mental qualities peculiar to any of these groups that our social order needs to consider in the government of this land. Today, more than ever, this question needs to be asked and the evidence sympathetically discussed, for we are today facing one of those recurring periods in the history of international relations in which payment is being exacted for our own mistakes as well as for those of earlier generations. Many of those mistakes are a matter of recent history. It will serve us not at all to lament them; they have been made and have redounded upon us. The monster that has been let loose upon the world is to a large extent of our own making, and whether we are willing to face the fact or not we are, all of us, individually and collectively, responsible for the ghastly form which he has assumed. Moreover, something of each of us has gone into the making of the Frankenstein, whose name is racism. If we are to combat this formidable problem successfully, we must become fully aware of the means by which we may do so. World War II, at home and abroad, was as much a war of ideas as of arms—ideas which were being made to infiltrate the mind in such a manner that the victim was, for the most part, unaware of what was happening until it was too late.

Let it be recalled that World War II was the first in which ideas were dropped from the skies, over the radio waves as well as from airplanes, before the bombs themselves began to wreak their inhuman havoc. Among these ideas, explicitly as well as in disguised form, racism played a prominent part. Linking "the Jews" with whatever it was desired to demonize was the first step in the process of the conquest and confusion of thought. It is an old and effective device used by unscrupulous politicians for distracting the attention of the people from vital issues and from their own nefarious activities. It was no less a monster than Hitler, who stated that racial propaganda was the most powerfully disruptive idea in the service of the Nazi ideology.

It is a matter of fairly recent history that in Europe the Nazis were able to impose a purely mythological dogma, first upon the Jews and then upon the Poles, a dogma which deprived all those who were not so-called Aryans of their civil rights and of the right to earn a living, even the right to life.[1] The Poles found themselves being beaten with their own stick, for their treatment of Jews in prewar days was based upon prejudices and discriminations similar to those the Germans put into effect against them.[2]

We have seen, and we see today, that what may at first be practiced on a local scale may spread until it is practiced nationally, and what is practiced nationally may spread until it becomes international. One nation learns from another. It is for us to decide whether it is the spirit of the racist or the spirit of democracy, of freedom and friendship, which is to become both national and international.

If people have acted upon ideas and beliefs which have brought the world to its present sorry state, then surely it should be clear that something is seriously wrong with such ideas and beliefs. And is there anywhere anyone who can for a moment entertain a doubt upon that score? If humanity is to be saved—and it is no less a matter than that—each of us must endeavor to clarify our thoughts upon this most urgent of all problems with which we, as humans beings, are today faced. We have too long taken things for granted and have lived too easily off our prejudices. If it is our privilege and our right to live and work upon this earth, then we must once more clearly recognize that with that privilege and that right is inseparably linked the obligation to make this earth an increasingly better and happier place for all who shall live on it. Toward that end it is particularly necessary at this time to be alive to the obligations of social inequality.

The race issue, as Harry Ashmore has said,

holds the undisputed American course record for public and private ambivalence. Nothing in our national experience remotely compares with the unresolved racial dilemma for the production of bloodshed, emotional trauma, rank injustice supercharged rhetoric dubious theology, unsound scientific research, bad legal theory, and perverse political practice.[3]

The right to difference, the legitimate right to collective singularities and identities, should be welcomed as fundamental for every people and every person. The problem of race is no longer limited to one or another country. The problem of race has assumed dimensions affecting the welfare, nay, the very continuation, of the whole world of humankind. When we speak of "undeveloped" versus "developed" countries, of "the Eastern bloc" versus "the Western bloc," "northern" versus "southern" hemisphere, what we are really talking about is a deep cleavage which has grown up, largely as a result of the misdoings of the western powers over the last two hundred and more years, between the white and non-white peoples of the world. Ronald Segal, in a brilliant book on this subject, has underscored the fact that it is this power of race which the circumstances of want in the world threaten to provoke beyond the most terrible experiences of the past. "By attempting to contain revolution, the white world . . . is driving the two powers together, in an alliance of unparalleled fury, which may well howl itself away only in the ruins of humanity. For if revolution is rational, race is not."[4]

In the United States of America, as Thomas Jefferson put it, "this government, the best hope of man," we have every opportunity open to us to make our lives a blessing to ourselves and to all the generations who follow us—in this great land first, and perhaps later, by our example, in all the rest of the world. Let it not be said that democracy is a form of government which most Americans are not yet good enough to deserve. Meanwhile, let us remember that democracy is a promise which each of us must keep.

Europe, the Europe from which many of us all escaped, whether our ancestors came on the Mayflower, cargo vessel, or other conveyance, shows us today where we shall end if we think that the color of the skin or the shape of the nose has anything whatever to do with human values or culture. The lights in Europe were almost all snuffed out, one by one, extinguished by the evil breath of bigoted and perverted men. Let us do everything in our power to secure the lights, long too dim here in America, from being entirely extinguished, that we may continue increasingly to live in enlightenment, and humanely, to know and enjoy the benefits of a free society, benefits which will ever increase, and will extend to the uttermost limits of the earth.

How may we achieve this? The answer is in two words: "enlightened action." Action without a thoroughly sound basis in thought, that is, analyzed fact, to support it is worthless, as is the soundest thought which is not realized in action. The first is dangerous, the second sterile. Thought without action and action without thought eventually lead to the same disastrous results.

In the preceding pages we have examined the concept of race—a conception which presupposes the existence of different groups of human beings, each believed to possess inborn physical and mental traits reflected in differences in national outlook, culture, social behavior, and so on.

We have seen that far too much significance has been attributed to both the physical and the mental differences existing between ethnic groups. Within certain broad limits we can demonstrate the physical differences, and we can observe those of culture and behavior. But the one thing we cannot do is to prove or demonstrate that differences in behavior and culture are for the most part determined by innate factors.

Certainly there appear to be differences in temperament, intellectual attitudes, and cultural behavior between ethnic groups; but there is no reason whatever to believe that these differences are inborn. As we have seen, for the most part they seem to be due to differences in cultural conditioning, different social backgrounds, differences in economic conditions, and idiosyncratic traits peculiar to the individual. The acquired nature of these differences should be strongly enough indicated to us in the United States, where such differences have been given a chance to emerge into a fairly similar character, there has developed, as a result, a typical American temperament or psychology, contrasting sharply with the British, French, German, and Italian psychology or temperament.

We have seen that the physical differences that exist between the various human groups cannot be intelligently discussed in terms of physical or cultural superiority to one another. There are no superior or inferior groups by birth. If there are any inborn mental differences associated with the physical differences which distinguish different ethnic groups, then science has been unable to discover them. Physical differences are purely external and are only superficially associated with cultural differences existing or imputed. Yet these external differences provide a convenient peg upon which to hang all sorts of imagined internal differences, moral, intellectual, mental, and emotional. In this way physical differences become the basis for social discrimination and the creation of social inequalities. But science is aware of no such association between external and internal traits, except, of course, such as are socially produced. In our own society such differences of behavior and character as seem to exist between ethnic groups are due principally to inequalities in the opportunities for social and economic betterment afforded them, not to unalterable inborn or hereditary differences. No ethnic group has a monopoly of good or bad hereditary qualities. The existence of any ethnic group at the present time is proof of the fact that it possesses a majority of desirable qualities, otherwise it could not have survived to the present time.

Democracy, like charity, begins at home. Give every ethnic group within our democracy equal social opportunities, and it may be predicted that one will find between minds only such differences as now exist between individuals of the same ethnic group who have enjoyed such opportunities. Every human being, whatever his or her ethnic affiliation, differs from every other in his or her make-up and has had a somewhat different inheritance and different opportunities. Would not this be a very dull world were we all poured to the same mold? As things are, the great reservoir of diversity upon which we can draw will always serve to enliven and enrich our interest in life.

As Kenneth Mather has remarked,

> education must be used to produce diversity because the essential of any organized system is the cooperation of unlikes, who because of the division of function which their unlikeness permits can jointly achieve more than would be possible by the sum of their undifferentiated activities and uncoordinated efforts.[5]

There need be no fear that a leveling process will ensue if all people, without discrimination, were afforded equal opportunities. Education increases differences—it does not diminish them. We may here recall the words of the great educational psychologist Professor E. L. Thorndike: "To the real work of man,—the increase of achievement through improvement of the environment,—the influence of heredity offers no barrier."

The important differences are not differences in racial averages, but between persons; and it is because of the existence of individual differences, which have little or nothing to do with race, that a true democracy must aim to devote its attention to individual differences regardless of whether the individual has a narrow nose or a broad one. A democracy must recognize differences and make every possible allowance for them—the differences that individuals exhibit, not as members of different ethnic groups but as individual citizens, individuals differing in innumerable ways and capable of making individualized contributions of all sorts to our common culture. It is for this reason that democracy must be actively concerned with the task of affording every individual, regardless of group affiliation, adequate opportunities for self-development, so that the best that every individual has it within him to give shall be given, both for his own happiness and for that of his fellows. We may here recall the words of a great American, Charles Sumner: "The true greatness of nations is in those qualities which constitute the greatness of the individual." In a speech made in the U.S. Senate on 6 February 1866, pleading for the granting of civil rights to the freedmen, Charles Sumner said:

> The populations of the earth—embracing Caucasians, Mongolians, Malays, Africans, and Americans—is about thirteen hundred million, of

whom only three hundred and seventy-five million are 'white men,' or little more than one-fourth, so that in claiming exclusive rights for 'white
men,' you degrade nearly three-quarters of the human family, made in
the 'image of God' and declared to be of 'one blood' while you sanction a
case offensive to religion, and oligarchy inconsistent with Republican government, and a monopoly which has the whole world as its footstool. . . .
Against this assumption, I protest with mind, soul, and heart. It is false in
religion, false to statesmanship, and false in economy. . . . You cannot
deny these rights without impiety. And so has God linked the material welfare with national duty, you cannot deny these rights without peril to the
Republic.

The freedman's civil rights were written into the law, but the freedman has
yet to be permitted those civil rights in his everyday life, over the length
and breadth of the land.

It was Woodrow Wilson who said: "America is not anything if it consists
of each of us. It is something only if it consists of all of us; and it can consist
of all of us only as our spirits are banded together in a common enterprise.
That common enterprise is the enterprise of liberty and justice and right."

What these distinguished men were saying is that it is our task to create
a sense of the common bond, as a commitment to a common humanity.

There are no minority groups in America, except those that bigots and
racists create with such racist terms. America is a nation made up of the
members of almost every ethnic group and every religion, all of which have
contributed toward its development. All of us are either the descendants of
immigrants or ourselves recent immigrants, and those who have voluntarily
chosen to be Americans have often had occasion to remark that they had
rather be foreign-born Americans than American-born foreigners. The important thing is to be an American, without being narrowly nationalistic,
and to grant all Americans the right to their Americanism, which implies
freedom of religion, freedom of speech, and freedom of opportunity. "As I
would not be a *slave* so I would not be a *master.* This expresses my idea of
democracy . . . Whatever differs from this, to the extent of the difference, is
no democracy . . ." Those are the simple words of Abraham Lincoln.

Many Americans, when they speak of democracy, make a pretense of a
creed in which they do not actually believe. "One nation indivisible, under
God, with liberty and justice for all." For blacks? For Hispanics? For the
American Indian? Not to mention other "minority" groups? The truth is
that many Americans are quite alienated from the creeds that, with incan-
tation and with ritual, on ceremonial occasions, they identify with the
essence of Americanism. But these are merely ceremonial credos, the
smoke of incense burnt before an empty shrine, for there is nothing in
those credos in which they, in fact, believe, for what one believes, is what
one does. On their treatment of blacks and American Indians most Ameri-

cans stand indicted before the bar of humanity, for they have made of color a badge of oppression, and in the case of the American Indians, genocide at its worst; at its best, abandonment. As former Secretary of State Dean Rusk, himself from the State of Georgia, wrote to Attorney General Kennedy on 29 May 1961:

> The efforts of the United States Government in international affairs to build the kind of world we want to live in . . . cannot be divorced from our ability to achieve these same purposes for all the people of our own country. The principles of racial equality and nondiscrimination are imperatives of the American society with its many racial strains. In the degree to which we ourselves practice these principles our voice will carry conviction . . . in the conduct of our foreign relations . . . American actions which fall short of Constitutional standards safeguarding individual freedom and dignity prejudice our position before the world.

Indeed, racism is the great American divide, American society's most exposed weakness. It is America's greatest domestic failure, and the worst of its international handicaps. As Professor Harold R. Isaacs has said, racism

> is so highly visible that when hundreds of millions of people all around the world look in our direction they often seem to be able to see little else. . . . The world's image of Americans as white racists is threatening to blot out the image of Americans as builders of the dream of the freest and most open society ever organized by man. Worse, it is blurring the image and sapping the strength of the very idea of the open society itself.[6]

Racism has damaged the reputation of Americans as the defenders of individual rights, and has provided the detractors of America with all the material they need to see to it that the image sticks. Racism is no longer a domestic issue, it has become a deeply involved problem of international relations, and a decisive element in the newly developing nations' opinion of the United States. Recall the not-so-distant past, when a Nigerian diplomat was refused service in a Charlottesville, Virginia, restaurant in December 1960. The National Council of Nigeria and the Cameroons issued a statement calling the United States "a country devoid of respect for human dignity, a country with a completely blank racial policy, a country which still lives in the dark ages, has no claim to leadership of free men."[7]

Incidents of this sort have done more damage to the prestige and standing of the United States in the eyes of the world than all the billions of dollars we are pouring into foreign aid can ever hope to repair. One Governor Faubus, one Governor Barnett, or one Governor Maddox, was worth more in propaganda value to the Russians than anything they themselves could supply. But not content with our domestic failures, we export them abroad. In December 1962, traveling in a United States Army Air Force plane, at the expense of the American taxpayer, Senator Ellender, "Democrat," of the State of Louisiana, delivered himself of the most deprecatory remarks concerning the abilities of Africans to govern themselves. At a news conference held in Southern Rhodesia, Senator Ellender announced to the press that "The average African is incapable of leadership except through the assistance of Europeans."[8]

What must Africans have thought of the United States when its "democratic" senators representing the American people uttered such insulting racist nonsense? America's historic future, its very survival as a great power in the world, depends upon its solution of the race problem. It is on that issue that the United States will ultimately stand or fall as a power in the world. The equal access to development, fulfillment, and citizenship is today no longer a pious wish—it is a practical political necessity, and a condition of civilized survival. The image the United States presents to the world is not an abstraction, but the extension of the conduct of its citizens. Every American represents America, and it is his or her individual conduct that is held responsible for racism in America. Whether responsible or not for racism, every American, as an American, must make himself responsible for the elimination of racism, for racism is inhuman, ethically wrong, constitutionally intolerable, and a denial of humanity. The very word race narrows the definition of humanity.

Stressing superficial differences between people only helps to maintain an illusion in our minds that there may be more fundamental differences behind them. What we, as informed and enlightened citizens living under a democratic form of government, ought to do is to stress the fundamental kinship of all humankind; to stress the likenesses that we all bear to one another; to reject divisive pluralism and recognize the essential unity of all humankind in the very differences which individuals of all ethnic groups display; and thus build that genuine democracy which is based on a unity of spirit in a diversity of minds. If we would preserve our unique differences, we must acknowledge our similarities. For "as we learn to see the common humanity showing through the accidental and finite differences in men we come to a practical recognition of human equality and learn to have a concern and regard for all mankind."[9] The fact that we are human beings is infinitely more important than all the peculiarities which may distinguish us from one another.

Every political system is capable of some improvement, and our democracy is no exception. We stand to profit immediately by giving up acting on racial mythology—the racial mythology that lurks in the minds of so many of us and contributes so much to social friction. We cannot, however, change the conditions of social friction merely by changing our minds. Changing our minds often amounts to no more than rearranging our prejudices. As members of an unregimented thinking democracy, we should study these things in order to keep them from adding to social friction, realizing that we have been and are being elitist and that there will be a price to pay if we continue. Let us by acting upon such facts and their interpretation as have been presented in the pages of this book afford the benefits of our democracy to all who live in it, so that we may truly "promote the general welfare and secure the blessings of liberty to ourselves and our posterity." This is the principle enshrined in the Constitution that created the government of the United States.

American democracy, at least in theory, is built upon the fundamental principle that all people should enjoy the same prerogatives and privileges because, by and large, they all possess the potentialities which would enable them to benefit by them, individually and mutually, and this is the first and greatest of the principles laid down in the Declaration of Independence, a document that represents the noblest and truest declaration of the principles of human liberty ever penned. Science and humane thought support this principle to the full, and it has been well called the genetic basis for democracy. The premise of racism, on the other hand, constitutes a negation of the very principle upon which the American Commonwealth is founded. The test of democracy in the United States must be measured by the degree to which it succeeds in applying the principles of the Declaration of Independence to the lives of all Americans. Democracy means cooperative living. It is a way of life in which men and women of different complexions, creeds, cultural origins, and customs can live together with mutual respect, understanding, and cooperation.

The flaring of latent racial enmities in times of economic stress is an association of events that has never been more painfully evident than it is today. Everywhere in the world under conditions of economic stress race prejudice has become a powerful weapon with which so-called "minority" groups have been attacked. Physical and cultural differences are seized upon and made the basis for group antagonism and discrimination. Trivial things, such as differences in manners, social backgrounds, religious beliefs, and the like, which if sympathetically understood would be points of interest and value, become the bases of distrust. Just as a child runs to its mother as a familiar refuge when in difficulties, so most of us run to our own group when we feel insecure, and fancy that anyone not of our own group is a bogeyman and the cause of all our troubles. In a democracy there should be no place for such immature conduct; nor should there be for the conditions which give rise to it, namely, improper education and economic insecurity. We can remedy these conditions. We can improve education and social and economic conditions so that all men may share in them equally. The power lies within our own hands; let us, then, use it.[10]

We are the result of the mixing of many different ethnic groups; every one of us is a much-mixed alloy, having all the added strength and qualities which the alloy possesses as compared with the unalloyed metal. Let us use that strength for the common good, so that the many may become truly one.

Equality is the condition of freedom. It is a fundamental tenet of democracy that it must balance the interests of all its component groups and citizens. As we have seen, there is nothing in the nature of any group, ethnic or otherwise, which gives it less weight in the balance of democracy than any other. That being the case, we must recognize and act upon this first principle set out in the Declaration of Independence that all human beings are

> created equal, that they are endowed by their Creator with certain un-alienable Rights, that among these are Life, Liberty, and the pursuit of Happiness. That to secure these rights, Governments are instituted among Men, deriving their just powers from the consent of the governed.

After more than two centuries science joins hands with humanity to ask Americans whether they will accept the challenge of those words.

Notes

1. See also Paul J. Massing, *Rehearsal for Destruction: A Study of Political Anti-Semitism in Imperial Germany* (New York: Harper, 1949); Leon Poliakov, *Harvest of Hate* (London: Elek Books, 1956); Joseph Tenenbaum, *Race and Reich: The Story of an Epoch* (New York: Twayne, 1957); Joshua Trachtenberg, *The Devil and the Jews* (New York: Meridian Books, 1961); Ervin Staub, *The Roots of Evil: The Origins of Genocide and Other Group Violence* (New York: Cambridge University Press, 1989).

2. It is regrettable to have to record that during World War II the Polish government in exile, its army, and official representatives maintained these prejudices unchanged. During the occupation of their country by the Germans, the Poles assisted the enemy in the task of maltreating and murdering Jews. As one Pole put it, "Fortune has come to us through Hitler. He is preparing for us a Poland without Jews." For a fully documented presentation of the facts see Jacob Lestchinsky, "The Jew in Ruined Europe," *Chicago Jewish Forum* 4 (1945): 10–16. There were, however, some noble exceptions; see Dabek-Szyszko, "The Great Bor Lie," *The Protestant* 6 (1946): 12–31. Following the liberation the elimination of the Jews in Poland seems to have met with the approval of the majority of Poles. See Meyer Levin, ed., "Journal of Kibbutz Buchenwald," *Commentary* 1 (1946): 31–39. In July 1946, a frightful anti-Semitic pogrom in Kielce where some 70 of the tiny community of 250 Jews were killed and more than a hundred injured. The Catholic Church in Poland, even after the war, continued to play the leading role in the encouragement and maintenance of anti-Semitism. See *Warsaw Correspondent,* "Jews and the Catholic Church in Poland;" *Jewish Chronicle* (London), 25 June 1948, 11.

In February 1957, Sydney Gruson, in a special communique from Warsaw to the *New York Times*, 17 February, 1957, reported that Jews were leaving Poland in great numbers owing to "the raving anti-Semitism" prevalent in that country. "All concerned have conceded that terror was being used until recently against Jews, particularly in small towns." For a victim's moving account see Oscar Pinkus, *The House of Ashes* (New York: World Publishing, 1964) "The Poles did not hide how they felt about the extermination. They said that they themselves would never have done such a thing. But since it had been done, and since they could not be held responsible, they were rather glad that it had happened" (p. 115). In 1968 the Polish Government mounted a vicious purge against "the Zionists." For an account of this and official cruelty toward Jews who seek to emigrate, see "Poland: Jewish Exodus," *Time*, 14 March 1969, 40–41. For the fullest and most judicious account of these matters see Yisrael Gutman and Smuel Krakowski, *Unequal Victims: Poles and Jews During World War I* (New York: Holocaust Library, 1986) See also Samuel Gruber, *I Chose Life* (New York: Shengold Publisher, 1978) on the murderous antisemitic peasants; also Michael Chesinski, *Poland: Communism, Nationalism, Anti-Semitism* (New York: Karz-Cohl Publishing, 1983) "Polish Jews Find a Haven in Denmark and Sweden," *New York Times*, 16 November 1969, 16. For the best and most authoritative account of these outrages see Gutman and Karakowski, *Unequal Victims*. Lest it be thought that the Poles were alone in their conduct toward the Jews, it should be stated that the Austrians of Gemütlichkeit, Strauss' waltzes, and the Blue Danube were not much better. Nor were the Slovaks. At Babi Yar the Ukrainians massacred more than 100,000 Jews. To this day a virulent anti-Semitism prevails throughout the nations of the former USSR. Contrast this with the magnificent behavior of the Danes who saved virtually the whole Jewish population from the murder-mills of the Nazis. See Harold Flander, *Rescue in Denmark* (New York: Simon & Schuster, 1962). For accounts of anti-Semitism in the former USSR and Poland, see the periodical, published since 1959 and edited by Emanuel Litvinoff, *Jews in Eastern Europe*. For an account of how some Poles strove to save Jews from the Nazis see Kazimierz Uranek-Osmecki, *He Who Saves One Life* (New York: Crown, 1971). In this connection see also Yisrael Gutman, *The Jews of Warsaw, 1939–1943: Ghetto, Underground Revolt* (Bloomington: Indiana University Press, 1982), also Wladyslaw Bartozewski and Zophia Lewin eds., *Righteous Among Nations: How Poles Helped the Jews, 1939–1945* (London: Elscourt, 1969); Nora Levin, *The Holocaust: The Destruction of European Jewry 1933–1945* (New York: Crowell, 1968). The story of a young Catholic Pole, Jan Karski, who saved the lives of so many Jews in Poland, and singlehandedly went the rounds of attempting to stop the Holocaust by giving an account of the murderous practices of the Nazis in interviews with Anthony Eden in England, Roosevelt, and others in the United States, and other American diplomats, who literally declined to believe the facts he placed before them. The book, in which Karski helped the authors tell his incredible story of this unforgettable hero, is by E. Thomas Wood and Stanslaw M. Janowski, *Karski: How One Man Tried to Stop the Holocaust* (New York: John Wiley, 1994).

    3. Harry Ashmore, *The Man in the Middle* (Columbia: University of Missouri Press, 1966).

    4. Ronald Segal, *The Race War* (New York: Viking, 1966), 374.

    5. Kenneth Mather, *Human Diversity* (Edinburgh: Oliver & Boyd, 1964).

6. Harold R. Isaacs. "American Race Relations and America's Image in World Affairs," *Human Relations* 10 (1962), 266–80; H. Isaacs, *The New World of Negro Americans* (New York: John Day, 1963).

7. UNESCO, *The Effect of the Existence of Segregation in the U.S. on the American Image in Africa*, U.S. National Commission for UNESCO (Press Release, Nat. Conf. 8/18, 25 October 1961).

8. *Time*, 14 December 1962, 22.

9. Lord Lindsay, *The Good and the Clever* (New York: Cambridge University Press), 18.

10. Eugene Hartley, *Problems in Prejudice* (New York: King's Crown Press, 1946); Frederick Hertz, *Nationality in History and Politics: A Study of the Psychology and Sociology of National Sentiment and Character* (London: Kegan Paul, 1944); Robert Hughes, *Culture of Complaint: The Fraying of America* (New York: New York Public Library and Oxford University Press, 1993); Nicholas N. Kittrie, *The War Against Authority: From the Crisis of Legitimacy to a New Social Contract* (Baltimore: Johns Hopkins University Press, 1995); Ian I. Mitroff and Warren Bennis, *The Unreality Industry: The Deliberate Manufacture of Falsehood and What it Does to Our Lives* (New York: Oxford University Press, 1993).

21

Racism and Social Action

The reaction of scientists to the propaganda of those who sought to convince the world of the truth of racism has had an interesting history. At first the errors and spurious arguments of the racists were duly exposed by the simple appeal to the facts of science. Facts, after all—it was felt—speak for themselves. With the unfolding of the monstrous Nazi racist policy of extermination of the Jews in Europe, and mounting racial tensions in America, the very real seriousness of the problem at last broke in on many scientists, and as a result we have witnessed a considerable increase in the literature devoted to the examination of the causes of race tensions and prejudice, and the refutation of racist ideas and dogmas. By this means scientists have hoped to arrest, at least, the spread of the infection of racism. Ideally they would have liked to render immune those who stood in danger of acquiring it, and to relieve those of the pathogens with which they were infected.

The attempt has been a noble one, and it has enjoyed something of a success, but that success, in the face of a growing intensification of race feeling, has been a strictly limited one. Many persons and groups have, gratifyingly, been influenced to think and behave more intelligently with respect to race relations, but the population as a whole, in this country— not to mention other lands—has made little progress but has, instead, remained measurably race conscious. It has become evident that to make the truth readily available is not enough. Facts, it appears, do not speak for themselves, nor, it seems, are they necessarily understood when they do, and when they are understood it far from follows that they will be accepted and acted upon. These are by no means new discoveries, but the responses which they define have come to most workers in the field of race relations with something of the shock of new discovery; and this because the seriousness of the issues at stake has given so much greater force to the errors and perversions of thought and conduct of which so many persons and groups are guilty. The stereotypes, the absurd beliefs, the vulgar errors, and the unfortunate attitudes, when multiplied several million times actually add

473

up to a tremendous social pathology. Western society, and our society in particular, is very sick indeed.

We have spent a fair amount of time inquiring into and investigating the causes of the social disease which is racism, and we have yet a great deal of work to do before we shall have brought such studies to completion. Investigations of this kind are invaluable and they must be encouraged to continue on an even larger scale than hitherto, but it should be quite obvious that investigation and the clearest analysis and description of causes will never succeed in curing the disease of racism. The better, however, we understand the causes of the disease the more efficiently it will be possible to prescribe the remedy for it. Hence, research into every aspect of the problem of prejudice and racism must continue on an ever-widening front. But it is now coming to be more and more widely understood that the prosecution of such researches and their publication in technical journals, periodicals, and books is not an end in itself, but a means to an end. The theoretical phase of the attack on racism has now reached the stage which renders it clear that not much more can be achieved by that means. What we now need is to enter upon the second, the applied, phase of the attack, in which, using our theoretical knowledge gained from the actual investigation of the necessary[1] conditions we embark upon the practical application of that knowledge.

We now know something of the nature of the causes of racism, and we know how spurious are the arguments that are used to support it, and of this we have heard a great deal. What we want to know now is what we can do about racism in a practical way in the form of social action in the attack upon this most critical of social problems.

One of the first things to be realized is that partial measures and measures which we know to have no more than a palliative effect are not going to accomplish very much. Education, full employment, and good housing will help, but they will not solve the race problem. Such measures are doomed to failure for the simple reason that race prejudice stems from sources which these remedies, for the most part, fail to reach. These sources are the internalized basic structures that determine the social functioning of the personality. The basic structures are those that are erected as the framework of the personality by the process of socialization; by the manner in which the socially undifferentiated human organism is turned into a socially differentiated human being. The basic personality structure of every human being is determined by the forms of social response that have been institutionalized in each society.

An analysis of the institutions determining such responses in American society makes it clear that in order to change any of those responses it will be necessary to change the character of some of our institutions. For example, perhaps the one value beyond all others which has become predominantly institutionalized in the United States is the value of success, success measured in terms of how many dollars a person possesses or how much he or she can "make" in a year, in a society in which *earning* a living has been turned into a *way* of living.

The emphasis is almost entirely upon material success in the open competitive market. Margaret Mead has discussed this trait of American culture at length in her book *And Keep Your Powder Dry*. The spirit of aggressive competition is inculcated in young Americans almost as soon as they are capable of understanding what is required of them. Many soon learn that their parents' love for them is conditional upon how they compare, measure up, with others; they must compete and be successful. The hunt for status and the impetus to obtain prestige by achievement of lots of dollars represents a very powerful drive indeed. All potential competing persons and groups, as a consequence of such a process of socialization, therefore come to be regarded as rivals, and inevitably they will be regarded with varying degrees of hostility and fear. The frustrations of infancy, childhood, adolescence, and adult life, which have been either wholly or partially repressed, find a very ready outlet in the sanctioned aggressiveness which the American competitive system of living encourages. Under such conditions racial prejudice and discrimination is inevitable, for in a society such as ours, in which there are distinctively recognized "in-groups" and "out-groups," that are regarded as in competition with each other hostility will always be directed toward the "out-group," since by its very presence it constitutes a threat to the security of the person whose personality is structured in terms of competition and the drive to succeed. In view of the fact that such persons spend a great part of their anxious lives in a state of actual or anticipated insecurity, it is not surprising that they should give their fears substantial form in the shape of some minority or ethnic—so-called racial—group, which may then serve as the object to which one may transfer or displace aggressions that have been directed to other frustrating objects, and thus serve as a convenient scapegoat.

The insecurities incident to life in highly industrialized societies continually produce frustrations, and race prejudices constitute a socially sanctioned outlet for the resulting accumulated aggressiveness. This in turn serves to explain the person's failure to himself and at the same time enables him to revenge himself upon the imagined cause of it.

As long as we maintain the kind of emphasis we do, in this country, upon competitive success, and as long as we continue to produce the kind of frustrations and insecurities that we do in infants, children, adolescents, and adults, active feelings of hostility towards members of "out-groups" will continue to plague our society no matter how well we succeed in restraining their expression by means of external constraints.

This is not to say that such external constraints are useless, they can, in fact, be of the first importance, and must be applied much more rigorously than any have yet been. But this *is* to say, that in order to eliminate the sickness of group hostility we must eliminate the conditions that give rise to it, and, as I have indicated, many of the most important conditions can be found in the character of some of our institutions.

In the first place, we must change our goal of success in terms of material achievement to one which will have as its goal the perfection of the human spirit, *humanitas*. We must change from the disoperative ideal of the American individualist, to the ideal of the cooperative citizen who is devoted to something other than himself—to his fellow men, and to the good of society. In other words, we must concentrate our energies on making *humane* beings out of humans. When we shall have achieved that we shall have solved not only the problem of group hostility but most of the social problems arising out of interpersonal relations. Obviously an ideal to be aimed at. But how is such an ideal to be practically achieved?

The answer is: By *social reform* and by *education,* and the two processes must proceed together, the development of one without the other will not be good enough. The person educated in certain values of behavior towards his fellows, must be given an opportunity to practice them. If the society in which he lives makes it difficult for him to do so, he will find himself at odds with far too many people for his conduct to make itself appreciably felt upon the masses, and if he makes any progress at all it will be slow, partial, and unsatisfying, and it is doubtful whether what little he may achieve at so great a cost will endure.

This is the lot of most would-be social reformers today. On the other hand, where conditions make it possible for the socially educated person to live life humanely and cooperatively, there can be little doubt of the great social progress that could be made within a single generation. If conditions could be made easier for the average person to cooperate in this way, even if, as in most cases, he or she would have to be directed by the imperatives of the law; we shall have made a very great advance in the right direction. And this brings me to the one great agency of social regulation which has thus far not been adequately utilized in the approach to the problem of group hostility. I mean the law. It has been said that one cannot legislate race prejudice out of existence. This may be true, but no more true than to say that one cannot legislate libel or slander out of existence.[2] The fact is that our laws of libel and slander exercise a most effective control over the publication, written or spoken, of malicious statements calculated to bring a person into group hostility of any kind based on race, religious, or ethnic prejudice. Race prejudice and race discrimination are not the same: Race prejudice is essentially an attitude of mind, but it does not always necessarily lead to race discrimination, though it usually does. Race discrimination is the active form of race prejudice as has been exhibited, for example, in exclusion laws against Jews, blacks, or others in educational institutions but more particularly as it functions in connection with business, housing, transportation, employment, voting, and so on. Race prejudice gives rise to race discrimination, and race discrimination serves to maintain and continually add fuel to race prejudice, and in this viciously circular manner to intensify and extend discriminative practices.

A law against group libel would obviously not necessarily affect the practice of race discrimination, while a law against race discrimination would not of itself eliminate race prejudice. The question arises whether both forms of group hostility should be approached, together or separately. This is ultimately a matter of strategy and the answer will vary for different areas. The strategy is a matter for those to determine who know their localities best. The case against group libel is clear: It should and must be enacted as a law by every State in the Union, at the same time, legislation should be passed against every form of discrimination on the basis of ethnic, religious or minority association. A concerted attack of this kind on group hostility will do more for the improvement of group relations than any other practical measures of which I can think. Coordinated with educational measures such a program will begin to produce results immediately.

Here, then, is something we can do in a practical way, here and now. We can not only begin thinking and working for State and Federal legislation against group hostility and discrimination, but the ground can be prepared for it, and local situations improved by working up sufficient interest to secure the passage of such legislation in one's own particular town.

With the establishment of a Federal Fair Employment Practice Commission, a first step was taken to deal with the problem of discrimination that still remains in our racist society, so that reinforcing our energies in this direction must be unflagging. As supplementary or perhaps as part of the task of securing this and allied legislation, we can, as has already been suggested, interest the proper people in our own particular localities in such legislation. But beyond all else it is legislation on a national scale that must be our objective.

With the passage of such anti-discriminatory legislation as FEPC the issue of group hostility, whether ethnic, religious or minority, would be squarely before the people. Let us then be prepared to meet the issue in the best possible manner, by paving the way now for the immediate passage of the bill making group libel a crime against society, a crime against the expressed ideal of this society: *"E pluribus unum,"* "out of the many one."

Education

From the viewpoint of the worker interested in the elimination of race prejudice, the early years of the developing person must receive far greater attention than has traditionally been bestowed upon this capitally important period. The mind of the preschool child—the first five years—is to a very large extent molded by its parents, particularly by the mother. Since within the first five years of life the foundations of many later attitudes are laid, and the antecedents of race prejudice can in most cases be clearly traced to this early period of life, the knowledge of how to help the child grow into a well-equilibrated cooperative human being must be put into the hands of all who are involved in the process of socialization.

The growth of the pre-school movement in this country provides an educational complement to education in the home, the potential importance of which cannot be overemphasized. It is through such schools that parents can be reached and educated in the cooperative task of educating their children. Because of the importance of the issues involved, the State should provide a preschool experience at no cost to the parents, to accommodate the population of children between the ages of 2 and 5 years. In this area of public instruction special emphasis should be placed upon the parents' obligation to cooperate with the school. Parent-teacher relationships should be an integral part of the educational program, and the school should be conducted as an integral part of the community, the child being a member of a community as well as of a family.

In spite of some doubts that have been expressed concerning the benefits of compensatory education, intensive research has shown that compensatory education is remarkably efficient in raising, for what it is worth, the IQ of underprivileged mothers as well as of children by as much as 30 points. These findings have been presented in two reports, one edited by Dr. Sally Ryan, the other written by Professor Urie Bronfenbrenner. Together the two reports—the former containing eight different studies recounted by the investigators and the second presenting authoritative answers to the questions "Is Early Intervention Effective?"–constitute a comprehensive rebuttal to those who prematurely claim the death of Headstart and compensatory education programs. What these studies show is that when one breaks through the walls of educational ghettos, which reflect the surrounding ghettos of daily existence, and succeeds in involving the parents in the education of their children (rather than acquiescing in the process of programming them to fail), it becomes possible to transform the school into both an effective center of learning and a focus for community activity and hope. In such schools, reading-score gains average 1.1 years—a full month above the national average; moreover, discipline is improved and vandalism is decreased. The program has been strikingly successful.[3]

It should be a prerequisite required of all teachers in such schools that they shall be adequately trained in the guidance of young children in laying the foundations of good habits in interpersonal and intergroup relationships. Such teachers should come to the school in the full awareness of the structure and problems of their society and of the particular community in which they serve. Especially must they be aware of their particular function in assisting the child to avoid all those developments which are later easily turned into group hostility. More positively, teachers must help the child to a sense of security within the family and the community, and must help to lay the foundations of that feeling of fellowship with people of all kinds that is the true basis of cultural democracy. In this task the co-operation of the parents is indispensable, and parents can, in most cases, be made to see the advantages of such cooperation.

Before we proceed to consider some of the practical steps that can be taken in this area of the educational program, let us briefly consider some of the antecedents of race prejudice encountered in preschool children.

In the first place, most pre-school children do not show any developed form of race prejudice, they can and do show potentialities that may develop into socially destructive race attitudes, although these attitudes are not likely to materialize until later in life. They do, however, quite often show race discrimination. Such discrimination, as Ruth Horowitz has shown,[4] is frequently made in relation to racial self-identification. The differences discriminated mostly relate to skin color, language, clothes, customs such as eating differently or different foods, and absence on certain festivals.

The primary bases out of which group prejudices may easily grow if not properly handled are present in the predispositions found in all children. Among the fears, for example, that children exhibit, are the fear of being left alone, fear of a strange person—which is really the same thing as the fear of being left alone—and fear of the dark. These fears may become the bases for insecurities of various sorts and aggressive feelings towards members of other groups, unless they are properly handled and directed.

Crying when left alone as exhibited, for example, by infants of 3 or 4 months, when physical contact is reduced, is perhaps the first social fear. The child is a highly dependent being, and as it develops it draws its feeling of security from those persons upon whom it has learned to grow dependent. Unless this social development is properly handled the child will tend to feel "alone" and insecure in the presence of strangers, will be afraid, and will dislike the object of his or her fear. Hence, an unreasoned prejudice against persons of all "out-groups" may easily develop from this kind of development. Good early conditioning in interpersonal relationships, and the insurance of the maximum of security for the child are the two primary generalizations which can be made here concerning the manner in which such fears may be handled. More particularly, where fears arise in the child as the result of the observation of striking differences in other people, such occasions must be converted into as pleasantly conditioning ones as possible.

As Jersild and Holmes have shown,[5] pre-school children may not only be afraid of strangers, and cling to mother when seeing a stranger on the street, but they are often afraid of familiar people when they look temporarily different. Thus, one child may show extreme fright when seeing its mother with a thick layer of cold cream on her face; another child may show fear seeing its father without a beard. Anyone who has carefully observed young children in unfamiliar situations will have been struck by the extreme sense of insecurity, which they exhibit. The unfamiliar lacks the supportive quality of the familiar, and hence induces a feeling of insecurity.

Such situations should be anticipated, as far as possible, by such devices as picture books and accompanying stories designed to introduce the child to the unfamiliar in a friendly and interested spirit. The natural curiosity of the child should be fully exploited. When the child inquires whether a African American is black all over, and whether the color will rub off, correct conditioning at this time is a simple matter, and it should be of the first importance. The child should be given a sensible explanation of the facts as we know them, and afforded every opportunity to play with children of various ethnic backgrounds.

Improperly handled fear of the dark may bring about a generalized fear of whatever is dark. Hence, special attention should be paid to this aspect of the child's development.

Since the antecedents of race prejudice manifested by the child at the preschool level have their roots primarily in parent-child and adult-child relationships, and are very definitely not something that grow autochthonously from within the child itself, we must see to it, whenever possible, and principally through the medium of the school-parent relationships that the necessary equipment for directing these antecedents into the proper sympathetic channels is made available.

We stand in need of a reevaluation of the place of the schools in our society. If children are to be properly educated their parents must be, too. The development of parent-teacher associations all over the country represents a spontaneous recognition of this need. Parents and teachers must become even more fully aware of the need for cooperation between them. They can mutually be of the greatest help to one another in the process of socializing the child, and thus, between them, the principal contributors to a happy harmonious society.

Education for democratic living in a unified society should begin in the pre-school. The cultural, ethnic, and religious differences at that age level must be treated as of no less importance than at any other age. Such group differences should be made the basis for creating an understanding, enriching, and enduring interest in other persons not only as persons but as members of different groups. The differences should be utilized to interest and educate rather than to antagonize and prejudice. In this way the natural curiosity of the child will be constructively satisfied and the proper attitudes initiated. At the same time the essential likenesses must be fully stressed. Children must be made to feel unqualifiedly secure in the presence of what is too often left as the strange and unfamiliar. In this direction no pupils are so apt as the very young.[6]

The great curiosity which all small children exhibit can be creatively utilized in getting them accustomed to and interested in others. At the preschool level the foundations can thus effectively be laid of what may later be developed as the truly cultivated human perspective, understanding of and appreciation for the other person's point of view.[7]

By the calculated and judicious choice of toys, books, and dolls representing a good selection of the peoples which have entered into the formation of this nation, group games with emphasis on cooperation, fair play, and respect for others, and similar means, we can hope to achieve much good in the conditioning and preconditioning of good interpersonal attitudes and relations. But again it must be emphasized that at this age level as well as at those that follow, the parents must be persuaded to cooperate with the schools, otherwise the best laid plans of philosophers and teachers will go astray.

Notes

1. The term "necessary" is here used in its logical sense as an indispensable condition entering into the group of conditions which together determine a cause.

2. Let us remember that there were men in the seventeenth and eighteenth centuries who held that it would be impossible to legislate slavery out of existence.

3. Sally Ryan, ed., *A Report on Longitudinal Evaluations of Preschool Programs* (Department of Health, Education and Welfare Publication No. OHD 74-24 and No. OHD 74-25), 19; Urie Brofenbrenner, ed., *Influences on Human Development* (Hinsdale, IL: Dryden Press, 1972).

4. Horowitz, Ruth, "Racial Aspects of Self Identification in Nursery School Children," *Journal of Psychology* 1 (1939): 91–99.

5. A. T. Jersild and F. B. Holms, *Children's Fears, Child Development* Monograph 20 (New York: Teachers College, Columbia University, 1935).

6. Ashley Montagu, *Touching: The Human Significance of the Skin* 3rd ed. (New York: Harper & Row, 1986).

7. Ashley Montagu, *Growing Young,* 2 ed. (Westport, CT: Bergin & Garvey, 1989).

22

Sociocultural Behavioral Influences

When the functions of the brain are disordered in neuromuscular, structural, chemical, electrical, or other observable ways, the tendency has been to look for the organic causes of the disorder or malformation. Function is the other face of structure. Functions are dependent upon organic structures, hence, the obvious, though not necessarily accurate conclusion is customarily drawn that disordered function must be caused by disordered structures, and frequently we tend to look no further.

We tend, in our thinking, to be limited to the idea that physical factors such as genetic, viral, bacterial, parasitic, chemical, iatrogenic, complications of pregnancy, prematurity, postmaturity, and the like are the kind of factors that must be involved in the brain damage that must be involved in the observable malfunction. This is often quite true, but it is also quite frequently not the whole story. No more the whole story than that pellagra is due to a deficiency of vitamins of the B complex, especially niacin (nicotinic acid) and its amide. It is quite true that under *any* conditions a diet deficient in nicotinic acid and other vitamins of the B complex will result in pellagra. In fact, however, under ordinarily normal sociocultural conditions the diet is likely to be more than adequate in B complex vitamins. Hence, the question must be asked whether or not the socioeconomic conditions in most cases constitute the principal factor in the causation of pellagra? Ever since 1915, we have known, thanks to the work of Joseph Goldberger, that pellagra is a disorder of extreme poverty, most unlikely to occur among those who can afford an adequate diet.[1]

While it should be obvious that no matter how inadequate the sociocultural conditions may be, if the diet is adequate, pellagra will not develop, nevertheless, it is almost exclusively under poor socioeconomic conditions that pellagra is most often encountered. In 1917–1918 there were over 200,000 cases of pellagra in the United States, and deaths from the condition numbered 10,000 annually. Between 1929 and 1949 the decrease in mortality in the southern states, where pellagra most frequently occurred, was striking: from 22.4 to 5.1 per 100,000. The number of acute cases and deaths from this disorder is today very low, largely as the result of an improvement in the dietary intake of people living in socioeconomically depressed environments. So it was not really the deficiency in niacin intake that was the principal cause of pellagra, but a socioeconomic environment which led to that deficiency. Indeed, it would appear that many, if not most, disorders are to a significant extent due to social conditions resulting from an environment impoverished in the elements necessary for the maintenance of health.

There is a class of sociocultural dysfunctions of the brain, the origin of which, it seems to me, has received insufficient attention. Functional expressions of this class of sociocultural injury are the deficits in behavior, and especially in motivation, learning ability, and intelligence which are its effects. It is generally agreed that the most important factor in the healthy development of the conceptus is nutrition—not merely the nutrition derived from the mother, but also the nutrition of the mother's mother, and probably also of the mother's father, not to mention the child's own father.[2]

I want to make it quite clear that when I use the word "damage" in this chapter I am not referring to any kind of physical injury or destruction to the brain, but to socially originating deprivation of schooling organization. This means, for example, if anyone is deprived of the opportunity to read, they will be unable to read, and suffer all the consequences associated with that damaging handicap in a society that places so high a premium upon the ability to read. That inability doe not mean that any physical damage has been done to the brain, but simply that the part of the brain involved in learning to read has not been adequately trained for reading. In short, what has occurred is perhaps best described as "delayed development." The outstanding species trait of human beings is their educability, a learning capacity which lasts well into old age. All that the brain needs for learning, for growth and development, is a stimulating and challenging educational environment.[3]

Our word "education," derived from the Latin *educare,* means, to "nourish and to cause to grow," from conception to the last days of our lives.

At twenty weeks fetal age to thirty weeks fetal age in the human female there are about seven million egg cells present in the ovary which, by about forty weeks fetal age become enveloped by granulosa cells, forming follicles containing ova which are already in the prophase of meiotic division. During later fetal life and childhood, these follicles undergo successive waves of development and atresia, the number of primordial follicles falling from a maximum of two million just before birth to about 300,000 in the adult.[4] Should the fetus suffer from inadequate nutrition, these egg-cells, like all tissues of the fetus, may be detrimentally affected. The process of mitosis, from interphase, through prophase, metaphase, anaphase, to telophase, takes about eighteen hours, and meiosis almost as long.[5] During those fundamental phases of genetic development, almost anything can happen to the cellular structures as a consequence of inadequate nutrition. Not alone the female, but the male who has himself suffered from malnutrition during his postnatal life may also have suffered some damage to his gonadal tissues. These are not conjectures. We know them to be very real possibilities.[6]

Morbidity, mortality, and teratogenic rates are significantly higher in the children of malnourished pregnant women than in those who were adequately nourished. Height, weight, and intelligence scores are also lower in the children of malnourished mothers. These are important facts, and they have long been known, even though the relation of fetal and childhood malnutrition to lowered intelligence does not seem to have stirred those who should have been most impressed by it. The physicalistic or biogenic bias seems to have been largely responsible for the failure to recognize the role played by social conditions in the causation of physical and behavioral deficiencies.

Maternal malnutrition in relation to impairment of the offspring has received some attention, but the role of paternal malnutrition in producing deficits in his offspring has been largely neglected. Stieve has shown, both in other animals and in man, that malnutrition may severely injure the sexual tissues in both male and female. Stieve found that stressful conditions of any kind may damage the development of sperm, and that such sperm fertilizing a normal ovum may jeopardize the healthy development of the conceptus. Stieve also found that at the very moment the female undergoes a stressful experience "and there is in the ovary a follicle ready to emerge or almost so, it does not erupt, but instead collapses and the whole follicle degenerates."[7]

Stress in the mother may have a more or less damaging effect upon the ovary as a whole or upon specific ova in it. Selye and others have produced abundant evidence that in rats the characteristic response of the female sex organs to systemic stress manifest itself mainly by ovarian atrophy and more or less permanent suppression of the female sex cycle.[8] Physiologically these changes are known to be due to decreased gonadotrophin production from the anterior lobe of the pituitary. It is highly probable that a similar mechanism, under similar conditions, is at work in the human female.[9]

To malnutrition, and as a factor entirely apart from it, resulting from the pressures of a disadvantaged sociocultural environment must be added stress. It is known that stress alone is capable of exerting all sorts of unfavorable effects upon the developing conceptus and child. Interaction of stress with the genotype is discussed is Joffe's book *Prenatal Determinants of*

Behavior, and in my own book *Prenatal Influences.*[10] Göllnitz has proposed a syndromic axis with the milder forms including over-reactivity, distractibility, stimulus domination, variability of mood, of motivation, and of bodily function, and general behavior disturbance. The more severe forms include emotional explosiveness, rage responses, passivity, loss of insight, slowing up of thought processes, and general personality disintegration.[11]

Birch speaks of brain damage as referring to a behavior syndrome and not to the fact of brain damage as such, and this may well apply to dysfunctional behavior resulting from temporary impairments of brain function, such as the conditions he describes, namely, developmental lag, behavior disturbance, motor awkwardness, minor perceptual disturbance, and distractibility;[12] to which malfunctions Stott would add a number of symptoms indicative of inefficient neural control or regulation of the soma: poor vocal articulation, faults of homeostasis, enuresis, excessive sweating or salivation, choroid movements, restless or over-heavy sleep, "hysterical" pains and disabilities

It would be quite misleading to suggest that we fully understand the nature of the morphological, metabolic or immunilogical counterparts of these phenomena. We do not, but we are making progress sufficient for us to be able to say that every kind of stress will affect the behavioral development of the conceptus and will do so to the end of our lives.

Early Malnourishment

There is a universal embryogenic law to the effect that the earlier the noxious influences to which the organism is exposed the more severe is the developmental injury. This law extends to the whole developmental period, and especially to the earlier stages of prenatal development. The living organism is so sensitive that even after it has achieved growth and development, unfavorable environmental influences may severely adversely affect it at any time during later life. This was tragically demonstrated by what happened to many concentration-camp victims of the Nazis during World War II. For example, among a group of Norwegians who had been prisoners of the Nazis, those who had been in the concentration camps the longest, and had suffered the severest deprivations and abuses, presented the most serious evidence of impairment of brain function and structure. "Late sequelae of the suffering and misery," writes Wolff, "were major behavior disturbances and even degenerative changes in the brain . . . Defects were roughly proportional to the duration and intensity of the abuse." Such were the effects of stress upon fully developed adults.[13] It would hardly be a bold speculation to suggest that similar stresses may be transmitted, in humoral and metabolic forms, through the placenta to the tissues of the developing conceptus and especially to the brain. The human's total number of brain cells, thirteen billion, appears to be established by twenty-five fetal weeks of age. On experimental animals, the evidence indicates that behavior disturbances as a consequence of damaging environmental effects may be irreversible.[14] There is some evidence that suggests that behavior may be seriously affected as a result of metabolic disturbances in the monoamines of the brain, the catecholamines, norepinephrine and dopamine, and the indole amine, serotonin, acting differentially in the different parts of the brain in which they are mostly found.[15]

That sociocultural environmental factors may determine the conditions that directly affect the very elements which influence the constitutional development of the individual, long before that individual is even conceived, and substantively after conception, is now no longer disputable. In the fourteen largest cities of the United States in 1950, approximately one child out of ten was culturally underprivileged or deprived. By 1960, this figure had risen to one in three.[16] In 1970, this figure approached almost one in two enrolled in the public schools of these large cities.

In the Santiago slums, in Chile, Dr. Fernando Mönckeberg found that 45 percent of the preschool children were mentally deficient, while between 60 and 70 percent of the children were malnourished.[17] There can be very little doubt that much the same conditions prevail in the slums of other impoverished regions virtually everywhere in the Americas. In the United States, in 1992, it is estimated that well over 20 million children were living under a subsistence level.[18]

Throughout the Americas there is a high positive correlation between poor socioeconomic conditions and malnutrition: Low per capita income, illiteracy, low cultural level, bad sanitary conditions, low intellectual performance of the underprivileged groups, and finally, racial and religious prejudices. Faced as we are with a coming world situation in which there will be less and less food for more and more people, a world in which the complexities of the social and political conditions thus exacerbated will render even more difficult the problems which will confront us, the challenge presented to us becomes urgently more pressing each hour, and with each hour the time grows short.

It has been conservatively estimated that the total number of malnourished children in the world between the ages of 1 and 6 years reached 269 million in 1966, 276 million in 1967, 329 million in 1968, well over 400 million in 1969, and well over 460 million in 1970.[19] By the end of this century, when world population is expected to double to over seven billion, it is more than likely, if present trends continue, that there will be more than a billion malnourished children on this earth, and that eighty percent of all inhabitants will be living in those parts of the world in which hunger is now a predominant every day fact of life.

Dr. Mönckeberg's findings in Santiago present a shocking example of conditions that are not only widespread throughout the Americas, but are also reported from many other parts of the world.[20] Furthermore, those findings present something of a forecast of the shape of things to come should we fail to take the proper measures in time. Hence, it is important to set out Dr. Mönckeberg's findings, and to reflect upon their meaning. Dr. Mönckeberg found that only 51 percent of his malnourished preschool children had a normal development quotient of over 85. The percentage of adequately nourished children rated as normal from the slums, 95 percent, was very similar, 97 percent, for the children from middle class homes in Santiago.

In 150 preschool children from a very low class homogeneous population in which malnutrition was prevalent, Dr. Mönckeberg found a marked difference in intellectual capacity in children whose weights were under the third percentile on a standard scale and had a marked growth retardation, as compared with those children whose weights were over the tenth percentile and were considered nutritionally normal. A very significant relationship was found between the degree of growth retardation, when outside the normal limits, and psychomotor development.

In addition to growth retardation, these children had smaller heads than those of 500 adequately nourished middle-class children. These deficits in cranial growth were significantly correlated with decreased mental ability. In infants with severe marasmus during the first months of life, not only is the head smaller, but the brain is disproportionately smaller than the head. In normal children, transillumination of the skull with a beam from a 500-watt bulb directed at the top of the head will show a zone of illumination approximately two centimeters wide around the point of contact between the light and the child's head. In children with marasmus, a much larger portion of the skull is illuminated, and in many cases, the entire skull, thus dramatically indicating the massive retardation of brain growth in these children.

In order to determine whether the early effects of malnutrition could be reversed, Dr. Mönckeberg conducted a follow-up study on fourteen children admitted to a hospital with severe malnutrition beginning during the first months of life. Following long periods of treatment in the hospital, the children continued to make outpatient visits and received liters of free milk per month. At three to six years of age, the clinical appearance and biochemical index of these children appear to be normal. Weight is within normal limits, but the children are short for their age. Head circumference is below normal, and the average IQ is only 62, significantly below the average of Chilean preschool children from low socio-economic areas. In no case was a child's IQ above 76. Since it is well established that brain growth, consisting largely of protein and lipid synthesis, takes place early in the life of the child, Dr. Mönckeberg concluded "it is logical to assume that the effects of malnutrition during this critical period are permanent."[21] The facts, however, have nothing to do with logic, but with the evidence that under improved conditions of life, such deficits are reversible.[22]

Cravioto, summarizing the results of many studies on the relation of malnutrition to development, concludes

> that the existence of an association between protein-calorie malnutrition in infancy and retardation in mental development has been established beyond reasonable doubt. It can also be stated that there is a high probability that this lag in mental development may have long lasting consequences if severe malnutrition is experienced at a very early age in the life of the child.[23]

In a similar survey, Eichenwald and Fry conclude, "Observations on animals and human infants suggest that malnutrition during critical period of early life results in short stature and may, in addition, permanently and profoundly affect the future intellectual and emotional development of the individual."[24]

Since in malnutrition it would be expected that the lack of adequate protein and the vitamin and calorie deficiencies, which are so often its accompaniments would affect the DNA and RNA which directs the formation of proteins, this has become the subject of inquiry. Winick and Rosso determined the amount of DNA in the brains of children who died of malnutrition as compared with the amount in the brains of normally nourished children. They found the amount of DNA in the brains of the malnourished children to be significantly less, thus indicating the presence of a substantially smaller number of brain cells. Head circumference, brain weight, and protein content, were all reduced.[25]

The protein-vitamin-calorie deficiencies may so affect DNA and RNA or both so that the mechanisms for incorporating amino acids into body proteins either cease to operate fully or function in abnormal ways.

Zamenhof and his co-workers have shown that deficient diets administered to female rats before and during pregnancy result in offspring that exhibit a substantial reduction in total brain DNA, and hence, they assumed, in a reduction in the total number of brain cells. Such offspring also show behavioral deficiencies.[26] Myelination, differentiation, development of arborizing collaterals between neurons may also be affected., the chemistry of the nervous system may all be seriously affected in the malnourished child, with more or less serious consequences for its ability to learn or develop into a normally competent human being.[27]

Stress factors of every sort are of the very essence of the life of the poor: physical illness, broken homes, malnutrition, emotional strain, and almost every kind of social deprivation. Every investigation that has ever been conducted on this subject has agreed in finding that poverty is the principal cause of most of the developmental retardation encountered in human beings.[28]

In addition to such stress factors there are the hazards of the physical environment: pollution of water and air, radiation, lead and other forms of poisoning, asbestos, and others; and then there are the effects upon the unborn of drug use, alcohol abuse, smoking, and many more, all affecting the growth and development of the body and mind.[29]

However, it cannot be too-often repeated that the evidence presented by such sources as Levitsky and Diamond incontrovertibly show that under enriched environments all deficits are reversible.[30]

Social Deprivation

Let us now turn our attention to a direct retardative influence on the development of the brain which is entirely the result of unfavorable social conditions. It has been known for many years that health, intelligence, achievement, and socially adequate behavior are highly correlated with socioeconomic factors: the better the socioeconomic environment the higher the scores achieved on all these parameters.[31] But more than that, the evidence is clear that the growth and development of the nervous system and the sense organs is greatly influenced by the social experience of the organism. One of the earliest, and now classical, experimental demonstrations of the effect of environmental experience on the development of the nervous system was George Ellett Coghill's investigation of the development of the salamander *Amblystoma punctatum,* set out in many papers and in his classic book *Anatomy and the Problem of Behaviour* (1929).[32] Coghill showed that neuronal development was markedly more developed in stimulated than in non-stimulated animals. Axon terminals and the growth of collaterals was much more active in the stimulated than in the nonstimulated animals. Coghill concluded his book with the memorable words, "The real measure of the individual ... whether lower animal or man, must include the element of growth as a creative power. Man is, indeed, a mechanism, but he is a mechanism which, within the limitations of life, sensitivity and growth, is creating and operating himself."[33]

The individual deprived of the stimulations necessary for the development of sensitivity and growth simply fails to develop in these modalities, and in the ability to create and operate himself.[34] For human beings, this is the greatest of all disasters. The greatest evil and the most enduring of all tragedies for the individual and his society lies in the difference between what he was capable of becoming and what he has in fact been caused to become.

It is of such sociogenically induced tragedies that I speak here. These tragedies and the mechanism of their production are of more than clinical interest, for there have always been those among us who have been eager to claim a genetic causation for such misfortunes, and to make such presumed and unsubstantiated genetic assumptions the basis for social policy. This has been especially so in connection with the problem-solving form of behavior we call intelligence, especially as allegedly measured by IQ tests.

Intelligence is something that develops as the result of the interaction of brain potentials with experience, nutritional and social. Fundamentally and functionally, intelligence is both a special and general abilities resulting primarily from the social organization of brain potentials for the making of adaptive responses to the particular challenges of the environment. At birth, the brain is continuing the accelerated rate of growth that commenced during the last two months of intrauterine development, gaining weight at the rate of between one and two milligrams a minute, a rate which is continued throughout the first six months. By the end of this period, the brain has virtually doubled in size, from a weight of 350 to 656 grams, a gain of 306 grams. The size of this increment exceeds by far anything ever achieved this way again (see Table 22.1).

By the end of the first year, the rate of increase has decelerated to half the rate of the first six months, when the brain attains a weight of 825 grams. The same decelerated rate is maintained during the whole of the second year, with the brain achieving a weight of 1010 grams. During the third year, there is a further deceleration to one-third the rate of the first six months. And by the end of the third year, the brain of the average 3-year-old has achieved more than four-fifths of its maximum adult size; the child's brain now weighs, on the average, 1115 grams. When the brain attains its maximum size, at between 20 and 29 years, it will have added, in the additional 17 or so years, no more than 281 grams to the grand total of 1396 grams.

All the evidence suggests that during the long period of brain growth, and especially during the first critical three years, it is probably the first six months, when the brain in its most rapid phase of growth and cell number is also increasing, that are the most critical.

Critical Periods In Brain Development

The evidence further suggests that at birth the human neonate is only half gestated, and that he completes his gestation, like the little marsupial, outside the womb. This latter developmental period I have called *exterogestation*. It terminates when the infant begins to crawl about for himself, at about 9 or 10 months.[35]

TABLE 22.1

GROWTH OF THE HUMAN BRAIN

Fetus Lunar Months	Weight in Grams	Gain in Grams	Percent of Gain	Rate of Increase
5	62.5	25.5	40.0	
6	88.0	25.5	29.0	
8	277.0	189.0	68.6	A threefold increase in weight in this two-month period
9 birth	350/392	73/115	30.0	An increment of about a third of the previous month's weight
½ year	656.0	306.0	47.0	Almost doubles in weight in first six months
1	825.0	169.0	20.5	Reduction to half rate of increase of first six months
2	1,010.0	185.0	18.3	Reduction to half rate of increase of first six months
3	1,115.0	105.0	9.4	Reduction to one-third rate of increase of first six months
4	1,180.0	75.0	6.4	Gradual deceleration of rate of growth
6	1,250.0	70.0	5.6	
9	1,307.0	57.0	4.3	
12	1,338.0	31.0	3.3	
20–29	1,396.0	58.0	4.0	

The human infant is much more precariously poised in relation to the environment than we have been accustomed to think. Humans are born biologically premature in every respect, and it is during the first six months of postnatal life that the brain, continuing its fetal rate of growth, accomplishes all that packaging of cellular materials which will serve it for the rest of its life. The whole of the first three years of postnatal life will constitute the period of the experiential, the social, organization of his brain. Almost the whole of the individual's later integrative behavioral abilities will depend upon it. It is during this critical period that purely social environmental deficiencies may seriously and detrimentally affect the organization of the brain.

Such deficiencies often result in what may be termed *the social deprivation syndrome.* This syndrome is principally characterized by a short attention span and learning difficulties resulting in poor test performance. This is usually measured in a lower than normal IQ test score, and in poor school and social performance. Such deficits are commonly attributed to genetic inadequacies. The difficulty is, indeed, that the social deprivation syndrome mimics the genetically influenced condition. Such mimicked conditions are known as phenocopies; that is to say, the apparent condition resembles the genetic one, but is in fact due to nongenetic causes. Much ink has been spilled and many a reputation lost in the sinuous convolutions of this difficult subject, in the endeavor by many writers to show that such behavioral deficits are principally due to genetic factors.

There can be not the least doubt that there exist many behavioral deficits of this sort that are due to genetic deficiencies.[36] It is therefore of great importance to be able to distinguish the genetic conditions from the phenocopies. We cannot, at present, do much to prevent the birth of genetically influenced poor learners, but we can do a great deal to prevent the development of poor learners who owe their disability to nothing more than a poor social environment.

With rather monotonous regularity there appear, at almost predictable intervals, elaborate studies that purport to show that certain racial or ethnic or social groups of other kinds are, on the whole, poorer learners and achievers and score significantly lower on IQ tests than the group to which the investigator happens to belong. Such reports invariably suffer the same eventual fate. They are lauded by those who prefer to believe what these studies purport to demonstrate, and are severely criticized and condemned by the experts. Following a period of perfervid discussion in the press, and partisan misuse in legislatures, the brouhaha generally dies down, and the entire incident is finally consigned to the archives in which such incidents are eventually preserved. In the meantime, aid and comfort has been given to racists, segregationists, those who perhaps should know better, and serve to fortify in their citadels of infallibility the half-educated and the many who have been "educated" beyond their intelligence.

The facts, derived from innumerable studies, indicate that what IQ tests measure are not the genetic potentials for intelligence, but a complex interacting of many other factors: the expression of the interaction between genetic potentials, nutritional, socioeconomic, emotional, motivational factors, and schooling, in addition to the developing individual's personal reorganization of his subjective and objective worlds to recreate his own environments.

One wonders whether those who are so ready to settle for the genetic factor as the principal cause of the differences in IQ between blacks and whites would also hold that the enormous overall differences, at every age level, in morbidity and mortality rates, between these two groups are also due to genetic factors.

Why is it that these racial ideologists refuse to acknowledge, even to consider, that social factors may be the principal causes responsible for the differences in learning abilities of different racial groups? Learning ability is highly correlated with social class within the same ethnic group.[37]

What racists fail to understand is that in man race is, for all practical purposes, a social myth and an institutionalized way of behavior, a special form of social class, a caste status, and that as such it is subject to all the influences and consequences that flow from such arrangements.

That a significant genetic element contributes to the basic intelligence potential of every individual is beyond dispute. It should, however, be clear that, like every other genetic potential, the development of intelligence is perhaps more than any other trait dependent on the kind of environmental stimulations to which it is exposed. Instead of dismissing such environmental factors as unimportant in order to sustain even the veriest semblance of his claims, the genetic reductionists should have carefully investigated the possible effects of such environmental factors upon IQ test results. This he conspicuously failed to do, and for this reason alone his claims would have to be wholly rejected. To assign, as the reductionists have been known to do, a good eighty percent of an individual's intelligence to genetic factors and a mere twenty percent to environmental influences constitutes not only a scientifically groundless assumption, but also a wholly indefensible one. For there exists a vast body of scientific evidence which indicates not that genetic potentials or environmental ones are more important than the other, but that both are of the greatest importance for the adequate development of intelligence, however constituted it may be.

Reference has already been made to some of the evidence indicating the damage that malnutrition can do to genetic potentials for intelligence. The evidence indicating the damage capable of being done by unfavorable socioeconomic conditions to the development of intelligence is even more extensive and conclusive.[38]

The universal conclusion to which these researches point is that no matter what the quality of the genetic potentials for intelligence may be in any individual, the expression of those potentials will be significantly influenced by his total environment. Poverty as such is not necessarily either a necessary or a sufficient condition in the production of intellectual deficits, for if nutrition and the home cultural environment are adequate, the child will suffer no handicapping effect.

But if nutrition is poor, health care deficient, housing debasing, family income low, family disorganization prevalent, discipline anarchic, ghettoization more or less complete, personal worth consistently diminished, expectations low, and aspirations frustrated, and these are combined with other environmental handicaps, then one may expect the kind of failures in intellectual development that are so often gratuitously attributed to genetic factors. Those who make such attributions fail to understand how dependent the development of intelligence is upon the reduction of such conditions of privation, frustration, and hopelessness.[39] When the effects of such postnatal environmental factors are combined with the adverse effects of prenatal ones, there emerges a continuum of psychosocial, as well as psychophysical casualty, which renders it utterly nonsensical to compare casualties of such environments with the products of average middle class environments by whom and on whom IQ tests were devised. It is not simply the culture of poverty or even the poverty of culture or any other one single factor, but the combination of many socioenvironmental factors, which produces the sociogenic deficits so irresponsibly attributed to genetic factors. As Gladys Schwesinger long ago pointed out at the conclusion of her book on *Heredity and Environment,* "the problem of heredity and environment is not a general problem, but is specific to each individual, to each of his characteristics, and to each environment."[40]

In the development of so complex an ability as intelligence, making every allowance for possible differences in genetic endowment, the environment is of paramount importance. Just as the individual learns to speak, with vocabulary, imagery, and accent according to environmental influences that have acted upon him, so he learns, within the limits of his genetic capacities, the vocabulary, imagery, and development of intelligence, according to the environmental influences with which he has interacted. As Bodmer and Cavalli-Sforza have put it, "any given test . . . depends on the ability acquired at a given age, which is inevitably the result of the combination of innate ability and the experience of the subject. Intelligence tests are therefore at most tests of achieved ability."[41]

And that is precisely the point. If seriously handicapping impediments are placed in the way of the development of any capacity, the individual will, to that extent, simply fail to achieve that ability, for abilities are trained capacities. Limiting environments place limits upon the development of abilities. In the matter of problem-solving, that is to say, thinking, intelligence, Harlow found that rhesus monkeys subjected to ambiguous rewards for tasks performed, so that no specific perceptual clues were available to the animals, were not nearly as effective problem-solvers as those in the control group who were consistently rewarded. Harlow thus showed that the learning sets which make insight possible do not come ready-made, but must be acquired, and that once acquired they increase the capacity of the organism to solve certain problems.[42]

Thompson and Heron have found that pet-reared dogs in a variety of situations behaved more intelligently than their litter-mates who were caged for the first eight months of their lives.[43] All animals thus far studied show the effects of early experience or its deprivation in much the same ways.[44]

Bennett, Rosenzweig, and Diamond showed that exposure of rats to different environments—enriched, colony, or impoverished—leads to characteristic changes in wet and dry weight of samples of rat brain, in enzymatic activity, and in depth of cerebral cortex. Impoverished animals were caged singly, colony animals two or three per cage, and enriched animals ten or twelve per larger cage including toys. In every case, dry weight, depth of cerebral cortex, enzymatic activity, and problem solving behavior, were increased by exposure to enriched environment as compared with standard colony and impoverished conditions.[45] In mice, Henderson found that an enriched environment resulted in an increase in brain weight.[46]

Since the internal consistency of the evidence for other animals fully agrees with that obtained in studies of humans, there can remain little doubt that for the development of innumerable behavioral traits, but especially for the development of intelligence, the stimulation of certain kinds of social experience is indispensably necessary.[47] It is, in a word, experiences of an encouraging kind, as contrasted to experiences of a discouraging kind that count.

When we consider the complexity of the factors operating upon the child, the sociocultural brain damage done in humans must be very considerable indeed, for there can be no question that damage is involved when size, weight, failure of cortical development, quantity and size of brain cells, and enzymatic activity of the brain are the effects of a socially impoverished environment. But we repeat, it is not irreversible under improved sociocultural environments.

The reductionists so completely failed to understand the nature of socially disadvantaging conditions that they actually believed children of blacks and whites of similar income level enjoy equal cultural and other environmental advantages. Hence, since these children, according to reductionists, enjoy similar environmental experiences, the differences in IQ test results must be due to genetic factors. What they fail to understand is that income level alone does not determine the quality of cultural background, and that it is quite unsound to equate the two. There is no income level at which blacks enjoy the same basic opportunities as whites. By basic opportunities I mean a sustaining cultural background of stimulation that encourages the growth and development of aspirations for achievement, a cultural background in which one does not suffer from malnutrition of the body or the mind, in which one has not suffered emotional, economic, social, or educational privations, but to which, in most of these respects, a positive rather than a negative sign is attached, and an environment free from susceptibility to virtually every disease and disorder from discrimination. See "Death by Discrimination? Of Prejudice and Heart Attacks" (*New York Times,* 24 November 1976).

The truth is that at no time have blacks of any income group enjoyed anything approaching equal basic opportunities with whites.[48] It is, therefore, quite unsound to attribute to genetic factors what may well be due to environmental ones.[49]

What is quite certain is that IQ scores vary with environmental experience. For example, it is well known that Native American children showed a spectacular rise in IQ scores after oil was discovered on tribal land and the Native Americans were permitted to share in the accruing profits. There is nothing mysterious about this. The oil simply facilitated the lubrication of intelligence potentials by creating conditions that enabled the children to enjoy a social and economic environment similar to that enjoyed by white children. Under such conditions, among the Osage Indians of Oklahoma, for example, Rohrer in 1942 found that on one test, the Goodenough "Draw-a-man" test, the white children obtained an average IQ of 103, and the Indian children an average of 104. On a second test, using language, the Indian children scored 100 and the white children scored 98.[50] Similarly, Garth found that a group of Indian children living in white foster homes scored an average IQ of 102, which is a quite significant improvement over the average IQ of their brothers and sisters still living on the Reservation who scored an average IQ of 87.5.[51]

Clearly, the environmental differences were principally responsible for the differences in the scores of these children. There is no question of brain damage being involved here—simply a difference in environment. Nor, for that matter was a difference in genetic intelligence involved, for clearly that is not what these test results reflected; what they reflected was a difference in environmental experience and personal development acting together with genetic potentials for the ability to respond to IQ tests. It is not that the lower testing siblings were any less intelligent than their higher testing siblings, but that they were less experienced in the requirements necessary to meet the challenges of those tests.

Since genetic factors are involved in virtually all forms of behavior, there can be little doubt that such factors may play a significant role in performance on IQ tests. But that is a very different thing from claiming that IQ tests measure the genetic contribution to intelligence. Scarr-Salapatek published a study in which she found differences in heritability of IQ scores in black and white and in social and class groups. The differences are in the expected directions and could have been predicted. Scarr-Salapatek sees the variance in performance as difference, not as deficit, and she welcomes these differences as contributing to the greater enrichment and variety of humanity.[52] "To the extent," she writes, "that better, more supportive environments can be provided for all children, genetic variance and mean scores will increase for all groups."[53] Indeed, "equality of opportunity" will lead "to bigger and better genotype-phenotype correlations," but meanwhile, it needs to be emphasized, that as long as the inequalities in opportunities remain, so will the misery and poor performance on IQ tests and in life situations remain for millions of the socially deprived. There are many flaws in IQ tests, and among those usually overlooked by those who administer and evaluate these tests is the fact that a difference of as much a twenty points can be produced in IQ scores depending upon the mood or attitude of the testee. Feelings toward the person administering the test can be an important factor in influencing performance on tests. Katz, Heuchy, and Allen found in 1968 that black boys of grade-school age performed better on verbal learning tasks with black examiners than with white examiners.[54] Watson found that West Indian students in a London secondary school in a working class neighborhood scored an average of ten points less on IQ tests than when the same tests were falsely described as an experiment to help curriculum. Watson, who is white, also found that when the tests were given by his assistant, a West Indian, with very dark skin, the scores typically climbed.

Similarly, Katz found that black students did better on IQ tests when they were deceived into believing that their intelligence was not being tested. Black students, when they were freed of anxiety about intellectual performance, achieved higher IQ scores under a white investigator than a black one.[55]

With little expectation of overcoming the judgment of their intellectual inferiority, which they knew to be held by many white Americans, the student's motivation was low, and so were their scores. But when the IQ test was disguised as something else, human ambition soared. As long as their intelligence was not being evaluated, they felt more challenged to show the white examiner what they could do than one of their own kind.

The expectation of inadequate performance on IQ tests undoubtedly contributed to the lower performance of blacks on these tests. Conversely, confidence bolstered by some successes raises scores by five to ten points.

I am not aware that either Scarr-Salapatek or any of the reductionists made any allowance for such factors.

Cooper and Zubek in an interesting experiment showed in 1958 how in different genetic lines different environments may serve either to develop or depress problem-solving capacities. They used two lineages of rats whose ability to find their way through a maze had been especially selected by selective breeding. When rats from the "bright" and "dull" lineages were raised for a whole generation in a restricted environment which differed from the normal laboratory environment, no differences between the lines could be found. The bright and dull performed at the same level. When both were raised in the same stimulating environment, both did almost equally well. In a normal environment, bright rats made 120 errors, whereas the dull ones made 168. In a restricted environment, both made about 170 errors, but in a stimulating environment, the bright made 112 errors while the dull made 120.[56]

Levitsky and Barnes[57] found that early malnutrition and isolation in rats during the first seven weeks of postnatal life led to various behavioral sequelae. Compared with the controls, the experimental animals showed a significant increase in open field locomotion, an increase, but not statistically significant, in mutual grooming, a reduction in following response, an increase in fighting time, and a marked depression in exploratory behavior. These investigators found that in all the observed responses, except fighting, whatever effect early malnutrition produced it was always exaggerated by environmental isolation and depressed by environmental stimulation. They found, also, that the behavioral effects of the malnutrition were completely eliminated in most cases by additional stimulation early in life.

The authors suggest two theoretical mechanisms as possibly explaining how malnutrition and environmental stimulation may interact to produce longterm behavioral changes. This explanation applies with equal cogency to the social deprivation syndrome.

Malnutrition may alter the experience or perception of the environment during early development by rendering the organism physiologically less capable of receiving and/or integrating environmental information. Decreases in brain size, brain DNA, myelinization, cortical dendritic growth, brain cholinesterase content, and brain norepinephrine control have all been reported in malnourished animals. Environmental stimulation produces changes in brain norepinephrine, cholinesterase, as well as cortical dendritic growth. Hence, malnutrition during a critical period of development may produce the changes which render inoperative the physiological mechanisms responsible for the long term effects of early stimulation.[58]

And, as Latham has suggested,

another mechanism through which early malnutrition and environmental variables may interact may be purely behavioral in nature. Malnutrition may produce behavior that is incompatible with the incorporation of environmental information necessary for optimum cognitive growth. In the case of a malnourished animal, the behavior may be primarily food oriented and in the case of a malnourished child, the behavior may be expressed as apathy and social withdrawal.[59]

In short, the specific kinds of information or specific behavioral responses which may be required for optimum cognitive development as reflected by test behavior or educational performance may be absent or depressed in the malnourished child as a result of a higher priority of responses elicited by the malnutrition.

The demonstration of a behavioral interaction between early nutritional conditions and the environment of young animals not only demonstrates the complexity of understanding determinants of behavior, but also points out the profundity of early experience and early nutrition as major contributions to ultimate adult behavior.[60]

The power of the environment is clearly very considerable indeed, and the earlier it affects the developing organism the more substantive are its effects. The point I wish to make here is that mental development is affected equally, whether by inadequate, ambiguous, or confusing social stimuli necessary for mental development; or by insufficient physical nutrition necessary for adequate cerebral development. The mental damage done by social deprivation, even though it may be more occult, is, in its behavioral consequences, at least as substantial as that done by physical malnutrition.

To conclude, the evidence clearly indicates that during the first three years, when the basic foundations and organization of the mind are in process of construction, inadequate provision and poor quality of experience may seriously affect the fabric of the brain, of which the mind is presumably a function. In such cases, the brain and mind are rendered incapable of later organization at levels of emotional and cognitive integration matching that achieved by others who have not suffered such sociogenic disturbance.

The brain may not have been damaged in quite the same manner, as it may be by physical malnutrition, but the damage done by social malnutrition is nonetheless real. This, we may postulate, consists in the disabling failure of organization which, both structurally and functionally, renders it extremely difficult if not impossible for individuals to respond appropriately to many of the challenges of the environment with the competence that their genetic potentials would, under the organizing stimulation of an adequate social environment, have permitted. Social malnourishment, both structurally, and functionally, can be just as brain/mind damaging as physical malnourishment. Such sociogenic malnourishment affects the brain in millions of human beings all over the world. It is a form of brain damage that has received far too little attention. Yet it constitutes an epidemic problem of major proportions. What it calls for is, first, the recognition that the problem is real, second that it can only be solved by those improvements in the environment that will assure every newborn baby the fulfillment of its birthright, which is development of its potentialities to the optimum.

Living in a culture of inequality, poverty, discrimination, racism, unemployment, and debasement of values, is humanly demeaning especially for blacks, a culture in which the very condition of being black is in some ways treated as a crime, a crime which leads to crime, because the only outlet for the resulting emotional frustration is its effect, namely, violence. In the culture of racism, where so many are scarred and criminalized, the victims are euphemistically called "the race problem," implying that the victims are the cause of it. The latest solution to the problem by government is the threatened enlistment of thousands more police, and the building of more overcrowded prisons.

In America racist policies have been pursued almost from the beginning of slavery, Jim Crow law has been the law, and justice has been lost in the law. In the last decade of the twentieth century there are more than 1,600,000 Americans in jail, of which number there are 4 times as many blacks behind bars than whites, all at a cost of $14 billion a year. Politicians habitually have no interest in discovering a humane solution to the "problem of racism." *May it not be that the white American is the problem?* In any event the failure of our politicians directly contributes to the maintenance and exacerbation of racism. and its consequences. This is especially true of the Washington demagogues who are always speaking of the welfare of "The American People," while cultivating their own self-interests as well as that of the National Rifle Association. By repeatedly blocking passage of handgun control bills they have been directly responsible for the fact that America has by far the highest number of handgun murders in the world. Combining the mean average of handgun homicides per 100,000 population in 1980, of the seven countries that control the availability and accessibility of handguns, the United States has a rate which is 77 times greater than that of all the countries combined![61]

May it not be that the staggering rates of murder, domestic violence against women, rape, drug abuse, as well as the general violence that pervades American culture—the fear of walking anywhere at night, the high rates of juvenile delinquency and violence, have some connection with the frustration that so many experience in their daily lives? The struggle to deal with that accumulation of frustration often finds expression against people of color, who have been so long wronged and suffered so much. It is time many Americans understand that in victimizing others they have themselves become the victims, of another demeaning sort.

Notes

1. Milton Terris, *Goldberger on Pellagra* (Baton Rouge: Louisiana State University Press, 1964); Elizabeth W. Elderidge, *The Butterfly Caste: A Social History of Pellagra in the South* (Westport, CT.: Greenwood Publishing, 1972).

2. Ashley Montagu, *Prenatal Influences* (Springfield, IL: Thomas, 1962); David A. Levitsky, ed., *Malnutrition, Environment, and Behavior* (Ithaca: Cornell University Press, 1979).

3. Marian C. Diamond, *Enriching Heredity: The Impact of the Environment on the Anatomy of the Brain* (New York: Free Press, 1988); Reuven Kohne-Raz, *Psychobiological Aspects of Cognitive Growth* (New York: Academic Press, 1977); Robert Ornstein and David Sobel, *The Healing Brain* (New York: Simon & Schuster, 1987); M. C. H. Dodgson, *The Growing Brain: An Essay in Dvelopmental Neurology* (Baltimore: Williams & Wilkins, 1962); James W. Trent, Jr., *Inventing the Feeble Mind* (Berkeley: University of California Press, 1994).

4. N. G. Kase, "The Ovary," in P. K. Duncan's *Diseases of Metabolism*, vol. 2, Garfield G. Duncan, P. K. Bondy, ed. (Philadelphia: Saunders, 1969), 1191–1226.

5. C. P. Swanson, *The Cell*, 2nd ed. (Englewood Cliffs, NJ: Prentice Hall, 1964).

6. Herbert G. Birch and Joan D. Gussow, *Disadvantaged Children* (New York: Harcourt, Brace & World, 1969).

7. H. Stieve, "Der Einfluss von Angst und Psychisher eregnung auf Bau und Funktion der Weiblicher Geschlechtsorgane," *Zentralblatt für Gynakologie* 66 (1942): 1698–1798; H. Stieve, "Anatomische nachweisbare Vorgange im Eirstock des Menschen und ihre Umweltbedingte Steuerung." *Geburtschiffe und Frauenheilkunde* 9 (1948): 639–44; H. Stieve, *Der Einfluss des Nervens Systems auf Bau und Totigkeit der Geschlechtsorgane des Menschen* (Stuttgart: Georg Thieme, 1951); M. Ingrashi, K. Tohma, and M. Ozama, "Pathogenesis of Psychogenic Amenorrhea and Anovulation," *International Journal of Fertility* 10 (1965): 311–19.

8. Hans Selye, *Stress* (Montreal: Acta Inc., 1950); George P. Chrousos et al., Stress: Basic Mechanisms and Clinical Implications, *Annals of the New York Academy of Sciences* (New York, 1995); Leo Goldberger and Shlomo Breznitz, eds., *Handbook of Stress; Theoretical and Clinical Aspects* (New York: Free Press, 1995).

9. W. Horsley Gantt, "Disturbances in Sexual Function During Periods of Stress," in *Life Stress and Bodily Disease*, eds., H. G. Wolff, S. G. Wolff, Jr., and C. C. Hare (Baltimore: Williams & Wilkins, 1950), 1030–50.; H. C. Taylor, in Wolff et al., ibid., 1051–56.

10. J. M. Joffe, *Prenatal Determinants of Behavior* (New York: Pergamon Press, 1969); Ashley Montagu, *Prenatal Influences* Springfield IL, Thomas, 1962); Christopher Norwood, *At Highest Risk: Environmental Hazards to Young and Unborn Children* (New York: McGraw-Hill, 1980).

11. G. Göllnitz, "Ueber die Problematik der Neurosen in Kindesalter." *Ideggyogyasazatio Szenle* 16 (1963–1964): 7–108.

12. Herbert B. Birch, ed., *Brain Damage in Children: Biological and Social Aspects* (Baltimore: William & Wilkins, 1964), 12; D. H. Stott, *Troublesome Children* (New York: Humanities Press, 1966).

13. Wolff, *Life Stress,* 209.

14. Urie Bronfenbrenner, "Early Deprivation in Mammals: A Cross-Species Analysis," in *Early Experience in Behavior,* eds. G. Newton and S. Levene (Springfield, IL: C. C. Thomas, 1968), 627–764.

15. J. J. Schildkraut and S. S. Kety, "Biogenic Amines and Emotion," *Science* 156 (1967): 21–30.

16. F. Reissman, *The Culturally Deprived Child* (New York: Harper & Row, 1962).

17. F. Mönckeberg, "Mental Retardation from Malnutrition," *Journal of the American Medical Association* 177: 2–4.

18. Urie Bronfenbrenner, ed., *Influences on Human Development* (Hinsdale, IL: Dryden Press, 1972); Urie Bronfenbrenner, *The Ecology of Human Development: Experiments by Nature and Design* (Cambridge: Harvard University Press: 1979); Marian C. Diamond, *Enriching Heredity: The Impact of the Environment on the Anatomy of the Brain* (New York: Free Press, 1988); Seymour Lustman, "Cultural Deprivation," *The Psychoanalytic Study of the Child* 25 (1970): 483–502; Ashley Montagu, ed., *Culture and Human Development: Insights Into Growing Human* (Englewood Cliffs, NJ: Prentice-Hall, 1974); Ashley Montagu, *On Being Human,* 2nd ed. (New York: Hawthorn Books, 1970); Ashley Montagu, *The Direction of Human Development,* 2nd ed. (New York: Hawthorn Books, 1970); Grant Newton and Seymour Levine, eds., *Early Experience and Behavior* (Springfield, IL: Thomas, 1968); Robert Gray Patton and Lytt I. Gardner, *Growth Failure in Maternal Deprivation* (Springfield, IL: Thomas, 1963); Albrecht Peiper, *Cerebral Function in Infancy and Childhood,* 3rd ed. (New York: Consultants Bureau, 1963); G. F. Powell, J. A. Brasel, and R. M. Blizzard, "Emotional Deprivation and Growth Retardation Simulating Idiopathic Hypopituitariam: Clinical Evaluation of the Syndrome," *New England Journal of Medicine* 276 (1967): 1271–8; John B. Reinhard and Alan R. Drash, "Psychological Dwarfism: Environmentally Induced Recovery," *Psychomatic Medicine* 31 (1969): 165–72; Barkev S. Sanders, *Environment and Growth* (Baltimore: Warwick & York, 1934); Richard Totman, *Social Causes of Illness* (New York: Pantheon, 1979); E. M. Widdowson, "Mental Contentment and Physical Growth," *Lancet* 1 (1951): 1316–8.

19. J. M. May and H. Lemons, "The Ecology of Malnutrition," *Journal of the American Medical Association* 207 (1969): 2401–05.

20. P. Gyorgy and O. L. Kline, eds., *Malnutrition is a Problem of Ecology* (Basel and New York: Karger, 1970).

21. F. Mönkeberg, op. cit., 30–31; F. Mönkeberg, "Factors Conditioning Malnutrition in Latin America with special reference to Chile," in Gyorgy and Kline, *Malnutrition,* 23.

22. David A. Levitsky, ed., *Malnutrition, Environment, and Behavior: New Perspectives* (Cornell University Press, 1979); Diamond, *Enriching Heredity.*

23. J. Cravioto, "Complexity of Factors Involved in Protein Calorie Malnutrition," in Gyorgy and Kline, *Malnutrition,* 7–22.

24. H. F. Eichenwald, and P. C. Fry, "Nutrition and Learning," *Science* 163 (1969): 139–41.

25. Myron Winick, "Nutrition and Cell Growth," *Nutrition Reviews* 26 (1969), 195–97; M. Winick and P. Rosso, "The Effect of Severe Malnutrition and Cellular Growth of the Human Brain," *Pediatric Research* 3 (1969): 181–84; M. Winick, "Fetal Malnutrition and Growth Processes" *Hospital Practice* (May 1970): 33–41; M. Winick, "Head Circumference and Cellular Growth of the Brain in Normal and Marasmic Children," *Journal of Pediatrics* 74 (1969), 774–78; Zena Stein et al., *Famine and Human Development* (New York: Oxford University Press, 1975); Bronfenbrenner, *Ecology of Human Dvelopment;* J. D.Lloyd-Still, ed., *Malnutrition & Intellectual Development* (Littleton, MA: Publishing Sciences Group, 1976); Nevin S. Scrimshaw and John E. Gordon, eds., *Malnutrition, Learning, and Behavior* (Cambridge: MIT Press, 1968); Bronfenbrenner, *Influences on Human Development;* Herbert L. Leff, Experience, *Environment, and Human Potentials* (New York: Oxford University Press, 1978); R. D. Lund, *Development and Plasticity of the Brain* (New York: Oxford University Press, 1978).

26. S. Zamenhof, E Van Marthens, and F. L. Margolis, "DNA (Cell Number) and Protein Deficiency in Neonatal Brain: Alteration by Dietary Maternal Protein Restriction," *Science* 140 (1968): 322–23; S. Zamenhoff, E. Van Marthens, and F. L. Margolis, "DNA (Cell Number) in Neonatal Brain: Second Generation (F2) Alteration by Maternal (F_o) Dietary Protein Restriction," *Science* 172 (1971): 850–51.

27. N. H. Bass, M. G. Netsky, and E. Young. "Effect of Neonatal Malnutrition on Developing Cerebrum," *Archives of Neurology* 23 (1970): 289–302; R. L. Hurley, *Poverty and Mental Retardation: A Causal Relationship* (New York: Random House, 1969); S. F. Osler and R. E. Cooke, eds., *The Biosocial Basis of Mental Retardation* (Baltimore: Johns Hopkins Press, 1965); E. Grotberg, ed., *Critical Issues in Research Related to Disadvantaged Children* (Princeton: Educational Testing Service, 1969); M. Deutsch, et al., *The Disadvantaged Child* (New York: Basic Books, 1967); M. Deutsch, I Katz, and R. Jensen., eds., *Social Class, Race, and Psychological Development* (New York: Holt, Rinehart and Winston, 1969); John Dobbing, "'Nutrition and the Developing Brain': A Critical Review," in *Malnutrition, Environment and Behavior,* ed. David Levitsky (Ithaca: Cornell University Press, 1979), 41–55.

28. Barkev S. Sanders, *Environment and Growth* (Baltimore: Warwick & York, 1934); J. McVicker Hunt, *Intelligence and Experience* (New York: Ronald Press, 1961); Lennart Levi, ed., *Society, Stress and Disease,* 5 vols., (New York: Oxford University Press, 1971–1987); Leo Goldberger and Shlomo Breznitz, eds., *Handbook of Stress,* 2nd. ed. (New York: The Free Press, 1981).

29. Norwood, *At Highest Risk.*

30. Diamond, *Enriching Heredity.*

31. Gerald S. Lesser, Gordon Fifer, and Donald H. Clark, "Mental Abilities of Children from Different Social Class and Cultural Groups," *Monographs of the Society for Research in Child Development* 30 (1965[4]): 1–115.

32. George Ellett Coghill, *Anatomy and the Problems of Behaviour* (Cambridge: Cambridge University Press, 1929).

33. Ibid., 110.

34. A. Ambrose, *Stimulation in Early Infancy* (New York: Academic Press, 1969); R. P. Michael, ed., *Endochrinology and Human Behavior* (New York: Oxford

University Press, 1968); E. Tobach, L. R. Aronson, and E. Shaw, eds., *The Biopsychology of Development* (New York: Academic Press, 1971).

35. Ashley Montagu, *Growing Young*, 2nd ed. (Westport, CT: Bergen & Garvey, 1989).

36. M. Levitan and Ashley Montagu, *Textbook of Human Genetics*, 2nd ed. (New York: Oxford University Press, 1977); Jerry Hirsch, *Behavior-Genetic Analysis* (New York: McGraw-Hill, 1967); Ashley Montagu, *Human Heredity*, 2nd ed. (New York: New American Library, 1963).

37. Helen H. Davidson, *Personality and Economic Background* (New York: King's Crown Press, 1843); J. M. Hunt, *The Challenge of Incompetence and Poverty* (Urbana: University of Illinois Press, 1969); Gerald L. Lesser et al. "Mental Abilities of Children from Different Social Class and Cultural Groups," *Monographs of the Society for Research in Child Development* 30 (1965 [4]): 1–115.

38. This evidence is set out in hundreds of independent studies ranging from Gladys Schwesinger's 1933 volume *Heredity and Environment* (New York: Macmillan, 1933) to R. Cancro's symposium on *Intelligence: Genetic and Environmental Influences* (New York: Grune & Stratton, 1971); as well as Herbert G. Birch and J. D. Gussow's book on *Disadvantaged Children* (New York: Harcourt, Brace & World, 1969), and R. L. Hurley's book on *Poverty and Mental Retardation: A Casual Relationship* (New York: Random House, 1969), and especially Stephen Jay Gould's *The Mismeasure of Man* (New York: Norton, 1981), not to mention many others.

39. P. Watson, "How Race Affects IQ" *New Society* (London), 16 July 1970, 103–104.

40. G. Schwesinger *Heredity and Environment* (New York: Macmillan, 1933), 45.

41. W. F. Bodmer and L. L. Cavalli–Sforza, "Intelligence and Race," *Scientific American* 223 (1970): 19–29.

42. Harry F. Harlow "The Formation of Learning Sets," *Psychological Review* 56 (1949), 51–56; Harlow, "Learning and Satiation of Response in Intrinsically Motivated Complex Puzzle Performance by Monkeys," *Journal of Comparative and Physiological Psychology* 43 (1995): 289–94.

43. W. R. Thompson and W. Heron, "The Effects of Restricting Early Eaxperience on the Problem-Solving Capacity of Dogs," *Canadian Journal of Psychology* 8 (1954): 17–31.

44. Urie Bronfenbrenner, "Early Deprivation in Mammals."

45. E. L. Bennett, M. R. Rosenberg, and M. C. Diamond, "Rat Brain: Effects of Environmental Enrichment on Wet and Dry Weights," *Science* 163, (1969): 825–26; M. R. Rosenzweig, D. Krech, E. L. Bennett, and M. C. Diamond, "Modifying Brain Chemistry and Anatomy by Enrichment or Impoverishment of Experience," in *Early Experience and Behavior* eds.G. Newton and S. Levine (Springfield, IL: C. C. Thomas, 1968), 258–98.

46. N. D. Henderson. "Brain Weight Increases Resulting from Environmental Enrichment: A Directional Dominance in Mice," *Science* 169 (1970): 776–78.

47. R. J. Light and P. V. Smith, "Social Allocation Models of Intelligence," *Harvard Educational Review* 39 (1969) 484–510; A. L. Stinchcombe, "Environment: The Cumulation of Events," *Harvard Educational Review* 39 (1969): 511–22.

48. Ashley Montagu, *The Direction of Human Development* (New York, Harper & Row, 1955).

49. Otto Klineberg, *Social Psychology*, rev. ed. (New York: Holt, Rinehart and Winston, 1954).

50. J. H. Rohrer, "The Intelligence of Osage Indians," *Journal of Social Psychology* 16 (1942): 99–105.

51. Thomas R. Garth, *Race Psychology* (New York: Whittlesey House, 1931); Thomas R. Garth, "A Study of the Foster Indian Child in the White Home," *Psychological Bulletin* 32 (1935): 708–09.

52. Sandra Scarr-Salapetek, "Unknowns in the IQ Equation," *Science* 174 (1971): 1223–28, and "Race, Social Class, and IQ," *Science* 174 (1971) 1285–95; Sandra Scarr, ed., *Race, Social Class, and Individual Differences in IQ* (Hillsdale, NJ: Erlbaum, 1981).

53. Scarr-Salapetek, "Race, Social Class, and IQ."

54. I. Katz, T. Heuchy, and H. Allen, "Effects of Race of Tester, Approval, Disapproval, and Need on Negro Children's Learning," *Journal of Personality and Social Research* 8 (1968): 38–42.

55. M. Deutsch, I. Katz, and R. Jensen, eds., *Social Class, Race, and Psychological Development* (New York: Holt, Rinehart, and Winston, 1968).

56. R. M. Cooper and J. P. Zubek. "Effects of Enriched and Restricted Early Environments on the Learning Ability of Bright and Dull Rats," *Canadian Journal of Psychology* 12 (1958): 159–64.

57. D. A. Levitzky and R. H. Barnes, "Nutritional and Environmental Interactions in the Behavioral Development of the Rat: Long Term Behavioral Effects," *Science* 176 (1972): 68–71.

58. Ibid.

59. M. C. Latham, in *Calorie and Protein Deficiencies*, eds., R. A. McCance and E. M. Widdowson (New York: Cambridge University Press, 1968).

60. See pages 70–71 of Levitsky, and Barnes, "Nutritional and Environmental Interactions."

61. See the Winter 1986 Washington Report of Handgun Control Inc. The figures per 100,000 population are, Australia 4, Canada 8, Sweden 18, Israel 23, Switzerland 24, Japan 27, United States 1,522.

23

Intelligence, IQ, and Race

What is intelligence? Most people would answer: "Intelligence is what IQ tests measure." But as we shall see, despite the claims of their proponents, IQ tests do not measure intelligence.

The truth is, IQ tests cannot possibly measure intelligence because no one really knows what the *structure* of intelligence is. Without knowing this structure in considerable detail, we cannot even approximate a quantitative measure of it. What is quite clear, except to IQ testers, is that many conditions enter into the making of intelligence. Without taking these conditions into consideration, IQ tests are quite valueless in arriving at an understanding of what intelligence really is. Even worse than valueless, IQ tests often unjustifiably brand childred with the mark of inferiority, especially when what they need beyond all else is encouragement.

Since my days, in the early 1920s, as a student of Charles Spearman, the noted pyschologist, whose novel theory of the nature of intelligence[1] has been put to perfidious use in recent years, psychologists have tried hard to reach some consensus as to the nature and expression of intelligence. Nonetheless, the unraveling of the structure of intelligence remains largely unaccomplished.

The cumulative research of the last seventy years suggests that a good working hypothesis would be to regard intelligence as constituted of a large assembly of highly varied overlapping and adaptive abilities, rather than as a single faculty. Somewhat independent of its elusive structure, however, intelligence appears to be largely the summation and personal incorporation of the learning experiences of each individual.

As for the relation of the structure of the brain to the nature and level of intelligence, many scientific reputations have been compromised in the sinuous twists of the human brain when insupportable racial differences were claimed to have been found in weight, size, convolutions, and its other structures. These racial differences in structure were believed to be sufficient to account for racial differences in intelligence.

Unfortunately, claims to racial structural differences resulting in racial differences in intelligence continue. Yet, all such claims of the higher phrenology, as it has been called, have repeatedly been shown to be wholly unsound and have been thoroughly discredited over the last several decades. Quite simply, within the normal range of variation in brain morphology, there exists no demonstrable relation to intelligence.

Furthermore, the brain as an organ is vastly more than a physical structure. Indeed, it is the most complex and functionally educable system of structures within the body. Made up of trillions of neurons and associated entities in an amazingly complicated network of environmentally educable interconnections, as well as a remarkable hormonal secretary activity and chemistry which it manages on its own,[2] the brain is the domain of the learned part of the environment. As functioning *human beings,* everything we know and come to do, we have had to learn from others and from the environment.

The evidence drawn from many relevant researches is now overwhelming; *individual experiences* literally shape the developing brain and subsequent behavior.[3] The quality of those experiences is fundamentally important for the development of the problem-solving behavior we call intelligence or thinking: that is, the ability to make the appropriately successful *responses* rather than reactions to the challenges of the environment. Just as differences between the cultural developments of different societies can be explained by differences in the histories of their experiences, so may differences in intelligence between individuals be explained, for the most part, by the histories of their experiences. The parenthetic "for the most part" allows for whatever genetic factors may be involved.

The culture of IQ testing over the last 70 years has become so routinized, and its influence upon education so powerful, that what was once a by-product of education has become a determinant of education and of social action. Schools often tailor their curricula to so-called IQ tests. Accordingly, narrow skills are taught; with the consequent neglect of the natural abilities of each child.

An enormous number of influences enter into each individual's learning experiences. To properly assess intelligence, these learning experiences must be evaluated for the roles they have played in its formulation. Otherwise, IQ advocates will vainly continue their search in a dark room for a black cat that is not there, all the while stubbing their toes.

For example, what is never considered in IQ testing are such variables as: maternal stimulations, parental dispositions, parental education, socioeconomic status, prenatal and perinatal birth experiences, early childhood, schooling, and mental and physical health. Without a thorough investigation of these conditions, regardless of the innate predispositions of each individual, all tests of intelligence, and especially IQ tests, are worthless as measures of intelligence.

To understand the nature of intelligence, one needs to appreciate the transformation of a predisposition into an ability. A predisposition is inborn, whereas an ability is evoked from a trained predisposition. By learning, which is the increase in the strength of any act by repetition, a predisposition is trained and becomes an ability. Among the innate prenatal and perinatal undeveloped predispositions are the basic behavioral needs. In any test of intelligence it would be necessary, at the very least, to acknowledge that such needs exist. An understanding of the history and satisfaction of those needs is indispensably requisite to arrive at a relatively accurate estimate of an individual's intelligence.

A basic behavioral need is an urge or drive toward the satisfaction of that need. The thwarting of an expected satisfaction during childhood, especially the need for love, generally leads to serious disorders in physical and mental development. Additionally, the unfulfillment of expected satisfaction can lead to aggressive or dysfunctional behavior, sometimes called failure to thrive, and may even lead to death.[4] Satisfaction of the basic behavioral needs leads to healthy behavioral growth and development. Healthy growth and development includes the ability to love, to work, to play, and to think soundly.

Satisfaction of the basic behavioral needs is also requisite for the healthy growth and development of the body and mind.[5] The basic behavioral needs are love, which means not only to be loved but also to love others, curiosity, creativity, imagination, learning, explorativeness, experimental-mindedness, open-mindedness, speech, sound thinking, flexibility, joyfulness, play, laughter, weeping, work, song, and dance.[6] These basic behavioral needs have not been formally recognized as playing major roles in the development of intelligence, largely because the whole subject of the development of intelligence has been approached in too intellectualized a manner. Furthermore, to fail to consider the roles that religious, spiritual, and emotional influences may play in the development of intelligence is to neglect among the most dominant influences relating to the intellectual development of the individual.

It is a great error to approach the investigation of human intelligence and IQ testing as if every individual were a product of purely informational conditioning. Yet, intelligence testers repeatedly commit this egregious error and, thereby, simultaneously forfeit the most basic understanding of some of the critical influences on the shaping of intelligence.

Since the acronym "IQ" has entered the language as a scientific measure of intelligence, as if indeed it were a real thing, it has done a great deal of damage to untold numbers of human beings. Lured into a false belief of the estimate of their capacities, the victims of IQ tests have suffered a loss of self esteem and of confidence in their abilities. Too frequently these victims have also suffered a devastating hopelessness which has marred so many lives. The psychometricians of humankind involved in such pernicious activities have rarely exhibited the least concern for the victims of their labors, but have often claimed, as in the latest case by the authors of *The Bell Curve,*[7] that their findings are for the good of us all.

The reprehensible thing about these taxonomists of the mind is a cluster of traits they generally display which disqualifies them from having any valid opinion on the nature of intelligence, especially when that opinion affects blacks. These traits include but are not limited to: obvious bias; general insensitivity; close-mindedness; failure to consider the evidence opposing their views; citation of views favorable to their kinds of arguments, though such views have long been discredited; and, abysmal ignorance of biological and cultural anthropology. Worst of all, their ignorance of *genetics* is pronounced, evoking innumerable rejections of both their methods and their conclusions.

An elementary example from agriculture may help illuminate the mistake so often made by the mental taxonomists. If we were to take corn seed from one source and plant half of the seed in an enriched field and the other half in an impoverished field, we would see two types of variation in the heights of the individual plants. The variation in plant heights within each field could be explained by very small and essentially unimportant genetic differences in the seed. The differences in plant heights between the fields would be due almost entirely to differing soil conditions and not to genetic differences. Nonetheless, and consistent with the history of IQ testing, the taxonomists of the mind would see the differences in crop heights between the fields as genetic in origin, never considering the conditions under which the corn plants were raised.

Beginning in 1923 with Walter Lippmann's[8] devastating attacks on the works and findings of the leading IQ testers of World War I army recruits,[9] and continuing to the most recent of these criticisms on the flaws and failures of IQ testing, the denunciations have been unceasing. Outstanding among the more recent critiques are Stephen Jay Gould's *The Mismeasure of Man* (1981),[10] Professor Albert Jacquard's *In Praise of Difference* (1984),[11] and Elaine and Harry Mensh's *The IQ Mythology* (1991).[12] These three works were published long enough before *The Bell Curve* to have given its authors plenty of time to deal with such critiques of IQ tests and their consequences. Instead, they, and innumerable others, were ignored.

The authors of *The Bell Curve,* like so many of their predecessors, apparently were determinedly uninterested in pursuing a balanced course, a course that every genuine scientist follows as part of the normal procedure of checking the validity of his work. Professor William Tucker in his book, *The Science and Politics of Racial Research* (1994),[13] published just one month after the appearance of *The Bell Curve,* has shown pointedly and unequivocally that the authors of such works as *The Bell Curve* have not been interested in the facts or the most reasonable interpretation of their findings. Rather, he shows, such authors are most interested in the use of such devices as IQ tests to represent social and political inequality as the unavoidable and ineradicable consequences of natural differences. One wonders why these so-called scientists have never tried standing the argument on its head by considering the possibility that, far from being due to natural differences, the differences are largely due to social and political inequalities? And that race is a product of the social history of an individual or group, not of nature?

One also wonders why the extraordinary accomplishments of American blacks, who traveled from slaves to affirmative action status in little more than a century, are not highlighted by these so-called scientists? Why are events such as the practically inconceivable redrawing of voting districts and membership of blacks on the United States Supreme Court in a white-ruled society absent from their works?

And, incredibly, one wonders why these so-called scientists never seemed to have considered it functionally irresponsible to publish views in the name of science which have been repeatedly shown to be unsound and disastrous for millions of people. Why is it that in the face of the Holocaust, "ethnic cleansing," and the endemic social and political inequalities that exist in the United States between whites and blacks that these so-called scientists have persisted in perpetuating demonstrably unsound views as an explanation for those inequalities and the evils to which these views lead? Their arguments are circular and are demonstrably wrong.

Blindness is not the affliction from which these enemies of humanity suffer. Rather, they suffer from an attitude of mind, however acquired, which causes them to perceive members of another group as belonging to a different race and thereby as inferior. These members of different races are considered to be threats to the continued integrity and welfare of society. I have called this viewpoint "man's most dangerous myth."[14] Hitler, by organizing the murder of millions of Jews, gypsies, and other targeted victims in the name of race, proved in the deeds of many of his loyal followers that the belief in race is indeed man's most dangerous myth.[15] In America, the myth of race has been endemic for several centuries, and remains America's primary public health problem.[16] It is therefore hardly surprising that the tide of passion whipped up by American public figures and windy writers overflowed its banks and surfaced on foreign shores.

The ideas and writing of American scientists' and writers on race have been widely influential in contributing support and endorsement for the ideologies of foreign reactionary politicians and demagogues. This situation was the case most notably in Germany, whose leaders found in the racist works of Americans an encouragement for and a reinforcement of their extreme racist programs. Racism in Germany had been deeply entrenched long before the advent of Hitler and Nazism. With Germany's defeat in World War I and the forced acceptance of a humiliating peace treaty in 1919, followed by a catastrophic national depression, anarchy in the streets, and the pressing cry for an explanation, a target was needed upon whom to fix the blame. The populace was easily led to believe that Germany had lost the war because it had been betrayed; the famous "stab in the back," a convenient scapegoat for the massive frustration was readily available: the Jews.

As a matter of historical record, the first prominent victim of the racist nationalists was Walther Rathenau, Foreign Minister and a Jew, who had served his country nobly and with great ability during and after the war. Rathenau, a charming man who believed in conciliation rather than confrontation, was assassinated in June 1922.

In November 1923, the failure of Hitler's Munich *putsch* landed him in jail, where, during the five months he was ensconced, he wrote *Mein Kampf*. During this comfortable situation, often euphemistically called his "incarceration," he read an account of the passage of the United States Immigration Restriction Act of 1924. In *Mein Kampf*, he wrote of the Immigration Restriction Act with the greatest enthusiasm, saying that it would serve as a model for his program of racial purification. Not only that, having read the American Madison Grant's, *The Passing of the Great Race*,[17] the popular racist tract of its time which spoke of Jews with especial malevolence, Hitler, who called his deep-seated hatred of Jews "the granite-firm foundation" of his ideology, wrote Grant thanking him for writing the book, saying that it was his Bible.

Grant's book, published in 1916, was well written, very easy to read, widely reviewed, enlarged, and quickly reprinted. Grant was a New Yorker, a bachelor, and a socialite who traced his ancestry back to colonial America. He was the founder of the New York Zoological Society and of the Galton Society, an exclusive group with monthly meetings in The American Museum of Natural History. The Galton Society, as its name implies, was chiefly interested in eugenic issues. Grant was also a luminary of the American Eugenics Society and a vice-president of the Immigration Restriction League.

Grant's book spawned others in rapid succession, many of which were greeted with enthusiasm in Germany, especially by German anthropologists.[18] The German sociologist Stefan Kühl has shown in his graphically titled book, *The Nazi Connection: Eugenics, American Racism, and German National Socialism*, that not only did the German anthropologists welcome the contributions of American authors to the cause of National Socialism but were, in fact, in regular contact with many of them.

Some Americans actually served on the editorial boards of well-known German racist journals while others traveled to Germany to accept honorary degrees from Nazi-controlled German universities. Among such degree recipients were Henry Fairfield Osborn, President of The American Museum of Natural History and Harry Laughlin, the instigator and drafter of the U.S. Restrictive Immigration Act of 1924 and Assistant Director of the Eugenics Record Office.[19]

In 1916 Osborn wrote an adulatory preface for the first edition of *The Passing of the Great Race*, in which he stated the function of

> the modern eugenics movement in relation to patriotism, namely, the conservation and multiplication for our country of the best spiritual, moral, intellectual, and physical forces of heredity," and that "thus only will the integrity of our institutions be maintained in the future." Osborn concluded with the words, "If I were asked: What is the greatest danger which threatens the American republic today? I would certainly reply: The gradual dying out among our people of those hereditary traits through which the principles of our religious, political, and social foundations were laid down, and their insidious replacement by traits of less noble character.

In the German translation of Grant's book, the word for "insidious" in Osborn's preface is *hinterlistig,* meaning "crooked," "underhanded," and "stealthy." Try to imagine the impression that Osborn's words made upon Hitler. Unlike Osborn, who lacked the courage to name explicitly who these "insidious" creatures might be, Grant left no doubt in the reader's mind who they were. They were "the Slovak, the Italian, the Syrian and the Jew." "The man of the old stock," Grant wrote, "is being crowded out of many country districts by these foreigners just as he is to-day being literally driven off the streets of New York City by the swarms of Polish Jews ... the Polish Jew, whose dwarf stature, peculiar mentality, and ruthless concentration on self-interest are being engrafted upon the stock of the nation."[20]

In December 1917, Osborn allowed his original preface to remain and added a completely new one for the 1918 enlarged new edition of Grant's book. With the then recent entry of the United States into World War I in mind, Osborn opened with the following ringing words: "History is repeating itself in America at the present time and incidentally is giving a convincing demonstration of the central thought in this volume, namely, that heredity and racial predisposition are stronger and more stable than environment and education." This portentous announcement was followed by an extended paean to "this strain of Anglo-Saxon life which has played so large a part in American history."[21]

To continue Osborn's history, it may seem ungracious to add the fact that in world history the American racist "strain of Anglo-Saxon" authors played a significant role in providing the Nazis, both before and during the Second World War, with support for a regime that was responsible for the monumental evil of the Holocaust and for the perpetration of many other genocides and acts of ruthlessness. It is estimated that those evils resulted in the deaths of more than fifty million human beings. The number of people indirectly subjected to unspeakable suffering was, of course, many times higher. All this was in the name of race.

It is generally held that anyone who cries "Fire!" in a crowded theater should be held responsible for the consequences of such conduct. The same rules should apply to anyone who, motivated by racism or callousness, publishes or utters inflammatory falsehoods concerning others. It should make no difference whether the perpetrators be individuals, groups, or populations; they should be held responsible for their conduct by law. More than 200 years of racial slander and libel are enough. The current use of IQ tests represents just such a continuing ethnic slander and libel by presenting demeaning falsehoods, regardless of the presence or absence of malicious intent. In the final analysis, what is involved is the matter of responsibility; that is, the welfare of human beings needs to be considered through the balancing of scientific responsibility by moral integrity and human concern.

It is important to understand that the whole concept of IQ is an arbitrary invention that has been given a spurious reality and an equally spurious quantification. In light of what is presently known and in fact has been known for quite some time, the persistent quantification of IQ is a travesty upon humanity, unleashed and maintained by irresponsible so-called scientists, for what are such scientists if they lack humanity?

Among the many weaknesses of IQ tests is that what they are said to measure—namely, intelligence—they do not in fact measure. For the most part IQ test results reflect the effects of socio-econimic background and schooling experience. What the test generally tells us is where a child stands in respect of his or her ability to respond to the test questions as compared with the performance of other children of similar chronologic age. Since, however, chronologic age is itself a poor index of developmental age, the value of the test even from the standpoint of its comparative value is more questionable than ever. IQ tests are, if anything, likely to be harmful to many children who happen to be slow developers who, when not condemned to a low IQ status, will catch up with and often outdistance the more rapid developers.

The future of humanity has its great diversity as its bedrock, not the categorization of humanity by IQ tests. It is in humanity's diversity that its greatest riches are stored, in the wonder of our individual differences seeking expression for the benefit of us all. We are born into a continuing social relationship. That relationship is the love shared between mother and child. The love is a bond and a relationship which is designed to grow and develop throughout our lives and by extension to the whole of humanity. Next to homicide, the greatest crime one can commit against others is to stand in the way of their development, to deprive them and society of the fulfillment of their unique individuality and their humanity.

The history of the concept of race is a truly dreadful one. From its beginning and by its very existence, the term has served to narrow the definition of humanity through the establishment of an hegemonic hierarchy of discrete entities. These entities, the so-called races, were primarily based on differences in physical traits. Such physical traits were soon linked with cultural and social differences, educability, and intelligence.

During the Victorian period, scientists were busily engaged in classifying the races of man, just as they had been classifying the races of animals. Books published as late as the latter half of the twentieth century still portrayed *typical* members of the races of mankind. The illustrations of the different races along with maps of their distributions were often attractively colored and, intended or not, served to reinforce two views of humankind. The first view was of an overall unity of humankind; and simultaneously, the second view confirmed the classifier's belief in the reality of "physical" races for all the world to see, and in the comforting uniformity of their beliefs they reigned supreme.

What the classifiers saw as they surveyed the peoples of the earth was a great deal of variability which, on the basis of the physical differences, they attempted to fit into the taxonomic pigeon-holes already available to them: *races*. In the pre-genetic age in which they lived and worked, the scientists of the day could hardly have done better than they did. Nonetheless, with the advent of genetics early in the twentieth century, it became quite clear where the classifiers had gone wrong; it was in treating populations as if they were composed of complexes of physical traits rather than of the distribution of the genes for the various traits they presented. When genetic explorations were done, it was found that the vast majority of genes for the various traits were shared by all the populations of humankind. In short, the genetic differences between human populations are very few. Furthermore, geneticists have found that the small extant differences are contributory to the welfare of us all, mentally as well as physically.

Classificatory ardor continued to the point of virtually excluding some peoples from the community of humankind and, like nationalism, succeeded in justifying enmity between nations.[22] Not only was the polarization of ethnicities between nations greatly facilitated by the idea of race, but race greatly justified and legitimized the stratifications of caste and class within nations. In Europe throughout the nineteenth century, especially during the kleptomaniac era of imperialism, slavery in America, and its offshoot called manifest destiny, it was customary to speak of higher and lower races. It is a mark of some progress that the use of these terms has been somewhat declining.

During the last 200 years, the work of anthropologists among the indigenous peoples of the earth incontrovertibly established the truth that if some groups of humanity are more advanced in some respects than others it is principally because the challenges of our highly technologized societies have been more complex. As such, more complex and challenging environments demand primarily different adaptive technologic inventions and social responses. Socially, the levels of complexity of a society, whether simple or complex, have everywhere elicited much the same kinds of responses by adapting to the requirements of the social pressures. In this way, intelligence, as measured by responses to the challenges of social and environmental pressures, does not seem hierarchically distributed but, instead, seems to be quite equally distributed among all of humankind.[23]

Every culture can be regarded as the historic result of a people's effort to adjust itself to its environment. Before the advent of the twentieth century, that environment was usually narrowly circumscribed. Today the boundaries which formerly divided people are crumbling before our eyes. Humankind is moving, in spite of occasional appearances to the contrary, toward greater understanding. This greater understanding means movement toward the condition whereby the differences that separate people today will be regarded as no more important than the differences that separate members of the same family. In a family, everyone, despite apparent differences, is ideally given the opportunity and encouragement to become a fully realized human being. Intra-family differences are not viewed as causes for suspicion, fear, discrimination, or pegs upon which to hang prejudices.

In 1920, H. G. Wells wrote in his *The Outline of History,* "Human history becomes more and more a race between education and catastrophe." Looking at the world that we have created since that time, it is clear that catastrophe has been winning out over education. Wells would have been appalled at what passes for education today. Wells thought of education as *humanitas,* the concern for and the involvement in humanity. What passes for education in our time is not education at all, but is, at best, instruction. Moreover, the instruction is all too often little more, and frequently less, than training in the traditional "three R's." Genuine education has been technologized by the technocrats of education to the point of being reduced to a handful of practical skills and routinized techniques.

Our love affair with technology, which was to have been our servant, has instead made willing servants of us.[24] We pride ourselves on having created machines that think much like human beings. What we have failed to understand is that, in the process, we have created human beings who think like machines. By any operative definition, that reductionism to cookbook skills and routine techniques is what, for the most part, we call education today.

The result is that we have turned our world into a technological disaster. We now have a citizenry that thinks in stereotypes and clichés, who have become the prisoners of their impoverished vocabularies. Having never been taught what thinking really is, we have "educated" a population into having little respect for those who do think.[25]

As Sir Joshua Reynolds put it, "Few have been taught to any purpose who have not been their own teachers." Thinking is a skill which can be taught as a searching and enchanting exercise which grows to be an immense and vitally important pleasure. Thinking can be taught in our schools, in all grades and at appropriately increasing levels of complexity. That teaching, however, does not appear to be one of the functions of today's educational institutions, for there we teach *what* to think, rather than *how* to think. The result has been catastrophic to the extent that we have become the most self-endangered species on this planet, composed as we are of so many ignorant minds and having the capacity to annihilate all life on Earth with the push of a few buttons.

We have a big challenge before us; namely, the complete revision of education and its replacement by a system that meets the basic needs of humanity. In the name of education our schools have become institutions for the promotion of illiteracy in the most important of all the areas: the art of being a warm, loving human being. Our educational system is largely responsible for producing a population of illiterates in a time when it has become imperative for each of us to care for others and think of the world not as full of strangers, but as full of friends we have not yet met.

To love our neighbors as we love ourselves is not enough. We must love others more than we love ourselves, for that is the true measure of love. In a world in which there is so much unloving love behind the show of love, it is necessary today more than ever before to understand that racism, in whatever form it may assume, represents and motivates the continuing dehumanizing loss of involvement in the welfare of our neighbors.

There is only one way to express a deeper truth or meaning than words themselves can do—by action! *The meaning of a word is the action it produces.* Think for a minute about the words *race* and *racism* and about the word *love.* For most people, what they do about these words is what they mean by them, and what they mean by them is, for the most part, thoroughly dehumanizing.

If we are ever to extricate ourselves from the slough of despond into which we have fallen, we must recognize that there is only one way; through education, education as love, the deep involvement in the welfare of others. It is only through learning to love that we find our own true identity. In giving love unconditionally, we fulfill ourselves and help others to do likewise.

When all is said and done, when all our scientific works have been published, when all our truths have been proven, we will not have made much more headway in dealing with racism than we have in the past unless we clearly understand the root cause and the cure of the disease which racism is. It is because scientists have shied away from the study of love that I have devoted so much attention to it. A scientist is one who believes in proof without certainty, while most other people believe in certainty without proof. Scientists are generally specialists who may have made invaluable contributions in their fields toward the better understanding of wider issues than those which they are not normally involved. They are not usually called upon to see the wood for the trees. Nonetheless, their contributions, when seen through the eyes of the thinking generalist, make the view of the wood highly rewarding.

It is largely through the anthropological investigations of the great and illuminating diversity of the peoples of the earth that we have come to understand the meaning of humanity. The remarkable discovery is of a common bond that unites us all in a kinship of wondrous variety and creativity, confirming the heart's profound feeling that every human is incomparable, unique, universal, and fundamentally alike in all the qualities that make us human. This discovery, cumulatively and repeatedly authenticated by anthropologists during the last seventy years, should encourage us to work in the belief that to the improvement of the environment, heredity offers no barrier. The news from both anthropology and genetics is truly heartening.

Finally, we need to appreciate that our genetic richness emanates directly from our diversity. As Saint-Exupery wrote in *A Letter to a Hostage*, "If I am different from you, I enrich rather than diminish you." That message contains a universal principle: you are precious to me because you are different, as I am to you.[26]

Notes

1. C. Spearman, *The Nature of Intelligence and the Principles of Cognition* (London & New York: Macmillan, 1922).

2. S. Rose, *The Conscious Brain* (New York: Knopf, 1973); S. Rose *Molecules and Minds* (Philadelphia: Open University Press, 1987); Marian C. Diamond, *Enriching Heredity: The Impact of the Environment on the Anatomy of the* Brain (New York: Free Press, 1988); J. Boddy, *Brain Systems and Psychological Concepts* (New York: Wiley, 1978).

3. Max Cynader, "Mechanisms of Brain Development and Their Role in Health and Well-Being," *Daedalus* 123 (4) (1995): 155–65.

4. Patton, R. G. & Gardner, L. I., *Growth Failure in Maternal Deprivation* (Springfield, IL: C. C. Thomas, 1963); G. F. Powell, Brasel, J. A., & Blizzard, R., "Emotional Deprivation and Growth Retardation, Simulating Idiopathic Hypopituitrism," *New England Journal of Medicine* 276 (1967): 1271–78; J. B. Reinhart & Drash, A. A., "Psychosocial Dwarfism: Environmentally Induced Recovery," *Psychosomatic Medicine,* 31 (1969) 165–72; A. Montagu, ed., *Culture and Human Development: Insights Into Growing Human* (Englewood Cliffs, NJ: Prentice-Hall, 1974).

5. R. H. Munroe, R. L. Munroe, & B. B. Whiting, eds., *Handbook of Cross-Cultural Human Development* (New York: Garland STM Press, 1981); A. Peiper, *Cerebral Function in Infancy and Childhood* (New York: Consultants Bureau, 1963).

6. Ashley Montagu, *Growing Young,* 2nd ed. (Westport, CT: Bergin & Garvey, 1989).

7. R. Herrnstein & C. Murray, *The Bell Curve* (New York: Free Press, 1994).

8. Walter A. Lippmann, "Future for the Tests," *New Republic,* 29 November 1922, 9–11; "The Mental Age of Americans," *New Republic,* 25 October 1922, 213–25; "Mr. Burt and the Intelligence Tests," *New Republic,* 2 May 1922, 263–64; "The Mystery of the 'A' Men," *New Republic,* 1 November 1922, 246–48; "The Reliability of Intelligence Tests," *New Republic,* 8 November 1922); 275–77; "Tests of Hereditary Intelligence," *New Republic,* 22 November 1922, 328–30; see also N. J. Block, & Gerald Dworkin, eds., *The IQ Controversy* (New York: Random House, 1976).

9. R. M. Yerkes, "Psychological Examining in the United States Army. Washington" *Memoir of the National Academy of Sciences* 15, pt. I (1922).

10. Stephen J. Gould, *The Mismeasure of Man* (New York: Norton, 1981).

11. A. Jacquard, *In Praise of Difference: Genetics and Human Affairs* (New York: Columbia University Press, 1984).

12. Elaine Mensh & Harry Mensh, *The IQ Mythology* (Carbondale: Southern Illinois University Press, 1991); C. G. Liungman, *What Is IQ?* (London: Gordon Cremonesi,1975).

13. W. H. Tucker, *The Science and Politics of Racial Research* (Urbana: University of Illinois Press, 1994); Richard E. Lewontin, Steven Rose, & Leon Kamin, *Not In Our Genes* (New York: Pantheon Books, 1984).

14. Ashley Montagu, *Man's Most Dangerous Myth: The Fallacy of Race,* 5th ed. (New York: Oxford University Press, 1974).

15. Martin Gilbert, *The Holocaust: A History of the Jews of Europe during the Second World War* (New York: Holt, Rinehart & Winston, 1986); Lucy S. Dawidowicz, *The War Against the Jews: 1933–1945* (New York: Holt, Rinehart & Winston, 1975).

16. *Crisis in Child Mental Health,* Joint Commission on Mental Health (New York: Harper & Row, 1970); C. V. Willie, B. M. Kramer, and B. S. Brown, eds., *Racism and Mental Health* (Pittsburgh:University of Pittsburgh Press, 1973).

17. Madison Grant, *The Passing of the Great Race* (New York: Scribner's, 1916): vii–ix, 14–15, 80–81.

18. Madison Grant, *Passing of the Great Race,* new edition (1918/19), 91–92.

19. Stefan Kühl, *The Nazi Connection: Eugenics, American Racism, and German National Socialism* (New York: Oxford University Press, 1994): 85–88; See most importantly also, R. Proctor, "From Anthropologie to Rassenkunde in the German Anthropological Tradition," in *Genes, Bodies and Behavior,* ed. G. W. Stocking Jr., (Madison, WI: University of Wisconsin Press, 1988), 138–79; R. N. Proctor, *Racial*

Hygiene: Medicine Under the Nazis (Cambridge: Harvard University Press, 1988); Benno Muller-Hill, *Murderous Science: Elimination by Scientific Selection of Jew, Gypsies, and Others* (New York: Oxford University Press, 1988).

20. Grant, ibid., 14.

21. H. F. Osborn, in Grant, *Passing of the Great Race,* xi–xiii.

22. Christine Bolt, *Victorian Attitudes to Race* (London: Routledge, 1971); L. Dumont, *Homo Hierarchicus* (Chicago: University of Chicago Press, 1970); George W. Stocking, Jr. *Victorian Anthropology* (New York: Free Press, 1987); J. W. Trent, Jr., *Inventing the Feeble Mind* (Berkeley: University of California Press, 1994); N. Wiener, *The Human Use of Human Beings* (Boston: Houghton-Mifflin, 1950).

23. Sander L. Gilman, *Difference and Pathology: Stereotypes of Sexuality, Race, and Madness* (Ithaca: Cornell University Press, 1985); Maurice Dumas, *A History of Technology and Invention: Progress Through the Ages* (New York: Crown, 1969); Ashley Montagu, *Culture and the Evolution of Man* (New York: Oxford University Press, 1962); Ashley Montagu, ed., *Culture, Man's Adaptive Dimension* (New York: Oxford University Press, 1968).

24. JoAnne Brown, *The Definition of a Profession: The Authority of Metaphor in the History of Intelligence Testing, 1890–1930* (Princeton: Princeton University Press, 1992); A. Alan Hanson, *Testing Testing: Social Consequences of the Examined Life* (Berkeley: University of California Press, 1993).

25. Ashley Montagu, "Education, Humanity, and Technology," in *Advances in Telematics,* ed. Jarice Hanson (Norwood, NJ: Ablex Publishing, 1994), 1–15; Ashley Montagu, *The Direction of Human Development* (New York: Harper & Row, 1955); Ashley Montagu, The Origin and Significance of Neonatal Immaturity in Man *Journal of the American Medical Association* 178 (1961): 156–57; William Stanton, *The Leopard's Spots: Scientific Attitudes Toward Race in America, 1815–1859* (Chicago: University of Chicago Press, 1960).

26. A. Montagu, *Growing Young,* 2nd ed. (Westport, CT: Bergin & Garvey, 1989).

Appendix A

Ethnic Group and Race

In the 1950 UNESCO Statement on Race, paragraph 6 reads as follows:

> National, religious, geographic, linguistic and cultural groups do not necessarily coincide with racial groups; and the cultural traits of such groups have no demonstrated genetic connection with racial traits. Because serious errors of this kind are habitually committed when the term 'race' is used in popular parlance, it would be better when speaking of human races to drop the term 'race' altogether and speak of ethnic groups.

The principal objection to the term "race" with reference to humans is that it takes for granted as solved problems which are far from being so, and tends to close the mind to problems to which it should always remain open. If, with ritual fidelity, one goes on repeating long enough that "the Nordics" are a race or that "the Armenoids" are, or that "the Jews" are, or that races may be determined by their blood group gene frequencies, we shall have already determined what a race is. Since there are today quite a number of physical anthropologists who question the validity of the term "race" when applied to man, and some biologists who question its value when applied to some nonhuman groups of animals,[1] the following discussion will not appear as revolutionary as it once did.

In 1936 Julian Huxley and Alfred Cort Haddon, the one a distinguished biologist, and the other a pioneer physical and cultural anthropologist, in their influential book on race, *We Europeans* (1936), repudiated the term race in favor of ethnic group,[2] and somewhat later Calman, a zoologist, recommended that the term "variety" should be avoided altogether and suggested that "Other terms such as 'geographical race,' 'form,' 'phase,' and so forth, may be useful in particular instances but are better not used until some measure of agreement is reached as to their precise meaning."[3] Kalmus, a geneticist, pointed out that, "A very important term which was originally used in systematics is 'race.' Nowadays, however, its use is avoided as far as possible in genetics."[4] In a later work Kalmus writes,

521

"It is customary to discuss the local varieties of humanity in terms of 'race.' However, it is unnecessary to use this greatly debased word, since it is easy to describe populations without it."[5] G. S. Carter, in his book on *Animal Evolution* (1951), wrote that the terms "'race,' 'variety,' and 'form' are used so loosely and in so many senses that it is advisable to avoid using them as infraspecific categories."[6] Professor Ernst Hanhart denies that there are any "true races" in man,[7] and Professor L. S. Penrose, in a review of Dunn and Dobzhansky's little book *Heredity, Race and Society* (1952), wrote that he was unable to

> see the necessity for the rather apologetic retention of the obsolete term 'race,' when what is meant is simply a given population differentiated by some social, geographical or genetic character, or . . . merely by a gene frequency peculiarity. The use of the almost mystical concept of race makes the presentation of the facts about the geographical and linguistic groups . . . unnecessarily complicated.[8]

Dr. J. P. Garlick, a physical anthropologist, reviewing two books on race, writes, "The use of 'race' as a taxonomic unit for man seems out-of-date, if not irrational."[9] Finally, Professor P. A. Parsons writes, "There are good arguments for abandoning the term race, as it is clearly arbitrary, undefinable, and without biological meaning. The term, population, although suffering from many of the same difficulties, at least has a lesser emotional content."[10]

In spite of these strictures many biologists will continue to use the term, and if they can use it in an adequately defined manner so that their meaning can be clearly understood by other scientists, erroneous though that usage may be, it will be all the more easy for the critic to direct attention to the sources of the error.

It cannot be too frequently emphasized that truly meaningful definitions cannot be achieved at the beginning of an inquiry but only at the end of one. Such inquiries have not yet been completed to the satisfaction of most scientists who have paid considered attention to the subject of race. The term, therefore, at best is at the present time not really scientifically permissible on any score for humankind. One may or may not be of the opinion that the term "race" ought to be dropped altogether from the vocabulary, because it is confusing and narrows the definition of humanity; and because biologists and other scientists are frequently guilty of using it incorrectly, and that therefore it would be better if they did not lend the aura of their authority to the use of so confusing a word. The term "subspecies" has been used as the equivalent of the term "race," but this suffers from the same disadvantages, and has been as misused as its equivalent.[11] The term "race" is so embarrassed by confused and mystical meanings, and accomodates so many blots upon its escutcheon, that a discouragement of its use would constitute an encouragement to clearer thinking.

In opposition to this view a number of objections have been raised. The hope that by trivial semantic changes we can exorcise prejudices and stereotypes is nothing but a pious delusion. One doesn't change anything by word magic, by changing names. It's an artful dodge. A subterfuge. Why not meet the problem head-on? If, in popular usage, the term "race" has been befogged and befouled, why not cleanse it of the smog and foulness and restore it to its pristine condition? Reeducation should be attempted by establishing the true meaning of race, not by denying its existence. The race problem is not merely a matter of faulty semantics. One cannot combat racism by enclosing the word in quotes. It is not the word that requires changing but people's ideas about it. It is a common failing to argue from the abuse of an idea to its total exclusion. And so on.

It was Francis Bacon who remarked that truth grows more readily out of error than it does out of confusion. The time may come when it may be possible to rehabilitate the term "race" in a legitimate scientific sense, with clarity and with reason. But that time is not yet. It does not appear to be generally realized that while stone walls do not a prison make, scientific terms, like any others, are capable of doing so. Words like "race" contain half-hidden implications that flow in and out of usage in uncharted ways. Until people are soundly educated to understand the muddlement of ideas represented by such terms as "race" they will continue to believe in absurdities. And as Voltaire so acutely remarked, "As long as people believe in absurdities they will continue to commit atrocities." Words are what men breathe into them. Men have a strong tendency to use words and phrases which cloak the unknown in the undefined or undefinable. As Housman put it, "calling in ambiguity of language to promote confusion of thought."[12]

Sooner or later most words tend to decay into imprecision, and the word "race" represents a conspicuous example of such a degeneration. The race problem is certainly not a matter of faulty semantics, but the faulty semantics implicit in the common conception of race certainly contributes to the exacerbation of that problem.

The layperson's conception of race is so confused and emotionally muddled that any attempt to modify it would seem to be met by the greatest obstacle of all, the term "race" itself. This is another reason why the attempt to retain the term "race" is popular parlance must fail. The term is a trigger word; utter it and a whole series of emotionally conditioned responses follow. The phrase "ethnic group" suffers from no such defect. If we are to clarify the minds of those who think in terms of race we must cease using the word primarily because in their minds the term defines conditions which do not in fact exist. There is no such thing as the kind of race in which most people believe. In spite of the shared comforting uniformity of their beliefs, if we are to re-educate them in a sound conception of the meaning of a population or distinguishable group, which we prefer to designate by the general and noncommittal term "ethnic group," then it would seem far more reasonable to convey to them the temporariness of the situation with a general rather than with a particular term. This is particularly desirable when it is sought to remove a prevailing erroneous conception and substitute one that clarifies without solidifying. Professor Henry Sigerist has well said that "it is never sound to continue the use of terminology with which the minds of millions of people have been poisoned even when the old terms are given new meanings."[13] And Professor George Gaylord Simpson has written,

> A word for which everyone has a different definition, usually unstated, ceases to serve the function of communication and its use results in futile arguments about nothing. There is also a sort of Gresham's Law for words; redefine them as we will, their worst or most extreme meaning is almost certain to remain current and to tend to drive out the meaning we might prefer.[14]

Bertrand Russell has suggested that for words that have strong emotional overtones we should substitute in our arguments the letters of the alphabet.

The biologist who has been largely concerned with the study of animal populations will be likely to take an oversimplified view of the problems here involved and to dismiss such attempts at re-education of the layman as unsatisfactory. By substituting one term for another, he will say, one solves nothing. It is quite as possible to feel "ethnic group prejudice" as it is to feel race prejudice. Perhaps. But this kind of comment indicates that the real point has been missed. The term "ethnic group" is not a substitute for the term "race." The grounds upon which it is suggested constitute a fundamental difference in viewpoint that significantly differentiates what the phrase stands for from what the term stands for. It is not a question of changing names, and there is no question of resorting to devices or artful dodges—the imputation is silly. If what the term "ethnic group" means is clearly understood and accepted, ethnic group prejudice would hardly require to be taken seriously. There have been some who have felt that the use of the phrase "ethnic group" was an avoidance of the main issue. On the other hand, most students of human nature would take the view that such a usage constitutes a more realistic and more promising approach to the problem of lay thinking on this subject than the method of attempting to put new meaning into the old bottle of race. It was Korzybski who remarked that because of the great semantic influence of the structure of language on the masses of mankind, leading, as it does, through lack of better understanding and evaluation to speculation on terms, it seems advisable to abandon completely terms which imply to the many the suggested elementalism, although these terms are used in a proper nonelementalistic way by the few.[15]

The premise on which the term "ethnic group" is principally suggested is that it is easier to re-educate people by introducing a new conception with a new distinctive term, particularly, I repeat, when it is desired to remove a prevailing erroneous conception and introduce a new and more correct one. Those who do not understand that the greatest obstacle to the process of re-education would be the retention of the old term *race,* which is itself a racist term, a term which enshrines the errors it is desired to remove, do not understand the deep implicit meanings which this word has inescapably come to possess for so many of its users.

The question may, then, be asked: Will the phrase *ethnic group* be sufficient to cause such persons to alter their ideas? The answer is for some "No," for others, "It will help"; and for still others, "Yes." No one should be so naive as to suppose that by this means alone one is going to solve the race problem! The suggestions here made are calculated to help; they can do no more at best. Each time the term *race* is used most individuals believe that it refers to a fact, a reality, which is beyond question, when in fact the chances are that what they understand by the term is false. Race is something so familiar that in speaking of it one takes one's private meaning completely for granted and one never thinks to question it. On the other hand, when the term "ethnic group" is used, the question is generally asked: "What do you mean by 'ethnic group'?" And that at once affords the opportunity to discuss the facts and to explain their meaning as well as the falsities of the prevailing conception of race. This, it seems to me, is one of the greatest educational advantages of the phrase *ethnic group* over the term *race.* Another advantage of the phrase is that it leaves all question of definition open, it refers specifically to human populations which are believed to exhibit a certain degree, amount, or frequency of undetermined physical likenesses or homogeneity. An ethnic group has already been described as one of a number of populations, which populations together comprise the species *Homo sapiens,* and which individually maintain their differences, physical and cultural, by means of isolating mechanisms such as geographic and social barriers. These differences vary as the power of the geographic and social barriers varies. Where these barriers are of high power, such ethnic groups will tend to remain distinct from each other geographically or ecologically.

English and English in their book *A Comprehensive Dictionary of Psychological and Psychoanalytical Terms* (1958), write as follows, "Ethnic group is an intentionally vague or general term used to avoid some of the difficulties of race. The ethnic group may be a nation, a people (such as the Jews), a language group (the Navajo Nation), a sociologically defined so-called race (the African American), or a group bound together in a coherent cultural entity by a religion (the Amish)."[16]

Yet another advantage of the phrase "ethnic group" is that it avoids the reductionist or "nothing but" fallacy, that is to say, the notion that people are nothing but the resultant of their biological heredity, that they are what they are because of their genes. The phrase "ethnic group" is calculated to provide the necessary corrective to this erroneous viewpoint by eliminating the question-begging emphases of the biologistic bias on purely physical factors and differences, and demanding that the question of definition be left open until the necessary scientific research and answers are available. The emphasis is shifted to the fact that the human is a uniquely cultural creature as well as a physical organism, and that under the influence of human culture the plasticity of humans, both mentally and physically, is greatly enhanced. Indeed, during the first half of the nineteenth century physical anthropologists were sometimes led to create races on the basis of physical traits which were subsequently discovered to be entirely due to cultural factors, as, for example, the head forms of the so-called Armenoid and Dinaric races, and the changes in head form in the offspring of Italian and Japanese immigrants into the United States.

Here, too, reply may be made to those who may object that the term "ethnic group" is too reminiscent of the cultural. But this is precisely why the term is so well found. The Greek word *ethnos* originally meant a number of people living together, and subsequently came to be used in the sense of a tribe, group, nation, or people. In modern times the term "ethnic" has occasionally been used to refer to a group identified by ties both of race and of nationality. This is pretty much what the phrase "ethnic group" ought to be taken to mean in the sense given in our description of an "ethnic group." If it be said that what the student of human variety is interested in is the way in which human groups came to be what they are, and that for this reason it is the biological fact and mechanisms in which such a student must be chiefly interested, the answer must be made that anyone who believes this must be disabused of his belief as quickly as possible. For it must be emphasized again that humans are not merely physical organisms but *human beings* who, as members of a cultural group have been greatly influenced by their culture. Human populations have had a remarkable assortment of marriage or breeding regulations, for instance, varying standards of sexual selection, different kinds of social barriers, mobility, and similar variables, all of which have probably played an appreciable part in the evolution of ethnic differences. These are the very kinds of factors that are most neglected by those who come to the study of humans with a biologistic bias. It would be to the advantage of such students, as well as for the layman, if they would look at the problem of human variety from the viewpoint of the ethnic group rather than from that of race. Where humans are concerned, the biologically biased need to add a cultural dimension to their horizons. That is what the term "ethnic group" will help them to do.

It has been argued that an "ethnic group," by its usual definition, is set off mainly by its cultural characteristics, and therefore is especially inept. What seems to me to be especially inept here is the failure of those who argue thus to perceive that it is because the differences between human populations are mainly cultural, that the term "ethnic group" is so well found. It is not a term which denies physical or biological differences, but recognizes them where they exist.

The term "ethnic group" denotes a self-perceived social grouping, within or without a larger social grouping, which is distinguished by a variety of traits. These include religious and linguistic characteristics, geographic or national origin, aesthetic cultural patterns, a socially transmitted way of life and sometimes more or less distinctive physical traits. None of these characteristics taken alone constitute an ethnic group. It is the association of all of them that does so.

An ethnic group represents a human population or part of one in process of undergoing genetic and socially unrelated cultural differentiation. It is a group of individuals capable of hybridizing genetically and culturally with other groups or members thereof to produce genetic and cultural recombination and differentiation, usually resulting in both cultural and physical vigor.

The concept of an "ethnic group" is quite different from that associated with the term *race*. The phrase *ethnic group* represents a different way of looking at populations, an open, non-question-begging way, a tentative, noncommittal, experimental way, based on the new understanding which the sciences of genetics and anthropology have made possible. A term is discontinued, retired, but another is not merely substituted for it; rather a new conception of human populations is introduced replacing the old one, which is now dropped, and a term or phrase suitable to this new conception is suggested. The old conception is not retained and a new name given to it, but instead a *new conception* is introduced under its own name. That is a very different thing from a mere change in names. It is important to be quite clear upon this point, for the new conception which defines an "ethnic group" renders the likelihood of the development of "ethnic group prejudice" quite impossible, for as soon as the nature of this conception is understood it cancels any such contingency. It is a noncontaminating neutral concept.

Perhaps the greatest advantage of the term "ethnic group" is that it is both noncommittal and flexible. It may be applied to any group concerning which physical and cultural traits, variable as they may be within the group, distinguish it from other groups. All that we say when we use the term "ethnic group" is that here is a group of people who physically, and perhaps in other additional ways, are more or less different, always remembering that on the basis of everything we know as scientists, and on the basis of historic experience, that the differences between ethnic groups are of the most superficial kind, and that whatever human beings have achieved anywhere, humans anywhere else, given the adequate opportunities, can also achieve, that no human anywhere weighs less in the scale of human values than any other. The great contribution of anthropology in the twentieth century has been to provide the evidence as well as the proof for this, surely the most important of all the discoveries for humanity, in this most perilous of centuries. In today's world the racist term "race" remains a monstrous fabrication and our most dangerous myth. As Ernest Haas has said, in his book *Beyond the Nation State: Functionalism and International Organization* (1969): "The tyranny of words is only less absolute than that of men; but whereas elections, revolutions, or just the dreary passage of time can do away with human tyranny, patient analysis and redefinition are required to remedy the linguistic affliction."[17]

The tyranny of race, the idea of which has enslaved so many people, and done so much damage to humanity, to the races as well as to the racists, should be abolished in order that humanity be emancipated from its corruption.

There are many parallels for this in science as well as in common usage. Possibly the most striking one was the dropping of the term "instinct" by psychologists and other behavioral scientists for reasons similar to those which make the term "race" undesirable.[18] Similarly, in anthropology the terms "savage" and "lower races" have been completely dropped, while the term "primitive" and "nonliterate" as referring to living peoples are largely being abandoned in favor of the term "indigenous" for much the same reason, namely, the inaccuracy and prejudiced nature of the earlier terms, and hence their unsuitability. In biology a long prevailing term like "atavism," meaning the recurrence in descendants of a trait which had been posessed by an ancestor, after an interval of several or many generations, has been abandoned because the phenomenon simply does not occur. And biologists no longer speak of "lower animals." In genetics the term "unit character," as erroneously referring to single genes as determining single characters or traits, has been forever banished from the scientific vocabulary. Retardative concepts like "phlogiston," the element believed to cause combustion, the concept of "ether" for the massless medium of propagation of electromagnetive waves, has also been abandoned. In medicine, from the days of Galen on, and even before, many errors concerning the construction and functioning of the human body endured for centuries until they were shown to be false. Among such beliefs, dropped by scientists with the advent of genetics, but which still lingers on in popular parlance, is that the carrier of heredity is the blood. People were of royal blood, blue blood, mixed blood, half-blood, and by racists usually, refined down to fractions of black blood (see Chapter 15 of this volume). And then there were those of good blood and others of bad blood, and so on. Terms like "Mongoloid Idiot" or "Mongolism," which were believed to be due to an atavistic recurrence of traits derived from an ancient ancestry, and so named by an English physician, Langdon Down in 1864, owing to what he thought was a resemblance to Mongoloid peoples. A book was even written in 1924 by another distinguished English physician, F. G. Crookshank, entitled *The Mongol in Our Midst* (London: Kegan Paul, 1924), in which he attempted to reinforce Down's Mongoloid theory. The terms "Mongoloid Idiocy," and "Mongolism" were dropped when, shortly after the discovery, in 1959, that "mongolism" was due to a chromosomal abnormality, and renamed "Down's Syndrome."

In common and institutional parlance terms like "Home for Incurables," "Home for Crippled Children," "bastard," illegitimate," "handicapped," "retarded," and the like have been dropped because they were unfeeling or otherwise inappropriate.

It is apparent, then, that the words we use act as psychophysical conditioners that determine the manner in which we shall think, feel, and behave. Hence, the importance of the careful use of our words, of sound thinking, and right feeling, as well as loving familial and educational goals. Hence, also, the importance of the teaching and the learning of language not so much as grammar or semantics, but as behavior, of experiencing and using language as a fine and sensitive instrument of communication designed to put us into touch with each other.

To conclude and summarize: The advantages of the phrase "ethnic group" are: first, while emphasizing the fact that one is dealing with a distinguishable group, this noncommittal term leaves the whole question of the precise status of the group on physical and other grounds open for further discussion and research; second, it recognizes the fact that it is a group that has been subject to the action of cultural influences; and third, it eliminates all obfuscating emotional implications.

The phrase "ethnic group" serves as a challenge to thought and as a stimulus to rethink the foundations of one's beliefs. It encourages the passage from ignorant certainty to thoughtful uncertainty. For the layperson, as for others, the term *race* closes the door on understanding: the phrase *ethnic group* opens it.

Notes

1. Ashley Montagu, ed., *The Concept of Race* (New York: Free Press, 1964); Frank R. Livingstone, "On the Non-Existence of Human Races," in Montagu, *Concept of Race*, 46–60; Jean Hiernaux, "Adaptation and Race," *Advancement of Science* (1967): 658–62.

2. Julian Huxley and Alfred Court Haddon, *We Europeans* (New York: Harper & Bros., 1936), 82–83.

3. W. T. Calman, *The Classification of Animals* (New York: Wiley, 1949), 14

4. H Kalmus, *Genetics* (London: Pelican Books, 1948), 45.

5. H. Kalmus, *Variation and Heredity* (London: Routledge, 1957), 30.

6. G. S. Carter, *Animal Evolution: A Study of Recent Views of Its Causes* (London: Sidgwick & Jackson; New York: Macmillan, 1951), 163.

7. Ernst Hanhart, "Infectious Diseases," in *Clinical Genetics*, ed. A. Sorsby (St. Louis: Mosby, 1953), 545.

8. Lionel Penrose, "Review of Dunn and Dobzhansky's 'Heredity, Race and Society,'" in *Annals of Eugenics* 17 (1952): 252–53.

9. J. P. Garlick, "Review," in *Annals of Human Genetics* 25 (1961): 169–70.

10. P. A. Parsons, "Genetic Determination of Behavior (Mice and Men)," in *Genetics, Environment, and Behavior*, eds. Lee Ehrman, Gilbert S. Omenn, and Ernst Caspari (New York: Academic Press, 1972), 94.

11. E. Raymond Hall, "Zoological Subspecies of Man at the Peace Table," *Journal of Mammalogy* 27(1946): 358–64.

12. A. E. Housman, *The Name and Nature of Poetry* (New York: Cambridge University Press), 31.

13. E. A. Sigerist, *A History of Medicine*, vol. 1 (New York: Oxford University Press, 1951), 101.

14. George G. Simpson, *The Major Features of Evolution* (New York: Columbia University Press), 268.

15. Alfred Korzybski, *Science and Sanity*, 2nd ed. (Lancaster: Science Press, 1941), 31.

16. H. B. English and A. C. English, *A Comprehensive Dictionary of Psychological and Psychoanalytical Terms* (New York: Longmans, 1958), 189.

17. Ernest B. Haas, *Beyond the Nation State: Functionalism and International Organization.* (Stanford: Stanford University Press, 1969), 3.

18. See L. L. Bernard, *Instinct: A Study in Social Psychology* (New York: Holt, 1924).

Appendix B

The Fallacy Of The Primitive[*]

From the rather self-conscious heights of our own state of equivocal civilization and of that of the community to which we belong, we of the latest period of human development have traditionally taken the view that whatever has preceded us was by so much the less advanced. Since we are the latest bearers of human development we reason, therefore, we are the most fully developed. This rather ortholinear view of development is widely held, and it is, of course, widely believed to be in harmony with the evolutionary facts.

The truth is that evolutionary processes do not proceed in straight lines but are more accurately observed to assume a reticulate form. And so it has been in the evolution of humans, both physically and culturally. So entrenched, however, have our beliefs become concerning the straight line (ortholinear) evolution of man that our conceptions of "progress," "development," and "evolution" have rendered the assumption automatic that what developed earlier was "less developed." From this the "logical" inference followed that what was less developed must be earlier than that which was more developed, and therefore the earlier was the more "primitive" and the later the more "advanced." Furthermore, since straight-line evolution is taken for granted by so many, it followed that the more advanced developed from the less advanced, from the "primitive," and the former was "superior" to the latter.

Since evolution from the less advanced to the more advanced or from the simpler to the complex (not quite the same thing) is a fact beyond dispute (although the reverse has sometimes occurred in evolution), it has been easy to fall into the habit of assuming that the later developed is not only the more evolved but also the better. "Better" is, of course, a value

[*]Reprinted from *The Journal of the American Medical Association* 179 (24 March, 1962): 962, 963. © 1962, by American Medical Association.

judgment, and value judgments are a quagmire in which one may get hopelessly stuck. And this seems to be the condition into which civilized man has fallen, with respect to those whom he chooses to call "primitive."

We speak of "primitive" peoples—the indigenous peoples of the earth. What do we mean when we use the term? We mean that such peoples are, in comparison with ourselves, undeveloped; in many respects that is true. For example, it would be true of reading and writing, of technological progress, and in various cultures it would be more or less true of certain aspects of moral and institutional development. But it is very necessary to point out that, in certain respects, such cultures are more highly developed than are most civilized cultures. By the standards of values in these matters prevailing in civilized societies, "primitive" cultures are "better" than civilized cultures.

For example, Eskimos and Australian aborigines, to take two of the so-called most "primitive" cultures known to anthropologists, are very much more generous, loving, and cooperative than are most of the members of civilized societies, their languages, and genealogical systems, very much more complex and efficient than those of the western world. By the measure of our own values in these matters, Eskimos, and Australian aborigines are better human beings than we are. Members of these "primitive" cultures are honest, dependable, generous, and courageous, in all these respects to a degree which comparatively few civilized humans manage to be. Who is more developed in these respects? Those who pay lip-service to these qualities or those who act them out in their lives?

An additional assumption widely made is that "primitive" peoples are "nearer" and more closely resemble prehistoric man than the so-called "more advanced" peoples. This, too, is an unsound assumption. The fact is that indigenous peoples have as long a history as civilized ones. Despite references to "living fossils," no human population can, even by the most extreme stretch of the imagination, be considered to be a fossil. All human societies change. The rate of change undoubtedly varies, some being slower than others, but changes must occur. They occur in language, religion, custom, and technology, and the changes will be considerably influenced by the varying experiences which each society undergoes. Those that are isolated from the mainstream of cultural change will change slowly; those that are exposed to the fertilizing effects of cultural interchange with other peoples will change rapidly. But even in the absence of such cultural stimulation, the very nature of cultural life involves more or less continuous adjustment to and encouragement of change to meet the requirements of changing conditions. We can, therefore, be certain that no culture, as we know it today, is as it was in prehistoric times. It may even be that some of the so-called "primitive" cultures are much less like those of prehistoric times than some that appear to be more advanced. It cannot be questioned that, in some respects, some indigenous cultures are closer to the conditions as they prevailed in prehistoric times than are civilized cultures. Examples are the egalitarian societies, such as the Australian aborigines, the pygmies of the Ituri Forest, the Hadza of Tanzania, This, however, does not mean that they are so in all, or even most, respects.

Each culture in the course of time makes the progress necessary to enable its members to live as comfortably as possible in the environment in which the culture functions. The environment generally sets certain limits beyond which it is impossible for the culture to develop unless radical changes are introduced from the outside. Metal tools, for example, will not be developed in an environment in which metal ores are unknown. As I have already said, cultures differ from one another in the history of the experiences they have undergone and, therefore, in the kind of development they have realized. In other words, given similar opportunities, human beings everywhere are capable of achieving similar degrees of development.

Too often we identify "primitive humans" with contemporary indigenous peoples when the only legitimate use of the phrase "primitive human" is when it is applied to prehistoric humans. But even here there are dangers in the use of terms which are so loaded with erroneous ideas. Primitive humans, that is, prehistoric humans, are too often thought of as beetle-browed monsters, with little brains, bull necks, knock-knees, and a nasty habit of dragging their womenfolk around by their hair. This is the "cartoon" idea of prehistoric humans and is utter nonsense. Beetle-brows there undoubtedly were, but it should have been explained that behind those beetle-brows beat a brain of considerable power and, as in the case of the Neandertal, larger in size than our noble own! The monster, the bull neck, the knock-knees, and the hair-dragging of women are all figments of the imaginations of those who wished to see these things the way they thought they ought to be. But the true scientist endeavors to see things the way they are, not the way they ought to be or what is considered desirable to fit some theory. It is never a matter of the facts fitting the theory, but rather the theory fitting the facts.

One of the consequences of the belief that primitive humans were so much less developed than ourselves is the failure to understand that prehistoric human of 15,000 years ago were in some aspects of their lives capable of achievements which have scarcely been surpassed since. An outstanding example of this is prehistoric art, especially the art of the Upper Old Stone Age. When this was first discovered at the beginning of the century, it was at first attributed to modern artists who, for some reason, had crept into a natural crypt and decorated its ceiling and walls in the manner of Michelangelo in the Sistine Chapel. But, as other discoveries were made in the dark recesses of caverns and caves under conditions which pointed to an extreme antiquity, the weight of evidence could no longer be resisted, and prehistoric humans were finally acknowledged as the creator of these wonderful works of art, paintings, sculpture, and engravings, As Sir Herbert Read has said, "The best paintings in the Altamira, Niaux, and Lascaux caves exhibit a degree of skill which is not less than that of a Pisanello or a Picasso." Anyone who has seen the originals or even reproductions will agree that this is no overstatement. In addition to the technical skill displayed by the artists, their work exhibits a vitality and expression which has seldom been surpassed in any age.

Be that as it may, in the works of art of prehistoric humans who lived between 15,000 and 30,000 years ago, we have the clearest evidence that these people, as artists, were as accomplished as any who have lived since. When it is remembered that these works were not really executed as works of art but as magico-religious rituals calculated to yield success in the hunt, that the conditions under which these works were created were often of the most difficult kind, high up on walls and ceilings, often with the artist lying on his back, and working by the uncertain light of a smoky oil lamp, the achievement becomes all the more remarkable. There can be little doubt that individuals capable of such skills were endowed with an intelligence potentially no less great than that possessed by contemporary civilized humans. Because the term "primitive" not only tends to obscure that fact, but also militates against the possibility of understanding the true significance of the facts, it will readily be understood why, if the term is used at all, it should be used with the greatest caution.

The primitive human as prehistoric human is most certainly a reality, and the more we learn to understand him, the better we understand ourselves. But to identify existing indigenous peoples with prehistoric humans is an error, when it is not an expedient fiction. In the rapidly changing world in which we live, in which the underdeveloped regions of the world will witness their most spectacular advances in the areas of human development, it is the first order of importance that the civilized peoples of the world understand and act upon these facts.[1]

Note

1. Mark S. Miller (ed.) and many associates, *State of the Peoples: A Global Human Rights Report on Societies in Danger* (Boston: Beacon Press, 1993). This book, which is dedicated to the thousands of cultures that have disappeared over the past five centuries, the victims of blindness and greed, draws attention to the many cultures all over the world that stand in need of our help. The literature on the "fatal impact" of the modern world upon indigineous cultures is very great. As I write innumerable cultures are being destroyed while the rest of the world stands by and

does nothing to stop the slaughter. See Jane and John Comaroff, *Of Revelation and Revolution*, vol. 1 (Chicago: University of Chicago Press, 1991); Martin Gilbert, *Auschwitz and the Allies* (New York: Holt, Reinhart & Winston, 1981), a devastating account of how the Allies responded to the news of Hitler's mass murder—it should be required reading in schools, colleges, universities and by all who have a heart left—similarly for Charlotte Delbo's *Auschwitz and After* (New Haven: Yale University Press, 1995).

Appendix C

The Term *Miscegenation*

The term *miscegenation* provides a remarkable exhibit in the natural history of nonsense. The term today is used in a pejorative sense as well as in a purely descriptive sense as referring to "race mixture." The prefix *mis* (from the Latin *mixcere,* "mix") has probably contributed its share to the misunderstanding of the nature of race mixture. Words that begin with the prefix "mis" suggest a "mistake," "misuse," "mislead," and similar erroneous ideas implying wrong conduct.

The word *miscegenation* was invented as a hoax, and published in an anonymous pamphlet at New York in 1864, with the title *Miscegenation: The Theory of the Blending of the Races, Applied to the White Man and Negro*. The pamphlet was almost certainly the joint product of two members of the *New York World* staff, David Goodman Croly,[1] an editor, and George Wakeman, one of the reporters. The purpose of the authors was to raise the race issue in aggravated form in the 1864 presidential campaign by attributing to the abolitionist Republicans and the Republican party the views set forth in *Miscegenation*. The pamphlet was intended to commit the Republican leaders to "the conclusions to which they are brought by their own principles," without any genuine hope of success but in the expectation that their folly would be made all the more clear to them in granting the blacks the franchise. The brief introduction sets the tone of the whole pamphlet:

> The word is spoken at last. It is Miscegenation—the blending of the various races of men—the practical recognition of all the children of the common father. While the sublime inspirations of Christianity have taught this doctrine, Christians so-called have ignored it in denying social equality to the colored man; while democracy is founded upon the idea that all men are equal, democrats have shrunk from the logic of their own creed, and refused to fraternize with the people of all nations; while science has demonstrated that the intermarriage of diverse races is indispensable to the progressive humanity, its votaries, in this country at least, have never had the courage to apply that rule to the relations of the white and colored races. But Christianity, democracy, and science are stronger

than the timidity, prejudice, and pride of short-sighted men; and they teach that a people, to become great, must become composite. This involves what is vulgarly known as amalgamation, and those who dread that name, and the thought and fact it implies, are warned against reading these pages.

The word "miscegenation" is defined by the authors as follows: "*Miscegenation*—from the Latin *Miscere,* to mix, and *Genus,* race, is used to denote the abstract idea of the mixture of two or more races."

Thus, the word "miscegenation" was invented by the well-meaning satirists to replace the vulgar term "amalgamation," as not being sufficiently elevated or distinguished.[2] Indeed, it seems to me that they deliberately hit upon "miscegenation" because it carried with it a sort of racialistic overtone, implying, approbium and unpalatability.[3] The extent of the prejudice inherent in and engendered by this word may be gathered from the fact that *Webster's New International Dictionary* illustrates the use of the word by the example of "one who is *guilty* of miscegenation."

In his book, *The Children of Caliban,* the sociologist Henriques (1974), perpetuates the term both in his title and throughout the text. Ali Mazrui writes in his book, *A World Federation of Cultures* (1976), that although he is aware of the racialistic origins of the term, his use of it is intended to be value free. Unfortunately terms having a tainted ancestry have a tendency to be reinforced by repetition. Joel Williamson, in his book *New People* (1980), subtitles his book "Miscegenation and Mulatoes in the United States."

The word should be replaced by ordinary English words such as "intermixture," "mixture," "admixture," or "intermarriage."

Notes

1. Croly's son Herbert was the author of *The Promise of American Life* (New York: Macmillan, 1912), the classic statement of the progressive movement in America. Herbert was also the founder of *The New Republic.*

2. The pamphlet is the subject of an excellent little book, J. M. Bloch, *Miscegenation, Melaleukation, and Mr. Lincoln's Dog* (New York: Schaum, 1958).

3. This is well illustrated by a remark made by former President Harry S. Truman. When asked whether he thought racial intermarriages would become widespread in the United States, he answered, "I hope not. I don't believe in it. What's that word about four feet long? Miscegenation?" *New York Times,* 12 September 1963.

Appendix D

Intelligence of Northern Blacks and Southern Whites in the First World War

In 1943[1] a comparison was made between the median scores obtained by blacks from three northern states and those obtained by whites from three southern states, scores made on the intelligence tests administered by the U.S. Army to draftees during World War I.[2] While neither the data nor the instruments used to obtain it represent the current methodology or standards for the so-called measuring of intelligence, I include it in this appendix for the information it provides. This chapter is derived from an article originally published in 1945, and although revised only slightly for the present edition of *Man's Most Dangerous Myth,* it is my hope that it will be of interest to the reader, if only as a matter of historical perspective.

When I wished to check on these scores I found, much to my astonishment, that though some medians had been calculated for some black and white groups, no complete list of medians had ever been published for all of them and that consequently the real facts were, twenty-three years after the original data had been published, still unknown. I therefore decided to compute the medians for all the relevant groups in order to discover precisely how the scores of northern blacks on these tests compared with those of southern whites.[3]

Before proceeding with the statement and analysis of the facts, certain matters pertaining to the groups examined and the tests used must be clarified. Four groups of men were examined, defined as follows:

Group I White: the white draft of the United States at large;[4]
Group II White: additional white draft;[5]
Group IV Negro: the black draft at large comparable to Group I;[6]
Group V Negro: additional black draft from the northern states;[7]

Three types of examinations were given, Alpha, Beta and Individual.

Alpha. The Alpha examination was given to all subjects who were not eliminated for illiteracy.[8] The highest number of points possible was 212.

Beta. The Beta examination was given to most of the men who had been eliminated from the Alpha examination because of relative illiteracy, and to most of the men who made a weighted score of less than 100 on the Alpha examination.[9] The highest number of points possible was 118.

Individual. The individual examination consisted of a list of tests provided for four types of subject: illiterate or non-English speaking, subnormal, psychotic, and supernormal, and also for those who made 19 points or less in the Alpha or Beta or both tests.[10] The highest number of points it was possible to secure on this test was 100. Finally, careful note must be made of the fact that data were available for only 23 states and the District of Columbia for blacks, while for whites data are available, in most cases, for all 48 states and the District of Columbia.

Beta Score

For the black draft, Groups IV and V, the Beta score medians are available for the District of Columbia, 14 southern and 9 northern states. In order to determine in which states the lowest median scores were made on this test by blacks these scores may be arranged in order beginning with the lowest and proceeding to the highest. This has been done in Table D.1.

From this table it will be seen that the lowest scores in the black draft were invariably made by blacks from the southern states, and, furthermore, that every one of the 14 southern states and the District of Columbia is associated with a low median Beta score, the average median Beta score for the black draft here being 17.58, with a median range of 8.95 to 23.90.

On the other hand, the black draft from 9 northern states invariably achieved a significantly higher median Beta score than the blacks from the South, the average median Beta score being 32.72 with a range from 27.60 to 39.65. It is of interest to note that in the northern group the lowest median scores come from the two states bordering on the South, namely, Pennsylvania with 27.60 and New Jersey with 29.45.

It is also of interest to note that the median Beta scores of the white draft, Groups I and II, for the 14 southern states and the District of Columbia listed in Table D.2 fall into the lower half of the rank order of scores for the 48 states and the District of Columbia. The exception is the District of Columbia in which the median Beta score for whites, 43.75, falls into the higher rank. It is also significant that the first, second, third, and fourth lowest median Beta scores made by whites were made in the four southern states of Kentucky 12.30, Virginia 16.60, Alabama 27.00, and North Carolina 27.00.

In Kentucky the 188 white draftees achieved a significantly lower score, 12.30, than the 330 colored draftees from the same state, the median Beta

TABLE D.1

BETA SCORE BY SCORE RANK: BLACKS

Groups IV and V. Computed from Mem. Nat. Acad. Sci., *15, 1921, 731, Table 267.*

Rank	State	Number	Range	Median
1	South Carolina	1,309	0– 99	8.95
2	Florida	123	0– 59	8.95
3	Alabama	1,059[a]	0– 99	10.95
4	Louisiana	1,012	0– 79	15.65
5	Virginia	1,220	0– 89	16.60
6	North Carolina	1,156	0–118	16.70
7	Kentucky	330	0– 84	17.20
8	Arkansas	686	0– 99	19.05
9	Georgia	1,868	0–114	20.00
10	West Virginia	91	0– 59	20.60
11	District of Columbia	168	0– 89	20.80
12	Texas	962	0–109	21.05
13	Maryland	340	0– 89	21.15
14	Mississippi	959	0– 84	22.10
15	Tennessee	419	0– 99	23.90
16	Pennsylvania	794	0–104	27.60
17	New Jersey	416	0–104	29.45
18	Oklahoma	201	5– 79	29.70
19	Illinois	661	0– 84	31.70
20	Indiana	116	0– 89	31.90
21	Missiouri	153	0– 74	33.50
22	New York	495	0– 89	33.55
23	Kansas	28	5– 84	37.50
24	Ohio	77	0– 94	39.65
	Total number and range	14,643	0–118	19.34

score of the latter being 17.20. Among the northern states it was in Ohio that 77 blacks obtained a median Beta score of 39.65, as compared with the score of 35.45 made by 68 white draftees from the same state.

With respect to the Beta scores it will be seen from Table D.3 that the average median score of the blacks from 6 northern states was 34.63, while that of the whites from 14 southern states was only 31.11, a difference of 3.52 points in favor of the blacks from these 6 northern states.

It has already been pointed out that comparable figures for black and white draftees are available for 23 states and the District of Columbia, as shown in Table D.1. From this table were selected the 6 states showing the highest median Beta scores obtained by the blacks from these states, and

TABLE D.2

BETA SCORE BY SCORE RANK: WHITES

Groups I and II. Computed from Mem. Nat. Acad. Sci., *15, 1921, 691, Table 206.*

Rank	State	Number	Range	Median
1	Kentucky	188	0– 84	12.30
2	Virginia	160	0–104	20.65
3	Alabama	402	0– 79	27.00
4	North Carolina	394	0– 84	27.00
5	Connecticut	214	0–104	29.35
6	New Jersey	367	5–104	30.45
7	Arizona	1	30– 34	32.00
8	Florida	12	0– 69	32.50
9	Mississippi	320	0– 84	32.85
10	New Mexico	392	0–114	32.95
11	West Virginia	573	0– 89	33.00
12	Arkansas	369	0– 99	33.55
13	Indiana	153	0– 89	33.80
14	South Carolina	447	0–109	34.30
15	Tennessee	473	0–104	34.45
16	Louisiana	359	0– 99	35.25
17	Ohio	68	0– 84	35.45
18	Massachusetts	420	0–104	35.90
19	Maryland	395	0–109	36.15
20	Delaware	19	5– 64	36.25
21	Georgia	297	0–104	36.25
22	Pennsylvania	602	0–114	36.25
23	Texas	317	0– 79	36.65
24	Oklahoma	302	0–109	37.35
25	Wisconsin	203	0–118	37.85
26	Michigan	349	0–104	38.60
27	Missouri	379	0–109	38.85
28	Rhode Island	328	0– 94	40.15
29	Vermont	215	5–104	42.10
30	New Hampshire	294	0– 99	43.10
31	New York	1,668	0–118	43.45
32	District of Columbia	36	5– 69	43.75
33	Colorado	116	0–109	44.00
34	Maine	302	0– 94	45.15
35	Iowa	161	0–109	46.25
36	Montana	366	10– 99	47.75
37	Kansas	153	0– 99	49.00
38	Illinois	772	0–144	49.45
39	Nebraska	329	15–118	49.80
40	North Dakota	240	10– 99	50.30
41	California	383	10–109	51.30
42	South Dakota	248	15– 99	54.10
43	Washington	241	5–104	57.20
44	Nevada	38	15– 94	58.53
45	Utah	258	5–104	59.10
46	Oregon	242	5–114	60.20
47	Idaho	248	0– 99	61.20
48	Wyoming	115	15– 99	62.15
49	Minnesota	380	0–114	63.25
	Total number and range	15,308	0–118	40.70

TABLE D.3

MEDIAN BETA SCORES FOR NORTHERN BLACKS AND SOUTHERN WHITES

Rank Order	Northern Blacks	Range	Median Score
1	Ohio	0– 94	39.65
2	Kansas	5– 84	37.50
3	New York	0– 89	33.55
4	Missouri	0– 74	33.50
5	Indiana	0– 89	31.90
6	Illinois	0– 84	31.70
		Average Median Score	34.63

Rank Order	Southern Whites	Range	Median Score
1	Kentucky	0– 84	12.30
2	Virginia	0–104	20.65
3	Alabama	0– 79	27.00
4	North Carolina	0– 84	27.00
5	Louisiana	0– 99	32.25
6	Florida	0– 69	32.50
7	Mississippi	0– 84	32.85
8	West Virginia	0– 89	33.00
9	Arkansas	0– 99	33.55
10	South Carolina	0–109	34.30
11	Tennessee	0– 79	34.45
12	Maryland	0–109	36.15
13	Georgia	0–104	36.25
14	Texas	0– 79	36.65
		Average Median Score	31.11

these have been listed in order of rank. There were then selected the states showing median Beta scores for white draftees which were lower than the highest made by the northern blacks. Altogether there were 24 states in which the median Beta scores of the whites were lower than the second highest median Beta scores achieved by the blacks. These states are the first 24 listed in table D.2. Of these 24 states, 14 are southern, 8 are northern, and 2 are southwestern.

Such a statement would not be very revealing were we content to stop with it. When, however, we plot the rank order of these 24 states on a map, as is done in Figure D.1, it will at once be seen that their distribution follows a strikingly interesting pattern. All the states in the southern part of the continent, in the Southeast, in the Northeast (with the exception of

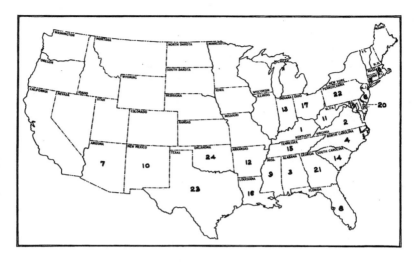

FIGURE D.1
DISTRIBUTION OF MEDIAN BETA SCORES OF ILLITERATE WHITES WHICH
WERE LOWER THAN THE SECOND BEST OBTAINED BY ILLITERATE BLACKS
Range of scores: 12.30–37.35

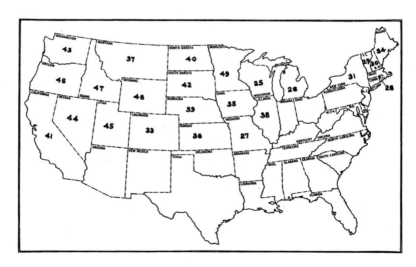

FIGURE D.2
DISTRIBUTION OF MEDIAN BETA SCORES OF ILLITERATE WHITES WHICH WERE
HIGHER THAN THE SECOND BEST OBTAINED BY ILLITERATE BLACKS
Range of scores: 37.85–63.25

New Hampshire, Maine, Vermont, and Rhode Island), and the northern states bordering on the South, Indiana, Ohio, and Pennsylvania, make up the states in which occurred Beta scores lower than the second best obtained by illiterate blacks in the North. All the extreme northern, all the middle western, and all the far western states fall into the upper rank on their median Beta scores. Their distribution is shown in Figure D.2. This upper rank distribution is as interesting as that of the lower rank, but let us deal with the distribution of the lower-rank scores first.

What did this remarkable geographic restriction of the lower-rank scores mean? There are probably a large number of factors that entered into the causation of this peculiarly limited distribution. The fact that the three lowest median Beta scores come respectively from Kentucky, Virginia, and Alabama, suggests that socioeconomic factors played a considerable part in determining these scores. Keeping the temporal context in mind, the poor white sections of these states represented socioeconomically very depressed groups indeed, their markedly low scores are not altogether unexpected. It seems probable that the median Beta score rank occupied by each state is to an appreciable extent associated with the socioeconomic status of the individuals examined from that state.

Observe how in Figure D.1 the arithmetical order of the score ranks occurs in clusters: 1 and 2, Kentucky and Virginia; 3 and 4, Alabama and North Carolina; 5 and 6, Connecticut and New Jersey; 7 and 10, Arizona and New Mexico; 9 and 8, Minnesota and Florida; and so on. In Figure D.2 this grouping is even more striking, as is shown by the following clusters: 25 and 26, Wisconsin and Michigan; 28, 29, 30 and 31, Rhode Island, Vermont, New Hampshire, and New York; 35 and 36, Kansas and Iowa; 44, 45, 46, 47 and 48, Nevada, Utah, Oregon, Idaho, and Wyoming. Adjacent states, on the whole, tend to have similar median Beta scores. In general, too, in states in which the whites did poorly on the Beta test the blacks also did badly. The question may be asked: Why did the illiterate blacks of Kentucky and Ohio do better on the Beta tests than the illiterate whites of the same states? It was difficult to say at the time of the original publication, but it is quite within the realm of possibility that the blacks had enjoyed a better socioeconomic environment than the illiterate whites.

What is important for our purposes here is the fact that any group of blacks from some states should have done better on the Beta tests than whites from some states. The illiterate blacks of Ohio with a Beta score of 39.65 achieved a better score than the whites from the first 27 states listed in Table D.2. Of these 27 states 14 are southern, and 13 are northern. The average median Beta score of the white illiterates for the 14 southern states is 30.85, while that for the white illiterates of the 13 northern states is 34.93. The illiterate blacks of Kansas with a score of 37.50 did better than the illiterate whites of 24 states. The illiterate blacks of New York with a

TABLE D.4

ALPHA SCORE BY SCORE RANK: BLACKS

For men who took Alpha only. Groups IV and V. Computed from Mem. Nat. Acad. Sci., *15,*
1921, 728, Table 262.

Rank	State	Number	Range	Median
1	Florida	499	0–114	9.25
2	Georgia	319	0–124	9.90
3	Mississippi	765	0–104	10.25
4	South Carolina	334	0– 99	14.20
5	North Carolina	210	0–154	16.40
6	Arkansas	181	0–104	17.10
7	Louisiana	401	0–129	19.00
8	Alabama	262	0–109	21.05
9	Kentucky	191	0–134	23.95
10	West Virginia	57	0– 69	25.30
11	Texas	412	0–114	25.65
12	Tennessee	502	0–159	29.80
13	Maryland	109	0–129	31.95
14	Missouri	167	0–134	33.25
15	New Jersey	724	0–144	34.30
16	Kansas	85	0–144	34.65
17	Oklahoma	87	5–114	35.30
18	District of Columbia	22	15– 89	37.50
19	Pennsylvania	661	0–149	40.40
20	Indiana	269	0–154	41.55
21	New York	1,021	0–164	44.55
22	Virginia	56	0–119	46.25
23	Illinois	704	0–184	46.85
24	Ohio	152	0–154	48.30
	Total number and range	8,190	0–184	28.40

score of 33.55 and those of Missouri with a score of 33.50 did better than
the illiterate whites of eleven states. The illiterate blacks of Indiana with a
score of 31.90 and those of Illinois with a score of 31.70 did better than the
illiterate whites of six states.

How is it that the illiterate blacks from these six states did so much better than the illiterate whites of these many other states? This question cannot be answered with any degree of certainty for the relevant data from
which it might be answered are lacking. The important fact, however, remains that these blacks did do so much better than the illiterate whites of
so many states. It must again be reiterated that data for Beta tests taken by

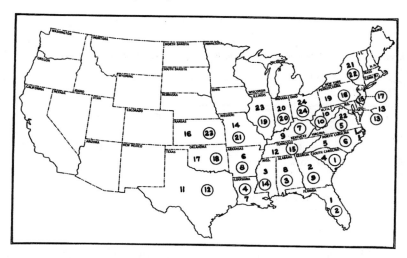

FIGURE D.3
AVERAGE RANK FOR ALPHA (UNENCIRCLED)
AND BETA (ENCIRCLED) SCORES: BLACKS

blacks are available for only 24 states. Had scores been available for blacks for all 48 states it is probable that we should have had several more states in which blacks did better on these tests than whites.

Alpha Score

For the black draft, Groups IV and V, the Alpha score medians are available for the same states as for the Beta scores, namely, the District of Columbia, 14 southern and 9 northern states. The facts are set out in tables D.4 and D.5. Table D.5 is principally of interest in that as an independent sampling of blacks from five of the states listed in Table D.4 it affords the reader an opportunity to reflect on the general accuracy of the tests. These medians are strikingly close to those for the same groups in Table D.4.

With the exception of the blacks from Virginia and those from the District of Columbia, the lowest scores were, as in the case of the Beta tests, made by blacks from the southern states. Twelve hundred and twenty blacks from Virginia and 168 from the District of Columbia were examined for the Beta tests, whereas only 56 of the former and 168 of the latter were examined for the Alpha tests. This difference in numbers may possibly explain the comparatively high place occupied by both Virginia and the District of Columbia on the Alpha tests. This inference is the more likely since, in general, the Alpha and Beta score ranks are fairly highly corre-

TABLE D.5

ALPHA SCORE BY SCORE RANK: BLACKS

For men who took Alpha only. Group V. Computed from Mem. Nat. Acad. Sci., *15, 1921, 725, Table 256.*

Rank	State	Number	Range	Median
1	New Jersey	621	0–144	34.20
2	Indiana	195	0–144	40.55
3	Pennsylvania	498	0–149	41.55
4	New York	850	0–164	45.20
5	Illinois	578	0–184	48.75
	Total number and range	2,742	0–184	42.50

lated. Where Alpha score is low, Beta score tends to be low; where Alpha is high, Beta tends to be high. The relation is well brought out in Figure D.3. Thus the rank order of Alpha and Beta scores of the following States is: Florida 1–2, South Carolina 4–6, North Carolina 5–6, Arkansas 6–8, Kentucky 7–9, West Virginia 10–10, Texas 11–12, Tennessee 12–15, Maryland 13–13, New Jersey 15–17, Oklahoma 17–18, Indiana 20–20, New York 21–22, Ohio 24–24. These fourteen states show a fairly close correlation for their ranks on Alpha and Beta. Where the ranks are not so close, in the remaining nine states and the District of Columbia, the trends are nevertheless similar. A like trend is seen in the Alpha and Beta scores of whites (see Figure D.4), but with this matter we shall deal later.

The average median Alpha score for literate blacks from the 14 southern states (including Virginia) and the District of Columbia is 21.31, with a range from 9.25 to 46.25. In contrast, the literate blacks from the nine northern states obtained an average median Alpha score of 39.90, with a range from 33.25 to 48.30.

The median Alpha scores of the white draft, Groups I and II, closely follows the pattern of distribution of the Beta scores. Thus, again, all 14 southern states fall into the lower rank order of scores for the 47 states (data are not available for Arizona) and the District of Columbia. Again, the exception is the District of Columbia in which the median Alpha score for whites, 78.75, falls into the higher rank. The first, second, third, and fourth lowest median Beta scores made by whites were achieved by the following States respectively: Kentucky, Virginia, Alabama, and North Carolina. On the Alpha tests these places are occupied, in the same order, by Mississippi, 41.20, Kentucky, 41.50, Arkansas, 41.55, and Georgia, 42.10. In other words, the lowest scores on the Beta and Alpha tests were made by the states of the Deep South.

TABLE D.6

ALPHA SCORE BY SCORE RANK: WHITES

For men who took Alpha only. Groups I and II. Computed from Men. Nat. Acad. Sci., *15, 1921, 682f.,*
Table 200.

Rank	State	Number	Range	Median
1	Mississippi	665	0–174	41.20
2	Kentucky	832	0–184	41.50
3	Arkansas	618	0–159	41.55
4	Georgia	702	0–194	42.10
5	North Carolina	607	0–159	43.15
6	Louisiana	641	0–174	45.20
7	Alabama	697	0–189	46.20
8	Tennessee	654	0–174	47.15
9	South Carolina	540	10–164	47.40
10	New Jersey	878	0–189	48.60
11	Delaware	126	0–184	50.00
12	Texas	1,169	0–189	50.80
13	Oklahoma	688	0–179	52.45
14	West Virginia	416	0–184	55.60
15	Indiana	1,169	5–189	56.05
16	Maryland	606	0–174	56.10
17	Virginia	505	0–174	56.25
18	Wisconsin	997	5–189	56.40
19	North Dakota	764	0–184	57.00
20	South Dakota	747	10–194	58.15
21	Florida	47	0–184	59.40
22	Missouri	1,227	15–184	59.55
23	New Mexico	184	15–179	60.00
24	New Hampshire	710	0–184	61.80
25	Rhode Island	690	0–212	62.85
26	Michigan	1,095	0–189	63.35
27	Illinois	2,056	0–194	63.75
28	Kansas	840	5–194	63.80
29	Minnesota	719	0–174	64.00
30	Nevada	81	15–174	64.40
31	Iowa	979	5–204	64.45
32	New York	2,843	0–204	64.50
33	Pennsylvania	3,089	0–199	65.05
34	Nebraska	676	5–199	66.10
35	Maine	664	10–189	66.90
36	Ohio	2,318	5–212	67.25
37	Vermont	802	0–212	67.45
38	Montana	632	10–189	68.40
39	Colorado	651	5–212	69.60
40	Massachusetts	1,134	0–212	71.50
41	Utah	602	10–184	72.15
42	Idaho	760	0–184	73.40
43	Connecticut	783	0–194	73.50
44	Wyoming	455	0–199	77.85
45	California	851	0–199	78.05
46	District of Columbia	77	0–194	78.75
47	Washington	794	0–189	79.20
48	Oregon	750	5–199	79.90
	Total number and range	40,530	0–212	61.25

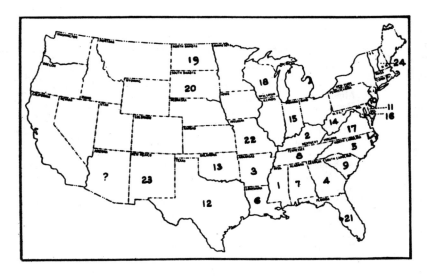

FIGURE D.4
DISTRIBUTION OF MEDIAN ALPHA SCORES OF LITERATE WHITES SHOWING
THE STATES IN WHICH THE RANK SCORES FALL INTO THE LOWER HALF
Range of scores: 41.20–61.80

A fact of interest is that while North and South Dakota ranked high on the Beta tests, 40th and 42nd respectively, on the Alpha tests they rank low, namely, 19th and 20th respectively. In general, however, as will be seen from figures 4 and 5, the states which ranked low on the Beta tests also ranked low on the Alpha tests.

It is of interest to note in examining the maps printed in this study that the illiterate and the literate white draftees from the Pacific Coast on the whole do better on both Alpha and Beta tests than the middle-western, western, and eastern draftees.

When the median Alpha and Beta scores made by the whites for each state are compared, as in Figure D.6, some most interesting distributions are seen to emerge. The Alpha ranks for the Pacific Coast states are always higher than the corresponding Beta ranks. On the other hand, with the exception of Montana, Colorado, and New Mexico, Beta ranks are higher than Alpha ranks in all the states east of the Pacific Coast, all the way to the western borders of Alabama, North Carolina, Kentucky, Indiana, and Michigan, that is to say, some 14 out of the 17 eastern States.

On the other hand, in 9 out of the 13 Eastern states Alpha ranks higher than Beta, while in one state, Michigan, the ranks are equal. In the South Beta are higher than Alpha ranks in eight States, while Alpha are

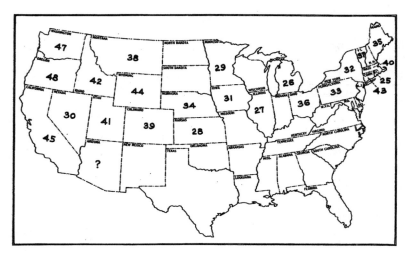

FIGURE D.5
DISTRIBUTION OF THE MEDIAN ALPHA SCORES OF LITERATE WHITES SHOWING
THE STATES IN WHICH THE RANK SCORES FALL INTO THE UPPER HALF
Range of scores: 62.85–79.90

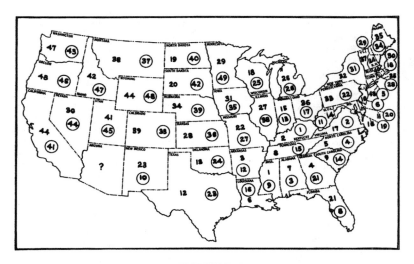

FIGURE D.6
AVERAGE RANK FOR ALPHA (UNENCIRCLED)
AND BETA (ENCIRCLED) SCORES: WHITES

TABLE D.6

ALPHA SCORE BY SCORE RANK: WHITES

For men who took Alpha only. Groups I and II. Computed from Men. Nat. Acad. Sci., 15, 1921, 682f., Table 200.

Rank	State	Number	Range	Median
1	Mississippi	665	0–174	41.20
2	Kentucky	832	0–184	41.50
3	Arkansas	618	0–159	41.55
4	Georgia	702	0–194	42.10
5	North Carolina	607	0–159	43.15
6	Louisiana	641	0–174	45.20
7	Alabama	697	0–189	46.20
8	Tennessee	654	0–174	47.15
9	South Carolina	540	10–164	47.40
10	New Jersey	878	0–189	48.60
11	Delaware	126	0–184	50.00
12	Texas	1,169	0–189	50.80
13	Oklahoma	688	0–179	52.45
14	West Virginia	416	0–184	55.60
15	Indiana	1,169	5–189	56.05
16	Maryland	606	0–174	56.10
17	Virginia	505	0–174	56.25
18	Wisconsin	997	5–189	56.40
19	North Dakota	764	0–184	57.00
20	South Dakota	747	10–194	58.15
21	Florida	47	0–184	59.40
22	Missouri	1,227	15–184	59.55
23	New Mexico	184	15–179	60.00
24	New Hampshire	710	0–184	61.80
25	Rhode Island	690	0–212	62.85
26	Michigan	1,095	0–189	63.35
27	Illinois	2,056	0–194	63.75
28	Kansas	840	5–194	63.80
29	Minnesota	719	0–174	64.00
30	Nevada	81	15–174	64.40
31	Iowa	979	5–204	64.45
32	New York	2,843	0–204	64.50
33	Pennsylvania	3,089	0–199	65.05
34	Nebraska	676	5–199	66.10
35	Maine	664	10–189	66.90
36	Ohio	2,318	5–212	67.25
37	Vermont	802	0–212	67.45
38	Montana	632	10–189	68.40
39	Colorado	651	5–212	69.60
40	Massachusetts	1,134	0–212	71.50
41	Utah	602	10–184	72.15
42	Idaho	760	0–184	73.40
43	Connecticut	783	0–194	73.50
44	Wyoming	455	0–199	77.85
45	California	851	0–199	78.05
46	District of Columbia	77	0–194	78.75
47	Washington	794	0–189	79.20
48	Oregon	750	5–199	79.90
	Total number and range	40,530	0–212	61.25

TABLE D.7

MEDIAN ALPHA SCORES FOR NORTHERN BLACKS AND SOUTHERN WHITES

Rank Order	Northern Blacks	Range	Median Score
1 (24)	Ohio	0–154	48.30
2 (23)	Illinois	0–184	46.85
3 (21)	New York	0–164	44.55
4 (20)	Indiana	0–154	41.55
	Average Median Score		45.31

Rank Order	Southern Whites	Range	Median Score
1	Mississippi	0–174	41.20
2	Kentucky	0–184	41.50
3	Arkansas	0–159	41.55
4	Georgia	0–194	42.10
5	North Carolina	0–159	43.15
6	Louisiana	0–174	45.20
7	Alabama	0–189	46.20
8	Tennessee	0–174	47.15
9	South Carolina	10–164	47.40
	Average Median Score		43.90
12	Texas	0–189	50.80
14	West Virginia	0–184	55.60
16	Maryland	0–174	56.10
17	Virginia	0–174	56.25
21	Florida (47)	0–184	59.40
	Average Median Score		48.11
	Without Florida		47.24

higher than Beta ranks in six others. Viewing this pattern of distribution as a whole, we may say that in the Pacific and Atlantic Coast states Alpha ranks tend to be more frequently higher than Beta, while the reverse tends to be true of the Western, Northwestern and Southwestern states. In Table D.7 the median Alpha scores obtained by the blacks from four northern states are shown, together with those obtained by whites from 14 southern states. Since the state of Florida supplied only 47 individuals for examination, it would be safer to omit the score for this state altogether. From Table D.7 it will be seen that on the Alpha tests the blacks from four Northern States did better than the whites from nine southern States, the average median

TABLE D.8

STATES IN WHICH BLACKS DID BETTER THAN WHITES ON BETA AND ALPHA TESTS

	BETA TESTS		ALPHA TESTS
Blacks from the State of	Did Better than the Whites from the Following Number of States	Blacks from the State of	Did Better than the Whites from the Following Number of States
Ohio	27	Ohio	9
Kansas	24	Illinois	7
New York	11	New York	5
Missouri	11		
Indiana	6	Indiana	2
Illinois	6		

score of the blacks being 45.31 while that of the whites from the nine southern States is 43.94. The blacks from Ohio with a score of 48.30 did better than the whites from nine northern states; those from Illinois with a score of 46.85 did better than the whites from seven southern states; those from New York with a score of 44.55 did better than the whites from five southern states; and those from Indiana with a score of 41.55 did better than the whites from two southern states.

In Table D.8 the states in which the blacks achieved a higher score than the whites from other states, and the number of states with such an inferior score, are shown for both Beta and Alpha tests. On the Beta tests there were six and on the Alpha tests four states in which blacks made a higher median score than the whites from many states. It is of interest to observe that four of these states are present in each list, namely, Ohio, New York, Indiana and Illinois.

Thus we find that literate as well as illiterate blacks did better on the tests than whites from a number of different states. Moreover, as will be seen from Table D.8, the illiterate blacks from six states achieved scores superior to those achieved by the illiterate whites in a greater number of states than the literate blacks did. The average number of states in which illiterate whites obtained a score inferior to that obtained by illiterate blacks from those six states is 14. The same figure for the literates is 6.

It is of interest to note that on the Alpha tests the literate blacks from the four northern states while doing better than the literate whites from nine states—all of them southern—failed, however, to do better than the literate whites from the four southern states of Texas, West Virginia, Maryland and Virginia.

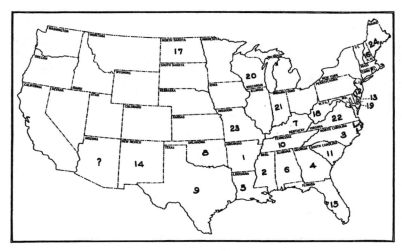

FIGURE D.7
AVERAGE RANK FOR THE COMBINED COMPREHENSIVE ALPHA,
ALPHA, AND BETA SCORES LOWER HALF
Range of scores: 35.60–57.95

The important point is that literate blacks from some northern states did do better than the literate whites from some other states, significantly enough all of them southern.

Comprehensive Alpha Score

In Tables D.9 and D.10 are shown the scores obtained by blacks and whites respectively who, in addition to Alpha examinations, may have taken Beta or an Individual Examination or all three. To distinguish this group from the preceding Alpha group this has been called the Median Comprehensive Alpha Score. Ratings for the same 23 states and the District of Columbia as were available for the other tests are also available for the blacks on this, but, since five states are represented by less than 100 draftees, there are for all practical purposes only 19 states. For the whites the only state for which figures are not available is Arizona, while Florida and the District of Columbia are represented by less than 100 men.

It will be seen from Tables D.9 and D.10 that both for blacks and whites the Southern States show the lowest ratings, and it is obvious that, conversely, the highest ratings for both blacks and whites occur almost exclusively in the northern states. The six northern states in which the median comprehensive Alpha scores fall into the lower rank are New Jersey,

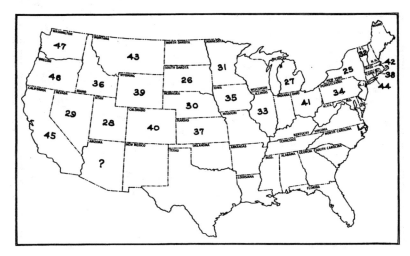

FIGURE D.8
AVERAGE RANK FOR THE COMBINED COMPREHENSIVE ALPHA,
ALPHA, AND BETA SCORES UPPER HALF: WHITES
Range of scores: 58.20–78.75

New Hampshire, North Dakota, Wisconsin, Indiana, and Maine. With the exception of Indiana and New Hampshire, these states stand uniformly in the higher rank on the Alpha and Beta tests. As will be seen from Figure D.7 the distribution of the states in the lower rank follows much the same pattern as that which we have observed for the other independent test material. The same holds true, as may be seen from Figure D.8, for the higher rank.

From Table D.11 it will be seen that the blacks from Ohio, with a median (comprehensive) Alpha score of 45.35 did better than the whites of 11 states, all of which, once more, happen to be southern! The blacks of Illinois with a score of 42.55 and those of Indiana with a score of 41.55 did better than the whites from seven southern states, while the blacks from New York with a score of 38.60 did better than the whites from three southern states. The average median score for the blacks from these four northern states is 41.94, while for the whites from the 11 southern states it is 40.93.

Average Rank of Blacks and Whites on All Tests

In Tables D.12 and D.13 the ranks attained by the black and white draftees from each state on the various tests are shown. "1" is the lowest and "48"

TABLE D.9

ALPHA SCORE BY SCORE RANK: BLACKS

For men who took Alpha only, Alpha and Beta only, Alpha and Individual Examination, and Alpha, Beta, and Individual Examination. Group IV and V. Computed from Mem. Nat. Acad. Sci., *15, 1921, 730, Table 266.*

Rank	State	Number	Range	Median
1	Florida	499	0–114	9.25
2	Georgia	416	0–124	10.00
3	Mississippi	773	0–104	10.25
4	Texas	854	0–114	12.15
5	Louisiana	538	0–129	13.40
6	South Carolina	334	0– 99	14.20
7	Arkansas	193	0–104	16.10
8	North Carolina	211	0–154	16.50
9	Alabama	271	0–109	19.90
10	Maryland	148	0–129	22.70
11	Kentucky	191	0–134	23.95
12	West Virginia	67	0– 74	26.80
13	Missouri	196	0–134	28.35
14	Tennessee	504	0–159	29.70
15	District of Columbia	30	0– 89	31.25
16	Oklahoma	98	5–114	31.45
17	New Jersey	748	0–144	33.00
18	Kansas	87	0–144	33.95
19	Pennsylvania	790	0–149	34.75
20	New York	1,188	0–164	38.60
21	Indiana	269	0–154	41.55
22	Illinois	804	0–184	42.25
23	Ohio	163	0–154	45.35
24	Virginia	57	0–119	45.60
	Total number and range	9,429	0–184	23.75

the highest rank. The average rank made on the three tests by the draftees from each state is shown in the fourth column of figures, while the average median score made on each of the tests is shown at the base of each column. The figures in the two tables are, of course, not comparable owing to the lack of data from 24 states for the blacks. It is the fourth column of figures which is the most significant in these two tables. In Table D.12, blacks, it will be seen that the first 13 states occupying the lowest average rank are all southern; next in order is the District of Columbia; then follow Missouri, New Jersey, Oklahoma, and Virginia. In Table D.13, whites, the

TABLE D.10

ALPHA SCORE BY SCORE RANK: WHITES

For men who took Alpha only, Alpha and Beta only, Alpha and Individual Examination, and Alpha, Beta, and Individual Examination. Group I and II. Computed from Mem. Nat. Acad. Sci., 15, 1921, 689f., Table 205.

Rank	State	Number	Range	Median
1	Arkansas	710	0–159	35.60
2	Mississippi	759	0–174	37.65
3	North Carolina	702	0–159	38.20
4	Georgia	762	0–194	39.35
5	Louisiana	702	0–174	41.10
6	Alabama	779	0–189	41.35
7	Kentucky	837	0–184	41.50
8	Oklahoma	865	0–179	43.00
9	Texas	1,426	0–189	43.45
10	Tennessee	710	0–174	44.00
11	South Carolina	581	0–164	45.05
12	New Jersey	937	0–189	47.90
13	Delaware	128	0–184	49.30
14	New Mexico	218	0–179	49.45
15	Florida	55	0–184	53.75
16	New Hampshire	817	0–184	53.80
17	North Dakota	799	0–199	54.75
18	West Virginia	423	0–184	54.90
19	Maryland	616	0–174	55.30
20	Wisconsin	1,012	0–189	55.90
21	Indiana	1,171	5–189	56.05
22	Virginia	506	0–174	56.15
23	Missouri	1,329	0–184	56.40
24	Maine	795	0–184	57.95
25	New York	3,288[a]	0–204	58.20
26	South Dakota	488	0–194	58.20
27	Michigan	1,196	0–189	58.80
28	Utah	786	0–184	58.95
29	Nevada	108	0–174	60.00
30	Nebraska	679	5–174	60.00
31	Minnesota	786	0–174	60.75
32	Vermont	856	0–199	61.60
33	Illinois	2,145	0–194	61.60
34	Pennsylvania	3,280	0–199	62.00
35	Iowa	1,029	0–204	62.25
36	Idaho	943	0–184	62.30
37	Kansas	861	0–194	62.85
38	Rhode Island	743	0–212	65.05

(continues)

TABLE D.10

(CONTINUED)

Rank	State	Number	Range	Median
39	Wyoming	567	0–199	65.10
40	Colorado	682	0–212	67.00
41	Ohio	2,318	0–199	67.25
42	Massachusetts	1,241	0–212	67.55
43	Montana	634	10–189	68.30
44	Connecticut	832	0–194	70.60
45	California	975	0–199	71.55
46	Oregon	888	0–199	71.65
47	Washington	910	0–189	72.10
48	District of Columbia	77	0–194	78.75
	Total number and range	44,223	0–212	57.00

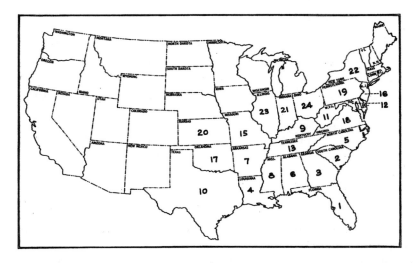

FIGURE D.9

AVERAGE RANK FOR THE COMBINED COMPREHENSIVE ALPHA,
ALPHA, AND BETA SCORES: BLACKS

TABLE D.11

MEDIAN COMPREHENSIVE ALPHA SCORE

For all men who took Alpha only, Alpha and Beta only, Alpha and Individual Examination, and Alpha, Beta, and Individual Examination.

Rank Order	Northern Blacks	Range	Median Score
1 (23)	Ohio	0–154	45.35
2 (22)	Illinois	0–184	42.25
3 (21)	Indiana	0–154	41.55
4 (20)	New York	0–164	38.60
	Average Median Score		41.94

Rank Order	Southern Whites	Range	Median Score
1	Arkansas	0–159	35.60
2	Mississippi	0–174	37.65
3	North Carolina	0–159	38.20
4	Georgia	0–194	39.35
5	Louisiana	0–174	41.10
6	Alabama	0–189	41.35
7	Kentucky	0–184	41.50
8	Oklahoma	0–179	43.00
9	Texas	0–189	43.45
10	Tennessee	0–174	44.00
11	South Carolina	0–164	45.05
	Average Median Score		40.93
18	West Virginia	0–184	54.90
19	Maryland	0–174	55.30
22	Virginia	0–174	56.15
	Average Median Score		44.04

lowest rank is occupied by southern states, with seventh position going to New Jersey, followed by six southern states, one shallow southern state (Delaware), followed by Florida, with Maryland occupying 19th place, and the District of Columbia 44th.

Figure D.9 shows the states for which data were available for the blacks. Data were also available for the District of Columbia, but it has not been possible to indicate this fact on the maps. Figure D.9 brings out very clearly how the higher ranks are distributed towards the North, while the lower ones cling to the South. The same facts are even more strikingly brought out in Figure D.10.

It is of such sociogenically induced tragedies that I speak here. These tragedies and the mechanism of their production are of more than clinical interest, for there have always been those among us who have been eager to claim a genetic causation for such misfortunes, and to make such presumed and unsubstantiated genetic assumptions the basis for social policy. This has been especially so in connection with the problem-solving form of behavior we call intelligence, especially as allegedly measured by IQ tests.

Intelligence is something that develops as the result of the interaction of brain potentials with experience, nutritional and social. Fundamentally and functionally, intelligence is both a special and general abilities resulting primarily from the social organization of brain potentials for the making of adaptive responses to the particular challenges of the environment. At birth, the brain is continuing the accelerated rate of growth that commenced during the last two months of intrauterine development, gaining weight at the rate of between one and two milligrams a minute, a rate which is continued throughout the first six months. By the end of this period, the brain has virtually doubled in size, from a weight of 350 to 656 grams, a gain of 306 grams. The size of this increment exceeds by far anything ever achieved this way again (see Table 22.1).

By the end of the first year, the rate of increase has decelerated to half the rate of the first six months, when the brain attains a weight of 825 grams. The same decelerated rate is maintained during the whole of the second year, with the brain achieving a weight of 1010 grams. During the third year, there is a further deceleration to one-third the rate of the first six months. And by the end of the third year, the brain of the average 3-year-old has achieved more than four-fifths of its maximum adult size; the child's brain now weighs, on the average, 1115 grams. When the brain attains its maximum size, at between 20 and 29 years, it will have added, in the additional 17 or so years, no more than 281 grams to the grand total of 1396 grams.

All the evidence suggests that during the long period of brain growth, and especially during the first critical three years, it is probably the first six months, when the brain in its most rapid phase of growth and cell number is also increasing, that are the most critical.

Critical Periods In Brain Development

The evidence further suggests that at birth the human neonate is only half gestated, and that he completes his gestation, like the little marsupial, outside the womb. This latter developmental period I have called *exterogestation*. It terminates when the infant begins to crawl about for himself, at about 9 or 10 months.[35]

TABLE 22.1

GROWTH OF THE HUMAN BRAIN

Fetus Lunar Months	Weight in Grams	Gain in Grams	Percent of Gain	Rate of Increase
5	62.5	25.5	40.0	
6	88.0	25.5	29.0	
8	277.0	189.0	68.6	A threefold increase in weight in this two-month period
9 birth	350/392	73/115	30.0	An increment of about a third of the previous month's weight
½ year	656.0	306.0	47.0	Almost doubles in weight in first six months
1	825.0	169.0	20.5	Reduction to half rate of increase of first six months
2	1,010.0	185.0	18.3	Reduction to half rate of increase of first six months
3	1,115.0	105.0	9.4	Reduction to one-third rate of increase of first six months
4	1,180.0	75.0	6.4	Gradual deceleration of rate of growth
6	1,250.0	70.0	5.6	
9	1,307.0	57.0	4.3	
12	1,338.0	31.0	3.3	
20–29	1,396.0	58.0	4.0	

TABLE D.12

RANK ORDER OF SCORES ON THE COMPREHENSIVE ALPHA, ALPHA, AND BETA TESTS: BLACKS

State	Compr. Alpha	Alpha	Beta	Average Rank
Florida	1	1	2	1
South Carolina	6	4	1	2
Georgia	2	2	9	3
Louisiana	5	7	4	4
North Carolina	8	5	6	5
Alabama	9	8	3	6
Arkansas	7	6	8	7
Mississippi	3	3	14	8
Kentucky	11	9	7	9
Texas	4	11	12	10
West Virginia	12	10	10	11
Maryland	10	13	13	12
Tennessee	14	12	15	13
District of Columbia	15	18	11	14
Missouri	13	14	22	15
New Jersey	18	15	17	16
Oklahoma	16	17	18	17
Virginia	24	22	5	18
Pennsylvania	17	19	16	19
Kansas	19	16	22	20
Indiana	21	20	20	21
New York	20	21	21	22
Illinois	22	23	19	23
Ohio	23	24	24	24
Totals	23.75	28.40	19.34	

Conclusion

In this chapter an analysis has been presented of the findings relative to the various categories of black and white draftees who took the intelligence tests administered by the United States Army during World War I. The findings are presented upon a total of 25,575 blacks drawn from 23 states and the District of Columbia, and upon 55,838 whites drawn from all the states in the Union and the District of Columbia.

This analysis had as its original purpose the answer to the question: Were there any states in which the blacks did better on the various tests than the whites in the same or any other state? The object in asking this question was to arrive at some sort of reasonable view as to the nature of

TABLE D.13

RANK ORDER OF SCORES ON THE COMPREHENSIVE ALPHA, ALPHA, AND BETA TESTS: WHITES

State	Compr. Alpha	Alpha	Beta	Average Rank
Kentucky	7	2	1	1
Mississippi	2	1	9	2
North Carolina	3	5	4	3
Alabama	6	7	3	4
Arkansas	1	3	12	5
Louisiana	5	6	16	6
New Jersey	12	10	6	7
Georgia	4	4	21	8
Tennessee	10	8	15	9
South Carolina	11	9	14	10
Virginia	22	17	2	11
Texas	9	12	23	12
West Virginia	18	14	11	13
Delaware	13	11	20	14
Florida	16	21	8	15
Oklahoma	8	13	24	16
New Mexico	14	23	10	17
Indiana	21	15	13	18
Maryland	19	16	19	19
New Hampshire	17	24	30	20
Missouri	23	22	27	21
Wisconsin	20	18	25	22
Michigan	27	26	26	23
North Dakota	15	19	40	24
Rhode Island	30	25	28	25
Pennsylvania	34	33	22	26
New York	25	32	31	27
South Dakota	28	20	42	28
Connecticut	44	43	5	29
Maine	30	35	34	30
Ohio	41	36	17	31
Vermont	31	37	29	32
Illinois	33	27	38	33
Iowa	35	31	35	34
Massachusetts	42	40	18	35
Kansas	37	28	36	36
Nevada	29	30	44	37
Nebraska	39	34	39	38
Utah	26	41	45	39
Colorado	40	39	33	40
Montana	43	38	37	41

(*continues*)

TABLE D.13

(CONTINUED)

State	Compr. Alpha	Alpha	Beta	Average Rank
Minnesota	32	29	49	42
Idaho	36	42	47	43
District of Columbia	48	46	32	44
Wyoming	38	44	48	45
California	45	45	41	46
Washington	47	47	43	47
Oregon	46	48	46	48
Totals	57.00	61.25	40.70	

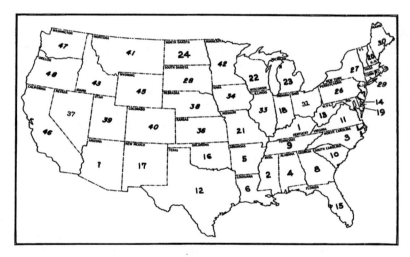

FIGURE D.10

AVERAGE RANK FOR THE COMBINED ALPHA, ALPHA, AND BETA SCORES: WHITES

the factors which the intelligence tests measured. Did they measure inherent ability, or did they measure, instead, the effects of socioeconomic conditions? What light do the results of these tests throw upon the intelligence, as measured by these tests, of the black as compared with that of the white?

The answers of these questions are clear and unequivocal so far as these tests go. On all tests and in practically every state whites do better than blacks, the exceptions being on the Beta tests where the blacks of Kentucky with a score of 17.20 did better than the whites from the same state with a score of 12.30, and Ohio where the blacks obtained a score of 39.65 while the white score from the same state was 35.45. For the rest whites always did better than blacks from the same state. Had data been available for all the states in the Union for the blacks, instead of only the 23 states and the District of Columbia for which they were available, it is possible that there might have been one or two more exceptions here. Even so the fact would still remain that in general the whites do better on the tests than the blacks.

Does this finding mean that the whites as a whole have greater intelligence than the blacks as a whole? Or does it mean that the socioeconomic condition in each state generally favor a better development of those qualities which are measured by the intelligence tests in the whites than in the blacks of that state? The answer to this question would seem to be very clearly returned by the finding that the median score made by the blacks of a number of states was better than that made by the whites of several other states. On the Beta tests the blacks of Ohio, for example, did better than the whites of 27 other States! On the Alpha tests they did better than the whites from nine states, and so on (see Table D.8). Does this finding mean, then, that the blacks of Ohio, for example, are, on the average, inherently more intelligent than the whites of the states who made a lower score? Of course not. It is more likely that the whites of those states did not, on the whole, enjoy as many socioeconomic advantages as the blacks who outranked them on the tests. The evidence of the geographic distribution of the test scores strongly supports this view. Thus, the lowest scores made on any test by blacks and whites are invariably to be found in the South—the deeper the South the lower the score. The depressed socioeconomic state of the South as compared with the greater part of the rest of the United States at the time of the original research fifty years ago was an unfortunate fact. It is, therefore, not surprising that both blacks and whites in the South should do worse on the tests than their fellows in any other part of the Union; and, since conditions are invariably worse for blacks than for whites, that the blacks should do worse than the whites. It is of interest to note that in such states as Delaware and New Jersey, the scores of blacks and whites should uniformly fall into the lower ranks.

In short, these findings show that, whatever differences may exist between blacks and whites, intelligence, or whatever it is that was measured by these tests, is to an appreciable extent determined by external factors, and that, when these external factors are favorable to one group and unfavorable to another, the favored group will do better than the unfavored one. The superior achievement of blacks from some states as compared with whites from others cannot be explained on any other grounds. From whatever position the matter is viewed, this is the only possible explanation. There are several possible positions: (1) blacks are inferior to whites in inherent abilities, (2) blacks are equal to whites in inherent abilities, (3) blacks are superior to whites in native abilities.

If for the purposes of discussion the first two possibilities are accepted, then in either case it becomes clear that external conditions played the most important part in determining the test scores, and not inherent ability; otherwise blacks could not in any case have done better than whites. This fact is further supported by the finding that blacks as a rule do not do better than whites of their own state, but better only than the whites in those states which are known to be somewhat less advanced than their own states. Thus, the evidence points to the fact that these conditions are of a socioeconomic nature. In general, socioeconomic conditions are more favorable to the white than to the black. That is why, it may be assumed, whites in general do better than blacks. In some states, however, particularly in the North, such conditions are better for blacks than they are for whites in some other states, as for example, in the South. That is why it may be assumed that the blacks from some northern states do better, on these tests, than the whites from so many other southern states.

Were blacks inherently superior to whites, the influence of socioeconomic conditions would still serve as the best explanation of the disparities in the respective performances of blacks and whites on these tests, since it is well known that such conditions may greatly alter the organization and expression of the qualities necessary to do well on such tests.[11]

The evidence, on the whole, indicates that there exist no significant inherent psychical differences between blacks and whites; hence differences in performance on these tests between blacks and whites, whether intra- or interstate, are best explained as due to the action upon native endowment of differences in socioeconomic history. And that is the conclusion which may most legitimately be drawn from the analysis of this data. Northern whites and blacks did better on these tests than southern whites and blacks because socioeconomic conditions in the North were, when the tests were made in 1917, superior to those which prevailed in the South for both blacks and whites. For the same reason, it may be assumed that blacks from certain northern states did better than whites from certain other states in addition to those in the South.

Notes

1. Ruth Benedict and Gene Weltfish, *The Races of Mankind* (New York: Public Affairs Committee, 1943).

2. R. M. Yerkes, ed., "Psychological Examining in the United States Army," *Memoirs of the National Acadademy of Science* 15, (1921).

3. My thanks are due to Professor E. A. Hooton for placing the facilities of his department at my disposal for the necessary statistical work.

4. Ibid., 555.

5. Ibid., 558.

6. Ibid., 560.

7. Ibid., 157–62.

8. Ibid., 162–67, 379.

9. Ibid., 167–82, 310.

10. Ibid.

11. See O. D. Duncan, D. Featherman, and Beverly Duncan, *Socioeconomic Background and Achievement* (New York: Seminar Press, 1972), and "The Cumulation of Handicaps," in *Success and Opportunity,* ed. Ephraim Harold Mizruchi (New York: Free Press, 1964).

Bibliography

Abbie, A. A. "A New Outlook on Physical Anthropology." *Proceedings of the New Zealand Association for the Advancement of Science* 28 (1951): 52–63.

———. *The Original Australians.* London: Frederick Muller, 1969.

Abecrombie, M., C. J. Hickman, and M. L. Johnson. *A Dictionary of Biology.* London and New York: Penguin Books, 1951.

Abel, Wolfgang. "Über Europäer-Annamiten-Kreuzungen." *Zeitschrift für Morphologie und Anthropologie,* 36 (1937): 311–29.

Abernethy, George L., ed. *The Idea of Equality: An Anthology.* Richmond: John Knox Press, 1959.

Abrahamson, Irving, ed. *Against Silence: The Voice and Vision of Elie Wiesel.* 3 vols. New York: Holocaust Library, 1986.

Abzug, Robert H. *Inside the Vicious Heart.* New York: Oxford University Press, 1985.

Ackerknecht, Erwin H. "White Indians." *Bulletin of the History of Medicine* 15 (1944): 15–36.

Ackerman, Nathan W. and Marie Jahoda. "Anti-Semitic Motivation in a Psychopathic Personality." *Psychoanalytic Review* 34 (1947): 76–101.

———. "Dynamic Basis of Anti-Semitic Attitudes." *Psychoanalytic Quarterly* 12 (1948): 240–60.

———. "Toward a Dynamic Interpretation of Anti-Semitic Attitudes." *American Journal of Orthopsychiatry* 18 (1948): 163–73.

———. *Anti-Semitism and Emotional Disorder.* New York: Harper, 1950.

Adachi, Buntaro. "Der Geruch der Europäer." *Globus* 83 (1903): 14–115.

Adam, Herbert. *Modernizing Racial Domination: The Dynamics of South African Politics.* Berkeley: University of California Press, 1971.

Adam, Herbert, and Kogila Moodley. *South Africa Without Apartheid: Dismantling Racial Domination.* Berkeley: University of California Press, 1986.

Adamastor. *White Man Boss.* Boston: Beacon Press, 1951.

Adamic, Louis. *A Nation of Nations.* New York: Harper, 1945.

Adams, Romanzo C. *Interracial Marriage in Hawaii.* New York: Macmillan, 1937.

Adinaryan, S. P. "Before and After Independence: A Study of Racial and Communal Attitudes in India." *British Journal of Psychology* 94 (1953): 108–15.

Adorno, T. W., E. Frenkel-Brunswik, D. J. Levenson, and R. Nevitt Sanford. *The Authoritarian Personality.* New York: Harper, 1950.

Agronsky, Martin. "Racism in Italy." *Foreign Affairs* 17 (1939): 391–401.

Alexander, Chester. "Antipathy and Social Behavior." *American Journal of Sociology* 51 (1946): 288–92.

Alexander, H. B. "A Comparison of the Ranks of American States in Army-Alpha and in Socio-economic Status." *School and Society* 16 (1922): 388–92.

Allee, Warder C. *Animal Aggregations.* Chicago: University of Chicago Press, 1931.

———. *The Social Life of Animals.* New York: Norton, 1938.

———. "Where Angels Fear to Tread: A Contribution from General Sociology to Human Ethics." *Science* 97 (1943): 518–25.

———. "Biology and International Relations." *New Republic* 112 (1945): 816–17.

———. *Cooperation Among Animals.* New York: Schuman, 1950.

Allee, Warder C., et al. *Principles of Animal Ecology.* Philadelphia: Saunders, 1949.

Allen, B., et al. "Social Awareness in a City High School." *Intercultural Educational News* 8 (1946): 1–7.

Allison, A. C. "Protection Afforded by the Sickle-Cell Trait Against Subtertian Malarial Infection." *British Medical Journal* 1 (1954): 290–94.

Allport, Gordon W. "Human Nature and the Peace." *Psychological Bulletin* 42 (1945): 37–78.

———. "Is Intergroup Education Possible?" *Harvard Educational Review* 15 (1945): 83–86.

———. "Controlling Group Prejudice." *Annals of the American Academy of Political and Social Science* 244 (1946): 1–240.

———. *The Nature of Prejudice.* Cambridge, MA: Addison-Wesley, 1953.

———. *Personality and the Social Encounter.* Boston: Beacon Press, 1960.

Allport, Gordon W., ed. *ABC's of Scapegoating.* Chicago: Central YMCA College, 1943.

Allport, Gordon W., and Bernard M. Kramer. "Some Roots of Prejudice." *Journal of Psychology* 22 (1946): 9–39.

Alpers, Edward A. *Ivory and Slaves in East Central Africa.* Berkeley: University of California Press, 1975.

Ambrose, A., ed. *Stimulation in Early Infancy.* New York: Academic Press, 1969.

Amery, Jean. *At the Mind's Limits: Contemplations by a Survivor on Auschwitz and its Realities.* Bloomington: Indiana University Press, 1966.

Anastasi, Anne. *Differential Psychology.* 3d ed. New York: Macmillan, 1958.

Anastasi, Anne, and Catherine Berndt. *The World of the First Australians.* Chicago: University of Chicago Press, 1965.

Anderson, Alan B., and George W. Pickering. *Confronting the Color Line.* Athens: University of Georgia Press, 1987.

Anderson, Robert T. "Lapp Racial Classifications as Scientific Myths." *Anthropological Papers of the University of Alaska* 11 (1962): 15–31.

Andrews, Charles F. "Racial Influences." In *The Causes of War,* edited by Arthur Porritt, 63–113. New York: Macmillan, 1932.

Angel, John. L. *Report on the Skeletons Excavated at Olynthus.* In *Excavations at Olynthus, Necrolynthia, a Study in Greek Burial Customs and Anthropology,* edited by David M. Robinson, part 9, 211–40. Baltimore: Johns Hopkins Press, 1942.

———. "A Racial Analysis of the Ancient Greeks." *American Journal of Physical Anthropology,* n.s., 2 (1944): 329–76.

———. "Skeletal Material from Attica." *Hesperia* 14 (1945): 279–363.

———. "Social Biology of Greek Culture Growth." *American Anthropologist,* n.s., 98 (1946): 493–533.

Anonymous. "Black Girl's Search." *Times Literary Supplement* 19 January 1967: 46.

Appleman, Philip, ed. *Darwin: Texts, Backgrounds, Contemporary Opinion, Critical Essays.* New York: W. W. Norton, 1970.

Apthekar, Herbert. *Essays in the History of the American Negro.* New York: International Publishers, 1945.

Arad, Yitzhak. *Belzec, Sobibor, Treblinka: The Operation Reinhard Death Camps.* Bloomington: Indiana University Press, 1987.

Ardrey, Robert. *African Genesis.* New York: Atheneum, 1961.

———. *The Territorial Imperative.* New York: Atheneum, 1966.

Arendt, Hannah. "Race—Thinking before Racism." *Review of Politics* 6 (1944): 36–73.

———. *The Origins of Totalitarianism.* New York: Harcourt, Brace, 1951.

———. *Eichman in Jerusalem.* New York: Viking Press, 1963.

———. *On Violence.* New York: Harcourt, Brace & World, 1970.

———. *The Jew as Pariah: Jewish Identity and Politics in the Modern Age.* New York: Grove Press, 1978.

Arensberg, Baruch. *The People in the Land of Israel from the Epipaleolithic to Present Times.* Ph.D. Dissertation, Tel Aviv University, 1973.

Argyris, Chris. *Personality and Organization.* New York: Harper, 1957.

Aristotle, *Politics.* Edited by Ernest Barker. New York: Oxford University Press, 1995.

Aristotle. *De generatione animalium.*

Armstrong, Virginia I., ed. *I Have Spoken: American History through the Voices of the Indians.* Chicago: Swallow Press, 1971.

Aronson, Lester R., Ethel Tobach, Jay S. Rosenblatt, and Daniel S. Lehrman, eds. *Development and Evolution of Behavior: Essays in Memory of T. C. Schneirla.* San Francisco: W. H. Freeman, 1970.

———. *Selected Writings of T. C. Schneirla.* San Francisco: Freeman & Co., 1972.

Asdell, S. A. "The Genetic Sex of Intersexual Goats and a Probable Linkage with the Gene for Hornlessness." *Science* 99 (1944): 124.

Ashcroft, Bill, Gareth Griffiths, and Helen Tiffin, eds. *The Post-Colonial Studies Reader.* New York: Routledge, 1995.

Ashmore, Harry S. *The Negro and the Schools.* Chapel Hill: University of North Carolina Press, 1954.

———. *An Epitaph for Dixie.* New York: Norton, 1958.

———. *The Other Side of Jordan.* New York: Norton, 1960.

———. *The Man in the Middle.* Columbia: University of Missouri Press, 1966.

———. *Hearts and Minds: The Anatomy of Racism From Roosevelt to Reagan.* New York: McGraw-Hill, 1982

Askenasy, Hans. *Hitler's Secret.* Laguna Beach, CA: P.O. Box 4197, 1984.

Astrov, Margot. *The Winged Serpent.* New York: John Day, 1946.

Augros, Robert, and George Stanciu. *The New Biology.* Boston: Shambhala, 1987.

Ausubel, David P. *Theory and Problems of Child Development.* New York: Grune & Stratton, 1958.

Ayers, Edward L. *The Promise of the New South: Life After Reconstruction.* New York: Oxford University Press, 1991.

Babington, William D. *Fallacies of Race Theories.* London: Longmans, 1895.

Bachman, C. L. *John Bachman, the Pastor of St. John's Lutheran Church.* Charleston, SC: Walker, Evans & Cogswell, 1888.

Baeumler, Alfred. "Race: A Basic Concept in Education." Translated from the original article in the *Internationale Zeitschrift für Erziehung* 8, 1939. *World Education* 4 (1939): 506–9.

Bagehot, Walter. *Physics and Politics.* London: H. S. Knight & Co., 1872. Reprint. New York: Alfred A. Knopf, 1948.

Bagley, Christopher and Gajendra K. Verma. *Racial Prejudice: The Individual and Society.* Lexington, MA: D.C. Heath, 1979.

Bain, Read. "Man, the Myth-Maker." *Scientific Monthly,* 65 (1947): 61–69.

Baker, Emily V. "Do We Teach Racial Intolerance?" *Historical Outlook* 24 (1933): 86–89.

Baker, Herschel. *The Dignity of Man.* Cambridge: Harvard University Press, 1947.

Baker, John. *Race.* New York: Oxford University Press, 1974.

Baker, Paul T., and J. S. Weiner, eds. *The Biology of Human Adaptability.* Oxford Clarendon Press, 1966.

Baldry, John. *The Unity of Mankind in Greek Thought.* New York: Cambridge University Press, 1947, 1965.

Baldwin, James. "Letter from a Region in My Mind." *The New Yorker,* 17 November 1962: 59–144.

———. *The Fire Next Time.* New York: Dial Press, 1963.

Ball, Ian. *Pitcairn: Children of Mutiny.* Boston: Little, Brown, 1973.

Baltzell, E. Digby. *The Protestant Establishment: Aristocracy and Caste in America.* New York: Random House, 1946.

Bandura, Albert. *Aggression: A Social Learning Analysis.* Englewood Cliffs, NJ: Prentice-Hall, 1973.

Banton, Michael. *The Coloured Quarter.* London: Cape, 1955.

———. "Beware of Strangers." *The Listener* (London) 3 April 1958: 565–67.

———. *White and Coloured.* London: Cape, 1959.

———. *Race Relations.* New York: Basic Books, 1967.

———. *Racial and Ethnic Competition.* Cambridge Univerity Press, 1983.

———. *Racial Theories.* New York: Cambridge University Press, 1987.

Barash, David P. "Review." *Animal Behaviour* 49(4)(1995): 1131–33.

Bardolph, Richard. *The Negro Vanguard.* New York: Vintage Books, 1961.

Barkan, Elazar. *From Race to Ethnicity: Changing Concepts of Race in England and the United States Between the Two World Wars.* Ph.D. Dissertation, Brandeis University, 1987.

———. *The Retreat of Scientific Racism.* Cambridge: Cambridge University Press, 1991.

Barker, Ernest. *National Character.* 4th ed. London: Methuen, 1948.

Barker, Martin. *The New Racism: Conservatism and the Ideology of the Tribe.* London: Junction, 1981.

Barkun, Michel. *Religion and the Racist Right: The Origins of the Christian Identity Movement.* Chapel Hill: University of North Carolina Press, 1994.

Bar-Levan, Reuven. *Thinking in the Shadow of Feelings.* New York: Simon & Schuster, 1988.

Barnes, E. W. "The Mixing of Races and Social Decay." *Eugenics Review* 41 (1949): 11–16.

Barnes, Harry E., and Negley K. Teeters. *New Horizons in Criminology.* New York: Prentice-Hall, 1943.

Barnes, I. "The Inheritance of Pigmentation in the Skin of the American Negro." *Human Biology* 1 (1929): 321–28.

Barnet, Richard. *The Roots of War.* Baltimore: Penguin Books, 1972.

Barnett, Anthony. *The Human Species.* New York: Norton, 1950.

Barnett, Louise K. *The Ignoble Savage: American Literary Racism, 1790—1890.* Westport, CT: Greenwood Press, 1975.

Barnow, David, and Gerrold Van Der Stroom, eds. *The Diary of Anne Frank.* Critical Edition. New York: Doubleday, 1989.

Baron, Salo W. *The Russian Jew Under Tsars and Soviets.* New York: Macmillan, 1976.

Barrett, David E., and Deborah A. Frank. *The Effects of Undernutrition on Children's Behavior.* London: Gordon & Breach, 1987.

Barton, Margaret, and Osbert Sitwell. *Victoriana.* London: Duckworth, 1949.

Bartoszewski, Wladyslaw and Zofia Lewin, eds. *Righteous Among Nations: How Poles Helped the Jews, 1939–1945.* London: Elscourt Publications, 1969.

Bartov, Omer. *Hitler's Army.* New York: Oxford University Press, 1992.

Barzun, Jacques. *Of Human Freedom.* Philadelphia: Lippincott, 1964.

———. *Race: A Study in Superstition.* New York: Harper & Row, 1965.

Bass, N. H., M. G. Netsky, and E. Young. "Microchemical and Histological Study of Myelin Formation in the Rat." *Archives of Neurology* 23 (1970): 303–13.

———. "Effect of Neonatal Malnutrition on Developing Cerebrum." *Archives of Neurology* 23 (1970): 289–302.

Bastide, Roger. *The African Religions of Brazil: Towards a Sociology of the Interpenetration of Civilization.* Baltimore & London: Johns Hopkins University Press, 1978.

Bastide, Roger and Pierre van den Berghe. "Stereotypes, Norms and Interracial Behavior in São Paulo, Brazil." *American Sociological Review* 22 (1957): 689–94.

Bates, Daisy. *The Passing of the Aborigines.* London: Murray, 1938.

———. *The Long Shadow of Little Rock.* New York: McKay, 1962.

Battaglia, Raffaello. "La Genetica Umana e l'Incrocio Razziale." In *Le Razzi e i Popoli della Terra,* edited by Renato Biasutti, 323–54. Torino: Unione-Tipografico, 1959.

Baudet, Henri. *Paradise on Earth: Some Thoughts on European Images of Non-European Man.* New Haven: Yale University Press, 1965.

Baughman, E. Earl. *Black Americans: A Psychological Analysis.* New York: Academic Press, 1971.

Baughman, E. Earl., and W. Grant Dahlstrom. *Negro and White Children.* New York: Academic Press, 1968.

Baum, Ratner. *The Holocaust and the German Elite.* London: Croom Heim, 1981.

Beaglehole, Ernest. "Race, Caste and Class." *Journal of the Polynesian Society* 62 (1943): 1–11.

Beaglehole, Ernest, and Pearl Beaglehole. *Some Modern Maoris.* Wellington: New Zealand Council for Education Research, 1946.

Beam, Lura. *They Called Them by the Lightning: A Teacher's Odyssey in the Negro South, 1908–1919.* Indianapolis: Bobbs-Merrill, 1967.

Bean, R. Bennett. "Some Racial Peculiarities of the Negro Brain." *American Journal of Anatomy* 5 (1906): 353—415.

Beaver, Harold. "On the Racial Frontier." *The Times Literary Supplement,* 20 May 1930: 619.

Becker, Gary S. *The Economics of Discrimination.* Chicago: University of Chicago Press, 1971.

Bedini, Silvio. *The Life of Benjamin Banneker.* New York: Charles Schribner's Sons, 1972.

Belknap, Michael R. *Federal Law and Southern Order.* Athens: University of Georgia Press, 1987.

Bell, Derrick. *Race, Racism and American Law.* 2d ed. Boston: Little, Brown, 1980.

———. *And We Are Not Saved.* New York: Basic Books, 1987.

———. *Faces at the Bottom of the Well.* New York: Basic Books, 1992.

Bellow, Barbara. "Prejudice in 'Seaside.'" *Human Relations* 1 (1947): 98–120.

Belth, N. C., ed. *Patterns of Discrimination Against Jews.* New York: Anti-Defamation League of B'nai B'rith, 1958.

Bender, David L., and Bruno Leone, eds. *War and Human Nature: Opposing Viewpoints.* St. Paul: Greenhaven Press, 1983.

Bender, Lauretta. "Genesis of Hostility in Children." *American Journal of Psychiatry* 105 (1948): 241–45.

———. *Aggression, Hostility, and Anxiety in Children.* Springfield: Thomas, 1953.

Bendyshe, Thomas. "The History of Anthropology." *Memoirs Read before the Anthropological Society of London* 1 (1863–1864): 335–458.

Benedict, Ruth. *Patterns of Culture.* Boston: Houghton Mifflin, 1934.

———. *Race: Science and Politics.* New York: Viking, 1943.

Benedict, Ruth, and Gene Weltfish. *The Races of Mankind.* New York: Public Affairs Committee, 1943.

Benjamin, Gerald. *Race Relations and the New York City Commission on Human Rights.* Ithaca: Cornell University Press, 1972.

Bennett, E. L., M. R. Rosenzweig, and M. C. Diamond. "Rat Brain: Effects of Environmental Enrichment on Wet and Dry Weights." *Science* 163 (1969): 825–26.

Bennett, Lerone, Jr. *Before the Mayflower: A History of the Negro in America, 1619–1692.* Chicago: Johnson Publishing, 1962.

Benoist, Jean. L'Etude de la Structure Génétique d'une Population Métisée." *Anthropologica,* n.s., 3 (1961): 1–10.

———. "Les Martiniquais: Anthropologie d'Une Population Metisee." *Bulletin et Memoires de la Societe d'Anthropologie Paris* 11 (1963): 241–432.

Benson, Mary. *Nelson Mandela.* New York: W. W. Norton, 1986.

Bentley, James. "The Most Irresistible Temptation." *The Listener* (London) 16 November 1978: 635–37.

Berg, Leo S. *Nomogenesis, or Evolution Determined by Law.* London: Constable, 1926.

Berger, Monroe. *Equality by Statute.* 2d ed. New York: Doubleday Inc., 1967.

Berger, Peter L., and Thomas Luckmann. *The Social Construction of Reality: A Treatise in the Sociology of Knowledge.* London Penguin Press 1967; New York: Penguin 1971.

Bergman, Peter, M. *The Chronological History of the Negro in America.* New York: Harper & Row, 1969.

———. *The Fabric of Mind: A Radical New Understanding of the Brain and How it Works.* New York: Viking, 1985.

———. *The Fabric of the Brain.* New York: Viking, 1986.

Bergmann, Martin S., and Milton E. Jucovy, eds. *Generations of the Holocaust*. New York: Basic Books, 1982.

Berkhofer, Jr., Robert F. *The White Man's Indian*. New York: Alfred A. Knopf, 1978.

Berkowitz, Leonard. *Aggression: A Social Psychological Analysis*. New York: McGraw-Hill, 1962.

———, ed. *Roots of Aggression*. New York: Atherton Press, 1969.

Berlin, Ira., et al. *Slaves No More: Three Essays on Emancipation and the Civil War*. New York: Cambridge University Press, 1991.

Bernal, Martin. *Black Athena: The Afroasiastic Roots of Classical Civilization*. New Brunswick: Rutgers University Press, 1987.

Bernard, Henry M. *Some Neglected Factors in Evolution*. New York: Putnam, 1911.

Bernard, L. L. "The Misuse of Instinct in the Social Sciences." *Psychological Review* 28 (1921): 96–118.

———. *Instinct: A Study in Social Psychology*. New York: Holt, 1924.

———. *War and Its Causes*. New York: Holt, 1944.

Berndt, Catherine H. "The Concept of the Primitive." *Sociologus* 10 (1960): 50–69.

Berndt, Ronald, and Catherine Berndt. *The World of the First Australians*. Sydney: Angus & Robertson, 1954.

Berndt, Ronald. *Australian Aboriginal Art*. New York: Macmillan, 1964.

———. *From Black to White in South Australia*. Chicago: University of Chicago Press, 1952.

Bernhardi, Friedrich von. *Germany and the Next War*. New York: Longmans, 1912.

Bernier [Bernier, François.] "Nouvelle division de la Terre, par les differentes Especes ou races d'hommes qui l'habitent, envoyée par un fameux Voyageur à Monsieur . . . à peu prés en ces termes." *Journal des Sçavans* 24 April 1684: 85–89.

Berreman, Gerald D. *Social Inequality*. New York: Academic Press, 1978.

———, ed. *Social Inequality: Comparative and Developmental Approaches*. New York: Academic Press, 1981.

Berry, Brewton. "The Concept of Race in Sociology Textbooks." *Social Forces* 18 (1940): 411–17.

———. *Race Relations: the Interaction of Ethnic and Racial Groups*. Boston: Houghton Mifflin, 1951.

———. *Almost White*. New York: Macmillan, 1963.

Berry, Wendell. *The Hidden Wound*. San Francisco: North Point Press, 1989.

Berson, Leonora, E. *The Negroes and the Jews*. New York: Random House, 1971.

Berwanger, Eugene H. *The Frontier Against Slavery*. Urbana: University of Illinois Press, 1971.

Bessel, Richard. *Germany After the First World War*. Oxford: Clarendon Press, 1993.

Best, Gary D. *To Free A People, American Jewish Leaders and the Jewish Problem in Eastern Europe, 1890–1914*. Westport, CT: Greenwood Press, 1982.

Bettelheim, Bruno, and Morris Janowitz. "Prejudice." *Scientific American* 183 (1950): 13.

———. *Dynamics of Prejudice*. New York: Harper, 1950.

———. *Social Change and Prejudice*. New York: Free Press, Collier-Macmillan, 1964.

Betts, Raymond F. *The False Dawn: European Imperialism in the Nineteenth Century*. Minneapolis: University of Minnesota Press, 1975.

Bhaba, Jacqueline, Francesca Klug, and Sue Shutter, eds. *Worlds Apart: Women under Immigration and Nationality Law.* London: Pluto Press, 1985.

Bibby, Cyril. *Race, Prejudice, and Education.* New York: Praeger, 1960.

Biddis, Michael D. *Father of Racist Ideology: The Social and Political Thought of Count Gobineau.* New York: Weybright & Talley, 1970.

————, ed. *Gobineau: Selected Political Writings.* New York: Harper & Row, 1970.

————, ed. *Images of Race.* Leicester: Leicester University Press, 1979.

Biddle, Francis. *Democracy and Racial Minorities.* New York: Institute for Religious Studies, 1943.

Bidney, David. "The Concept of Myth and the Problem of Psychocultural Evolution." *American Anthropologist* 62 (1950): 16–26.

————. *Theoretical Anthropology.* New York: Columbia University Press, 1953.

Bidwell, Sidney. *Red, White & Black.* London: Gordon & Cremonesi, 1976.

Biesheuvel, S. *African Intelligence.* Johannesburg: South African Institute of Race Relations, 1943.

————. *Race, Culture and Personality.* Johannesburg: South African Institute of Race Relations, 1959.

Bigelow, Karl W. *Cultural Groups and Human Relations.* New York: Columbia University Press, 1951.

Bilden, Ruediger. "Racial Mixture in Latin America—With Special Reference to Brazil." In *The Role of the Races in Our Future Civilization,* edited by Harry W. Laidler, 49–54. New York: League for Industrial Democracy, 1942.

Billig, Michael. *Social Psychology and Intergroup Relations.* New York: Academic Press, 1966.

Birch, Herbert G. "Psychological Differences as among Races." *Science* 101 (1945): 173–74.

————, ed. *Brain Damage in Children: Its Biological and Social Aspects.* Baltimore: Williams & Wilkins, 1964.

Birch, Herbert G., and J. D. Gussow. *Disadvantaged Children.* New York: Harcourt, Brace & World, 1969.

Birdsell, Joseph B. "Some Implications of the Genetical Concept of Race in Terms of Spatial Analysis." *Proceedings of the Cold Spring Harbor Symposia on Quantitative Biology* 15 (1950): 259–314.

————. "The Problem of the Early Peopling of the Americas as Viewed from Asia." In *Papers on the Physical Anthropology of the American Indian,* edited by William S. Laughlin, 1–68a. New York: The Viking Fund, 1951.

————. *Human Evolution: An Introduction to the New Physical Anthropology.* 2d ed. New York: Rand McNally, 1975.

Bishop, L. K. "Democracy Demands Co-operative Living." *Education* 68 (1946): 12–18.

Blackburn, Robin. *The Overthrow of Colonial Slavery, 1776–1848.* London and New York: Verso, 1988.

Blackett, R. J. M. *Building an Antislavery Wall: Black Americans in the Atlantic Abolitionist Movement, 1830–1860.* Baton Rouge: Louisiana State University Press, 1983.

Blainey, Geoffrey. *Triumph of the Nomads.* Woodstock, NY: Overlook Press, 1976.

Blair, Lewis, H. *The Prosperity of the South Dependent on the Elevation of the Negro.* Richmond, VA: Everett and Waddy, 1889. Republished and edited with an introduction by C. Vann Woodward as *A Southern Prophecy.* Boston: Little, Brown, 1964.

Blalock, H. M., Jr. "A Power Analysis of Racial Discrimination." *Social Forces* 39 (1961): 53–59.

———. *Toward a Theory of Minority-Group Relations.* New York: Capricorn Books, 1970.

Blassingame, John W. *The Slave Community.* Revised. New York: Oxford University Press, 1979.

Blauner, Bob. *Racial Oppression in America.* Berkeley: University of California Press, 1972.

———. *Black Lives, White Lives.* Berkeley: University of California Press, 1989.

Blinkov, Samuil, and Il'ya M. Glezer. *The Human Brain in Figures and Tables.* New York: Basic Books. 1968.

Bloch, J. M. *Miscegenation, Melaleukation, and Mr. Lincoln's Dog.* New York: Schaum, 1958.

Block, N. J. and Gerald Dworkin, eds. *The IQ Controversy: Critical Readings.* New York: Pantheon Books, 1976.

Bloom, Jack M. *Class, Race, and the Civil Rights Movement.* Bloomington: Indiana University Press, 1987.

Bloom, Leonard. *The Social Psychology of Race Relations.* Cambridge, MA: Schenckman, 1972.

Bloom, Leonard, and Ruth Riemer. *Removal and Return.* Berkeley: University of California Press, 1949.

Blue, John T., Jr. "The Relationship of Juvenile Delinquency, Race, and Economic Status." *Journal of Negro Education* 17 (1948): 469–77.

Blum, Harold F. "The Physiological Effects of Sunlight on Man." *Physiological Reviews* 25 (1945): 483–530.

———. "Does the Melanin Pigment of Human Skin Have Adaptive Value?" *Quarterly Review of Biology* 36 (1961): 50–63.

Blum, Jeffrey M. *Pseudoscience and Mental Ability: The Origins and Fallacies of the IQ Controversy.* New York: Monthly Review Press, 1978.

Blumberg, Abraham. "The Ghost in Poland." *New York Review of Books,* 2 June 1983, 37–42.

———. "Poland and the Jews: An Exchange." *New York Review of Books,* 18 August 1983, 51–52.

Blumberg, Rhoda G. and Wendell J. Roye, eds. *Interracial Bonds.* Bayside, NY: General Hall 1979.

Blumenbach, Johann F. *Anthropological Treatises.* Translated by T. Bendyshe. London: Anthropological Society, 1865.

———. Die generis humani varietate nativa. Göttingen, 1775. Translated by T. Bendyshe, "On the Natural Variety of Mankind." In *The Anthropological Treatises of Johann Friedrich Blumenbach.* London: Anthropological Society, 1865.

Blumer, Herbert. "Race Prejudice as a Sense of Group Position." In *Race Relations,* edited by Jitsuichi Masuoka and Preston Valien, 217–27. Chapel Hill: University of North Carolina Press, 1961.

Boas, Franz. "Human Faculty as Determined by Race." *Proceedings, American Association for the Advancement of Science* 43rd Annual Meeting, Brooklyn (1894): 311–27

————. "The Half-Blood Indian: an Anthropometric Study." *Popular Science Monthly* 14 (1894): 761–70; reprinted in Franz Boas, *Race, Language and Culture.* New York: Macmillan (1940): 138–48.

————. *Changes in Bodily Form of Descendants of Immigrants.* Final Report. 61st Congress, 2d sess., 1911. S. Doc. 208. Reprint. New York: Columbia University Press, 1912.

————. *Anthropology and Modern Life.* New York: Norton, 1928.

————. "Race and Progress." *Science* 74 (1931): 1–8.

————. "History and Science in Anthropology: A Reply." *American Anthropologist* 38 (1936): 137–41.

————. "Race." In *Encyclopedia of the Social Sciences* 13, 25–26. New York: Macmillan, 1937.

————. *The Mind of Primitive Man.* New York: Macmillan, 1938.

————. "Heredity and Environment." *Jewish Social Studies* 1 (1939): 5–14.

————. *Race, Language and Culture.* New York: Macmillan, 1940.

————. "Racial Purity." *Asia* 40 (1940): 231–34.

————. "Class Consciousness and Race Prejudice." *Christian Register* 122 (1943): 5–6.

————. *Race and Democratic Society.* New York: Augustin, 1945.

————, ed. *General Anthropology.* Boston: Heath, 1938.

Boddy, J. *Brain Systems and Psychological Concepts.* New York: Wiley, 1978.

Bodley. John. H. *Victims of Progress.* 2d ed. Menlo Park, CA: The Benjamin/Cummings Publishing Co., 1982.

Bodmer, W. F., and L. L. Cavalli-Sforza. "Intelligence and Race." *Scientific American* 223 (1970): 19–29.

————. *Genetics, Evolution, and Man.* San Francisco: W. H. Freeman, 1976.

Bogardus, Emory S. *Immigration and Race Attitudes.* Boston: Health, 1938.

Bogart, Ernest L. *Direct and Indirect Costs of the Great World War.* New York: Oxford University Press, 1919.

Bolk-Fetlkamp, A. J. van. "Physical Anthropology in the Netherlands Indies since 1939." *Man* 44 (1949): 43–45.

Bolt, Christine. *Victorian Attitudes to Race.* London: Routledge & Kegan Paul, 1971.

Bond, Horace M. "What the Army 'Intelligence' Tests Measured." In *The Bell Curve Debate: History, Documents, Opinions,* edited by Russell Jaacoby and Naomi Glauberman, 583–98. New York: Times Books, 1995.

Bondy, Ruth. *Elder of the Jews.* New York: Grove Press, 1989.

Bonger, Willem A. *Race and Crime.* Translated by M. M. Hordyk. New York: Columbia University Press, 1943.

Bonifacy, A. "Les Métis Franco-Tonkinois." *Revue Anthropologique* 21 (1911): 259–66.

Bonin, Gerhardt von. "On the Size of Man's Brain, as Indicated by Skull Capacity." *Journal of Comparative Neurology* 59 (1934): 1–28.

————. "On Racial Inequality." *The Interne* (1948).

Bonne, Batsheva. "Are There Hebrews Left?" *American Journal of Physical Anthropology* 24 (1966): 135–45.

Bonner, John T. *The Evolution of Culture in Animals.* Princeton: Princeton University Press, 1980.

Bonta, Bruce D., ed. *Peaceful Peoples.* Metuchen, NJ: Scarecrow Press, 1987.

Bookchin, Murray. *The Ecology of Freedom.* Palo Alto, CA: Cheshire Books, 1981.

Borden, Morton. *Jews, Turks, and Infidels.* Chapel Hill: University of North Carolina Press, 1984.

Bordewich, Fergus M. *Killing the White Man's Indian.* New York: Doubleday, 1996.

Bosmajian, Hamida. *Metaphors of Evil: Contemporaty German Literature and the Shadow of Nazism.* Iowa City: University of Iowa Press, 1967, 1979.

Bosworth, Allen, R. *America's Concentration Camps.* New York: W. W. Norton, 1967.

Boucher, Jerry, Dan Landis and Karen A. Clark. *Ethnic Conflict: International Perspectives.* Thousand Oaks, CA: Sage Publications, 1987.

Bourlière, François. *The Natural History of Animals.* New York: Alfred A. Knopf, 1954.

Bowers, David F., ed. *Foreign Influences in American Life.* Princeton: Princeton University Press, 1944.

Boxer, C. R. *The Golden Age of Brazil, 1695–1750: Growing Pains of a Colonial Society.* Berkeley: University of California Press, 1963.

———. *Race Relations in the Portuguese Colonial Empire.* New York: Oxford University Press, 1963.

Boyd, William C. "Critique of Methods of Classifying Mankind." *American Journal of Physical Anthropology* 27 (1940): 333–64.

———. *Genetics and the Races of Man, An Introduction to Modern Physical Anthropology.* Boston: Little, Brown, 1950.

Brace, C. Loring. "A Four-Letter Word Called 'Race.'" In *Race and Other Misadventures: Essays in Honor of Ashley Montegu in His Ninetieth Year,* edited by Larry T. Reynolds and Leonard Lieberman, 106–141. Dix Hill, NY: General Hall, 1996.

———. "Racialism and Racist Agendas." *The American Anthropologist* 98(1) (1996): 36–37.

———. "Review of *The Bell Curve.*" *Current Anthropology* 37 (1996) (Supplement): S156–S161.

Brace, C. Loring, and Ashley Montagu. *Man's Evolution.* New York: Macmillan, 1965.

Brace, C. Loring, G. R. Gamble, and J. T. Bond, eds. *Race and Intelligence.* Washington, D.C.: American Anthropological Association, 1971.

Brady, Terrence, and Evan Jones. *The Fight Against Slavery.* New York; W. W. Norton, 1977.

Braham, Randolph L. *The Politics of Genocide: The Holocaust in Hungary.* 2 vols. New York: Columbia University Press, 1981.

Braham, Randolph L., ed. *The Origins of the Holocaust: Christian Anti-Semitism.* New York: Columbia University Press, 1986.

Brain, Robert. *Into the Primitive Environment.* Englewood Cliffs, NJ: Prentice-Hall, 1972.

Braithwaite, E. R. *Honorary White.* New York: McGraw-Hill, 1975.

Bram, Joseph. "The Social Identity of the Jews." *Transactions of the New York Academy of Sciences,* ser. 2, 7 (1944): 1194–99.

———. "Change and Choice in Ethnic Identification." *Transactions of the New York Academy of Sciences* 28 (1965): 241–48.

Brameld, Theodore. *Minority Problems in the Public Schools.* New York: Harper, 1946.

Brandes, Georg. *Hellas: Travels in Greece.* Translated by Jacob W. Hartmann. New York: Adelphi, 1926.

Brandon, William. *The Last Americans: The Indian in American Culture.* New York: McGraw-Hill, 1974.

Brandt, B., ed. *Social Justice.* Englewood Cliffs, NJ: Prentice-Hall, 1962.

Brass, Paul R. *Ethnicity and Nationalism: Theory and Comparison.* Thousand Oaks, CA: Sage Publications, 1996.

Braunstein, Baruch. *The Chuetas of Majorca.* Columbia University Oriental Series, 28/29. New York: Columbia University Press, 1936.

Breasted, James H. *The Dawn of Conscience.* New York: Scribner's Sons, 1934.

Brenan, Gerald. *The Spanish Labyrinth.* New York: Macmillan, 1943.

Brend, William A. *Foundations of Human Conflicts.* London: Chapman & Hall, 1944.

Brenman, Margaret. "Urban Lower-Class Negro Girls." *Psychiatry* 6 (1943): 307–24.

Bridenbaugh, Carl. *Jamestown, 1544–1699.* New York: Oxford University Press, 1980.

Bridges, E. Lucas. *Uttermost Part of the Earth.* London: Hodder & Stoughton, 1948.

Bridgman, Jon M. *The Revolt of the Hereros.* Berkeley: University of California Pres, 1981.

Briffault, Robert. "You Can't Change Human Nature." *Scribner's Magazine* 92 (1932): 27–29.

Briggs, Jean L. "The Origins of Nonviolence : Aggression in Two Canadian Eskimo Groups." In *The Psychoanalytic Study of Society* vol. 6., edited by Warner Muensterberger and Aaron H. Esman, 134–203. New York: International Universities Press, 1975.

Brink, William, and Louis Harris. *The Negro Revolution in America.* New York: Simon & Schuster, 1964.

———. *Black and White: A Study in U.S. Racial Attitudes Today.* New York: Simon & Schuster, 1967.

Brislin, Richard W., Stephen Bochner, and Walter J. Lonner, eds. *Cross-Cultural Perspectives on Learning.* New York: John Wiley, 1975.

Brittan, Arthur, and Mary Maynard. *Sexism, Racism, and Oppression.* New York: Basil Blackwell, 1984.

Broca, Paul. *On the Phenomena of Hybridity in the Genus Homo.* London: Longman, Green, 1864.

Brody, Eugene, B. *Minority Group Adolescents in the United States.* Baltimore: Williams & Wilkins, 1968.

———. *The Lost Ones: Social Forces and Mental Illness in Rio de Janeiro.* New York: International Universities Press, 1974.

Brody, Eugene, B., and Nathan Brody. *Intelligence: Nature, Determinants, and Consequences.* New York: Academic Press, 1976.

Bromberg, Norbert, and Verna V. Small. *Hitler's Psychopathology.* New York: International Universities Press, 1983.

Bronfenbrenner, Urie. "Early Deprivation in Mammals: A Cross-Species Analysis." In *Early Experience and Behavior,* edited by G. Newton and S. Levene, 627–764. Springfield, IL: C. C. Thomas, 1968.

———. *A Report on Longitudinal Evaluations of Preschool Programs II. Is Early Intervention Effective?* Washington, D.C.: US Department of Health, Education and Welfare Publication No. (OHD): 74–25, 1974.

———. *The Ecology of Human Development: Experiments by Nature and Design.* Cambridge: Harvard University Press: 1979.

————, ed. *Influences on Human Development*. Hinsdale, IL: Dryden Press, 1972.

Brookfield, H. C. *Colonism, Development, and Independence: The Case of the Melanesian Islands in the South Pacific*. Cambridge: Cambridge University Press, 1992.

Brooks, Roy L. *Rethinking the American Race Problem*. Berkeley: University of California Press, 1990.

Broom, Leonard, et al. *The Inheritance of Inequality*. London & Boston: Routledge & Kegan Paul, 1980.

Brotz, Howard, ed. *Negro Social and Political Thought, 1850–1920*. New York: Basic Books, 1966.

Brown, Douglas. *Against the World*. New York: Doubleday, 1968.

Brown, F. Martin. "Studies of Nearctic Coenonympha tullia." *Bulletin of the American Museum of Natural History* 105(4) (1955): 361–409.

Brown, Fred. "A Sociopsychological Analysis of Race Prejudice." *Journal of Abnormal and Social Psychology* 27 (1932–1933): 364–74.

Brown, Ina C. *National Survey of the Higher Education of Negroes*. Publications of the U.S. Office of Education, Misc. 6. I. Washington, D.C., 1942.

————. *Race Relations in a Democracy*. New York: Harper, 1949.

————. *Understanding Race Relations*. Englewood Cliffs, NJ: Prentice-Hall, 1973.

Brown, JoAnne. *The Definition of a Profession: The Authority of Metaphor in the History of Intelligence Testing, 1890–1930*. Princeton: Princeton University Press, 1992.

Brown, Leonard, and G. Norval. *Transformation of the American Negro*. New York: Harper & Row, 1965.

Brown, Spencer. *They See for Themselves*. New York: Harper, 1944.

Brown, W. O. "Rationalization of Race Prejudice." *International Journal of Ethics* 63 (1933): 299–301.

Browne, Robert S. *Race Relations in International Affairs*. Washington, D.C.: Public Affairs Press, 1961.

Browne, Thomas. *Pseudodoxia Epidemica*. London: Dod, 1646.

Browning, Christopher R. *The Path to Genocide: Essays on Launching the Final Solution*. New York: Cambridge University Press, 1993.

Bruce, Philip A. *Social Life in Old Virginia*. New York: Capricorn Books, 1938.

Brückner, G. H. "Untersuchungen zur Tiersoziologie, insbesondere zur Auflösung der Familie." *Zeitschrift für Psychologie* 128 (1933): 1–110.

Bruns, Roger, ed. *Am I Not a Man and a Brother*. New York: Chelsea House, 1977.

Brutzkus, J. "Jewish Anthropology." *The Jewish People* 1 (1946): 10–26.

Bryce, James, Viscount. *The Relations of the Advanced and Backward Races of Mankind*. Oxford: Clarendon Press, 1902.

————. *Race Sentiment as a Factor in History*. London: University of London Press, 1915.

Bryson, Gladys. *Man and Society*. Princeton: Princeton University Press, 1945.

Bryson, Lyman, Louis Finkelstein, and Robert M. MacIver, eds. *Approaches to Group Understanding*. New York: Harper, 1947.

————, eds. *Aspects of Human Equality*. New York: Harper, 1956.

Budd, Edward C., ed. *Inequality and Poverty*. New York: W. W. Norton, 1966.

Buffon, Georges, L. L. *Natural History, General and Particular (Historie naturelle, générale et particulière*. Paris, 1749). Translated by William Smellie, corrected by William Wood (London, 1812): III, 302 ff.

Bugner, Ladislas, ed. *The Image of the Black in Western Art.* 3 vols. New York: William Morrow, 1979–80.

Bullard, Robert D., ed. *In Search of the New South.* Tuscaloosa: University of Alabama Press, 1989.

Bullock, Alan. *Hitler: A Study in Tyranny.* New York: Harper & Row, 1964.

Bunak, V. V., et al. "Contemporary Raciology and Racism." *International Journal of American Linguistics* 27 (1961): 1–146.

Burger, John. *The Black Man's Burden.* London: Gollancz, 1943.

Burlew, A. Kathleen H., et al., eds. *African American Psychology: Theory, Research, and Practice.* Thousand Oaks, CA: Sage Publications, 1992.

Burman, Sanda, and Pamela Reynolds. *Growing Up in a Divided Society: The Contexts of Childhood in South Africa.* Evanston, IL: Northwestern University Press, 1986.

Burns, Alan. *Colour Prejudice.* London: Allen & Unwin, 1948.

Burrows, Edwin G. *Hawaiian Americans.* New Haven: Yale University Press, 1947.

Burton-Bradley, B. G. "Mixed-Race Society in Port Moresby." *New Guinea Research Bulletin* 23 (1968): 1–51.

Buss, Arnold H. *The Psychology of Aggression.* New York: Wiley, 1961.

Butcher, H. J. *Human Intelligence: Its Nature and Assessment.* New York: Harper & Row, 1968.

Butcher, Margaret J. *The Negro in American Culture.* New York: Alfred A. Knopf, 1956.

Butler, Leonard, Leonard Thompson, and Jeffrey Butler, eds. *Change in Contemporary South Africa.* Berkeley: University of California Press, 1975.

Butler, Rohan D'O. *The Roots of National Socialism.* New York: Dutton, 1942.

Buxton, L. H. Dudley. "Cross Cousin Marriages, the Biological Significance." In R. S. Rattray, *Religion and Art in Ashanti.* Oxford: Oxford University Press, 1927.

Cabell, J. L. *The Testimony of Modern Science to the Unity of Mankind.* New York: R. Carter & Bros., 1859.

Cable, Mary. *Black Odyssey.* New York: Viking Press, 1971.

Cahn, Edgar S., and David W. Hearne, eds. *Our Brother's Keeper: The Indian in White America.* New York: New American Library, 1975.

Calas, Nicholas. "Myth and Initiation." *Chimera* 4 (1946): 21–24.

Caldwell, W. E., and H. C. Moloy. "Anatomical Variations in the Female Pelvis and Their Effects in Labor, with a Suggested Classification." *American Journal of Obstetrics and Gynecology* 26 (1933): 479–514.

Calman, W. T. *The Classification of Animals.* New York: Wiley, 1949.

Cameron, V. K., and H. Smith. "The Physical Form of Mississippi Negroes." *American Journal of Physical Anthropology* 16 (1931): 193–201.

Campbell, Angus. *White Attitudes toward Black People.* Ann Arbor: Institute for Social Research, 1971.

Campbell, Bernard. *Human Evolution.* Chicago: Aldine, 1966.

Cancro, R., ed. *Intelligence: Genetic and Environmental.* New York: Grune & Stratton, 1971.

Carey, Alexander Timothy. *Colonial Students.* London: Secker & Warburg, 1956.

Carey, M. D., and R. H. Warmington. *The Ancient Explorers.* London: Meithen, 1929.

Carmichael, Emmet B. "Josiah Clark Nott." *Bulletin of the History of Medicine* 22 (1948): 249–62.

Carmichael, Joel. *Satanizing the Jews.* New York: Fromm International, 1989.

Carpenter, Edmund. "Space Concepts of the Aivilik Eskimos." *Explorations* (Toronto) 5 (1955): 131–45.

Carson, Clayborne. *In Struggle: SNCC and the Black Awakening of the 1960s.* Cambridge: Harvard University Press, 1981.

Carson, Hampton L. *Heredity and Human Life.* New York: Columbia University Press, 1963.

Carter, G. S. *Animal Evolution: A Study of Recent Views of Its Causes.* London: Sidgwick & Jackson; New York: Macmillan, 1951.

Caruana, Wally. *Aboriginal Art.* New York: Thames & Hudson, 1993.

Cash, W. J. *The Mind of the South.* New York: Alfred A. Knopf, 1941.

Cashmore, E. Ellis. *Dictionary of Race and Ethnic Relations.* Boston: Routledge & Kegan Paul, 1984.

Casillo, Robert. *The Genealogy of Demons: Anti-Semitism, Facism and the Myths of Ezra Pound.* Evanston: Northwestern University Press, 1988.

Cassirer, Ernst. *An Essay on Man.* New Haven: Yale University Press, 1944.

———. *The Myth of the State.* New Haven: Yale University Press, 1946.

Castle, William E. "Biological and Social Consequences of Race Crossing." *American Journal of Physical Anthropology* 9 (1926): 145–56.

———. "Race Mixture and Physical Disharmonies." *Science* 71 (1930): 603–6.

———. "Dog Crosses and Human Crosses." *Journal of Heredity* 23 (1942): 249–52.

Catton, William R., Jr., and Sung Chick Hong. "The Relation of Apparent Minority Ethnocentrism to Majority Antipathy." *American Sociological Review* 27 (1962): 178–91.

Caute, David. *Under the Skin: The Death of White Rhodesia.* Evanston: Northwestern University Press, 1983.

Cavalli-Sforza, L. L., and W. P. Bodmer. *The Genetics of Human Populations.* San Francisco: W. H. Freeman & Co., 1971.

Cavalli-Sforza, L. L., Paolo Menozzi, and Albert Piazza. *The History and Geography of Human Genes.* Princeton: Princeton University Press, 1994.

Cecil, Robert. *The Myth of the Master Race: Alfred Rosenberg and Nazi Ideology.* New York: Dodd, Mead, 1972.

Chaloner, W. H., and W. O. Henderson. "Marx/Engels and Racism." *Encounter* 45 (1975): 18–23.

Chamberlain, Houston S. *The Foundations of the Nineteenth Century.* 2 vols. Translated by John Lees, with an introduction by Lord Redesdale. London and New York: Lane, 1910.

Chambers, Frank P., Christina Phelps Grant, and Charles C. Bayley. *This Age of Conflict: A Contemporary World History 1914–1943.* New York: Harcourt Brace, 1943.

Champagne, Duane. *Native America Portrait of the Peoples.* Detroit: Visible Ink Press, 1994.

———. *Native North American Almanac.* Detroit: Gale Research, Inc., 1994.

———. *Chronology of Native North American History.* Detroit: Gale Research, Inc., 1995.

Chandler, Albert R. *Rosenberg's Nazi Myth.* Ithaca: Cornell University Press, 1945.

Chapman, Malcolm, ed. *Social and Biological Aspects of Ethnicity.* New York: Oxford University Press, 1993.

Chapman, Paul D. *Schools as Sorter: Lewis M. Terman, Applied Psychology, and the Intelligence Testing Movement, 1890–1930.* New York: New York University Press, 1988

Chappat, Janine S. A. "Race Prejudice and Preschool Education." Ms. Harvard School of Education, Cambridge, Mass., n.d.

Chase, Allan. *The Legacy of Malthus: The Social Costs of the New Scientific Racism.* New York: Alfred A. Knopf, 1977

Chase, Stuart. *The Tyranny of Words.* New York: Harcourt, Brace, 1938.

Chaudhuri, Nirad C. *Scholar Extraordinary: Frederich Max Müller.* New York: Oxford University Press.

Chen, Jack. *The Chinese of America.* San Francisco: Harper & Row, 1980.

Chesinski, Michael. *Poland: Communism, Nationalism, Anti-Semitism.* New York: Karz-Cohl Publishing, 1983.

Chewings, Charles. *Back in the Stone Age.* Sydney: Angus & Robertson, 1936.

Childe, V. Gordon. *Man Makes Himself.* New York: Oxford University Press, 1940.

———. "War in Prehistoric Societies." *Sociological Review* 33 (1941): 126–38.

———. *The Dawn of European Civilization.* 4th ed. New York: Alfred A. Knopf, 1947.

———. *What Happened in History.* New York: Mentor Books, 1948.

Chinweizu. *The West and the Rest of Us: White Predators, Black Slavers, and the African Elite.* New York: Random House, 1975.

Chorover, Stephen L. *From Genesis to Genocide: The Meaning of Human Behavior and the Power of Behavior Control.* Cambridge: MIT, 1979.

Chrousos, George P., et al., "Stress: Basic Mechanisms and Clinical Implications." *Annals of the New York Academy of Sciences.* New York, 1995.

Chuman, Frank F. *The Bamboo People: The Law and Japanese Americans.* Del Mar, CA: Publishers Inc., 1976.

Churchill, Ward. *Since Predator Came: Notes from the Struggle for American Indian Liberation.* Littleton, CO: Aigis Publications, 1995.

Cioran, E. M. *A Short History of Decay.* New York: Viking, 1975.

Cipriani, Lidio. *Un assurdo etnico: L'Impero Etiopico.* Firenze: R. Bemporad & F.O., 1936.

Clark, Colin. "What's Wrong with Economics?" *Encounter* 10 (1958): 14–23.

Clark, E., and R. H. Lhamon. "Observations on the Sweat Glands of Tropical and Northern Races." *Anatomical Record* 12 (1917): 139–47.

Clark, Kenneth B. *Prejudice and Your Child.* Boston: Beacon Press, 1955.

———. *Dark Ghetto.* New York: Harper & Row, 1965. Reprint. Middletown, CT: Wesleyan University Press, 1989.

Clark, Thomas Blake. "One World on an Island." *Research in Race Relations* 47, I (1947): 14–21.

Clark, W. W. *Los Angeles Negro Children.* Educational Research Bulletin, Los Angeles, 1923.

Clarkson, Jesse D., and Thomas C. Cochran, eds. *War as a Social Institution.* New York: Columbia University Press, 1941.

Clarkson, Thomas. *Thoughts on the Necessity of Improving the Condition of the Slaves in the British Colonies, with a View to Their Ultimate Emancipation.* London: Richard Taylor, 1823.

Clift, Virgil A., A. W. Anderson, and C. G Hullfish, eds. *Negro Education in America.* New York: Harper, 1962.

Clinchy, Everett R. *Intergroup Relations Centers.* New York: Farrar, Straus, 1949.

Cloudsely-Thompson, J. L. *Animal Conflict and Adaptation.* London: Foulis, 1965.

Clutterbuck, Richard. *Britain in Agony: The Growth of Political Violence.* London & Boston: Faber & Faber, 1978.

Coamy, Joan. *The Diaspora Story: The Epic of the Jewish People Among the Nations.* New York: Harper & Row, 1972.

Coates, James. *Armed and Dangerous: The Rise of the Survivalist Right.* New York: Hill & Wang, 1987.

Cobb, Thomas R. R. *An Inquiry into the Law of Negro Slavery in the United States of America.* Philadelphia: Johnson & Co., 1858.

Cobb, William M. "The Physical Constitution of the American Negro." *Journal of Negro Education* 3 (1934): 340–88.

———. "Your Nose Won't Tell." *Crisis* 45 (1938): 332–36.

———. "Race and Runners." *Journal of Health and Physical Education* 7 (1936): 1–8.

———. "Physical Anthropology of the American Negro." *American Journal of Physical Anthropology* 29 (1942): 113–223.

Coben, Stanley. *Rebellion Against Victorianism.* New York: Oxford University Press, 1991.

Coghill, G. E. *Anatomy and the Problems of Behavior.* Cambridge: Cambridge University Press, 1929.

Cohen, David W., and Jack P. Greene, eds. *Neither Slave nor Free.* Baltimore: Johns Hopkins University Press, 1972.

Cohen, Lester. "Letters to the Editor" [On the Jews]. *Saturday Review of Literature* 31 (1948): 19–21.

Cohen, Richard I. *The Burden of Conscience: French Jewry's Response to the Holocaust.* Bloomington: Indiana University Press, 1987

Cohen, Robert, and Ken Heyman. *The Color of Man.* New York: Random House, 1968.

Cohen, Steven M. *American Modernity and Jewish Identity.* London and New York: Tavistock/Metheun, 1983.

Cohn, Margaret. "The Truth About Asian Americans." In *The Bell Curve Debate: History, Documents, Opinions,* edited by Russell Jacoby and Naomi Glauberman. New York: Times Books, 1995.

Cohn, Norman. *Warrant for Genocide: The Myth of the Jewish World Conspiracy and the Protocols of the Elders of Zion.* London: Eyre & Spottiswoode, 1967.

Cohodas, Nadine. *The Band Played Dixie: Race and the Liberal Conscience at Ole Miss.* New York: Free Press, 1997.

Cole, Ernest. *House of Bondage.* New York: Random House, 1967.

Cole, M., J. Gay, J. A. Glick, and D. W. Sharp. *The Cultural Context of Learning and Thinking.* New York: Basic Books, 1971.

Cole, Stewart G., and Mildred Wise Cole. *Minorities and the American Promise.* New York: Harper, 1954.

Coleman, E. L. *New England Captives Carried to Canada between 1677 and 1760.* 2 vols. Portland, ME: Southworth Press, 1925.

Coleman, James S., et al. *Equality of Educational Opportunity.* Washington, D.C.: Government Printing Office, 1966.

Coles, Kenneth. *The Desegregation of Southern Schools: A Psychiatric Study.* New York: Anti-Defamation League of B'nai B'rith, 1963.

Coles, Robert. *Children of Crisis.* Boston: Little, Brown, 1967.

Collias, Nicholas E. "Aggressive Behavior among Vertebrate Animals." *Physiological Zoology* 17 (1944): 83–123.

Collier, John. "The Creative Value of Cultural Diversity." *Trend & Tides* 2 (1946): 5–6.

Collingwood, R. G., and J. N. L. Myres. *Roman Britain and the English Settlements.* 2nd. ed. Oxford: Clarendon Press, 1936.

Collins, Sydney. *Coloured Minorities in Britain.* London: Lutterworth Press, 1957.

———. "The Status of Coloured People in Britain." *Phylon* 18 (1957): 82–87.

Comaroff, Jane, and John Comaroff. *Of Revelation and Revolution* vol. 1. Chicago, University of Chicago Press, 1991.

Comas, Juan. "'Scientific' Racism Again?" *Current Anthropology* 2 (1961): 303–40.

Comay, Joan. *The Diaspora Story: The Epic of the Jewish People Among the Nations.* New York: Random House, 1980.

Commission on Mixed Marriages in South Africa. *Report.* Pretoria: Government Printer, 1939.

Conant, Melvin, ed. *Race Issues on the World Scene.* Honolulu: University of Hawaii Press, 1955.

Condliffe, J. B. *New Zealand in the Making.* London: Allen & Unwin, 1930.

Conklin, Edwin G. *Heredity and Environment.* Princeton: Princeton University Press, 1939.

———. *What is Man?* Rice Institute Pamphlet, 28: 163. Houston, 1941.

———. *Man: Real and Ideal.* New York: Scribner, 1943.

Connolly, Cornelius J. *External Morphology of the Primate Brain.* Springfield, IL: Thomas, 1950.

Conquest, Robert. *The Great Terror.* New York: Viking, 1990.

———. *Stalin: Breaker of Nations.* New York, Viking, 1991.

Cook, Cecil. *Report of the 27th of June, 1933, by the Chief Protector of Aboriginals in the Northern Territory of Australia. Darwin, 1933.* Reprinted in the Report of the Commission on Mixed Marriages in South Africa. Pretoria: Government Printer, 1939.

Cook, James G. *The Segregationists.* New York: Appleton-Century-Crofts, 1962.

Cooley, John H., Robert R. Angell, and Julliard Carr. *Introductory Sociology.* New York: Schribner's Sons, 1933.

Coomaraswamy, Ananda K. *Am I My Brother's Keeper?* New York: John Day, 1947.

Coombs, Norman. *The Black Experience.* New York: Twayne, 1972.

Coon, Carleton S. *The Races of Europe.* New York: Macmillan, 1939.

———. "Have the Jews a Racial Identity?" In *Jews in a Gentile World,* edited by I. Graeber and Steuart H. Britt. New York: Macmillan, 1942.

———. *The Origin of Races.* New York: Alfred A. Knopf, 1962.

Coon, Carleton S., Stanley M. Garn, and Joseph B. Birdsell. *Races: a Study of the Problems of Race Formation in Man.* Springfield: Thomas, 1950.

Cooper, Jr., William, J. *The South and the Politics of Slavery. 1828–1856.* Baton Rouge: Louisiana State University Press, 1980.

Cooper, R. M., and J. P. Zubek. "Effects of Enriched and Restricted Early Environments on the Learning Ability of Bright and Dull Rats." *Canadian Journal of Psychology* 12 (1958): 159–64.

Corner, George W. *Ourselves Unborn.* New Haven: Yale University Press, 1944.

Cornfield, Gaalyahu. *Archaeology of the Bible*. New York: Harper & Row, 1961.

Corrigan, J. W., ed. *Scientific Aspects of the Race Problem*. New York: Longmans, 1941.

Coser, Lewis A. "Europe's Neurotic Nationalism." *Commentary* 1 (1946): 59–63.

Cotton, W. A. *The Race Problem in South Africa*. London: Student Christian Movement, 1926.

Cottrell, Leonard. *The Anvil of Civilization*. New York: New American Library, 1957.

Coudenhove-Kalergi, Heinrich. *Anti-Semitism through the Ages*. London: Hutchinson, 1935.

Count, Earl, ed. *This Is Race*. New York: Schuman, 1950.

Coupland, Reginald. *Wilberforce: A Narrative*. Oxford: Oxford University Press, 1923.

Courtet de l'Isle, Victor. *La Science Politique Fondee sur la Science de l'homme*. Paris: A. Betrano, 1838.

Cover, Robert M. *Justice Accused: Antislavery and the Judicial Process*. New Haven: Yale University Press, 1975.

Cowdry, Edmund H., ed. *Human Biology and Racial Welfare*. New York: Hoeber, 1930.

Cowley, Geoffrey. "It's Time to Rethink Nature and Nurture." *Newsweek*, 27 March 1955: 52–53.

Cox, Oliver C. "Race and Caste: A Distinction." *American Journal of Sociology* 50 (1945): 360–68.

———. *Race Relations: Elements and Social Dynamics*. Detroit: Wayne State University Press, 1976.

Craey, A. T. *Colonial Students*. London: Secker & Warburg, 1956.

Crain, Robert L., and Carol S. Weisman. *Discrimination, Personality, and Achievement*. New York: Seminar Press, 1972.

Crane, Jonathan. "Exploding the Myth of Scientific Support for the Theory of Black Intellectual Inferiority." *Journal of Black Psychology* 20 (1994): 189–209.

Cranston, Maurice. *Freedom*. New York: Basic Books, 1967.

Crapanzano, Vincent. *Waiting: The Whites of South Africa*. New York: Random House, 1985.

Cravens, Hamilton. *The Triumph of Evolution: American Scientists and the Heredity-Environment Controversy 1900–1941*. Philadelphia: University of Pennsylvania Press, 1978.

Cravioto, J. "Complexity of Factors Involved in Protein-Calorie Malnutritin." In *Malnutrition is a Problem of Ecology*, edited by P. Gyorgy and O. L. Kline, 7–22. Basel and New York: Karger, 1970.

Creyveld, M. Van. "Beyond the Fini-Contini Garden: Mussolini's 'Fascist Racism.'" *Encounter* 42 (1974): 42–47.

Crichton, J. M. "A Multiple Discriminant Analysis of Egyptian and African Negro Crania." *Papers of the Peabody Museum of Archaeology and Ethnology, Harvard University* 57 (1966): 47–67.

Crisis in Child Mental Health: Challenge for the 1970's. Report of the Joint Commission on Mental Health of Children. New York: Harper & Row, 1970.

Crocker, Chester A. *High Noon in Southern Africa: Making Peace in a Rough Neighborhood*. New York: W. W. Norton, 1992.

Crocker, William. "Botany of the Future." *Science* 88 (1938): 391.

Crockett, Charis. *The House in the Rain Forest*. Boston: Houghton Mifflin, 1942.

Crockett, Harry J., and Jerome L. Schulman. *Achievement Among Minority Americans.* Cambridge MA: Schenckman, 1973.

Croly, Herbert. *The Promise of American Life.* New York: McMillan, 1912.

Crosby, Alfred W., Jr. *The Columbian Exchange: Biological and Cultural Consequences of 1492.* Westport, CT: Greenwood Press, 1972.

Cross, F. L., and E. A. Livingstone, eds. *The Oxford Dictionary of the Christian Church.* 2d ed. New York: Oxford University Press.

Cross, Theodore, ed. "On Racial Sensitivity Training for College Freshman: A Survey of International Opinions and Practices." *The Journal of Blacks in Higher Education* 1 (Spring 1994): 77–79.

Crow, Games F. "Mechanisms and Trends in Human Evolution." In *Evolution and Man's Progress,* edited by Hudson Hoagland and Ralph W. Burhoe, 6–21. New York: Columbia University Press, 1962.

Cummings, Michael R. *Human Heredity: Principles and Issues.* St. Paul, MN: West, 1991.

Current, Richard N., ed. *Reconstruction (1865–1877).* Englewood Cliffs, NJ: Prentice-Hall, 1965.

Curriculum Office, Philadelphia Public Schools. *Open-Mindedness Can Be Taught.* Philadelphia, 1946.

Curtin, Philip D. "The Origin of the 'White Man's Burden.'" *The Listener* 66 (1961): 412–15.

Cuvier, Georges. *Le Règne Animal.* Vol. 1. Paris: Deterville, 1817.

Cyander, Max S. "Mechanisms of Brain Development and Their Role in Health and Wellbeing." *Daedalus* 123 (4) (1995): 155–65.

Dabek-Szyszko, M. "The Great Bor Lie." *The Protestant* 6 (1946): 12–31.

Dahlberg, Gunnar. "An Analysis of the Conception of Race and a New Method of Distinguishing Races." *Human Biology* 14 (1942): 372–85.

———. *Race, Reason and Rubbish: a Primer of Race Biology.* New York: Columbia University Press, 1942.

———. "Notes on the Conception of Type." *Acta Genetica et Statistica Medica* 1 (1949): 174–78.

Danforth, C. H. "Distribution of Hair on the Digits in Man." *American Journal of Physical Anthropology* 4 (1921): 189–204.

Daniel, Pete. *The Shadow of Slavery: Peonage in the South, 1901–1969.* Urbana: University of Illinois Press, 1972.

Daniels, Farrington Jr. "Man and Radiant Energy: Solar Radiation." In *Adaptation to the Environment,* edited by D. B. Dill et al. 969–87. Washington, D.C.: American Physiological Society, 1964.

Dark, Eleanor. *The Timeless Land.* New York: Macmillan, 1941.

Darlington, Cyril D. "The Genetic Understanding of Race in Man." *International Social Science Bulletin* (UNESCO): 2 (1950): 479–88.

———. *The Evolution of Man and Society.* New York: Simon & Schuster, 1969.

Dart, Raymond. "The Predatory Transition from Ape to Man, *International Anthropological and Linguistic Review* 1 (1954): 207–08.

Darwin, Charles. *The Origin of Species.* London: Murray, 1859.

———. *Variation of Animals and Plants under Domestication.* London: Murray, 1867.

———. *The Descent of Man.* London: Murray, 1871.

———. *Heredity of Skin Color in Negro-White Crosses.* Publication of the Carnegie Institution of Washington, No. 188. Washington, D.C., 1913.

———. "The Mingling of Races." In *Human Biology and Racial Welfare,* edited by E. V. Cowdry. New York: Hoeber, 1930.

———. "Some Criticisms of 'Race Crossing in Jamaica.'" *Science* 62 (1930): 501–2.

Davenport, Charles B. "Heredity of Hair Form in Man." *American Naturalist* 42 (1908): 341.

Davenport, Charles. *Heredity of Skin Color in Negro-White Crosses.* Washington, D.C.: Carnegie Institution, 1913.

Davenport, Charles B., and A. G. Lowe. *Army Anthropology: Based on Observations Made on Draft Recruits 1917–1918, and on Veterans at Demobilization, 1919.* Medical Department of the U.S. Army in the World War. Vol. 15, Part 1. Washington, D.C.: Government Printing Office, 1921.

Davenport, Charles B., and Morris Steggerda. *Race Crossing in Jamaica.* Washington, D.C.: Carnegie Institution, 1929.

David Milner. *Children and Race, Ten Years On.* London: Ward Lock Educational, 1983.

David, Jay, ed. *The American Indian: The First Victim.* New York: William Morrow, 1972.

David, Jay, and Elaine Crane. *Living Black in White America.* New York: William Morrow, 1971.

David, Paul R., and Laurence S. Snyder. "Genetic Variability and Human Behavior." In *Social Psychology at the Crossroads,* edited by John H. Rohrer and Muzafer Sherif, 53–82. New York: Harper, 1951.

David, Richard J., and James W. Collins, Jr. "Racism and Bad Pregnancy Outcomes Among African-Americans: The Case Against the Biological Concept of Race in Prenatal Epidemiology." In *Race and Other Misadventures,* edited by L. Reynolds and L. Lieberman, 206–16. Dix Hills, NY: General Hall, 1996.

Davidio, John L., and Samuel Gaertner, eds. *Prejudice, Discrimination, and Racism.* Orlando: Academic Press, 1986.

Davidson, Basil. *Black Mother: The African Slave Trade.* Boston: Little, Brown, 1961.

———. *The African Past.* Boston: Little, Brown, 1964.

———. *The African Genius.* Boston: Little, Brown, 1969.

Davidson, Helen H. *Personality and Economic Background.* New York: King's Crown Press, 1943.

Davidson, Henry A. "The Anatomy of Prejudice." *Common Ground* 1 (1941): 3–12.

Davie, Maurice R. *Negroes in American Society.* New York: McGraw-Hill, 1950.

Davies, Alan. *Infected Christianity: A Study of Modern Racism.* Kingston & Montreal: McGill-Queen's University Press, 1988.

———, ed. *Antisemitism and The Foundations of Christianity.* Mahwah, NJ: Paulist Press, 1979.

Davies, Horton. "Race Tensions in South Africa." *Hibbert Journal* 49 (1951): 118–27.

Davis, Allison. "Racial Status and Personality Development." *Scientific Monthly* 57 (1934): 354–62.

———. "The Distribution of the Blood Groups and the Concept of Race." In *Political Arithmetic,* edited by Lancelot Hogben. New York: Macmillan, 1938.

Davis, Allison, Burleigh B. Gardner, and Mary R. Gardner. *Deep South; A Social Anthropological Study of Caste and Class.* Chicago: University of Chicago Press, 1941.

Davis, David Brion. *The Problem of Slavery in the Age of Revolution, 1770–1823.* Ithaca, Cornell University Press, 1966, 1975.

———. *Slavery and Human Progress.* New York: Oxford University Press, 1984.

———. *Revolutions: Reflections on American Equality and Foreign Liberation.* Cambridge: Harvard University Press, 1991.

Davis, Frank. *Livin' the Blues: Memoirs of a Black Journalist and Poet.* Madison: University of Wisconsin Press, 1992.

Davis, Mary B., ed. *Native America in the Twentieth Century: An Encyclopedia.* New York: Garland, 1996.

Davis, Ossie. "The Language of Racism." In *Language in America,* edited by Neil Postman, Charles Weingartner, and Terence P. Moran. New York: Pegasus, 1969.

Davis, S. *Race-Relations in Ancient Egypt.* New York: Philosophical Library, 1952.

Davison, A. N., and J. Dobbing. "Myelination as a Vulnerable Period in Brain Development." *British Medical Bulletin* 22 (1968): 40–44.

Dawidowicz, Lucy S. *The War Against the Jews.* New York: Holt, Rinehart & Winston, 1975.

———. *The Holocaust and the Historians.* Cambridge: Harvard University Press, 1981.

Day, Beth. *Sexual Life Between Blacks and Whites.* New York: Crowell, 1974.

Day, Caroline B. *A Study of Some Negro-White Families in the United States.* Cambridge: Peabody Museum, Harvard University, 1932.

de Azurara, Gomes Eannes. *The Chronicle of the Discovery and Conquest of Guinea.* London: Hakluyt Society, 1896.

De Fleur, Melvin, and Frank R. Westie. "The Interpretation of Interracial Situations." *Social Forces* 38 (1959): 17–23.

de Huszar, George B. *Anatomy of Racial Intolerance.* New York: The H.W. Wilson Co., 1946.

De Lone, Richard H. *Small Futures: Children, Inequality and the Limits of Social Reform.* New York: Harcourt Brace Jovanovich, 1979.

de Menil, Hermione, ed., *The Images of the Black in Western Art.* 4 vols. Cambridge: Harvard University Press, 1976.

de Rueck, Anthony and Julie Knight eds. *Caste and Race: Comparative Approaches.* New York: Little, Brown, 1967.

De Verone, Cesar de l'Escale. *Observations sur les Hommes de Couleur des Colonies.* Paris: Bailly, 1790.

De Vries, James E. *Race and Kinship in a Midwestern Town.* Urbana: University of Illinois Press, 1984.

Deakin, Nicholas. *Colour and the British Electorate, 1964.* London: Pall Mall, 1965.

Dean, John P., and Alex Rosen. *A Manual of Intergroup Relations.* Chicago: University of Chicago Press, 1955.

Deane, Dee Shirley. *Black South Africans: A Who's Who. 57 Profiles of Natal's Leading Blacks.* New York: Oxford University Press, 1978.

Debo, Angie. *And Still the Waters Run.* Princeton: Princeton University Press, 1972.

Decter, Moshe. *Israel and the Jews in the Soviet Mirror.* Conference on Soviet Jews. New York, 1967.

Dees, Morris. *Gathering Storm.* New York: Harper-Collins, 1996.

Dees, Morris, with Steve Fiffer. *A Season for Justice: The Life and Times of Civil Rights Lawyer Morris Dees.* New York: Schribner's Sons, 1991.

Degler, Carl N. *Neither Black nor White: Slavery and Race Relations in Brazil and the United States.* New York: Macmillan, 1971.

Delage, Yves, and Marie Goldsmith. *The Theories of Evolution.* London: Palmer, 1912.

Delbo, Charlotte. *Auschwitz and After.* New Haven: Yale University Press, 1995.

Deloria, Vine, Jr. *Custer Died for Your Sins.* New York: Macmillan, 1969.

———. *We Talk, You Listen.* New York: Macmillan, 1970.

———. *God Is Red.* New York: Grossett & Dunlap, 1973.

———. *Behind the Trail of Broken Treaties.* New York: Delacorte, 1974.

———. *American Indian Policy in the Twentieth Century.* Norman: University of Oklahoma Press, 1995.

Demiashkevich, Michael. *The National Mind: English, French and Germans.* New York: American Book Co., 1938.

Demolins, Edmond. *Anglo-Saxon Superiority: To What is it Due.* 10th ed. New York: R. F. Frenno, 1898.

Denitch, Bogdan. *Ethnic Nationalism: The Tragic Death of Yugoslavia.* Minneapolis: University of Minnesota Press, 1994.

DeParle, Jason. "Daring Research or 'Social Science Pornography?'" *New York Times Magazine,* 9 October 1994: 50.

Des Pres, Terrence. *The Survivor.* New York: Oxford University Press, 1976.

Detweiler, Frederick G. "The Rise of Modern Race Antagonisms." *American Journal of Sociology* 38 (1932): 738–47.

Deutsch, M., and M. E. Collins. *Interracial Housing.* Minneapolis: University of Minnesota Press, 1952.

Deutsch, M., et al. *The Disadvantaged Child.* New York: Basic Books, 1967.

Deutsch, M., and I. Katz, and R. Jensen, eds. *Social Class, Race, and Psychological Development.* New York: Holt, Rinehart & Winston, 1968.

DeVore, Irven, ed. *Primate Behavior.* New York: Holt, Rinehart & Winston, 1965.

Dew, Thomas R. *Review of the Debates in the Virginia Legislature of 1831 and 1832.* Richmond, VA: Randolph, 1832.

———. *An Essay on Slavery.* Richmond, VA: Randolph, 1849.

Dewey, John. "Does Human Nature Change?" In *Problems of Men.* New York: Philosophical Library, 1946.

Diamond, Marian C. *Enriching Heredity: The Impact of Environment on the Anatomy of the Brain.* New York: Free Press, 1988.

Diaz-mas, Paloma. *Sephardim: The Jews from Spain.* Chicago: University of Chicago Press, 1992.

Dickinson, A. "Race Mixture: a Social or a Biological Problem?" *Eugenics Review* 41 (1949): 81–85.

Diller, Aubrey. *Race Mixture among the Greeks before Alexander.* Illinois Studies in Language and Literature, University of Illinois, vol. 20. Urbana, 1937.

Dillon, Morton L., *The Abolitionists.* De Kalb: Northern Illinois University Press, 1974.

———. *Slavery Attacked: Southern Slaves and Their Allies, 1619–1865.* Baton Rouge: Louisiana State University Press, 1990.

Dinnerstein, Leonard. *American and the Survivors of the Holocaust.* New York: Columbia University Press, 1982.

Dinnerstein, Leonard, and Frederic C. Jaher, eds. *The Aliens: A History of Ethnic Minorities in America.* New York: Appleton-Century-Crofts, 1970.

Diop, Cheikh Anta. *The African Origin of Civilization. Myth or Reality?* New York: Lawrence Hill, 1974.

Dixon, N. E. *On the Psychology of Military Incompetence.* London: Jonathan Cape, 1988.

Dixon, Pierson. *The Iberians of Spain.* London: Oxford University Press, 1939.

Dobbing, J. "The Influence of Nutrition on the Development of the Brain." Proceedings of the Royal Society, London, ser. B. *Biological Science* 160 (1964): 503–09.

———. "Effects of Experimental Undernutrition of the Development of the Nervous System." In *Malnutrition, Learning and Behavior,* edited by N. S. Scrimshaw and J. E. Gordon, 181–202. Cambridge: MIT Press, 1968.

———. "Food for Thinking." *New Scientist,* 46 (1970): 636–37.

———. "Undernutrition and the Developing Brain." *American Journal of Diseases of Childhood* 120 (1970): 411–15.

Dobroszycki, Lucjan, ed. *The Chronicle of the Lodz Ghetto, 1941–1944.* New Haven: Yale University Press, 1984.

Dobzhansky, Theodosius. *Genetics and the Origin of Species.* New York: Columbia University Press, 1937; 2d ed., 1941; 3d ed., 1951.

———. "The Race Concept in Biology." *The Scientific Monthly* 52 (1941): 161–65.

———. "Races and Methods of Their Study." *Transactions of the New York Academy of Sciences,* ser. 2, 4 (1942): 115–23.

———. "Genetics and Human Affairs." *Teaching Biologist* 12 (1943): 97–106.

———. "Rules of Geographic Variation." *A Review of Darwinism and Geographic Regularities in Variation in Organisms,* by E. I. Lukin (in Russian). Moscow-Leningrad Academy of Sciences of the U.S.S.R., 1943. *Science* 99 (1944): 127–28.

———. "On Species and Races of Living and Fossil Man." *American Journal of Physical Anthropology,* n.s., 2 (1944): 251–65.

———. "The Genetic Nature of Differences among Men." In *Evolutionary Thought in America,* edited by S. Persons, 86–155. New Haven: Yale University Press, 1950.

———. *Evolution, Genetics, and Man.* New York: Wiley & Sons, 1955.

———. "Comment." *Current Anthropology* 3 (1962): 279–80.

———. *Mankind Evolving.* New Haven: Yale University Press, 1962.

———. "The Present Evolution of Man." In *Biology and Culture in Modern Perspective,* edited by Joseph G. Jorgensen, 87–90. San Francisco: W. H. Freeman, 1972.

———. *Genetic Diversity and Human Dignity.* New York: Basic Books, 1973.

Dobzhansky, Theodosius, Francisco J. Ayala, G. Ledyard Stebbins, and James W. Valentine. *Evolution.* San Francisco: W. H. Freeman, 1977.

Dobzhansky, Theodosius, and Carl Epling. *Contributions to the Genetics, Taxonomy, and Ecology of Drosophila Pseudooscura and Its Relatives.* Publication No. 554. Washington, D.C.: Carnegie Institution, 1944.

Dobzhansky, Theodosius, and M. F. Ashley Montagu. "Natural Selection and the Mental Capacities of Mankind." *Science* 105 (1947): 587–90.

Dodd, William E. *The Cotton Kingdom.* New Haven: Yale University Press, 1919.

Dodge, Ernest S. "Early American Contacts in Polynesia and Fiji." *Proceedings of the American Philosophical Society* 117 (1963): 102–106.

Dodgson, M. C. H. *The Growing Brain: An Essay in Developmental Neurology.* Baltimore: Williams & Wilkins, 1962.

Dollard, John. *Caste and Class in a Southern Town.* New Haven: Yale University Press, 1937.

———. "Hostility and Fear in Social Life." *Social Forces* 17 (1938): 15–26.

Dollard, John, et al. *Frustration and Aggression.* New Haven: Yale University Press, 1939.

Donald, James and Ali Rattansi, eds. *"Race," Culture and Difference.* Thousand Oaks, CA: Sage Publications, 1992.

Donaldson, Henry H. "The Significance of Brain Weight." *Archives of Neurology and Psychiatry* 13 (1925): 385–86.

Donnan, Elizabeth, ed. *Documents Illustrative of the History of the Slave Trade to America.* 4 vols. Publication No. 409. Washington, D.C.: Carnegie Institution, 1930.

Dorn, Edwin. *Rules and Racial Equality.* New Haven: Yale University Press, 1979.

Dornfeldt, Walter. "Studien über Schädelform und Schadelveranderung von Berliner Ostjunden und ihren Kindern." *Zeitschrift für Morphologie und Anthropologie* 39 (1941): 290–372.

Dorsen, Norman, ed. *The Evolving Constitution.* Middletown: Wesleyan University Press, 1989.

Dorsey, George A. "Race and Civilization." In *Whither Mankind,* edited by Charles A. Beard, 229–63. New York: Longmans, 1928.

Dostoevski, Feodor. *The Brothers Karamazov.*

Dover, Cedric. *Half-Caste.* London: Secker & Warburg, 1937.

———. "Race." *Man,* art. 95 (1951): 1.

———. "Antar for the Anthropologist." *The Eastern Anthropologist* 5 (1952): 165–69.

———. "The Classification of Man." *Current Science* 21 (1952): 209–13

———. "The Racial Philosophy of Ibn Khaldun." *Phylon* 13 (1952): 107–9.

———. "The Racial Philosophy of Johann Herder." *British Journal of Sociology* 3 (1952): 124–33.

Dower, John W. *War Without Mercy: Race and Power in the Pacific War.* New York: Pantheon Books, 1986.

Downs, Donald A. *Nazis in Skokie: Freedom, Community, and the First Amendment.* Notre Dame: Notre Dame University Press, 1985.

Doyle, Bertram W. *The Etiquette of Race Relations in the South.* Chicago: University of Chicago Press, 1937.

Dozier, E. P. "The Concepts of 'Primitive' and 'Native' in Anthropology." In *Yearbook of Anthropology* (1955): 187–202. New York: Wenner-Gren Foundation, 1955.

Drago, Edmund L. *Black Politicians and Reconstruction in Georgia: A Splendid Failure.* Baton Rouge: Louisiana State University Press, 1982.

Drew, Charles R. *Banked Blood: A Study in Blood Preservation.* New York: Columbia University Press, 1945.

Driberg, Tom. *Ruling Passions.* London: Jonathan Cape, 1977, 202–3.

Drillien, C. M., and E. M. Wilkinson, "Emotional Stress and Mongoloid Births." *Developmental Medicine and Child Neurology* 6 (1964): 140–43.

Drimmer, Melvin. *Black History: A Reappraisal.* New York: Doubleday, 1967.

———. *Issues in Black History.* Dubuque: Iowa, Kendall/Hunt, 1987.

Drinnon, Richard. *Facing West: The Metaphysics of Indian-Hating and Empire-Building.* Minneapolis: University of Minnesota Press, 1980.

Duberman, Martin. *The Antislavery Vanguard.* Princeton: Princeton University Press, 1965.

DuBois, W. E. B. *The Suppression of the African Slave Trade, 1638–1870.* Baton Rouge: Louisiana State University Press, 1969.

Dudley, Edward, and Maximillian E. Novak. *The Wild Man Within: An Image in Western Thought From the Renaissance to Romanticism.* Pittsburgh: University of Pittsburgh Press, 1972.

Duguid, Charles. *No Dying Race.* Sydney: Angus & Robertson, 1964.

Duijker, H. C.J., and N. H. Frijda. *Confluence: National Character and National Stereotypes.* Vol. 1. New York: The Humanities Press; Amsterdam: North Holland Publishing Co., 1960.

Dumas, Maurice. *A History of Technology and Invention: Progress Through the Ages.* New York: Crown, 1969.

Dummet, A. *A Portrait of English Racism.* London: Penguin, 1973.

Dumond, Dwight L. *Antislavery Origins of the Civil War in the United States.* Ann Arbor: University of Michigan Press, 1960.

———. *Antislavery.* Ann Arbor: University of Michigan Press, 1961.

———. *America's Shame and Redemption.* Marquette: Northern Michigan University Press, 1965.

Duncan J. McLeod. *Slavery, Race and the American Revolution.* London, New York: Cambridge University Press, 1974.

Duncan, O. D., D. L. Featherman, and B. Duncan. "The Cumulation of Handicaps," in *Success and Opportunity,* ed. Ephraim Harold Mizruchi. New York: Free Press, 1964.

———. *Socioeconomic Background and Achievement.* New York: Seminar Press, 1972.

Dunham, Barrows. *Man against Myth.* Boston: Little, Brown, 1947.

Dunlap, Knight. "Are There Any Instincts?" *Journal of Abnormal and Social Psychology* 14(1919–20): 307–11.

Dunlop, D. M. *The History of the Jewish Khazars.* New York: Schocken Books, 1967.

Dunn, Leslie C., and Theodosius Dobzhansky. *Heredity, Race, and Society.* New York: Mentor Books, 1946.

Dunn, Leslie C., and A. M. Tozzer. "An Anthropometric Study of Hawaiians of Pure and Mixed Blood." *Papers of the Peabody Museum of American Archaeology and Ethnology, Harvard University* 9 (1928): 90–211.

Dunn, R. "On the Physiological and Psychological Evidence in Support of the Unity of the Human Species." *Transactions of the Ethnological Society of London:* n.s., 1 (1861): 186–202.

Durbin, E. F. M., and John Bowlby. *Personal Aggressiveness and War.* New York: Columbia University Press, 1939.

Durden, Robert F. *The Gray and the Black.* Baton Rouge: Louisiana State University Press, 1972.

Dvorin, E. P. *Racial Separation in South Africa.* Chicago: University of Chicago Press, 1952.

Dworkin, Ronald. *A Matter of Principle.* Cambridge: Harvard University Press, 1985.

Dye, Thomas R. *The Politics of Equality.* Indianapolis: Bobbs-Merrill, 1971.

Dykeman, Wilma, and James Stokely. *Seeds of Southern Change.* Chicago: University of Chicago Press, 1962.

Dykes, Eva B. *The Negro in English Romantic Thought.* Washington, D.C.: Associated Publishers, 1942.

Dyre, Thomas G., *Theodore Roosevelt and the Idea of Race.* Baton Rouge: Louisisana State University Press,

Eagles, Charles W. *Outside Agitator: John Daniels and the Civil Rights Movemant in Alabama.* Chapel Hill: University of North Carolina Press, 1993.

East, E. M., and D. F. Jones. *Inbreeding and Outbreeding.* Philadelphia: Lippincott, 1919.

Ebling, F. J., ed. *Racial Variation in Man.* New York: Wiley, 1975.

Eckhardt, A. Roy. *Black—Woman—Jew.* Bloomington: University of Indiana Press, 1989.

Edelman, Marian Wright. *Portrait of Inequality: Black and White Children in America.* Washington, D.C.: Children's Defense Fund, 1980.

Edelstein, Alan. *An Unacknowledged Harmony—Philo-Semitism and the Survival of European Jewry.* Westport, CT: Greenwood Press, 1982.

Edgerton, Robert R. *Mau Mau.* New York: Free Press, 1989.

Edinger, Ludwig. *Vorlesungen über den Bau der nervüsen Zentralorgane des Menschen und der Tiere.* Leipzig: Vogel, 1911.

Editorial. "Aleuts WWII Tragedy." *Indian Affairs* 192 (March 1981): 4

Edmondson, Munro S. "A Measurement of Relative Racial Differences." *Current Anthropology* 4 (1965): 167–68.

Edson, L. "The Theory that I.Q. is Largely Determined by the Genes." *New York Times Magazine,* 31 August 1969: 10–11, 40–41, 43–47.

Edwards, Edward A., and S. Quimby Duntley. "The Pigments and Color of Living Human Skin." *American Journal of Anatomy* 45 (1939): 1–33.

Edwards, Paul, and James Walvin. *Black Personalities in the Era of the Slave Trade.* Baton Rouge: Louisiana State University Press, 1983.

Edwards, T. Bentley, and Frederick M. Wirt. *School Desegregation in the North.* New York: Academic Press, 1968.

Efron, David. *Gesture, Race and Culture.* 2d ed. The Hague: Mouton, 1972.

Ehle, John. *Trail of Tears: The Rise and Fall of the Cherokee Nation.* New York: Doubleday, 1988.

Ehrlich, Paul R., and Shirley Feldman. *The Race Bomb: Skin Color, Prejudice and Intelligence.* New York: Quadrangle, 1977.

Eichenwald, H. F., and P. C. Fry. "Nutrition and Learning." *Science* 163 (1969): 644–48.

Eiseley, Loren. *The Firmament of Time.* New York: Atheneum, 1960.

Eisen, Nathaniel H. "Ethnic Differences." *Perspectives in Biology and Medicine* 5 (1961): 139–41.

Eisenberg, J. F., and Wilton S. Dillon, eds. *Man and Beast: Comparative Social Behavior.* Washington, D.C.: Smithsonian Institution Press, 1971.

Eisler, Robert. "Metallurgical Anthropology in Hesiod and Plato and the Date of a 'Phoenician Lie.'" *Isis* 40 (1949): 108–12.

Ekberg, Douglas L. *Intelligence and Race.* New York: Praeger, 1979.

Eleftheriou, B. E., and J. P. Scott, eds. *The Physiology of Aggression and Defeat.* New York: Plenum Press, 1971.

Eliach, Yaffa. *Hasidic Tales of the Holocaust.* New York: Oxford University Press, 1982.

Elias, Robert, and Jennifer Turpin, eds. *Rethinking Peace.* Boulder, CO: Lynne Reinner, 1994.

Elkin, A. P. "Science, Society and 'Everyman.'" *Journal of the Royal Society of New South Wales* 75 (1941): 11–20.

———. *Society, the Individual and Change.* Sydney: Camden College, 1940–45.

———. *The Australian Aborigines.* 2d ed. Sydney: Angus & Robertson, 1954.

Elkins, Stanley M. *Slavery.* Chicago: University of Chicago Press, 1959.

———. "Culture Contacts and Negro Slavery." *Proceedings of the American Philosophical Society* 107 (1963): 107–9.

Elliach, Vaffa. *Hasidic Tales of the Holocaust.* New York: Oxford University Press, 1982.

Ellinger, Tage U. H. "On the Breeding of Aryans." *Journal of Heredity* 33 (1942): 141–43.

Ellis, Havelock. *The Philosophy of Conflict.* London: Constable, 1919.

Ells, Kenneth, et al. *Intelligence and Cultural Differences.* Chicago: University of Chicago Press, 1951.

Elton, Lord. *Saint George or the Dragon.* London: Collins, 1942.

Elwin, Verrier. *The Tribal World of Verrier Elwin.* New York: Oxford University Press, 1964.

Emerson, Alfred E. "Basic Comparisons of Human and Insect Societies." *Biological Symposia* 13 (1942): 163–77.

———. "The Biological Basis of Social Cooperation." *Illinois Academy of Science Transactions* 39 (1946): 9–18.

Emerson, Ralph Waldo. *English Traits.* Boston: Phillips, Sampson & Co., 1856.

Emigh, T. H., "Statistical Methodology of the Nature—Nurture Controversy in Human Intelligence." Ph.D. Dissertation, Iowa State University, 1974.

Endelman, Todd M. *The Jews of Georgian England 1714–1830: Tradition and Change in a Liberal Society.* Philadelphia: The Jewish Publication Society of America, 1979.

Engerman, Stanley L., and Eugene D. Genovese. *Race and Slavery in The Western Hemisphere: Quantitative Studies.* Princeton: Princeton University Press, 1990.

English, H. B., and A. C. English. *A Comprehensive Dictionary of Psychological and Psychoanalytical Terms.* New York: Longmans, 1958.

Engram, Eleanor. *Science, Myth, Reality: The Black Family in One-Half Century of Research.* Westport, CT: Greenwood Press, 1982.

Epstein, Benjamin R., and Arnold Foster. *The Troublemakers.* New York: Doubleday, 1952.

———. *The Radical Right.* New York: Random House, 1956.

———. *Some of My Best Friends . . .* New York: Farrar, Straus & Cudahy, 1962.

Epstein, Helen. *Children of the Holocaust.* New York: Putnam, 1979.

Eric Foner. *Reconstruction: America's Unfinished Revolution 1863–1877.* New York: Harper & Row, 1988.

Eron, Leonard D., Leopold O. Walder, and Monroe M. Lefkowitz. *Learning of Aggression in Children*. Boston: Little, Brown & Co., 1971.

Esman, Milton J., ed. *Ethnic Conflict in the Western World*. Ithaca: Cornell University Press, 1977.

Essed, Philomena. *Understanding Everyday Racism*. Thousand Oaks, CA.: Sage Publications, 1992.

Essien-Udom, E. U. *Black Nationalism: A Search for an Identity in America*. Chicago: University of Chicago Press, 1970.

Estel, L. "Race as an Evolutionary Concept." *American Journal of Physical Anthropology*, n.s., 15 (1956): 378.

Etheridge, E. W. *The Butterfly Caste: A Social History of Pellagra in the South*. Westport, CT: Greenwood, 1972.

European Race Audit Bulletin No. 16. Institute of Race Relations. November, 1995. London.

Evans, Bergen. *The Natural History of Nonsense*. New York: Alfred A. Knopf, 1964.

Evans, Richard J. *Hitler's Shadow: West German Historians and the Attempt to Escape from the Nazi Past*. New York: Pantheon Books, 1989.

Evans, Robley D. "Quantitative Inferences concerning the Genetic Effects of Radiation on Human Beings." *Science* 109 (1949): 299–304.

Ewing, Quincy, "The Heart of the Race Problem." Atlantic Monthly (1909) 389–397. Reprinted in *Forgotten Voices: Dissenting Southerners in an Age of Conformity*, edited by Charles E. Wynes. Baton Rouge: Louisiana State University Press, 1967.

Eyferth, V. K. "Eine Untersuchung der Neger-Mischlingskinder in Westdeutschland." *Vita Humana* 2 (1959): 102–114.

Ezekiel, Raphael S. *Voices from the Corner: Poverty and Racism in the Inner City*. Philadelphia: Temple University Press, 1984.

———. *The Racist Mind*. New York: Viking, 1995.

Fabregat, Claudio Esteva. *Mestizaje in Ibero-America*. Tucson: University of Arizona Press, 1994.

Fagan, Brian M. *The Great Journey: The Peopling of Ancient America*. New York: Thames & Hudson, 1987.

Fahey, Joseph J., and Richard Armstrong. *A Peace Reader: Essential Readings on War, Justice, Non-Violence and World Order*. New York/Mahah: Paulist Press, 1992.

Fairchild, Henry P. *The Prodigal Century*. New York: Philosophical Library, 1950.

Fairchild, Hoxie N. *The Noble Savage*. New York: Columbia University Press, 1928.

Fairclough, Adam *To Redeem the Soul of America: The Southern Christian Leadership Conference and Martin Luther King*. Athens: University of Georgia Press, 1987.

Fairclough, H. Rushton. "Early Racial Fusion in Mediterranean Lands." In *So to Live the Works of Man*, edited by Brand & Brand, 131–45. Albuquerque: University of New Mexico Press, 1939.

Fancher, Raymond E. *The Intelligence Men: Makers of the IQ Controversy*. New York: Norton, 1985.

Fanon, Frantz. *Black Skin White Masks*. New York: Grove Press, 1967.

———. *The Wretched of the Earth*. New York: Grove Press, 1968.

Faris, Ellsworth. "Are Instincts Data or Hypotheses?" *American Journal of Sociology* 27 (1921–22): 184–96.

Farmer, James. *Freedom—When?* New York: Random House, 1965.

Farrison, William Edward. *William Wells Brown: Author and Reformer.* Chicago: University of Chicago Press, 1969.

Faust, Drew G., ed. *The Ideology of Slavery: Pro-Slavery Thought in the Antebellum South, 1830–1860.* Baton Rouge: Louisiana State University Press, 1981.

Faverty, Frederic E. *Matthew Arnold the Ethnologist.* Evanston: Northwestern University Press, 1951.

February, V. A. *Mind Your Colour: The Coloured Stereotype in South African Literature.* London & Boston: Routledge & Kegan Paul, 1981.

Febvre, Lucien. *A Geographical Introduction to History.* New York: Knopf, 1925.

Fehrenbacher, Don E. *Slavery, Law & Politics.* New York: Oxford University Press, 1981.

Fein, Helen. *Accounting for Genocide: National Responses and Jewish Victimization During the Holocaust.* New York: Free Press, 1979.

Feingold, Henry L. *The Politics of Rescue.* New Brunswick: Rutgers University Press, 1970.

Feldman, M. W., and L. L. Cavalli-Sforza. *Cultural Transmission and Evolution: A Quantitative Approach.* Princeton: Princeton University Press, 1981.

Feldman, M. W., and R. C. Lewontin, "The Heritability Hangup." *Science* 290 (1975): 1163–68.

Feldstein, Stanley. *Once a Slave: The Slave's View of Slavery.* New York: Morrow, 1971.

———, ed. *The Poisoned Tongue: A Documentary History of American Racism and Prejudice.* New York: Morrow, 1972.

Feldstein, Stanley, and Lawrence Costello, eds. *The Ordeal of Assimilation.* New York: Anchor Books, 1974.

Fellows, Lawrence. "Laborities Slate a Racial Inquiry." *New York Times,* 17 October 1964: 9.

Fenichel, Otto. "A Psychological Approach to Anti-Semitism." *Commentary* 2 (1946): 36–44.

Ferencz, Benjamin B. *Less Than Slaves.* Cambridge: Harvard University Press, 1979.

Fernandes, Florestan. *The Negro in Brazilian Society.* New York: Columbia University Press, 1969.

Fetterman, David M. *Excellence & Equality.* Albany: State University of New York Press, 1988.

Feuer, Lewis S. "Political Myths and Metaphysics." *Philosophy and Phenomenological Research* 15 (1955): 332–50.

Field, Geoffrey G., "Nordic Racism." *Journal of the History of Ideas* 38 (1977): 523–40.

———. *Evangelist of Race: The Germanic Vision of Houston Stewart Chamberlain.* New York: Columbia University Press, 1981.

Filler, Louis. *The Crusade against Slavery, 1830–1860.* New York: Harper & Brothers, 1960.

Finch, E. "The Effects of Racial Miscegenation." In *Papers on Inter-Racial Problems,* 108–12. New York: 1911.

Fincher, Jack. *Human Intelligence.* New York: Putnam's Sons, 1976.

Finkelman, Paul, ed. *Slavery, Race, and the American Legal System, 1700—1872.* 16 vols. New York: Garland Publishing, 1988.

Finkelstein, Louis, ed. *The Jews: Their History, Culture, and Religion.* 2 vols. New York: Harper, 1949.

Finley, M. I. "Race Prejudice in the Ancient World." *The Listener* (London) (February 1968): 146–47.

Finney, D. J. "The Detection of Linkage." *Journal of Heredity* 33 (1942): 156–60.

Finot, Jean. *Race Prejudice.* New York: Dutton, 1907; Los Angeles: Zeitlin & ver Brugge, 1944.

Fischer, Eugen. "Die Rehobother Bastards und das Bastardierungsproblem beim Menschen." *Jena,* 1913.

———. "Rasse und Rassenentstehung beim Menschen." *Wege zum Wissen* 62 (1927): 1–137. Berlin: Ulstein.

———. "Variable Characters in Human Beings." In *Human Heredity,* edited by Edwin Baur, Eugen Fischer, and Fritz Lenz, 114–66. New York: Macmillan, 1931.

Fishberg, Maurice. *The Jews.* New York: Scribner, 1911.

Fisher, Ronald A. *The Genetical Theory of Natural Selection.* Oxford: Clarendon Press, 1930.

———. "Limits to Intensive Production in Animals." *British Agriculture Bulletin* 4 (1951): 317–18.

Fitzgerald, C. P. "Once More in the Yellow Peril." *The Nation* 202 (1966): 606–9.

Fitzhugh, George. *Sociology for the South, or the Failure of Free Society.* Richmond, VA: A Morris, 1985.

Fitzpatrick, Thomas B., M. Seiji, and A. David McGugan. "Melanin Pigmentation." *New England Journal of Medicine* 265 (1961): 328–32, 374–78, 430–34.

Fladeland, Betty. *Men and Brothers.* Urbana: University of Illinois Press, 1972.

Fleming, Gerald. *Hitler and the Final Solution.* Berkeley: University of California Press, 1984.

Fleming, R. M. "Physical Heredity in Human Hybrids." *Annals of Eugenics* 9 (1939): 55–81.

Flender, Harold. *Rescue in Denmark.* New York: Simon & Schuster, 1963.

Fletcher, Ronald. *Instinct in Man.* New York: International Universities Press, 1957.

Fleure, Herbert J. "Some Biological Considerations in Social Evolution." *Eugenics Review* 41 (1949): 134–40.

Fleure, Herbert J. "The Distribution of Types of Skin Colour." *Geographical Review* 35 (1945): 580–95.

Flood, Charles B. *Hitler: The Path to Power.* Boston: Little, Brown, 1980.

Flower, William H. "On the Classification of the Varieties of the Human Species." In *Essays on Museums.* London: Macmillan, 1898.

———. "The Study of Race." In *Essays on Museums.* London: Macmillan, 1898.

Flynn, James R. *Race, IQ, and Jensen.* Boston & London: Routledge, 1980.

Flynn, Kevin, and Gary Gerhardt. *The Silent Brotherhood: Inside America's Racist Underground.* New York: Free Press, 1989.

Fodor, Nandor. *In Search of the Beloved: A Clinical Investigation of the Trauma of Birth and Pre-Natal Conditioning.* New York: Hermitage Press, 1949.

Foner, Eric, ed. *America's Black Past.* New York: Harper & Row, 1970.

Foner, Philip S., ed. *Basic Writings of Thomas Jefferson.* New York: Halcyon House, 1950.

Foot, Paul. *Immigration and Race in British Politics.* London: Penguin Books, 1965.

Forbes, Jack D. *Black Africans and Native Americans.* New York: Blackwell, 1988.

Forster, Arnold, and Benjamin R. Epstein. *Cross Currents.* New York: Doubleday, 1956.

———. *The Trouble Makers.* Garden City, NY: Doubleday, 1952.

———. *Danger on the Right.* New York: Random House, 1964.

Forster, E. M. "Jew Consciousness." In *Two Cheers for Democracy,* edited by E. M. Forster, 12–14. New York: Harcourt, Brace & Co., 1951.

———. "Racial Exercise." In *Two Cheers for Democracy,* edited by E. M. Forster, 17–20. New York: Harcourt, Brace & Co., 1951.

Fortuyn, A. B. D. "The Origin of Human Races." *Science* 90 (1939): 352–53.

Fossey, Dian. *Gorillas in the Mist.* Boston: Houghton Mifflin, 1983.

Foster, T. S. *Travels and Settlements of Early Man.* London: Benn, 1929.

Fox, Robin. "The Abolition of Race." In *Encounter with Anthropology,* Robin Fox. New York: Harcourt Brace Jovanovich, 1973.

Francis, E. K. "The Nature of the Ethnic Group." *American Journal of Sociology* 52 (1947): 393–400.

———. "Minority Groups—A Revision of Concepts." *British Journal of Sociology* 2 (1951): 219–30.

Frank C. J. McGurk. *Comparison of the Performance of Negro and White High School Seniors on Cultural and Noncultural Psychological Test Questions.* Washington, D.C.: Catholic University Press, 1951. Microcard. 12 July 1996.

Frank, Lawrence K. *Nature and Human Nature.* New Brunswick: Rutgers University Press, 1951.

Frankel, Ellen, et al., eds. *Equal Opportunity.* Oxford: Blackwell, 1988.

Franklin, Benjamin. *The Autobiography.* Edited by Leonard Larabee, Ralph L. Ketcham, Helen C. Boatfield, and Helen H. Fineman, New Haven: Yale University Press, 1964.

Franklin, John Hope. *The Militant South.* Cambridge: Harvard University Press, 1956.

———. *From Slavery to Freedom: A History of Negro Americans.* 3d. ed. New York: Alfred A. Knopf, 1961.

———, ed. *Color and Race.* Boston: Houghton Mifflin, 1968.

Franzblau, R. N. "Race Differences in Mental and Physical Traits." *Archives of Psychology* 177 (1935).

Fraser, Steven, ed. *The Bell Curve Wars: Race, Intelligence, and the Future.* New York: Basic Books, 1995.

Frazier, E. Franklin. "A Comparison of Negro-White Relations in Brazil and in the United States." *Transactions of the New York Academy of Sciences,* ser. 2, 6 (1944): 251–69.

———. *The Negro in the United States.* New York: Macmillan, 1949.

———. *Race and Culture Contacts in the Modern World.* New York: Alfred A. Knopf, 1957.

Frederickson, George M. *The Black Image in the White Mind.* New York: Harper & Row, 1971.

———. *White Supremacy: A Comparative Study in American & South African History.* New York: Oxford University Press, 1981.

———. *The Arrogance of Race: Historical Perspectives on Slavery, Racism and Social Inequality.* Middletown: Wesleyan University Press, 1988.

Freedman, David N., and Edward F. Campbell, Jr. *The Biblical Archaeological Reader,* vol. 2. New York: Anchor Books, 1964.

Freedman, Maurice, ed. *A Minority in Britain.* London: Valentine, Mitchell, 1955.

Freedman, Theodore. "Oberammergau: Christian Folk Religion and Anti-Judaism." *Face to Face* 12 (1985): 1–35.

Freehling, Alison G. *Drift Toward Dissolution: The Virginia Slavery Debate of 1831–1832.* Baton Rouge: Louisiana State University Press, 1982.

Freimarch, V., and B. Rosenthal, eds. *Race and the American Romantics.* New York: Schocken Books, 1971.

Fremont-Smith, Frank. "The Physiological Basis of Aggression." *Child Study* 15 (1938): 1–8.

———. "The Influence of Emotional Factors upon Physiological and Pathological Processes." *Bulletin of the New York Academy of Medicine* 15 (1939): 560–69.

Frenchman, D. "Mixing of Races." *Eugenics Review* 41 (1949): 98.

Frenkel-Brunswik, Else. "Patterns of Social and Cognitive Outlook in Children and Parents." *American Journal of Orthopsychiatry* 21 (1951): 543–58.

Frenkel-Brunswik, Else, and R. Nevitt Sanford. "Some Personality Factors in Anti-Semitism." *Journal of Psychology* 20 (1945): 271–91.

Freud, Sigmund. *Beyond the Pleasure Principle.* London: Hogarth Press, 1922.

———. *Group Psychology and the Analysis of the Ego.* London: Hogarth Press, 1922.

———. *Introductory Lectures on Psycho-Analysis.* London: Allen & Unwin, 1922.

———. *The Future of an Illusion.* London: Hogarth Press, 1928.

———. *Civilization and Its Discontents.* London: Hogarth Press, 1930.

Freund, Philip. *Myths of Creation.* London: W. H. Allen, 1964.

Freye, William R. *In Whitest Africa: The Dynamics of Apartheid.* Englewood Cliffs, NJ: Prentice-Hall, 1968.

Freyre, Gilberto. *The Masters and the Slaves* (Casa-Grande & Senzala). New York: Alfred A. Knopf, 1946.

———. *The "Mansions" and the "Shanties."* New York: Alfred A. Knopf, 1963.

———. *Order and Progress.* New York: Alfred A. Knopf, 1970.

Fried, Morton H. "A Four-Letter Word That Hurts." *Saturday Review,* 48 (1965): 21–23, 35.

Friedenthal, H. "Die Sonderstellung des Menschen in der Natur." *Wege zum Wissen* 8 (1925). Berlin: Ulstein.

Friedlich, Otto. *The Kingdom of Auschwitz.* New York: Harper Perennial, 1994.

Friedman, Lawrence J. *The White Savage: Racial Fantasies in the Postbellum South.* Englewood Cliffs, NJ: Prentice-Hall, 1970.

Friedman, Leon, ed. *Southern Justice.* New York: Pantheon Books, 1965.

Friedman, Saul F. *The Oberammergau Play.* Carbondale: Southern Illinois University Press, 1984.

Friedman, Saul S. *No Haven For the Oppressed.* Detroit: Wayne State University Press, 1973.

Friedrich, Otto. *Before the Deluge: A Portrait of Berlin in the 1920's.* New York: Harper & Row, 1960.

Fromm, Erich. *Escape from Freedom.* New York: Farrar & Rinehart, 1942.

———. "Sex and Character." *Psychiatry* 11 (1943): 21–31.

————. *The Anatomy of Human Destructiveness.* New York: Holt, Rinehart & Winston, 1973.

Fry, H. K. "Aboriginal Mentality." *Medical Journal of Australia* 1 (1935): 353–60.

Frye, William. *In Whitest Africa: The Dynamics of Apartheid.* Englewood Cliffs, NJ: Prentice-Hall, 1968.

Fuller, J. L. *Nature and Nurture: A Modern Synthesis.* New York: Doubleday, 1954.

Fuller, L. *The Crusade Against Slavery.* New York: Harper, 1960.

Fuller, Renee. *In Search of the IQ Correlation.* Stony Brook NY: Ball-Sick-Bird Publications, 1975.

Furet, Francois, ed. *Unanswered Questions.* New York: Schocken Books, 1989.

Furnas, J. C. *Goodbye to Uncle Tom.* New York: William Sloane, 1956.

————. *The Road to Harpers Ferry.* New York: William Sloane, 1959.

Fyfe, William Hamilton. *The Illusion of National Character.* London: Watts, 1946.

————. "Colonial University Colleges." *The Listener* 45 (1951): 531–32.

Gager, John G. *The Origins of Anti-Semitism: Atitudes Toward Judaism in Pagan and Christian Antiquity.* New York: Oxford University Press, 1983.

Gallagher, Buell G. *Color and Conscience.* New York: Harper, 1946.

Galton, Francis. *The Narrative of an Explorer in Tropical South Africa.* London: John Murray, 1853.

————. *Inquiries into the Human Faculty and Its Development.* London: Macmillan, 1883.

Gann, L. H., and Peter Duignan, eds. *Colonialism in Africa, 1870–1960.* 3 vols. London and New York: Cambridge University Press, 1969.

Gantt, W. Horsley. "Disturbances in Sexual Function During Periods of Stress." In *Life Stress and Bodily Disease,* edited by H. G. Wolff, S. G. Wolff, Jr, and C. C. Hare, 1030–50. Baltimore: Williams & Wilkins, 1950.

Garcia, John. "IQ: The Conspiracy." *Psychology Today* September 1972: 40–43, 92–93.

Gardiner, Robert. *A World of People.* New York and London: Oxford University Press, 1966.

Garlick, J. P. "Review of Human Races and Readings on Race by S. M. Garn." *Annals of Human Genetics* 25 (1961): 169–70.

Garn, Stanley M. *Human Races.* 2d ed. Springfield, IL: Thomas, 1969.

Garn, Stanley, and Carleton Coon, "On the Number of Races of Mankind." *American Anthropologist* 67 (1955): 997.

Garrett, Henry E. "The Equalitarian Dogma." *Perspectives in Biology and Medicine* 4 (1961): 480–84.

————. "The Scientific Racism of Juan Comas." *The Mankind Quarterly* 2 (1961): 100–106.

Garrett, Henry E., and W. C. George. "Findings on Race Cited." *New York Times,* 10 October 1962: 46.

Garrow, David J. *The FBI and Martin Luther King, Jr.* New York: Norton, 1981.

Garth, Thomas R. *Race Psychology.* New York: Whittlesey House, 1931.

————. "A Study of the Foster Indian Child in the White Home." *Psychological Bulletin* 32 (1935): 708–9.

Gasman, Daniel. *The Scientific Origins of National Socialism.* New York: Neale Watson Academic Publications, 1971.

Gaston, Paul M. *The New South Creed: A Study in Southern Mythmaking.* New York: Alfred A. Knopf, 1970.

Gates, Henry Louis, ed. *"Race," Writing, and Difference.* Chicago: University of Chicago Press, 1985.

Gates, R. Ruggles. "A Pedigree Study of Amerindian Crosses in Canada." *Journal of the Royal Anthropological Institute* 58 (1928): 511–32.

———. "Phylogeny and Classification of Hominids and Anthropoids." *American Journal of Physical Anthropology* n.s., 2 (1944): 279–92.

———. *Human Ancestry.* Cambridge: Harvard University Press, 1948.

———. "Disadvantages of Race Mixture." *Nature* 170 (1952): 896.

———. "Studies in Race Crossing." *Zeitschrift für Morphologie und Anthropologie* 47 (1956): 233–315.

———. "Studies in Race Crossing: The Japanese War Children." *Zeitschrift für Morphologie und Anthropologie* 49 (1958): 129–47.

———. "The Genetics of the Australian Aborigines." *Acta Geneticae Medicae et Gemellologiae* 9 (1960): 7–50.

Gatewood Jr, William B. *Black Americans and the white Man's Burden, 1898–1903.* Urbana: University of Illinois Press, 1975.

Gattegno, Caleb. *What We Owe Children.* New York:Avon Books, 1971.

Gay, Ruth. *The Jews of Germany.* New Haven: Yale University Press, 1992.

Geddes, Patrick, and J. Arthur Thomson. *Sex.* London: William & Norgate, 1911.

———. *Evolution.* New York: Holt, 1911.

Geertz, Clifford. "The Growth of Culture and the Evolution of Mind," In *Theories of the Mind,* edited by Jordan Scher. New York: Free Press, 1962.

Geist, Valerius. *Life Strategies, Human Evolution, Environmental Design: Toward a Biological Theory of Health.* New York: Springer-Verlag, 1978.

Gelb, S. A., G. E. Allen, A. Futterman, and B. Mehler, "Rewriting Mental Testing History: The View from the American Psychologist." *Sage Race Relations Abstracts* (1986): 18–31.

Gell, Frank. *Black Badge: Confessions of a Case Worker.* New York: Harper & Row, 1969.

Gellner, Ernest. *Nations and Nationalism.* Ithaca: Cornell Univeristy Press, 1983.

———. *Conditions of Liberty: Civil Society and its Rivals.* New York: Penguin Press, 1994.

Genovese, Eugene D. "The Slave South: An Interpretation." *Science & Society* 25 (1962): 320–37.

———. *The Political Economy of Slavery.* New York: Pantheon Books, 1965. Reprint. Middletown, CT: Wesleyan University Press, 1989.

———. *The World the Slaveholders Made.* New York: Pantheon Books, 1969.

George, Katherine. "The Civilized West Looks at Primitive Africa: 1400–1800. A Study in Ethnocentrism." *Isis* 49 (1958): 62–72.

Gerard, Ralph. "Higher Levels of Integration." *Biological Symposia* 8 (1942): 67–87.

Gerhart, Gail M. *Black Power in South Africa: The Evolution of an Ideology.* Berkeley: University of Calfornia Press, 1978.

Gernet, Louis. *The Anthropology of Ancient Greece.* Baltimore: Johns Hopkins University Press, 1981.

Getches, David H., Charles F. Wilkinson, and Robert A. Williams, Jr. *Federal Indian Law: Cases and Materials*. 3d ed. St Paul, MN: West Publishing, 1993.

Gibbs, Henry. *Twilight in South Africa*. New York: Philosophical Library, 1950.

Gibson, R. W. *The Morality of Nature*. New York: Putnam, 1923.

Gilbert, Martin. *Auschwitz and the Allies*. New York: Holt, Rinehart & Winston, 1981.

———. *The Holocaust: A History of the Jews of Europe During the Second World War*. New York: Holt, Rinehart & Winston, 1986.

Gill, Anton. *The Journey Back From Hell*. New York: William Morrow, 1989.

Gill, Dawn, Barbara Mayor, and Maud Blair, eds. *Racism and Education*. Thousand Oaks, CA: Sage Publications, 1992.

Gill, Owen, and Barbara Jackson. *Adoption and Race: Black, Asian, and Mixed Race Children in White Families*. London: Batsford/St. Martin's, 1983.

Gillham, Nicholas W. "Geographical Variation and the Subspecies Concept in Butterflies." *Systematic Zoology* 5(3) 1956): 110–20.

Gillin, John. "'Race' Relations without Conflict: A Guatemalan Town." *American Journal of Sociology* 53 (1948): 337–43.

———, ed. *For a Science of Social Man*. New York: Macmillan, 1954.

Gilman, Sander L. *Jewish Self-Hatred: Anti-Semitism and the Hidden Languages of the Jews*. Baltimore: John Hopkins University Press, 1986.

Ginsberg, Morris. *Sociology*. London: Butterworth, 1932.

———. "Anti-Semitism." *Sociological Review* 35 (1943): 1–11.

———. "National Character." *British Journal of Psychology* 32 (1942): 196–204.

Ginsburg, Benson E., and William Laughlin. "The Multiple Bases of Human Adaptability and Achievement: A Species Point of View." *Eugenics Quarterly* 13 (1966): 240–57.

Ginzberg, Elie, and Alfred S. Eichner. *The Troublesome Presence: American Democracy and the Negro*. New York: The Free Press, 1964.

Ginzberg, Elie, et al. *The Middle Class Negro in the White Man's World*. New York: Columbia University Press, 1967.

Ginzburg, Ralph. *100 Years of Lynchings*. New York: Lancer Books, 1962.

Gioseffi, Daniela. *On Prejudice: A Global Perspective*. New York: Anchor Books, 1993.

Girant, Marcel. *Le Métis canadien*. Paris: Institut d'Ethnologie, 1950.

Girdner, Audrie, and Anne Loftis. *The Great Betrayal*. New York: Macmillan, 1960.

Gittler, Joseph B., ed. *Social Thought Among the Early Greeks*. Athens: University of Georgia Press, 1941.

———, ed. *Understanding Minority Groups*. New York: Wiley, 1956.

Gladwin, Thomas. *Slaves of the White Myth: The Psychology of Neocolonialism*. Atlantic Highlands, NJ: Humanities Press, 1980.

Glaser, S. "Sweat Glands in the Negro and the European." *American Journal of Physical Anthropology* 17 (1934): 371–76.

Glasgow, Douglass G. "Brazil's Black Underclass." *New York Times*, 30 November 1984, A30.

Glass, Bentley. *Genes and the Man*. New York: Teachers College, Columbia University, 1943.

Glass, Bentley, and C. C. Li. "The Dynamics of Racial Intermixture—An Analysis Based on the American Negro." *American Journal of Human Genetics* 5 (1953): 1–20.

Glassman, Bernard. *Anti-Semitic Stereotypes without Jews: Images of the Jews in England, 1290–1700*. Detroit: Wayne State University Press, 1975.

Glazer, N. "Ethnic Groups in America." In *Freedom and Control in Modern Society*, edited by M. Berger, et al., 156–73. New York: Van Nostrand, 1944.

———. *Affirmative Discrimination*. New York: Basic Books, 1976.

Glazer, Nathan, and Daniel P. Moynihan. *Beyond the Melting Pot*. Cambridge: MIT Press and Harvard University Press, 1963.

———, eds. *Ethnicity: Theory and Experience*. Cambridge: Harvard University Press, 1975.

Glicksberg, Charles I. "Intercultural Education." *Common Ground* 6 (1946): 61–68.

Glock, Charles Y., and Rodney Stark. *Christian Beliefs and Anti-Semitism*. New York: Harper & Row, 1966.

Glock, Charles Y., Gertrude J. Selznick, and Joe L. Spaeth. *The Apathetic Majority: A Study Based on Public Responses to the Eichmann Trial*. New York: Harper & Row, 1966.

Gobineau, Joseph A. de, Count. *Essai sur l'inégalité des races humaines*. Translated by H. Hotz, *The Moral and Intellectual Diversity of Races*. Philadelphia: Lippincott, 1856; Paris, 1853–55.

———. *The Renaissance*, with an introductory essay by Oscar Levy. Translated by Paul V. Cohn. London: Allen & Unwin, 1927.

Goddard, H. H. *The Kallikak Family, a Study in the Heredity of Feeblemindedness*. New York: Macmillan, 1912.

Goddard, H.H. "Mental Tests and the Immigrant." *Journal of Delinquency* 2 (1917): 243–77.

Godsell, Philip H. "Is There Time To Save the Eskimo?" *Natural History* 61 (1952): 56–62.

Goldberg, Michel. *Namesake*. New Haven: Yale University Press, 1982.

Goldberger, Leo. *The Rescue of the Danish Jews: Moral Courage Under Stress*. New York: New York University Press, 1987.

Goldberger, Leo, and Shlomo Breznitz, eds. *Handbook of Stress; Theoretical and Clinical Aspects*. New York; Free Press, 1995.

Goldhagen, Daniel Jonah. *Hitler's Willing Executioners: Ordinary Germans and the Holocaust*. New York: Alfred A. Knopf, 1996.

Golding, William. *Lord of the Flies*. New York: Harcourt, Brace & Co., 1954.

Goldschmidt, E., ed. *Genetics of Isolate and Migrant Populations*. Baltimore: Williams & Wilkins, 1963.

Goldschmidt, Richard. "Anthropological Determination of 'Aryanism.'" *Journal of Heredity* 33 (1942): 215–16.

Goldsmith, Oliver. "On National Prejudices." *The Miscellaneous Works*. New York: Putnam, 1850.

Goldstein, Marcus S. *Demographic and Bodily Changes in Descendants of Mexican Immigrants*. Austin: Institute of Latin-American Studies, 1943.

Goldstein, Nathaniel L. "New York Proves It: Laws CAN Cut Discrimination." *Christian Century* 127 (1948): 30–32.

Goleman, Daniel, "Anti-Semitism: A Prejudice that Takes Many Guises." *New York Times*, 4 September 1984, C1–C2.

Golin, Milton. "How Deadly the Thought." *Journal of the American Medical Association* 171 (1959): 148–54.

Gollnitz, G. "Uber die Problematik der Neurosen im Kindesalter." *Ideggyogyasazatio Szemle* 16 (1963–64): 97–108.

Good, Paul. "Blue Notes from Dixie." *The Nation* 203 (1966): 570–75.

Goodall, Jane. "My Life among Wild Chimpanzees." *National Geographic* 124 (1963): 272–308.

Goodman, Alan. "Bred in the Bone?" *The Sciences*. March/April 1997: 20–25.

Goodman, Mary E. *Race Awareness in Young Children*. New York: Collier Books, 1964.

Goodman, Richard M. "Various Genetic Traits and Diseases Among the Jewish Ethnic Groups." In *Medical Genetics Today*, edited by Daniel Bergsma, 205–19. Baltimore: Johns Hopkins University Press, 1974

Goodwin, June. *Cry Amandla!: South African Women and the Question of Power.* New York: Africana Publishing, 1984.

Gordon, Albert. *Intermarriage*. Boston: Beacon Press, 1964.

Gordon, Bertram M. *Collaborationism in France During the Second World War.* Ithaca: Cornell University Press, 1980.

Gordon, Charles. "Ineligible Aliens." *New Republic* 112 (1945): 502–3.

Gordon, M. M. "Social Structure and Goals in Group Relations." In *Freedom and Control in Modern Society*, edited by M. Berger et al., 141–57. New York: Van Nostrand, 1944.

———. *Assimilation in American Life*. New York: Oxford University Press, 1964.

———. *Human Nature, Class and Ethnicity*. New York: Oxford University Press, 1978.

Gordon, M. M., and J. P. Roche. "Segregation—Two Edged Sword." *New York Times Magazine*, 25 April 1954.

Gordon, Paul, and Francesca Klug. *New Right New Racism*. London: Searchlight, 1986.

Gorer, G. *African Dances*. New York: Alfred A. Knopf, 1935.

———. "Some Notes on the British Character." *Horizon* 29 (1949–50): 369–79.

Gossett, Thomas F. *Race: The History of an Idea in America*. Dallas: Southern Methodist University Press, 1963.

Gould, Stephen Jay. *The Mismeasure of Man*. New York: Norton, 1981.

———. "The Geometer of Race." *Discover* 15, 1994, 64–69.

Gowen, John W. *Heterosis*. New York: Hafner Publishing, 1964.

Graeber, Isacque, and Steuart H. Britt, eds. *Jews in a Gentile World*. New York: Macmillan, 1942.

Grambs, Jean D. *Group Processes in Intergroup Education*. New York: National Council of Christians and Jews, 1953.

Grant, Douglas. *The Fortunate Slave: An Illustration of African Slavery in the Eighteenth Century*. New York: Oxford University Press, 1968.

Grant, Madison. *The Passing of the Great Race*. New York: Scribner, 1st ed., 1916; 2d ed., 1918; 3d ed., 1919; 4th ed., 1921.

Grant, Michael, ed. *The Birth of Western Civilization*. New York: McGraw-Hill, 1965.

Graubard, Mark. *Man, the Slave and Master.* New York: Covici, Friede, 1938.

Graubard, Stephen R., ed. "The Negro American." *Daedalus,* Fall 1965.

Grebler, Leo, Joan W. Moore, and Ralph C. Guzman. *The Mexican-American People.* New York: Macmillan, 1970.

Green, Graham. "African Chequerboard." *The Listener* (London) 74 (1965): 421–22.

Green, Peter. "Downtreading the Demos." *The Times Literary Supplement* (London) 11 February 1983.

Green, Philip. *The Pursuit of Inequality.* New York: Pantheon, 1981.

Greenberg, Jack. *Race Relations and American Law.* New York: Columbia University Press, 1959.

Greenberg, Jonathan. *Staking A Claim.* New York: Atheneum, 1990.

Greene, Jack P. and J. R. Pole, eds. *Colonial British America: Essays in the New History of the Modern Era.* Baltimore: Johns Hopkins University Press, 1984.

Greene, John C. "The American Debate on the Negro's Place in Nature." *Journal of the History of Ideas* 15 (1954): 384–96.

———."Some Early Speculations on the Origin of Human Races." *American Anthropologist* 46 (1954): 31–41.

———. *Science, Ideology, and World View: Essays in the History of Evolutionary Ideas.* Berkeley: University of California Press, 1982.

Greene, Lorenzo J. *The Negro in Colonial New England.* New York: Atheneum, 1968.

Greene, Mary F., and Orletta Ryan. *The Schoolchildren: Growing Up in the Slums.* New York: Pantheon, 1966.

Greenfield, L. *Nationalism: Five Roads to Modernity.* Cambridge: Harvard University Press, 1992.

Greer, Colin, ed. *Divided Society: The Ethnic Experience in America.* New York: Basic Books, 1974.

Gressman, Eugene. "The Unhappy History of Civil Rights Legislation." In *Michigan Law Review* 50(8): 1323–58.

Grier, William H., and Price M. Cobbs. *Black Rage.* New York; Basic Books, 1968.

Griffin, John H. *Black Like Me.* Boston: Houghton Mifflin Co., 1961.

Grimes, Alan P. *Equality in America.* New York: Oxford University Press, 1964.

Grimshaw, Allen D., ed. *Racial Violence in the United States.* Chicago: Aldine Publishing, 1969.

Grobman, Arnold B., ed. *Social Implications of Biological Education.* Princeton: Darwin Press, 1970.

Grodzins, Milton M. *Americans Betrayed.* Chicago: University of Chicago Press, 1949.

Gross, Leonard. *The Last Jews in Berlin.* New York: Simon & Schuster, 1982.

Grotberg, E., ed. *Critical Issues in Research Related to Disadvantaged Children.* Princeton: Educational Testing Service, 1969.

Gruber, Samuel. *I Chose Life.* New York: Shengold Publishers, 1978.

Guillaume-Louis, P., and Louis Dubreuil-Chambardel. "Le Cerveau d'Anatole France." *Bulletin de l'Academie de Médecine* (Paris) 98 (1927): 328–36.

Gussman, Boris. *Out in the Mid-day Sun.* New York: Oxford University Press, 1963.

Guthrie, James W., et al. *Schools and Inequality.* Cambridge: MIT Press, 1971.

Gutman, Amy. *Democratic Education.* Princeton: Princeton University Press, 1987.

Gutman, Herbert G. *The Black Family in Slavery & Freedom, 1750–1925.* New York: Pantheon, 1976.

Gutman, Yisrael. *The Jews of Warsaw, 1939–1943: Ghetto, Underground, Revolt.* Bloomington: Indiana University Press, 1982.

Gutman, Israel, editor-in-chief. *Encyclopedia of the Holocaust.* 4 vols. New York: Macmillan, 1990.

Gutman, Yisrael and Michael Berenbaum. *Anatomy of the Auschwitz Death Camp.* Bloomington: Indiana University Press, 1994.

Gutman, Yisrael and Shmuel Krakowski. *Unequal Victims: Poles and Jews During World War II.* New York: Holocaust Library, 1986.

Guyette, Susan. *Planning for Balanced Development: A Guide for Native American Communities.* Sponsored by the Pueblo of Pojoaque. Santa Fe: Clear Light Publications, 1996.

Gyorgy, P., and O. L. Kline, eds. *Malnutrition is a Problem of Ecology.* Basel and New York: Karger, 1970.

Haarhoff, T. J. *The Stranger at the Gate.* New York: Macmillan, 1948.

Haas, Ernest B. *Beyond the Nation State: Functionalism and International Organization.* Stanford: Stanford University Press, 1969.

Hacker, Andrew. *The Persistence of Inequality: Black and White, Separate, Hostile, Unequal.* New York: Scribner's (Macmillan), 1992.

Haddon, Alfred C. *The Races of Man.* Cambridge: Cambridge University Press, 1924.

———. *History of Anthropology.* London: Watts, 1934.

Hagmeier, Edwin M. "Inapplicability of the Subspecies Concept to North American Marten." *Systematic Zoology* 7(1) (1958): 1–7.

Hahn, Eduard. *Die Haustiere.* Leipzig: Duncker und Humbolt, 1896.

Haksar, Vinit. *Heredity and Politics.* New York: Norton, 1938.

———. *New Paths in Genetics.* New York: Harper, 1942.

———. "The Interaction of Nature and Nurture." *Annals of Eugenics* 13 (1946): 196–205.

———. *Equality, Liberty, and Perfectionism.* New York: Oxford University Press, 1979.

Haldane, J. B. S. *The Causes of Evolution.* New York: Longmans, 1932.

———. *Heredity and Politics.* New York: Norton, 1938.

———. "The Argument from Animals to Men." In *Culture and the Evolution of Man,* edited by Ashley Montagu, 65–83. New York: Oxford University Press, 1962.

Hall, E. Raymond. "Zoological Subspecies of Man at the Peace Table." *Journal of Mammalogy* 27 (1946): 358–64.

Hall, William S., and Roy O. Freedle. *Culture and Language: The Black American Experience.* New York: Wiley, 1975.

Halle, Louis J. "Myths and Hopes." *Encounter* 22 (1962): 25.

———. *The Ideological Imagination.* New York: Oxford University Press, 1972.

Haller, John S., Jr. "The Species Problem: Nineteenth-Century Concepts of Racial Inferiority in the Origin of Man Controversy." *American Anthropologist* 72 (1970): 1319–29.

———. *Outcasts from Evolution: Scientific Attitudes of Racial Inferiority.* Urbana: University of Illinois Press, 1971.

Haller, Mark H. *Eugenics: Hereditarian Attitudes in American Thought.* New Brunswick: Rutgers University Press, 1963.

Halligan, Alice L. "A Community's Total War Against Prejudice." *Journal of Educational Sociology* 16 (1943): 374—80.

Hallowell, A. Irving. "Some Psychological Characteristics of the Northeastern Indians." In *Man in Northeastern North America.* Papers of the R. S. Peabody Foundation for Archaeology 3 (1946): 195–225.

———. *Culture and Experience.* Philadelphia: University of Pennsylvania Press, 1955.

Halpern, Ben. *The American Jew: A Zionist Analysis.* New York: Schocken Books, 1983.

Halpern, Florence. *Survival: Black/White.* New York: Pergamon Press, 1973.

Halsell, Grace. *Black-White Sex.* New York: William Morrow, 1972.

Hambly, Wilfrid D. "Primitive Warfare." *Chicago Natural History Museum Bulletin* 17(1946): 4–5.

————*The Origins of Education Among Primitive People.* London: Macmillan, 1926.

Hampden-Turner, Charles. *From Poverty to Dignity: A Strategy for Poor Americans.* New York: Doubleday, 1974.

Hance, William A., ed. *Southern Africa and the United States.* New York: Columbia University Press.

Handlin, Oscar and Lilian Handlin. *Liberty and Equality 1920–1924.* New York: HarperCollins, 1994.

Handlin, Oscar. *Race and Nationality in American Life.* Boston: Little, Brown, 1957.

Hanhart, Ernst. "Infectious Diseases." In *Clinical Genetics,* edited by Arnold Sorsby. St. Louis: Mosby, 1953.

Hanke, Lewis. *Aristotle and the American Indians.* Bloomington: Indiana University Press, 1959.

————. "The Dawn of Conscience in America: Spanish Experiments and Experiences with Indians in the New World." *Proceedings of the American Philosophical Society* 107 (1963): 83–92.

Hankins, Frank H. *The Racial Basis of Civilization.* New York: Alfred A. Knopf, 1931.

Hanlon, Joseph. *Beggar Your Neighbors: Apartheid Power in South Africa.* Bloomington: Indiana University Press, 1987.

Hannerz, Ulf. *Soulside: Inquiries into Ghetto Culture and Community.* New York: Columbia University Press, 1969.

Hardin, Russell. *One for All: The Logic of Group Conflict.* Princeton: Princeton University Press, 1995.

Harding, Robert S. O., and Geza Teleki, eds. *Omniverous Primates.* New York: Columbia University Press, 1981.

Harding, Vincent. *There is a River: The Black Struggle for Freedom in America.* New York: Harcourt, Brace, & Jovanovich, 1981.

Harlan, Louis R. *Separate and Unequal.* New York: Atheneum, 1968.

Harlow, H. F. "The Formation of Learning Sets." *Psychological Review* 56 (1949): 51–65.

————. "Learning and Satiation of Response in Intrinsically Motivated Complex Puzzle Performance by Monkeys." *Journal of Comparative and Physiological Psychology* 43 (1958): 289–94.

Harper, Ida H. *The Life and Works of Susan B. Anthony.* Indianapolis: Bowen-Merrill Co., 1898. Reprint. Indianapolis: The Hollenbeck Press, 1908.

Harper, William. *A Memoir on Slavery.* Charleston: Burges, 1838.

Harris, Dale. *The Concept of Behavior: An Issue in the Study of Human Behavior.* Minneapolis: University of Minnesota Press, 1957.

Harris, D. B., H. G. Gough, and W. E. Martin. "Children's Ethnic Attitudes: II, Relationships to Parental Beliefs Concerning Child Training." *Child Development* 21 (1950): 169–81.

Harris, Marvin. *Town and Country in Brazil.* New York: Columbia University Press, 1956.

————. "Caste, Class, and Minority." *Social Forces* 37 (1958): 246–54.

————. *Patterns of Race in the Americas.* New York: Walker & Co., 1964.

Harrison, David. *The White Tribe of Africa: South Africa in Perspective.* Berkeley: University of California Press, 1981.

Harrison, G. A. "The Biological Effects of Miscegenation." In *Patterns of Dominance,* P. Mason. New York: Oxford University Press, 1970.

Harrison, G., et al. *Human Biology.* 2d ed. New York: Oxford University Press, 1977.

Harrisson Barbara. *Orang-Utan.* New York: Doubleday, 1963.

Harrrison, John. *The Reactionaries.* New York: Schocken Books, 1967.

Hart, C. W. M. "The Race Myth." *University of Toronto Quarterly* 11 (1942): 180–88.

Hart, Liddell. *Through the Fog of War.* New York: Random House, 1938.

Hartley, Eugene. *Problems in Prejudice.* New York: King's Crown Press, 1946.

Hartman, Walter. "Ethnic Differences." *Perspectives in Biology and Medicine* 5 (1961): 136–38.

Hartmann, H., E. Kris, and M. Lowenstein. "Notes on the Theory of Aggression." *The Psychoanalytic Study of the Child* 3/4. (1949): 9–36.

Hatfield, Henry, "The Myth of Nazism." In *Myth and Mythmaking,* edited by Henry R. Murray, 199–220. New York: George Braziller, 1960.

Havelock, Ellis. *Man & Woman.* 8th ed. London: A. & C. Black, 1934.

Hawkes, Jacquetta. *Early Britain.* London: William Collins, 1945.

Hawkins, David. *The Science and Ethics of Equality.* New York: Basic Books, 1977.

Hay, Malcolm Vivian. *The Foot of Pride.* Boston: Beacon Press, 1950.

————. *Europe and the Jews.* Boston: Beacon Press, 1960.

Hayakawa, S. I. *Language in Action.* New York: Harcourt, Brace, 1941.

————. "Race and Words." *Common Sense* 12 (1943): 231–35.

Hayes, Peter. *Lessons and Legacies: The Meaning of the Holocaust in a Changing World.* Evanston, IL: Northwestern University Press, 1991.

Haynal, Andre, Miklos Molnar, and Gerard de Puymege. *Fanaticism: A Historical and Psychoanalytical Study.* New York: Schocken Books, 1983.

Haynes, Robert V., ed. *Blacks in White America Before 1865.* New York: David McKay, 1972.

Heath, Dwight, and Richard Adams, eds. *Contemporary Cultures and Societies of Latin America.* New York: Random House, 1965.

Hechst, Bela. "Über einen Fall von Mikroencephalie ohne Geistigen Defekt." *Archiv für Psychiatrie und Nervenkrankheiten* 97 (1932): 64–76.

Heiser, Victor. *An American Doctor's Odyssey.* New York: Norton, 1936.

Heiss, Jerold. *The Case of the Black Family: A Sociological Study.* New York: Columbia University Press, 1975.

Heizer, Robert F., and Alan F. Almquist. *The Other Californians.* Berkeley: University of California Press, 1971.

Heller, Celia S. *On the Edge of Destruction: The Jews of Poland Between the Two World Wars.* New York: Columbia University Press, 1977.

Hellman, Ellen, and Leah Abrahams. *Handbook on Race Relations in South Africa.* London: Oxford University Press, 1949.

Hellman, Peter. *The Auschwitz Album.* New York: Random House, 1981.

Helm, J. D., and M. H. Jacobs. "Some Apparent Differences between the Erythrocytes of White and Negro Subjects." *Journal of Cellular and Comparative Physiology* 22 (1943): 43–50.

Henderson, N. D. "Brain Weight Increases Resulting from Environmental Enrichment: A Directional Dominance in Mice." *Science* 169 (1970): 776–78.

Henriques, Fernando. *Children of Caliban.* New York: Dutton, 1974.

Hentoff, Nat. *The New Equality.* New York: Viking Press, 1964.

Herbert, Xavier. *Capricornia.* New York: Appleton-Century, 1943.

Herder, Johann G. von. *Outlines of a Philosophy of the History of Man.* Translated by T. Churchill from *Ideen zur Philosophie der Geschichte der Menschheit.* Riga, 1784; London: J. Johnson, 1803.

Herford, H. Travers. "The Meaning of Anti-Semitism." *The Hibbert Journal* 42 (1944): 341–47.

Hernton, Calvin C. *Sex and Racism in America.* Garden City, N.Y.: Doubleday, 1965.

Herrick, C. Judson. "A Neurologist Makes up His Mind." *Scientific Monthly* 50 (1939): 99–110.

Herrnstein, Richard J. *I.Q. in the Meritocracy.* Boston: Atlantic Monthly Press/Little Brown, 1973.

Herrnstein, Richard J., and Charles Murray. *The Bell Curve: Intelligence and Class Structure in American Life.* New York: Free Press, 1994.

Herskovits, Melville J. *The American Negro.* New York: Alfred A. Knopf, 1928.

———. "Social Selection and the Formation of Human Types." *Human Biology* 1 (1929): 250–62.

———. *The Anthropometry of the American Negro.* New York: Columbia University Press, 1930.

———. "Domestication." *Encyclopedia of the Social Sciences.* Vol. 3. (1937): 206–08. New York.

———. *The Myth of the Negro Past.* New York: Harper, 1941.

———. "Who Are the Jews?" In *The Jews: Their History, Culture, and Religion II,* edited by Louis Finkelstein, 1151–71. New York: Harper, 1949.

———. "Rear-Guard Action." *Perspectives in Biology and Medicine* 5 (1961): 122–28.

Hertz, Friedrich. *Race and Civilization.* London: Kegan Paul, 1928.

———. *Nationality in History and Politics: A Study of the Psychology and Sociology of National Sentiment and Character.* London: Kegan Paul, 1944.

———. *Nationalism.* London: Routledge, 1944.

Hiernaux, Jean. "The Concept of Race and the Taxonomy of Mankind." In *The Concept of Race,* edited by Ashley Montagu, 30–45. New York: Free Press, 1964.

———. "Hétérosis et Dominance dans les Populations Humaines." *Comptes Rendus Académie des Sciences* 209 (1964): 4357–60.

———. "Adaptation and Race." *Advancement of Science* (1967): 658–62.

———. "Ethnic Differences in Growth and Development." *Eugenics Quarterly* 15 (1968): 12–21.

———. *Égalité ou Inègalité des Races.* Paris: Hachette, 1969.

———. "The Analysis of Multivariate Biological Distances Between Human Populations: Principles and Applications to Subsaharan Africa. " In *The Assessment of*

Population Affinities in Man, edited by J. S. Weiner and J. Huizinga, 96–114. Oxford: Clarendon Press, 1972.

———. "Numerical Taxonomy of Man: An Application of a Set of Thirty-Two African Populations." In *Physical Anthropology and its Extending Horizons,* edited by A. Basu, et al. Calcutta: Orient Longman, 1973.

———. *The Peoples of Africa.* London: Weidenfeld & Nicolson, 1974.

———. "Le Decoupage de l'Humanité Actuelle en Taxons." *Bulletin et Memoires de la Société d'Anthropologie de Paris* 5, Ser. 13 (1978): 281–85.

Hiernaux, Jean, and Heintz N. Hiernaux. "Croissance Biometrique des Franco-Vietnamiens." *Bulletins et Mémoires de la Sociétié d' Anthropologie de Paris* 1, Série XIIe, (1967): 55–89.

Higginbotham, A. Leon, Jr. *In the Matter of Color: Race and The American Legal Process: The Colonial Period.* New York: Oxford University Press, 1978.

Higham, John. *Send These to Me: Immigrants in Urban America.* Revised. Baltimore: Johns Hopkins University Press, 1984.

———. *Strangers in the Land.* New Brunswick, NJ: Rutgers University Press, 1955.

———, ed. *Ethnic Leadership in America.* Baltimore & London: Johns Hopkins University Press, 1978.

Highet, Gilbert. *Man's Unconquerable Mind.* New York: Columbia University Press, 1954.

Hilberg, Raul. *The Destruction of the European Jews.* Revised and definitive ed. New York: Holmes & Mier, 1985.

Hill, J. Eric. "A Zoologist Looks at Raciology: A Reply to Dr. E. Raymond Hall's 'Zoological Subspecies at the Peace Table.'" *Journal of Mammalogy* 28 (1947): 87–89.

Hill, Robert, ed. *The F. B. I.'s Racon: Racial Conditions in the United States During World War II.* Boston: Northeastern University Press, 1995.

Himmelfarb, Gertrude. *Lord Acton: A Study in Conscience and Politics.* Chicago: University of Chicago Press, 1952.

Hippocrates. *Airs, Waters, and Places.* Vol. 1. Translated by W. H. S. Jones. Cambridge: Harvard University Press, 1923.

Hiro, Dilip. *Black British, White British.* New York: Monthly Review Press, 1974.

Hirsch, Arnold R. *Making the Second Ghetto: Race and Housing in Chicago: 1940–1960.* New York: Cambridge University Press, 1983.

Hirsch, Jerry, "To 'Unfrock the Charlatans.'" *Sage Race Relations Abstracts* 6 (1981): 1–68.

———, ed. *Behavior-Genetic Analysis.* New York: McGraw-Hill, 1967.

Hirschfeld, Magnus. *Men and Women.* New York: Putnam, 1935.

———. *Racism.* London: Gollancz, 1938.

Hirschfelder, Arlene. *Happily May I Walk: American Indians and Alaska Natives Today.* New York: Scribners, 1986.

Hitler, Adolf. *Mein Kampf.* Originally published in Munich, 1925. Translated by Ralph Manheim. Boston: Houghton Mifflin, 1943.

Hoagland, Jim. *South Africa: Civilizations in Conflict.* Boston: Houghton Mifflin, 1972.

Hobson, J. A. *Imperialism: A Study.* 2d ed. London: Allen & Unwin, 1965; Ann Arbor: University of Michigan Press Press, 1965.

Hochschild, Jennifer L. *The New American Dilemma: Liberal Democracy and School Desegregation.* New Haven: Yale University Press, 1984.

Hodgkinson, Harold L. *The Demographics of American Indians,* 24 (Washington, D.C.: Institute for Educational Leadership, 1990).

———. *The Current Condition of Native Americans.* ERIC Digest 348202. Charleston: ERIC Clearinghouse on Rural Education and Small Schools, 1992.

Hoetink, Harmannus. *Slavery and Race Relations in the Americas.* New York: Harper & Row, 1973.

Hoffman, Frederick L. "Miscegenation in Hawaii." *Journal of Heredity* 8 (1917): 12.

Hofstadter, Richard. *Social Darwinism in American Thought, 1860–1915.* Boston: Beacon Press, 1961.

Hogben, Lancelot. *Genetic Principles in Medicine and Social Science.* London: Williams & Norgate 1931.

———. *Nature and Nurture.* New York: W. W. Norton, 1933.

———. *Dangerous Thoughts.* New York: Norton, 1940.

———, ed. *Political Arithmetic.* New York: Macmillan, 1938.

Hokanson, Jack E. "The Effects of Guilt Arousal and Severity of Discipline on Adult Aggressive Behavior." *Journal of Clinical Psychology* 17 (1961): 29–32.

Holbé T. V. "Métis de Cochinchine." *Revue Anthropologique* 24 (1914): 281–93; 26 (1916): 449–66.

Holleman, J. F. *African Interlude.* Johannesburg: National Bockhandel, 1959.

Holmes, Colin. *Anti-Semitism in British Society, 1876–1939.* London, Edward Arnold, 1979.

Holmes, S. J. *The Negro's Struggle for Survival.* Berkeley: University of California Press, 1937.

———. *Life and Morals.* New York: Macmillan, 1948.

Holsti, Rudolf. *The Relation of War to the Origin of the State.* Helsingfors: New Printing Co., 1913.

Holt, Anne. *Walking Together.* London: Allen & Unwin, 1938.

Homel, Michael W. *Down from Equality.* Urbana: University of Illinois Press, 1984.

Homma, H. "On Apocrine Sweat Glands in White and Negro Men and Women." *Johns Hopkins Hospital Bulletin* 38 (1926): 367–71.

Honig, Emily. *Creating Chinese Ethnicity: Subei People in Shanghai 1850–1980.* New Haven; Yale University Press, 1992.

Honigsheim, Paul. "Voltaire as Anthropologist." *American Anthropologist* 47 (1945): 104–8.

Hood, M. S. F. "The Aegean Before the Greeks." In *The Dawn of Civilization,* edited by Stuart Piggott. New York: McGraw Hill, 1961, 219–28.

Hook, Sidney. *Reason, Social Myths, and Democracy.* New York: John Day, 1941.

———. "Naturalism and Democracy." In *Naturalism and the Human Spirit,* edited by Y. V. Krikorian, 40–64. New York: Columbia University Press, 1944.

Hooton, Earnest. "Racial Types in America and Their Relation to Old World Types." In *The American Aborigines: Their Origin and Antiquity,* edited by Diamond Jenness, 133–63. Toronto: University of Toronto Press, 1933.

Hopson, Darlene P., and Derek S. Hopson. *Different and Wonderful: Raising Black Children in a Race-Conscious Society.* New York: Prentice-Hall, 1990.

Horowitz, Donald L. *Ethnic Groups in Conflict.* Berkeley: University of California Press, 1985.

Horowitz, E. "The Development of Attitudes Toward the Negro." *Archives of Psychology* 194 (1936).

Horowitz, Ruth. "Racial Aspects of Self Identification in Nursery School Children." *Journal of Psychology* 1 (1939): 91–99.

Horrell, Muriel. *A Survey of Race Relations in South Africa.* Johannesburg: South African Institute of Race Relations, 1962.

Horsman, Reginald. *Race and Manifest Destiny: The Origins of American Racial Anglo-Saxonism.* Cambridge: Harvard University Press, 1981.

Housman, A. E. *The Name and Nature of Poetry.* New York: Cambridge University Press, 1933.

Howe, Harold, Elinor L. Gordon, et al. *Racism and American Education.* New York: Harper & Row, 1970.

Howe, Irving, and B. J. Widick. "The U.A.W. Fights Race Prejudice." *Commentary* 8 (1949): 261–68.

Howell, Signe, and Roy Willis. *Societies at Peace: Anthropological Perspectives.* London and New York: Routledge, 1989.

Howells, W. W., ed. *Ideas on Human Evolution.* Cambridge: Harvard University Press, 1962.

Hoyle, Fred. *The Nature of the Universe.* New York: Harper, 1951.

Hrdlička, Aleš. *The Old Americans.* Baltimore: Williams & Wilkins, 1925.

Hsu, F.L.K. *Clan, Castle, and Club.* Princeton: Van Nostrand, 1963.

Huard, P., and A. Bigot. "Recherches sur Quelques Groupes Ethniques Observés en Indochine." *Travaux de l'Institut Anatomique de l'école Superieure de Médicine de l'Indochine* (Hanoi), 6 (1939).

Huddleston, Trevor. *Naught for Your Comfort.* New York: Doubleday, 1956.

Hughes, Charles C. *Eskimo Boyhood.* Lexington: University of Kentucky Press, 1974.

Hughes, Everett C., and H. M. Hughes. *Where Peoples Meet: Ethnic and Racial Frontiers.* Glencoe, IL: Free Press, 1952.

Hughes, Langston, and Milton Meltzer. *A Pictorial History of the Negro in America.* Revised. New York: Crown, 1963.

Hughes, Robert. *The Fatal Shore: The Epic of Australia's Founding.* New York: Alfred A. Knopf, 1987.

———. *Culture of Complaint: The Fraying of America.* New York: New York Public Library and Oxford University Press, 1993.

Huie, William B. *Three Lives for Mississippi.* New York: Basic Books, 1965.

Hulse, Frederick S. "Exoganie et Hétéosis." *Archives Suisse d'Anthropologie Générale* 22 (1957): 103–25.

———. "Exogamy and Heterosis." *Yearbook of Physical Anthropology* 9 (1964): 241–57.

———. "Race as an Evolutionary Episode." *American Anthropologist* 64 (1962): 929–45.

———. "Ethnic, Caste and Genetic Miscegenation." *Journal of Biosocial Science* Supp. 1 (1969): 31–41.

Humboldt, Alexander von. *Cosmos: A Sketch of a Physical Description of the Universe.* Vol. 1. Translated from the German by E. C. Otté. London: Bohn, 1849.

Humboldt, Wilhelm von. *Über die Kawi-Sprache auf der Insel Java.* Vol. 3. Berlin: Königlichen Akademie der Wissenschaften, 1836.

Hume, David. *Treatise on Human Nature,* 1720.

Humphrey, Norman D. "American Race and Caste." *Psychiatry* 4 (1941): 159–60.

————. "American Race Relations and the Caste System." *Psychiatry* 8 (1945): 379–81.

Hunt, Earl. "On the Nature of Intelligence." Science 109 (1983): 141–42.

Hunt, J. McVicker. *Intelligence and Experience.* New York: Ronald Press, 1961.

————. *The Challenge of Incompetence and Poverty.* Urbana: University of Illinois Press, 1969.

Hunt, James. "The Negro's Place in Nature." *Memoirs of the Anthropological Society* (London) 1 (1863): 1–64.

Hunt, Leigh. "Negro Civilization." *The Examiner* (London), 118 (1811).

Hunting, Claudine. "The *Philosophes* and Black Slavery: 1748–1765." *Journal of the History of Ideas* 39 (1978): 405–18.

Hurley, Denis E. *Apartheid: A Crisis of Christian Conscience.* Johannesburg: South African Institute of Race Relations, 1964.

Hurley, R. L. *Poverty and Mental Retardation: A Casual Relationship.* New York: Random House, 1969.

Huttenback, Robert A. *Racism and Empire.* Ithaca, NY: Cornell University Press, 1976.

Hutton, J. H. *Caste in India.* New York: Cambridge University Press, 1946.

Huxley, Elspeth. "Australia's Aborigines Step out of the Stone Age." *New York Times,* 20 June 1965: 10sq.

Huxley, George. "The Genesis of Greece." In *The Birth of Western Civilization,* edited by Michael Grant, 27–50. New York: McGraw-Hill, 1965).

Huxley, Julian S. *Man Stands Alone.* New York: Harper, 1941.

————. *Evolution: The Modern Synthesis.* New York: Harper, 1942.

————. *On Living in a Revolution.* London: Chatto & Windus, 1944.

————. *Heredity East and West.* New York: Schuman, 1949.

————. *Evolution in Action.* New York: Harper, 1953.

————. "Clines: An Auxiliary Taxonomic Principle." *Nature* 142: 219–20.

————, ed. *The New Systematics.* New York: Oxford University Press, 1940.

Huxley, Julian S., and Alfred S. Haddon. *We Europeans: A Survey of "Racial" Problems.* New York: Harper & Bros. 1936.

Huxley, Thomas H. "Emancipation—Black and White." *The Reader,* 20 May, 1865, 561–62.

————. "On the Methods and Results of Ethnology. " In *Man's Place in Nature,* T. H. Huxley. London: Williams & Norgate; New York: Appleton, 1865; Ann Arbor: University of Michigan Press, 1959.

————. *Man's Place in Nature and Other Anthropological Essays.* New York: Appleton & Co., 1890.

————. "Emancipation—Black and White." In *Science and Education,* T. H. Huxley, 64–71. New York: Collier, 1901.

Huxley, Thomas H., and Julian S. Huxley. *Touchstone for Ethics.* New York: Harper, 1948.

Iagrashi, M., K. Tohma, and M. Ozama. "Pathogenesis of Psychogenic Amenorrhea and Anovulation." *International Journal of Fertility* 10 (1965): 311–19.

Idriess, Ion L. *Over the Range.* Sydney: Angus & Robertson, 1937.

Ignatieff, M. *Blood and Belonging: Journeys into the New Nationalism.* New York: Viking, 1993.

Imamura, Yutaka. "What is Race?" *Hiroshima Journal of Medical Sciences* 1 (1951): 1–10.

Ingle, Dwight J. "Racial Differences and the Future." *Science* 146 (1944): 375–79.

Ingold, Tim, David Riches, and James Woodburn. *Hunters and Gatherers.* 2 vols. Oxford: Berg, 1988.

Iranek-Osmecki, Kazimierz. *He Who Saves One Life.* New York: Crown, 1971.

Irons, Peter. *Justice at War.* New York: Oxford University Press, 1983.

Irvine, S. H., and J. W. Berry, eds. *Human Assessment and Cultural Factors.* New York: Plenum, 1983.

Isaac, Jules. *The Teaching of Contempt: The Christian Roots of Anti-Semitism.* New York: Holt, Rinehart & Winston, 1964.

Isaacs, Harold R. "World Affairs and U.S. Relations: A Note on Little Rock." *The Public Opinion Quarterly* 22 (1958): 364–70.

———. "Back to Africa." *The New Yorker* 13 May 1961.

———. "American Race Relations and the United States Image in World Affairs." *Human Relations* 1 (1962): 266–80.

———. *The New World of Negro Americans.* New York: John Day, 1963.

———. *India's Untouchables.* New York: John Day, 1964.

———. *Idols of the Tribe: Group Identity and Political Change.* New York: Harper & Row, 1975.

———. *India's Ex-Untouchables.* New York: John Day, 1974.

Isaacs, Jennifer. *Australian Dreaming.* Sydney: Lansdowne Press, 1980.

Isocrates. *Panegyricus.* 4, 50. Translated by George Norlin. Loeb Classical Library, 1: xxiv, 149. Cambridge: Harvard University Press, 1928.

Jackman, Jarrell C., and Carla M. Borden, eds. *The Muses Flee Hitler: Cultural Transfer and Adaptation, 1930–1945.* Washington, D.C.: Smithsonian Institution Press, 1983.

Jackman, Mary R., and Robert W. Jackman. *Class Awareness in the United States.* Berkeley: University of California Press, 1983.

Jacks, L. P. *The Confessions of an Octogenarian.* London: Allen & Unwin, 1942.

Jackson, Fatima L. C. "Race and Ethnicities as Biological Constructs." *Ethnicity & Disease* 2 (1992): 120–25.

Jackson, Helen H. *A Century of Dishonor: A Sketch of the United States Government's Dealings with Some of the Indian Tribes.* New York: Harper Bros., 1881. Reprinted in Harper Torchbooks, 1965.

Jackson, Henry F. *From the Congo to Soweto: U.S. Foreign Policy Toward Africa Since 1960.* New York: Quill, 1984.

Jackson, Lydia. *Aggression and Its Interpretation.* London: Methuen, 1954.

Jackson, Richard L. *The Black Image in Latin American Literature.* Albuquerque: University of New Mexico Press, 1976.

Jackson, Walter A. *Gunnar Myrdal and America's Conscience.* Chapel Hill: University of North Carolina Press, 1990.

Jacob, Paul. *Prelude to Riot.* New York: Random House, 1968.

Jacob, Paul, Saul Landau, and Eve Pell. *To Serve the Devil.* 2 vols. New York: Random House, 1971.

Jacobs, Harriet A. *Incidents in the Life of a Slave Girl: Written by Herself.* Bloomington: Indiana University Press, 1987.

Jacobs, Melville, and Bernhard J. Stern. *Outline of Anthropology.* New York: Barnes & Noble, 1947.

Jacobs, Wilbur R. *Dispossessing the American Indian.* New York: Scribner's Sons, 1972.

Jacoby, Russell, and Naomi Glauberman, eds. *The Bell Curve Debate: History, Documents, Opinions.* New York: Times Books, 1995.

Jacquard, A. "Inne et acquis: mots, choses et concepts." *Bulletin et Memoires de la Societe d'Anthropologie de Paris* 5, ser. 13 (1978): 117–37.

———. *Eloge de la Difference.* Paris, Editions de Seuil, 1978. Translated into English as *In Praise of Difference.* New York: Columbia University Press, 1984

———. *Endangered by Science?* New York: Columbia University Press, 1985.

———. "Science and Racism." In *Racism, Science and Pseudo Science,* 15–49. Paris: UNESCO, 1981.

Jaimes, M. Annette. *The State of Native America: Genocide, Colonization, and Resistance.* Boston: South End Press, 1992.

James, Alice. *The Diary of Alice James.* Edited by Leon Edel. New York: Dodd, Mead, 1964.

James, H. E. O., and Cora Tenen. "Grievances and Their Displacement." *Occupational Psychology* (1946): 1–7.

James, Patricia. *Population Malthus: His Life and Times.* London: Routledge & Kegan Paul, 1979.

James, Thomas. *Exile Within: The Schooling of Japanese Americans, 1942–1945.* Bloomington: Indiana University Press, 1987.

Jamieson, Kathleen Hall. *Dirty Politics, Deception, Distraction, and Democracy.* New York: Oxford University Press, 1992.

Janowsky, Oscar I. *Nationalities and National Minorities.* New York: Macmillan, 1945.

Jaspers, Karl. *The Question of German Guilt.* New York: Dial Press, 1947.

Jastrow, Joseph. *The Story of Human Error.* New York: Appleton-Century, 1936.

Javits, Jacob J. *Discrimination—U.S.A.* New York: Harcourt, Brace, 1960.

Jefferson, Thomas. "Notes on the State of Virginia, 1781–1785." In *The Complete Jefferson,* edited by Saul K. Padover, 567–97. New York: Tudor Publishing.

Jell-ahlsen, Sabine. "Ethnology and Fascism in Germany." *Dialectical Anthropology* 9 (1985): 313–35.

Jencks, Christopher. *Inequality.* New York: Basic Books, 1972.

Jenkins, Daniel. *Equality and Education.* London: SCM Press, 1961.

Jenkins, William S. *Pro-slavery Thought in the Old South.* Chapel Hill: University of North Carolina Press, 1935.

Jenks, Albert E. *Indian-White Amalgamation: an Anthropometric Study.* University of Minnesota Studies in the Social Sciences No. 6. Minneapolis, 1916.

Jennings, Francis. *The Invasion of America.* Chapel Hill: University of North Carolina Press, 1975.

Jennings, Herbert S. *Prometheus.* New York: Dutton, 1925.

————. *The Biological Basis of Human Nature*. New York: Norton, 1930.

————. *Genetics*. New York: Norton, 1935.

————. "The Laws of Heredity and Our Present Knowledge of Human Genetics on the Material Side." In *Scientific Aspects of the Race Problem*, edited by J. W. Corrigan, 71–72. New York: Longmans, 1941.

Jensen, Arthur R. "How Much Can We Boost IQ Scores and Scholastic Achievement?" *Harvard Educational Review* 39 (1969): 1–123.

————. *Educability & Group Differences*. New York: Harper & Row, 1973.

————. *Genetics and Education*. New York: Harper & Row, 1973.

————. *Bias in Mental Testing*. New York: Free Press, 1980.

Jersild, A. T., and F. B. Holms. "Children's Fears." *Child Development Monographs* 20. New York: Teachers College, Columbia University, 1935.

Joffe, J. M. *Prenatal Determinants of Behavior*. New York: Pergamon Press, 1969.

Johnson, Alvin. "Race in the World to Come." *Yale Review* 33 (1943): 193–200.

Johnson, Charles S. "Race Relations and Social Change." In *Race Relations and the Race Problem*, edited by Edgar T. Thompson, 271–303. Durham: Duke University Press, 1939.

————. *Patterns of Negro Segregation*. New York: Harper, 1943.

————. *Being & Race: Black Writing Since 1970*. Bloomington: Indiana University Press, 1989.

Johnson, F. Ernest, ed. *Foundations of Democracy*. New York: Harper, 1947.

Johnson, Roger N. *Aggression in Man and Animals*. Philadelphia: Saunders, 1972.

Johnson, Shaun, ed. *South Africa: No Turning Back*. Bloomington: Indiana University Press, 1989.

Johnston, Harry H. *The Story of My Life*. Indianapolis: Bobbs-Merrill, 1943.

Jones, Greta. *Social Darwinism and English Thought*. Sussex: Harvester Press; Atlantic Highlands, NJ: Humanities Press, 1980.

Jones, James H. *Bad Blood*. New York: Free Press, 1981.

Jordan, Winthrop D. "Modern Tensions and the Origins of American Slavery." *Journal of Southern History* 28 (1962): 18–30.

————. *White over Black*. Chapel Hill: University of North Carolina Press, 1968.

————. *The White Man's Burden*. New York: Oxford University Press, 1974.

Jorgensen, Joseph G. *Biology and Culture in Modern Perspective*. San Francisco: W. H. Freeman, 1972.

Joseph, Gloria I., and Jill Lewis. *Common Differences: Conflicts in Black and White Feminist Perspectives*. New York: Anchor Press/Doubleday, 1981.

Josephy, Alvin *Now that the Buffalo's Gone*. University of Oklamoma Press, 1989.

Jost, Hudson. "Some Physiological Changes During Frustration." *Child Development* 12 (1941): 9–15.

Joyner, Charles. *Down by the Riverside: A South Carolina Slave Community*. Urbana: University of Illinois Press, 1984.

July, Robert W. *A History of the African People*. 2d ed. (New York: Charles Scribners, 1971)

Kahler, Erich. *Man the Measure*. New York: Braziller, 1943.

————. *The Jews Among the Nations*. New York: Ungar, 1967.

Kahn, Jr., E. J. *The Separated People*. New York: W. W. Norton, 1966.

Kalmus, H. *Genetics*. London: Pelican Books, 1948.

———. *Variation and Heredity*. London: Routledge, 1957.

Kames, Lord (Henry Home). *Sketches of the History of Man*. Edinburgh: Tourneiseu, 1774; 2d ed. 1796.

Kamin, Leon J. *The Science and Politics of IQ*. Potomac, MD: Lawrence Erlbaum Associates, 1974.

Kane, Martin. "An Assessment of 'Black is Best.'" *Sports Illustrated*, 18 January 1971: 73–83.

Kaplan, Chaim A. *The Scroll of Agony*. New York: Macmillan, 1981.

Kaplan, Sidney. *The Black Presence in the Era of the American Revolution 1770–1800*. New York: New York Graphic Society, 1973.

Kardiner, Abram, and Lionel Ovesey. *The Mark of Oppression*. New York: Norton, 1951.

Kartman, Leo. "Sociological Excursions of Biologists." *Scientific Monthly* 62 (1943): 337–46.

Kase, N. G. "The Ovary. " In *Diseases of Metabolism*, edited by Philip K. Bondy, vol. 2, 1191–1226. Philadelphia: Saunders, 1969.

Katsh, Abraham I., ed. *The Scroll of Agony: The Warsaw Diary of Chaim A. Kaplan*. New York: Macmillan, 1981.

Katz, I., T. Heuchy, and H. Allen. "Effects of Race of Tester, Approval, Disapproval, and Need on Negro Children's Learning." *Journal of Personality and Social Research* 8 (1968): 38–42.

Katz, Irwin, and Patricia Gurin, eds. *Race and the Social Sciences*. New York: Basic Books, 1969.

Katz, Jacob. *From Prejudice to Destruction: Anti-Semitism, 1700–1933*. Cambridge: Harvard University Press, 1980.

Katz, Phyllis A., ed. *Towards the Elimination of Racism*. New York: Pergamon Press, 1976.

Kaufman, Harold F., J. Kenneth Morland, and Herbert F. Fockler, eds., *Group Identity in the South*. State College: Mississippi State University, 1975.

Kaufman, Jonathan. *A Hole in the Heart of the World: Being Jewish in Eastern Europe*. New York: Viking, 1997.

Kaus, Mickey. *The End of Equality*. New York: Basic Books, 1992.

Kautsky, Karl. *Are the Jews a Race?* New York: International Publishers, 1926.

Kearney, G. E., P. R. de Lacey, and G. R. Davidson, eds. *The Psychology of Aboriginal Australians*. New York: John Wiley, 1973.

Keen, Sam. *Faces of the Enemy*. New York: Harper & Row, 1986.

Keesing, Felix M. *The Changing Maori*. New Plymouth, NZ: Avery & Sons, 1928.

Keil, Charles. *Urban Blues*. Chicago: University of Chicago Press, 1966.

Keith, Arthur. *Nationality and Race*. London: Oxford University Press, 1919.

———. *The Place of Prejudice in Modern Civilization*. New York: John Day, 1931.

———. "Must a Rationalist Be a Pacifist?" *Truth Seeker* 67 (1939): 33–34.

———. "Nationalism." *Sunday Express* (London), 27 August 1939.

———."Darwinian Exhibition in Moscow." *Nature* 140 (1942): 393.

———. "An Anthropologist in Retirement." I-XV. *Literary Guide and Rationalist Review* 57 (1943); 59 (1944).

―――. *Essays on Human Evolution.* New York: Putnam, 1947.

―――. *A New Theory of Human Evolution.* New York: Philosophical Library, 1948.

―――. *An Autobiography.* New York: Philosophical Library, 1950.

Kellogg, Vernon L. *Military Selection and Race Deterioration.* New York: Oxford University Press, 1916.

Kelly, Alfred. *The Descent of Darwin: The Popularization of Darwinism in Germany, 1960–1914.* Chapel Hill: University of North Carolina Press, 1981.

Kelly, Caroline. "The Reaction of White Groups in Country Towns of New South Wales to Aborigines." *Social Horizons* 1 (1943): 34–40.

Kelly, Lawrence C. *The Assault on Assimilation: John Collier and the Origins of Indian Policy Reform.* Albuquerque: University of New Mexico Press, 1983.

Kennard, Margaret A., and John F. Fulton. "Age and Reorganization of the Central Nervous System." *Journal of the Mount Sinai Hospital* 9 (1942): 594–606.

Kennedy, Kenneth A. R. *Human Variation in Space and Time.* Dubuque: William C. Brown, 1976.

Kennedy, Theodore R. *You Gotta Deal With It.* New York: Oxford University Press, 1980.

Kerridge, Roy. *Real Wicked Guy: A View of Black Britain.* London: Basil Blackwell, 1983.

Kevles, Daniel J. *In the Name of Eugenics: Genetics and the Uses of Human Heredity.* New York: Alfred A. Knopf, 1985.

Khaldûn, Ibn. *The Muquaddimah.* 3 vols. Translated and edited by Franz Rosenthal. New York: Pantheon Books, 1958.

Khan, Peter, J., ed. *The Promise of World Peace.* Oxford: One World Publications, 1996.

Kiernan, V. G. *The Lords of Human Kind.* Boston: Little, Brown, 1969.

Kikuchi, Charles, ed. *The Kikuchi Diary: Chronicle from an American Concentration Camp.* Edited and with an introduction by David Modell. Urbana: University of Illinois Press, 1992.

"The Killer Game." *New York Times,* 2 June 1981: A A 14. (See also *Wall Street Journal*).

Killian, Lewis, and Charles Gregg. *Racial Crisis in America.* Englewood Cliffs, NJ: Prentice-Hall, 1964.

Kimble, George H. T. "Racialism in South Africa is a Sickness too." *New York Times Magazine* 11 October, 1964: 38 sq.

Kincheloe, Joe L., Shirley R. Steinberg, and Aaron D. Gresson III, eds. *Measured Lies: The Bell Curve Examined.* New York: St. Martin's Press, 1996.

King, Bert T., and Eliott McGinnies, eds. *Attitudes, Conflict and Social Change.* New York: Academic Press, 1972.

King, James C. "Inbreeding, Heterosis and Information Theory." *American Naturalist* 95 (1962): 345–64.

―――. *The Biology of Race.* New York: Harcourt Brace Jovanovich, 1971.

Kirp, David L. *Just Schools: The Idea of Racial Equality in American Education.* Berkeley: University of California Press, 1982.

Kitagawa, Daisuke. *Issei and Nissei.* New York: Seabury Press, 1967.

Kittrie, Nicholas N. *The War Against Authority: From the Crisis of Legitimacy to a New Social Contract.* Baltimore: Johns Hopkins University Press, 1995.

Klama, John. (pseudonym). *Aggression: The Myth of the Beast Within.* New York: John Wiley, 1988.

Klatt, B. "Mendelismus, Domestikation und Kraniologie." *Archiv für Anthropologie,* n.s., 18 (1921): 225–50.

Klein, Barry T. *Reference Encyclopedia of the American Indian.* 7th edition. West Nyak, NY: Todd, 1995.

Klein, Herbert S. *Slavery in the Americas.* Chicago: University of Chicago Press, 1967.

———. *The Middle Passage: Comparative Studies in the Atlantic Slave Trade.* Princeton: Princeton University Press, 1978.

Klein, R. E., B. M. Lester, C. Yarbrough, and J. R. Hibicht. "Crosscultural Evolution of Human Intelligence." In *Malnutrition in the Developing Brain,* edited by K. Elliott and J. Knight, 249–65. New York: Elsevier, 1972.

Klineberg, Otto. *Negro Intelligence and Selective Migration.* New York: Columbia University Press, 1935.

———. *Race Differences.* New York: Harper, 1935.

———. "Mental Testing of Racial and National Groups." In *Scientific Aspects of the Race Problem,* edited by J. W. Corrigan. New York: Longmans, 1941.

———. "Race Differences: the Present Position of the Problem." *International Social Science Bulletin* (UNESCO) 2 (1950): 460–66.

———. *Social Psychology.* Revised. New York: Holt, Rinehart & Winston, 1954.

———, ed. *Characteristics of the American Negro.* New York: Harper, 1944.

Klingberg, Frank J. *The Anti-Slavery Movement in England.* New Haven: Yale University Press, 1926.

Kloepfer, H. W. "An Investigation of 171 Possible Linkage Relationships in Man." *Annals of Eugenics* 13 (1946): 35–71.

Klopfer, Peter H. *Behavioral Aspects of Ecology.* 2d ed. Englewood Cliffs, NJ: Prentice-Hall, 1973.

Kluckhohn, Clyde. "Anthropological Research and World Peace." In *World Peace: A Symposium,* 143–66. 4th Congress on Philosophy, Science and Religion. New York: Harper, 1944.

———. "The Myth of Race." In *Religion and Our Racial Tensions,* edited by Willard R. Sperry, 3–27. Cambridge: Harvard University Press, 1945.

———. *Culture and Behavior.* New York: Free Press, 1962.

———. *Mirror for Man.* New York: Whittlesey House, 1949; Tucson: University of Arizona Press, 1985.

Kluckhohn, Clyde, and William H. Kelly. "The Concept of Culture." In *The Science of Man in the World Crisis,* edited by Ralph Linton, 78–106. New York: Columbia University Press, 1945.

Klug, Francesca, and Paul Gordon. *Different Worlds: Racism and Discrimination in Britain.* London: The Runnymede Trust, 1983.

Klug, Francesca. *Racist Attacks.* London: The Runnymede Trust, 1982.

Kluger, Richard. *Simple Justice.* New York: Alfred A. Knopf, 1976.

Knobloch, Hilda, and Benjamin Pasamanick. "A Developmental Questionnaire for Infants Forty Weeks of Age: An Evaluation." *Monographs of the Society for Research in Child Growth and Development* 20 (1956): No. 2.

———. "The Relationship of Race and Socioeconomic Status to the Development of Motor Behavior Patterns in Infancy." *Psychiatric Research Reports* 10 (1958): 123–33.

Kochman, Thomas. *Styles in Conflict*. Chicago: University of Chicago Press, 1981.

Koenig, Frederick W., and Morton B. King, Jr. "Cognitive Simplicity and Prejudice." *Social Forces* 40 (1962): 220–22.

Koestler, Arthur. *Thieves in the Night*. New York: Macmillan, 1946.

Kohl, Herbert. *36 Children*. New York: New American Library, 1967.

Kohl, Johann G. *England, Wales, and Scotland*. London: Chapman & Hall, 1844.

Kohn, Hans. "Race Conflict." In *Encyclopaedia of the Social Sciences* 13: 40. New York: Macmillan, 1937.

Kohne-Raz, Reuven. *Psychobiological Aspects of Cognitive Growth*. New York: Academic Press, 1977.

Kolb, Edith A. *Runnin' Down Some Line: The Language and Culture of Black Teenagers*. Cambridge: Harvard University Press, 1980.

Korzec, Pawl, "Antisemitism in Poland as an Intellectual, Social and Political Movement." In *Studies on Polish Jewry, 1919–1939*, edited by Joshua A. Fishman. New York: YIVO Institute for Jewish Research, 1974.

Korzybski, Alfred. *Science and Sanity*. 2d ed. Lancaster: Science Press, 1941.

Kotkin, Joel. *Tribes: How Race, Religion, and Identity Determine Success in the New Global Economy*. New York: Random House, 1992.

Koumaris, John. "On the Morphological Variety of Modern Greeks." *Man* 48 (1948): 126–27.

Kousser, J. Morgan, and James M. McPherson, eds. *Region, Race and Reconstruction*. New York: Oxford Univesity Press, 1982.

Kovel, Joel. *White Racism: A Psychohistory*. New York: Pantheon Books, 1970.

Kozol, Jonathan. *Death at an Early Age: The Destruction of the Hearts and Minds Negro Children in the Boston Public Schools*. New York: Houghton Mifflin, 1967.

Kraditor, Aileen S. *Means and Ends in American Abolitionism*. New York: Pantheon Books, 1969.

Krall, Hanna. *Shielding the Flame*. New York: Henry Holt, 1986.

Kramer, Fritz W. "Empathy—Reflections on the History of Ethnology in Pre-Fascist Germany: Herder, Creutzer, Bastan, Bachofen, and Frobenius." *Dialectical Anthropology* 9 (1985): 337–47.

Kramer, Samuel. *History Begins at Sumer*. New York: Doubleday, 1959.

Kraus, Michael. *Immigration: The American Mosaic*. Princeton: Van Nostrand, 1966.

Krauss, William. "Race Relations in the Islands of the Pacific," *Journal of Heredity* 32 (1941) 371–78.

Krech, David, and Richard S. Crutchfield. *Theory and Problems of Social Psychology*. New York: McGraw-Hill, 1948.

Kretschmer, Ernst. *The Psychology of Men of Genius*. New York: Harcourt, Brace, 1931.

Krieger, Nancy, and Stephen Sydney. "Racial Discrimination and Blood Pressure: The CARDIA Study of Young Black and White Adults." *American Journal of Public Health* 86 (1996): 1370–78.

Kroeber, Alfred L. "The Superorganic." *American Anthropologist* 19 (1917): 163–213.

Kroeber A. L. *The Nature of Culture*. Chicago: University of Chicago Press, 1952.

Krogman, Wilton M. "The Concept of Race." In *The Science of Man in the World Crisis*, edited by Ralph Linton. New York: Columbia University Press, 1944.

———. *The Physical Anthropology of the Seminole Indians*. Comitato Italiano per lo studio dei problemi della populazione, serie 3 II, ix–199. Roma, 1935.

Kropotkin, Petr. *Mutual Aid, a Factor in Evolution*. Revised. New York: McClure, 1904.

Kühl, Stefan. *The Nazi Connection: Eugenics, American Racism, and German National Socialism*. New York: Oxford University Press, 1994.

Kujichagulia, Phavia. *Recognizing and Resolving Racism*. Vol. 1. Oakland, CA: A. Wisdom Co., 1994.

Kuno, Yas. *Human Perspiration*. Springfield, IL: Thomas, 1956.

Kuper, Leo. *Race, Class and Power*. London: Duckworth, 1975.

———. *Race, Science and Society*. Revised. Paris & New York: UNESCO Press/Columbia University Press, 1975.

———. *The Pity of It All: Polarisation of Racial and Ethnic Relations*. Minneapolis: University of Minnesota Press, 1977.

———. *Genocide: Its Political Use in the Twentieth Century*. New Haven: Yale University Press, 1981.

———. *The Prevention of Genocide*. New Haven: Yale University Press, 1985.

Kuper, Leo, Hilstan Watts, and Ronald Davies. *Durban: A Study in Racial Ecology*. New York: Columbia University Press, 1958.

Kupka, Karel. *Dawn of Art: Painting and Sculpture of Australian Aborigines*. Translated by John Ross. New York: Viking, 1965.

Kuttner, Robert E. "Biochemical Anthropology." In *Race and Modern Science*, edited Robert E. Kuttner. New York: Social Science Press, 1967, 197–222.

———. "Writers on the Grassy Knoll: A Reader's Guide." *New York Times Book Review* (2 February 1992): 23–25.

La Barre, Weston. "The Cultural Basis of Emotions and Gestures." *Journal of Personality* 16 (1947): 49–68.

———. *The Human Animal*. Chicago: University of Chicago Press, 1954

La Farge, Oliver. "The Newest Frontier: Last Hope of the American Indians." *Country Beautiful* 3 (1964): 26–31.

La Guma, Alex, ed. *Apartheid: A Collection of Writings on South African Racism*. New York: International Publishers, 1972.

Lader, Lawrence. *The Bold Brahmins*. New York: E. P. Dutton, 1961.

Ladner, Joyce A. *Mixed Families: Adopting Across Racial Boundaries*. New York: Anchor Press, 1977.

Laidler, Harry W., ed. *The Role of the Races in Our Future Civilization*. New York: League for Industrial Democracy, 1942.

Lamont, Corliss. "National and Racial Minorities." In *USSR: a Concise Handbook*, edited by Ernest J. Simmons. Ithaca: Cornell University Press, 1947.

Landau, Ronnie S. *The Nazi Holocaust*. Chicago: Dee, 1994.

Lander, Ernest M., and Richard J. Calhoun, eds. *Two Decades of Change: The South Since the Supreme Court Desegregation Decision*. Columbia: University of South Carolina Press, 1975.

Landes, R. "A Preliminary Statement of a Survey of Negro-White Relationships in Britain." *Man* 52 (1952): 133.

Landry, Stuart O. *The Cult of Equality*. New Orleans: Pelican Pubishing, 1945.

Lane, Anne J., ed. *The Debate over Slavery.* Urbana: University of Illinois Press, 1971.

Lane, Charles. "The Tainted Sources of *The Bell Curve.*" *New York Review of Books,* 1 December 1994: 14–19; 14

Langmuir, Irving. "Science, Common Sense and Decency." *Science* 97 (1943): 1–7.

Lapiere, R. T. "Race Prejudice: France and England." *Social Forces* 7 (1928): 102–11.

Lapping, B. *Apartheid: A History.* London: Grafton Books, 1986.

Laqueur, Walter. *The Terrible Secret: The Suppression of the Truth about Hitler's "Final Solution."* Boston: Little, Brown, 1980.

Larsen, Stein U., Bernt Hagtvet, and Jan P. Myklebust, eds., *Who Were the Facists: Social Roots of European Fascism.* Bergen: Universitetsforlaget, 1980.

Larson, Sidner J. *Catch Colt.* Lincoln: University of Nebraska Press, 1955.

Lasch, Christopher. "The Anti-Imperialists, the Philippines, and the Inequality of Man." *Journal of Southern History* 24 (1958): 319–31.

Lasker, Bruno. *Race Attitudes in Children.* New York: Holt, 1929.

Lasker, Gabriel W. "Migration and Physical Differentiation." *American Journal of Physical Anthropology,* n.s., 4 (1946): 273–300.

Laslett, Peter, ed. *The Physical Basis of Mind.* New York: Macmillan, 1950.

Lassek, A. M. *The Human Brain.* Springfield: Thomas, 1957.

Latham, M. C. In *Calorie and Protein Deficiencies,* edited by R. A. McCance and E. M. Widdowson. New York and London: Cambridge University Press, 1968.

Laufer, Berthold. "Methods in the Study of Domestications." *Scientific Monthly* 25 (1927): 251–55.

Laughlin, William S. "Races of Mankind." *Anthropological Papers of the University of Alaska* 8 (1960): 89–99.

———. "Race: A Population Concept." *Eugenics Quarterly* 13 (1966): 326–40.

———, ed. *Papers on the Physical Anthropology of the American Indian.* New York: The Viking Fund, 1951.

Laurence, John. *The Seeds of Disaster.* London: Gollancz, 1968.

Layzer, David. "Science or Superstition? A Physical Scientist Looks at the IQ Controversy." In *The IQ Controversy: Critical Readings,* edited by N. J. Block and Gerald Dworkin. New York: Pantheon, 1976.

Le Gros Clark, W. E. *Fitting Man to His Environment.* Newcastle-upon-Tyne: King's College, 1949.

Le Jeune, Paul. *Quebec and Hurons: 1640.* Jesuit Relations, vol. 19. Cleveland: Burrows Bros., 1898.

League of Coloured Peoples. *Race Relations and the Schools.* London: 1944.

Leake, Chauncey D. "Ethicogenesis." *Proceedings of the Philosophical Society of Texas* 10 (1944): 7–34.

Lee, Alfred L. *Fraternities Without Brotherhood.* Boston: Beacon Press, 1955.

Lee, Alfred, and Norman D. Humphrey. *Race Riot.* New York: Dryden Press, 1943.

Lee, Richard B., and Irven De Vore, eds. *Kalahari Hunter-Gatherers.* Cambridge: Harvard University Press, 1976.

Leer, Richard B. *The !Kung San: Men, Women and Work in a Foraging Society.* Cambridge: Cambridge University Press, 1979.

Leff, Herbert L. *Experience, Environment, and Human Potentials.* New York: Oxford University Press, 1978.

Lefroy, C. E. C. "Australian Aborigines: a Noble-Hearted Race." *Contemporary Review* 135 (1929): 22.

Lehrman, Daniel S. "Semantic and Conceptual Issues in the Nature-Nurture Problem" In *Development and Evolution of Behavior,* edited by Lester R. Aronson, Ethel Tobach, Daniel S. Lehrman and Jay S. Rosenblatt, 17–52. San Francisco: Freeman & Co., 1970.

Leibnitz, Gottfried W. von. *Otium Hanoveriana; sive, Miscellanea.* Leipzig, 1718.

Leighton, Alexander. *The Governing of Men.* Princeton: Princeton University Press, 1945.

Lelyveld, Joseph. *Move Your Shadow: South Africa: Black and White.* New York: Basic Books, 1995.

Lemann, Nicholas. *The Promised Land.* New York: Alfred A. Knopf, 1991.

Leschi, Jeanne. *Races Mélanodermes et Leucodermes: Pigmentation et Fonctionnement Cortico-Surrénalien.* Paris: Mason, 1952.

Leschnitzer, Adolf. *The Magic Background of Modern Anti-Semitism: An Analysis of the German-Jewish Relationship.* New York: International Universities Press, 1969.

Lesser, Gerald L., et al. "Mental Abilities of Children from Different Social Class and Cultural Groups." *Monographs of the Society for Research in Child Development* 30(4)(1965): 1–115.

Lesser, Gerald S., Gordon Fifer, and Donald H. Clark. "Mental Abilities of Children from Different Social Class and Cultural Groups." *Monographs of the Society for Research in Child Development* 3 (1965) No. 4: 1–115.

Lesser, Jeff H. "Brazil Pretends to Have No Race Problem." *The New York Times,* 10 October 1991: A26.

Lestchinsky, Jacob. "The Jew in Ruined Europe." *Chicago Jewish Forum* 4 (1945): 10–16.

Lester, Anthony, and Geoffrey Bindman. *Race and Law in Great Britain.* Cambridge: Harvard University Press, 1972.

Levi, Lennart, ed. *Society, Stress and Disease.* 5 vols. New York: Oxford University Press, 1971–1987.

Levi, Primo. *Moments of Reprieve.* New York: Summit Books, 1986.

———. *Survival in Auschwitz.* New York: Collier Books, 1961.

Levin, G. "Racial and 'Inferiority' Characters in the Human Brain." *American Journal of Physical Anthropology* 22 (1937): 345–80.

Levin, Meyer, ed. "Journal of Kibbutz Buchenwald." *Commentary* 1 (1946): 31–39.

Levin, Nora. *The Holocaust: The Destruction of European Jewry 1933–1945.* New York: Crowell, 1968.

Levine, Donald M., and Mary Jo Bane, eds. *The "Inequality" Controversy: Schooling and Distributive Justice.* New York: Basic Books, 1975.

Levins, Richard, and Richard Lewontin. *The Dialectical Biologist.* Cambridge: Harvard University Press, 1985.

Levitan, M., and A. Montagu. *A Textbook of Human Genetics.* New York: Oxford University Press, 1971, 3d ed. 1988.

Levitan, Sar A., and Barbara Hetrick. *Big Brother's Indian Programs—With Reservations.* New York: Harper & Row, 1926.

Levitan, Sar A., William B. Johnston, and Robert Taggart, eds. *Still a Dream: The Changing Status of Blacks Since 1960*. Cambridge: Harvard University Press, 1975.

Levitsky, David A., ed. *Malnutrition, Environment, and Behavior.* Ithaca: Cornell University Press, 1979.

Levitsky, D. A., and R. H. Barnes. "Nutritional and Environmental Interactions in the Behavioral Development of the Rat: Long Term Behavioral Effects." *Science* 176 (1972): 68–71.

Lewin, Kurt. *Resolving Social Conflicts*. New York: Harper, 1948.

Lewis, Anthony. "Never Again." *New York Times*, 1 October: A17.

Lewis, B. *Race and Color in Islam*. New York: Harper & Row, 1977.

———. *Semites and Anti-Semites*. New York: Norton, 1986.

Lewis, David L. *The Race to Fashoda: European Colonialism and African Resistance in the Scramble for Africa*. New York: Weidenfeld & Nicolson, 1987.

Lewis, David L., and W. E. B. Du Bois. *Biography of a Race*. New York: Henry Holt, 1993.

Lewis, Julian H. *The Biology of the Negro*. Chicago: University of Chicago Press, 1942.

Lewis, Michael. *The Culture of Inequality*. Amherst: University of Massachusetts Press, 1978, 1992.

———, ed. *Origins of Intelligence*. New York: Plenum, 1983.

Lewis, Wyndham. *The Art of Being Ruled*. New York: Harper Bros., 1926.

———. *The Lion and the Fox*. London: Grant Richards, 1927.

Lewontin, Richard C. "The Apportionment of Human Diversity." In *Evolutionary Biology*, edited by T. Dobzhansky, Max K. Hecht and William C. Steere, vol. 6, 381–98. New York: Appleton Century-Cotts, 1972.

———. *Human Diversity*. New York: W. H. Freeman, 1982.

Lewontin, Richard C., Steven Rose, and Leon Kamin. *Not in Our Genes: Biology, Ideology, and Human Nature*. New York, Pantheon, 1984.

Lieberman, Leonard. An Attempted Revival of the Race Concept. *American Anthopologist* 97 (1995): 590–92.

———. "IQ Deja Vu: Phases of IQ Controversy and Their Social Context." In *Race & IQ*, 2d ed., edited by A. Montagu. New York: Oxford University Press, 1995.

Lieberman, Leonard, and Larry T. Reynolds. *Race and Other Misadventures*. Dix Hills, NY: General Hall, 1996.

Lieberman, Leonard, Blaine W. Stevenson, and Larry T. Reynolds. "Race and Anthropology: A Core Concept Without Consensus." *Anthropology and Education Quarterly* 20 (1989): 67–73.

Lieberson, Stanley. "A Societal Theory of Race and Ethnic Relations." *American Sociological Review* 26 (1961): 902–10.

———. *A Piece of the Pie: Blacks and White Immigrants Since 1880*. Berkeley: University of California Press, 1981.

———. *Ethnic Patterns in American Cities*. New York: Free Press, 1963.

Liebman, Robert C., and Robert Wuthnow, eds. *The New Christian Right*. New York: Aldine, 1983.

Lifton, Robert J. *The Nazi Doctors*. New York: Basic Books, 1986.

———. *The Protean Self: Human Resilience in an Age of Fragmentation*. New York: Basic Books, 1993.

Light, R. J., and P. V. Smith. "Social Allocation Models of Intelligence." *Harvard Educational Review* 39 (1969): 484–510.

Lillie, Ralph S. "The Psychic Factor in Living Organisms." *Philosophy of Science* 10 (1943): 262–70.

Limson, Marciano. "Observations on the Bones of the Skull in White and Negro Fetuses and Infants." *Contributions to Embryology* 136 (1932): 204–22.

Lincoln, C. Eric. *The Black Muslims in America.* Boston: Beacon Press, 1961.

Lind, Andrew W. *Hawaii's Japanese: An Experiment in Democracy.* Princeton: Princeton University Press, 1946.

———. *Race Relations in the Islands of the Pacific.* Research in Race Relations, New York: UNESCO Publication Center, 1966.

———, ed. *Race Relations in World Perspective.* Honolulu: University of Hawaii Press, 1955.

Lind, Michael. "Rev. Robertson's Grand International Conspiracy Theory." *The New York Review of Books* 42(3) (2 February 1995): 21–25.

———. "On Pat Robertson: His Defenders." *New York Review of Books* 42(7) (20 April 1995): 67–68.

Lindsay, Lord. *The Good and the Clever.* New York: Cambridge University Press, 1945.

Linnaeus, Carolus. *Systema naturae.* Leyden, 1735, 1753.

Linton, Ralph. "Error in Anthropology." In *The Story of Human Error,* edited by Joseph Jastrow, 292–321. New York: Appleton-Century, 1935.

———. *The Study of Man.* New York: Appleton-Century, 1936.

———. *The Science of Man in the World Crisis.* New York: Columbia University Press, 1944.

———, ed. *Most of the World.* New York: Columbia University Press, 1949.

Lintott, Andrew. *Violence, Civil Strife, and Revolution in the Celestial City.* 2d ed. London: Croon-Helm, 1987.

Lippitt, R., and M. Radke. "New Trends in the Investigation of Prejudice." *Annals of the American Academy of Political and Social Science* 244 (1946): 167–76.

Lippmann, W. A. "Mr. Burt and the Intelligence Tests." *New Republic* (2 May 1922): 263–64.

———. "The Mental Age of Americans." *New Republic* (25 October 1922): 213–25.

———. "The Mystery of the 'A' Men." *New Republic* (1 November 1922): 246–48.

———. "The Reliability of Intelligence Tests." *New Republic* (8 November 1922): 275–77.

———. "Tests of Hereditary Intelligence." *New Republic* (22 November 1922): 328–30.

———. "Future for the Tests." *New Republic* (29 November 1922): 9–11.

———. *Public Opinion.* New York: Signet Books, 1946.

———. "The Mystery of the 'A' Men." In *The IQ Controversy: Critical Readings,* edited by N. J. Block and Gerald Dworkin. New York: Pantheon, 1976.

Lipschütz, Alejandro. *El Indoamericanismo y el problema racial en las Américas.* 2d ed. Santiago: Editorial Nascimento, 1944.

Lipset, Seymour M., and Earl Raab. *The Politics of Unreason: Right- Wing Extremism in America, 1790–1970.* New York: Harper & Row, 1970.

Lipsitz, George. *A Life in the Struggle: Ivory Perry and the Culture of Opposition.* Philadelphia: University of Pennsylvania Press, 1988.

Lipstadt, Deborah E. *Denying the Holocaust: The Growing Assault on Truth and Memory.* New York: Free Press, 1993.

Littel, S. Harrington. "All Races Necessary." *New York Times,* 3 September 1944.

Little, Kenneth L. The Study of Racial Mixture in the British Commonwealth." *Eugenics Review* 32 (1941): 141–20.

———. "London Square." *Sociological Review* 34 (1942): 119–46.

———. "Race Relations in English Society." *Man* 42 (1942): 90–91.

———. "Some Anthropological Characteristics of Anglo-Negro Children." *Journal of the Royal Anthropological Institute* 73 (1943): 57–73.

———. "A Note on Colour Prejudice amongst the English 'Middle Class." *Man* 42 (1943): 104–7.

———. "The Psychological Background of White-Coloured Contacts in Britain." *Sociological Review* 35 (1943): 12–28.

———. *Negroes in Britain.* London: Kegan Paul, 1948.

———. *Race and Society.* New York: UNESCO/ Columbia University Press, 1952.

Littlefield, Alice, Leonard Lieberman, and Larry T. Reynolds. "Redefining Race: The Potential Demise of a Concept in Physical Anthropology." *Current Anthropology* 23 (1982) 641–55.

Litvinoff, Emanuel, ed. "The Anti-Semitism of Soviet and Polish Communism." *Jews in Eastern Europe* 4 (1969): 1–71

Litwack, Leon F. *Been in the Storm So Long: The Aftermath of Slavery.* New York: Alfred A. Knopf, 1979.

Liu, William T. "The Community Reference System, Religiosity, and Race Attitudes." *Social Forces* 39 (1961): 324–28.

Liungman, C. G. *What Is IQ? Heredity, Intelligence, and Environment.* London: Gordon Cremonesi, 1970, 1975.

Livingston, Sigmund. *Must Men Hate?* New York: Harper, 1944.

Livingstone, Frank B. "Anthropoligical Implications of Sickle Cell Gene Distribution in West Africa." *American Anthropologist* 60 (1958): 533–62.

———. "Who Gave Whom Hemoglobin S: The Use of Restriction Site Haplogype Variation For the Interpretation of the Evolution of the (^{s}-globin gene." *American Journal of Human Biology* 1 (1989): 289–302.

Livingstone, Frank B., and James N. Spuhler. "Cultural Determinants in Natural Selection." *International Social Science Journal* 17 (1965): 118–20.

Livingstone, Frank R. "On the Non-Existence of Human Races." *Current Anthropology* 3 (1962): 279–81.

———. "On the Non-Existence of Human Races." In *The Concept of Race,* edited by A. Montagu, 46–60. New York: Free Press, 1964.

Livingstone, R. W. *The Greek Genius and Its Meaning to Us.* Oxford: Oxford University Press, 1924.

Lloyd, Arthur Y. *The Slavery Controversy 1831–1860.* Chapel Hill: University of North Carolina Press, 1939.

Lloyd, F., and D. A. Pidgeon. "An Investigation into the Effects of Coaching on Nonverbal Test Material With European, Indian, and African Children." *British Journal of Educational Psychology* 21 (1961): 145–51.

Lloyd-Still, J. D., ed. *Malnutrition & Intellectual Development.* Littleton, MA: Publishing Sciences Group, 1976.

Locke, Alain, and Bernhard J. Stern. *When Peoples Meet.* New York: Progressive Education Association, 1942.

Locke, Mary Stoughton. *Anti-Slavery in America From the Introduction of African Slaves to the Prohibition of the Slave Trade 1619–1808.* Gloucester, MA: P. Smith, 1965.

Loehlin, John C., Gardner Lindzey and J. N. Spuhler. *Race Differences in Intelligence.* San Francisco: W. H. Freeman, 1975.

Logan, Rayford W. And Michel R. Winston, eds. *Dictionary of American Negro Biography.* New York: W. W. Norton, 1984.

Logan, Spencer. *A Negro's Faith in America.* New York: Macmillan, 1946.

Lomax, Louis E. *The Reluctant African.* New York: Harper, 1960.

———. *The Negro Revolt.* New York: Harper, 1962.

Long [Long, Edward]. *The History of Jamaica.* 3 vols. London: 1774.

———. "Observations on the Gradation in the Scale of Being Between the Human and the Brute Creation. Including Some Curious Particulars Respecting Negroes." *The Columbia Magazine or Monthly Miscellany* 2 (1788): 15.

Long, Herman H. "Race Prejudice and Social Change." *American Journal of Sociology* 57 (1951): 15–19.

Loram, T. C., and T. F. McIlwraith, eds. *The North American Indian.* Toronto: University of Toronto Press, 1943.

Lorenz, Konrad. *Man Meets Dog.* Boston: Houghton Mifflin, 1955.

———. *On Aggression.* New York: Harcourt, Brace & World, 1966.

Lorimer, Frank, and Frederick Osborn. *Dynamics of Population.* New York: Macmillan, 1934.

Lotsy, J. P., and W. A. Goddijn. "Voyages of Exploration to Judge of the Bearing of Hybridization upon Evolution. I. South Africa." *Genetica* 10 (1928): viii–315.

Loumala, K. "California Takes Back Its Japanese Evacuees." *Applied Anthropology* 3 (1946): 25–39.

Love, J. R. B. *Stone Age Bushman of To-Day.* London: Blackie, 1936.

Love, Spencie. *One Blood: The Death and Resurrection of Charles R. Drew.* Chapel Hill: University of North Carolina Press, 1996.

Low, Alfred D. *Jews in the Eyes of Germans: From the Enlightenment to Imperial Germany.* Philadelphia: Institute for the Study of Human Issues, 1979.

Lowenstein, Alfred K. *Brutal Mandate.* New York: Macmillan, 1962.

Lowenthal, Leo, and Norbert Guterman. *Prophets of Deceit.* New York: Harper, 1949.

Lowie, Robert H. *Are We Civilized?* New York: Harcourt Brace, 1919.

———. "Intellectual and Cultural Achievements of Human Races." In *Scientific Aspects of the Race Problem,* by H. H. Jennings, preface by Bishop J. W. Corrigan, 189–249. Washington, D.C., The Catholic University of America Press; London and New York: Longmans, Green & Co., 1941. Freeport, NY: Books for Libraries Press, 1970.

Lowy, Samuel. *Co-operation, Tolerance, and Prejudice.* London: Routledge, 1948.

Loye, David. *The Healing of a Nation.* New York: W. W. Norton, 1971.

———. *The Leadership Passion.* San Francisco: Jossey-Bass, 1977.

Lubell, Samuel. "Racist Dress Rehearsal for November." *Commentary* 13 (1952): 307–15.

———. *White and Black: Test of a Nation.* New York: Harper & Row, 1964.

Ludmerer, Kenneth M. *Genetics and American Society.* Baltimore: John Hopkins University Press, 1972.

Ludwig, Emil. *Talks with Mussolini.* Boston: Little, Brown, 1933.

Lukas, J. Anthony. *Common Ground: A Turbulent Decade in the Lives of Three American Families.* New York: Alfred A. Knopf, 1985.

Lukas, Richard C. *The Forgotten Holocaust: The Poles Under German Occupation, 1939–1944.* Lexington: University Press of Kentucky, 1986.

Lund, R. D. *Development and Plasticity of the Brain.* New York: Oxford University Press, 1978.

Lundsgarde, Henry P. "Racial and Ethnic Classification: An Appraisal of the Role of Anthropology in the Lawmaking Process." *Houston Law Review* 10 (1973): 641–54.

Lurie, Edward. "Louis Agassiz and the Races of Man." *Isis* 45 (1954): 227–42.

Luthuli, Albert. *Let My People Go.* New York: McGraw-Hill, 1962.

Lutz, Alma. *Crusade for Freedom: Women in the Anti-Slavery Movement.* Boston: Beacon Press, 1968.

Lyman, Stanford M. *Color, Culture, Civilization: Race and Minority Issues in American Society.* Urbana: University of Illinois Press, 1994.

Lynch, John R. *The Facts of Reconstruction.* Indianapolis: Bobbs-Merrill, 1970.

Mabee, Carleton. *Black Freedom: The Nonviolent Abolitionists from 1830 through the Civil War.* New York: Macmillan, 1970.

MacCaughey, V. "Race Mixture in Hawaii." *Journal of Heredity* 10 (1919): 41–47, 90–95.

MacCrone, I. D. *Race Attitudes in South Africa.* London: Oxford University Press, 1937.

———. *Group Conflicts and Race Prejudice.* Johannesburg: South Africa Institute of Race Relations, 1947.

———. "Reaction to Domination in a Colour-Caste Society: A Preliminary Study of the Race Attitudes of a Dominated Group." *Journal of Social Psychology* 26 (1947): 69–98.

Macdonald, Callum. *The Killing of SS Obergruppenfurer Richard Heydrich.* New York: Free Press, 1989.

MacDougall, Hugh A. *Racial Myth in English History: Trojans, Teutons, and Anglo-Saxons.* Hanover: University Press of New England, 1983.

Mace, C. A. "National Stereotypes—Their Nature and Function." *Sociological Review* 35 (1943): 29–36.

Macfarlane, John M. *The Causes and Course of Organic Evolution.* New York: Macmillan, 1918.

MacIver, Robert M. *Unity and Difference in American Life.* New York: Harper, 1947.

———. *The More Perfect Union.* New York: Macmillan, 1948.

———, ed. *Discrimination and National Welfare.* New York: Harper, 1949.

Mack, Raymond W., ed. *Prejudice and Race Relations.* Chicago: Quadrangle, 1970.

Maclean, Joan C., ed. *Africa: The Racial Issue.* New York: Wilson, 1954.

MacLeod, Duncan J. *Slavery, Race and the American Revolution.* New York and London: Cambridge University Press, 1975.

Macleod, James C. *The American Indian Frontier.* New York: Alfred A. Knopf, 1928.

MacMunn, G. F. *Slavery through the Ages.* Philadelphia: Saunders, 1938.

Mahalanobis, Prasanta A. "Analysis of Race Mixture in Bengal." *Journal of the Asiatic Society of Bengal* 23 (1927): 301–33.

———."Anthropological Observations on the Anglo-Indians of Calcutta." *Records of the Indian Museum* 23 (1922–40): 1–187.

Maier, Norman R. F. *Frustration.* Ann Arbor: University of Michigan Press, 1961.

———. *Principles of Human Relations.* New York: Wiley, 1952.

Maier, Norman R. F., and Theodore C. Schneirla. *Principles of Animal Psychology.* New York: McGraw-Hill, 1935.

Mair, L. P. *Australia in New Guinea.* London: Christophers, 1948.

Maizlish, Stephen E., "Race and Politics in the Northern Democracy." In *New Perspectives on Race and Slavery in America,* edited by R. H. Abzug and S. E. Maizlish, 79–80. Lexington: University Press of Kentucky, 1986.

Malafa, R. *On the Bodily Differences between Sprinters and Non-Sportsmen.* Brno: Publications de la Faculté des Sciences de la Université Masaryk, 1933.

Malinowski, Bronislaw. "War—Past, Present, and Future." In *War as a Social Institution,* edited by in J. D. Clarkson and T. C. Cochran, 23–24. New York: Columbia University Press, 1941.

———. *A Scientific Theory of Culture and Other Essays.* Chapel Hill: University of North Carolina Press, 1944; New York: Oxford University Press, 1960.

Mall, Franklin P. "On Several Anatomical Characters of the Human Brain, Said to Vary According to Race and Sex." *American Journal of Anatomy* 9 (1909): 1–32.

Malone, Dumas. *Jefferson and His Time: The Sage of Monticello.* Vol. 6. Boston: Little, Brown, 1981–1984.

Mandel, Bernard. *Labor: Free and Slave.* New York: Associated Authors, 1955.

Mandela, Nelson. *Long Walk to Freedom.* Boston: Little, Brown, 1994.

Mandelbaum, David G. *Soldier Groups and Negro Groups.* Berkeley: University of California Press, 1953.

Manning, Kenneth B. *Black Apollo of Science.* New York: Oxford University Press, 1983.

Mannix, Daniel P., and Malcolm Cowley. *Black Cargoes.* New York: Viking Press, 1962.

Mannoni, O. *Prospero and Caliban: A Study of the Psychology of Colonization.* New York: Praeger, 1956.

Manschreck, Clyde L., "Religion in the South: Problems and Promise." In *The South in Perspective,* edited by F. B. Simkins, 81–90. Farmville, VA: Longwood College, 1959.

Manteggazza, P. *Physiognomy and Expression.* New York: Scribner's, 1910.

Manuel, Frank E. "From Equality to Organicism." *Journal of the History Ideas* 13 (1956): 54–69.

Manwell, Roger, and Heinrich Fraenkel. *The Incomparable Crime: Mass Extermination in the Twentieth Century: The Legacy of Guilt.* New York: Putnam's, 1967.

Manypenny, George W. *Our Indian Wards.* Cincinnati: Robert Clarke & Co., 1880; reprinted New York: Praeger Publishers, 1973.

Marcum, John A. *Education, Race, and Social Change in South Africa.* Berkeley: University of California Press, 1981.

Marcuse, F. L., and M. E. Bitterman. "Notes on the Results of Army Intelligence Testing in World War I." *Science* 104 (1946): 231–32.

Marden, Charles F. *Minorities in American Society*. New York: American Book Company, 1952.

Mariott, Michael. "A World Defined by Dread." *The New York Times* (27 April 1992): B1, 4.

Mark, Bert. *Uprising in the Warsaw Ghetto*. New York: Schocken Books, 1975.

Markides, Kyriakos S., and Charles H. Mindel. *Aging & Ethnicity*. Thousand Oaks, CA: Sage Publications, 1987.

Marks, Jonathan. *Human Biodiversity: Genes, Race, and History*. New York: Aldine de Gruyter, 1995.

———. "The Anthropology of Science: Part I: Science as Humanities." *Evolutionary Anthropology* 5 (1996): 6–10

———. The Anthropology of Science: Part II: Science as Humanities. *Evolutionary Anthropology*.

———. "Science and Race." *American Behavioral Scientist* 40 (1996): 123–33.

Marks, Sheila and Trapido Stanley, eds. *The Politics of Race, Class and Nationalism in Twentieth Century South Africa*. London: Longman, 1987.

Marquand, Leo. *Peoples and Policies of South Africa*. New York: Oxford University Press, 1952.

Marret, R. R., ed. *Anthropology and the Classics*. Oxford: Clarendon Press, 1908

Marrow, Alfred J. *Living Without Hate*. New York: Harper, 1951.

———. *Changing Patterns of Prejudice*. New York: Chilton, 1962.

Marrus, Michael R., and Robert O. Paxton. *Vichy France and the Jews*. New York: Basic Books, 1981.

Marshall, Lorna. *The !Kung of Nyae Nyae*. Cambridge: Harvard University Press, 1976.

Martin, James G. "Intergroup Tolerance—Prejudice." *Journal of Human Relations* 10 (1961): 197–204.

———. "Tolerant and Prejudiced Personality Syndromes." *Journal of Intergroup Relations* 2 (1961): 171–75.

———. "Racial Ethnocentrism and Judgement of Beauty." *Journal of Social Psychology* 63 (1964): 59–63.

———. *The Tolerant Personality*. Detroit: Wayne State University Press, 1964.

Martin, James G., and Frank R. Westie. "The Tolerant Personality." *American Sociological Review* 24 (1959): 521–28.

Marvin, Francis S., ed. *Western Races and the World*. London: Oxford University Press, 1922.

Mascoe-Taylor, C. G. N., and Barry Bogin, eds. *Human Variability and Plasticity*. New York: Cambridge University Press, 1995.

Maslow, Will. "The Law and Race Relations." In *Controlling Group Prejudice*, edited by Gordon Allport, 75–81. Annals of the American Academy of Political and Social Science No. 244 (1946).

———. "Civil Rights Legislation and the Fight for Equality, 1862–1952." *University of Chicago Law Review* 20 (1952): 363–413.

Mason, Philip. *An Essay on Racial Tension*. London: Royal Institute of National Affairs, 1954.

———. *Christianity and Race*. London: Lutterworth Press, 1956.

———. *Common Sense About Race.* New York: Macmillan, 1961.

———. *Patterns of Dominance.* New York: Oxford University Press, 1970.

Massey, Douglass S. *American Apartheid: Segregation and the Making of the Underclass.* Cambridge: Harvard University Press, 1993.

Massing, Paul W. *Rehearsal for Destruction: A Study of Political Anti-Semitism in Imperial Germany.* New York: Harper, 1949.

Masuoka, J., and R. L. Yokley. "Essential Structural Requisites in Race Relations." *Social Forces* 33 (1954): 30–35.

Masuoka, J.,and Preston Valien, eds. *Race Relations.* Chapel Hill: University of North Carolina Press, 1961.

Mather, Kenneth. *The Measurement of Linkage in Heredity.* 2d ed. London: Methuen, 1951.

———. *Human Diversity.* Edinburgh: Oliver & Boyd, 1964.

Mathew, J. *Eaglehawk and Crow.* London: Nutt, 1899.

Mathews, A. S. *Law, Order and Liberty in South Africa.* Berkeley: University of California Press, 1972.

Mathews, Donald G. *Slavery and Methodism.* Princeton: Princeton University Press, 1965.

Matson, Floyd W. *The Broken Image: Man, Science and Society.* New York: Braziller, 1964.

Matthews, Z. K. "The Black Man's Outlook." *Saturday Review* 36 (2 May 1953): 13–14, 51–52.

Maude, H. E. *Slavers in Paradise: The Peruvian Slave Trade in Polynesia, 1862–1874.* Stanford: Stanford University Press, 1981.

Maxwell, Roger, and Heinrich Fraenkel. *The Incomparable Crime.* New York: Putnam, 1967.

May, J. M., and H. Lemons. "The Ecology of Malnutrition." *Journal of the American Medical Association* 207 (1969): 2401–05.

Maybury-Lewis, David. "Societies on the Brink." *Harvard Magazine* Jan–Feb. 1977: 56–61.

Mayer, Arno J. *Why Did the Heavens Not Darken? The Final Solution in History.* New York: Pantheon, 1988.

Mayer, Susan and Christopher Jencks. "Growing Up in Poor Neighborhoods." *Science* 243 (1989): 1441–45.

Mayr, Ernst. "Speciation Phenomena in Birds." *Biological Symposia* 2 (1941): 59–88.

———. *Systematics and the Origin of Species.* New York: Columbia University Press, 1942.

———. *Animal Species and Evolution.* Cambridge: Harvard University Press, 1963.

———. *Populations, Species, and Evolution.* Cambridge: Harvard University Press, 1970.

———. *The Growth of Biological Thought.* Cambridge: Harvard University Press, 1982.

Mazrui, Ali A. *A World Federation of Cultures: An African Perspective.* New York: Free Press, 1976.

Mazur, Allan, and Leon S. Robertson. *Biology and Social Behavior.* New York: Free Press, 1972.

McAdoo, Harriette P., ed. *Black Families.* 2d ed. Thousand Oaks, CA: Sage Publications, 1988.

McAdoo, Harriette P., and John L. McAdoo, eds. *Black Children: Social, Educational, and Parental Environments.* Thousand Oaks: Sage Publications, 1985.

McCarthy, Frederick D. *Australia's Aborigines.* Melbourne: Colorgravure Publications, 1959.

McClosky, Herbert and Alida Brill. *Dimensions of Tolerance: What Americans Believe About Civil Liberties.* New York: Russell Sage Foundation/Basic Books, 1983.

McClure, Matthew Thompson. "Greek Genius and Race Mixture." *Studies in the History of Ideas,* vol. 3. New York: Columbia University Press, 1935, 25–35.

McCord, Jane and Alan Howard. "Early Familial Experiences and Bigotry." *American Sociological Review* 25 (1960): 717–22.

McCord, William, and Nicholas J. Demerath, III. "Negro v. White Intelligence: A Continuing Controvery." *Harvard Educational Review* 28 (1958): 120–35.

McCord, William, Jane McCord, and Alan Howard. "Early Familial Experiences and Bigotry." *American Sociological Review* 25 (1960): 717–22.

McCown, Theodore D., and Arthur Keith. *The Stone Age of Mount Carmel.* Vol. 2. Oxford: Clarendon Press, 1939. (See the review of this work by M. F. Ashley Montagu, *American Anthropologist* 42 [1940]: 518–22).

McCready, William C., ed. *Culture, Ethnicity and Identity.* New York: Academic Press, 1983.

McCuen, Gary E. *The Religious Right.* Hudson, WI: G. E. McCuen, 1989.

McDill, Edward. "Anomie, Authoritarianism, Prejudice, and Socio-Economic Status: An Attempt at Clarification." *Social Forces* 39 (1961): 239–45.

McDonagh, Edward C. "Status Levels of American Jews." *Sociology and Social Research* 32 (1948): 944–53.

McDonald, Marjorie. *Not by the Color of Their Skin.* New York: International Universities Press, 1970.

McDougall, William. *An Introduction to Social Psychology.* 14th ed. New York: Barnes & Noble, 1960.

McElroy, W. A. "Aesthetic Appreciation in Aborigines of Arnhemland. A Comparative Experimental Study." *Oceania* 23 (1952): 81–94.

McFie, J. "The Effect of Education on African Performance on a Group of Intellectual Tests." *British Journal of Educational Psychology* 30 (1961): 232–40.

McGary, Howard, and Bill E. Lawson. *Between Slavery and Freedom.* Bloomington: Indiana University Press, 1992.

McGurk, Frank C. J. "On White and Negro Test Performance and Socioeconomic Factors." *Journal of Abnormal and Social Psychology* 48 (3) (1952): 448–50.

McInnes, Colin. *City of Spades.* New York: Macmillan, 1958.

McKay, Vernon. *Africa in World Politics.* New York: Harper & Row, 1963.

McKitrick, Eric L., ed. *Slavery Defended: The Views of the Old South.* Englewood Cliffs, NJ: Prentice-Hall, 1963.

McLaren, Jack. *My Crowded Solitude.* London: Newnes, 1926.

McLaurin, Melton A. *Celia: A Slave.* Athens: University of Georgia Press, 1991.

———. *Separate Pasts: Growing Up White in the Segregated South.* Athens: University of Georgia Press, 1987.

McLoughlin, William G. *Champions of the Cherokees: Evan and John B. Jones.* Princeton: Princeton University Press, 1990.

McManus, Edgar J. *A History of Negro Slavery in New York.* Syracuse: Syracuse University Press, 1966.

McMillen, Neil R. *The Citizens' Council: Organized Resistance to the Second Reconstruction, 1954–1964.* Urbana: University of Illinois Press, 1971.

——. *Dark Journey.* Urbana: University of Illinois Press, 1989.

McNeill, William H. *Polyethnicity and National Unity in World History.* Toronto: University of Toronto, 1986; New York: Cambridge University Press, 1995.

McPherson, James M. *The Struggle for Equality.* Princeton: Princeton University Press, 1964.

——. *The Negro's Civil War.* New York: Pantheon Books, 1964.

——. "How U.S. Historians Falsified Slave Life." *University* [Princeton] (Summer 1967): 6–10.

——. *The Abolitionist Legacy.* Princeton: Princeton University Press, 1975.

McPherson, James M., et al. *Blacks in America: Bibliographical Essays.* New York: Doubleday, 1971.

McQueen, Robert, and Churn Browning. "The Intelligence and Educational Achievement of a Matched Sample of Negro and White Students." *School and Society* 88 (1960): 327–29.

McWilliams, Carey. "Race Discrimination and the Law." *Science and Society* 9 (1945): 1–22.

——. *A Mask for Privilege.* Boston: Little, Brown, 1948.

——. *Prejudice—the Japanese-Americans: Symbol of Racial Intolerance.* Boston: Little, Brown, 1944.

——. *Brothers under the Skin.* Revised. Boston: Little, Brown, 1964.

Mead, J. E., and A. S. Parkes. *Genetic and Environmental Factors in Human Ability.* New York: Plenum Press, 1966.

——, eds. *Biological Aspects of Social Problems.* New York: Plenum Press, 1955.

Mead, Margaret, T. Dobzhansky, Ethel Tobach, and R. E. Light, eds. *Science and the Concept of Race.* New York: Columbia University Press, 1968.

Mead, Margaret. *Peoples and Places.* Cleveland & New York: World Publishing Co., 1959.

——. "Warfare Is Only an Invention—Not a Biological Necessity." *Asia* 40 (1940): 402–5.

Meek, Ronald. *Social Science and the Ignoble Savage.* London & New York: Cambridge University Press, 1976.

Meggers, Betty J. "Environmental Limitation on the Development of Culture." *American Anthropologist* 56 (1954): 801–24.

Mehler, Barry. "The New Eugenics: Academic Racism in the U.S. Today." *Science for the People* 15 (1983): 18–23.

——. "Foundation for Fascism: The New Eugenics Movement in the United States." *Patterns of Prejudice* 23 (1989): 17–25.

Meier, August, and Elliot M. Rudwick. *From Plantation to Ghetto.* New York: Hill & Wang, 1966.

Meier, Matt S., and Feliciano Rivera. *The Chicanos: A History of Mexican Americans.* New York: Hill & Wang, 1972.

Meisler, Stanley. "Our Stake in Apartheid." *The Nation* 201 (1965): 71–73.

Mekeel, Scudder. "Cultural Aids to Constructive Race Relations." *Mental Hygiene* 29 (1945): 177–89.

Melendy, H. Brett. *The Oriental Americans.* New York: Twayne Publishers, 1972.

Menander. Translated by Francis G. Allinson. Cambridge: Harvard University Press, 1921: 345.

Mendelson, Wallace. *Discrimination.* Englewood Cliffs: NJ: Prentice-Hall, 1962.

Mendez-Flohr, Paul R., and Jehuda Reinharz. *The Jew in the Modern World: A Documentary History.* New York: Oxford University Press, 1980.

Menil Foundation. *The Image of the Black in Western Art.* 7 vols. Cambridge: Harvard Universitiy 1976.

Menschreck, Clyde L. "Religion in the South: Problems and Promise" In *The South in Perspective,* edited by Francis B. Simkins, 84–89. Farmville, VA: Longwood College, 1959.

Mensh, Elaine and Harry Mensh. *The IQ Mythology.* Carbondale: Southern Illinois University Press, 1991.

Merck, Frederick. *Manifest Destiny and Mission in American History.* New York: Alfred A. Knopf, 1963.

———. *Slavery and the Annexation of Texas.* New York: Alfred A. Knopf, 1972.

Meredith, James. *Three Years in Mississippi.* Bloomington, Indiana University Press, 1966.

Meredith, M. *In the Name of Apartheid.* London: Hamilton, 1988.

Merkl, Peter H. *Political Violence Under the Swastika, 581 Early Nazis.* Princeton: Princeton University Press, 1975.

———. *The Making of a Stormtrooper.* Princeton: Princeton University Press, 1980.

Mermelstein, David, ed. *The Anti-Apartheid Reader: South Africa and the Struggle Against White Racist Rule.* New York: Grove Press, 1987.

Merton, Robert K. "Social Structure and Anomie." *American Sociological Review* 3 (1938): 680.

———. "Discrimination and the American Creed." In *Discrimination and National Welfare,* edited by Robert MacIver, 99–126. New York: Harper, 1959.

Merton, Robert K., and M. F. Ashley Montagu. "Crime and the Anthropologist." *American Anthropologist* 42 (1940): 384–408.

Meyer, D. H. *The American Moralists: Academic Moral Philosophy in the United States, 1835–1880.* Unpublished Ph.D. dissertation. University of California, Berkeley, 1967.

Michael, R. P., ed. *Endocrinology and Human Behavior.* New York: Oxford University Press, 1968.

Middleton, John, ed. *From Child to Adult.* New York: American Museum of Natural History, 1970.

Mielche, Hakon. *Journey to the World's End.* New York: Doubleday, 1941.

Miles, Robert, and Annie Phizacklea, eds. *Racism and Political Action in Britain.* London and Boston: Routledge & Kegan Paul, 1978.

Milikovsky, J., and J. A. Novák, eds. *Evolution and Morphogenesis,* 2 vols. *Proceedings of the International Symposium, Plezen, Czochoslovak Academy of Sciences.* Prague, 1985).

Mill, John Stuart. *Autobiography.*

———. *Principles of Political Economy.* 2 vols. London: Longmans, 1848.

Miller, Alice. *Prisoners of Childhood*. New York: Basic Books, 1981.

———. *For Your Own Good: Hidden Cruelty in Child-Rearing and the Roots of Violence*. New York: Farrar, Straus & Giroux, 1982.

———. *Thou Shalt Not Be Aware: Society's Betrayal of the Child*. New York: Farrar Straus, 1984.

———. *The Untouched Key*. New York: Doubleday, 1988.

Miller, Arthur. *Focus*. New York: Arbor House, 1945.

Miller, Clyde R. "Community Wages Total War on Prejudice." *The Nation's Schools* 33 (1944): 16–18.

Miller, Donald E., and Lorna Touryan Miller. *Survivors: An Oral History of the Armenian Genocide*. Berkeley: University of California Press, 1993.

Miller, Elizabeth W., ed. *The Negro in America: A Bibliography*. Cambridge: Harvard University Press, 1967.

Miller, Floyd J. *The Search for a Black Nationality: Black Colonization and Emigration, 1787–1863*. Urbana: University of Illinois Press, 1975.

Miller, Hugh. *The Community of Man*. New York: Macmillan, 1949.

———. *Progress and Decline*. Los Angeles: Ward Ritchie Press, 1963.

Miller, John C. *The Wolf by the Ears: Thomas Jefferson and Slavery*. New York: Free Press, 1977; New American Library, 1980.

Miller, John. *Egotopia: Narcissism and the New American Landscape*. Tuscaloosa: University of Alabama Press, 1997.

Miller, Judith. *One by One: Facing the Holocaust*. New York: Simon and Schuster, 1990.

Miller, Kelley. "Is Race Prejudice Innate or Acquired?" *Journal of Applied Sociology* 11 (1927): 516–24.

Miller, Kent S., and Ralph M. Dreger, eds. *Comparative Studies of Whites and Blacks in the United States*. New York: Seminar Press, 1973.

Miller, Loren. *The Petitioners*. New York: Pantheon Books, 1965.

Miller, Marc S., ed. *State of the Peoples: A Global Human Rights Report on Societies in Danger*. Boston: Beacon Press, 1993.

Miller, Mary D., and Florence Rutter. *Child Artists of the Australian Bush*. London: Harrap, 1952.

Miller, Michael. "Outlawing Anti-Semitism." *Ideas for Action* June, 1946.

Miller, Randall M., and John David Smith, eds. *Dictionary of Afro-American Slavery*. Westport, CT: Greenwood Press, 1988.

Miller, Sarah. *The People of South Africa*. New York: Alfred A. Knopf, 1954.

Miller, Stuart C. *The Unwelcome Immigrant: American Images of Chinese, 1785–1882*. Berkeley: University of California Press, 1969.

Milner, David. *Children and Race*. Thousand Oaks, CA: Sage Publications, 1965.

Milner, Lucille B. "Miscegenation in South Africa." *Nature* 7 (1940): 357.

———. "Jim Crow in the Army." *New Republic* 110 (1944): 339–42.

Miner, Horace. *Timbuctoo*. Princeton: Princeton University Press, 1953.

Minton, Henry M., and Lewis M. Terman. *Pioneers in Psychological Testing*. New York: New York University Press, 1988.

Mintz, Sydney W., ed. *Slavery, Colonialism, and Racism*. New York: W. W. Norton, 1974.

Mintzer, George J., and Newman Levy. *The International Anti-Semitic Conspiracy*. New York: The American Jewish Committee, 1946.

Mitchell, William E. *The Bamboo Fire: An Anthropologist in New Guinea*. New York: W. W. Norton, 1978.

Mitroff, Ian I., and Warren Bennis. *The Unreality Industry: The Deliberate Manufacture of Falsehood and What it Does to Our Lives*. New York: Oxford University Press, 1993.

Mizruchi, Ephraim H. *Success and Opportunity*. New York: Free Press, 1964.

Modder, Montagu F. *The Jew in the Literature of England: To the End of the 19th Century*. Philadelphia: The Jewish Publication Society of America, 1939.

Mokgatle, Naboth. *The Autobiography of an Unknown South African*. Berkeley: University of California Press, 1971.

Molnar, Stephen. *Races, Types, and Ethnic Groups*. Englewood Cliffs, NJ: Prentice-Hall, 1976.

Moloney, James C. "Authoritarianism and Intolerance." *International Journal of Psychoanalysis* 29 (1948): 2–4.

Momigliana, Amaldo. *On Pagans, Jews, and Christians*. Middletown, CT: Wesleyan University Press, 1989.

Mönckeberg, F. "Mental Retardation from Malnutrition: 'Irreversible. . . . '" *Journal of the American Medical Association* 177 (1961): 56–57.

———. "Factors Conditioning Malnutrition in Latin America with special reference to Chile." In *Malnutrition is a Problem of Ecology*, edited by P. Gyorgy and O. L. Kline. Basel and New York: Karger, 1970.

Money-Kyrle, R. E. *Psychoanalysis and Politics*. London: Duckworth, 1951; New York: Norton, 1952.

Monro, D. H. "The Concept of Myth." *Sociological Review* 42 (1950): 115–32.

Montagu, Ashley. "*Intelligence Tests and the Negro in America*." *WASU* (West African Students' Union, London) 1 (1926): 5–7.

———. "On the Primate Thumb." *American Journal of Physical Anthropology* 15 (1931): 291–314.

———. "The Premaxilla in the Primates." *Quarterly Review of Biology* 10 (1935): 182–84.

———. "The Premaxilla in Man." *Journal of the American Dental Association* 23 (1936): 2043–57.

———. "The Future of the Australian Aborigines." *Oceania* 8 (1938): 343–50.

———. "Social Time: a Methodological and Functional Analysis." *American Journal of Sociology* 44 (1938): 282–84.

———. "A Cursory Examination of the Relations between Physical and Social Anthropology." *American Journal of Physical Anthropology* 26 (1940): 41–61.

———. "The Significance of the Variability of the Upper Lateral Incisor Teeth in Man." *Human Biology* 12 (1940): 323–58.

———. "The Socio-Biology of Man." *Scientific Monthly* 50 (1940): 483–90.

———. "The Biologist Looks at Crime." *Annals of the Academy of Political and Social Science* 217 (1941): 46–57.

———. "The Concept of Race in the Human Species in the Light of Genetics." *Journal of Heredity* 23 (1941): 243–47.

———. "Physical Anthropology and Anatomy." *American Journal of Physical Anthropology* 28 (1941): 261–71.

———. "Race, Caste and Scientific Method." *Psychiatry* 4 (1941): 337–38.

————. "Escape from Freedom." *Psychiatry* 5 (1942): 122–29.

————. "The Nature of War and the Myth of Nature." *The Scientific Monthly* 54 (1942): 342–53.

————. "On the Breeding of 'Aryans.'" *Psychiatry* 6 (1943): 254–55.

————. "Edward Tyson, M.D., F.R.S. (1650–1708), and the Rise of Human and Comparative Anatomy in England." *Memoirs of the American Philosophical Society* 20, xxix–488. Philadelphia, 1943.

————. "Genetics and the Antiquity of Man in the Americas." *Man* 43 (1943) [nos. 103–124] 105: 131–35.

————. "Comments on Comparative Studies in Human Biology." *Science* 100 (1944): 383–84.

————. "The Intelligence of Southern Whites and Northern Negroes." *Psychiatry* 7 (1944): 184–89.

————. "On the Relation between Body Size, Waking Activity, and the Origin of Social Life in the Primates." *American Anthropologist* 66 (1944): 141–45.

————. "Physical Anthropology." In *Medical Physics,* edited by Otto Glasser. Chicago: Year Book Publishers, Vol. I, 1944; Vol. II, 1950.

————. "Some Anthropological Terms: A Study in the Systematics of Confusion." *American Anthropologist* 47 (1945): 119–33.

————. "The Intelligence of Northern Negroes and Southern Whites in the First World War." *American Journal of Psychology* 58 (1945): 161–88.

————. "The Negro's Problem: The White Man." *Bulletin of Negro History* 8 (1945): 177–79.

————. "On the Phrase 'Ethnic Group' in Anthropology." *Psychiatry* 8 (1945): 27–33.

————. *One World or None* [a film]. New York: The American Federation of Scientific Workers/Washington: The National Committee on Atomic Information, 1946.

————. "Anti-feminism and Race Prejudice." *Psychiatry* 9 (1946): 69–71.

————. *Studies and Essays in the History of Science and Learning.* New York: Schuman, 1946.

————. "The Nature of Race Relations." *Social Forces* 25 (1947): 336–42.

————. "The Origin and Nature of Social Life and the Biological Basis of Coöperation." *Journal of Social Psychology* 29 (1949): 267–83.

————. "A Consideration of the Concept of Race." *Cold Spring Harbor Symposia on Quantitative Biology* 15 (1950): 315–36.

————. "Constitutional and Prenatal Factors in Infant and Child Health." In *The Healthy Personality,* edited by M. J. E. Senn, 148–210. New York: Josiah Macy, Jr., Foundation, 1950.

————. "A Hybrid Gibbon." *Journal of Mammalogy* 31 (1950): 150–53.

————. "'Social Instincts.'" *Scientific American* 182 (1950): 54–56.

————. *On Being Intelligent.* New York: Schuman, 1951.

————. "Answer by an Anthropologist to a Geneticist about the Understanding of Race in Man." *International Social Science Bulletin* (UNESCO) 3 (1951): 1007–10.

————. *The Biosocial Nature of Man.* New York: Grove Press, 1956.

————. *Education and Human Relations.* New York: Grove Press, 1958.

————. *An Introduction to Physical Anthropology*. 3d ed. Springfield, IL: Thomas, 1960.

————. "The Origin and Significance of Neonatal Immaturity in Man." *Journal of the American Medical Association* 178 (1961): 156–57.

————. "Science Versus Value Commitments." *Perspectives in Biology and Medicine* 5 (1961): 131–35.

————. *Man in Process*. Cleveland & New York: World Publishing Co., 1961.

————. *Culture and the Evolution of Man*. New York: Oxford University Press, 1962.

————. "Prehistoric Hybridization." *Man* 62 (1962): 25.

————. "The Concept of Race." *American Anthropologist* 64 (1962): 919–28.

————. *Prenatal Influences*. Springfield IL: Thomas, 1962.

————. *The Humanization of Man*. New York: World Publishing, 1962.

————. *Human Heredity*. Cleveland & New York: World Publishing Co., 1959; 3d ed., New York: New American Library, 1963.

————. *Race, Science and Humanity*. Princeton: Van Nostrand, 1963.

————. *Human Heredity*. New York: New American Library, 1963.

————. *Life Before Birth*. New York: New American Library, 1964.

————. *The Science of Man*. New York: Odyssey Press, 1964.

————. "A Non-Racial Approach Towards the Understanding of Human Diversity." In *The Concept of Race*, edited by A. Montagu, 103–52. New York: Free Press, 1964.

————. *The Human Revolution*. New York: World Publishing, 1965; New York: Bantam, 1967.

————. *The Idea of Race*. Lincoln: University of Nebraska Press, 1965.

————. *On Being Human*. New York: Dutton world Publishing, 1966. 2d ed. New York: Hawthorn Books, 1969, 1970.

————. "The Concept of the 'Primitive' and Related Anthropological Terms: A Study in the Systematics of Confusion." In *The Concept of the Primitive*, edited by Ashley Montagu, 148–68. New York: Free Press, 1968.

————. "The Language of Self-Deception." In *Language in America*, edited by Neil Postman, Charles Weingartner, and Terence P. Moran, 82–95. New York: Pegasus Press, 1969.

————. *Man: His First Two Million Years*. New York: Columbia University Press, 1969.

————. *The Direction of Human Development*. 2d ed. New York: Hawthorn Books, 1970.

————. "Just What is Equal Opportunity?" *Vista* 6 (1970): 23–25, 56.

————. *Touching: The Human Significance of the Skin*. New York: Columbia University Press, 1971.

————. *Statement on Race*. 3d ed. New York: Oxford University Press, 1972.

————. *Darwin, Competition and Cooperation*. New York: Schuman, 1952; Westport CT: Greenwood Press, 1973.

————. *Man's Most Dangerous Myth: The Fallacy of Race*. 5th edition. New York: Oxford University Press, 1974.

————. *Coming into Being among the Australian Aborigines*. 2d ed. London & Boston: George Routledge, 1974.

————. *Learning Non-Aggression: The Experience of Non-Literate Societies*. New York: Oxford University Press, 1976.

———. *The Nature of Human Aggression.* New York: Oxford University Press, 1976.

———. Toolmaking, Hunting, and the Origin of Language. In *Annals of the New York Academy of Sciences,* 280 edited by S. Harnad and H. D. Steklis, 266–72. New York: New York Academy of Sciences, 1976.

———. "On the Nonperception of 'Race' Differences." *Current Anthropology* 18 (1977): 743–44.

———. "Not By Bread Alone." *The Sciences* (September 1979): 23–24.

———. *Growing Young.* 2d ed. Westport, CT: Bergin & Garvey, 1989.

———. *The Natural Superiority of Women.* 4th ed. New York: Collier Books, 1992.

———. "Education, Humanity, and Technology," in *Advances in Telematics,* ed. Jarice Hanson, 1–15. Norwood, NJ: Ablex Publishing, 1994.

———. "Education, Humanity, and Technology." In *Advances in Telematics,* vol. 2, edited by Jarice Hanson, 1–15. Norwood, NJ: Ablex Publishing, 1994.

———. *Race and IQ.* 2d ed. New York: Oxford University Press, 1996.

———, ed. *Culture and the Evolution of Man.* New York: Oxford University Press, 1962.

———, ed. *The Concept of Race.* New York: Free Press, 1964.

———, ed. *Culture: Man's Adaptive Dimension.* New York: Oxford University Press, 1968.

———, ed. *The Concept of the Primitive.* New York: Free Press, 1968.

———, ed. *Man and Aggression.* 2d ed. New York: Oxford University Press, 1973.

———, ed. *The Origin and the Evolution of Man.* New York: Crowell, 1973.

———, ed. *Culture and Human Development: Insights Into Growing Human.* Englewood Cliffs, NJ: Prentice-Hall, 1974.

———, ed. *Frontiers of Anthropology.* New York: G. P. Putnam, 1974.

———, ed. *Learning Non-Aggression: The Experience of Non-Literate Societies.* New York: Oxford University Press, 1978.

Montagu, Ashley, and Theodosius Dobzhansky. "Natural Selection and the Mental Capacities of Mankind." *Science* 105 (1947): 587–90.

Montagu, Ashley, and Floyd Matson. *The Dehumanization of Man.* New York: McGraw-Hill, 1983.

———. *The Human Connection.* New York, McGraw-Hill, 1989.

Montellano, B. R. O. de. "Melanin, Afrocentricity, and Pseudoscience." *Yearbook of Physical Anthropology,* vol. 26: 33–58, 1953.

Montesquieu, Charles de Secondat. *The Spirit of the Laws,* bk. XV, chap. V. Translated by Thomas Nugent. New York: Hafner, 1949.

Moodie, T. Dunbar. *The Rise of Afrikanerdom.* Berkeley: University of California Press, 1975.

Moore, Barrington, Jr. *Reflections on the Causes of Human Misery and Upon Certain Proposals to Eliminate Them.* Boston: Beacon Press, 1972.

———. *Social Origins of Dictatorship and Democracy.* Boston: Beacon Press, 1993.

Moore, Doris L. *The Vulgar Heart.* London: Cassell, 1945.

Moore, George H. *Notes on the History of Slavery in Massachusetts.* New York: Appleton, 1866.

Moore, Gilbert. *A Special Rage.* New York: Harper & Row, 1971.

Moore, Joan W., with Harry Pachon. *Mexican Americans.* Englewood Cliffs, NJ: Prentice-Hall, 1976.

Moore, John A. "Geographic Variations of Adaptive Characters in *Rana pipiens* Schraber." *Evolution* 3(1) (1943): 1–23.

Moore, R. *Racism and Black Resistance in Britain.* London: Pluto Press, 1975.

Moore, Wilbert E. *American Negro Slavery and Abolition.* New York: The Third Press, 1971.

Moorhead, Alan. *The Fatal Impact: An Account of the Invasion of the South Pacific 1767–1840.* New York: Harper & Row, 1966.

Moquin, Wayne and Charles van Doren, eds. *Great Documents in American Indian History.* New York: Praeger, 1973.

———, eds. *A Documentary History of the Mexican Americans.* New York: Praeger, 1971.

Morais, Vamberto. *A Short History of Anti-Semitism.* New York: Norton, 1976.

Moran, Emilio F. *Human Adaptability: An Introduction to Ecological Anthropology.* Belmont, CA: Wadsworth, 1979.

Morant, Geoffrey M. *The Races of Central Europe.* New York: Norton, 1939.

———. "Racial Theories and International Relations." *Journal of the Royal Anthropological Institute of Great Britain and Ireland* 69 (1939): 151–62.

———. "The Future of Physical Anthropology." *Man* 44 (1944): 16–18.

Morgan, Thomas H. *Evolution and Genetics.* Princeton: Princeton University Press, 1925.

Morlan, G. K. "An Experiment on the Identification of Body Odor." *Journal of Genetic Psychology* 77 (1950): 257–65.

Morland, J. Kenneth. "Racial Recognition by Nursery School Children in Lynchburg, Va." *Social Forces* 37 (1958): 132–37.

Mörner, Magnus, ed. *Race and Class in Latin America.* New York: Columbia University Press, 1971.

Morris, Desmond. *The Naked Ape.* New York: McGraw-Hill, 1968.

Morse, Arthur D. *While Six Million Die: A Chronicle of American Apathy.* New York: Random House, 1967.

Morse, J. Mitchell. *Prejudice and Literature.* Philadelphia: Temple University Press, 1976.

Morton, Newton E. "Genetics of Interracial Crosses in Hawaii." *Eugenics Quarterly* 9 (1962): 23–24.

Morton, Newton E., Chin S. Chung, and Ming-Pi Mi. *Genetics of Interracial Crosses in Hawaii.* New York: Karger, 1967.

Moscati, Sabatino. *The Face of the Ancient Orient.* Chicago: Quadrangle Books, 1961.

———, ed. *The Phoenecians.* New York: Abbeville Press, 1988.

Moskovitz, Sarah. *Love Despite Hate: Child Survivors of the Holocaust and Their Adult Lives.* New York: Schocken Books, 1983.

Mosse, George L. *Toward the Final Solution: A History of European Racism.* New York: Howard Fertig, 1978.

Motley, Mary P., ed. *The Invisible Soldier: The Experience of the Black Soldier, World War II.* Detroit: Wayne State University Press, 1975.

Mountford, Charles P. *The Art of Albert Namatjira.* Melbourne: Bread & Cheese Club, 1944.

———. *Brown Men and Red Sand.* London: Phoenix House, 1950.

———. *Nomads of the Australian Desert.* Rigby: Adelaide, 1976.

Mourant, A. E. *The Distribution of the Human Blood Groups.* Springfield, IL: Thomas, 1954.

Mourant, Arthur E., A. C. Kopec, and K. Domaniewska-Sobczak. *Blood Groups and Disease: A Study of the Association of Diseases with Blood Groups and Other Polymorphisms.* New York: Oxford University Press, 1978.

Mudgett, Helen P. *Democracy for All.* Minneapolis: General Extension Division, University of Minnesota, 1945.

Muensterberger, Warner, and Aaron H. Esman, eds. *The Psychoanalytic Study of Society.* Vol. 6. New York: International Universities Press, 1975.

Muhsam, H. V. "The Genetic Origin of the Jews." *Genus* 20 (1964): 53–54.

Muller, Filip. *Eyewitness Auschwitz: Three Years in the Gas Chambers.* New York: Stein & Day, 1979.

Muller, Hermann J. "Genetics in the Scheme of Things." Proceedings of the Eighth International Congress of Genetics. *Hereditas,* supp. vol., 1949: 96–127.

———. *Out of the Night.* New York: Vanguard Press, 1935.

———. "On the Variability of Mixed Races." *American Naturalist* 70 (1936): 409–42.

Muller-Hill, Benno. *Murderous Science: Elimination by Scientific Selection of Jew, Gypsies, and Others.* Germany, 1953, New York: Oxford University Press, 1988.

Mullin, Michael, ed. *American Negro Slavery: A Documentary History.* Columbia: University of South Carolina Press, 1976.

Munroe, Ruth H., Robert L. Munroe, Beatrice B. Whiting, eds. *Handbook of Cross-Cultural Development.* New York: Garland, 1981.

Murdock, K., and Louis R. Sullivan. "A Contribution to the Study of Mental and Physical Measurements in Normal Children." *American Physical Educational Review* 28 (1923): 209–15, 278–88, 328.

Murphy, Douglas. *Congenital Malformations.* 2d ed. Philadelphia: Lippincott, 1947.

Murphy, Gardner. *Personality.* New York: Harper, 1947.

Murphy, John. *Lamps of Anthropology.* Manchester: Manchester University Press, 1943.

Murphy, T. D. *Ambassadors in Arms.* Honolulu: University of Hawaii Press, 1954.

Murray, Albert. *The Omni-Americans: Some Alternatives to the Folklore of White Supremacy.* New York: Random House, 1970.

Murray, Charles. *Losing Ground: American Social Policy, 1950–1980.* New York: Basic Books, 1984.

Murray, Harry A., ed. *Myth and Mythmaking.* New York: Braziller, 1960.

Murray, Pauli. *States' Laws on Race and Color.* Cincinnati: Methodist Woman's Division of Christian Service, 1950.

Mwase, George S. *Strike a Blow and Die: A Narrative of Race Relations in Colonial Africa.* Cambridge: Harvard University Press, 1967.

Myers, Gustavius. *History of Bigotry in the United States.* New York: Random House, 1943.

Myers, Henry A. *Are Men Equal?* New York: Putnam, 1945.

Myrdal, Gunnar. *An American Dilemma: The Negro Problem and Modern Democracy.* 2 vols. New York: Harper, 1944.

Myres, John L. *Who Were the Greeks?* Berkeley: University of California Press, 1930.

Nabakov, Peter, ed. *Native American Testimony.* New York: Viking Penguin, 1991.

Nabours, R. K. "Emergent Evolution and Hybridism." *Science* 71 (1930): 371–75.

Nagel, Joane. American Indian Ethnic Renewal. Oxford University Press, 1996.

Nagler, Michael N. America Without Violence: Why Violence Persists and How You Can Stop It. Covelo, CA: Island Press, 1982.

Nairn, Tom. The Break-Up of Britain. New York: Schocken, 1981.

Namais, June. White Captives! Gender and Ethnicity on the American Frontier. Chapel Hill: University of North Carolina Press, 1993.

Nash, E., H. Nash, B. Pasamanick, and H. Knobloch. "Further Observations on the Development of Negro Children: Status at Seven Years." Unpublished material.

Nash, Manning. "Race and the Ideology of Race." Current Anthropology 3 (1962): 285–88.

Nash, Philleo. "An Introduction to the Problem of Race Tension." In The North American Indian Today, edited by C. T. Loram and T. F. McIlwraith, 331–35. Toronto: University of Toronto Press, 1943.

Nash, Walter. "Democracy's Goal in Race Relationships—with Special Reference to New Zealand." In The Role of the Races in Our Future Civilization, edited by Harry W. Laidler, 12–16. New York: League for Industrial Democracy, 1942.

Nasmyth, George. Social Progress and the Darwinian Theory. New York: Putnam, 1916.

National Spiritual Assembly of Bahá'í of the United States: The Vision of Race Unity: America's Most Challenging Issue. Wilmette, IL: 1995.

Ndem, Eyo B. "The Status of Coloured People in Britain." Phylon 58 (1957): 82–87.

Nef, John U. War and Human Progress. Cambridge: Harvard University Press, 1950.

Neilsen, Melany. Even Mississippi. Tuscaloosa: University of Alabama Press, 1989.

Nelli, Humbert S. From Immigrants to Ethnics: The Italian Americans. New York: Oxford University Press, 1983.

Nelson, Dana D. The Word in Black and White: Reading "Race" in American Literature 1638–1867. New York: Oxford University Press, 1994.

Nelson, William, ed. William Golding's Lord of the Flies: A Source Book. New York: Odyssey, 1963.

Netanyahu, B[enzion]. The Origins of the Inquisition in Fifteenth Century Spain. New York: Random House, 1995.

Neumann, Franz L. Behemoth: the Structure and Practice of National Socialism. New York: Oxford University Press, 1942.

Neuville, Henri. L'Espèce, la race et le métissage en anthropologie. Archives de L'Institut de Paléontologie Humaine, Mémoire II. Paris, 1933.

———. "Les Métissages de l'Isle Pitcairn." L'Anthropologie 43 (1933): 267, 485.

Neville, A. O. Australia's Coloured Minority. Sydney: Currawong Press, 1947.

Nevo, Eviator. "Genetic diversity and the Evolution of Life and Man." In Racism, Science and Pseudo Science, 77–92. Paris, UNESCO, 1981.

Newby, I. A. Challenge to the Court: Social Scientists and the Defense of Segregation, 1954–1966. Baton Rouge: Louisiana State University Press, 1969.

———. Jim Crow's Defense. Baton Rouge: Louisiana State University Press, 1965.

Newby, Robert G. "The Bell Curve: Laying Bare the Resurgence of Scientific Racism." American Behavioral Scientist 39 (1995): 6–108.

Newhall, Richard A. The Columbus Letter. Williamstown, MA: Chapin Library, Williams College, 1953.

Newman, Dorothy K., et al. *Protest, Politics, and Prosperity*. New York: Pantheon, 1978.

Newman, M. T. "The Application of Ecological Rules to the Racial Anthropology of the Aboriginal New World." *American Anthropologist* 55 (1955): 309–27.

Newton, Grant, and Seymour Levine, eds. *Early Experience and Behavior*. Springfield, IL: Thomas, 1968.

Nichols, Charles H. *Many Thousand Gone*. Leiden: Brill, 1963.

Nichols, Lee. *Breakthrough on the Color Front*. New York: Random House, 1954.

Niewyk, Donald L. *Socialist, Anti-Semite and Jew: German Social Democracy Confronts the Problem of Anti-Semitism*. Baton Rouge: Louisiana State University Press, 1971.

———. *The Jews in Weimar Germany*. Baton Rouge: Louisiana State University Press, 1980.

Nilsson, Martin P. "The Race Problem of the Roman Empire." *Hereditas* 2 (1921): 370–90.

Njeri, Itabari. *The Last Plantation: Color, Conflict, and Identity*. Boston: Houghton-Mifflin, 1997.

Nolen, Claude H. *The Negro's Image in the South*. Lexington: University of Kentucky Press, 1967.

Norgren, Jill, and Nanda Serena. *American Cultural Pluralism and Law*. New York: Praeger, 1988.

Norlin, George. *Things in the Saddle*. Cambridge: Harvard University Press, 1940.

———. *The Quest of American Life*. University of Colorado Studies, Series B. *Studies in the Humanities*, vol. 2. Boulder, 1945.

Norrell, Robert J. *Reaping the Whirlwind: The Civil Rights Movement in Tuskegee*. New York: Alfred A. Knopf, 1985.

Northrup, Solomon. *Twelve Years a Slave*. Baton Rouge: Louisiana State University Press, 1968.

Norwood, Christopher. *At Highest Risk: Environmental Hazards to Young and Unborn Children*. New York: McGraw-Hill, 1980.

Nott, Josiah C. *Types of Mankind*. Philadelphia: Lippincott, 1854.

Nott, Josiah C., and George R. Gliddon. *Indigenous Races of the Earth*. Philadelphia: Lippincott, 1857.

Novák, Vladimir J. *The Principles of Sociogenesis*. Prague: Academia Czechoslovak Academemy of Sciences, 1982.

Numelin, Ragnar. *The Beginnings of Diplomacy*. New York: Philosophical Library, 1950.

Nye, Russel B. "Civil Liberties and the Anti-Slavery Controversy." *Science & Society* 9 (1945): 125–46.

———. *Fettered Freedom*. East Lansing: Michigan State College Press, 1949.

O'Brien, S. J., D. E. Wildt, and Bush, M. "The Cheetah in Genetic Peril." *Scientific American* 254, 1986, 84–92.

O'Brien, S. J., D. E. Wildt, D. Goldman, C. R. Merril, and M. Bush. "The Cheetah is Depauparate in Genetic Variation." *Science* 221: 459–462.

O'Reilly, Kenneth. *Racial Matters: The FBI's Secret File on Black America, 1960–1972*. New York: Free Press, 1989.

Oakes, James. *The Ruling Class: A History of American Slaveholders*. New York: Alfred A. Knopf, 1982.

Oakesmith, John. *Race and Nationality*. London: Heinemann, 1919.

Odum, Howard. *Race and Rumors of Race.* Chapel Hill: University of North Carolina Press, 1943.

Ofari, Earl. *Let Your Motto Be Resistance.* Boston: Beacon Press, 1972.

Ogbu, John U. *The Next Generation: An Ethnography of Education in an Urban Neighborhood.* New York: Academic Press, 1974.

———. *Minority Education and Caste.* New York: Academic Press, 1978.

Ogden, C. K., and I. A. Richards. *The Meaning of Meaning.* New York: Harcourt, Brace, 1923.

Oishi, Gene, "The Anxiety of Being a Japanese-American." *The New York Times Magazine* 28 April 1985: 54sq.

Okubo, Mine. *Citizen 13660.* New York: Columbia University Press, 1946.

Oldham, Joseph H. *Christianity and the Race Problem.* London: Student Christian Movement Press, 1925.

Oliver, Douglas. *The Pacific Islands.* Cambridge: Harvard University Press, 1951.

Olivier, Georges. "Hétérosis et Dominance dans les Populations Humaines." *Comptes Rendus de l'Académie des Sciences,* 259 (1964): 4357–60. Paris.

———. "Émigration et Métissage." *Bulletin et Mémoires de la Société d'Anthropologie de Paris* 7 (1965): 193–208.

———. "La Responsibilite Scientifique des Anthropologistes Biologiques." Garcia de Orta, *Ser. Antrobio* 2 (1986): 35–40. Lisbon

Olivier, Sidney. "Colour Prejudice." *Contemporary Review* 124 (1923): 448–57.

———. *Jamaica the Blessed Island.* London: Faber & Faber, 1936.

Olson, Bernard E. *Faith and Prejudice.* New Haven: Yale University Press, 1963.

Olzak, Susan and Joane Nagel, eds. *Competitive Ethnic Relations.* Orlando: Academic Press, 1987.

Omi, Michael, and Howard Winant. *Racial Formation in the United States.* New York: Routeledge, 1986.

Onions, R. B. *The Origins of Human Thought.* Cambridge: Cambridge University Press, 1951

Opler, Morris E. "Cultural and Organic Conceptions in World History." *American Anthropologist* 46 (1944): 448–60.

———. "The Use and Abuse of the Word 'Aryan.'" *El Palacio* 103 (1946): 9–12.

Orleans, Peter, and William E. Russell, eds. *Race, Change, and Urban Society.* Thousand Oaks, CA: Sage Publications, 1971.

Ornstein, Robert, and David Sobel. *The Healing Brain.* New York: Simon & Schuster, 1987.

Osborn, Frederick. *A Preface to Eugenics.* New York: Harper, 1940.

Osler, S. F., and R. E. Cooke, eds. *The Biosocial Basis of Mental Retardation.* Baltimore: Johns Hopkins Press, 1965.

Osofsky, Gilbert, ed. *The Burden of Race: A Documentary History of Negro-White Relations in America.* New York: Harper & Row, 1967.

———, ed. *Puttin' On Ole Massa.* New York: Harper & Row, 1969.

Owen, David. *Human Rights.* New York: Norton, 1978.

Padover, Saul K. "Who Are the Germans?" *Foreign Affairs* 13 91935): 509–18.

———, ed. *A Jefferson Profile.* New York: John Day, 1956.

———, ed. *The Complete Jefferson.* New York: Tudor Publishing Co., 1943.

Paine, Thomas. *African Slavery in America. The Writings of Thomas Paine.* Vol. 1. Edited by Moncure Daniel Conway. New York: G. P. Putnam's Sons (1894).

Palmer, Colin A. *Human Cargoes: The British Slave Trade to Spanish America, 1700–1739.* Urbana: University of Illinois Press, 1981.

Panichas, George A., ed. *Promise of Greatness: The War of 1914–1918.* New York: John Day, 1968.

Park, Robert E. "The Bases of Race Prejudice." *Annals of the American Academy of Political and Social Science* 140 (1928): 11–20.

Parkes, James. *An Enemy of the People: Antisemitism.* New York: Pelican Books, 1946.

———. *Antisemitism: A Concise World History.* Chicago: Quadrangle Books, 1946.

———. *The Jewish Problem in the Modern World.* New York: Oxford University Press, 1946.

Parsons, P. A. "Genetic Determination of Behavior (Mice and Men)." In *Genetics, Environment, and Behavior,* edited by Lee Ehrman, Gilbert S. Omenn, and Ernst Caspari. New York: Academic Press, 1972.

Parsons, Talcott. "Certain Primary Sources and Patterns of Aggression in the Social Structure of the Western World." *Psychiatry* 10 (1947): 167–81.

Pasamanick, Benjamin. "A Comparative Study of the Behavioral Development of Negro Infants." *Journal of Genetic Psychology* 69 (1946): 3–44.

———. "Some Misconceptions Concerning Differences in the Racial Prevalence of Mental Disease." *American Journal of Orthopsychiatry* 33 (1963): 72–86.

———. "Myths Regarding Prevalence of Mental Disease in the American Negro." *Journal of the National Medical Association* 56 (1964): 6–17.

———. "Some Sociological Aspects of Science, Race, and Racism." *American Journal of Orthospsychiatry* 39 (1969): 7–15.

———. "A Child is Being Beaten." *American Journal of Orthopsychiatry* 41 (1971): 540–56.

Pastore, Nicholas. *The Nature-Nurture Controversy.* New York: King's Crown Press, 1949.

Patai, Raphael. *The Jewish Mind.* New York: Scribner's, 1977.

Patai, Raphael, and Jennifer P. Wing. *The Myth of the Jewish Race.* New York: Scribner's, 1975.

Paterson, Donald G. *Physique and Intellect.* New York: Century, 1930.

Paton, D. M., ed. *Church and Race in South Africa.* London: Student Christian Movement Press, 1958.

Patten, William. *The Grand Strategy of Evolution.* Boston: Badger, 1920.

Patterson, Orlando. *Slavery and Social Death.* Cambridge: Harvard University Press, 1982.

Patterson, Sheila. *Colour and Culture in South Africa.* London: Routledge, 1953.

———. *Dark Strangers.* London: Tavistock, 1963.

Patton, Robert Gray, and Lytt I. Gardner. *Growth Failure in Maternal Deprivation.* Springfield, IL: Thomas, 1963.

Peacock, George. *Life of Thomas Young.* London: Murray, 1855.

Pearce, Roy H. *The Savages of America.* Revised. Baltimore: Johns Hopkins Press, 1965.

Pearce, W. Barnett. *Communication and the Human Condition.* Carbondale: Southern Illinios University, 1989.

Pearl, Raymond. "On the Correlation between Intelligence and the Size of the Head." *Journal of Comparative Neurology and Psychology* 16 (1906): 189–99.

———. "The Biology of Superiority." *American Mercury* 12 (1927): 257–66.

———. "Some Biological Considerations about War." *American Journal of Sociology* 66 (1941): 487–503.

Pearson, Egon S. *Karl Pearson: An Appreciation of Some Aspects of His Life and Work.* Cambridge: University Press, 1938.

Pearson, Jr., Willie, and H. Kenneth Bechtel, eds. *Blacks, Science and American Education.* New Brunswick: Rutgers University Press, 1989.

Pearson, Karl, and Margaret Moul. "The Problem of Alien Immigration into Great Britain, Illustrated by an Examination of Russian and Polish Children." *Annals of Eugenics* 1 (1925): 5–91, 126–27.

Pearson, Karl. "Relationship of Intelligence to Size and Shape of the Head and Other Mental and Physical Characters." *Biometrika* 5 (1906): 105–46.

———. "The Problem of Alien Immigration into Great Britain, Illustrated by an Examination of Russian and Polish Jewish Children." *Annals of Eugenics* 1 (1925): 1–127.

———. *The Grammar of Science.* London: Walter Scott, 1892; Final revised edition, London: J.M. Dent, 1937.

———. *The Life, Letters and Labours of Francis Galton.* 3 vols in 4. Cambridge University Press, 1914–1930.

Pearson, Karl., and A. G. Davin. "On the Biometric Constants of the Human Skull." *Biometrika* 16 (1942): 328–64.

Pearson, Karl., and T. L. Woo. "Further Investigation of the Morphometric Characters of the Individual Bones of the Human Skull." *Biometrika* 27 (1935): 424–66.

Pease, William H., and Jane H. Pease. "Antislavery Ambivalence: Immediatism, Expediency, Race." *American Quarterly* 17 (1965): 682–95.

Peckham, Howard H. *Captured by Indians.* New Brunswick, NJ: Rutgers University Press, 1954.

Peiper, Albrecht. *Cerebral Function in Infancy and Childhood.* 3d ed. New York: Consultants Bureau, 1963.

Penfield, Wilder. "Letter to the Editor." *Perspectives in Biology and Medicine* 6 (1963): 540–41.

Penkower, Monty N. *The Jews Were Expendable: Free World Diplomacy and the Holocaust.* Urbana: University of Illinois Press, 1984.

Penrose, Lionel S. "Review of Dunn and Dobzhansky's Heredity, Race and Society." *Annals of Eugenics* 17 (1952): 252–53.

———. "Evidence of Heterosis in Man." *Proceedings of the Royal Society,* B, 144 (1955): 203–13.

Perl, William R. *The Four Front War: From the Holocaust to the Promised Land.* New York: Crown, 1978.

Perlmutter, Nathan, and Ruth Perlmutter. *The Real Anti-Semitism in America.* New York: Arbor House, 1982.

Perry, Lewis. *Radical Abolitionism.* Ithaca: Cornell University Press, 1973.

Perry, Lewis, and Fellman, Michael, eds. *Antislavery Reconsidered: New Perspectives on the Abolitionists.* Baton Rouge: Louisiana State University Press, 1979.

Perry, Richard J. *From Time Immemorial: Indigenous Peoples and State Systems.* Austin: University of Texas Press, 1996.

Perry, W. J. "Man the Primeval Pacifist." *Vincula* (University of London Student Journal) (14 December 1925): 64.

Persell, Caroline H. *Education and Inequality.* New York: Free Press, 1977.

Persons, Stow, ed. *Evolutionary Thought in America.* New Haven: Yale University Press, 1950.

Petersen, William. "Prejudice in American Society." *Commentary* 26 (1958): 342–48.

———. *Japanese Americans: Oppression and Success.* New York: Random House, 1971. Reprint. Washington, D.C.: University Press of America, 1981.

Peterson, Robert W., ed. *South Africa and Apartheid.* New York: Facts on File, 1975.

Pettigrew, Thomas F. *A Profile of the Negro American.* Princeton: Van Nostrand, 1964.

Pettman, Ralph. *Biopolitics and International Values: Investigating Liberal Norms.* New York: Pergamon Press, 1981.

Peukert Detlev. *Germany: Conformity, Opposition, and Racism in Everyday Life.* New Haven: Yale University Press, 1987.

Peukert, Detlev J. K. *Inside Nazi Germany.* New Haven: Yale University Press, 1987.

Pfeffer, Leo. *This Honorable Court.* Boston: Beacon Press, 1967.

Phelan, Gloria. "Aboriginal Children in New South Wales Schools." *Integrated Education* 3 (1965): 36–41.

Phillips, Norman. *The Tragedy of Apartheid.* New York: McKay, 1960.

Phillips, Ulrich B. *American Negro Slavery.* Baton Rouge: Louisiana State University Press, 1966.

———. *The Slave Economy of the Old South.* Baton Rouge: Louisiana State University Press, 1968.

Phinney, Jean S., and Mary Jane Rotheram. *Children's Ethnic Socialization.* Thousand Oaks, CA: Sage, 1987.

Pickens, Donald K. *Eugenics and the Progressives.* Nashville: Vanderbilt University Press, 1968.

Pickering, S. P. "Correlation of Brain and Head Measurements and Relation of Brain Shape and Size to Shape of Size of the Head." *American Journal of Physical Anthropology* 15 (1931): 1–52.

Pierson, Donald. *Negroes in Brazil.* Chicago: University of Chicago Press, 1942.

Pierson, George W. *Tocqueville in America.* New York: Anchor Books, 1958.

Pinkney, Alphonso. *The Myth of Black Progress.* New York: Cambridge University Press, 1984.

Pinkus, Oscar. *The House of Ashes.* New York: World Publishing Co., 1964.

Pisar, Samuel. *Of Blood and Hope.* Boston: Little, Brown, 1980.

Pittard, Eugene. *Race and History.* New York: Alfred A. Knopf, 1926.

Pitt-Rivers, Julian. "Who are The Indians?" *Encounter* 25 (1965): 44–49.

Plato. *The Republic.*

Platt, Lord, and A. S. Parkes. *Social and Genetic Influences on Life and Death.* New York: Plenum Press, 1967.

Plimpton, Ruth T. *Operation Crossroads.* New York: Viking Press, 1962.

Pliny. *Natural History.*

Plomer, Willliam. *Double Lives.* London: Jonathan Cape, 1943; New York: Noonday Press, 1956.

Polanyi, Karl. *The Great Transformation*. New York: Rinehart, 1944.

Polenberg, Richard. *One Nation Divisible: Class, Race, and Ethnicity in the United States Since 1938*. New York, Viking Press, 1980.

Poliakov, Leon. *Harvest of Hate*. London: Elek Books, 1956.

———. *The History of Anti-Semitism*. 4 vols. New York: Vanguard, 1973/1983.

———. *The Aryan Myth*. New York: Basic Books, 1974.

Pollard, Albert F. "The War of Nature and a Peace of Mind." *Vincula* (University of London Student Journal) (14 December 1925): 60–61.

Pope, Liston. *Millhands and Preachers*. New Haven: Yale University Press, 1942.

———. *The Kingdon Beyond Caste*. New York: Friendship Press, 1957.

Pope-Hennessy, James. *Sins of the Fathers: A Study of the Atlantic Slave Traders, 1441–1807*. New York: Alfred A. Knopf, 1968.

Popper, Karl R. *The Open Society and Its Enemies*. Princeton: Princeton University Press, 1950.

———. "Prediction and Prophecy in the Social Sciences." In *Theories of History*, edited by Patrick Gardiner. New York: Free Press; London: Collier-Macmillan, 1959.

Porteous, S. D. *The Psychology of a Primitive People*. New York: Longmans, 1931.

Porter, Judith D. R. *Black Child, White Child*. Cambridge: Harvard University Press, 1971.

Postman, Neil, Charles Weingartner, and Terence P. Moran, eds. *Language in America*. New York: Pegasus, 1969.

Potter, Joan. *African American Firsts*. Elizabeth, NY: Pinto Press, 1994.

Pourchet, Maria J. "Brazilian Mestizo Types." In *Handbook of South American Indians* V, edited by Julian H. Steward, 111–20. Washington, D.C.: Smithsonian Institution, 1950.

Powdermaker, Hortense. *Probing Our Prejudices*. New York: Harper, 1944.

———. *After Freedom*. New York: Atheneum, 1968.

Powell, G. F., J. A. Brasel, and R. M. Blizzard. "Emotional Deprivation and Growth Retardation Simulating Idiopathic Hypopituitariam: Clinical Evaluation of the Syndrome." *New England Journal of Medicine* 276 (1967): 1271–8.

Powell, William P. *Tree of Hate: Propaganda and Prejudices Affecting United States Relations with the Hispanic World*. New York: Basic Books, 1971.

Power, Margaret. *The Egalitarians: Human and Chimpanzee*. New York: Cambridge University Press, 1991.

Powers, Mabel. *The Indian as Peacemaker*. New York: Revell, 1932.

Powers, William K. *Beyond the Vision: Essays on American Indian Culture*. Athens: University of Georgia Press, 1987.

Poynter, C. W. M., and J. J. Keegan. "A Study of the American Negro Brain." *Journal of Comparative Neurology* 25 (1915): 183–202.

Prager, Dennis, and Joseph Tolushkin. *Why the Jews?* New York: Simon & Schuster, 1983.

Price, Gwilym A. "Racial Integration in Industry." *New York Herald Tribune*, 1 November 1955: 16.

Price, Willard. "Race Barriers Broken." *The Spectator* 5 September 1952: 291–92.

Prichard, James Cowles. *Researches into the Physical History of Man*. 3d ed. London: Ballière, 1836.

Proctor, R. "From Anthropologie to Rassenkunde in the German Anthropological Tradition." In *Genes, Bodies and Behavior* edited by G. W. Stocking, Jr. Madison: University of Wisconsin Press, 1988: 138–79.

Proctor, Robert. *Racial Hygiene: Medicine Under the Nazis.* Cambridge: Harvard University Press, 1988.

Provine, William B. "Geneticists and the Biology of Race Crossing." *Science* 182 (1973): 790–96.

Pushkin, Isidore, and Thelma Veness. "The Development of Racial Awareness and Prejudice in Children." In *Psychology and Race,* edited by Peter Watson. Chicago: Aldine, 1973.

Putnam, Carleton. *Race and Reason.* Washington, D.C.: Public Affairs Press, 1961.

Quarles, Benjamin. *The Negro in the Making of America.* New York: Collier Books, 1965.

———. *Black Abolitionists.* New York: Oxford University Press, 1969.

Quiggin, A. Hingston. *Haddon the Head Hunter.* Cambridge: Cambridge University Press, 1942.

Quigley, Carroll. "Review of Darlington's 'The Evolution of Man and Society.'" *American Anthropologist* 73 (1971): 434–39.

Quinley, Harold E., and Charles Y. Glock. *Anti-Semitism in America.* New York: Free Press, 1979.

Raab, Earl, ed. *American Race Relations Today.* New York: Anchor Books, 1962.

Raboteau, Albert J. *Slave Religion: The "Invisible Institution" in the Antebellum South.* New York: Oxford University Press, 1978.

Race, R. R., and Ruth Sanger. *Blood Groups in Man.* 3d ed. Springfield, IL: Thomas, 1958.

Radin, Paul. *The Racial Myth.* New York: Whittlesey House, 1934.

Radke, Marian, and Helen Trager. "Children's Perceptions of the Social Roles of Negroes and Whites." *Journal of Psychology* 29 (1950): 3–33.

Radke-Yarrow, M., H. Trager, and Jean Miller. "The Role of Parents in the Development of Children's Ethnic Attitudes." *Child Development* 23 (1952): 13–53.

Rae, Douglas. *Equalities.* Cambridge: Harvard University Press, 1981.

Ramos, Arthur. *The Negro in Brazil.* Translation of O Negro Brasileiro, Rio de Janeiro, 1934, made by Richard Pattee. Manuscript. Washington, D.C., 1939.

———. *Introdução à antropologia Brasileira.* Rio de Janeiro. Casa de Estudiante do Brasil, 1943–1947, 1951.

Ramsey, Paul. *Christian Ethics and the Sit-In.* New York: Association Press, 1961.

Randal, Judith. "Hunger: Does it Cause Brain Damage?" *Think* 32 (1967): 2–7.

Randel, William P. *The Ku Klux Klan.* Philadelphia: Chilton Books, 1965.

Ranson, Stephen W. *The Anatomy of the Nervous System.* 7th ed. Philadelphia: Saunders, 1939.

Rau, R. E. "Additions to the Revised List of Preserved Material of the Extinct Cape Colony Quagga and Notes on the Relationship and Distribution of Southern Plains Zebras." *Annals of the South African Museum* 77(2) (1978): 27–45.

Rauschning, Hermann. *The Voice of Destruction.* New York: Putnam, 1940.

Ravenstein, E. G., ed. *A Journal of the First Voyage of Vasco da Gama, 1497–1499.* London: Hakluyt Society, 1897.

Ravitch, Diane. "Multiculturalism: E Pluribus Plures." *American Scholar* (Summer 1990): 337–54.

Rawley, James A. *Race and Politics: "Bleeding Kansas" and the Coming Civil War.* Philadelphia: Lippincott, 1969.

———. *The Trans-Atlantic Slave Trade.* New York: Norton, 1981.

Rayner, William. *The Tribe and its Successors.* London: Faber, 1962.

Read, Herbert, and Charles P. Mountford, eds. *Australia: Aboriginal Painting from Arnhemland.* UNESCO World Art Series. New York: Columbia University Press, 1955.

Reader's Digest. *Through Indian Eyes, The Untold Story of Native American Peoples.* Pleasantville, New York, 1995.

Reasons, Charles E., and Jack L. Kuykendall, eds. *Race, Crime and Justice.* Pacific Palisades, CA: Goodyear, 1972.

Redding, J. Saunders. *They Came in Chains.* Philadelphia: Lippincott, 1950.

Reddy, Maureen T. *Crossing the Line.* New Brunswick, NJ: Rutgers University Press, 1994.

Redfield, Robert. "Race and Class in Yucatan." In *Cooperation in Research,* 511–32. Publication No. 501. Washington, D.C.: Carnegie Institution of Washington, 1938.

———. "Culture Contact without Conflict." *American Anthropologist* 41 (1939): 514–17.

Reed, Ismael, ed. *MultiAmerica: Essays on Cultural Wars and Cultural Peace.* New York: Viking, 1997.

Reed, John Shelton. *The Enduring South.* Chapel Hill: University of North Carolina Press, 1975.

Reed, T. Edward. "Caucasian Genes in American Negroes." *Science* 165 (1969): 762–88.

Reel, Frank A. *The Case of General Yamashita.* Chicago: University of Chicago Press, 1949.

Reid, Ira De A., ed. "Racial Desegregation and Integration." *Annals of the Academy of Political and Social Science* 24 (March 1956): 1–211.

Reid, R. R., and J. H. Mulligan. "Relation of Cranial Capacity to Intelligence." *Journal of the Royal Anthropological Institute of Great Britain and Ireland* 53 (1923): 322–32.

Reinemann, J. O. "The Mulatto Children in Germany." *Mental Hygiene* 37 (1953): 365–76.

Reinhard, John B., and Alan R. Drash. "Psychological Dwarfism: Environmentally Induced Recovery." *Psychomatic Medicine* 31 (1969): 165–72.

Reinheimer, Hermann. *Evolution by Coöperation: A Study in Bioeconomics.* London: Kegan Paul, 1913.

———. *Symbiosis: A Socio-physiological Study of Evolution.* London: Headley, 1920.

Reissman, F. *The Culturally Deprived Child.* New York: Harper & Row, 1962.

Renan, Ernest. *The Future of Science.* Translated by Albert D. Vandam and C. B. Pitman. London: Chapman & Hall, 1891.

———. "Judaism: Race or Religion." [1883]. *Contemporary Jewish Record* 6 (1943): 436–48.

Renard, G. *Life and Work in Prehistoric Times.* New York: Alfred A. Knopf, 1929.

Report of the Commission on Mixed Marriages in South Africa. Pretoria: Government Printer, 1939.

Report of the Joint Commission on Mental Health in Children: *Crisis in Child Mental Health: Challenge for the 1970's.* New Youk: Harper & Row, 1970.

Reuck, Anthony de, and Julie Knight, eds. *Caste and Race: Comparative Approaches.* Boston: Little, Brown, 1967.

Reuter, Edward B. "Competition and the Racial Division of Labor." In *Race Relations and the Race Problem,* edited by Edgar T. Thompson, ed., 47–60. Durham: Duke University Press, 1939.

———. *The American Race Problem.* Introduction and revision by Jitsuichi Masuoka. New York: Crowell, 1970.

Rex, John. *Race Relations in Sociological Theory.* New York: Schocken Books, 1970; Boston: Routledge & Kegan Paul, 1984.

———. *Race, Colonialism and the City.* London and Boston: Routledge & Kegan Paul, 1973.

Reynolds, Donald E. *Editors Make War: Southern Newspapers in the Secession Crisis.* Nashville: Vanderbilt University Press, 1970.

Reynolds, Lacey T. "A Retrospective on 'Race': The Career of a Concept." *Sociological Focus* 25 (1992): 1–14.

Reynolds, Lacey T. and Leonard Lieberman, eds. *Race and Other Misadventures: Essays in Honor of Ashley Montagu in His Ninetieth Year.* Dix Hills, NY: General Hall, 1996.

Reynolds, Vernon, Vincent S. E. Flagler, and Ian Vine. *The Sociobiology of Ethnocentrism.* London: Croom Helm, 1987.

Rhoodie, N. J., ed. *South African Dialogue.* Johannesburg, New York: McGraw-Hill Book Co., 1972; Philadelphia: Westminister Press, 1972.

Ribeiro, Rene. "Situação Etnica do Nordeste." *Sociologia 15* (1953): 210–59.

Rice, C. Duncan. *The Rise and Fall of Black Slavery.* Baton Rouge: Louisiana State University Press, 1975.

Rice, David T., ed. *The Dawn of European Civilization.* New York: McGraw-Hill, 1965.

Richards, Leonard L. *Gentlemen of Property and Standing.* New York: Oxford University Press, 1970.

Richardson, Ken, David Spears, and Martin Richards, eds. *Race, Culture, and Intelligence.* Baltimore: Penguin Books, 1972.

Richarz, Monika, ed. *Jewish Life in Germany.* Bloomington: Indiana University Press, 1991.

Richmond, Anthony H. "Racial Relations in England." *Midwest Journal* 2 (1951): 1–13.

Richmond, Arthur. "Economic Insecurity and Stereotypes as Factors in Colour Prejudice." *Sociological Review* 42 (1950): 147–70.

———. *Colour Prejudice in Britain.* London: Routledge, 1954.

———. *The Colour Problem.* New York: Penguin Books, 1955.

———. "Memories of South Africa." *The Listener* 60 (1958): 736–39.

Ride, L. T. "The Problem of Depopulation with Special Reference to British North Borneo." *The Caduceus* (University of Hong Kong) 13 (1934): 182–83.

Rife, David C. *Hybrids.* Washington, D.C.: Public Affairs Press, 1965.

Riggins, Stephen H. *Ethnic Minority Media.* Thouand Oaks, CA.: Sage, 1992.

Ringelblum, Emanuel. *Notes From the Warsaw Ghetto.* New York: McGraw-Hill, 1952.

Ringer, Benjamin. *"We the People" and Others: Duality and America's Treatment of its Racial Minorities.* London & New York: Tavistock/Methuen, 1983.

Risdon, D. L. "A Study of the Cranial and Other Human Remains from Palestine Excavated at Tell Duweir (Lachish)." *Biometrika* 31 (1939): 99–166.

Rist, Ray C. *The Invisible Children: School Integration in American Society.* Cambridge: Harvard University Press, 1978.

Ritchie, Jane, and James Ritchie. *Growing Up in Polynesia.* Sydney: Allen & Unwin, 1979.

Ritner, Peter. *The Death of Africa.* New York: Macmillan, 1960.

Rivers, W. H. R., ed. *Essays on the Depopulation of Melanesia.* Cambridge: Cambridge University Press, 1922.

Roback, A. A. *A Dictionary of International Slurs.* Cambridge: Sci-Art Publishers, 1944.

Robateau, Albert J. *Slave Religion: The "Invisible Institution" in the Ante-bellum South.* New York: Oxford University Press, 1978.

Robb, James H. *Working-Class Anti-Semite.* London: Tavistock Publications, 1955.

Robertson, J. M. *The Germans.* London: Williams & Norgate, 1916.

Robertson, Pat. *The New World Order.* New York: Word Publishing: 1991.

Robertson, T. C. "Racism Comes to Power in South Africa." *Commentary* 6 (1948): 423–29.

Robeson, Eslanda G. *African Journey.* New York: John Day, 1945.

Robins, Ashley H. *Biological Perspectives on Human Pigmentation.* New York: Cambridge University Press, 1991.

Robinson, David M. *Excavations at Olynthus.* Pt. XI, *Necrolynthia, a Study in Greek Burial Customs and Anthropology.* Baltimore: Johns Hopkins Press, 1942.

Robinson, Donald. *Slavery in the Structure of American Politics, 1765–1820.* New York: W. W. Norton, 1979.

Robson, Lloyd. *A History of Tasmania.* Melbourne: Oxford University Press, 1983.

Rodenwaldt, Ernst. *Die Mestizen auf Kisar.* 2 vols. The Hague: Martinus Nijhoff, 1927.

Roe, Anne, and George G. Simpson, eds. *Behavior and Evolution.* New Haven: Yale University Press, 1958.

Roen, S. R. "Personality and Negro-White Intelligence." *Journal of Abnormal and Social Psychology* 61 (1960): 148–50.

Rohrer, J. H. "The Test Intelligence of Osage Indians." *Journal of Social Psychology* 16 (1942): 99–105.

Rokeach, M. E. *The Open and Closed Mind.* New York: Basic Books, 1960.

Root, Maria, P. P. *Racially Mixed People in America.* Thousand Oaks, CA: Sage Publications, 1992.

Roquette-Pinto, Edgardo. "Contribuição à antropologia do Brasil." *Revista de Imigração, e Colonização.* Ano I, III, no. 3. Rio de Janeiro, 1940.

Rose, Arnold M., ed *Race Prejudice and Discrimination.* New York: Alfred A. Knopf, 1951.

———, ed. *Assuring Freedom to the Free.* Detroit: Wayne University Press, 1964.

Rose, Arnold M., and Caroline Rose. *America Divided.* New York: Alfred A. Knopf, 1948.

Rose, Peter, ed. *Old Memories, New Moods.* New York: Atherton Press, 1970.

———, ed. *Slavery and Its Aftermath.* New York: Atherton Press, 1970.

Rose, Peter I., Stanley Rothman and William J. Wilson, eds. *Through Different Eyes: Black and White Perspectives on American Race Relations.* New York: Oxford University Press, 1974.

Rose, S. *Molecules and Minds.* Philadelphia: Open University Press, 1987.

———. *The Conscious Brain.* New York: Alfred A. Knopf, 1973.

———, ed. *Against Biological Determinism.* London: Allison & Busby, 1982.

Rose, Willie Lee. *Rehearsal for Reconstruction*. Indianapolis: Bobbs-Merrill, 1964.

————, ed. *A Documentary History of Slavery in North America*. New York: Oxford University Press, 1976.

Rosen, Bernard C. "Race, Ethnicity, and the Achievement Syndrome." *American Sociological Review* 24 (1959): 47–60.

Rosenberg, Alfred. "Der Mythus des 20." *Jahrhunderts*. Munich: Hoeneichen-Verlag, 1930.

————. *Memoirs of Alfred Rosenberg*. New York: Ziff-Davis, 1949.

————. *Race and History*. New York: Harper & Row, 1970.

Rosenberg, Karen R. "The Evolution of Modern Human Childbirth." *Yearbook of Physical Anthropology* 35 (1992): 89–124.

Rosenberg, Karen R., and Wenda Trevathen. "Bipedalism and Human Birth: The Obstetrical Dilemma Revisited." *Evolutionary Anthropology* 4 (1995–96): 161–68.

Rosenberg, Morris, and Ralph H. Turner. *Social Psychology: Sociological Perspectives*. New York: Basic Books, 1981.

Rosenberg, Tina. "Recovering from Apartheid." *The New Yorker* (18 November 1996): 86–95.

Rosenfeld, Alvin H. *A Double Dying: Reflections on Holocaust Literature*. Bloomington: University of Indiana Press, 1980.

Rosenfeld, Alvin, and Irving Greenberg, eds. *Confronting the Holocaust: The Impact of Elie Wiesel*. Bloomington: University of Indiana Press, 1978.

Rosenstiel, Annette. *Red and White: Indian Views of the White Man. 1492–1892*. New York: Universe Books, 1983.

Rosenzweig, M. R., D. Krech, E. L. Bennett, and M. C. Diamond. "Modifying Brain Chemistry and Anatomy by Enrichment or Impoverishment of Experience." *Early Experience and Behavior*, edited by G. Newton and S. Levine, 258–98. Springfield, IL: C. C. Thomas, 1968.

Ross, E. Dennison. *Both Ends of the Candle*. London: Faber & Faber, 1943.

Ross, Robert W. *So It Was True: The American Protestant Press and the Nazi Persecution of the Jews*. Minneapolis: University of Minnesota Press, 1980.

Ross, Robert. *Cape of Torments: Slavery and Resistance in South Africa*. Boston: Routledge & Kegan Paul, 1984.

Rossiter, Clinton. *The American Quest, 1790–1860*. New York: Harcourt Brace Jovanovich, 1971.

Rotberg, Robert I., and Ali A. Mazuri, eds. *Protest and Power in Black Africa*. New York: Oxford University Press, 1970.

Roth, H. Ling. *The Aborigines of Tasmania*. Halifax, England: King 7 Sons, 1899. Reprint. Hobart, Tasmania: Fullers Bookshop, 1969.

Roth, John K., ed. *American Diversity, American Identity*. New York: Henry Holt, 1995.

Rothwell, J. Dan. *Telling It Like It Isn't*. Englewood Cliffs, NJ: Prentice-Hall, 1982.

Rousseau, Jean J. *The Social Contract*. Translated by G. D. H. Cole. New York: Dutton, 1932.

Rout, Jr., Leslie B. *The African Experience in Spanish America: 1502 to the Present Day*. Cambridge & New York: Cambridge University Press, 1976.

Roux, Edward. *Time Longer than Rope: A History of the Black Man's Struggle for Freedom in Africa*. Madison: University of Wisconsin Press, 1964.

Rowley, C. D. *The Destruction of Aboriginal Society.* Vol. 1. Canberra: Australian National University Press, 1970.

———. *Outcasts in White Australia.* Vol. 2. Canberra: Australian National University Press, 1971.

———. *The Remote Aborigines.* Vol. 3. Canberra: Australian National University Press, 1971.

Rowse, A. L. *Appeasement: A Study in Political Decline, 1933–39.* New York: Norton, 1961.

Roy W. Meyer: *History of the Santee Sioux: United States Indian Policy on Trial.* Lincoln: University of Nebraska Press, 1967.

Royce, Anya P. *Ethnic Identity: Strategies of Diversity.* Bloomington, Indiana University Press, 1982.

Rubin, Theodore I. *Anti-Semitism: A Disease of the Mind.* New York: Continuum, 1990.

Rubin, Vera, and Arthur Tuden, eds. "Comparative Perspectives on Slavery in the New World Plantation Societies." *Annals of the New York Academy of Sciences* vol. 202, 1977.

Rubinoff, Lionel. *The Pornography of Power.* New York: Quadrangle Books, 1968.

Ruchames, Louis. *Race, Jobs, and Politics.* New York: Columbia University Press, 1953.

———, ed. *Racial Thought in America.* Amherst: University of Massachusetts Press, 1969.

———, ed. *The Abolitionists: A Collection of their Writings.* New York: Putnam's, 1963.

Rumney, Jay, and Joseph Maier. *The Science of Society.* London: Duckworth, 1953.

Rury, John L. "Race, Region, and Education: An Analysis of Black and White Scores on the 1917 Army Alpha Intelligence Test." *Journal of Negro Education* 57 (1988): 51–65.

Rushton, J. Philippe. *Race, Evolution, and Behavior: A Life History Perspective.* New Brunswick: Transaction Publishers, 1995.

———. Review. *Current Anthropology* 37 (Supplement): S168–S172.

Russell, A. G. *Colour, Race and Empire.* London: Gollancz, 1944.

Russell, Bertrand. *Fact and Fiction.* New York: Simon and Schuster, 1962.

Russell, George L. *American Indian Digest.* Phoenix: Thunderbird Enterprises, 1994.

Russell, Howard S. *Indian New England Before the Mayflower.* Hanover, NH: University Press of New England, 1980.

Russell, Kathy, Midge Wilson, and Ronald Hall. *The Color Complex: The Politics of Skin Color Among African Americans.* New York: Harcourt Brace Jovanovich, 1992.

Russell, Margo, and Martin Russell. *Afrikaners of the Kalahari: White Minority in a Black State.* Cambridge: Cambridge University Press, 1979.

Russell, Richard J., and Fred B. Kniffen. *Culture Worlds.* New York: Macmillan, 1951.

Ryan, Jr., W. Carson. "Special Capacities of American Indians." In *A Decade of Progress in Eugenics,* edited by C. B. Davenport, 159–163. Baltimore: Williams & Wilkins, 1934.

Ryan, Lyndall. *The Aboriginal Tasmanians.* Vancouver: University of British Columbia Press, 1953. 1981.

Ryan, Sally. A *Report on Longitudinal Evaluations of Preschool Programs, I: Longitudinal Evaluations.* Department of Health, Education and Welfare Publication Nos. (OHD) 74–24 and (OHD) 74–25. Washington, D.C., 1974.

Ryan, William. *Blaming the Victim.* New York: Pantheon Books, 1971.

————. *Equality.* New York: Pantheon Books, 1981.

Ryle, Gilbert. *The Concept of Mind.* New York: Barnes & Noble, 1949.

Sachar, Abram L. *Sufferance is the Badge: The Jew in the Contemporary World.* New York: Alfred A. Knopf, 1939.

Sachar, Howard M. *Diaspora.* New York: Harper & Row, 1985.

Sachs, Albie. *Justice in South Africa.* Berkeley: University of California Press, 1973.

Sachs, Bernard. "South Africa: Life on a Volcano." *Commentary* 9 (1950): 530–37.

Sachs, Wulf. *Black Anger.* Boston: Little, Brown, 1947.

Sacks, Benjamin. *South Africa: An Imperial Dilemma.* Albuquerque: University of New Mexico Press, 1967.

Sacuto, Salamea Antonio. *The Indian in the Ecuadorian Novel.* New York: Las Americas Publishing, 1976.

Saenger, Gerhart. *The Social Psychology of Prejudice.* New York: Harper, 1953.

Saffin, John. *A Brief and Candid Answer to a Late Printed Sheet, Entitled, The Selling of Joseph.* Boston, 1701.

Sahlins, Marshall. *The Use and Abuse of Biology: An Anthropological Critique of Sociobiology.* Ann Arbor: University of Michigan Press, 1976.

Sahlins, Marshall, and Elman R. Service, eds. *Evolution and Culture.* Ann Arbor: University of Michigan Press, 1960.

Said, Edward W. *Culture and Imperialism.* New York: Vintage Books, 1994.

Saint-Simon, Claude-Henri de. "Lettre d'un Habitant de Genève a ses Contemporains, 1803." In *Oeuvres de Claude-Henri de Saint-Simon,* vol. 5, 55. Paris: Editions Anthropos, 1966.

Saldanha, P. H. "The Genetic Effects of Immigration in a Rural Community of São Paolo, Brazil." *Acta Geneticae Medicae et Gemellologiae* 11 (1962): 158–224.

Sale, Kirkpatrick. *The Conquest of Paradise.* New York: Alfred A. Knopf, 1990.

Samuel, Maurice. *The Great Hatred.* New York: Alfred A. Knopf, 1948.

Sanchez, G. "The American of Mexican Descent." *Chicago Jewish Forum* 20 (1961–62): 120–24.

Sancton, Thomas. "Trouble in Dixie." *New Republic* 108 (1943): 51.

Sanday, Peggy R. "On the Causes of I.Q. Differences between Groups, and Implications for Social Policy." *Human Organization* 21 (1973): 411–24.

Sanders, Barkev S. *Environment and Growth.* Baltimore: Warwick & York, 1934.

Sanders, Ronald. *Lost Tribes and Promised Lands: The Origins of American Racism.* New York: Little, Brown, 1978.

Sanford, Charles L., ed., *Manifest Destiny and the Imperialism Question.* New York: Wiley, 1974.

Sanford, Nevitt and Craig Comstock, eds. *Sanctions for Evil.* San Francisco: Jossey Bass, 1971.

Sarason, Seymour B. *Psychology Misdirected.* New York: Free Press, 1983.

Sargent, C. W., C. H. Westfall, and F. M. Adams. "The Obstetric Risk of the Japanese Woman with a Caucasoid Husband." *American Journal of Obsterics and Gynecology* 76 (1958): 137–40.

Sartre, Jean P. "Portrait of the Anti-Semite." *Partisan Review* 13 (1946): 163–78.

————. *Anti-Semite and Jew.* New York: Schocken Books, 1965.

Satz, Ronald N. *American Indian Policy in the Jacksonian Era.* Lincoln: University of Nebraska Press, 1975.

Sauer, Norman J. "Forensic Anthropology and the Concept of Race." *Social Science and Medicine* 34(2)(1992): 107–11.

Sautman, Barry. "Theories of East Asian Superiority" In *The Bell Curve Debate: History, Documents, Opinions,* edited by Russell Jacoby and Naomi Glauberman, 210–21. New York: Times Books, 1995.

Savitt, Todd L. *Medicine and Slavery: The Diseases and Health Care of Blacks in Antebellum Virginia.* Urbana: University of Illinois Press, 1978.

Savitz, L. D., and R. F. Tomasson. "The Identifiability of Jews." *American Journal of Sociology* 64 (1959): 468–75.

Saxton, Alexander. *The Indispensable Enemy: Labor and the Anti-Chinese Movement in California.* Berkeley: University of California Press, 1971.

Scarr, Sandra, ed. *Race, Social Class, and Individual Differences in I.Q.* Hillsdale, NJ: Erlbaum, 1981.

Scarr-Salapetek, Sandra. "Race, Social Class and I.Q." *Science* 174 (1971): 1285–95.

———. "Unknowns in the I.Q. Equation." *Science* 174 (1971): 1223–28.

Schaar, John H. "The Case for Egalitarianism." In *Philosophy and Contemporary Issues,* edited by John R. Burr and Milton Goldinger, 293–302. 2nd ed. New York: Macmillan, 1976.

Schaer, K. Fritz. *Charakter, Blutgruppe and Konstitution, Grundriss einer Gruppentypologie auf philosophischer Grundlage.* Zurich and Leipzig: Rascher, 1941.

Schaller, George. *The Mountain Gorilla: Ecology and Behavior.* Chicago: University of Chicago Press, 1963.

———. *The Year of the Gorilla.* Chicago: University of Chicago Press, 1964.

Schapera, I. *The Khoisan People of South Africa.* London: Routledge, 1930.

Schapiro, S., and K. R. Vukovich. "Early Experience Effects upon Cortical Dendrites: A Proposed Model for Development." *Science* 165 (1970): 293–94.

Scheick, William J. *The Half-Breed.* Lexington: University Press of Kentucky, 1980.

Scheinfeld, Amram. *The New You and Heredity.* Philadelphia: Lippincott, 1950.

Schemann, Ludwig. *Die Rasse in den Geistwissenschaften.* 3 vols. München, 1928–37.

———. *Die Rassenfrage im Schrifttum der Neuzeit.* Munich: Lehmann's Verlag, 1931.

———, ed. *Correspondence entre Alexis de Tocqueville et Arthur de Gobineau, 1843–1859.* 2d ed. Paris: 1908.

Scherer, Lester B. *Slavery and the Churches in Early America.* Grand Rapids, MI: Erdmans, 1975.

Schermerhorn, R. A. *Comparative Ethnic Relations.* Chicago: Univesity of Chicago Press, 1978.

Schiff, Fritz, and William C. Boyd. *Blood Grouping Technic.* New York: Interscience Publishers, 1942.

Schildkraut, J. J., and S. S. Kety. "Biogenic Amines and Emotion." *Science* 156 (1967): 21–30.

Schlaifer, Robert. "Greek Theories of Slavery from Homer to Aristotle." *Harvard Studies in Classical Philology* 47 (1936): 165–204.

Schlegel, Freidrich von. *Uber die Sprache und Weisheit der Indier.* 1808.

Schmidt, Royal J. "Cultural Nationalism in Herder." *Journal of the History of Ideas* 12 (1956): 407–17.

Schneirla, Theodore C. "'Cruel' Ants—and Occam's Razor." *Journal of Comparative Psychology* 34 (1942): 79–83.

———. "Problems in the Biopsychology of Social Organization." *Journal of Abnormal and Social Psychology* 41 (1946): 385–402.

Schrier, Allan M., Harry F. Harlow, & Fred Stollnitz, eds. *Behavior of Nonhuman Primates.* 2 vols. New York: Academic Press, 1965.

Schrödinger, Erwin. *What Is Life?* New York: Macmillan, 1945.

Schubert, Grace. "To Be Black is to be Offensive: Racist Attitudes in San Lorenzo." In *Cultural Transformations and Ethnicity in Modern Ecuador,* edited by Norman E. Whitten, Jr. Urbana: University of Illinois Press, 1981.

Schull, W. J. "Inbreeding and Maternal Effects in the Japanese." *Eugenics Quarterly* 5 (1962): 14–22.

Schultz, Adolph H. "Fetal Growth in Man." *American Journal of Physical Anthropology* 6 (1923): 389–400.

———. "Fetal Growth of Man and Other Primates." *Quarterly Review of Biology* 1 (1926): 465–521.

———. "The Skeleton of the Trunk and Limbs of Higher Primates." *Human Biology* 2 (1930): 381–83.

Schwartz, Barry N., and Robert Disch, eds. *White Racism: Its History, Pathology, and Practice.* New York: Dell, 1970.

Schwartz, M., and J. Schwartz. "Evidence Against a Genetical Component to Performance on IQ Tests." *Nature* 148 (1974): 84–85.

Schwartz, Solomon. "The New Anti-Semitism of the Soviet Union." *Commentary* 7 (1949): 535–45.

Schwesinger, Gladys C. *Heredity and Environment.* New York: Macmillan, 1933.

———. Minutes of the Conference on Genetics and Social Behavior. *Roscoe B. Jackson Memorial Laboratory.* Bar Harbor, 1947.

———. "The Magnification of Differences by a Threshold." *Science* 100 (1944): 569–70.

———. *Aggression.* Chicago: University of Chicago Press, 1958.

Scott, James C. *Domination and the Arts of Resistance.* New Haven: Yale University Press, 1990.

Scrimshaw, Nevin S., and John E. Gordon, eds. *Malnutrition, Learning, and Behavior.* Cambridge: MIT Press, 1968.

Seagrim, G. N., and R. J. Lendon. *Furnishing the Mind.* New York: Academic Press, 1981.

Searle, G. R. *Eugenics and Politics in Britain, 1900–1914.* Leyden: Nordhoff, 1976.

Seeber E. *Anti-Slavery Opinions in France During the Second Half of the Eighteenth Century.* New York: Greenwood Press, 1969.

Segal, Ronald. *The Race War.* New York: Viking, 1967.

Selden, Steven. "Education Policy and Biological Science: Genetics, Eugenics, and the College Textbook, c. 1908–1931." *Teachers' College Record* 87 (1985): 35–51.

———. *The Capturing of Science, Eugenics, Race Betterment, and American Education, 1903–1949.* In Press, 1997.

Seligmann, Herbert J. *Race against Man.* New York: Putnam, 1939.

Selye, H. *Stress.* Montreal: Acta, Inc., 1950.

Selzer, Michael. *"Kike!"* New York: World Publishing Co., 1972.

———. *Deliverance: The Last Days at Dachau.* Philadelphia: Lippincott, 1978.

Selznick, Gertrude J., and Stephen Steiberg. *The Tenacity of Prejudice: Anti-Semitism in Contemporary America*. New York: Harper & Row, 1969.

Semprun, Jorge. *The Long Voyage*. New York: Penguin Books, 1997.

Sen, Mihir. "The Calamity of Colour." *Mankind* (Hyderabad) 6 (1961): 48–55.

Senna, Carl, ed. *The Fallacy of IQ*. New York: The Third Press, 1973.

Service, Elman R. *The Hunters*. Englewood Cliffs, NJ: Prentice-Hall, 1966.

Sexton, Patricia C. *Spanish Harlem*. New York: Harper & Row, 1965.

Shade, William G., and Roy C. Herrenkohl. *Seven on Black: Reflections on the Negro Experience in America*. Philadelphia: Lippincott, 1969.

Shafer, Boyd C. *Nationalism: Myth and Reality*. New York: Harcourt, Brace, 1955.

Shannon, A. H. *The Negro in Washington*. New York: Webb, 1930.

Shapiro, Harry L. *Descendants of the Mutineers of the Bounty*. Memoirs of the Bernice P. Bishop Museum (Honolulu) 11 (1929): 1–106.

———. *The Heritage of the Bounty*. New York: Simon & Schuster, 1936.

———. *Migration and Environment*. New York: Oxford University Press, 1939.

———. *Race Mixture*. Paris: UNESCO, 1953.

Shapiro, Miles. *Charles Drew: Founder of the Blood Bank*. Austin: Raintree Steck-Vaughan, 1997.

Sharp, Evelyn. *The IQ Cult*. New York: Coward, McCann & Geoghegan, 1972.

Shelley, Walter B., Harry J. Hurley, and Anna Nichols. "Axillar Odor," *Archives of Dermatology and Syphilology* 68 (1953): 430.

Sherif, Muzafer, and Carolyn W. Sherif. *Groups in Harmony and Tension*. New York: Harper, 1953.

Sherif, Muzafer, and M. O. Wilson. *Group Relations at the Crossroads*. New York: Harper, 1953.

Sherrington, Charles. *Man On His Nature*. New York: Macmillan, 1941.

Sherwin, Oscar. "The Founding Fathers." *Negro History Bulletin* 8 (1945): 173–76, 189–91.

Sherwin-White, A. N. *Racial Prejudice in Imperial Rome*. London and New York: Cambridge University Press, 1968.

Sherwood, Rae. *The Psychodynamics of Race: Vicious and Benign Spirals*. Atlantic Highlands, NJ: Humanities Press, 1980.

Shibutani, Tomotsu, and Kian M. Kwan. *Ethnic Stratification*. New York: Macmillan, 1965.

Shiloh, Ailon, and Ida Cohen Selavan, eds. *Ethnic Groups of America: Their Morbidity, Mortality and Behavior Disorders*. Vol. 2, *The Blacks*. Springfield, IL: Thomas, 1974.

Shirer, William L. *The Rise and Fall of the Third Reich*. New York: Simon & Schuster, 1960.

Shoemaker, Don, ed. *With All Deliberate Speed*. New York: Harper, 1957.

Shore, Brad. "Is Language a Prisonhouse." *Cultural Anthropology* 2 (1987): 115–36.

Shorris, Earl. *The Death of the Great Spirit: An Elegy for the American Indian*. New York: Simon & Schuster, 1971.

Shufeldt, R. W. *The Negro: A Menace to American Civilization*. Boston: Badger, 1907.

Shulman, Steven., and William J. Darity, Jr., eds. *The Question of Discrimination: Racial Inequality in the U.S. Labor Market*. Middletown, CT: Wesleyan University Press, 1989.

Sichrovsky, Peter. *Strangers in Their Own Land*. New York: Basic Books, 1986.

Siegal, Saul M. "The Relationship of Hostility to Authoritarianism." *Journal of Abnormal and Social Psychology* 52 (1956): 368–72.

Siemens, G. J. "Anthropometric Effects of Recorded Cases of Miscegenation among Certain Caucasian Sub-Groups." *Ohio Journal of Science* 50 (1950): 45–52.

Sigerist, Henry E. A. *History of Medicine*. Vol. I. New York: Oxford University Press, 1951.

Sikes, E. E. *The Anthropology of the Greeks*. London: Nutt, 1914.

Silberman, C. E. "The City and the Negro." *Fortune* 65 (1962): 88ff.

———. *Crisis in Black and White*. New York: Random House, 1964.

Silberman, Leo, and Betty Spice. *Colour and Class in Six Liverpool Schools*. Liverpool: University of Liverpool Press, 1951.

Silone, Ignazio. *Bread and Wine*. New York: Penguin Books, 1946.

Silvandan, A. "From Resistance to Rebellion: Asian and Afro-Caribbean Struggles in Britan." *Race and Class* (Autumn/Winter, 1981/1982).

Silverman, Jason H. *Unwelcome Guests: Canada West's Response to American Fugitive Slaves, 1800–1865*. Millwood, NY: Associated Faculty Press, 1984.

Simar, Théophile. *Etude critique sur la fondation de la doctrine des races au 18e et son expansion au 19e siècle*. Brussels: Lamertin, 1922.

Simkins, Francis B., ed. *The South in Perspective*. Farmville, VA: Longwood College, 1959.

Simmel, Ernst, ed. *Anti-Semitism: A Social Disease*. New York: International Universities Press, 1946.

Simmons, Katherine. "Cranial Capacities by Both Plastic and Water Techniques with Cranial Linear Measurements of the Reserve Collection, White and Negro." *Human Biology* 14 (1942): 473–98.

Simon, Rita, and Howard Alstein. *Transracial Adoption: A Follow-Up*. Lexington, MA: Heath, 1981.

Simon, Yves R. "Secret Sources of the Success of the Racist Ideology." *Review of Politics* 7 (1945): 74–105.

———. *Community of the Free*. New York: Holt, 1947.

Simons, H. J. "Mental Disease in Africans: Racial Determinism." *Journal of Mental Science* 104 (1958): 377–88.

Simons, R. D. G. *The Colour of the Skin in Human Relations*. New York: Elsevier, 1961.

Simpson, George E., and Milton J. Yeager. *Racial and Cultural Minorities*. 5th ed. New York: Plenum Press, 1985.

Simpson, George G. "Behavior and Evolution." In *Behavior and Evolution*, edited by Ann Roe and George G. Simpson, 597–635. New York: Yale University Press, 1958.

———. "The Biological Nature of Man." *Science* 152 (1966): 472–78.

———. *Biology and Man*. New York: Harcourt Brace & World, 1969.

———. *The Major Features of Evolution*. New York: Columbia University Press, 1953.

Sinclair, Andrew. *The Savage: A History of Misunderstanding*. London: Weidenfield & Nicolson, 1977.

Sinkler, George. *The Racial Attitudes of American Presidents*. New York: Doubleday & Co., 1971.

Sinnott, Edmund W. "The Biological Basis of Democracy." *Yale Review* 35 (1945): 61–73.

Sitkoff, Harvard. *A New Deal for Blacks.* New York: Oxford University Press, 1978.

Skidmore, Thomas E. *Black Into White: Race and Nationality in Brazilian Thought.* New York: Oxford University Press, 1974.

Sleeper, Jim. *The Closet of Strangers: Liberalism and the Politics of Race in New York.* New York: W. W. Norton, 1990.

Small, Stephen. "Attaining Racial Parity in the United States and England." *Race Relations Abstracts* 16 (1991): 3–55.

Smedley, Audrey. *Race in North America: Origin and Evolution of a World View.* Boulder, CO: Westview Press, 1993.

———. *The Origin and Evolution of the Idea of Race.* Boulder, CO: Westview Press, 1988.

Smith, Elbert B. *The Death of Slavery: The United States, 1837–65.* Chicago: University of Chicago Press, 1967.

Smith, G. Elliot. "The Influence of Racial Admixture in Egypt." *Eugenics Review* 57 (1915): 163–83.

———. "The Aryan Question." *The Rationalist Annual* (1935): 30–34.

Smith, Lillian. *Now is the Time.* New York: Viking, 1955.

Smith, Page. *John Adams.* 2 vols. New York: Doubleday, 1963.

Smith, Samuel S. *An Essay on the Causes of the Variety of Complexion and Figure in the Human Species.* Philadelphia, 1787 2d ed., New Brunswick, NJ: Simpson, 1810. Reprint. Harvard University Press, 1965.

Smoke Rising: The Native North American Literary Companion. Detroit, MI: Visible Ink Press, 1995.

Smyth, Albert H., ed. *The Writings of Benjamin Franklin.* 10 vols. New York: Macmillan, 1905–7.

Snell, George D. "Hybrids and History. The Role of Race and Ethnic Crossing in Individual and National Achievement." *Quarterly Review of Biology* 26 (1951): 331–47.

Snitow, Virginia L. "I Teach Negro Girls." *New Republic* 107 (1942): 603–5.

Snowden, F. M., Jr. "The Negro in Classical Italy." *American Journal of Philology* 68 (1947): 266–92.

———. *Blacks in Antiquity.* Cambridge: Harvard University Press, 1970.

Snyder, Louis L. *Race: A History of Modern Ethnic Theories.* New York: Longmans, 1939.

———. *German Nationalism: The Tragedy of a People.* Harrisburg: Stackpole, 1952.

———. *The Idea of Racialism.* Princeton: Van Nostrand, 1962.

———. *Encyclopedia of the Third Reich.* New York: McGraw-Hill, 1976.

———. *Varieties of Nationalism.* New York: Holt, Rinehart & Winston, 1976.

———. *The Roots of German Nationalism.* Bloomington: University of Indiana Press, 1978.

———. *Encyclopedia of Nationalism.* New York: Paragon House, 1990.

———. *World War II.* Academic American Encyclopedia, vol. 29. Danbury, CT, 1996: 280.

———, ed. *The Imperialism Reader.* Princeton: Van Nostrand, 1962.

———, ed. *The Dynamics of Nationalism.* Princeton: Van Nostrand, 1964.

Solaun, Mauricio, and Sidney Kronus. *Discrimination Without Violence: Miscegenation and Racial Conflict in Latin America.* New York: Wiley, 1973.

Sollors, Werner. *Beyond Ethnicity: Consent and Descent in American Culture.* New York: Oxford University Press, 1986.

Solomon, Robert C. *History and Human Nature.* New York: Harcourt Brace Jovanovich, 1979.

Sorokin, Pitirim A. *Sociocultural Casuality, Space, Time.* Durham: Duke University Press, 1943.

———. "The Roles of Similarity and Dissimilarity in Social Solidarity and Antagonism." *Journal of Legal and Political Sociology* 3 (1944): 34–55.

———. "What Is a Social Class?" *Journal of Legal and Political Sociology* 4 (1946): 15–28.

Sorokin, Pitirim A., and Robert K. Merton. "Social Time: A Methodological and Functional Analysis." *American Journal of Sociology* 42 (1937): 615–29.

Southern, David W. *Gunnar Myrdal and Black-White Relations: The Use and Abuse of An American Dilemma, 1944–1969.* Baton Rouge: Louisiana State University Press, 1987.

Southwick, Charles H., ed. *Primate Social Behavior.* Princeton: Van Nostrand, 1963.

Sowden, Lewis. *The Union of South Africa.* New York: Doubleday, Doran, 1943.

Sowell, Thomas. *Race and Economics.* New York: McKay, 1975.

———. *Ethnic America: A History.* New York: Basic Books, 1991.

Spearman, C. *The Nature of Intelligence and the Principles of Cognition.* London & New York: Macmillan, 1922.

Spencer, Margaret B., Catherine K. Brookins, and Walter R. Allen, eds. *Beginnings: The Social and Affective Development of Black Children.* Hillsdale, NJ: Lawrence Erlbaum, 1985.

Spicer, Edward H., A. Hasen, A. T. Luomala, and M. K. Opler. *Impounded People.* Tucson: University of Arizona Press, 1969.

———, ed. *Human Problems in Technological Change.* New York: Russell Sage Foundation, 1952.

Spickard, Paul R. *Mixed Blood.* Madison, University of Wisconsin Press, 1989.

Spindler, George D., ed. *Education and Culture: Anthropological Approaches.* New York: Holt, Rinehart & Winston, 1963.

Spitz, David. *Patterns of Anti-Democratic Thought.* New York: Macmillan, 1949.

Sponsel, Leslie E., and Thomas Gregor, eds. *The Anthropology of Peace and Nonviolence.* Boulder: Rienner, 1994.

Spuhler, James N. "An Estimate of the Number of Genes in Man." *Science* 108 (1948): 279.

———, ed. *The Evolution of Man's Capacity for Culture.* Detroit: Wayne State University Press, 1959.

Stace, Walter T. *What Are Our Values?* Lincoln: University of Nebraska Press, 1950.

Stalvey, Lois M. *The Education of a Wasp.* Madison: University of Wisconsin Press, 1989.

Stampp, Kenneth. *The Peculiar Institution.* New York: Alfred A. Knopf, 1956.

Stanfield, John H., II. "The Myth of Race and the Human Sciences." *Journal of Negro Education* 64 (1995).

Stannart, David E. *American Holocaust.* Cambridge: Oxford University Press, 1992.

Stanton, William. *The Leopard's Spots: Scientific Attitudes Toward Race in America, 1815–1859.* Chicago: University of Chicago Press, 1960.

Stapleton, Laurence. *Justice and World Society.* Chapel Hill: University of North Carolina Press, 1944.

Starobin, Robert S. *Industrial Slavery in the Old South.* New York: Oxford University Press, 1970.

Stasz, Clarice. *The American Nightmare: Why Inequality Persists.* New York: Schocken Books, 1981.

Staub, Ervin. *The Roots of Evil: The Origins of Genocide.* New York: Cambridge University Press, 1989.

Staudinger, Hans. *The Inner Nazi: A Critical Analysis of* Mein Kampf. Baton Rouge: Louisiana State University Press, 1981.

Steggerda, Morris. "The McAdory Art Test Applied to Navaho Indian Children." *Journal of Comparative Psychology* 22 (1936): 283–86.

Stegner, Wallace. *One Nation.* Boston: Houghton Mifflin, 1945.

Stein, Leon. *The Racial Thinking of Richard Wagner.* New York: Philosophical Library, 1950.

Stein, Zena, et al. *Famine and Human Development.* New York: Oxford University Press, 1975.

Steinberg, Milton. *A Partisan Guide to the Jewish Problem.* New York: Bobbs-Merrill, 1945.

Steinberg, Stephen. *Turning Back: The Retreat from Racial Justice in American Thought and Policy.* Boston: Beacon Press, 1995.

Steiner, Stan. *The New Indians.* New York: Harper & Row, 1968.

———. *La Raza: The Mexican Americans.* New York: Harper & Row, 1970.

Stember, Charles H. *Sexual Racism: The Emotional Barrier to an Integrated Society.* New York: Elsevier, 1976. Paperback, Harper & Row, 1978.

Stember, Charles H., ed. *Jews in the Mind of America.* New York: Basic Books, 1966.

Stepan, Nancy. *The Idea of Race in Science: Great Britain 1800–1960.* Hamden, CN: (Archon) Shoe String Press, 1982.

Sterman, M. B., D. J. McGinty, and A. M. Adinolfi, eds. *Brain Development and Behavior.* New York: Academic Press, 1971.

Stern, Curt. "The Biology of the Negro." *Scientific American* 191 (1954): 80–85.

———. *Principles of Human Genetics.* San Francisco: Freeman, 1973.

Sternthrom, Stephan, Ann Orlov, and Oscar Handlin, eds. *The Harvard Encyclopedia of American Ethnic Groups.* Cambridge: Harvard University Press, 1980.

Stevens, F. S., ed. *Racism: The Australian Experience.* 3 vols. Sydney: Australian & New Zealand Book Co., 1971–72.

Stewart, James B. *Holy Warriors: The Abolitionists and American Slavery.* New York: Hill & Wang, 1976.

Stieve, H. "Der Einfluss von Angst und Psychischer eregnung auf Bau und Funktion der Weiblichen Geschlechtsorgane." *Zentralblatt für Gynakologie* 66 (1942): 1698–1708.

———. "Anatomisch nachweisbare Vorgange in Eirstock des Menschen und ihre Umweltbedingte Steuerung." *Geburtschiffe und Frauenheilkunde* 9 (1948): 639–44.

———. *Der Einfluss des Nervens Systems auf Bau und Totigkeit der Geschlechtsorgane des Menschen.* Stuttgart: Georg Thieme, 1951.

Stinchcombe, A. L. "Environment: The Cumulation of Events." *Harvard Educational Review* 39 (1969): 511–22.

Stockard, Charles R. *The Genetic and Endocrine Basis for Differences in Form and Behavior.* Philadelphia, Wistar Institute of Anatomy and Biology, 1941.

Stocking, George W., Jr. "American Social Scientists and Race Theory." Ph.D. diss., University of Pennsylvania, 1960.

———. "French Anthropology in 1800." *Isis* 65 (1964): 134–50.

———. *Race, Culture and Evolution.* New York: The Free Press, 1968.

———. *Victorian Anthropology.* New York: The Free Press, 1987

Stoddard, Lothrop. *The Rising Tide of Color.* New York: Scribner's Sons, 1920.

———. *The Revolt Against Civilization: The Menace of the Under Man.* New York: Scribner's Sons, 1922.

Stomfay-Stitz, Aline M. *Peace Education in America, 1828–1990: Sourcebook for Education and Research.* Metuchen, NJ: Scarecrow Press, 1993.

Stone, Vernon W. "The Interaction Component Is Critical." *Harvard Educational Review* 39 (1969): 628–39.

Stonequist, Everett V. *The Marginal Man: A Study in Personality and Culture Conflict.* New York: Scribner, 1937.

Stott, D. H. "Mongolism Related to Emotional Shock in Early Pregnancy." *Vita Humana* 4 (1961): 57–76.

———. *Troublesome Children.* New York: Humanities Press, 1966.

Strandskov, Herluf H. "The Distribution of Human Genes." *Scientific Monthly* 52 (1942): 203–15.

———. "The Genetics of Human Populations." *American Naturalist* 76 (1942): 156–64.

———. "Further Comments on Comparative Studies in Human Biology." *Science* 100 (1944): 146–47.

Strenio, Jr., Andrew J. *The Testing Trap.* New York: Rawson Wade, 1980.

Stroop, Juergen. *The Stroop Report: The Jewish Quarter of Warsaw is No More.* New York: Pantheon Books, 1979.

Strouhal, Eugene. "Anthropometric and Functional Evidence of Heterosis from Egyptian Nubia." *Human Biology* 43 (1971): 271–87.

Stuart, Donald. *Yandy.* Melbourne: Georgian House, 1959.

Stuart, Irving, and Lawrence E. Abt, eds. *Interracial Marriage: Expectations and Realities.* New York: Grossman Publishers, 1973.

Stubbs, Dacre. *Prehistoric Art of Australia.* New York: Scribners, 1980.

Stuckert, Robert P. "African Ancestry of the White American Population." *Ohio Journal of Science* 58 (1958): 155–60.

Study Commission on U.S. Policy Toward Southern Africa. *South Africa: Time Running Out.* Berkeley: University of California Press, 1981.

Sullivan, Louis R. "Anthropometry of Siouan Tribes." *Proceedings of the National Academy of Sciences* 6 (1920): 131–34.

Sullivan, Louis R., and K. Murdock. "A Contribution to the Study of Mental and Physical Measurements in Normal Children." *American Physical Education Review* 28 (1923): 209–15, 278–88, 328.

Sung, Betty L. *Mountain of Gold: The Story of The Chinese in America.* New York: Macmillan, 1967.

Suransky, Valerie Polakow. *The Erosion of Childhood.* Chicago: University of Chicago Press, 1982.

"Survey of the National Opinion Research Center of the University of Denver." *Pacific Citizen* 21 (31 August 1946), 3.

Suttie, Ian D. *The Origins of Love and Hate.* New York: Julian Press, 1966.

Sutton, Peter et al. *Dreamings: The Art of Aboriginal Australia.* New York: Braziller, 1988.

Svoray, Yavon, and Nick Taylor. *In Hitler's Shadow.* New York: Doubleday, 1994.

Swann, Elsie. *Christopher North.* Edinburgh: Oliver Boyd, 1934.

Swanson, C. P. *The Cell.* 2d ed. Englewood Cliffs, NJ: Prentice-Hall, 1964.

Sweet, David G., and Gary B. Nash, eds. *Struggle and Survival in Colonial America.* Berkeley: University of California Press, 1981.

Swiebocka, Teresa, Jonathan Webber, and Connie Wilsack. *Auschwitz: A History in Photographs.* Bloomington: Indiana University Press, 1993.

Swisher, Karen. *American Indian/Alaskan Native Learning Styles: Research and Practice.* ERIC Digest 335175. Charleston: ERIC Clearinghouse on Rural Education and Small Schools, 1991.

Sydnor, Charles S. *Slavery In Mississippi.* Gloucester, MA: P. Smith, 1965.

Symonds, Percival M. "How Teachers Solve Personal Problems." *Journal of Educational Research* 2 (1941): 80–93.

———. *The Dynamics of Human Adjustment.* New York: Appleton-Century, 1946.

Synder, Laurence H. "The Principles of Gene Distribution in Human Populations." *Yale Journal of Biology and Medicine* 19 (1947): 817–33.

———. "The Genetic Approach to Human Individuality." *Science* 108 (1948): 586.

———. "The Study of Human Heredity." *Scientific Monthly* 51 (1940): 536–41.

Szamuely, T. "Jews in Russia: The Semi-Final Solution." *Spectator* (London) (11 August 1967): 153–54.

Tachibana, K. "A Study of Racial Preference." *Proceedings of the 8th Annual Meeting of the Japanese Psychological Association* (1941): 64–65. Abstracted from the Japanese *Far Eastern Science Bulletin* 3, no. 3 (Sept. 1943): 35.

Tadman, Michael. *Speculators and Slaves.* Madison: University of Wisconsin Press, 1989.

"Taft, Donald R." Cultural Opportunities through Race Contacts." *Journal of Negro History* 14 (1929): 12–20.

Tajfel, H. "Experiments in Intergroup Discrimination." *Scientific American* 223 (1970): 96–102.

———. "The Psychology of Intergroup Relations." *Annual Review of Psychology* 33 (1982): 1–39.

Takaki, Ronald T. *Iron Cages: Race and Culture in 19th Century America.* New York: Alfred A. Knopf, 1979.

Tal, Uriel. *Christians and Jews in Germany: Religion, Politics, and Ideology in the Second Reich, 1870–1914.* Ithaca: Cornell University Press, 1975.

Tanner, J. M. *The Physique of the Olympic Athlete.* London: Allen & Unwin, 1964.

Tao, Yun-Juei. "Chinesen-Europäerinnen-Kreuzung." *Zeitschrift für Morphologie und Anthropologie* 33 (1935): 349–408.

Taut, François. *Trésor de la langue française.* Edited by Jean Nicot. Paris: P. Doucer, 1600.

Tawney, R. H. *Equality.* 4th ed. London: Allen & Uniwn, 1952.

Taylor, Griffith. *Race and Environment.* Oxford: Oxford University Press, 1927.

Taylor, H. C. "Life Situations, Emotions and Gynecological Pain Associated with Congestion." In *Life Stress and Bodily Disease,* edited by H. G. Wolff, S. G. Wolff, Jr., and C. C. Hare, 1051–56. Baltimore: Williams & Wilkins, 1950.

Taylor, Joe G. *Negro Slavery in Louisiana.* Baton Rouge: Louisiana Historical Association, 1963.

Taylor, Joshua. *Paved with Good Intentions: The Failure of Race Relations in Contemporary American.* New York: Carroll & Graf, 1994.

Tekiner, Roselle. "Race and the Issue of National Identity." *International Journal of Middle East Studies* 23 (1991): 39–55.

Teller, Judd L. *Scapegoat of Revolution.* New York: Scribner, 1954.

Temperley, Howard. *British Anti-Slavery 1833–1870.* London: Longman, 1973.

Tenenbaum, Joseph. *Race and Reich: The Story of an Epoch.* New York: Twayne, 1957.

Tenenbaum, Samuel. *Why Men Hate.* New York: Jewish Book Guild of America, 1947.

Terris, Milton. *Goldberger on Pellagra.* Baton Rouge: Louisiana State University Press, 1964.

Terry, Michael. *Hidden Wealth and Hiding People.* New York: Putnam, 1934.

Terry, Wallace. *Bloods: An Oral History of the Vietnam War by Black Veterans.* New York: Random House, 1985.

Thalmann, Rita, and Emanual Feinermann. *Crystal Night.* New York: Columbia University Press, 1971.

Thernstrom, Stephan, Ann Orlov, and Oscar Handlin, eds. *Harvard Encyclopedia of American Ethnic Groups.* Cambridge: Harvard University Press, 1980.

Thomas, Alexander. *Racism and Psychiatry.* New York: Brunner/Mazel, 1972.

Thomas, Dorothy S., and Richard S. Nishimoto. *The Spoilage.* Berkeley: University of California Press, 1946.

Thomas, John L., ed. *Slavery Attacked: The Abolitionist Crusade.* Englewood Cliffs, NJ: Prentice-Hall, 1965.

Thomas, William I. "The Relative Mental Endowment of Races." In *Primitive Behavior,* by William I. Thomas, 770–800. New York: McGraw-Hill, 1937.

Thompson, Charles H. Racial Minorities and the Present International Crisis. *Journal of Negro Education* 10 (1941): 305–622.

———, ed. The Physical and Mental Abilities of the American Negro. *Journal of Negro Education* 3 (1934): 317–564.

Thompson, David. *Equality.* London & New York: Cambridge University Press, 1949.

Thompson, Edgar T., ed. *Race Relations and the Race Problem.* Durham: Duke University Press, 1939.

Thompson, Edgar T., and Everett C. Hughes, eds. *Race: Individual and Collective Behavior.* New York: The Free Press, 1958.

Thompson, Leonard. *The Political Mythology of Apartheid.* New Haven: Yale University Press, 1985.

Thompson, Leonard, and Jeffrey Butler, eds. *Change in Contemporary South Africa.* Berkeley & Los Angeles: University of California Press, 1975.

Thompson, Richard A. *The Winds of Tomorrow: Social Change in a Maya Town.* Chicago: University of Chicago Press, 1944.

Thompson, W. R., and W. Heron. "The Effects of Restricting Early Experience on the Problem-solving Capacity of Dogs." *Canadian Journal of Psychology* 7 (1954): 17–31.

Thomson, Arthur, and L. H. Dudley Buxton. "Man's Nasal Index in Relation to Certain Climatic Conditions." *Journal of the Royal Anthropological Institute of Great Britain and Ireland* 53 (1923): 92–122.

Thomson, David. *England in the Nineteenth Century.* New York: Penguin Books, 1950.

Thomson, M. L. "Relative Efficiency of Pigment and Horny Layer Thickness in Protecting Skin of Europeans and Africans Against Solar Ultraviolet Radiation." *Journal of Physiology* 127 (1955): 236–46.

Thorne, Frederick E. "The Attitudinal Pathoses." *Journal of Clinical Psychology* 5 *(1949): 1–21.*

———. "The Frustration-Anger-Hostility States: A New Diagnostic Classification." *Journal of Clinical Psychology* 9 (1953): 334–39.

———. "Epidemiological Studies of Chronic Frustration-Hostility-Aggression States." *American Journal of Psychiatry* 113 (1957): 717–21.

Thornton, Russell. *American Indian Holocaust and Survival: A Population History Since 1492.* Athens: University of Georgia Press, 1987.

Thorpe, W. H. "Biological Races in *Hyponemeuta Padella L." Journal of the Linnaean Society (Zoölogy):* 36 (1928): 621.

———. "Biological Races in Insects and Allied Groups." *Biological Reviews* 5 (1930): 177.

———. "Ecology and the Future of Systematics." In *The New Systematics,* edited by Julian Huxley, 340–64. Oxford: Clarendon Press, 1940.

———. *Animal Nature and Human Nature.* New York: Anchor-Press/Doubleday, 1974.

Tilman, David, and Johannes Knops. "Productivity and Sustainability Influenced by Biodiversity in Grassland Ecosystems." *Nature* 379 (1966): 718–20.

Tinbergen, Niko. *The Study of Instinct.* Oxford: Clarendon Press, 1951.

Tindale, Norman B. "Survey of the Half-Caste Problem in South Australia." *Proceedings of the Royal Geographical Society, South Australian Branch* (1940–41): 66–161.

Tindall, George B. *The Ethnic Southerners.* Baton Rouge: Louisiana State University Press, 1976.

Tirala, Lothar G. *Rasse, Geist und Seele.* Munich: Lehmann's Verlag, 1935.

Tise, Larry E. *Proslavery: A History of the Defense of Slavery in America, 1700–1840.* Athens: University of Georgia Press, 1988.

To Secure These Rights: the Report of the President's Committee on Civil Rights. Washington, D.C.: Government Printing Office: 1947.

Tobach, E., L. R. Aronson, and E. Shaw, eds. *The Biopsychology of Development.* New York: Academic Press, 1971.

Tobias, Phillip V. "On a Bushman-European Hybrid Family." *Man* 54 (1955): 179–82.

———. "Brain Size, Grey Matter and Race–Fact or Fiction?" *American Journal of Physical Anthropology* 32 (1970): 3–26.

———. *The Brain in Hominid Evolution.* New York: Columbia University Press, 1971.

———, ed. *The Bushmen.* Cape Town: Human & Rousseau, 1978.

Tocqueville, Alexis de. *The European Revolution and Correspondence with Gobineau.* Edited by John Lukacs. New York: Anchor Books, 1959.

Todd, T. Wingate. "Cranial Capacity and Linear Dimensions." *American Journal of Physical Anthropology* 6 (1923): 97–194.

———. "Entrenched Negro Physical Features." *Human Biology* 1 (1929): 57–69.

———. "The Skeleton." In *Growth and Development of the Child, Part II* (White House Conference on Child Health and Protection): 26–130. New York: Century, 1933.

Todd, T. Wingate, and Anna Lindala. "Dimensions of the Body: Whites and American Negroes of Both Sexes." *American Journal of Physical Anthropology* 12 (1928): 35–119.

Todd, T. Wingate, and D. W. Lyon. "Cranial Suture Closure; Its Progress and Age Relationship. Part IV. Ectocranial Closure in Adult Males of Negro Stock." *American Journal of Physical Anthropology* 8 (1925): 149–68.

Todd, T. Wingate, and L. van Gorder. "The Quantitative Determination of Black Pigmentation in the Skin of the American Negro." *American Journal of Physical Anthropology* 4 (1921): 239–60.

Todorov, Tzvetan. *On Human Diversity: Nationalism, Racism and Exoticism in French Thought.* Cambridge: Harvard University Press, 1963, 1993.

Todorov, Tzvetan. "'Race,' Writing and Culture." In *"Race," Writing, and Difference,* edited by Henry Louis Gates. Chicago: University of Chicago Press, 1985.

Tolles, Frederick B. "Nonviolent Contact: The Quakers and the Indians." *Proceedings of the American Philosophical Society* 107 (1963): 93–101.

Tolman, Edward C. "A Stimulus-Expectancy Need—Cathexis Psychology." *Science* 101 (1945): 160–66.

Topinard, Paul. "La Notion de race en anthropologie." *Revue d'Anthropologie* 2d ser., II (1879): 589–660.

Totman, Richard. *Social Causes of Illness.* New York: Pantheon, 1979.

Townsend, Joseph. *A Dissertation on the Poor Laws: By a Well-Wisher to Mankind.* London: C. Dilly, 1786. Reprinted with Foreword by Ashley Montagu and Afterword by Clark Neuman. Berkeley: University of California Press, 1971.

Toynbee, Arnold J. *A Study of History.* Vol. 1. New York: Oxford University Press, 1934.

Trachtenberg, Joshua. *The Devil and the Jews.* New York: Meridian Books, 1961.

Trager, H. G., and M. R. Yarrow. *They Learn What They Live: Prejudice in Young Children.* New York: Harper, 1952.

Trelease, Allen W. *White Terror: The Ku Klux Klan Conspiracy and Southern Reconstruction.* New York: Harper & Row, 1971.

Trembley, Francis J. "Evolution and Human Affairs." *Proceedings of the Pennsylvania Academy of Science* 23 (1949): 181–95.

Trent, J. W., Jr. *Inventing the Feeble Mind*. Berkeley: University of California Press, 1994.

Trevor, Jack C. "Some Anthropological Characteristics of Hybrid Populations." *Eugenics Review* 30 (1938): 21–31.

———. "Race Crossing in Man." *Eugenics Laboratory Memoirs* 36 (1953): iv–45.

Trotter, Mildred. "A Study of Facial Hair in White and Negro Races." *Washington University Studies* (Scientific Studies) 10 (1922): 273–89.

Trudeau, Arthur G. "Army Experience and Problems of Negro Education." In *Education for Victory, III*, 13–16. Washington, D.C.: U.S. Office of Education, 1945.

Tucker, Frank H. *The White Conscience*. New York: Frederick Ungar, 1968.

Tucker, William H. *The Science and Politics of Racial Research*. Urbana: University of Illinois Press, 1994.

Tuker, M. A. R. *Past and Future of Ethics*. London & New York: Oxford University Press, 1938.

Tumin, Melvin M. *Desegregation: Readiness and Resistance*. Princeton: Princeton University Press, 1958.

———., ed. *Race and Intelligence*. New York: Anti–Defamation League of B'nai B'rith, 1963.

Turgot, Robert J. "Tableaux Philosophique des Progrès Successifs de L'Esprit Humains." In *Œuvres de Turgot*, edited by Gustave Schelle, 214. Paris: Alcan, 1913.

Turnbull, Clive. *Black War: The Extermination of the Tasmanian Aborigines*. Melbourne: F. W. Cheshire, 1948.

Turner, Frederick. *Beyond Geography. The Western Spirit Against Geography*. New York: Viking, 1980.

Turner, Jr., Henry A., ed. *Hitler: Memoirs of a Confidant*. New Haven: Yale University Press, 1985.

Turner, Lorenzo D. "The Negro in Brazil." *Chicago Jewish Forum* 15 (1957): 232–36.

Turner, Paul R., and David Pitt. *The Anthropology of War and Peace*. Granby, MA: Bergin & Garvy, 1989.

Tusnet, Leonard. *The Uses of Adversity*. South Brunswick: Thoman Yoseloff, 1966.

Tuttle, Russell. *The Functional and Evolutionary Biology of Primates*. Chicago/New York: Aldine, 1972.

Tuveson, Ernest L. *Redeemer Nation*. Chicago: University of Chicago Press, 1969.

Twombley, Robert C., ed. *Blacks in White America Since 1865*. New York: David McKay, 1971.

Ulich, Robert. *The Human Career*. New York: Harper, 1955.

Ullmann, Stephen. "The Prism of Language." *The Listener* (London) (22 July 1954): 131–32.

Underwood, Jane H. *Human Variation and Human Microevolution*. Englewood Cliffs NJ: Prentice Hall, 1979.

UNESCO. *Human Rights: Comments and Interpretations*. New York: Columbia University Press, 1949.

———. *The Race Concept: Results of an Inquiry. Comments by Anthropologists on the Second UNESCO Statement*. Paris: UNESCO, 1952.

———. *The Nature of Conflict: Studies on the Sociological Aspects of International Relations*. Paris: UNESCO, 1957.

———. *The Race Concept*. New York: UNESCO, Unipub., 1958.

———. *The Effect of the Existence of Segregation in the U.S. on the American Image in Africa.* U.S. National Commission for UNESCO (Press Release, Nat. Conf. 8/18, 25 October 1961).

———. *Race and Science.* New York: Columbia University Press, 1961.

———. *Research on Race Relations.* New York: Unipub., Inc., 1966.

———. *Some Suggestions About Human Rights.* Paris: UNESCO, 1968.

———. *Apartheid.* New York: Unipub. Inc., 1969.

———. *Four Statements on the Race Question.* Paris: UNESCO, 1969.

———. *Birthright of Man.* Paris: UNESCO, 1970.

———. *Apartheid: Its Affects on Education, Science, Culture, and Information* 2d ed. New York: Unipub., 1972.

———. *Statement on Race 1950 and 1952.* New York: UNESCO. See A. Montagu *Statement on Race.* 3d ed. New York: Oxford University Press, 1972.

———. *Declaration of Race and Racial Prejudice.* Paris: UNESCO, 1979.

———. *The General History of Africa.* 8 vols. Berkeley: University of California Press, 1981.

———. *Racism, Science, and Pseudo-Science.* Paris: UNESCO, 1983.

"Unwanted Heroes." *New Republic* 106 (1942): 655.

Uranek-Osmecki, Kazimirz. *He Who Saves One Life.* New York: Crown, 1971.

Utter, Jack. *American Indians: Answers to Today's Questions.* Lake Ann, MI: National Woodlands Publishing, 1993.

Uya, Okon Edet. *From Slavery to Public Service: Robert Smalls, 1839–1915.* New York: Oxford University Press, 1971.

Valentine, Charles A., and Bettylou Valentine. "Brain Damage and the Intellectual Defense of Inequality." *Current Anthropology* 1 (1975): 117–50.

Van Creveld, M. "Beyond the Fini-Contini Garden: Mussolini's 'Fascist Racism.'" *Encounter* 42 (1974): 42–7.

Van den Berghe, Pierre L. "The Dynamics of Racial Prejudice: An Ideal-Type Dichotomy." *Social Forces* 37 (1958): 138–41.

———. *South Africa: A Study in Conflict.* Middletown, CT: Wesleyan University Press, 1965.

———. *Race and Racism.* New York: Wiley, 1967.

———. *Race and Ethnicity.* New York: Basic Books, 1970.

Van den Berghe, Pierre L., and George P. Primov. *Inequality in the Peruvian Andes.* Columbia: University of Missouri Press, 1977.

Van Dijk, T. A. *Communicating Racism: Ethnic Prejudice in Thought and Talk.,* Thousand Oaks, CA: Sage Publications, 1987.

Van Every, Dale. *Disinherited: The Lost Birthright of the American Indian.* New York: William Morrow, 1966.

Van Rensburg, Patrick. *Guilty Land: The History of Apartheid.* New York: Praeger, 1962.

Van Til, William, John J. DeBoer, R. Will Burnett, and Kathleen C. Ogden. *Democracy Demands It.* New York: Harper, 1947.

Van Walsem, G. C. "Ueber das Gewicht des Schwersten bis jetzt Gescriebenen Gehirns." *Neurologisches Centrallblatt* (1899): 578–80.

Vayda, Andrew P., ed. *Environment and Cultural Behavior.* New York: American Museum of Natural History, 1969.

Verma, Gajendra K., and Christopher Bagley, eds. *Race, Education and Identity.* New York: St. Martin's, 1979.

Vernier, Chester G. *American Family Laws.* Stanford: Stanford University Press, 1931: I, Sec. 44, 204–9; 1938 Supp., Stanford University Press, 1938: 24–25.

Viaud, Gaston. *Intelligence: Its Evolution and Forms.* New York: Harper & Bros., 1960.

Vickery, William. "A Redefinition of Prejudice for Purposes of Social Science Research." *Human Relations* 1 (1948): 419–28.

Vickery, William, and Stewart G. Cole. *Intercultural Education in American Schools.* New York: Harper, 1943.

Vidal, David. "Many Blacks Shut Out of Brazil's Racial 'Paradise.'" *New York Times,* 5 June 1978: 1, 10.

Vidal-Naquet, Pierre. *Assassins of Memory, Essays on the Denial of the Holocaust.* New York: Columbia University Press, 1992.

Viereck, Peter. *Metapolitics: The Roots of the Nazi Mind.* New York: Capricorn Books, 1961.

Virchow, Rudolf. "Gesammtbericht über die von der deutschen anthropologischen Gesellschaft veranlassten Erhebungen über die Farbe der Haut, der Haare und der Augen der Schulkinder in Deutschland." *Archiv für Anthropologie* 16 (1886): 275–475.

Vital, David. *The Future of the Jews.* Cambridge: Harvard University Press, 1990.

Vogel, Joseph O. *The Encyclopedia of Precolonial Africa.* Walnut Creek, CA: Altamira Press, 1997.

Vogel, Virgil J. *This Country Was Ours: A Documentary History of the American Indian.* New York: Harper & Row, 1972.

Vogelin, Eric. "The Growth of the Race Idea." *Review of Politics* 2 (1940): 283–317.

von Kutschera, Hugo. *Die Chazaren: Historische Studie.* 2d ed. Vienna: Adolf Holtzhausen, 1910.

Waal, F. B. M. de. *Chimpanzee Politics: Power and Sex Among Apes.* New York: Harper and Row, 1982.

———. *Good-Natured: The Origins of Right and Wrong in Humans and Other Animals.* Cambridge: Harvard University Press, 1996.

———. *Peacemaking Among Primates.* Cambridge: Harvard University Press, 1989.

Wachs, Theodore D., and Gerald E. Gruen. *Early Experience and Human Development.* New York: Plenum, 1983.

Waddington, C. H. "Human Ideals and Human Progress." *World Review* (August 1946): 29–36.

———. *The Ethical Animal.* New York: Atheneum, 1960.

Wade, Richard C. *Slavery in the Cities: The South 1810–1860.* New York: Oxford University Press, 1964.

Wagley, Charles. "On the Concept of Social Race in the Americas." In *Contemporary Cultures and Societies of Latin America,* edited by Dwight Heath and Richard Adams. New York: Random House, 1965.

———. *An Introduction to Brazil.* New York: Columbia University Press, 1971.

———, ed. *Race and Class in Rural Brazil.* New York: Columbia University Press, 1952; New York: Unipub, 1963.

Wagley, Charles, and Marvin Harris. *Minorities in the New World.* New York: Columbia University Press, 1958.

Waldmeir, Patti. *Anatomy of a Miracle: the End of Apartheid and the Birth of the New South Africa.* New York: W. W. Norton, 1997.

Wallace, Anthony F. C. "The Psychic Unity of Human Groups." In *Studying Personality Cross-Culturally,* edited by Bert Kaplan, 128–163. Evanston: Northwestern University Press, 1961.

Wallace, Bruce. "Heterotic Mutation." *In Molecular Genetics and Human Disease,* edited by Lytt I. Gardner, 212–30. Springfield, IL: Thomas, 1960.

———. "Race and Reason." *Eugenics Quarterly* 9 (1962): 161—65.

Wallace, Henry A. *The Genetic Basis for Democracy.* New York: American Committee for Democracy and Intellectual Freedom, 1939.

———. "Racial Theories and the Genetic Basis for Democracy." *Science* 89 (1939): 140–43.

Wallas, Graham. *Human Nature in Politics.* 3d ed. London: Constable, 1920.

Wallis, Wilson D. "Variability in Race Hybrids." *American Anthropologist* 40 (1938): 680–97.

———. "Some Phases of the Psychology of Prejudice." *Journal of Abnormal and Social Psychology* 24 (1939): 418–29.

Walpole, Hugh R. *Semantics: The Nature of Words and Their Meanings.* New York: Norton, 1941.

Walsem, G. C. Van. "Ueber das Gewicht des Schwersten bis jetzt Beschribenen Gehirns. *Neurologisches Centralblatt* 13 (1899): 578–80.

Walter, W. Grey. *The Living Brain.* New York: Norton, 1953.

Walters, Ronald G. *The Antislavery Appeal: American Abolitionism After 1830.* Baltimore: Johns Hopkins University Press, 1976.

Walvin, James. *Slavery and British Society, 1776–1846.* Baton Rouge: Louisiana State University Press, 1983.

Walzer, Michael. *Just and Unjust Wars: A Moral Argument with Historical Illustrations.* New York: Basic Books, 1977.

Ward, Geoffrey E., Ric Burns, and Ken Burns, *The Civil War.* New York: Alfred A. Knopf, 1990.

Ward, W. E. F. *The Royal Navy and the Slavers.* New York: Pantheon Books, 1969.

Warden, Carl J. *The Evolution of Human Behavior.* New York: Macmillan, 1932.

———. *The Emergence of Human Culture.* New York: Macmillan, 1936.

Warner, W. Lloyd, and Allison Davis. "A Comparative Study of American Caste." In *Race Relations and the Race Problem,* edited by Edgar T. Thompson, 219–45. Durham: Duke University Press, 1939.

Warner, W. Lloyd, Allison Davis, and Leo Srole. *The Social Systems of American Ethnic Groups.* New Haven: Yale University Press, 1945.

Warner, W. Lloyd, et al. *Democracy in Jonesville.* New York: Harper, 1949.

Warren, Robert Penn. *Who Speaks for the Negro?* New York: Random House, 1965.

Warsaw Correspondent. "Jews and the Catholic Church in Poland." *Jewish Chronicle* (London) 25 June 1948: 11.

Warwick, Donald P. "The Politics and Ethics of Cross-Cultural Research." In *Handbook of Cross-Cultural Psychology,* vol. 1, edited by H. C. Triandis and W. W. Lambert, 319–71. Boston: Allyn & Bacon, 1980.

Washburn, Sherwood L. "The Study of Race." *American Anthropologist* 65 (1963): 521–31.

————, ed. *Social Life of Early Man*. Chicago: Quadrangle Books, 1961.

Washburn, Sherwood L., and C. S. Lancaster, "The Evolution of Hunting." In *Man the Hunter*, edited by Richard B. Lee and Irven De Vore. Chicago: Aldine Publishing, 1968.

Washburn, Wilcomb E. *Red Man's Land-White Man's Law*. New York: Scribner's Sons, 1971.

————. *The Indian in America*. New York: Harper & Row, 1975.

Washington, Joseph R., Jr. *Marriage in Black and White*. Boston: Beacon Press, 1970.

Washow, Arthur I. *From Race Riot to Sit-In 1919–1960's*. New York: Doubleday, 1966.

Wasserstein, Bernard. *Britain and the Jews of Europe 1939–1945*. New York: Oxford University Press, 1979.

Wasserstein, Bruce, and Mark J. Green eds. *With Justice for Some: An Indictment of the Law by Young Advocates*. Boston: Beacon Press, 1970.

Waters, Ethan. "Claude Steele Has Scores to Settle." *New York Times Magazine*, 17 September 1995: 44–47; 6.

Waters, Mary C. *Ethnic Options*. Berkeley: University of California Press, 1990.

Watson, Goodwin. *Action for Unity*. New York: Harper, 1947.

Watson, P. "How Race Affects I.Q." *New Society* (London): 16 July 1970: 103–4.

————, ed. *Psychology and Race*. Chicago: Aldine Publishing, 1974.

Watt, David. "Colour and the Election." *The Spectator* (28 August 1964): 261–62.

Waxman, Julia. *Race Relations: A Selected List of Readings on Racial and Cultural Minorities in the United States with Special Emphasis on Negroes*. Chicago: Julius Rosenwald Fund, 1945.

Webb, Beatrice, and Sidney Webb. *Soviet Communism: a New Civilization*. 2 vols. New York: Longmans, 1935.

Webber, Thomas L. *Deep Like the Rivers*. New York: Norton, 1978.

Weglyn, Michi. *Years of Infamy: The Untold Story of America's Concentration Camps*. New York: Morrow, 1976.

Weidenreich, Franz. *Rasse und Kürperbau*. Berlin: Springer, 1927.

————. "The Brachycephalization of Recent Mankind." *Southwestern Journal of Anthropology* 1 (1945): 1–54.

————. *Apes, Giants, and Man*. Chicago: University of Chicago Press, 1946.

Weinberg, Albert K. *Manifest Destiny: A Study of Nationalist Expansion in American History*. Baltimore: Johns Hopkins University Press, 1935.

Weinberg, Meyer. *Desegregation Research: An Appraisal*, Bloomington, IN: Phi Delta Kappa 1968.

Weinberg, Robert L. "Group Libel and the Law." *Chicago Jewish Forum* 6 (1948): 85–90.

Weiner, Marc A. *Richard Wagner and the Anti-Semitic Imagination*. Lincoln: University of Nebraska Press, 1995.

Weinert, Hans. *Der Geistige Aufstieg der Menschheit vom Ursprung bis zur Gegenwart*. Stuttgart: Ferdinand Enke, 1951.

Weinreb, Lloyd L. *Natural Law and Justice*. Cambridge: Harvard University Press, 1987.

Weinreich, Max. *Hitler's Professors: the Part of Scholarship in Germany's Crimes against the Jewish People*. New York: Yiddish Scientific Institute, 1946.

Weisbord, Robert G., and Richard Kazarian, Jr. *Israel in the Black American Perspective*. Westport, CT: Greenwood Press, 1985.

Weisborg, Robert C., and Arthur Stein. *Bittersweet Encounter: The Afro-American and the American Jew.* Westport, CT: Negro Universities Press, 1970.

Weiss, John. *Ideology of Death: Why the Holocaust Happened in Germany.* Chicago: Ivan R. Dee, 1996.

Weiss, K. M., and T. Marayama. "Archeology, Population Genetics, and Studies of Human Racial Ancestry." *American Journal of Physical Anthropology* 44 (1976): 31–49.

Weiss, Sheila F. *Race, Hygiene and National Efficiency.* Berkeley: University of California Press, 1987.

Weizäcker, C. F. von. *The History of Nature.* Chicago: University of Chicago Press, 1950.

Wells, H. G. *The Outline of History.* London: Newnes, 1920.

Went, F. W. "The Ecology of Desert Plants." *Scientific American* 192 (1955): 68–75.

Weslager, Clinton A. *Delaware's Forgotten Folk.* Philadelphia: University of Pennsylvania Press, 1943.

———. *The Delaware Indians: A History.* New Brunswick: Rutgers University Press, 1972.

Wesley, John. *Thoughts upon Slavery.* London [n.d.]

Westerman, George W. *A Study of Socio-Economic Conflicts on the Panama Canal Zone.* Panamá: Liga Cívica Nacional, 1949.

Westermann, W. L. "Slavery and the Elements of Freedom in Ancient Greece." *Quarterly Bulletin of the Polish Institute of Arts and Sciences in America* 1 (1943): 332–47.

———. "The Slave Systems of Greek and Roman Antiquity." *Memoirs of the American Philosophical Society* 40 (1955): xi–180.

Westie, Frank R. "Negro-White Status Differentials and Social Distance." *American Sociological Review* 18 (1952): 550–58.

Weston, Rubin F. *Racism in U.S. Imperialism.* Columbia: University of South Carolina Press, 1962.

Whalen, Richard E., ed. *The Neurophysiology of Aggression.* New York: Plenum Press, 1974.

Wheaton, Elizabeth. *Code Name Greenkill: The 1979 Greensboro Killings.* Athens: University of Georgia Press, 1987.

Wheeler, William M. *Social Life among Insects.* New York: Harcourt, Brace, 1923.

———. "Social Evolution." In *Human Biology and Racial Welfare*, edited by E. V. Cowdry, 139–55. New York: Hoeber, 1930.

Whimbey, Arthur, and Linda S. Whimbey. *Intelligence Can Be Taught.* New York: Dutton, 1975.

White, Charles. *An Account of the Regular Gradation in Man.* London: Dilly, 1799.

White, Garvin. "Canadian Apartheid." *Canadian Forum* 31 (1951): 102–3.

White, Leslie. *The Evolution of Culture.* New York: McGraw-Hill, 1949.

———. *The Science of Culture.* New York: Farrar, Straus, 1949.

White, Walter. *A Rising Wind.* New York: Doubleday, 1945.

———. "Why I Remain a Negro." *Saturday Review of Literature* 30 (1947): 13–49, 50–52.

Whitfield, Stephen J. *Jews in American Life and Thought.* Hamden, CT: Shoestring Press, 1984.

674 MAN'S MOST DANGEROUS MYTH

Whitten, Jr., Norman, ed. *Cultural Transformations and Ethnicity in Modern Ecuador.* Urbana: University of Illinois Press, 1981.

Widdowson, E. M. "Mental Contentment and Physical Growth," *Lancet* 1 (1951): 1316–8.

Widney, Joseph P. *Mankind: Racial Values and Racial Prospects,* I. Los Angeles: Pacific Publishing, 1917.

Wiecek, William M. *The Sources of Antislavery: Constitutionalism in America, 1760–1848.* Ithaca: Cornell University Press, 1979.

Wiedemann, Thomas. *Greek and Roman Slavery.* Baltimore: Johns Hopkins University Press, 1981.

Wiener, N. *The Human Use of Human Beings.* Boston: Houghton-Mifflin, 1950.

Wiesel, Elie. *Night.* New York: Avon Books, 1960.

Wieseltier, Leon. "History and the Holocaust." *Times Literary Supplement* (London): 25 February 1977: 220–21.

Wiggam, Albert E. *The New Decalogue of Science.* Garden City, NY: Garden City Publishing, 1925.

———. *The Fruits of the Family Tree.* Garden City, NY: Garden City Publishing, 1926.

Wilde, Oscar. "The True Function and Value of Criticism." *Nineteenth Century* 28 (1890): 123–47.

Wilder, Burt G. *The Brain of the American Negro.* New York: First National Negro Conference, 1909.

Wilkins, George H. *Undiscovered Australia.* London: Benn, 1928.

Wilkins, Roy, with Tom Mathew. *Standing Fast: The Autobiography of Roy Wilkins.* New York: Viking, 1982.

Wilkinson, Harvie III. *From Brown to Bakke: The Supreme Court and School Integration, 1954–1978.* New York: Oxford University Press, 1979.

Wilkomirski, Binjamin. *Fragments: Memories of a Wartime Childhood.* New York: Schocken Books, 1997.

Willerman, L., A. F. Naylor, and N. C. Myrianthopoulos. "Intellectual Development of Children from Interracial Matings." *Science* 170 (1970): 1329–31.

Williams, Eric. *Capitalism and Slavery.* Chapel Hill: University of North Carolina Press, 1944.

Williams, G. D. "Maya-Spanish Crosses in Yucatan." *Papers of the Peabody Museum of American Archaeology and Ethnology, Harvard University* 13 (1931): 1–256.

Williams, J., and R. Scott. "*Growth and Development of Negro Infants. IV. Motor Development and its Relationship to Child Rearing Practices in Two Groups of Negro Infants.*" Child Development 24 (1953): 103–21.

Williams, John E., and Kenneth Morland. *Race, Color, and the Young Child.* Chapel Hill: University of North Carolina Press, 1976.

Williams, Jr., Robin M. *The Reduction of Intergroup Tensions: a Survey of Research on Problems of Ethnic, Racial, and Religious Group Relations.* New York: Social Science Research Council, 1947.

———. *Strangers Next Door: Ethnic Relations in American Communities.* Englewood Cliffs, NJ: Prentice-Hall, 1964.

———. *Mutual Accommodation: Ethnic Conflict and Cooperation.* Minneapolis: University of Minnesota Press, 1977.

Williams, Patricia. *The Alchemy of Race and Rights.* Cambridge: Harvard University Press, 1991.

Williams, Robert L. "Scientific Racism and IQ: The Silent Mugging of the Black Community," *Psychology Today* (May 1974): 32–41, 101.

Williams, Walter E. *The State Against Blacks.* New York: McGraw-Hill, 1982.

Williams, Watkins. "Heterosis and the Genetics of Complex Characters." *Nature* 184 (1959): 527–30.

Williamson, Joel. *New People: Miscegenation and Mulattoes in the United States.* New York: Free Press, 1980.

———. *The Crucible of Race: Black-White Relations in the American South Since Emancipation.* New York: Oxford University Press, 1984.

Willie, C. V., B. M. Kramer, and B. S. Brown, eds. *Racism and Mental Health.* Pittsburgh: University of Pittsburgh Press, 1973.

Wills, Garry. *Inventing America: Jefferson's Declaration of Independence.* Garden City, NY: Doubleday, 1978.

Wilson, E. O., and William L. Brown, Jr. "The Subspecies Concept and its Taxonomic Application." *Systematic Zoology* 2(3) (1953): 97–111.

Wilson, Glenn D., ed. *The Psychology of Conservatism.* New York: Academic Press,1973.

Wilson, Janet. "The Early Anti-Slavery Propaganda." *More Books* (Bulletin of the Boston Public Library): Nov/Dec. 1944: 3; Feb. 1945: 51–56.

Wilson, John A. "Egypt." In *The Intellectual Adventure of Ancient Man,* edited by H. A. Frankfort et al.: 33–34. Chicago: University of Chicago Press, 1946.

Wilson, Mitchell. *American Science and Invention.* New York: Simon & Schuster, 1954.

Wilson, Theodore B. *The Black Codes of the South.* University of Alabama Press, 1965.

Wilson, William J. *Power, Racism and Privilege.* New York: Free Press, 1973.

———. *The Declining Significance of Race.* Chicago: University of Chicago Press, 1978.

Wilson. E. O. *Sociobiology: The New Synthesis.* Cambridge: Belknap Press of Harvard University Press, 1975.

Wimbley, Arthur, and Linda S. *Intelligence Can Be Taught.* New York: Dutton, 1975.

Winant, Howard. *Racial Conditions.* Minneapolis: University of Minnesota Press, 1994.

Winick, M. "Nutrition and Cell Growth." *Nutrition Reviews* 26 (1968): 195–97.

———. "Head Circumference and Cellular Growth of the Brain in Normal and Marasmic Children." *Journal of Pediatrics* 74 (1969): 774–78.

———. "Fetal Malnutrition and Growth Processes." *Hospital Practice* (May 1970): 33–41.

———. *Malnutrition and Brain Development.* New York: Oxford University Press, 1975.

Winick, M., and P. Rosso. "The Effect of Severe Malnutrition on Cellular Growth of the Human Brain." *Pediatric Research* 3 (1969): 181–84.

Winks, Robin W. *The Blacks in Canada.* New Haven: Yale University Press, 1971.

Wirth, Andrzej, ed. *The Stroop Report: The Jewish Quarter of Warsaw is No More.* New York: Pantheon Books, 1979.

Wish, Harvey, ed. *Ante-Bellum: Three Classic Works of Slavery in the Old South.* New York: Putnam's Sons, 1960.

Wisniewski, Bronislaw. "How a 'Historical Haven' Has Treated Jews." *New York Times,* 11 May 1984: A30.

Wissler, Clark. "Growth of Children in Hawaii; Based on Observations by Louis R. Sullivan." *Bernice P. Bishop Museum Memoirs* (Honolulu, 1930): 105–257.

Witherspoon, Gary. *Language and Art in the Navajo Universe.* Ann Arbor: University of Michigan Press, 1977.

Witherspoon, Joseph P. *Administrative Implementation of Civil Rights.* Austin: University of Texas Press, 1968.

Wittenberg, Philip. "Miscegenation." In *Encyclopedia of the Social Sciences* 5 (1938): 531–34. New York: Macmillan.

———. "Individual Recovery for Defamation of a Group." *Ohio State Law Journal* Summer (1954).

Witty, Paul A. "New Evidence on the Learning Ability of the Negro." *Journal of Abnormal and Social Psychology* 40 (1945): 401–4.

Witty, Paul A., and Harvey C. Lehman. "Racial Differences: the Dogma of Superiority." *Journal of Social Psychology* 1 (1930): 394–418.

Witzig, Ritchie. *"The Medicalization of Race: Scientific Legitimization of a Flawed Social Concept."* Annals of Internal Medicine 125 (1996): 675–79

Wolanski, N., E. Jarosz, and M. Pyzik. "Heterosis in Man: Growth in Offspring and Distance Between Parents' Birthplaces." *Social Biology* 17 (1970): 1–16.

Wolfenstein, Eugene V. *The Victims of Democracy: Malcolm X and the Black Revolution.* Berkeley: University of California Press, 1981.

Wolff, H. G. *Stress and Disease.* 2d ed. Springfield, IL: C. C. Thomas, 1968.

Wolfgang, Marvin E. *Crime and Race; Conceptions and Misconceptions.* New York: Institute of Human Relations, 1964.

Wolters, Raymond. *The Burden of Brown: Thirty Years of School Desegregation.* Knoxville: University of Tennessee Press, 1984.

Woo, T. L., and G. M. Morant. "A Biometric Study of the 'Flatness' of the Facial Skeleton in Man." *Biometrika* 26 (1934): 196–250.

Wood, E. Thomas, and Stanslaw M. Janowski. *Karski: How One Man Tried to Stop the Holocaust.* New York: John Wiley, 1994.

Wood, Forrest G. *Black Scare.* Berkeley: University of California Press, 1968.

———. *The Arrogance of Faith: Christianity and Race in America from the Colonial Era to the Twentieth Century.* New York: Alfred A. Knopf, 1990.

———. *The Era of Reconstruction, 1863–1877.* New York: Alfred A. Knopf, 1975.

Woods, Donald. *Biko.* New York: Paddington Press, 1978.

Woods, Frances J. *Cultural Values of American Ethnic Groups.* New York: Harper, 1956.

Woodward, C. Vann. *The Strange Case of Jim Crow.* 2d ed. New York: Oxford University Press, 1966.

———. *American Counterpoint: Slavery and Racism in the North-South Dialogue.* Boston: Little, Brown, 1970.

Wootton, Barbara. *Testament for Social Science.* New York: Norton, 1951.

Worden, N. *Making of Modern South Africa.* Oxford, Cambridge: Blackwell, 1993.

Wright, G. Ernest, and David N. Freedman, eds. *The Biblical Archaeological Reader.* Vol. 1. New York: Anchor Books, 1961.

Wright, George C. *Racial Violence in Kentucky: Lynchings, Mob Rule, and "Legal Lynchings."* Baton Rouge: Louisiana State University Press, 1990.

Wright, Jr., J. Leitch. *The Only Land They Knew: The Tragic Story of the American Indians in the Old South.* New York: Free Press, 1981.

Wright, Quincy. *A Study of War.* 2 vols. Chicago: University of Chicago Press, 1942.

Wright, Richard. *The Color Curtain.* Cleveland & New York: World Publishing Co., 1956.

Wright, Sewall. *Principles of Live Stock Breeding.* U.S. Department of Agriculture Bulletin 905. Washington, D.C.: Government Printing Office, 1920.

————. "The Roles of Mutation, Inbreeding, Crossbreeding, and Selection in Evolution." In *Proceedings of the Sixth International Congress of Genetics* I, 356–66. Ithaca, NY, 1932.

Wu, Chang-Tsu. *"Chink!"* New York: World Publishing Co., 1972.

Wunder, John R. *Retained by The People: A History of American Indians and the Bill of Rights.* New York: Oxford University Press, 1994.

Wundt, Wilhelm. *Philosophische Studien.* Vol. 3. Leipzig: Englemann, 1883.

Wyatt-Brown, Bertram. *Southern Honor: Ethics & Behavior in the Old South.* New York: Oxford University Press, 1982.

Wyman, David S. *Paper Walls: America and the Refugee Crisis, 1938–1941.* Amherst: University of Massachussetts Press; New York: Pantheon Books, 1968.

————. *The Abandonment of the Jews: America and the Holocaust 1941–1945.* New York: Pantheon, 1984.

Wynes, Charles E. *Race Relations in Virginia 1870–1902.* Charlottesville: University of Virginia Press, 1961.

————, ed. *Forgotten Voices: Dissenting Southerners in an Age of Conformity.* Baton Rouge: Louisiana State University Press, 1967.

Wynot, Edward D. "'A Necessary Cruelty': The Emergence of Official Anti-Semitism in Poland, 1936–1939." *American Historical Review* (1971).

Yarmolinsky, Adam, Lance Liebman, and Corinne S. Schelling, eds. *Race and Schooling in the City.* Cambridge: Harvard University Press, 1981.

Yee, Albert H. "Ethnicity and Race: Psychological Perspectives." *Educational Psychologist* 18 (1983): 14–24.

Yerkes, Robert M., ed. "Psychological Examining in the United States Army." *Memoirs of the National Academy of Sciences* 15 (1921): 690–91.

Yetman, Norman R. ed. *Voices from Slavery.* New York: Holt, Rinehart, & Winston, 1970.

Young, Donald. *American Minority Peoples.* New York: Harper, 1932.

————. "Techniques of Race Relations." *Proceedings of the American Philosophical Society* 91 (1947): 150–61.

Young, Kimball. "Prejudices: An Outgrowth of Subjective Environment." In *Source Book for Social Psychology.* New York: Alfred A. Knopf, 1927.

Young, Warren L. *Minorities and the Military: A Cross-National Study in World Perspective.* Westport, CT: Greenwood Press, 1982.

Zamenhof, S., E. Van Marthens, and F. L. Margolis. "DNA (Cell Number) and Protein Deficiency in Neonatal Brain: Alteration by Maternal Dietary Protein Restriction." *Science* 160 (1968): 322–23.

————. "DNA (Cell Number) in Neonatal Brain: Second Generation (F2) Alteration by Maternal (F0) Dietary Protein Restriction." *Science* 172 (1971): 850–51.

Zanden, J. W. Vander. "The Ideology of White Supremacy." *Journal of the History of Ideas* 20 (1959): 355–402.

Ziegler, Herbert. *Nazi Germany's New Aristocracy.* Princeton: Princeton University Press, 1938.

Zirkle, Conway. "Father Adam and the Races of Man." *Journal of Heredity* 45 (1954): 29–34.

Zmarlik, Hans-Gunter. "Der Sozialdarwinismus in Deutschland as Gesichtliches Problem." *Vierteljahreshefte für Zeitgeschichte* 11 (1963): 246–73.

———. "Social Darwinism in Germany—An Example of Socio-Political Abuse of Scientific Knowledge." In *The Human Creature,* edited by Gunter Altner, 346–77. New York: Anchor Books, 1974.

Zolla, Elémire. *The Writer and the Shanman: A Morphology of the American Indian.* New York: Harcourt Brace Jovanovich, 1973.

Zollschan, I. *Racialism against Civilization.* London: New Europe Publishing Co., 1942.

———. *Das Rassenproblem.* Berlin: Baumueller, 1910; 5th edition, 1924.

Zubaida, Sami, ed. *Race and Racialism.* New York: Barnes & Noble, 1970.

Zuccotti, Susan. *The Italians and the Holocaust.* New York: Basic Books, 1987.

Zuckerman, Yitzhak ("Antek"). *A Surplus of Memory: Chronicle of the Warsaw Ghetto Uprising.* Berkeley: University of California Press, 1993.

Zweigenhaft, Richard L., and G. William Domhoff. *Blacks in the White Establishment? A Study of Race and Class in America.* New Haven: Yale University Press, 1991.

Index